PABLO

First published in English in 2015
by SelfMadeHero
139–141 Pancras Road
London NW1 1UN
www.selfmadehero.com

This edition is collected from four volumes originally published in
France by Dargaud.

Pablo 1 – Max Jacob
© DARGAUD 2012, by Birmant/Oubrerie
Pablo 2 – Apollinaire
© DARGAUD 2012, by Birmant/Oubrerie
Pablo 3 – Matisse
© DARGAUD 2013, by Birmant/Oubrerie
Pablo 4 – Picasso
© DARGAUD 2014, by Birmant/Oubrerie
www.dargaud.com
All rights reserved.

Written and Illustrated by: Julie Birmant and Clément Oubrerie
Coloured by: Sandra Desmazières
Translated by: Edward Gauvin
Publishing Assistant: Guillaume Rater
Layout: Lizzie Kaye
Sales & Marketing Manager: Sam Humphrey
Publishing Director: Emma Hayley
With thanks to: Nick de Somogyi, Dan Lockwood, Jane Laporte
and Kate McLauchlan

A CIP record for this book is available from the British Library.

ISBN: 978-1-906838-94-2

10 9 8 7 6 5 4 3 2 1

Printed and bound in Slovenia.

PABLO

by

Julie Birmant & Clément Oubrerie

Translated by Edward Gauvin
Coloured by Sandra Desmazières

SELF MADE HERO

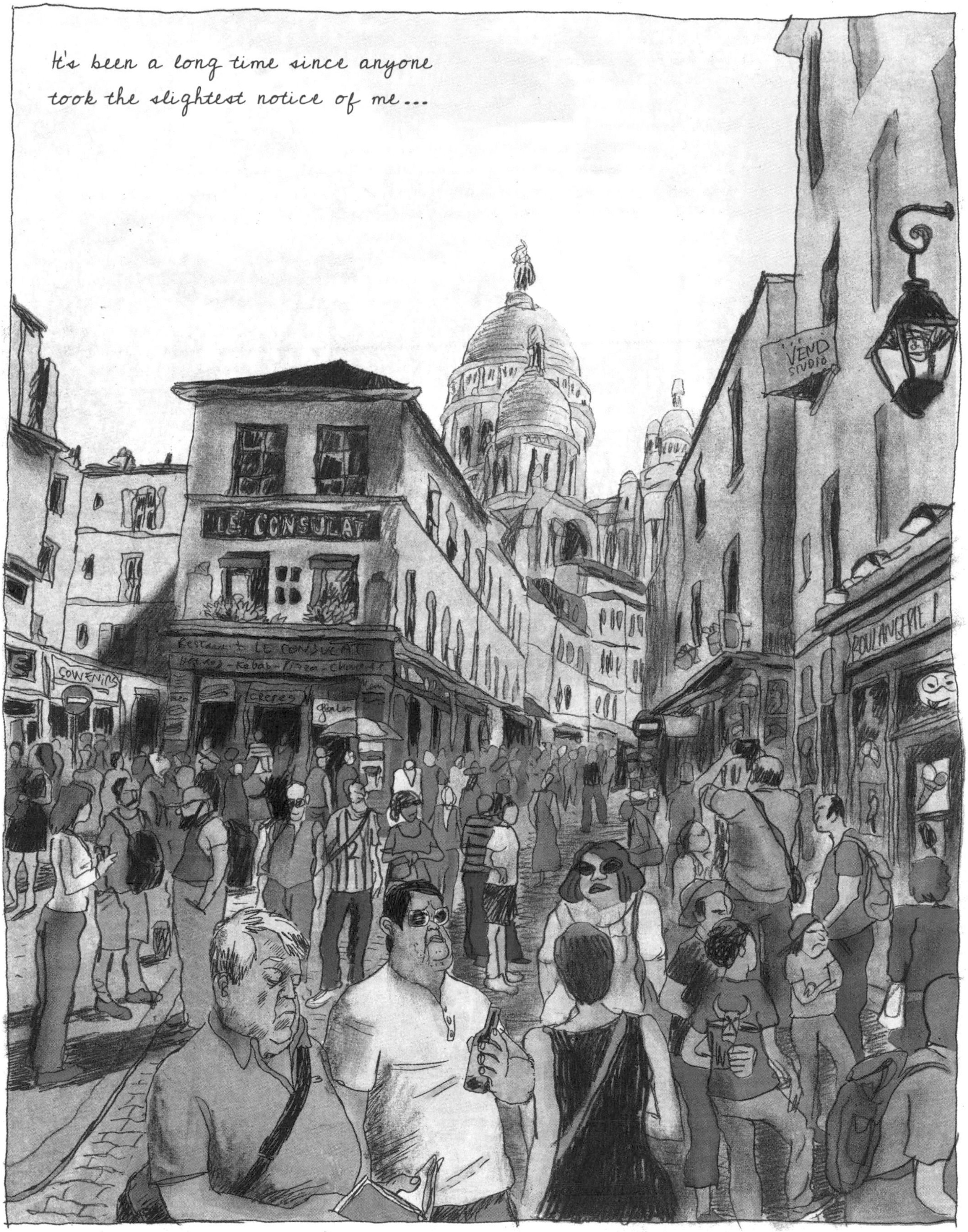
It's been a long time since anyone took the slightest notice of me....
LE CONSULAT
VEND STUDIO

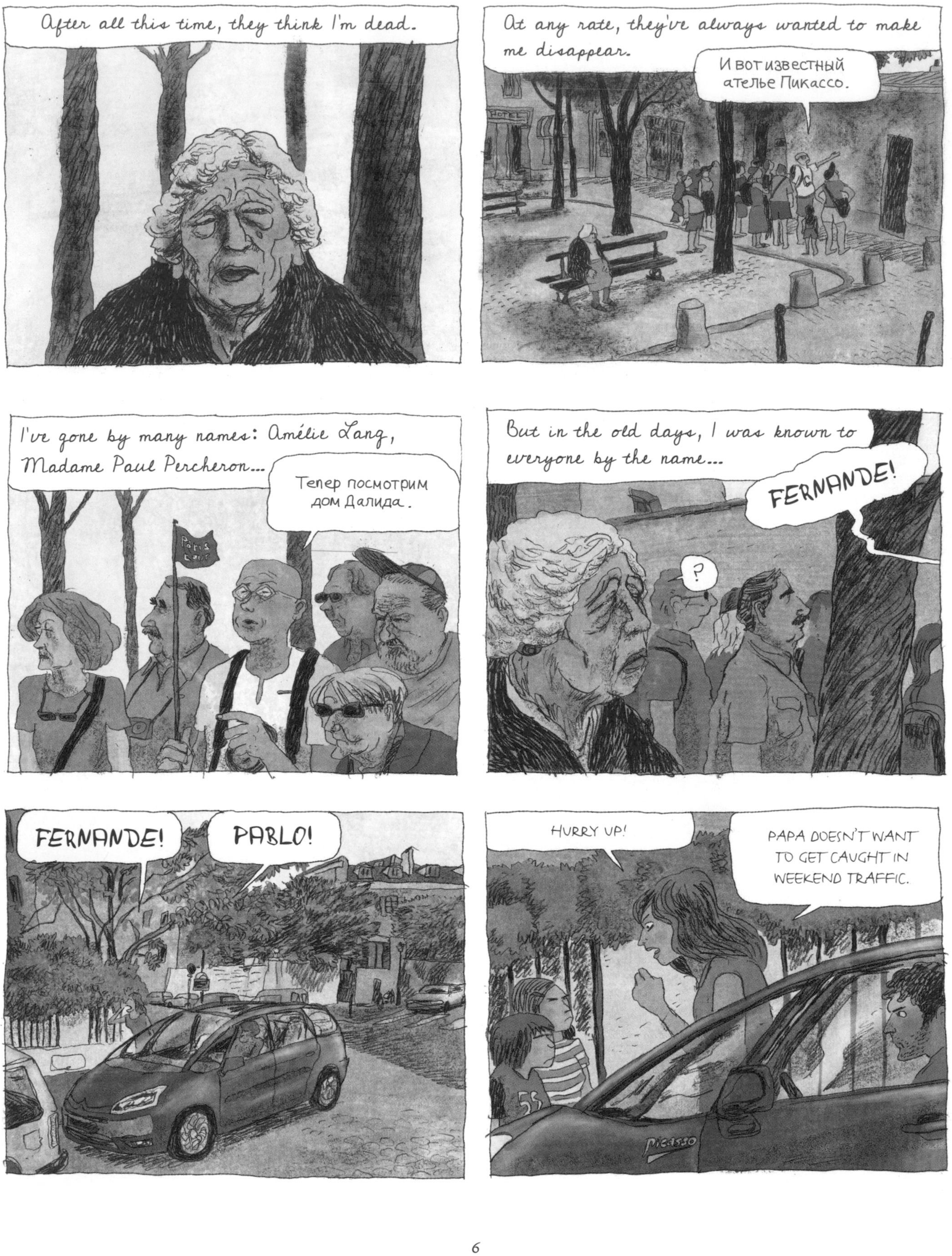
After all this time, they think I'm dead.
At any rate, they've always wanted to make me disappear.
И вот известный ателье Пикассо.
I've gone by many names: Amélie Lang, Madame Paul Percheron...
Тепер посмотрим дом Далида.
But in the old days, I was known to everyone by the name...
FERNANDE!
?
FERNANDE!
PABLO!
HURRY UP!
PAPA DOESN'T WANT TO GET CAUGHT IN WEEKEND TRAFFIC.

OH, PABLO! STOP PESTERING YOUR SISTER!

To be young in Montmartre in 1900 was to know cruelty, violence, madness.

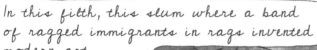

In this filth, this slum where a band of ragged immigrants in rags invented modern art...

Picasso loved me. Picasso painted me.

He always wanted to erase me from sight...

Instead, he made me eternal.

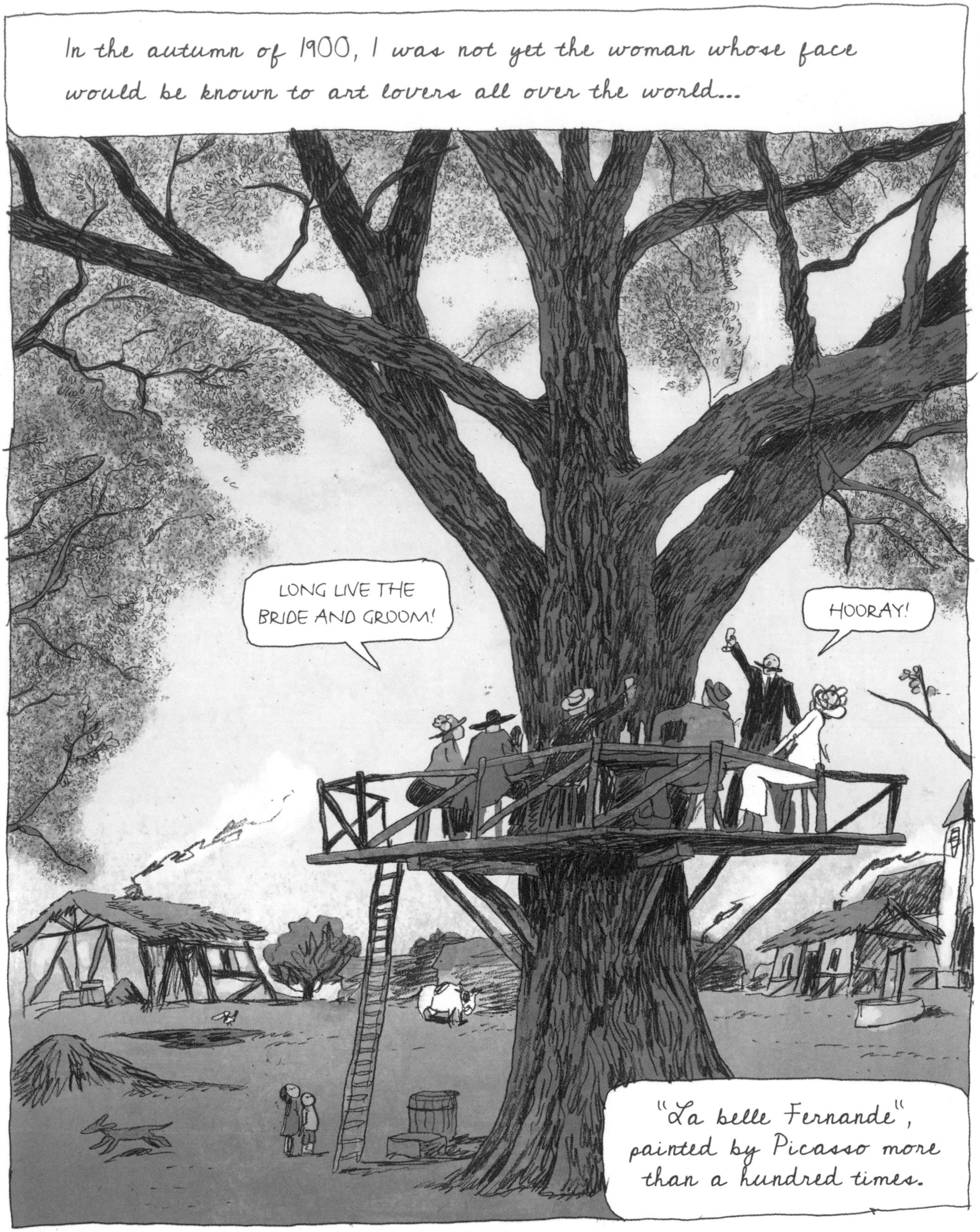
In the autumn of 1900, I was not yet the woman whose face would be known to art lovers all over the world...
LONG LIVE THE BRIDE AND GROOM!
HOORAY!
"La belle Fernande", painted by Picasso more than a hundred times.

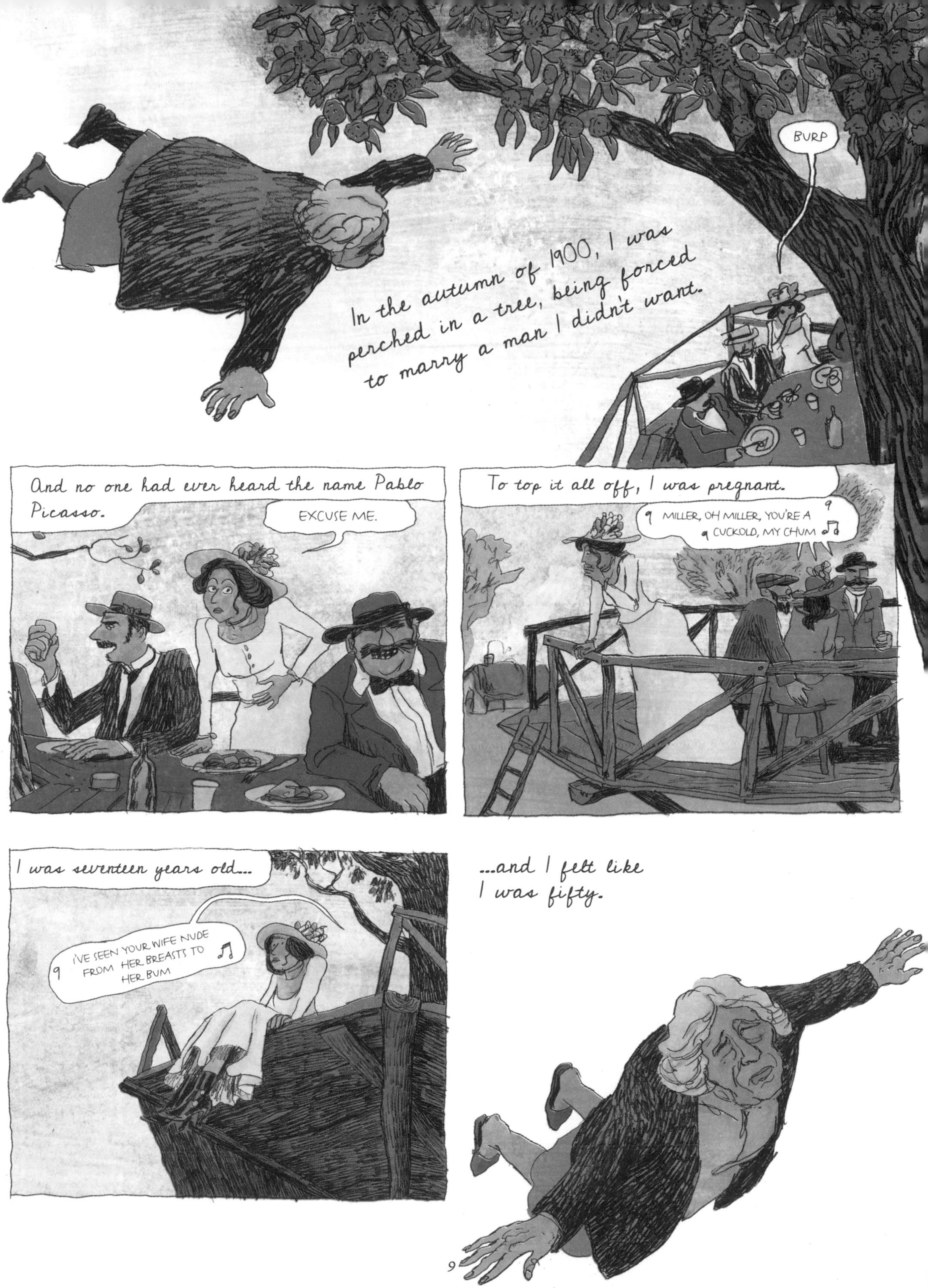

BURP
In the autumn of 1900, I was perched in a tree, being forced to marry a man I didn't want.
And no one had ever heard the name Pablo Picasso.
EXCUSE ME.
To top it all off, I was pregnant.
MILLER, OH MILLER, YOU'RE A CUCKOLD, MY CHUM
I was seventeen years old...
I'VE SEEN YOUR WIFE NUDE FROM HER BREASTS TO HER BUM
...and I felt like I was fifty.

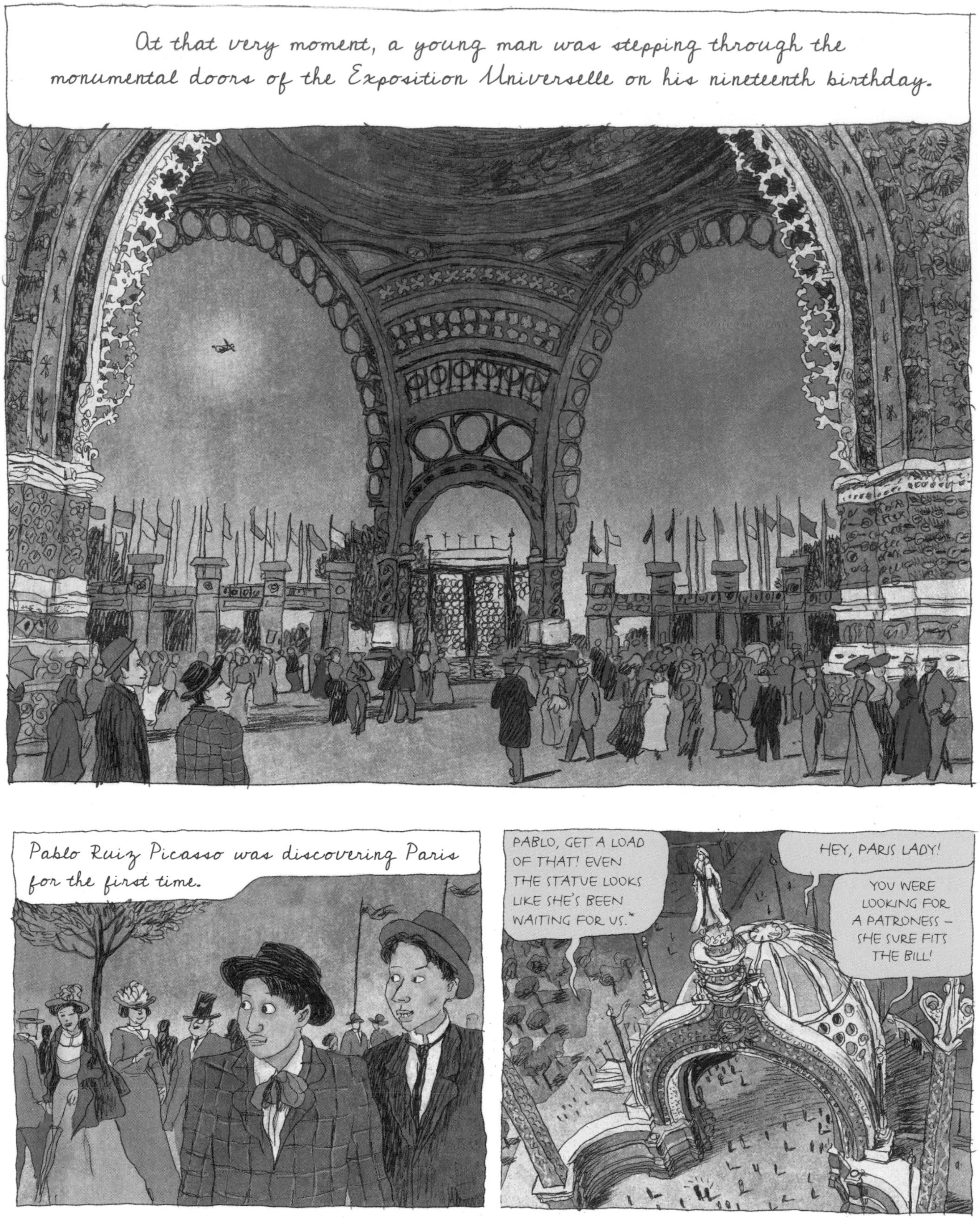
At that very moment, a young man was stepping through the monumental doors of the Exposition Universelle on his nineteenth birthday.
Pablo Ruiz Picasso was discovering Paris for the first time.
PABLO, GET A LOAD OF THAT! EVEN THE STATUE LOOKS LIKE SHE'S BEEN WAITING FOR US.*
HEY, PARIS LADY!
YOU WERE LOOKING FOR A PATRONESS – SHE SURE FITS THE BILL!

*THE GREY BALLOONS INDICATE CATALAN

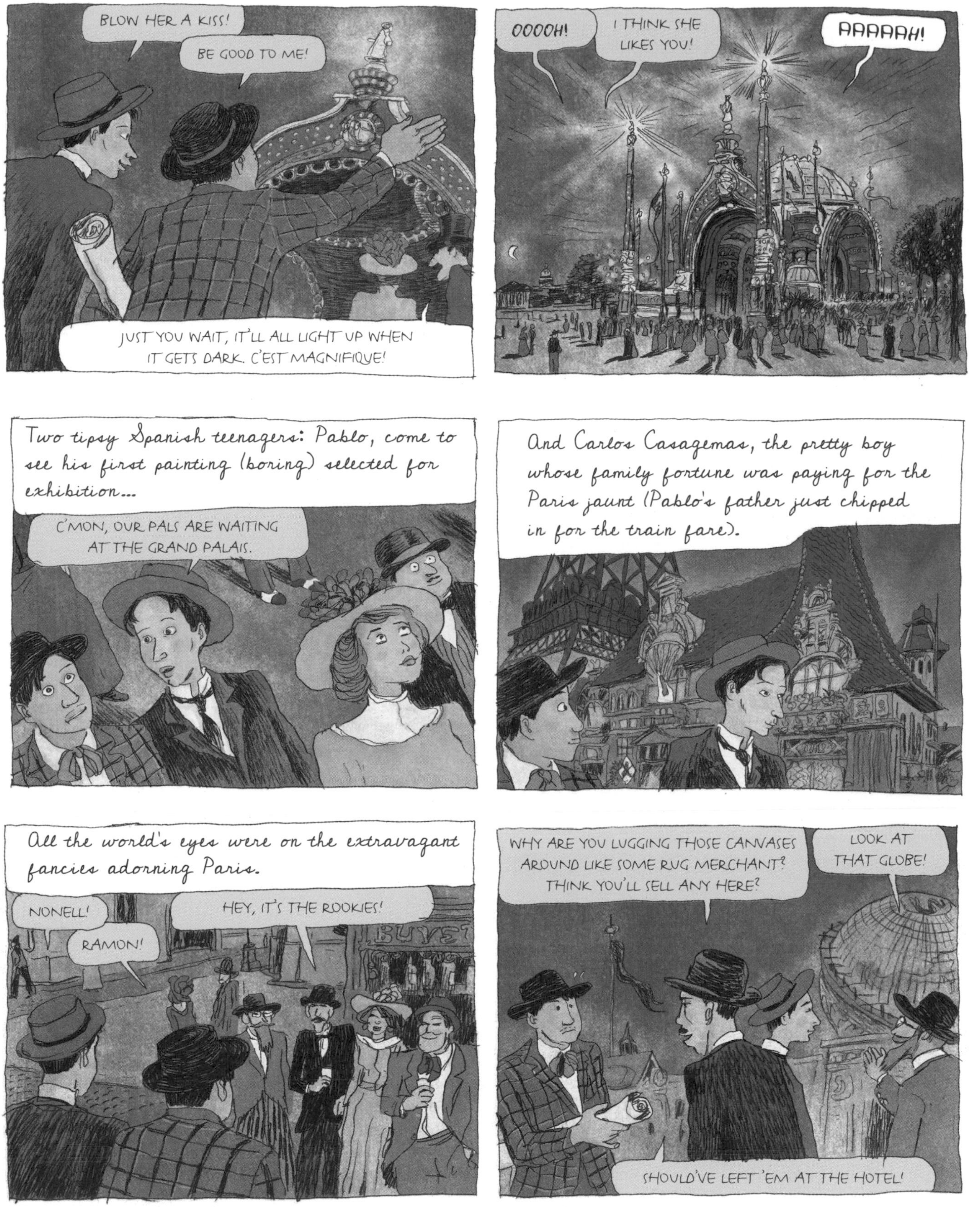
BLOW HER A KISS!
BE GOOD TO ME!
JUST YOU WAIT, IT'LL ALL LIGHT UP WHEN IT GETS DARK. C'EST MAGNIFIQUE!
OOOOH!
I THINK SHE LIKES YOU!
AAAAAH!
Two tipsy Spanish teenagers: Pablo, come to see his first painting (boring) selected for exhibition...
C'MON, OUR PALS ARE WAITING AT THE GRAND PALAIS.
And Carlos Casagemas, the pretty boy whose family fortune was paying for the Paris jaunt (Pablo's father just chipped in for the train fare).
All the world's eyes were on the extravagant fancies adorning Paris.
NONELL!
RAMON!
HEY, IT'S THE ROOKIES!
BUVET
WHY ARE YOU LUGGING THOSE CANVASES AROUND LIKE SOME RUG MERCHANT? THINK YOU'LL SELL ANY HERE?
LOOK AT THAT GLOBE!
SHOULD'VE LEFT 'EM AT THE HOTEL!

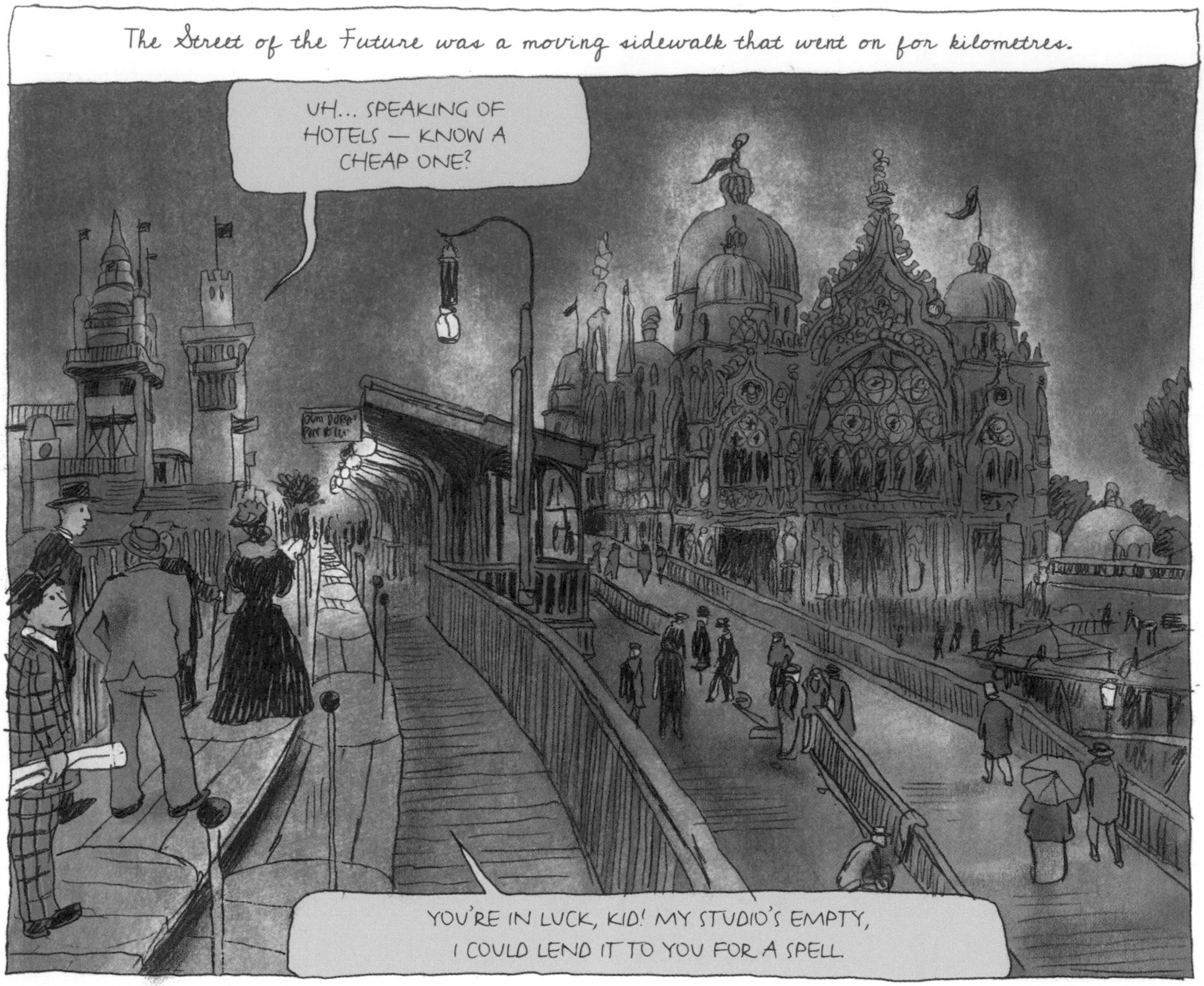
The Street of the Future was a moving sidewalk that went on for kilometres.
UH... SPEAKING OF HOTELS — KNOW A CHEAP ONE?
YOU'RE IN LUCK, KID! MY STUDIO'S EMPTY, I COULD LEND IT TO YOU FOR A SPELL.

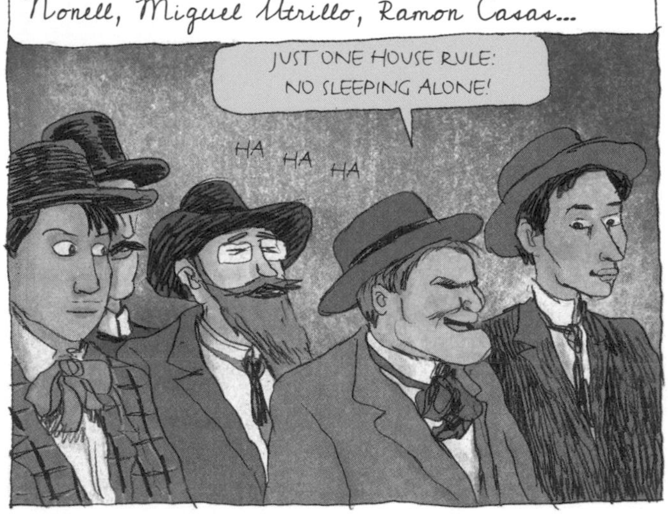
Nonell, Miquel Utrillo, Ramon Casas...
JUST ONE HOUSE RULE: NO SLEEPING ALONE!
HA HA HA

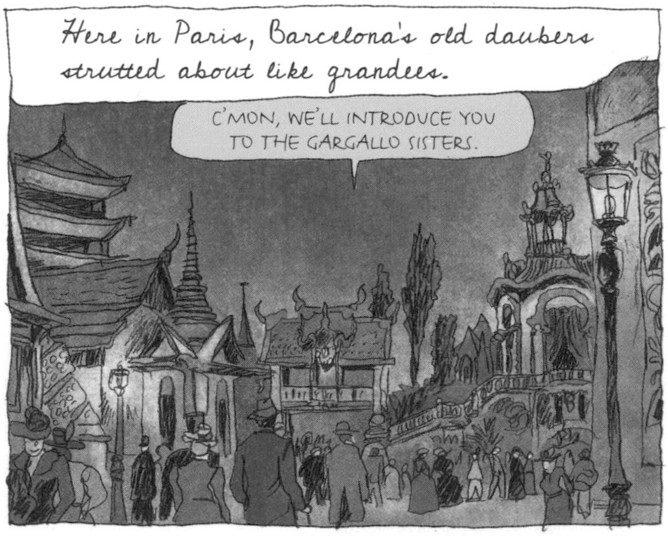
Here in Paris, Barcelona's old daubers strutted about like grandees.
C'MON, WE'LL INTRODUCE YOU TO THE GARGALLO SISTERS.

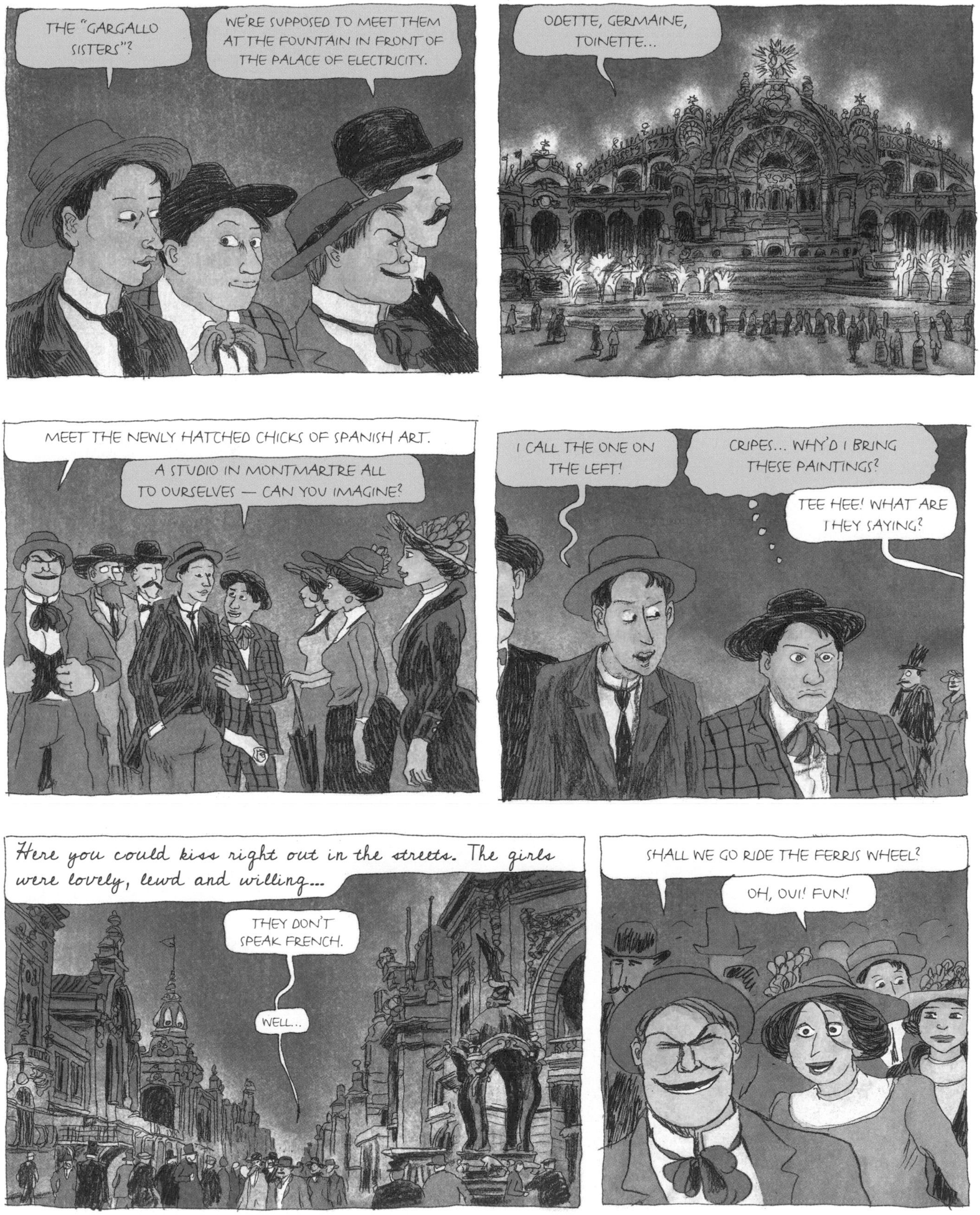
THE "GARGALLO SISTERS"?
WE'RE SUPPOSED TO MEET THEM AT THE FOUNTAIN IN FRONT OF THE PALACE OF ELECTRICITY.
ODETTE, GERMAINE, TOINETTE...
MEET THE NEWLY HATCHED CHICKS OF SPANISH ART.
A STUDIO IN MONTMARTRE ALL TO OURSELVES — CAN YOU IMAGINE?
I CALL THE ONE ON THE LEFT!
CRIPES... WHY'D I BRING THESE PAINTINGS?
TEE HEE! WHAT ARE THEY SAYING?
Here you could kiss right out in the streets. The girls were lovely, lewd and willing...
THEY DON'T SPEAK FRENCH.
WELL...
SHALL WE GO RIDE THE FERRIS WHEEL?
OH, OUI! FUN!

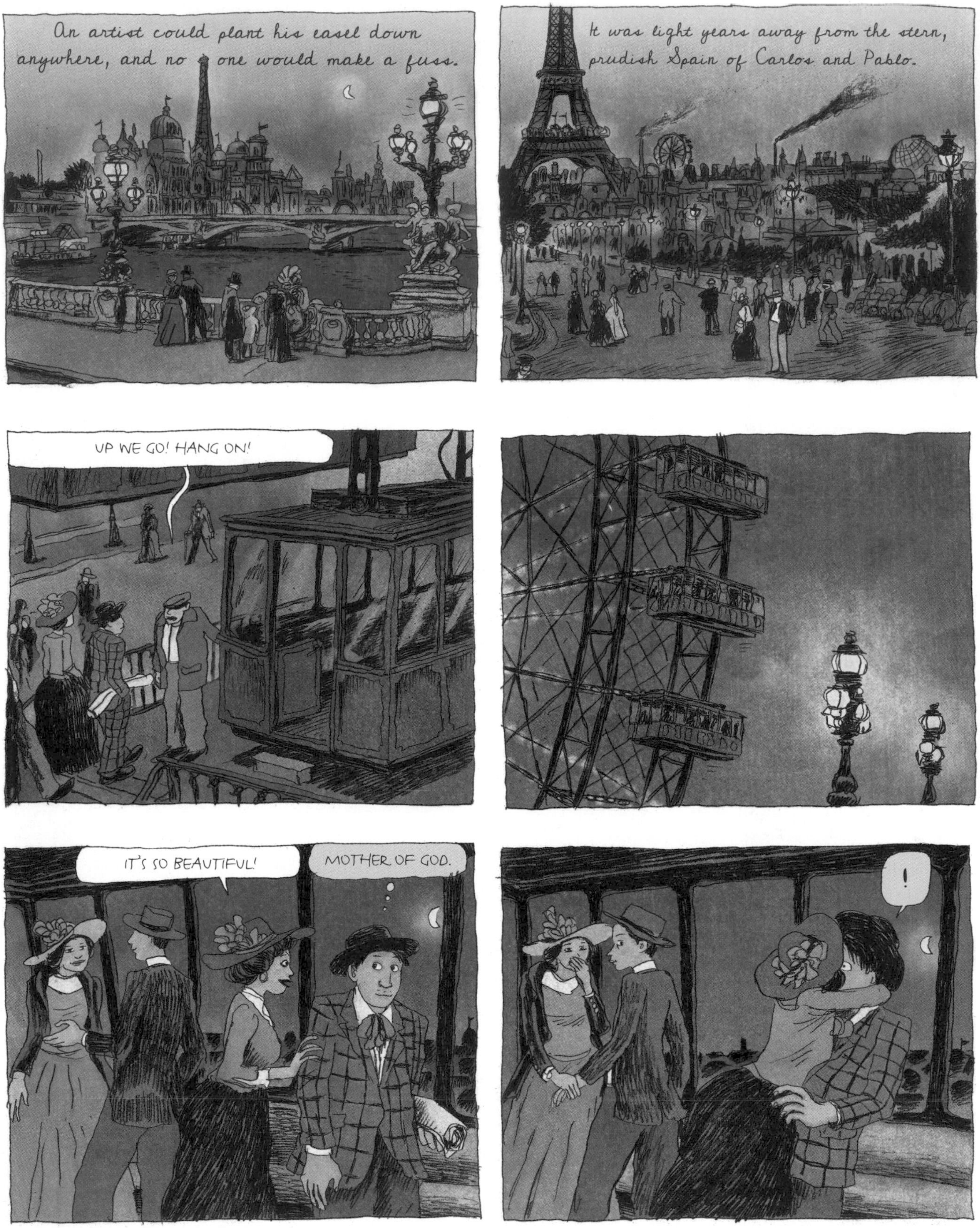
An artist could plant his easel down anywhere, and no one would make a fuss.
It was light years away from the stern, prudish Spain of Carlos and Pablo.
UP WE GO! HANG ON!
IT'S SO BEAUTIFUL!
MOTHER OF GOD.
!

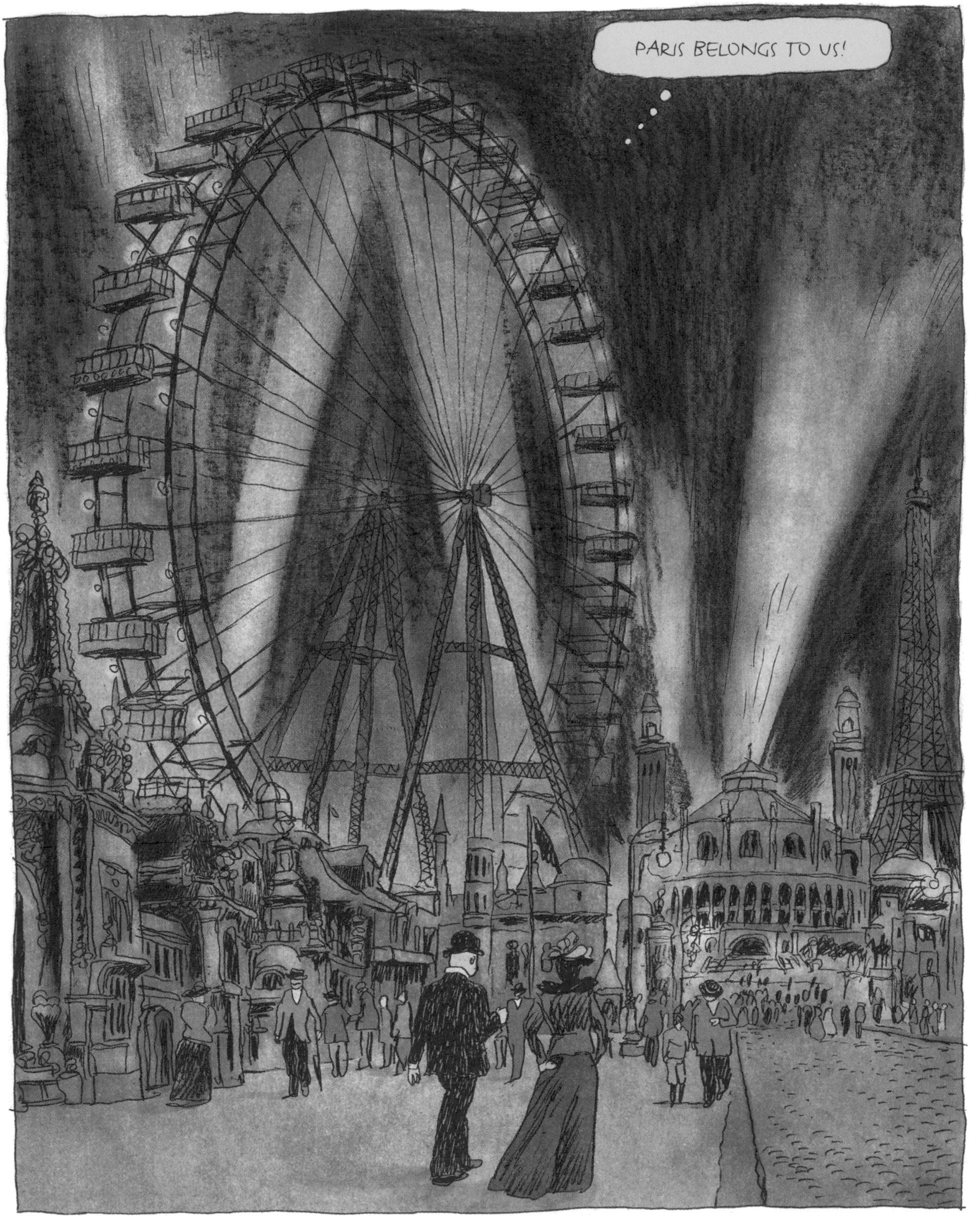
PARIS BELONGS TO US!

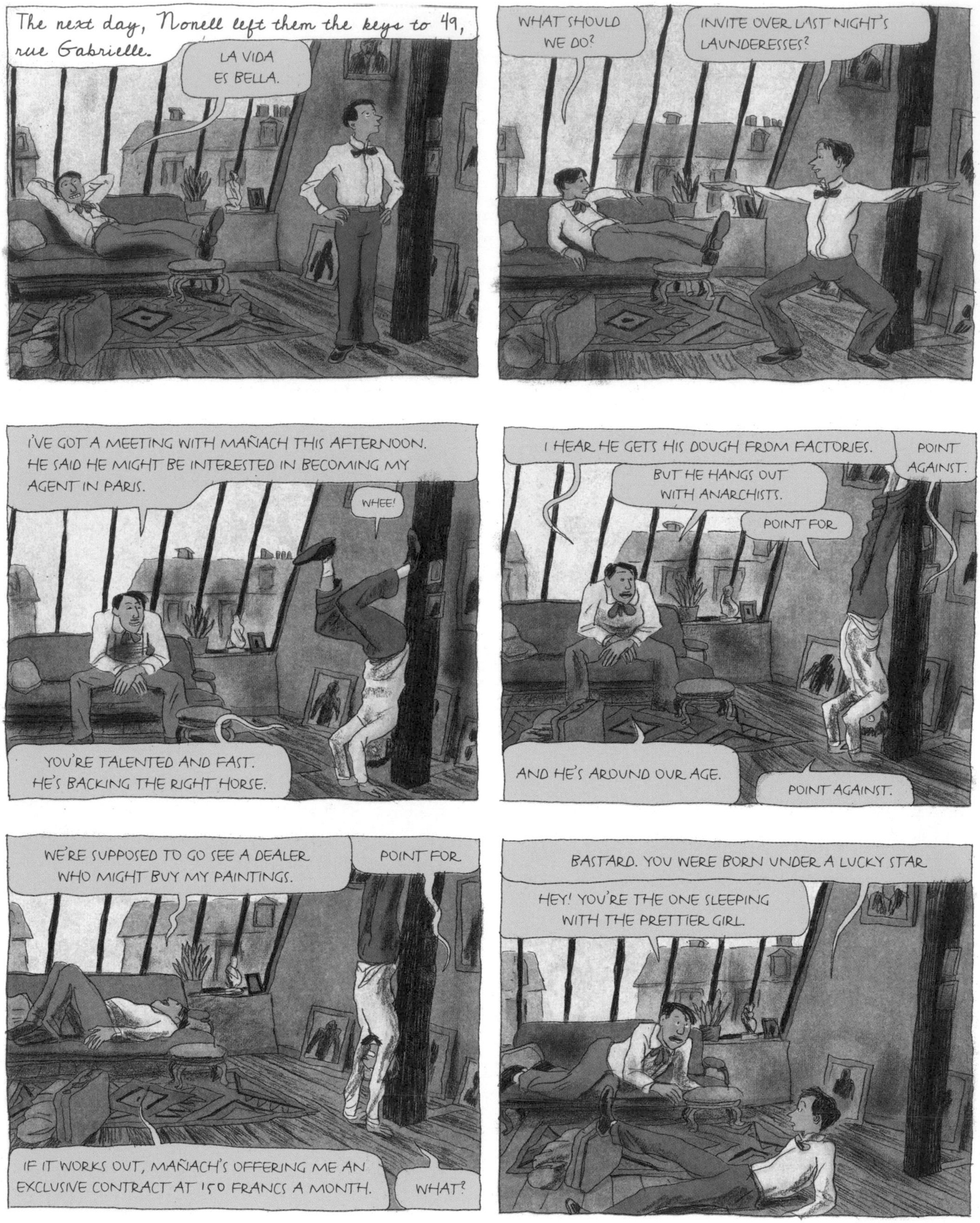

The next day, Nonell left them the keys to 49, rue Gabrielle.
LA VIDA ES BELLA.
WHAT SHOULD WE DO?
INVITE OVER LAST NIGHT'S LAUNDERESSES?
I'VE GOT A MEETING WITH MAÑACH THIS AFTERNOON. HE SAID HE MIGHT BE INTERESTED IN BECOMING MY AGENT IN PARIS.
WHEE!
YOU'RE TALENTED AND FAST. HE'S BACKING THE RIGHT HORSE.
I HEAR HE GETS HIS DOUGH FROM FACTORIES.
POINT AGAINST.
BUT HE HANGS OUT WITH ANARCHISTS.
POINT FOR
AND HE'S AROUND OUR AGE.
POINT AGAINST.
WE'RE SUPPOSED TO GO SEE A DEALER WHO MIGHT BUY MY PAINTINGS.
POINT FOR
IF IT WORKS OUT, MAÑACH'S OFFERING ME AN EXCLUSIVE CONTRACT AT 150 FRANCS A MONTH.
WHAT?
BASTARD. YOU WERE BORN UNDER A LUCKY STAR
HEY! YOU'RE THE ONE SLEEPING WITH THE PRETTIER GIRL.

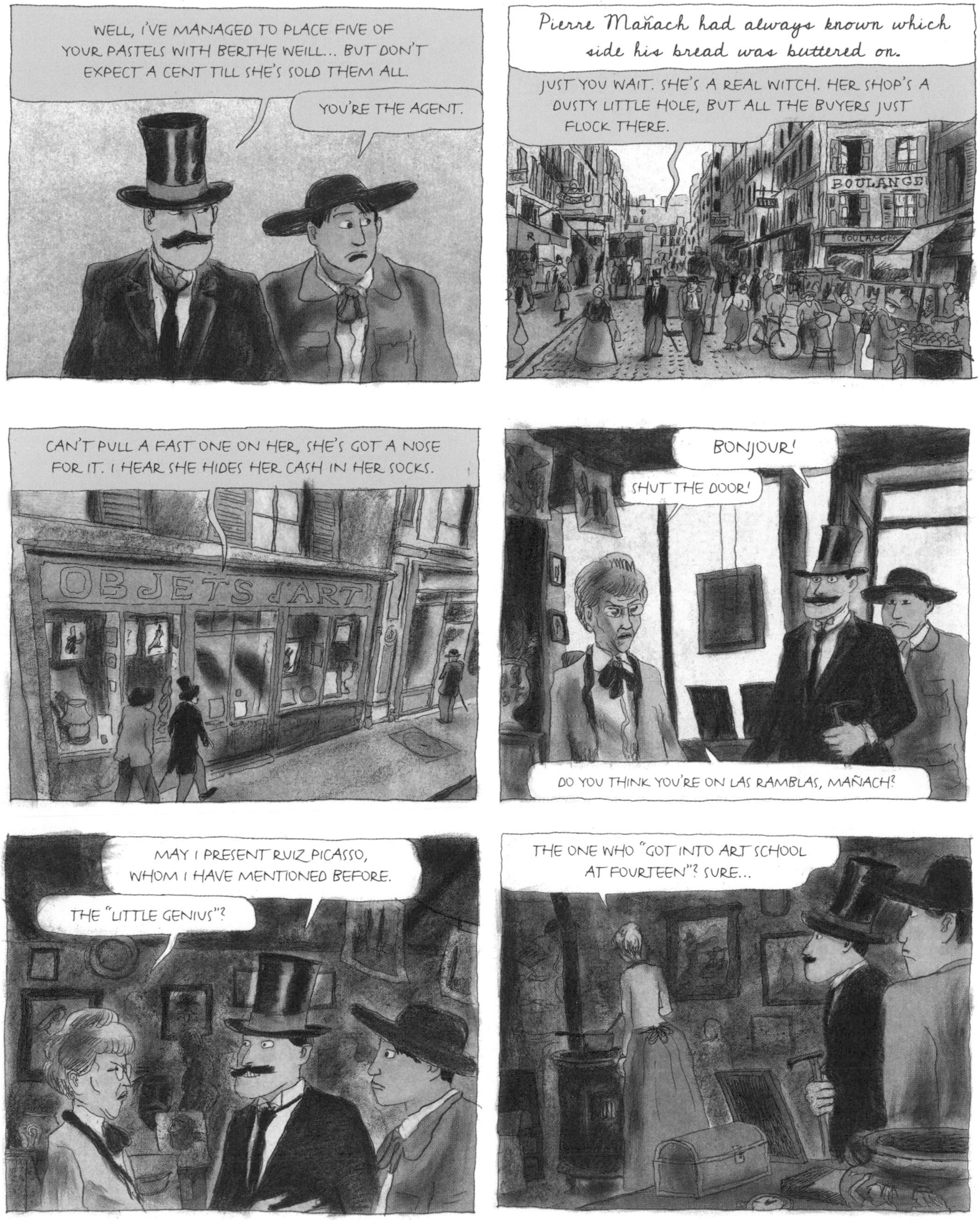
WELL, I'VE MANAGED TO PLACE FIVE OF YOUR PASTELS WITH BERTHE WEILL... BUT DON'T EXPECT A CENT TILL SHE'S SOLD THEM ALL.
YOU'RE THE AGENT.
Pierre Mañach had always known which side his bread was buttered on.
JUST YOU WAIT. SHE'S A REAL WITCH. HER SHOP'S A DUSTY LITTLE HOLE, BUT ALL THE BUYERS JUST FLOCK THERE.
BOULANGE
CAN'T PULL A FAST ONE ON HER, SHE'S GOT A NOSE FOR IT. I HEAR SHE HIDES HER CASH IN HER SOCKS.
OBJETS d'ART
BONJOUR!
SHUT THE DOOR!
DO YOU THINK YOU'RE ON LAS RAMBLAS, MAÑACH?
MAY I PRESENT RUIZ PICASSO, WHOM I HAVE MENTIONED BEFORE.
THE "LITTLE GENIUS"?
THE ONE WHO "GOT INTO ART SCHOOL AT FOURTEEN"? SURE...

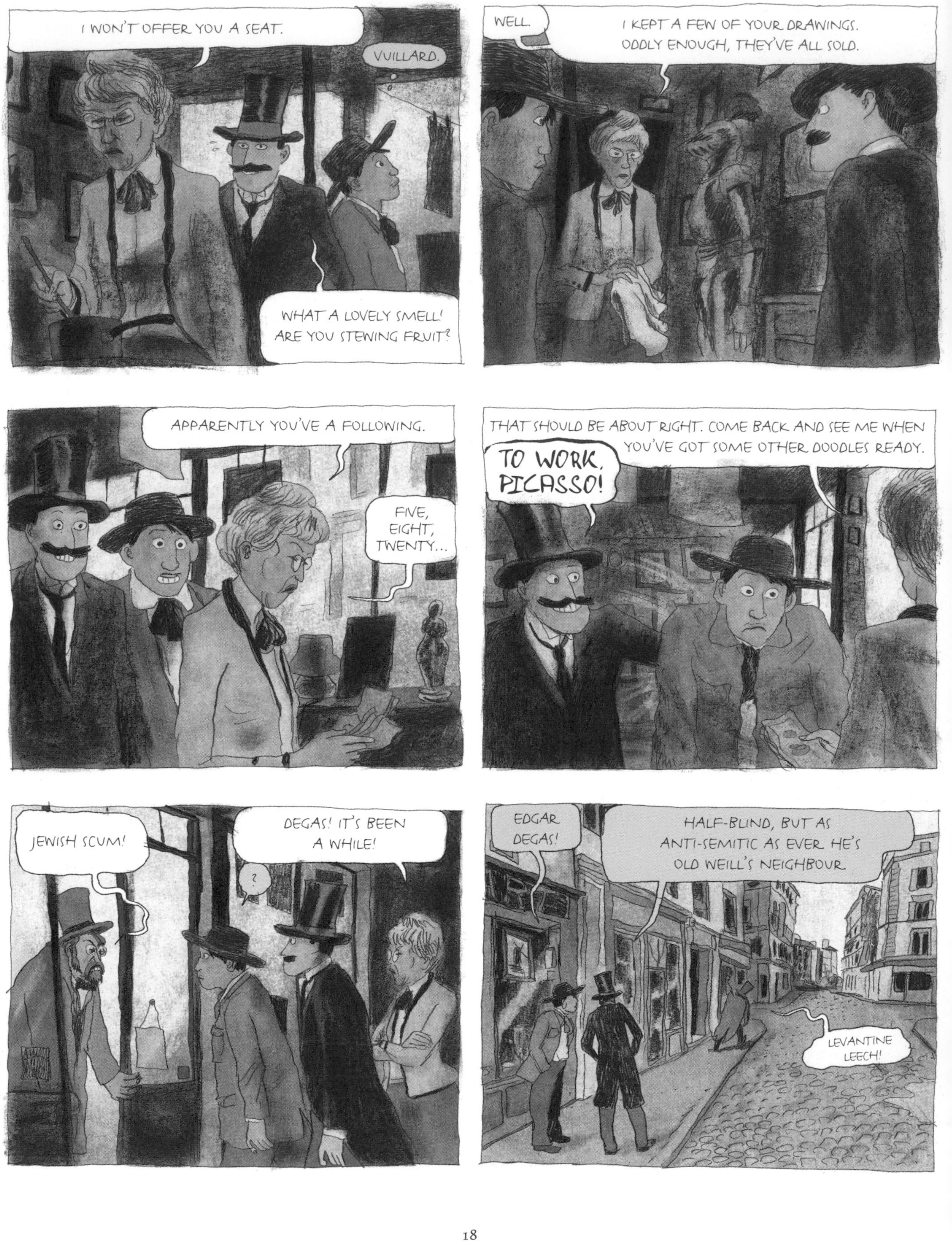
I WON'T OFFER YOU A SEAT.
VUILLARD.
WHAT A LOVELY SMELL! ARE YOU STEWING FRUIT?
WELL.
I KEPT A FEW OF YOUR DRAWINGS. ODDLY ENOUGH, THEY'VE ALL SOLD.
APPARENTLY YOU'VE A FOLLOWING.
FIVE, EIGHT, TWENTY...
THAT SHOULD BE ABOUT RIGHT. COME BACK AND SEE ME WHEN YOU'VE GOT SOME OTHER DOODLES READY.
TO WORK, PICASSO!
JEWISH SCUM!
DEGAS! IT'S BEEN A WHILE!
?
EDGAR DEGAS!
HALF-BLIND, BUT AS ANTI-SEMITIC AS EVER. HE'S OLD WEILL'S NEIGHBOUR.
LEVANTINE LEECH!

An agent, a fiancée: Picasso was ready to face life in Paris.

ME, I JUST LOVE PABLO. HE'S SO FUNNY WHEN HE TRIES TO SPEAK FRENCH.

OH?

YOU'RE JUST SAYING THAT 'CAUSE HE'S RAKING IT IN RIGHT NOW.

WELL, YOUR CARLOS ISN'T JUST LOADED, HE'S HANDSOME, TOO!

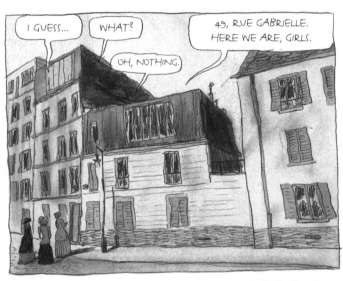

I GUESS...

WHAT?

OH, NOTHING.

49, RUE GABRIELLE. HERE WE ARE, GIRLS.

WHO'S THEIR THIRD WHEEL?

OH, ANOTHER SPIC FROM ART SCHOOL: PALLARÈS.

A HOT-TEMPERED SOUTHERNER, LIKE THE OTHERS — JUST YOUR TYPE.

IT'S THE LAUNDRY LADIES!

HI, SWEETHEARTS!

I CAME WITH MY SISTER, ODETTE.

WELCOME TO THE TEMPLE OF ART AND SMUT.

I DIDN'T CATCH A WORD.

BRANDY?

LOOK AT THOSE PAINTINGS!

19

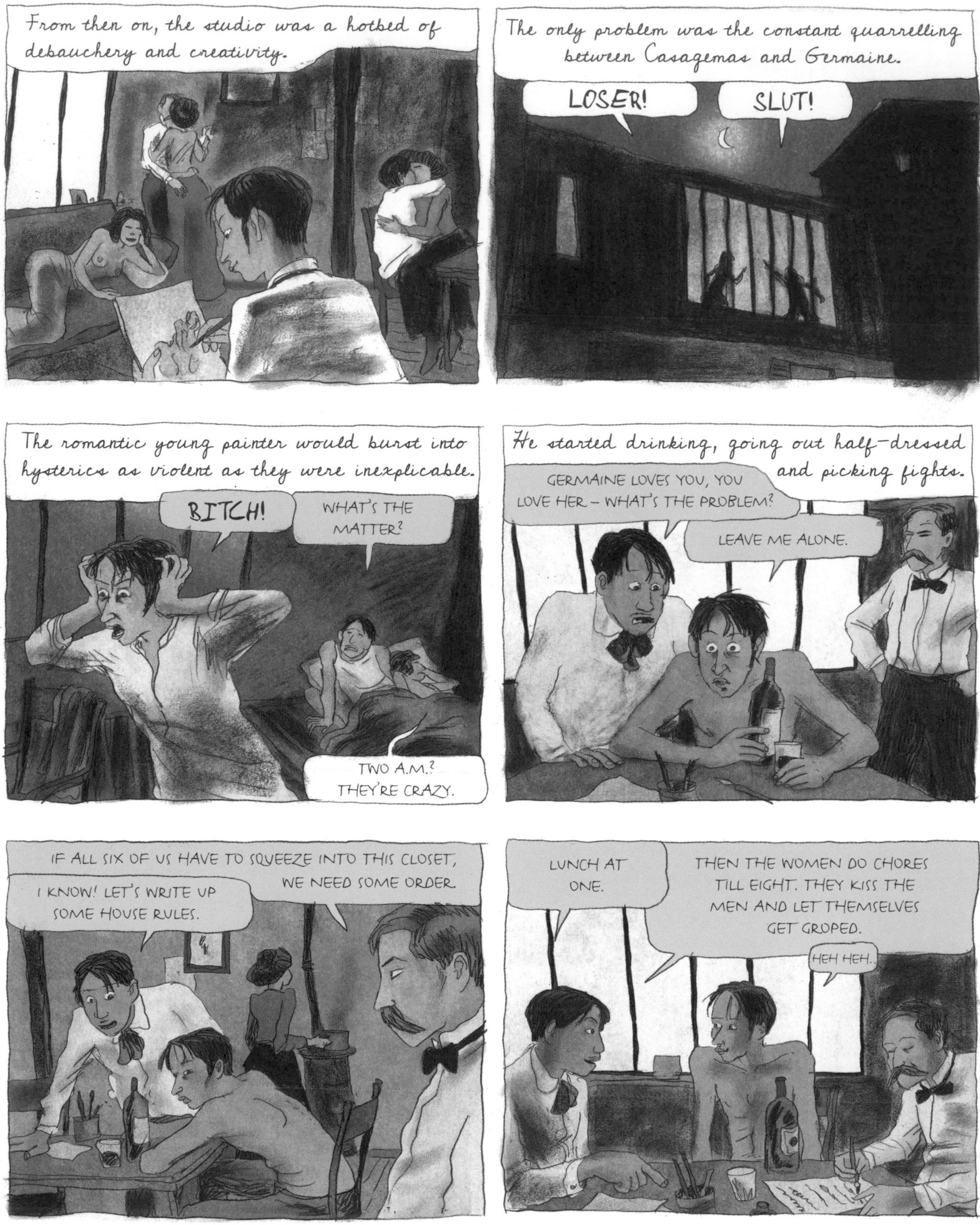
From then on, the studio was a hotbed of debauchery and creativity.
The only problem was the constant quarrelling between Casagemas and Germaine.
LOSER!
SLUT!
The romantic young painter would burst into hysterics as violent as they were inexplicable.
BITCH!
WHAT'S THE MATTER?
TWO A.M.? THEY'RE CRAZY.
He started drinking, going out half-dressed and picking fights.
GERMAINE LOVES YOU, YOU LOVE HER – WHAT'S THE PROBLEM?
LEAVE ME ALONE.
IF ALL SIX OF US HAVE TO SQUEEZE INTO THIS CLOSET, WE NEED SOME ORDER.
I KNOW! LET'S WRITE UP SOME HOUSE RULES.
LUNCH AT ONE.
THEN THE WOMEN DO CHORES TILL EIGHT. THEY KISS THE MEN AND LET THEMSELVES GET GROPED.
HEH HEH.

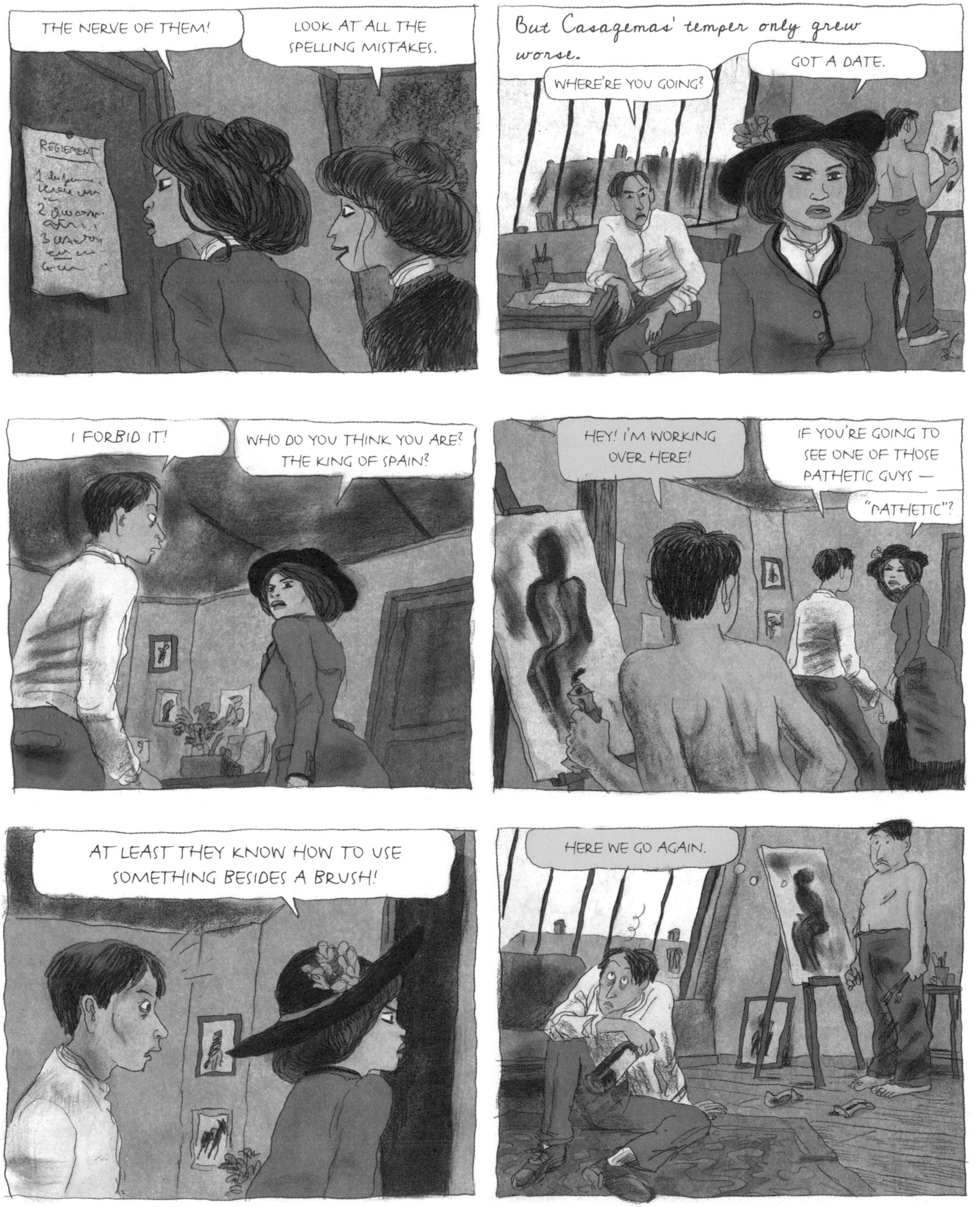
THE NERVE OF THEM!
LOOK AT ALL THE SPELLING MISTAKES.
REGLEMENT
But Casagemas' temper only grew worse.
WHERE'RE YOU GOING?
GOT A DATE.
I FORBID IT!
WHO DO YOU THINK YOU ARE? THE KING OF SPAIN?
HEY! I'M WORKING OVER HERE!
IF YOU'RE GOING TO SEE ONE OF THOSE PATHETIC GUYS —
"PATHETIC"?
AT LEAST THEY KNOW HOW TO USE SOMETHING BESIDES A BRUSH!
HERE WE GO AGAIN.

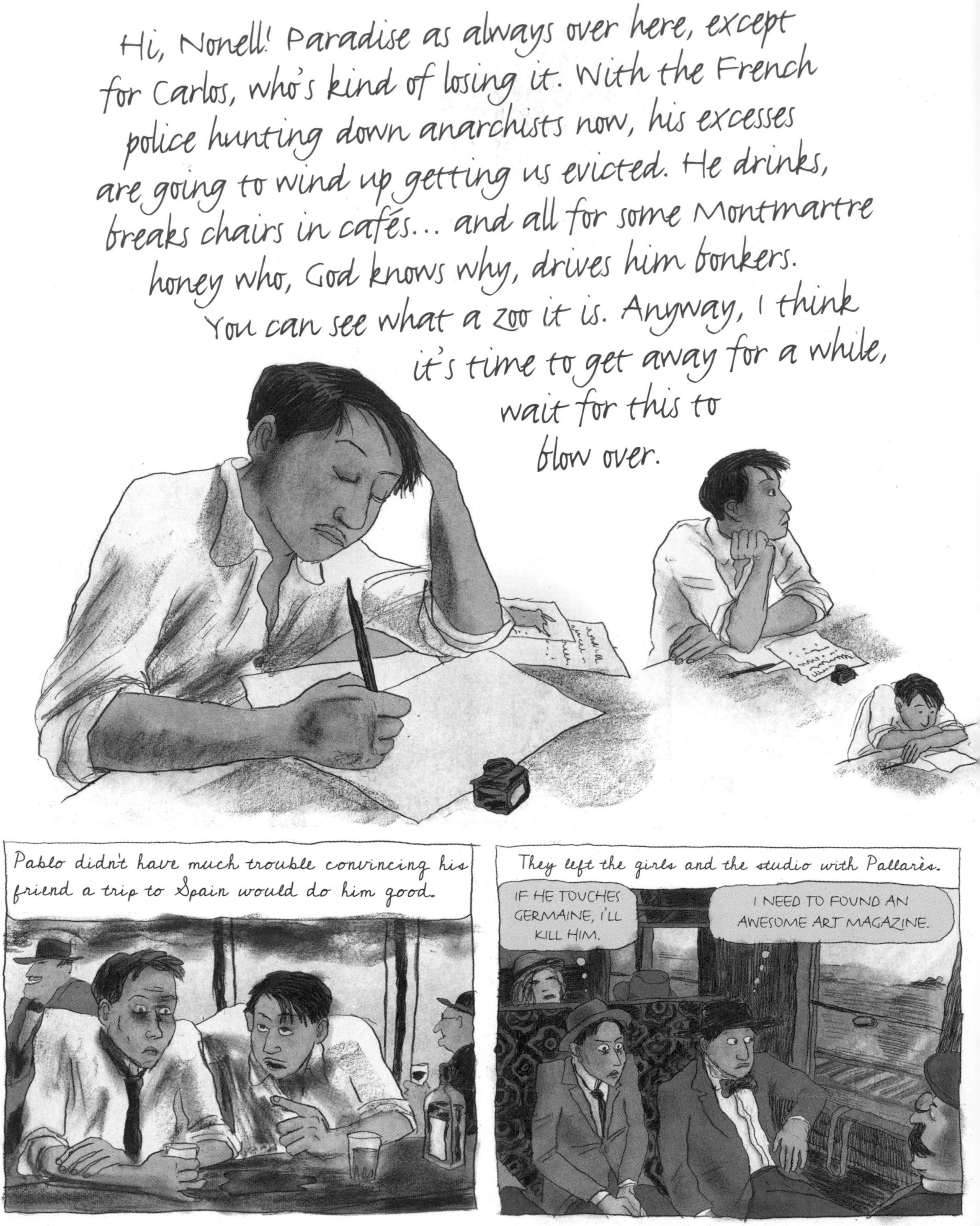
Hi, Nonell! Paradise as always over here, except for Carlos, who's kind of losing it. With the French police hunting down anarchists now, his excesses are going to wind up getting us evicted. He drinks, breaks chairs in cafés... and all for some Montmartre honey who, God knows why, drives him bonkers. You can see what a zoo it is. Anyway, I think it's time to get away for a while, wait for this to blow over.
Pablo didn't have much trouble convincing his friend a trip to Spain would do him good.
They left the girls and the studio with Pallarès.
IF HE TOUCHES GERMAINE, I'LL KILL HIM.
I NEED TO FOUND AN AWESOME ART MAGAZINE.

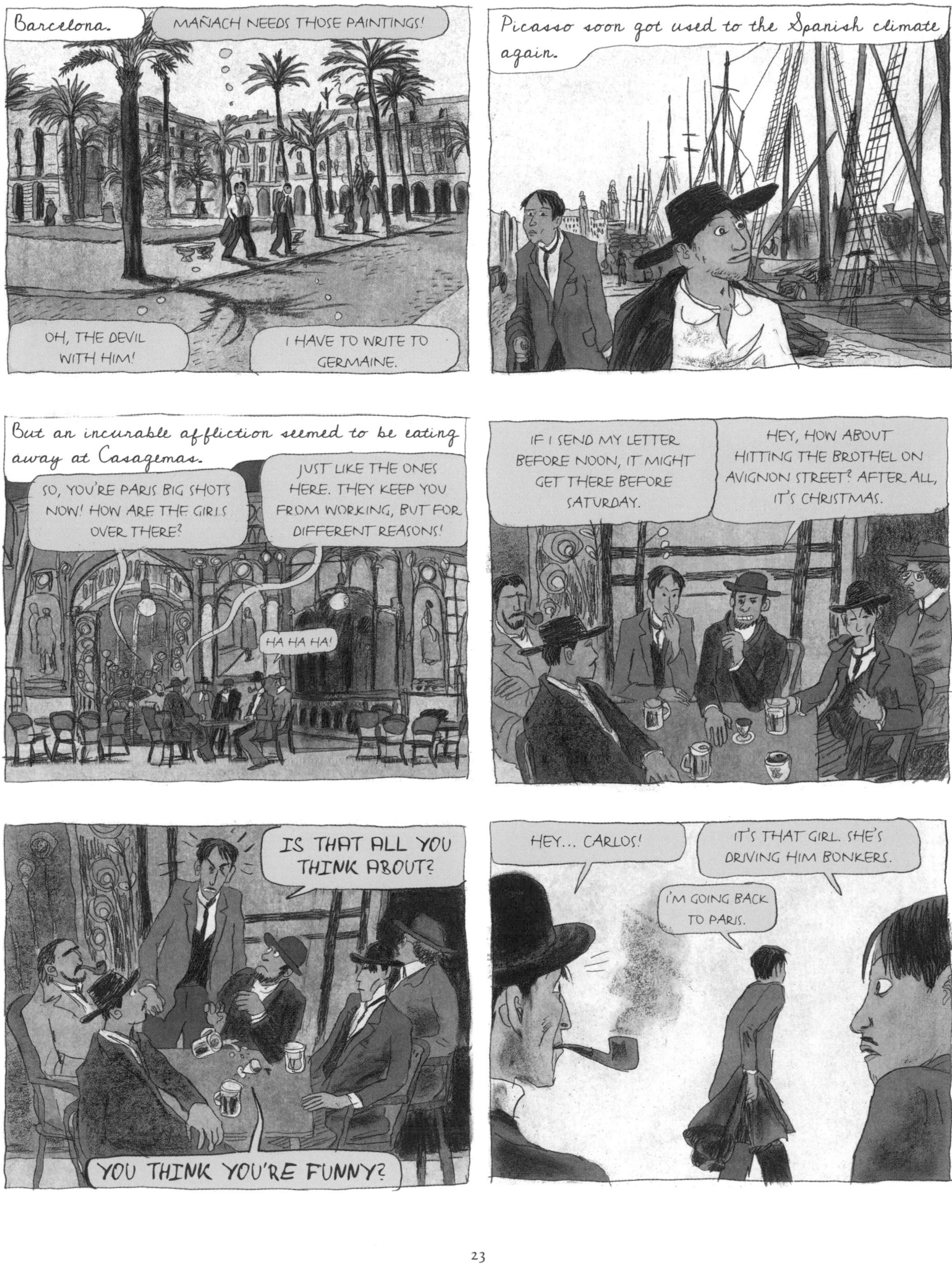

Barcelona.
MAÑACH NEEDS THOSE PAINTINGS!
OH, THE DEVIL WITH HIM!
I HAVE TO WRITE TO GERMAINE.
Picasso soon got used to the Spanish climate again.
But an incurable affliction seemed to be eating away at Casagemas.
SO, YOU'RE PARIS BIG SHOTS NOW! HOW ARE THE GIRLS OVER THERE?
JUST LIKE THE ONES HERE. THEY KEEP YOU FROM WORKING, BUT FOR DIFFERENT REASONS!
HA HA HA!
IF I SEND MY LETTER BEFORE NOON, IT MIGHT GET THERE BEFORE SATURDAY.
HEY, HOW ABOUT HITTING THE BROTHEL ON AVIGNON STREET? AFTER ALL, IT'S CHRISTMAS.
IS THAT ALL YOU THINK ABOUT?
YOU THINK YOU'RE FUNNY?
HEY... CARLOS!
IT'S THAT GIRL. SHE'S DRIVING HIM BONKERS.
I'M GOING BACK TO PARIS.

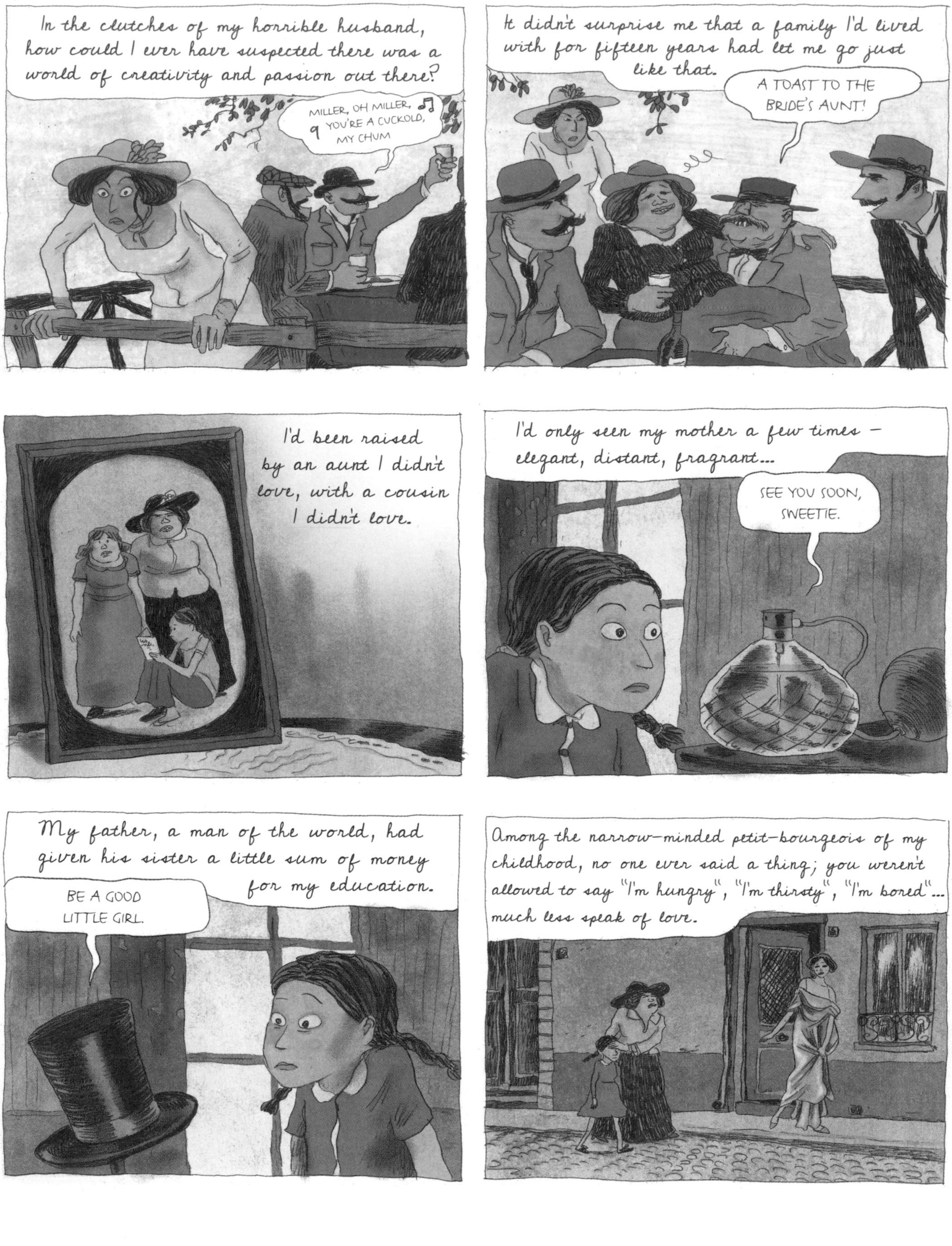
In the clutches of my horrible husband, how could I ever have suspected there was a world of creativity and passion out there?
MILLER, OH MILLER, YOU'RE A CUCKOLD, MY CHUM
It didn't surprise me that a family I'd lived with for fifteen years had let me go just like that.
A TOAST TO THE BRIDE'S AUNT!
I'd been raised by an aunt I didn't love, with a cousin I didn't love.
I'd only seen my mother a few times – elegant, distant, fragrant...
SEE YOU SOON, SWEETIE.
My father, a man of the world, had given his sister a little sum of money for my education.
BE A GOOD LITTLE GIRL.
Among the narrow-minded petit-bourgeois of my childhood, no one ever said a thing; you weren't allowed to say "I'm hungry", "I'm thirsty", "I'm bored"... much less speak of love.

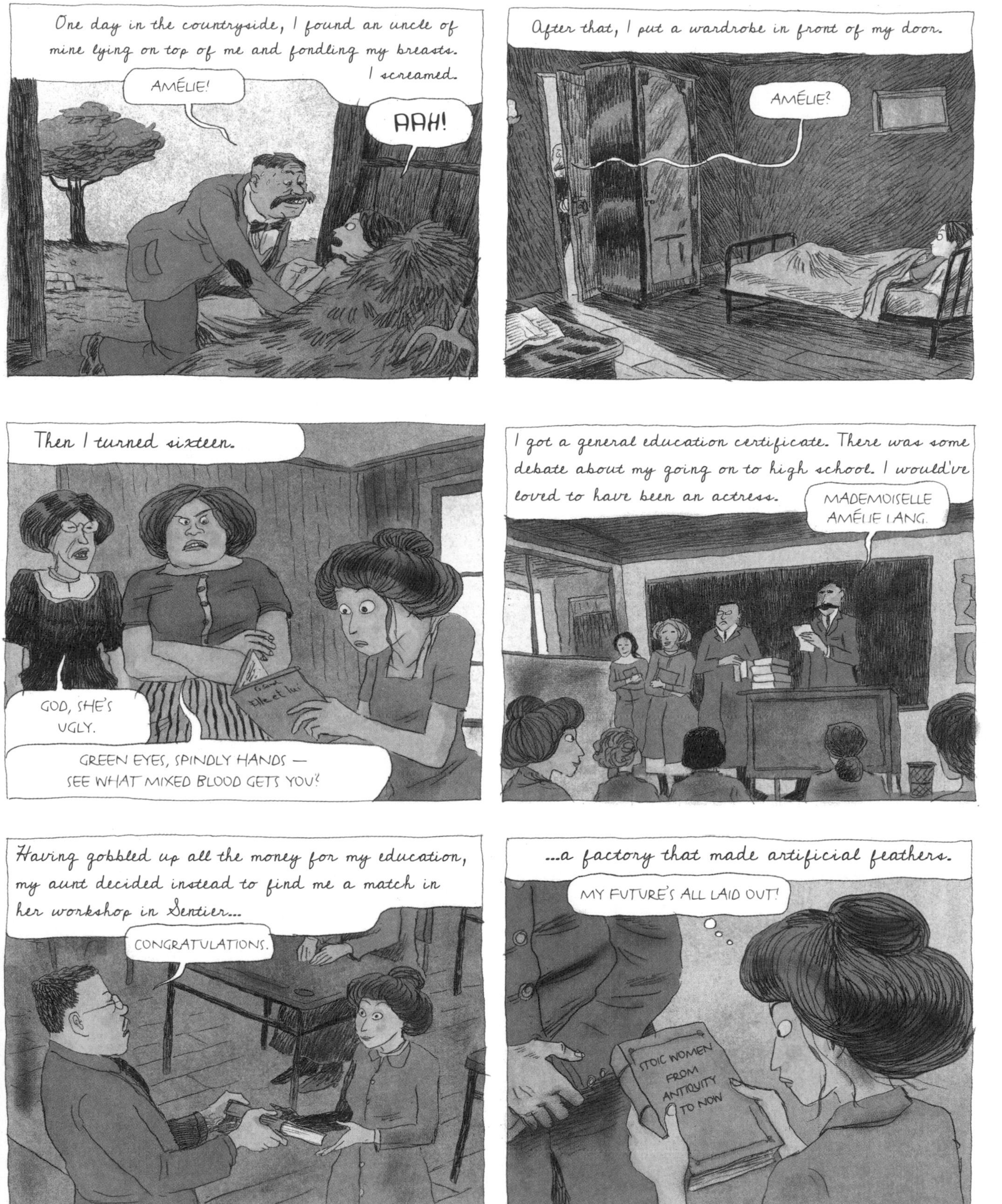

One day in the countryside, I found an uncle of mine lying on top of me and fondling my breasts. I screamed.
AMÉLIE!
AAH!
After that, I put a wardrobe in front of my door.
AMÉLIE?
Then I turned sixteen.
GOD, SHE'S UGLY.
GREEN EYES, SPINDLY HANDS — SEE WHAT MIXED BLOOD GETS YOU?
I got a general education certificate. There was some debate about my going on to high school. I would've loved to have been an actress.
MADEMOISELLE AMÉLIE LANG.
Having gobbled up all the money for my education, my aunt decided instead to find me a match in her workshop in Sentier...
CONGRATULATIONS.
...a factory that made artificial feathers.
MY FUTURE'S ALL LAID OUT!
STOIC WOMEN FROM ANTIQUITY TO NOW

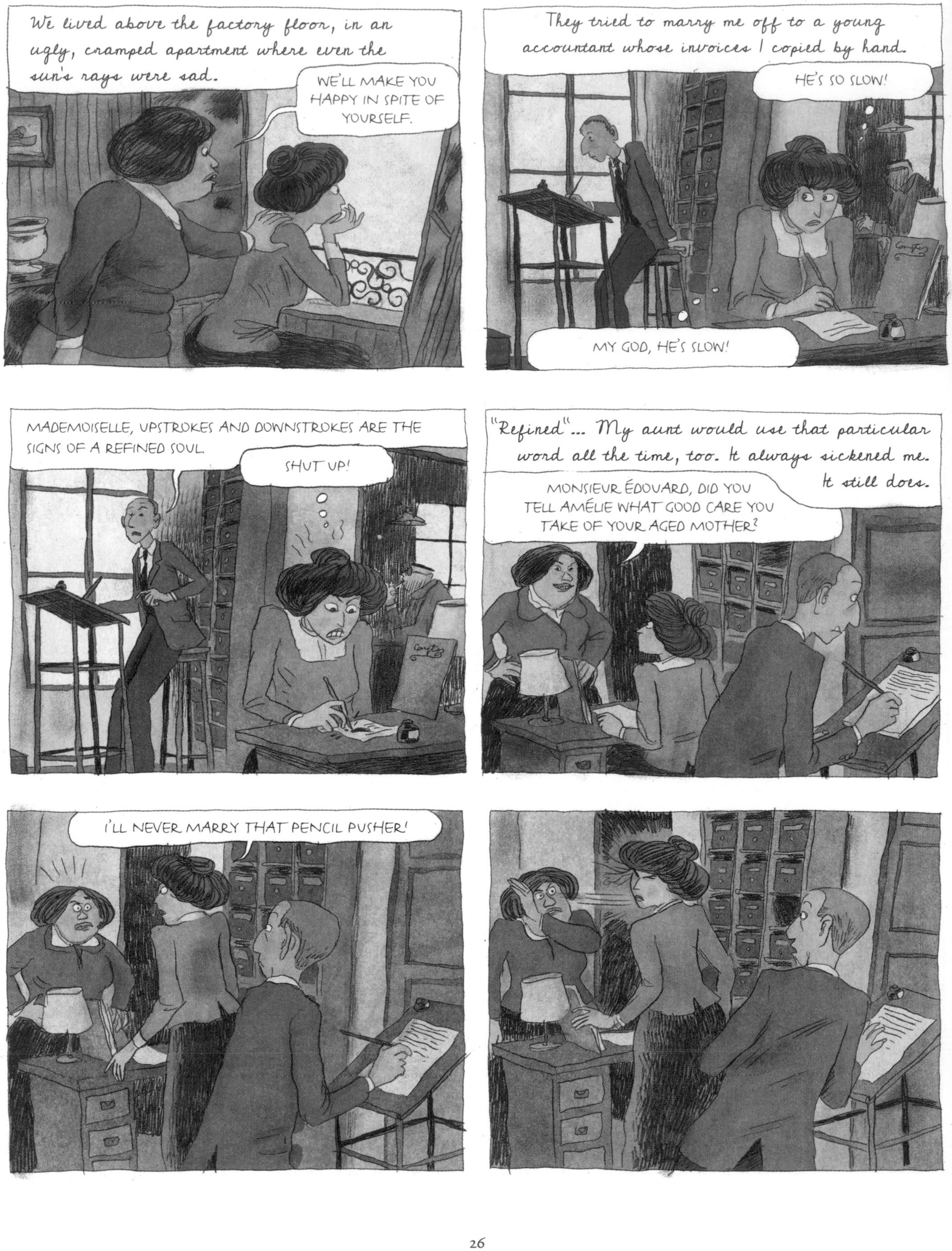
We lived above the factory floor, in an ugly, cramped apartment where even the sun's rays were sad.
WE'LL MAKE YOU HAPPY IN SPITE OF YOURSELF.
They tried to marry me off to a young accountant whose invoices I copied by hand.
HE'S SO SLOW!
MY GOD, HE'S SLOW!
MADEMOISELLE, UPSTROKES AND DOWNSTROKES ARE THE SIGNS OF A REFINED SOUL.
SHUT UP!
"Refined"... My aunt would use that particular word all the time, too. It always sickened me. It still does.
MONSIEUR ÉDOUARD, DID YOU TELL AMÉLIE WHAT GOOD CARE YOU TAKE OF YOUR AGED MOTHER?
I'LL NEVER MARRY THAT PENCIL PUSHER!

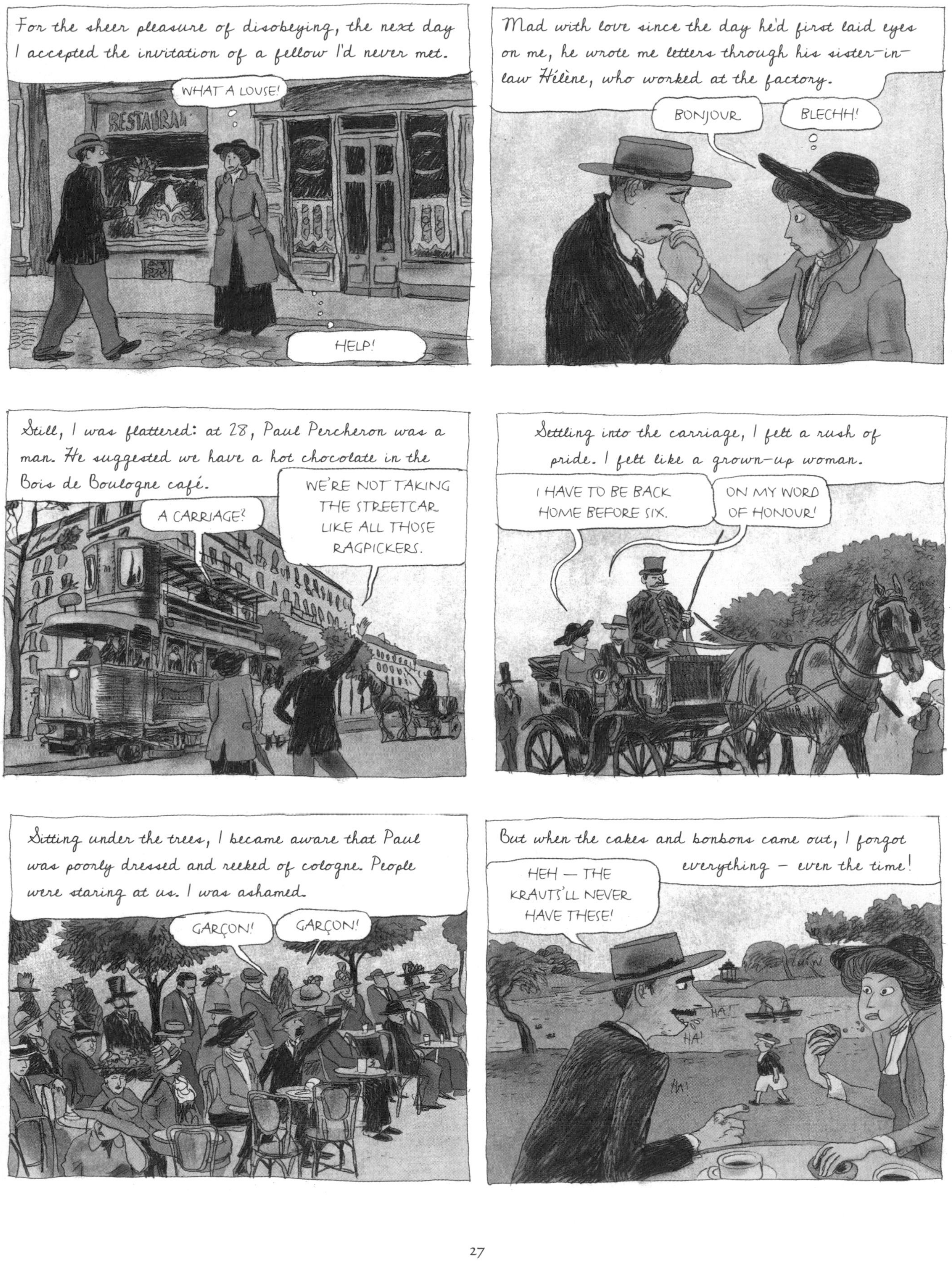
For the sheer pleasure of disobeying, the next day I accepted the invitation of a fellow I'd never met.
WHAT A LOUSE!
HELP!
Mad with love since the day he'd first laid eyes on me, he wrote me letters through his sister-in-law Hélène, who worked at the factory.
BONJOUR
BLECHH!
Still, I was flattered: at 28, Paul Percheron was a man. He suggested we have a hot chocolate in the Bois de Boulogne café.
A CARRIAGE?
WE'RE NOT TAKING THE STREETCAR LIKE ALL THOSE RAGPICKERS.
Settling into the carriage, I felt a rush of pride. I felt like a grown-up woman.
I HAVE TO BE BACK HOME BEFORE SIX.
ON MY WORD OF HONOUR!
Sitting under the trees, I became aware that Paul was poorly dressed and reeked of cologne. People were staring at us. I was ashamed.
GARÇON!
GARÇON!
But when the cakes and bonbons came out, I forgot everything – even the time!
HEH — THE KRAUTS'LL NEVER HAVE THESE!
HA!
HA!
HA!

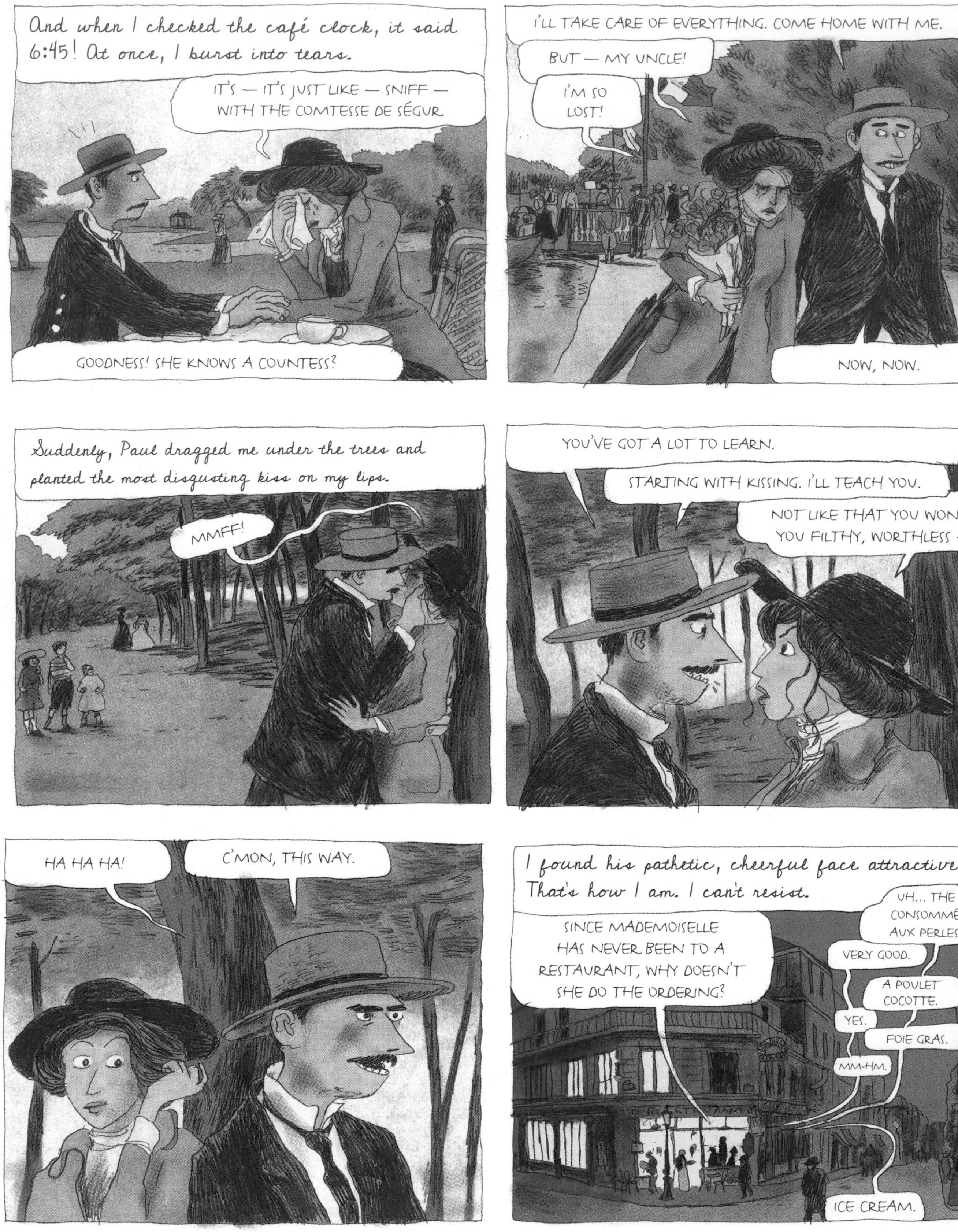
And when I checked the café clock, it said 6:45! At once, I burst into tears.
IT'S — IT'S JUST LIKE — SNIFF — WITH THE COMTESSE DE SÉGUR
GOODNESS! SHE KNOWS A COUNTESS?
I'LL TAKE CARE OF EVERYTHING. COME HOME WITH ME.
BUT — MY UNCLE!
I'M SO LOST!
NOW, NOW.
Suddenly, Paul dragged me under the trees and planted the most disgusting kiss on my lips.
MMFF!
YOU'VE GOT A LOT TO LEARN.
STARTING WITH KISSING. I'LL TEACH YOU.
NOT LIKE THAT YOU WON'T! YOU FILTHY, WORTHLESS —
HA HA HA!
C'MON, THIS WAY.
I found his pathetic, cheerful face attractive. That's how I am. I can't resist.
SINCE MADEMOISELLE HAS NEVER BEEN TO A RESTAURANT, WHY DOESN'T SHE DO THE ORDERING?
UH... THE CONSOMMÉ AUX PERLES.
VERY GOOD.
A POULET COCOTTE.
YES.
FOIE GRAS.
MM-HM.
ICE CREAM.

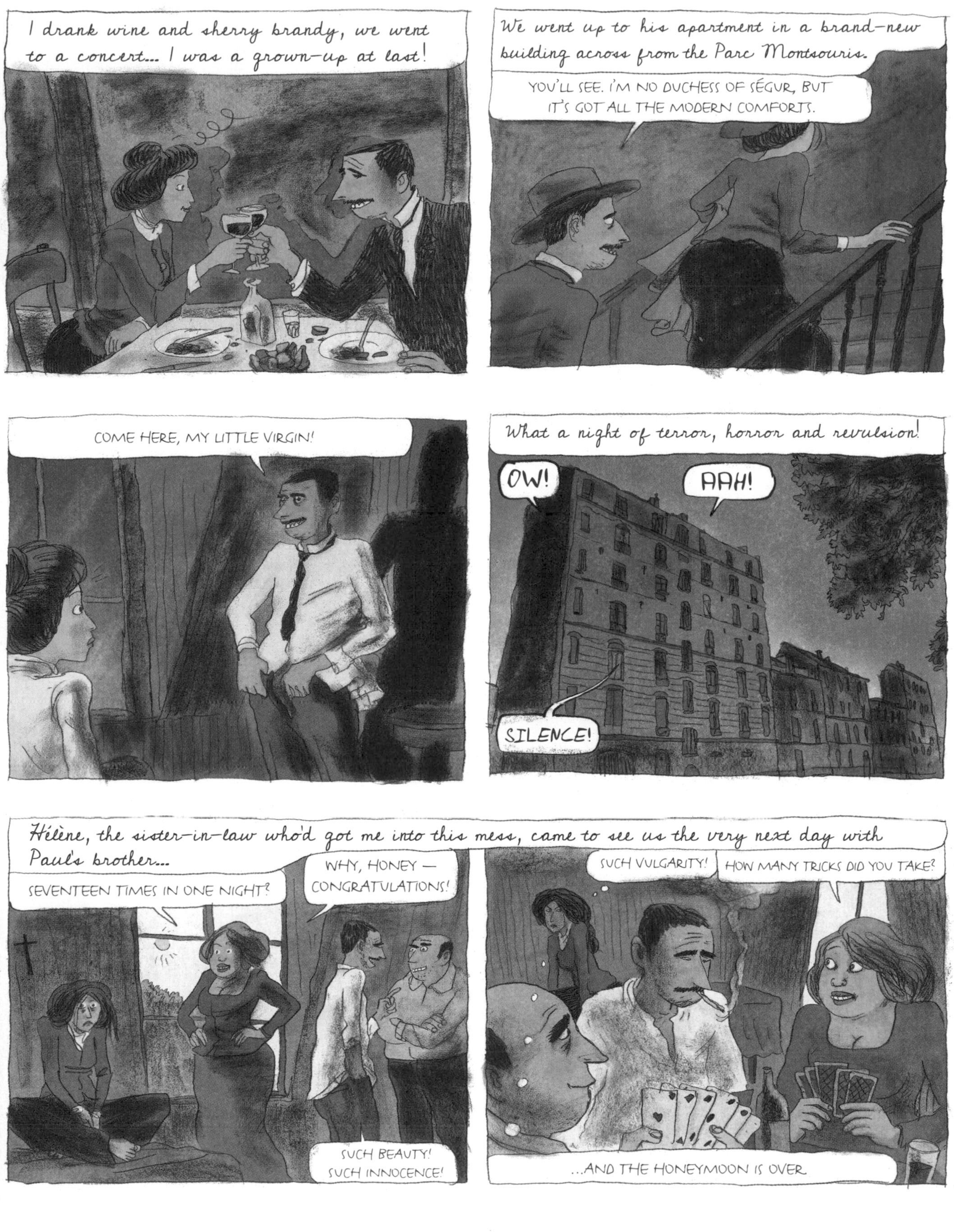
I drank wine and sherry brandy, we went to a concert... I was a grown-up at last!
We went up to his apartment in a brand-new building across from the Parc Montsouris.
YOU'LL SEE. I'M NO DUCHESS OF SÉGUR, BUT IT'S GOT ALL THE MODERN COMFORTS.
COME HERE, MY LITTLE VIRGIN!
What a night of terror, horror and revulsion!
OW!
AAH!
SILENCE!
Hélène, the sister-in-law who'd got me into this mess, came to see us the very next day with Paul's brother...
SEVENTEEN TIMES IN ONE NIGHT?
WHY, HONEY — CONGRATULATIONS!
SUCH BEAUTY! SUCH INNOCENCE!
SUCH VULGARITY!
HOW MANY TRICKS DID YOU TAKE?
...AND THE HONEYMOON IS OVER

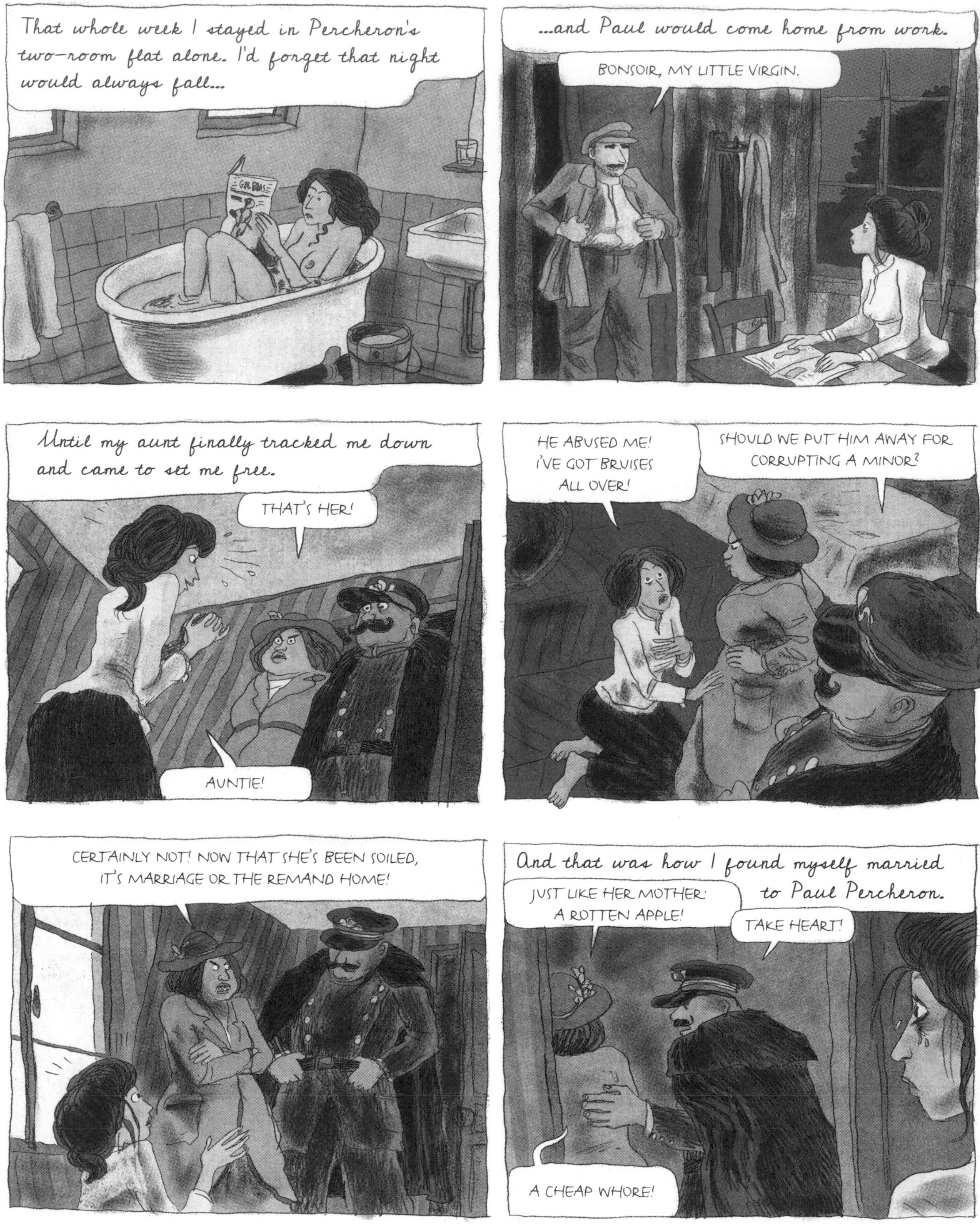
That whole week I stayed in Percheron's two-room flat alone. I'd forget that night would always fall...
...and Paul would come home from work.
BONSOIR, MY LITTLE VIRGIN.
Until my aunt finally tracked me down and came to set me free.
THAT'S HER!
AUNTIE!
HE ABUSED ME! I'VE GOT BRUISES ALL OVER!
SHOULD WE PUT HIM AWAY FOR CORRUPTING A MINOR?
CERTAINLY NOT! NOW THAT SHE'S BEEN SOILED, IT'S MARRIAGE OR THE REMAND HOME!
And that was how I found myself married to Paul Percheron.
JUST LIKE HER MOTHER: A ROTTEN APPLE!
TAKE HEART!
A CHEAP WHORE!

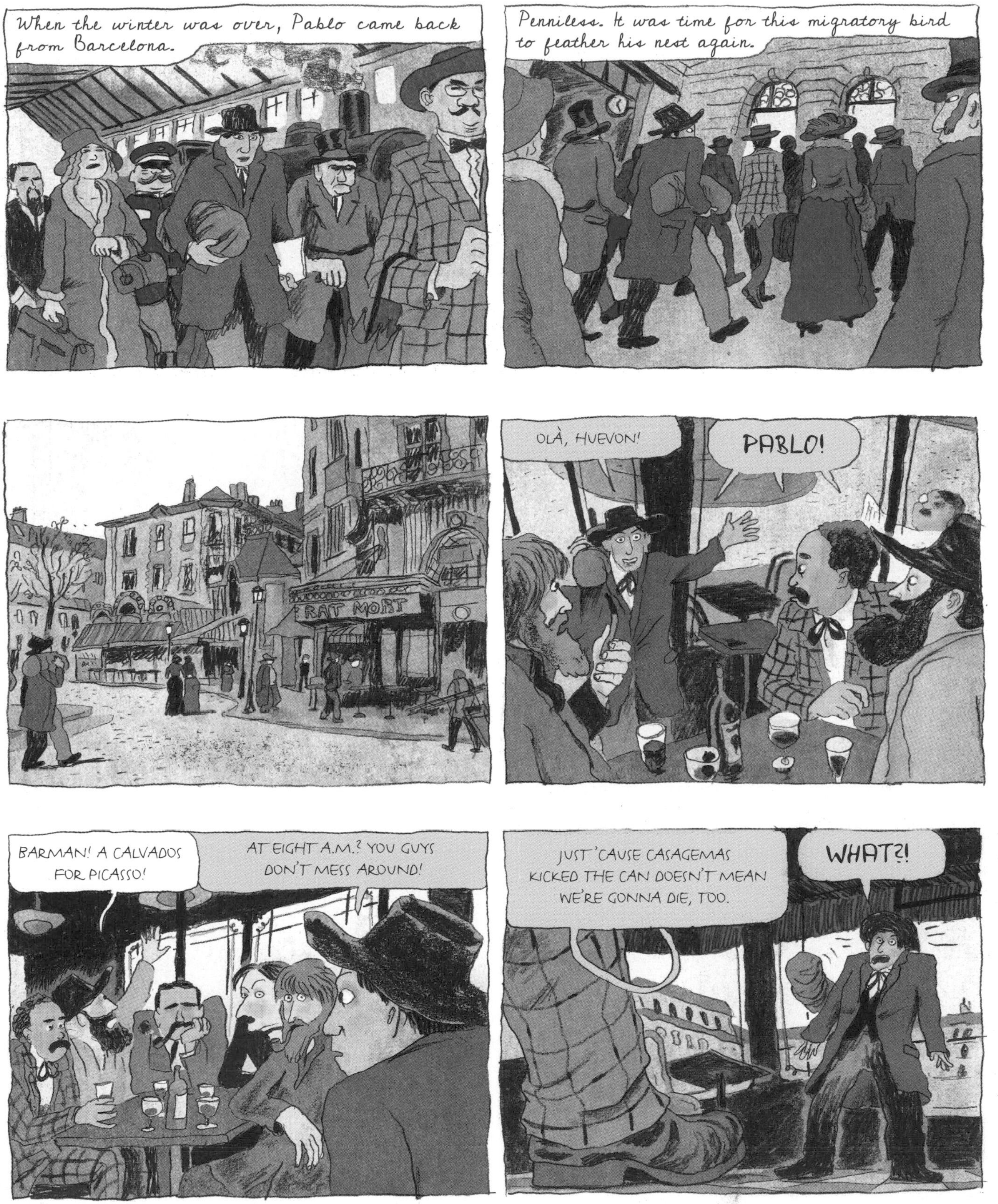
When the winter was over, Pablo came back from Barcelona.
Penniless. It was time for this migratory bird to feather his nest again.
RAT MORT
OLÀ, HUEVON!
PABLO!
BARMAN! A CALVADOS FOR PICASSO!
AT EIGHT A.M.? YOU GUYS DON'T MESS AROUND!
JUST 'CAUSE CASAGEMAS KICKED THE CAN DOESN'T MEAN WE'RE GONNA DIE, TOO.
WHAT?!

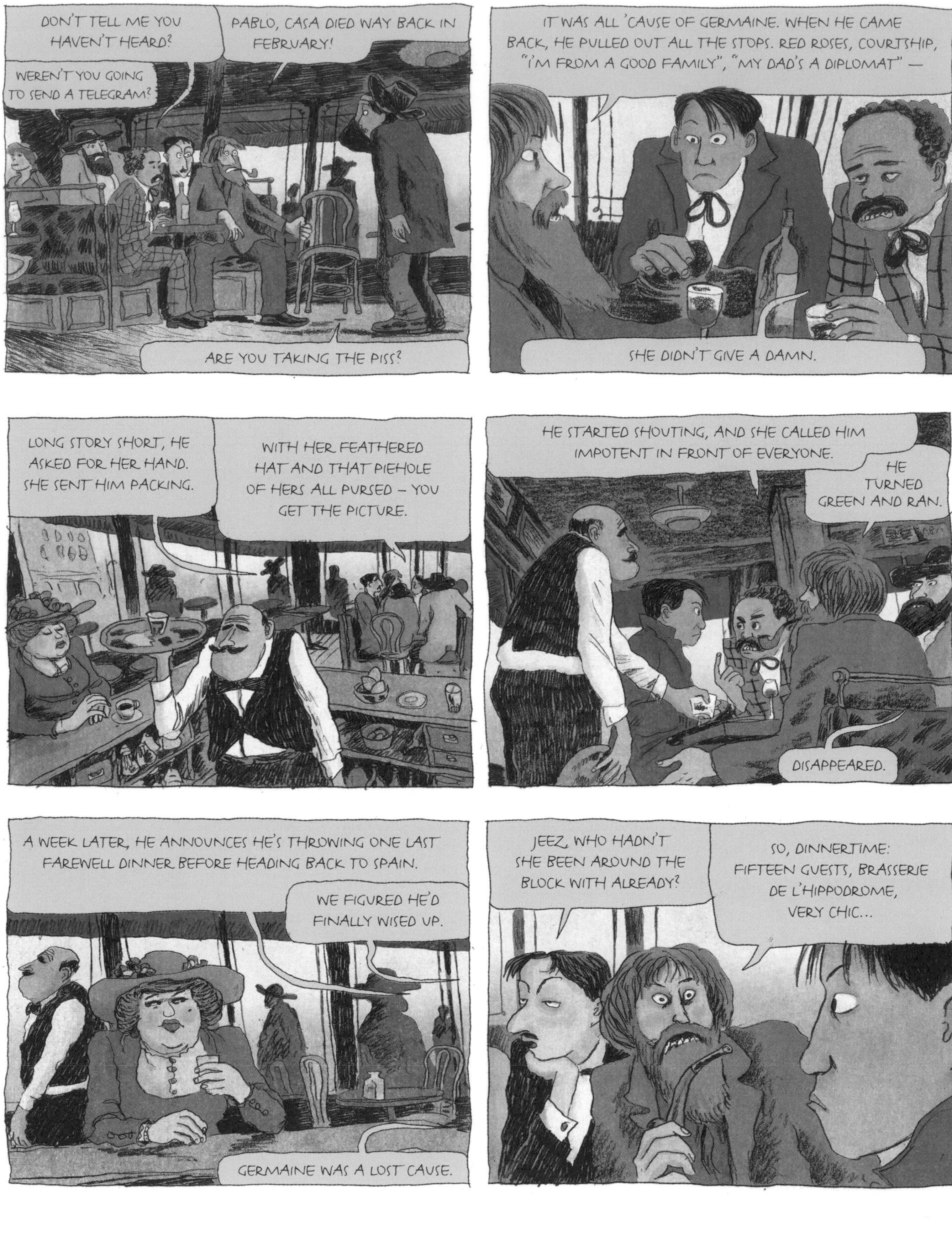
DON'T TELL ME YOU HAVEN'T HEARD?
WEREN'T YOU GOING TO SEND A TELEGRAM?
PABLO, CASA DIED WAY BACK IN FEBRUARY!
ARE YOU TAKING THE PISS?
IT WAS ALL 'CAUSE OF GERMAINE. WHEN HE CAME BACK, HE PULLED OUT ALL THE STOPS. RED ROSES, COURTSHIP, "I'M FROM A GOOD FAMILY", "MY DAD'S A DIPLOMAT" —
SHE DIDN'T GIVE A DAMN.
LONG STORY SHORT, HE ASKED FOR HER HAND. SHE SENT HIM PACKING.
WITH HER FEATHERED HAT AND THAT PIEHOLE OF HERS ALL PURSED – YOU GET THE PICTURE.
HE STARTED SHOUTING, AND SHE CALLED HIM IMPOTENT IN FRONT OF EVERYONE.
HE TURNED GREEN AND RAN.
DISAPPEARED.
A WEEK LATER, HE ANNOUNCES HE'S THROWING ONE LAST FAREWELL DINNER BEFORE HEADING BACK TO SPAIN.
WE FIGURED HE'D FINALLY WISED UP.
GERMAINE WAS A LOST CAUSE.
JEEZ, WHO HADN'T SHE BEEN AROUND THE BLOCK WITH ALREADY?
SO, DINNERTIME: FIFTEEN GUESTS, BRASSERIE DE L'HIPPODROME, VERY CHIC...

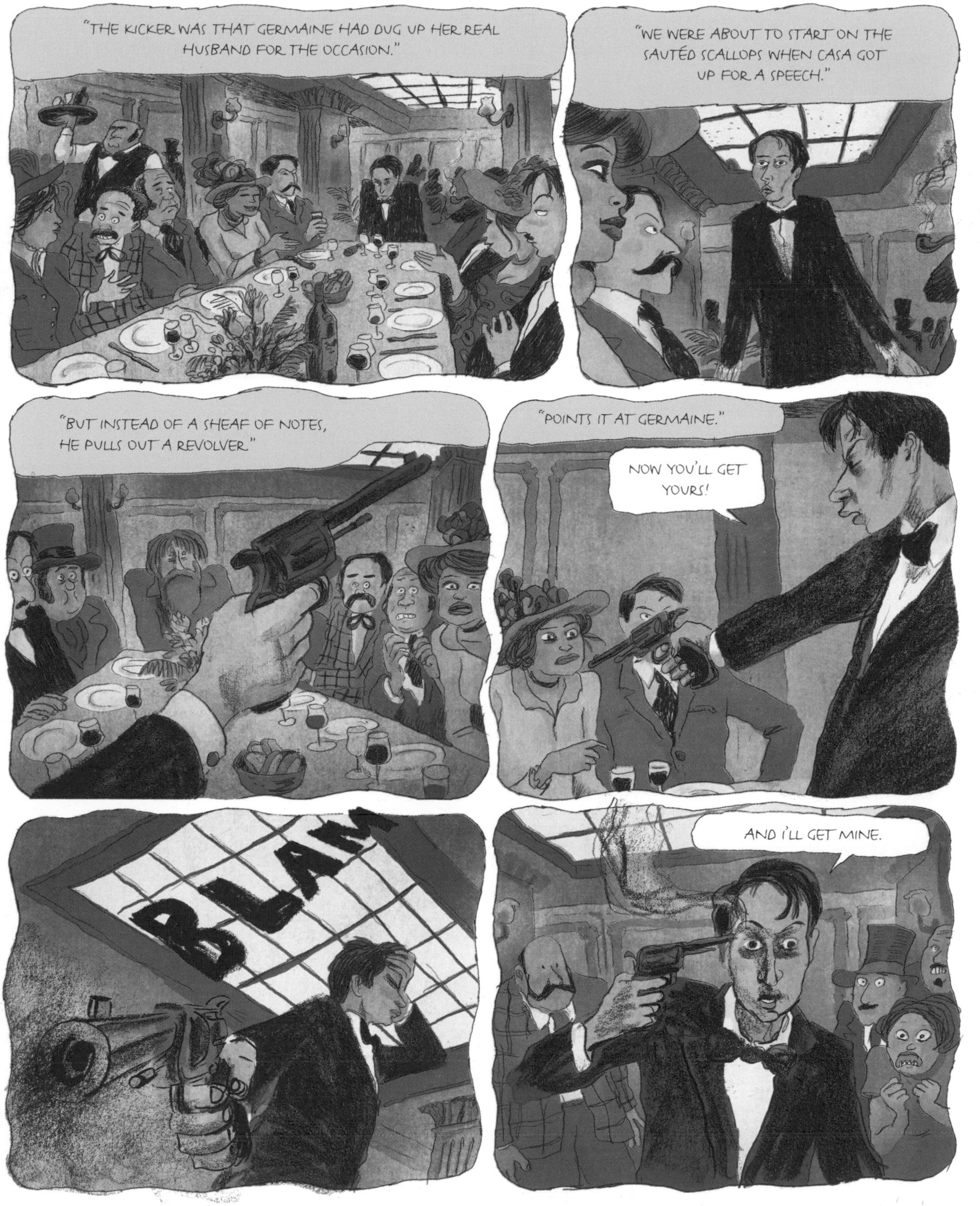
"THE KICKER WAS THAT GERMAINE HAD DUG UP HER REAL HUSBAND FOR THE OCCASION."
"WE WERE ABOUT TO START ON THE SAUTÉD SCALLOPS WHEN CASA GOT UP FOR A SPEECH."
"BUT INSTEAD OF A SHEAF OF NOTES, HE PULLS OUT A REVOLVER."
"POINTS IT AT GERMAINE."
NOW YOU'LL GET YOURS!
BLAM
AND I'LL GET MINE.

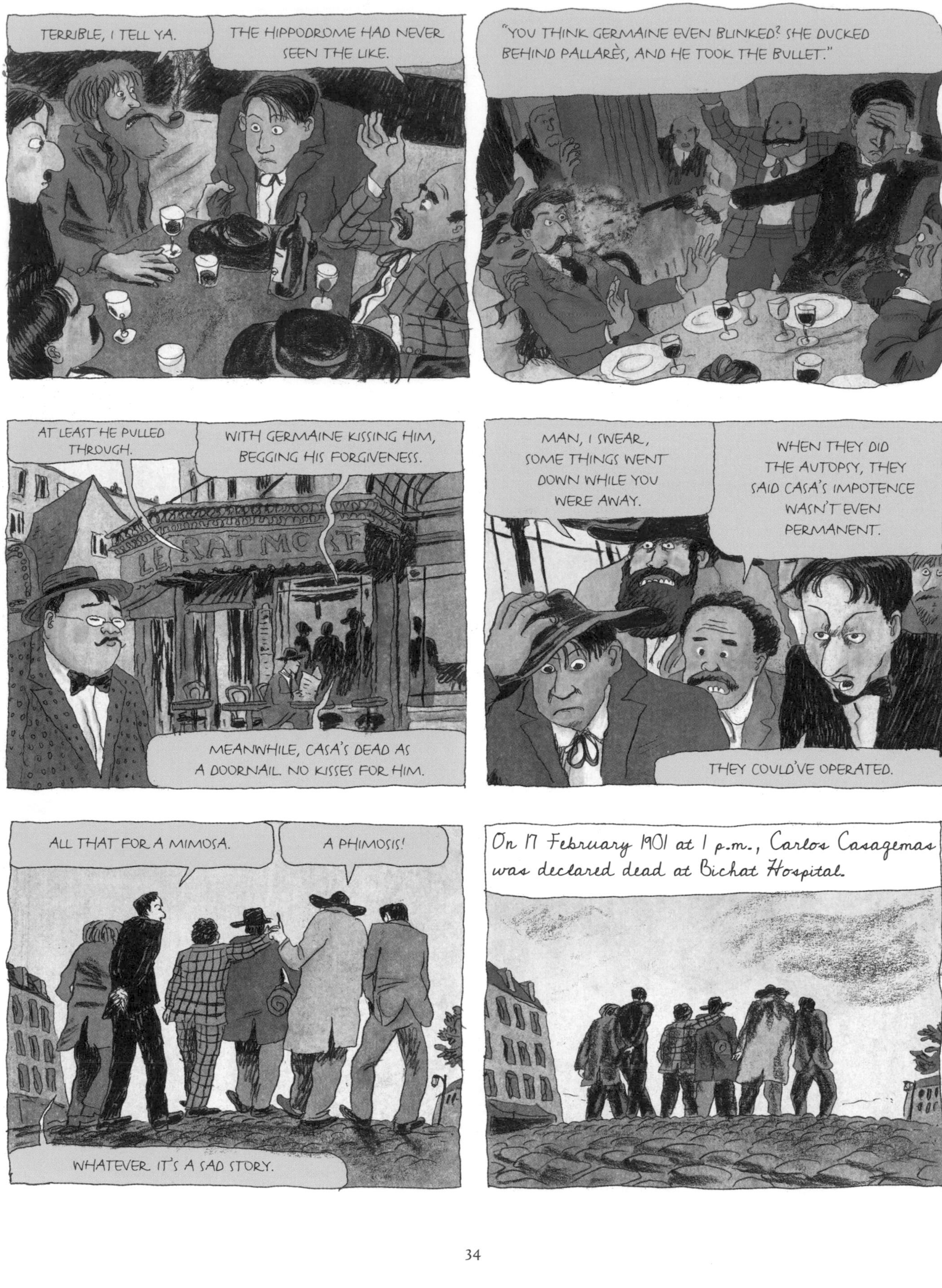
TERRIBLE, I TELL YA.
THE HIPPODROME HAD NEVER SEEN THE LIKE.
"YOU THINK GERMAINE EVEN BLINKED? SHE DUCKED BEHIND PALLARÈS, AND HE TOOK THE BULLET."
AT LEAST HE PULLED THROUGH.
WITH GERMAINE KISSING HIM, BEGGING HIS FORGIVENESS.
MEANWHILE, CASA'S DEAD AS A DOORNAIL. NO KISSES FOR HIM.
MAN, I SWEAR, SOME THINGS WENT DOWN WHILE YOU WERE AWAY.
WHEN THEY DID THE AUTOPSY, THEY SAID CASA'S IMPOTENCE WASN'T EVEN PERMANENT.
THEY COULD'VE OPERATED.
ALL THAT FOR A MIMOSA.
A PHIMOSIS!
WHATEVER. IT'S A SAD STORY.
On 17 February 1901 at 1 p.m., Carlos Casagemas was declared dead at Bichat Hospital.

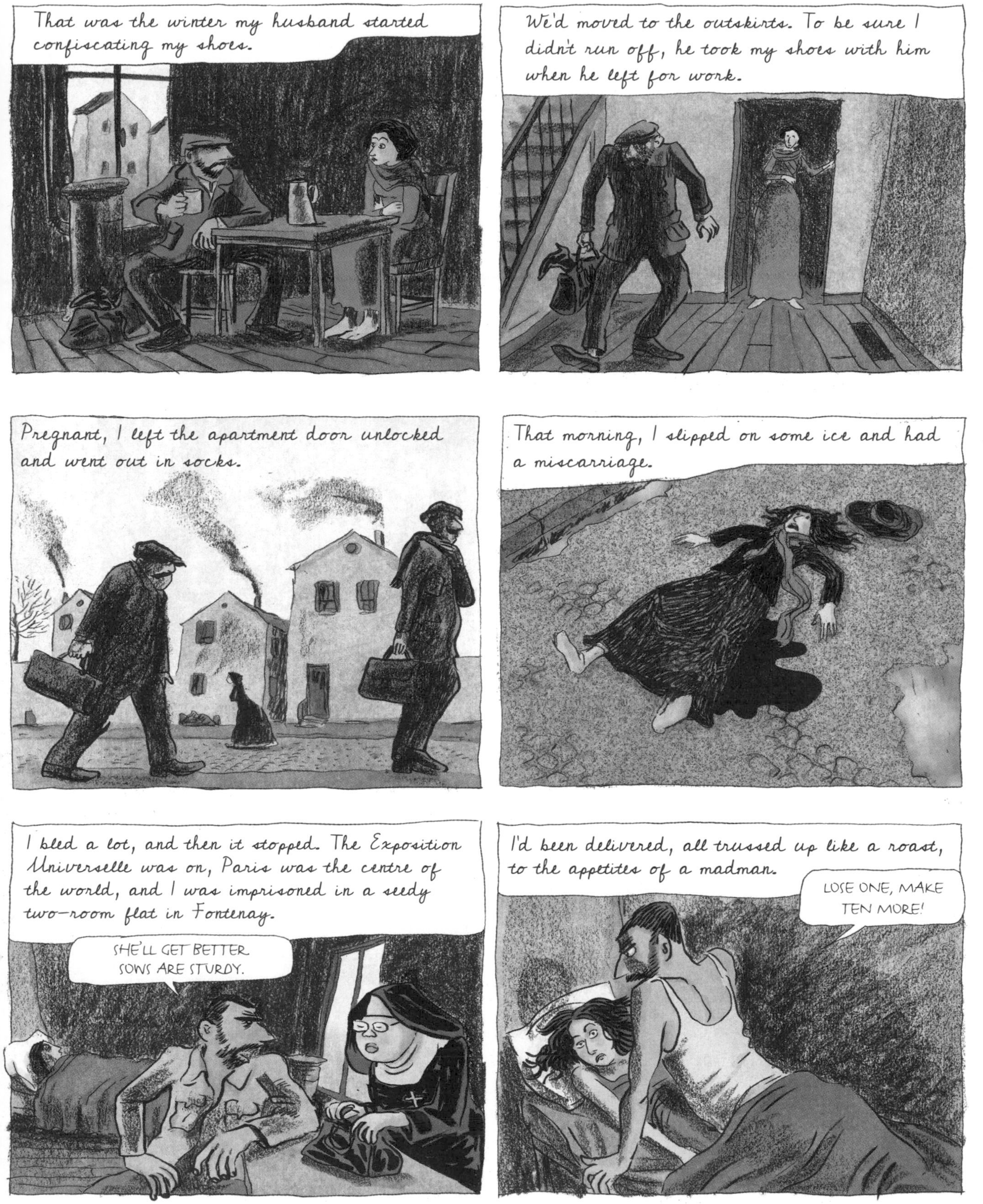
That was the winter my husband started confiscating my shoes.
We'd moved to the outskirts. To be sure I didn't run off, he took my shoes with him when he left for work.
Pregnant, I left the apartment door unlocked and went out in socks.
That morning, I slipped on some ice and had a miscarriage.
I bled a lot, and then it stopped. The Exposition Universelle was on, Paris was the centre of the world, and I was imprisoned in a seedy two-room flat in Fontenay.
SHE'LL GET BETTER SOWS ARE STURDY.
I'd been delivered, all trussed up like a roast, to the appetites of a madman.
LOSE ONE, MAKE TEN MORE!

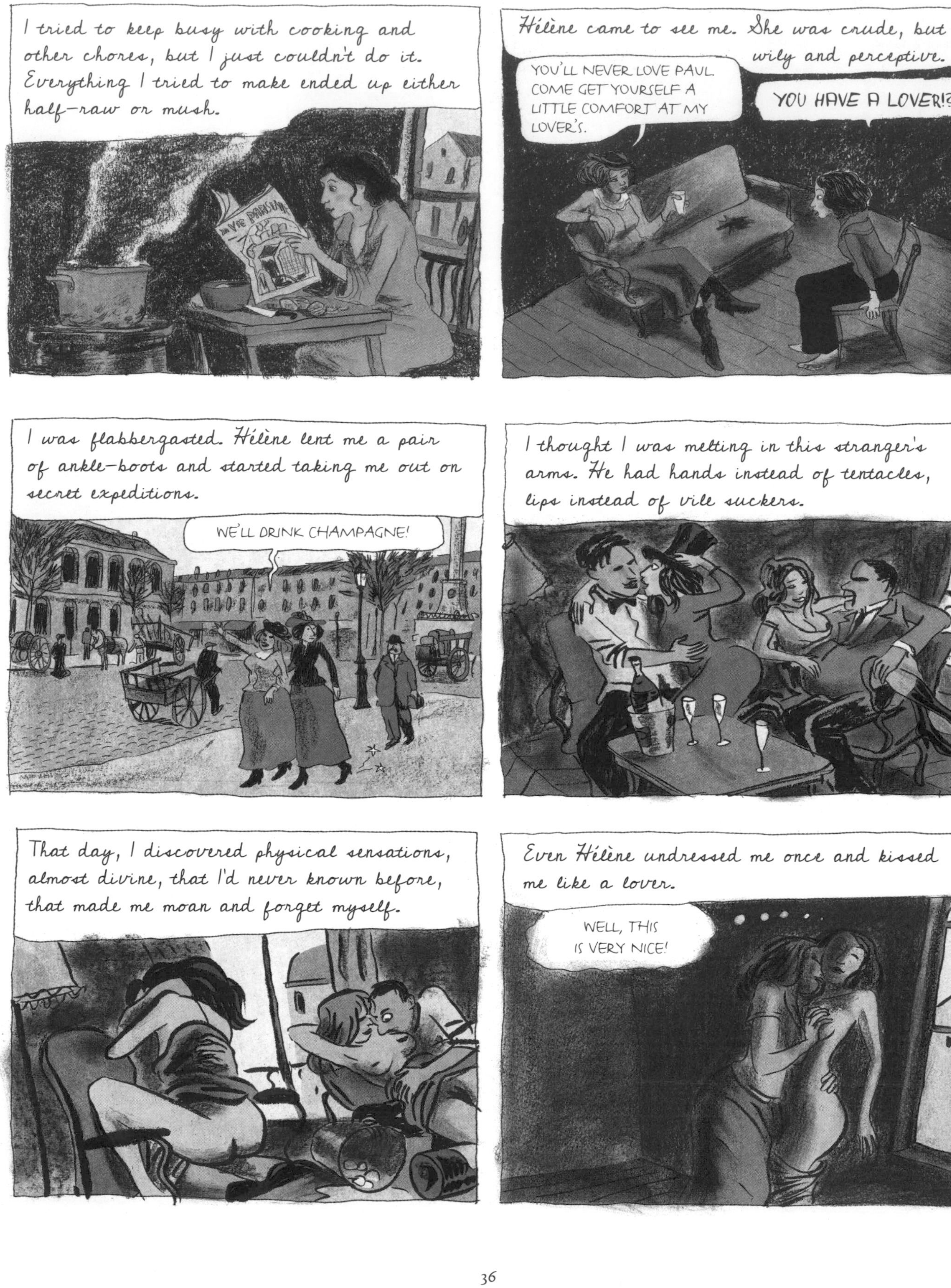
I tried to keep busy with cooking and other chores, but I just couldn't do it. Everything I tried to make ended up either half-raw or mush.
Hélène came to see me. She was crude, but wily and perceptive.
YOU'LL NEVER LOVE PAUL. COME GET YOURSELF A LITTLE COMFORT AT MY LOVER'S.
YOU HAVE A LOVER!?
I was flabbergasted. Hélène lent me a pair of ankle-boots and started taking me out on secret expeditions.
WE'LL DRINK CHAMPAGNE!
I thought I was melting in this stranger's arms. He had hands instead of tentacles, lips instead of vile suckers.
That day, I discovered physical sensations, almost divine, that I'd never known before, that made me moan and forget myself.
Even Hélène undressed me once and kissed me like a lover.
WELL, THIS IS VERY NICE!

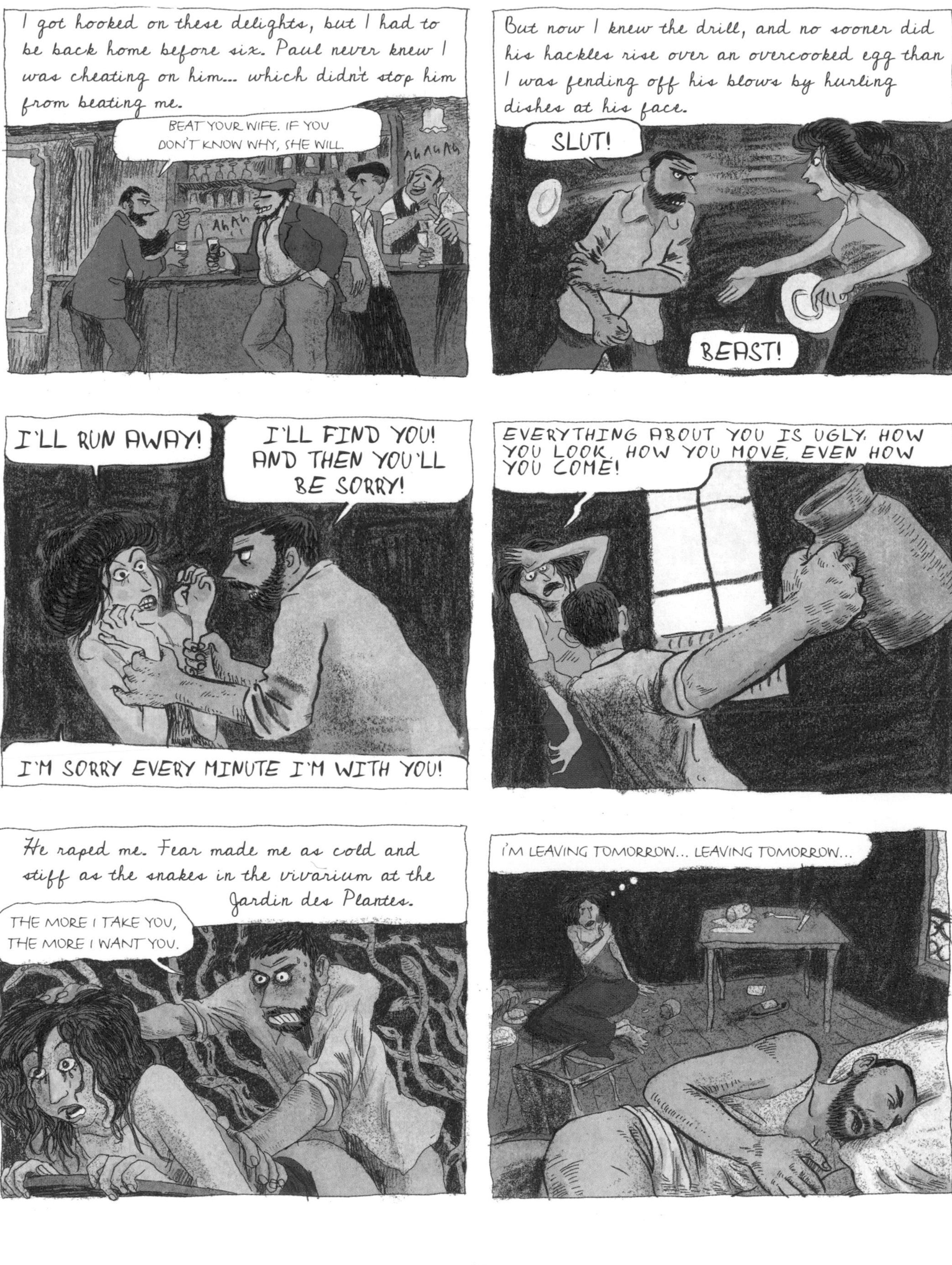
I got hooked on these delights, but I had to be back home before six. Paul never knew I was cheating on him... which didn't stop him from beating me.
BEAT YOUR WIFE. IF YOU DON'T KNOW WHY, SHE WILL.
But now I knew the drill, and no sooner did his hackles rise over an overcooked egg than I was fending off his blows by hurling dishes at his face.
SLUT!
BEAST!
I'LL RUN AWAY!
I'LL FIND YOU! AND THEN YOU'LL BE SORRY!
I'M SORRY EVERY MINUTE I'M WITH YOU!
EVERYTHING ABOUT YOU IS UGLY. HOW YOU LOOK, HOW YOU MOVE, EVEN HOW YOU COME!
He raped me. Fear made me as cold and stiff as the snakes in the vivarium at the Jardin des Plantes.
THE MORE I TAKE YOU, THE MORE I WANT YOU.
I'M LEAVING TOMORROW... LEAVING TOMORROW...

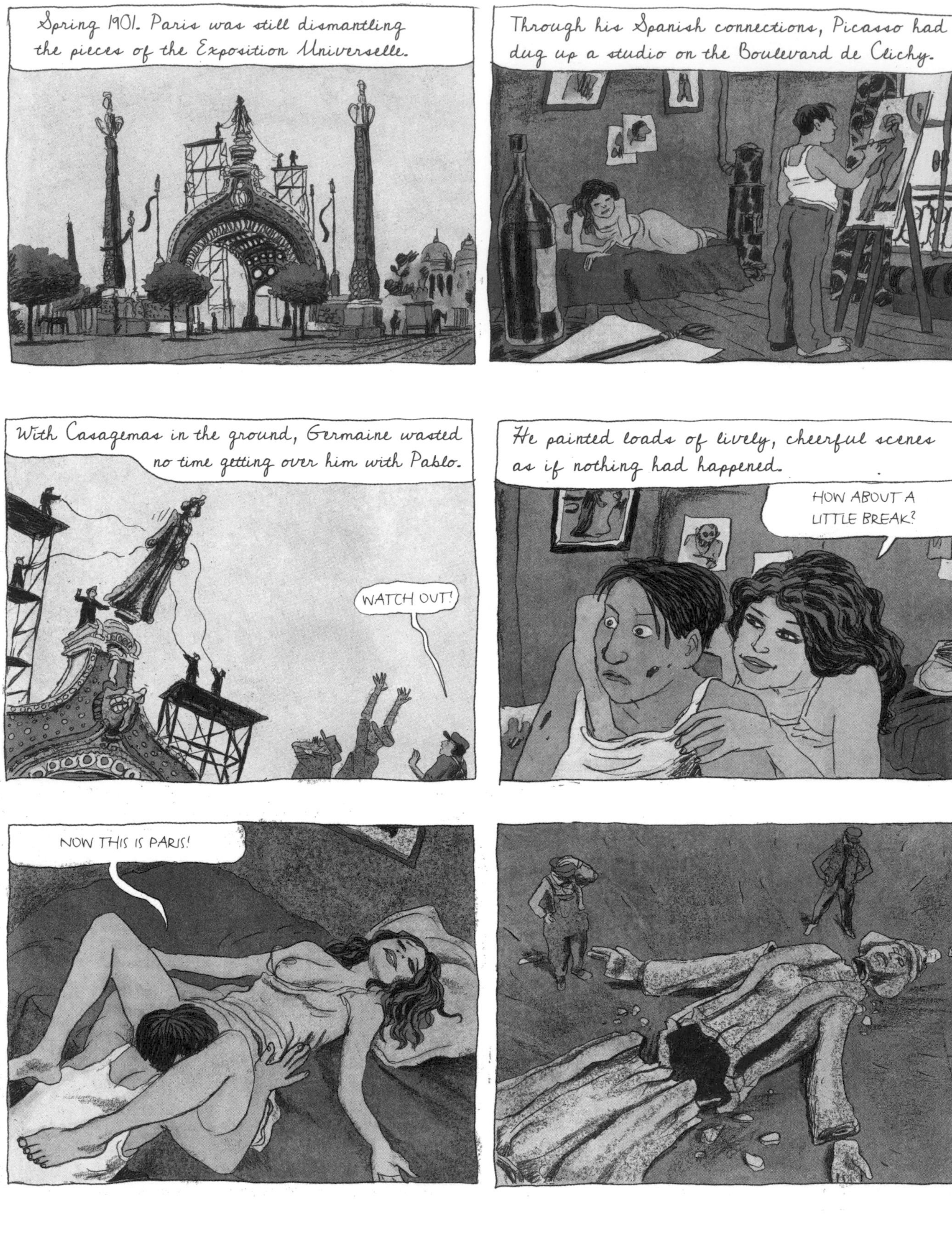
Spring 1901. Paris was still dismantling the pieces of the Exposition Universelle.
Through his Spanish connections, Picasso had dug up a studio on the Boulevard de Clichy.
With Casagemas in the ground, Germaine wasted no time getting over him with Pablo.
WATCH OUT!
He painted loads of lively, cheerful scenes as if nothing had happened.
HOW ABOUT A LITTLE BREAK?
NOW THIS IS PARIS!

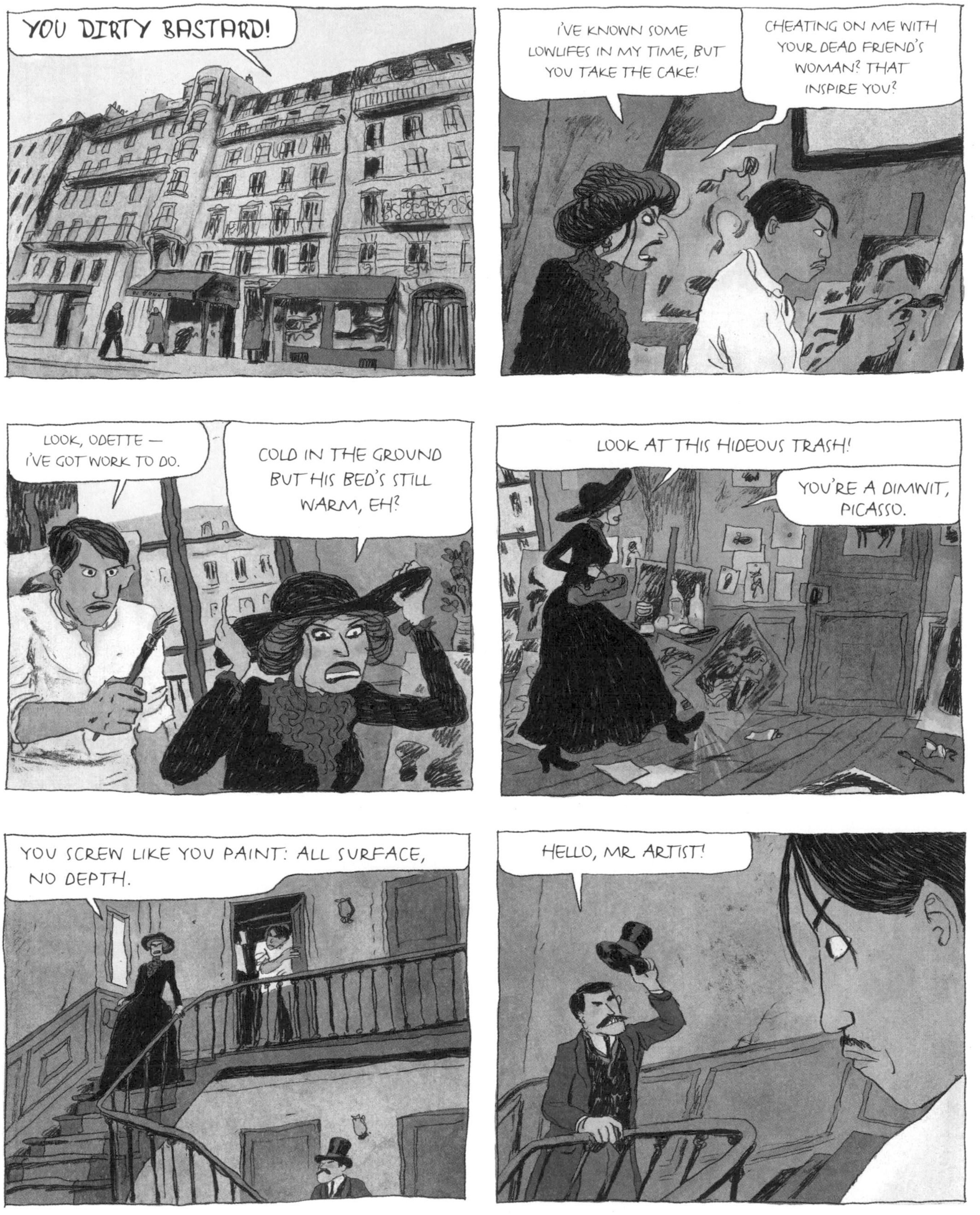
YOU DIRTY BASTARD!
I'VE KNOWN SOME LOWLIFES IN MY TIME, BUT YOU TAKE THE CAKE!
CHEATING ON ME WITH YOUR DEAD FRIEND'S WOMAN? THAT INSPIRE YOU?
LOOK, ODETTE — I'VE GOT WORK TO DO.
COLD IN THE GROUND BUT HIS BED'S STILL WARM, EH?
LOOK AT THIS HIDEOUS TRASH!
YOU'RE A DIMWIT, PICASSO.
YOU SCREW LIKE YOU PAINT: ALL SURFACE, NO DEPTH.
HELLO, MR. ARTIST!

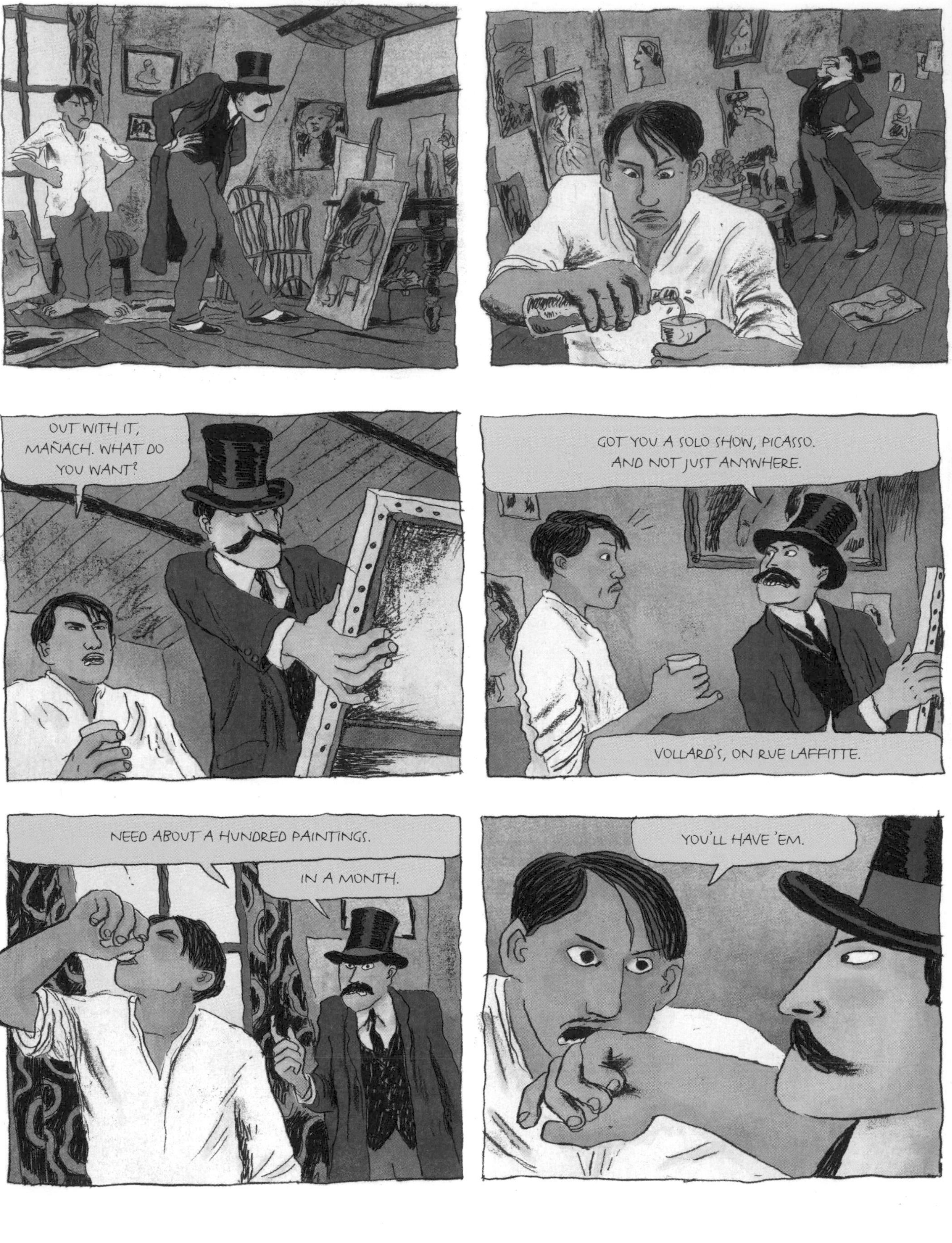
OUT WITH IT, MAÑACH. WHAT DO YOU WANT?
GOT YOU A SOLO SHOW, PICASSO. AND NOT JUST ANYWHERE.
VOLLARD'S, ON RUE LAFFITTE.
NEED ABOUT A HUNDRED PAINTINGS.
IN A MONTH.
YOU'LL HAVE 'EM.

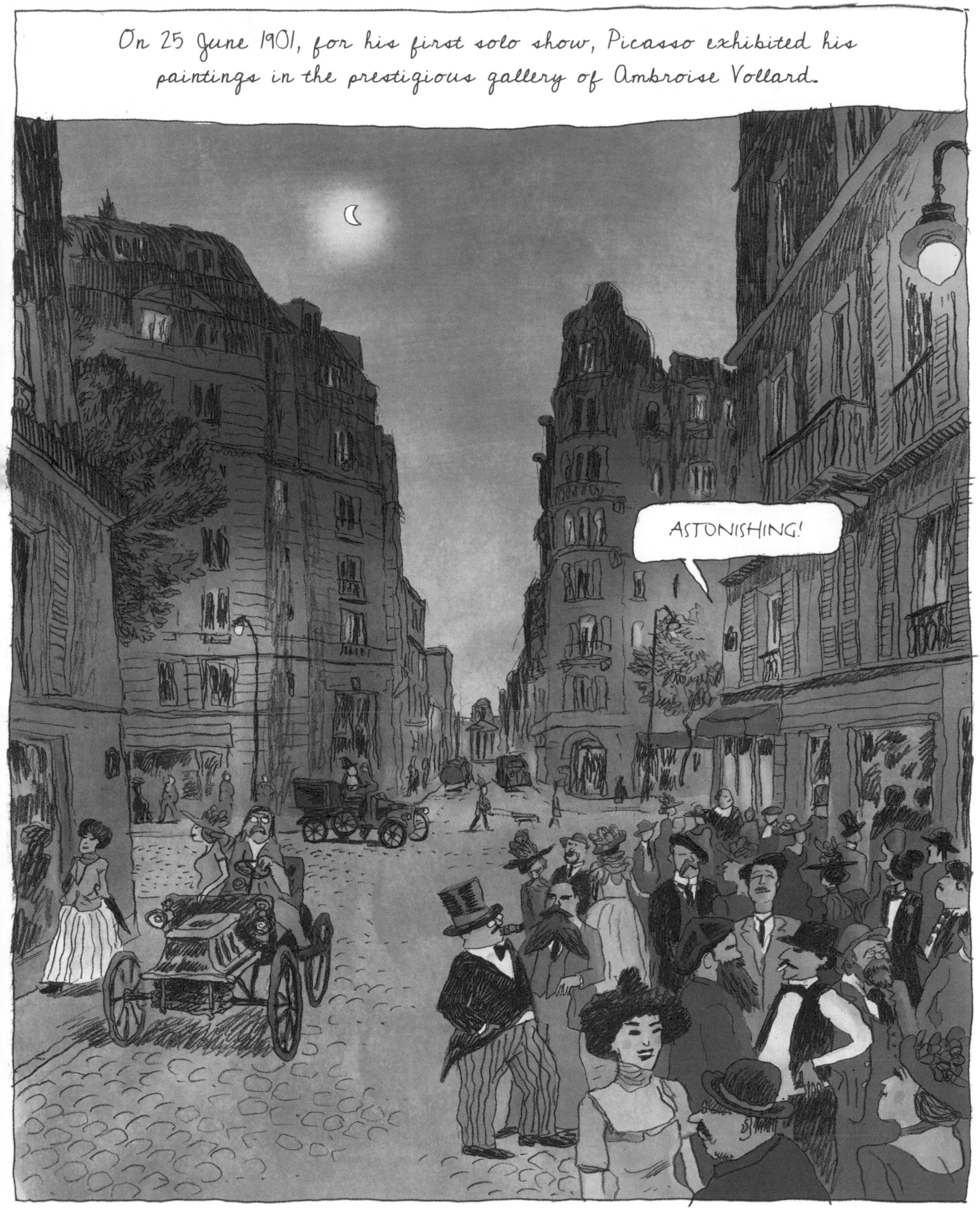
On 25 June 1901, for his first solo show, Picasso exhibited his paintings in the prestigious gallery of Ambroise Vollard.
ASTONISHING!

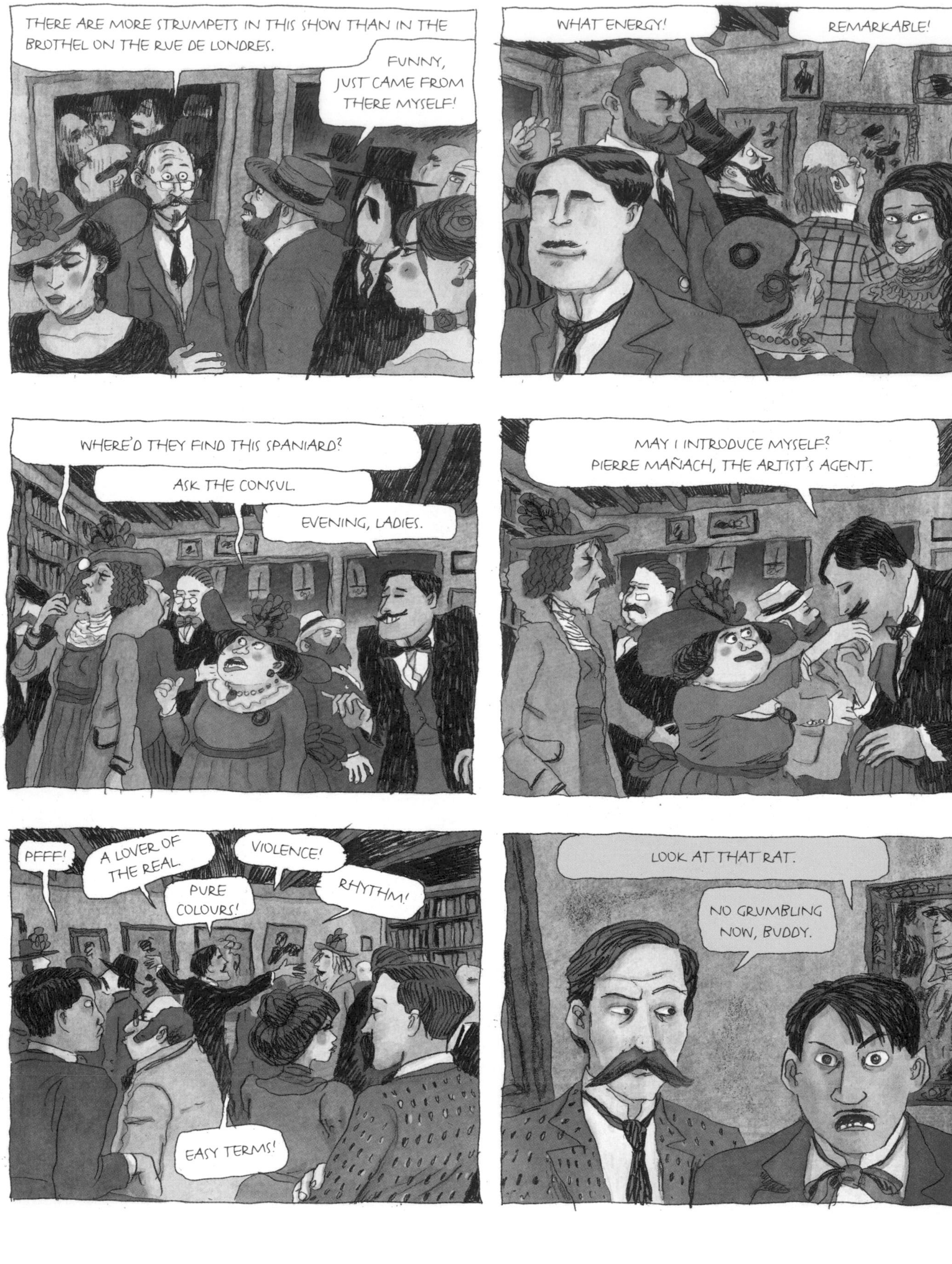
THERE ARE MORE STRUMPETS IN THIS SHOW THAN IN THE BROTHEL ON THE RUE DE LONDRES.
FUNNY, JUST CAME FROM THERE MYSELF!
WHAT ENERGY!
REMARKABLE!
WHERE'D THEY FIND THIS SPANIARD?
ASK THE CONSUL.
EVENING, LADIES.
MAY I INTRODUCE MYSELF? PIERRE MAÑACH, THE ARTIST'S AGENT.
PFFF!
A LOVER OF THE REAL.
VIOLENCE!
PURE COLOURS!
RHYTHM!
EASY TERMS!
LOOK AT THAT RAT.
NO GRUMBLING NOW, BUDDY.

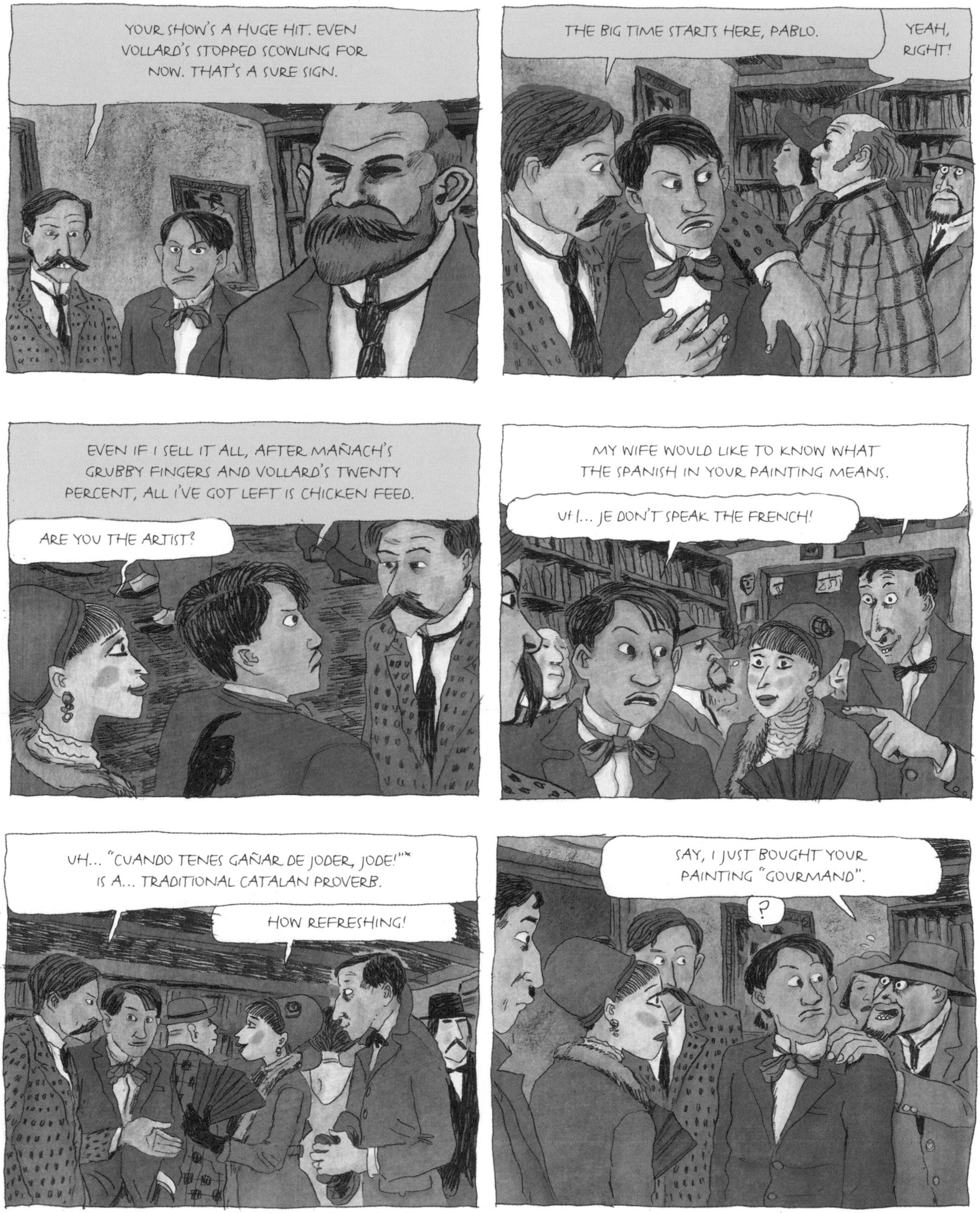
YOUR SHOW'S A HUGE HIT. EVEN VOLLARD'S STOPPED SCOWLING FOR NOW. THAT'S A SURE SIGN.
THE BIG TIME STARTS HERE, PABLO.
YEAH, RIGHT!
EVEN IF I SELL IT ALL, AFTER MAÑACH'S GRUBBY FINGERS AND VOLLARD'S TWENTY PERCENT, ALL I'VE GOT LEFT IS CHICKEN FEED.
ARE YOU THE ARTIST?
MY WIFE WOULD LIKE TO KNOW WHAT THE SPANISH IN YOUR PAINTING MEANS.
UH... JE DON'T SPEAK THE FRENCH!
UH... "CUANDO TENES GAÑAR DE JODER, JODE!"* IS A... TRADITIONAL CATALAN PROVERB.
HOW REFRESHING!
SAY, I JUST BOUGHT YOUR PAINTING "GOURMAND".
?

* "WHEN YOU WANT TO FUCK, FUCK!"

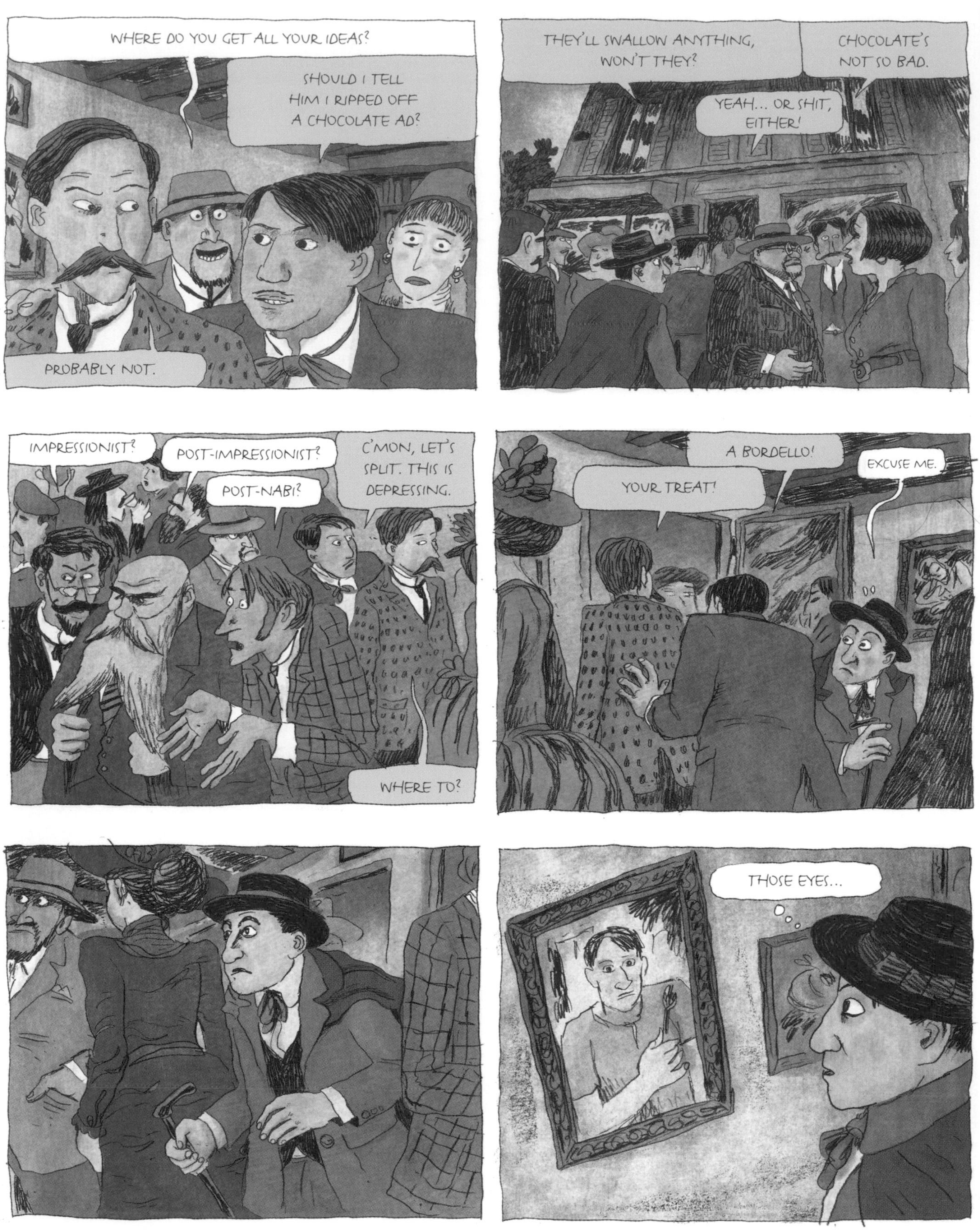

WHERE DO YOU GET ALL YOUR IDEAS?
SHOULD I TELL HIM I RIPPED OFF A CHOCOLATE AD?
PROBABLY NOT.
THEY'LL SWALLOW ANYTHING, WON'T THEY?
CHOCOLATE'S NOT SO BAD.
YEAH... OR SHIT, EITHER!
IMPRESSIONIST?
POST-IMPRESSIONIST?
POST-NABI?
C'MON, LET'S SPLIT. THIS IS DEPRESSING.
WHERE TO?
A BORDELLO!
YOUR TREAT!
EXCUSE ME.
THOSE EYES...

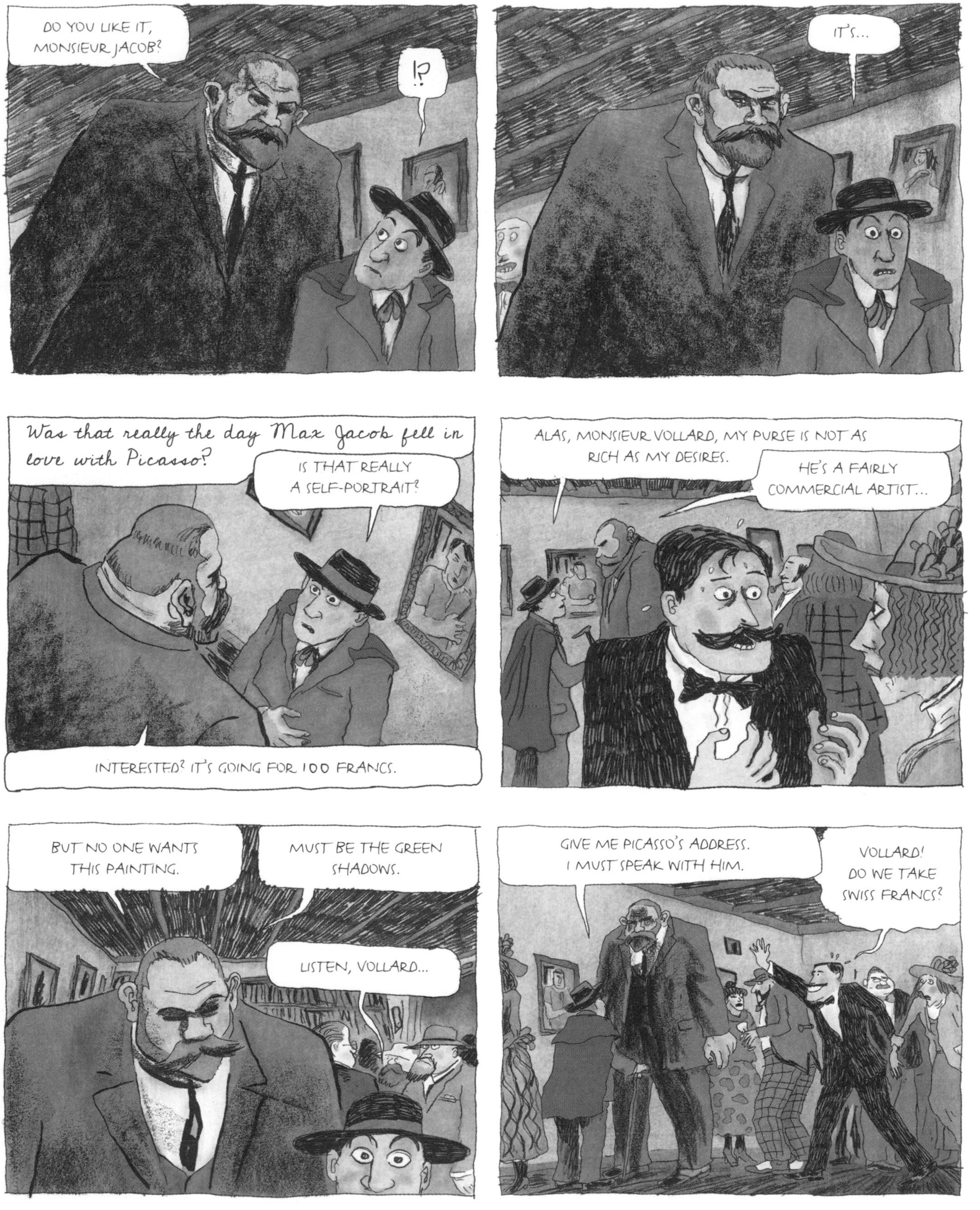
DO YOU LIKE IT, MONSIEUR JACOB?
!?
IT'S...
Was that really the day Max Jacob fell in love with Picasso?
IS THAT REALLY A SELF-PORTRAIT?
INTERESTED? IT'S GOING FOR 100 FRANCS.
ALAS, MONSIEUR VOLLARD, MY PURSE IS NOT AS RICH AS MY DESIRES.
HE'S A FAIRLY COMMERCIAL ARTIST...
BUT NO ONE WANTS THIS PAINTING.
MUST BE THE GREEN SHADOWS.
LISTEN, VOLLARD...
GIVE ME PICASSO'S ADDRESS. I MUST SPEAK WITH HIM.
VOLLARD! DO WE TAKE SWISS FRANCS?

He couldn't help it.

Max Jacob had to meet Picasso.

HEAVENS...

I SHOULD'VE WORN PAPA'S CAPE.

IF IT'S ODETTE AGAIN, I'M THROWING HER OUT.

KNOCK

YES?

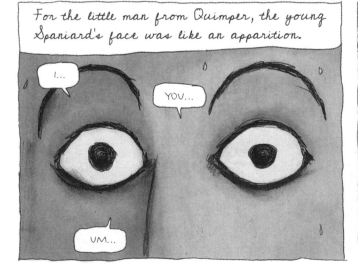
For the little man from Quimper, the young Spaniard's face was like an apparition.

I...

YOU...

UM...

A face like ivory, unblemished, fiery eyes beneath a lock of crow-black hair.

PLEASE BE SO KIND AS TO PARDON MY PRESUMPTUOUSNESS...

SHIT, I CAN'T UNDERSTAND A WORD...

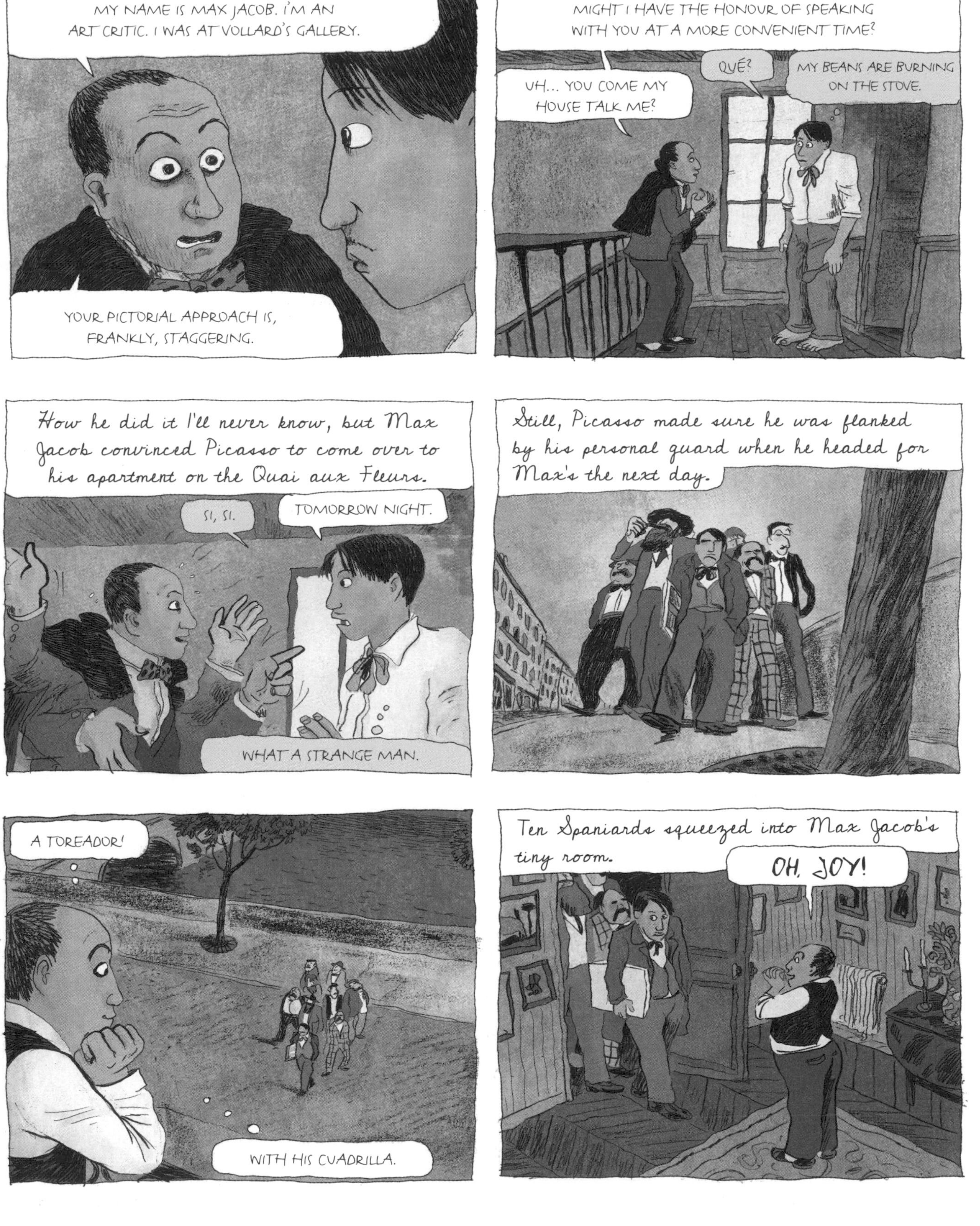
MY NAME IS MAX JACOB. I'M AN ART CRITIC. I WAS AT VOLLARD'S GALLERY.
YOUR PICTORIAL APPROACH IS, FRANKLY, STAGGERING.
MIGHT I HAVE THE HONOUR OF SPEAKING WITH YOU AT A MORE CONVENIENT TIME?
UH... YOU COME MY HOUSE TALK ME?
QUÉ?
MY BEANS ARE BURNING ON THE STOVE.
How he did it I'll never know, but Max Jacob convinced Picasso to come over to his apartment on the Quai aux Fleurs.
SI, SI.
TOMORROW NIGHT.
WHAT A STRANGE MAN.
Still, Picasso made sure he was flanked by his personal guard when he headed for Max's the next day.
A TOREADOR!
WITH HIS CUADRILLA.
Ten Spaniards squeezed into Max Jacob's tiny room.
OH, JOY!

PABLO BROUGHT STUFF TO DRAW YOUR PORTRAIT.

FOUND THE GLASSES!

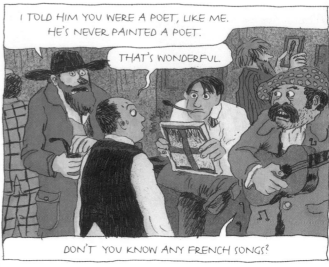

I TOLD HIM YOU WERE A POET, LIKE ME. HE'S NEVER PAINTED A POET.

THAT'S WONDERFUL.

DON'T YOU KNOW ANY FRENCH SONGS?

NO... BUT I CAN RECITE VERLAINE, IF YOU WISH.

GARLIC SAUSAGE!

HOORAY!

DA DEE DA DUM DUM

"IT RAINS IN MY HEART / AS IT RAINS ON THE TOWN / WHAT LANGUOR SO DARK / THAT SOAKS TO MY HEART?"

DA DEE DA DUM DUM

STOP PLAYING BEETHOVEN, CABRÓN!

"OH, SWEET SOUND OF RAIN / ON THE EARTH AND THE ROOFS! / FOR THE HEART DULL AGAIN / OH THE SONG OF THE RAIN!"

TO ANARCHY!

TO WOMEN!

SALUD!

"IT RAINS FOR NO REASON / IN THIS HEART LACKING HEART. / WHAT? AND NO TREASON? / IT'S GRIEF WITHOUT REASON."

HEY, THAT'S NOT BAD.

"AND NOTHING PAINS ME SO / WITH NEITHER LOVE NOR HATE / AS SIMPLY NOT TO KNOW / WHY MY HEART SUFFERS SO."

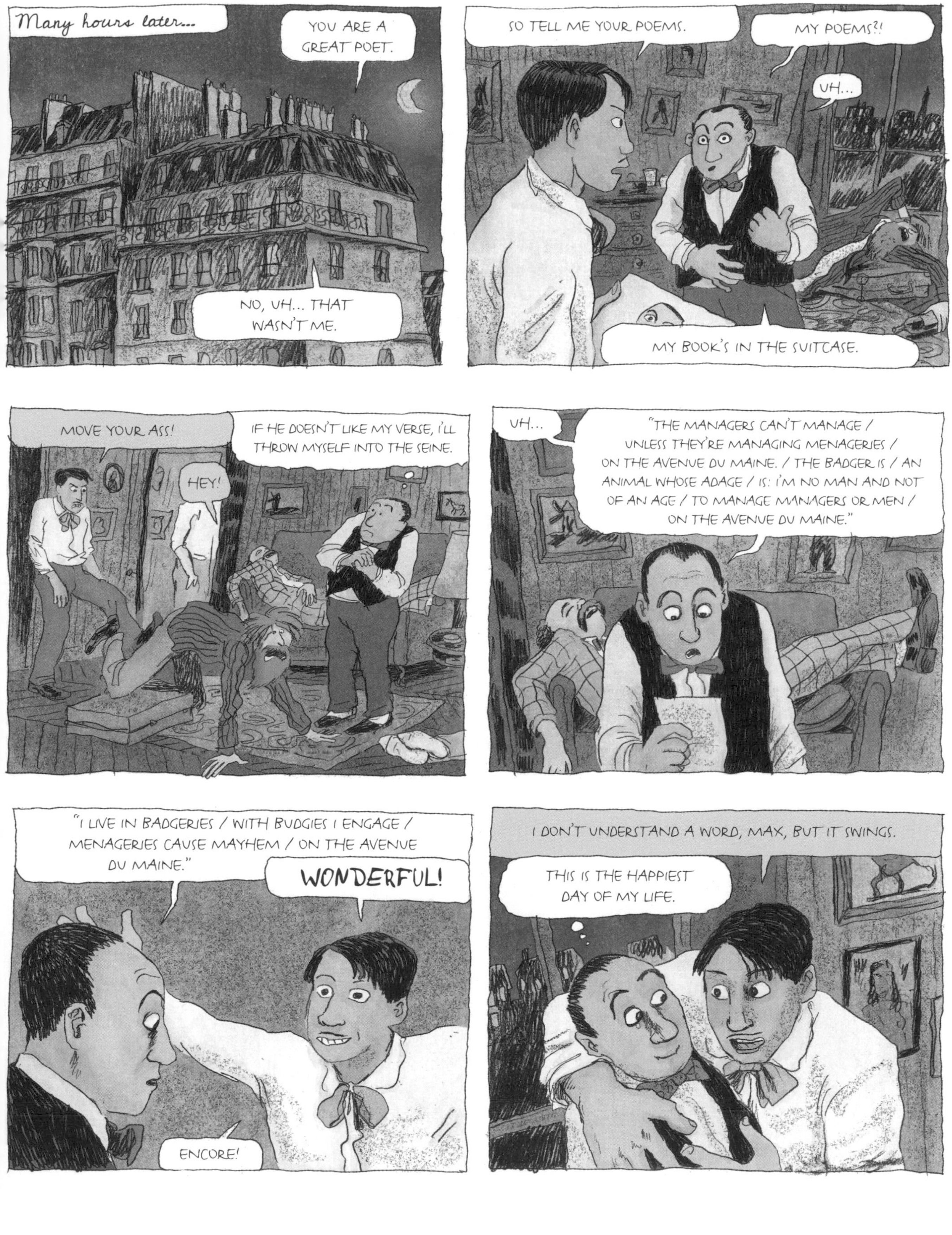
Many hours later...
YOU ARE A GREAT POET.
NO, UH... THAT WASN'T ME.
SO TELL ME YOUR POEMS.
MY POEMS?!
UH...
MY BOOK'S IN THE SUITCASE.
MOVE YOUR ASS!
IF HE DOESN'T LIKE MY VERSE, I'LL THROW MYSELF INTO THE SEINE.
HEY!
UH...
"THE MANAGERS CAN'T MANAGE / UNLESS THEY'RE MANAGING MENAGERIES / ON THE AVENUE DU MAINE. / THE BADGER IS / AN ANIMAL WHOSE ADAGE / IS: I'M NO MAN AND NOT OF AN AGE / TO MANAGE MANAGERS OR MEN / ON THE AVENUE DU MAINE."
"I LIVE IN BADGERIES / WITH BUDGIES I ENGAGE / MENAGERIES CAUSE MAYHEM / ON THE AVENUE DU MAINE."
WONDERFUL!
ENCORE!
I DON'T UNDERSTAND A WORD, MAX, BUT IT SWINGS.
THIS IS THE HAPPIEST DAY OF MY LIFE.

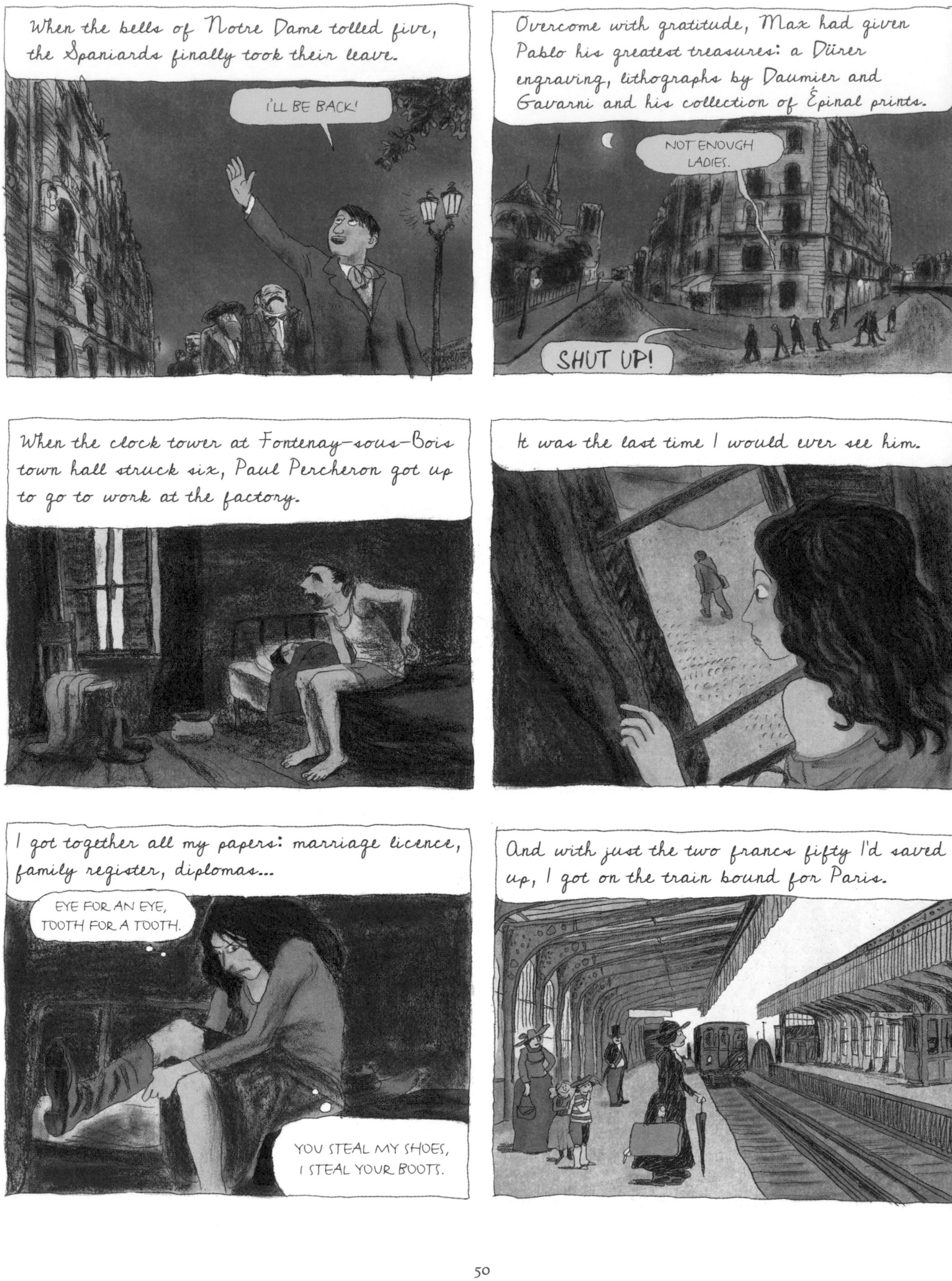
When the bells of Notre Dame tolled five, the Spaniards finally took their leave.
I'LL BE BACK!
Overcome with gratitude, Max had given Pablo his greatest treasures: a Dürer engraving, lithographs by Daumier and Gavarni and his collection of Épinal prints.
NOT ENOUGH LADIES.
SHUT UP!
When the clock tower at Fontenay-sous-Bois town hall struck six, Paul Percheron got up to go to work at the factory.
It was the last time I would ever see him.
I got together all my papers: marriage licence, family register, diplomas...
EYE FOR AN EYE, TOOTH FOR A TOOTH.
YOU STEAL MY SHOES, I STEAL YOUR BOOTS.
And with just the two francs fifty I'd saved up, I got on the train bound for Paris.

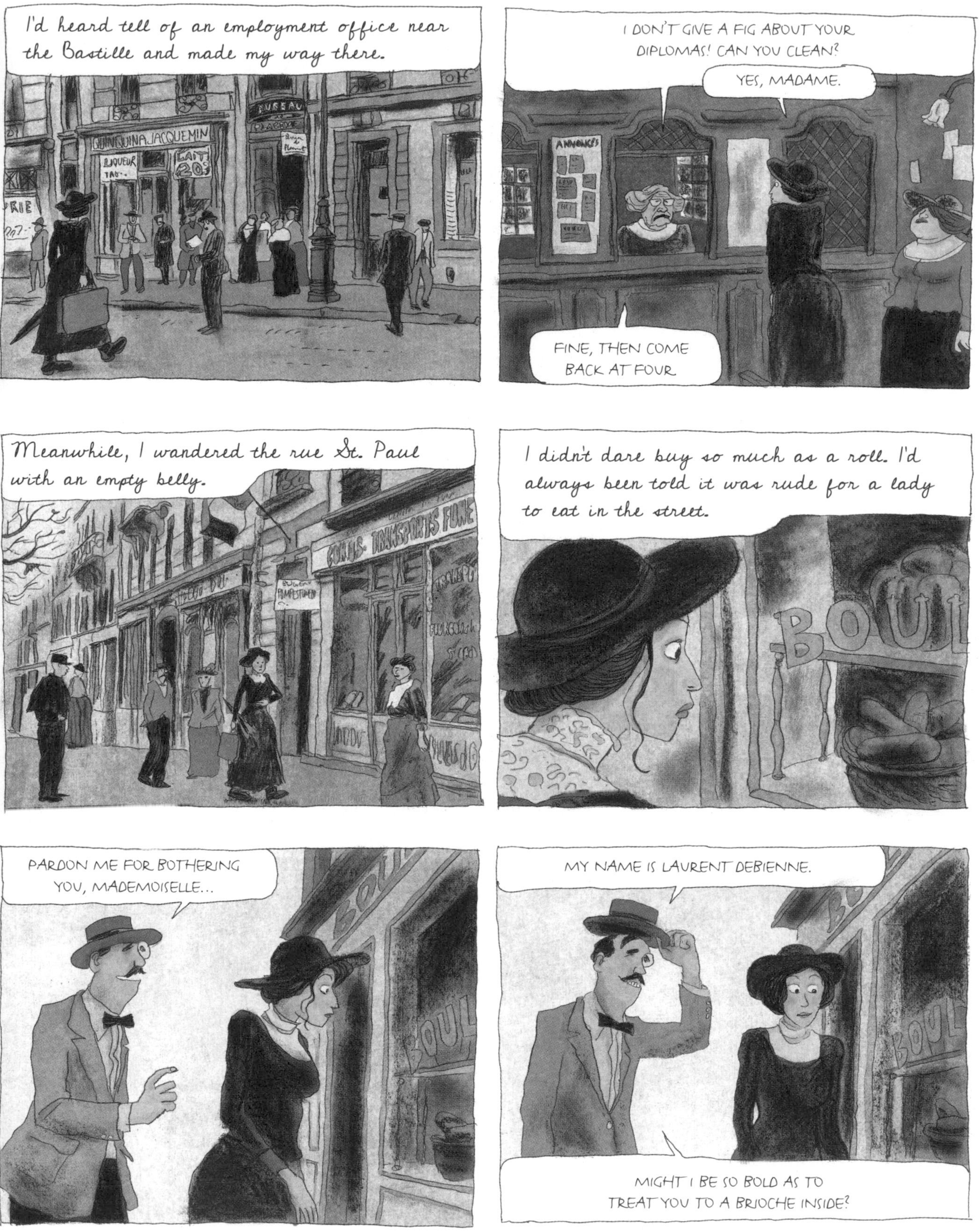
I'd heard tell of an employment office near the Bastille and made my way there.
QUINQUINA JACQUEMIN
LIQUEUR
LAIT 20c
BUREAU
I DON'T GIVE A FIG ABOUT YOUR DIPLOMAS! CAN YOU CLEAN?
YES, MADAME.
ANNONCES
FINE, THEN COME BACK AT FOUR
Meanwhile, I wandered the rue St. Paul with an empty belly.
TRANSPORTS FUNE
I didn't dare buy so much as a roll. I'd always been told it was rude for a lady to eat in the street.
BOUL
PARDON ME FOR BOTHERING YOU, MADEMOISELLE...
MY NAME IS LAURENT DEBIENNE.
MIGHT I BE SO BOLD AS TO TREAT YOU TO A BRIOCHE INSIDE?

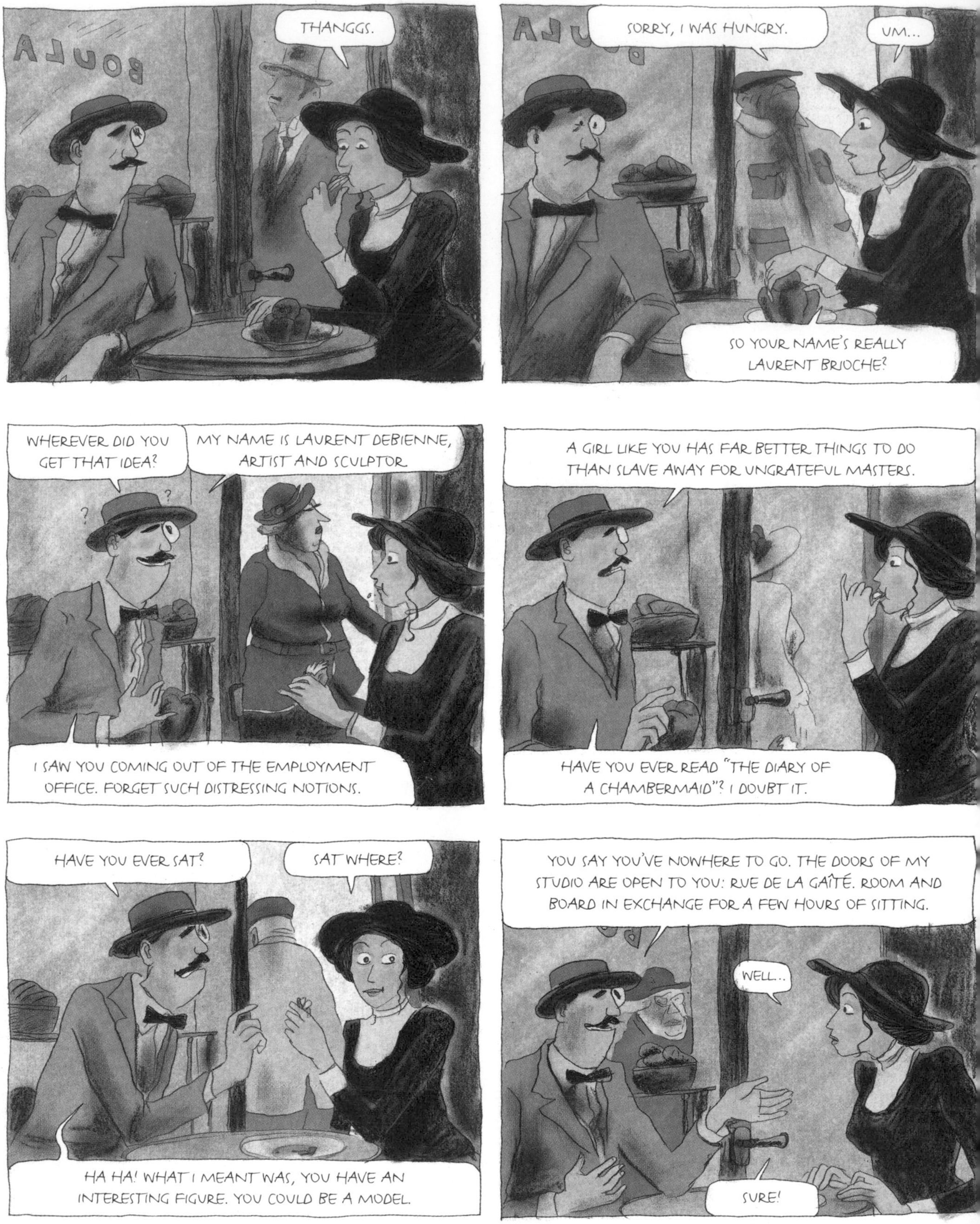
THANGGS.
SORRY, I WAS HUNGRY.
UM...
SO YOUR NAME'S REALLY LAURENT BRIOCHE?
WHEREVER DID YOU GET THAT IDEA?
MY NAME IS LAURENT DEBIENNE, ARTIST AND SCULPTOR.
I SAW YOU COMING OUT OF THE EMPLOYMENT OFFICE. FORGET SUCH DISTRESSING NOTIONS.
A GIRL LIKE YOU HAS FAR BETTER THINGS TO DO THAN SLAVE AWAY FOR UNGRATEFUL MASTERS.
HAVE YOU EVER READ "THE DIARY OF A CHAMBERMAID"? I DOUBT IT.
HAVE YOU EVER SAT?
SAT WHERE?
HA HA! WHAT I MEANT WAS, YOU HAVE AN INTERESTING FIGURE. YOU COULD BE A MODEL.
YOU SAY YOU'VE NOWHERE TO GO. THE DOORS OF MY STUDIO ARE OPEN TO YOU: RUE DE LA GAÎTÉ. ROOM AND BOARD IN EXCHANGE FOR A FEW HOURS OF SITTING.
WELL...
SURE!

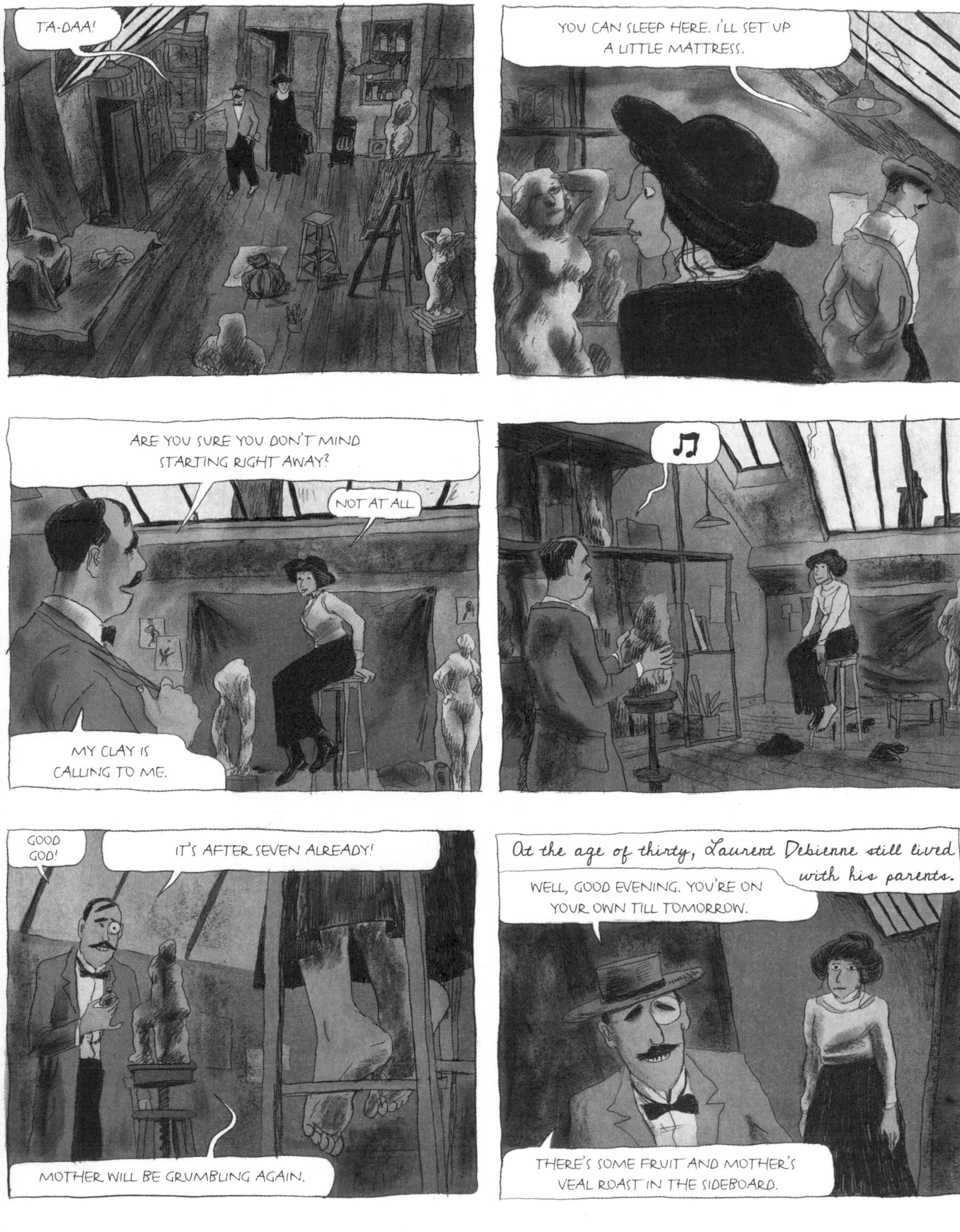
TA-DAA!
YOU CAN SLEEP HERE. I'LL SET UP A LITTLE MATTRESS.
ARE YOU SURE YOU DON'T MIND STARTING RIGHT AWAY?
NOT AT ALL.
MY CLAY IS CALLING TO ME.
♫
GOOD GOD!
IT'S AFTER SEVEN ALREADY!
MOTHER WILL BE GRUMBLING AGAIN.
At the age of thirty, Laurent Debienne still lived with his parents.
WELL, GOOD EVENING. YOU'RE ON YOUR OWN TILL TOMORROW.
THERE'S SOME FRUIT AND MOTHER'S VEAL ROAST IN THE SIDEBOARD.

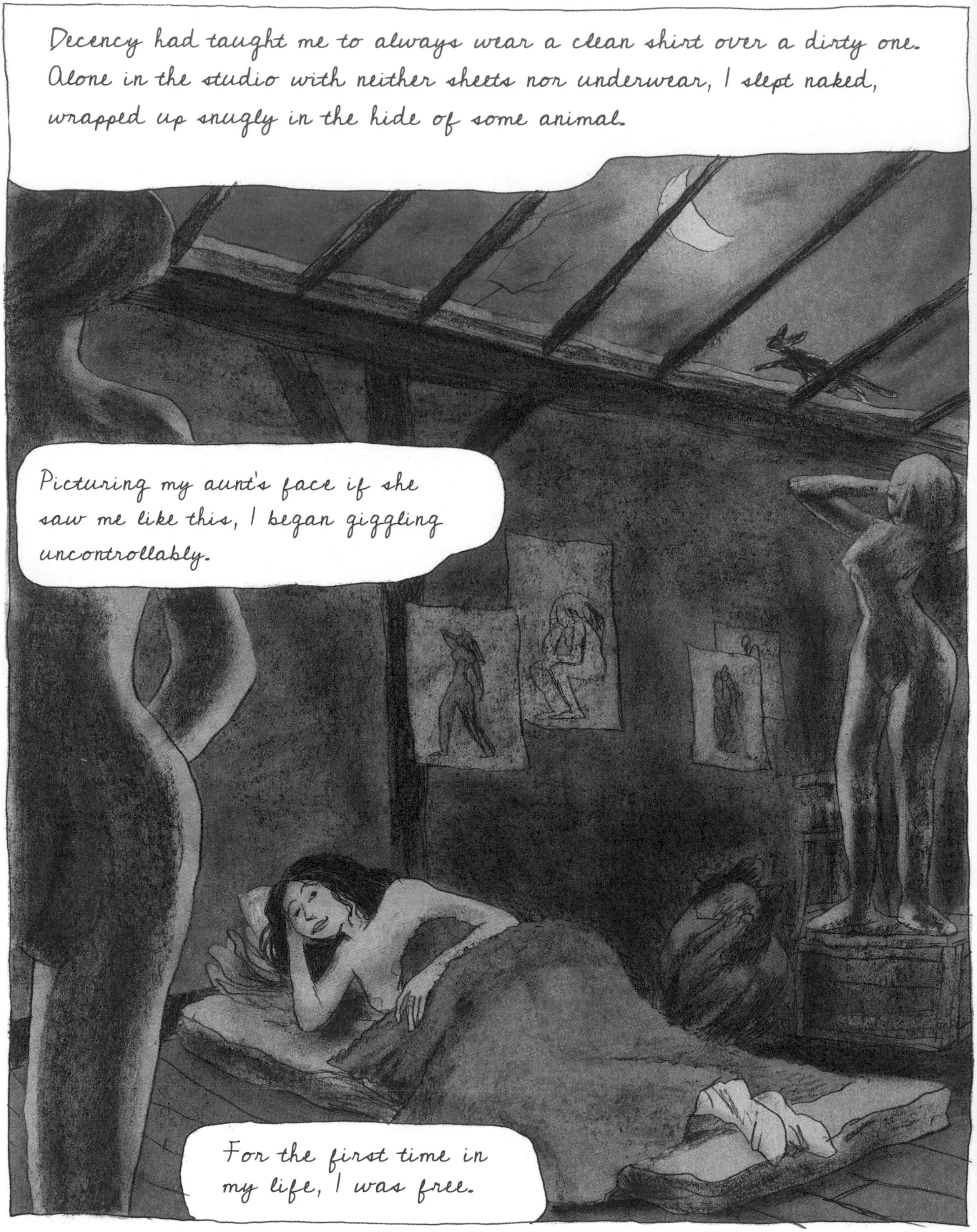
Decency had taught me to always wear a clean shirt over a dirty one. Alone in the studio with neither sheets nor underwear, I slept naked, wrapped up snugly in the hide of some animal.
Picturing my aunt's face if she saw me like this, I began giggling uncontrollably.
For the first time in my life, I was free.

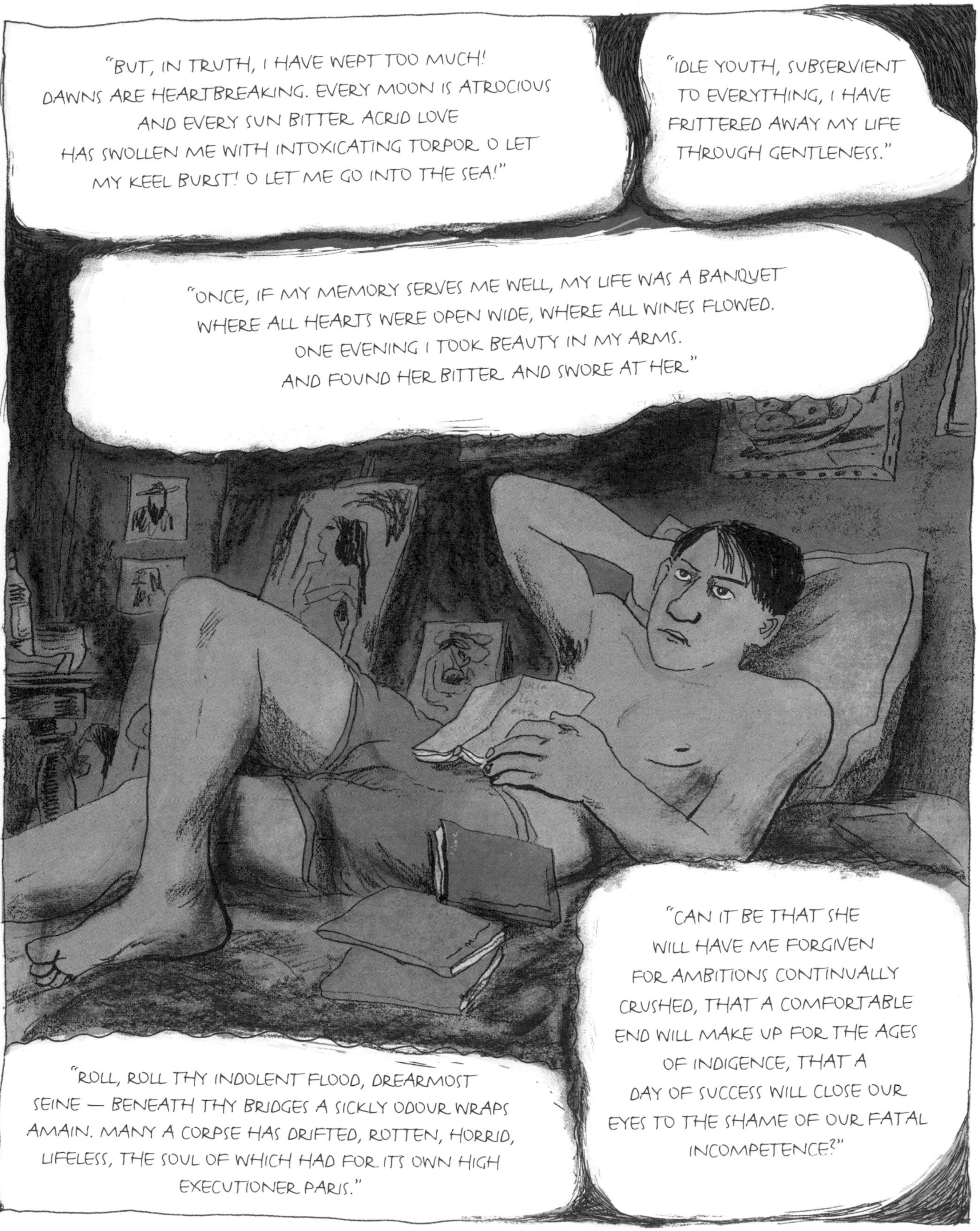
"BUT, IN TRUTH, I HAVE WEPT TOO MUCH! DAWNS ARE HEARTBREAKING. EVERY MOON IS ATROCIOUS AND EVERY SUN BITTER. ACRID LOVE HAS SWOLLEN ME WITH INTOXICATING TORPOR. O LET MY KEEL BURST! O LET ME GO INTO THE SEA!"
"IDLE YOUTH, SUBSERVIENT TO EVERYTHING, I HAVE FRITTERED AWAY MY LIFE THROUGH GENTLENESS."
"ONCE, IF MY MEMORY SERVES ME WELL, MY LIFE WAS A BANQUET WHERE ALL HEARTS WERE OPEN WIDE, WHERE ALL WINES FLOWED. ONE EVENING I TOOK BEAUTY IN MY ARMS. AND FOUND HER BITTER. AND SWORE AT HER."
"ROLL, ROLL THY INDOLENT FLOOD, DREARMOST SEINE — BENEATH THY BRIDGES A SICKLY ODOUR WRAPS AMAIN. MANY A CORPSE HAS DRIFTED, ROTTEN, HORRID, LIFELESS, THE SOUL OF WHICH HAD FOR ITS OWN HIGH EXECUTIONER PARIS."
"CAN IT BE THAT SHE WILL HAVE ME FORGIVEN FOR AMBITIONS CONTINUALLY CRUSHED, THAT A COMFORTABLE END WILL MAKE UP FOR THE AGES OF INDIGENCE, THAT A DAY OF SUCCESS WILL CLOSE OUR EYES TO THE SHAME OF OUR FATAL INCOMPETENCE?"

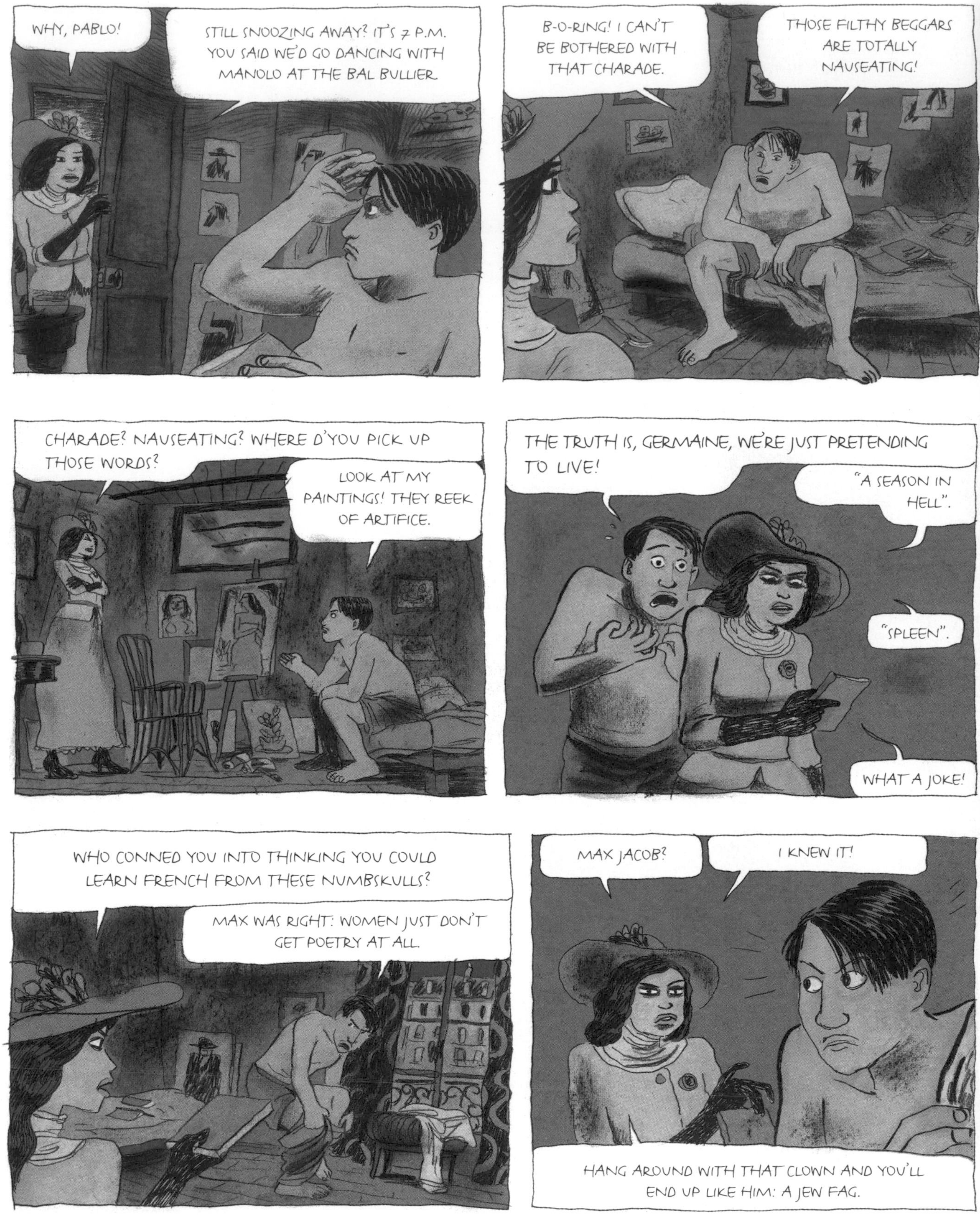
WHY, PABLO!
STILL SNOOZING AWAY? IT'S 7 P.M. YOU SAID WE'D GO DANCING WITH MANOLO AT THE BAL BULLIER.
B-O-RING! I CAN'T BE BOTHERED WITH THAT CHARADE.
THOSE FILTHY BEGGARS ARE TOTALLY NAUSEATING!
CHARADE? NAUSEATING? WHERE D'YOU PICK UP THOSE WORDS?
LOOK AT MY PAINTINGS! THEY REEK OF ARTIFICE.
THE TRUTH IS, GERMAINE, WE'RE JUST PRETENDING TO LIVE!
"A SEASON IN HELL".
"SPLEEN".
WHAT A JOKE!
WHO CONNED YOU INTO THINKING YOU COULD LEARN FRENCH FROM THESE NUMBSKULLS?
MAX WAS RIGHT: WOMEN JUST DON'T GET POETRY AT ALL.
MAX JACOB?
I KNEW IT!
HANG AROUND WITH THAT CLOWN AND YOU'LL END UP LIKE HIM: A JEW FAG.

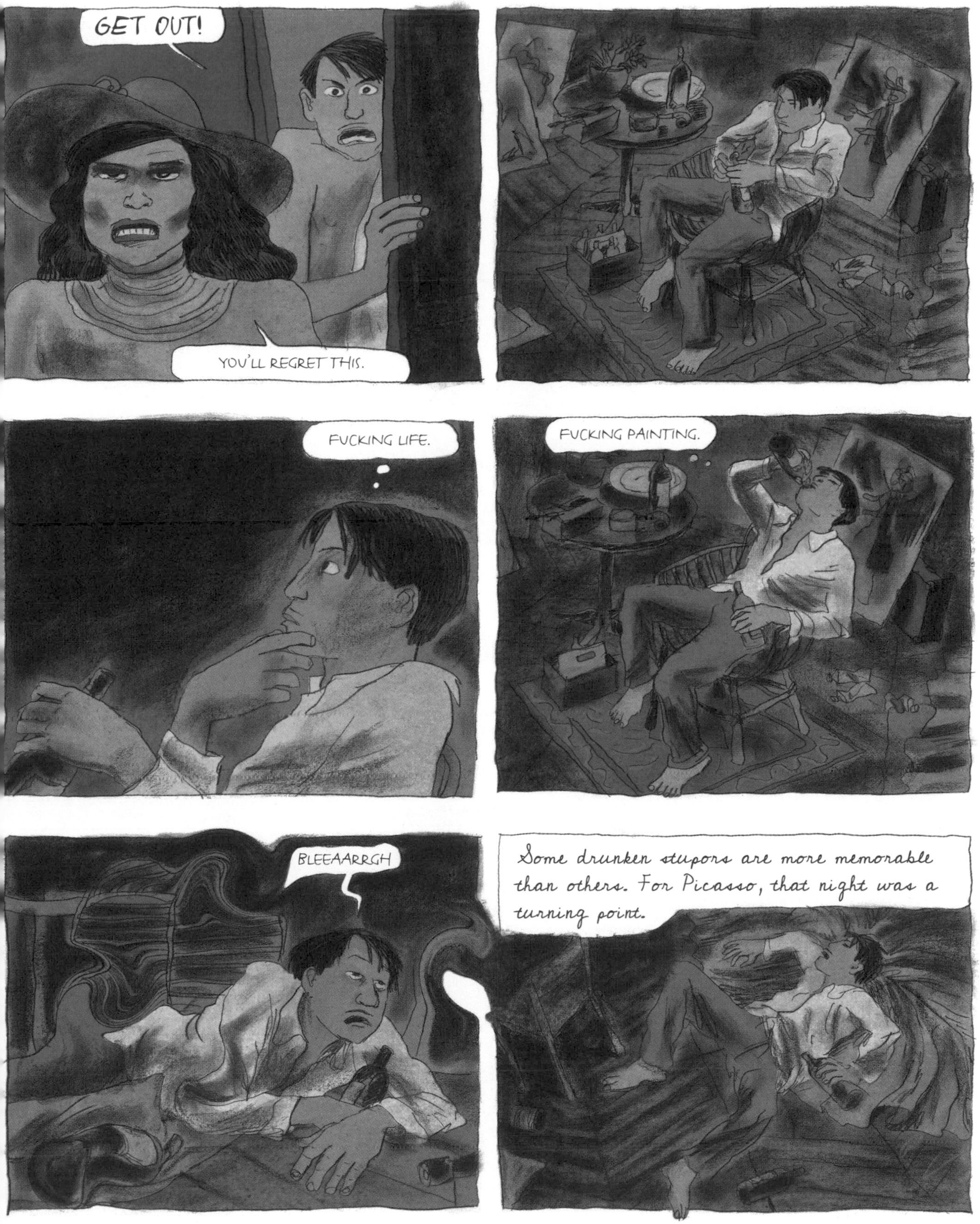

GET OUT!
YOU'LL REGRET THIS.
FUCKING LIFE.
FUCKING PAINTING.
BLEEAARRGH
Some drunken stupors are more memorable than others. For Picasso, that night was a turning point.

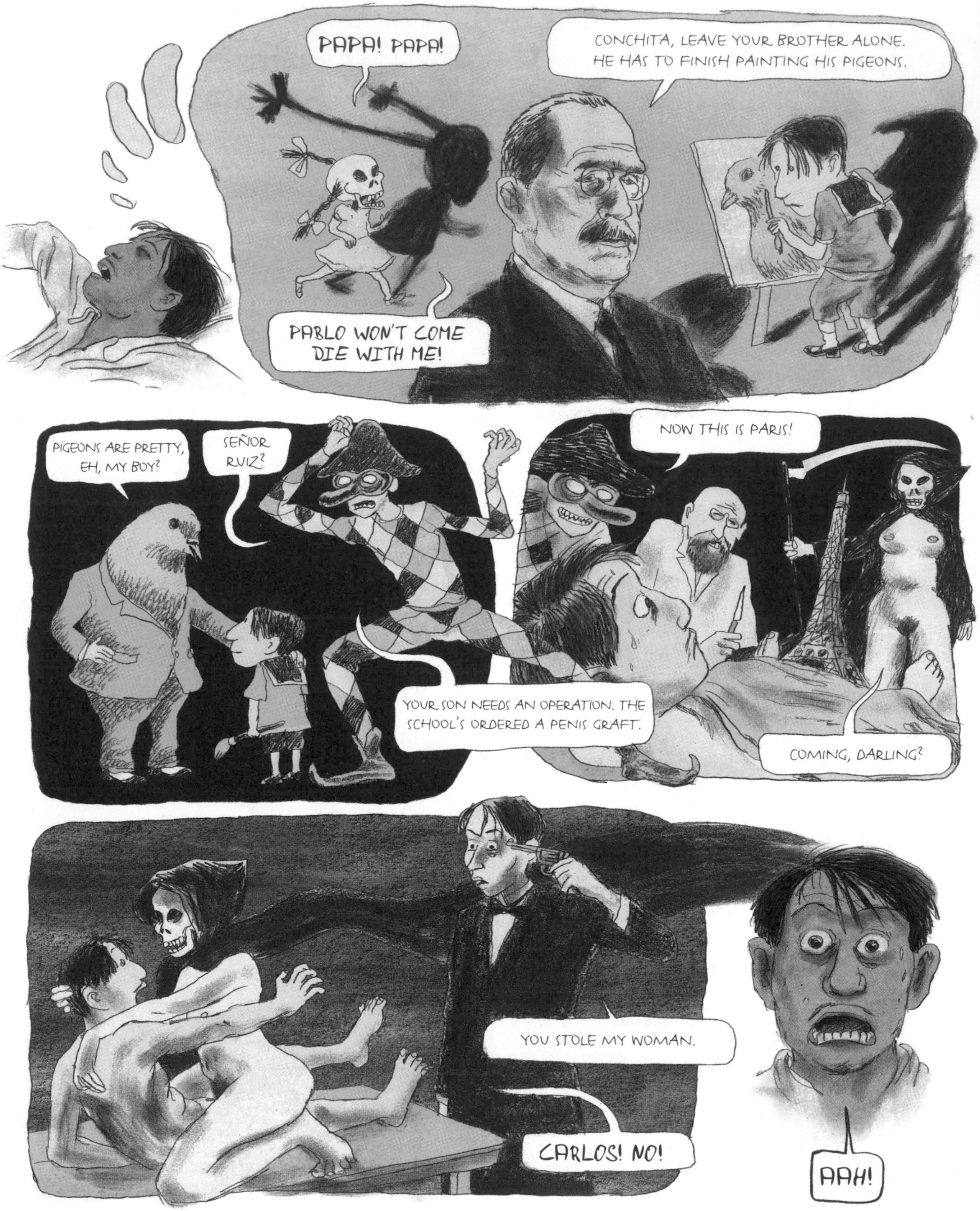
PAPA! PAPA!
PABLO WON'T COME DIE WITH ME!
CONCHITA, LEAVE YOUR BROTHER ALONE. HE HAS TO FINISH PAINTING HIS PIGEONS.
PIGEONS ARE PRETTY, EH, MY BOY?
SEÑOR RUIZ?
YOUR SON NEEDS AN OPERATION. THE SCHOOL'S ORDERED A PENIS GRAFT.
NOW THIS IS PARIS!
COMING, DARLING?
YOU STOLE MY WOMAN.
CARLOS! NO!
AAH!

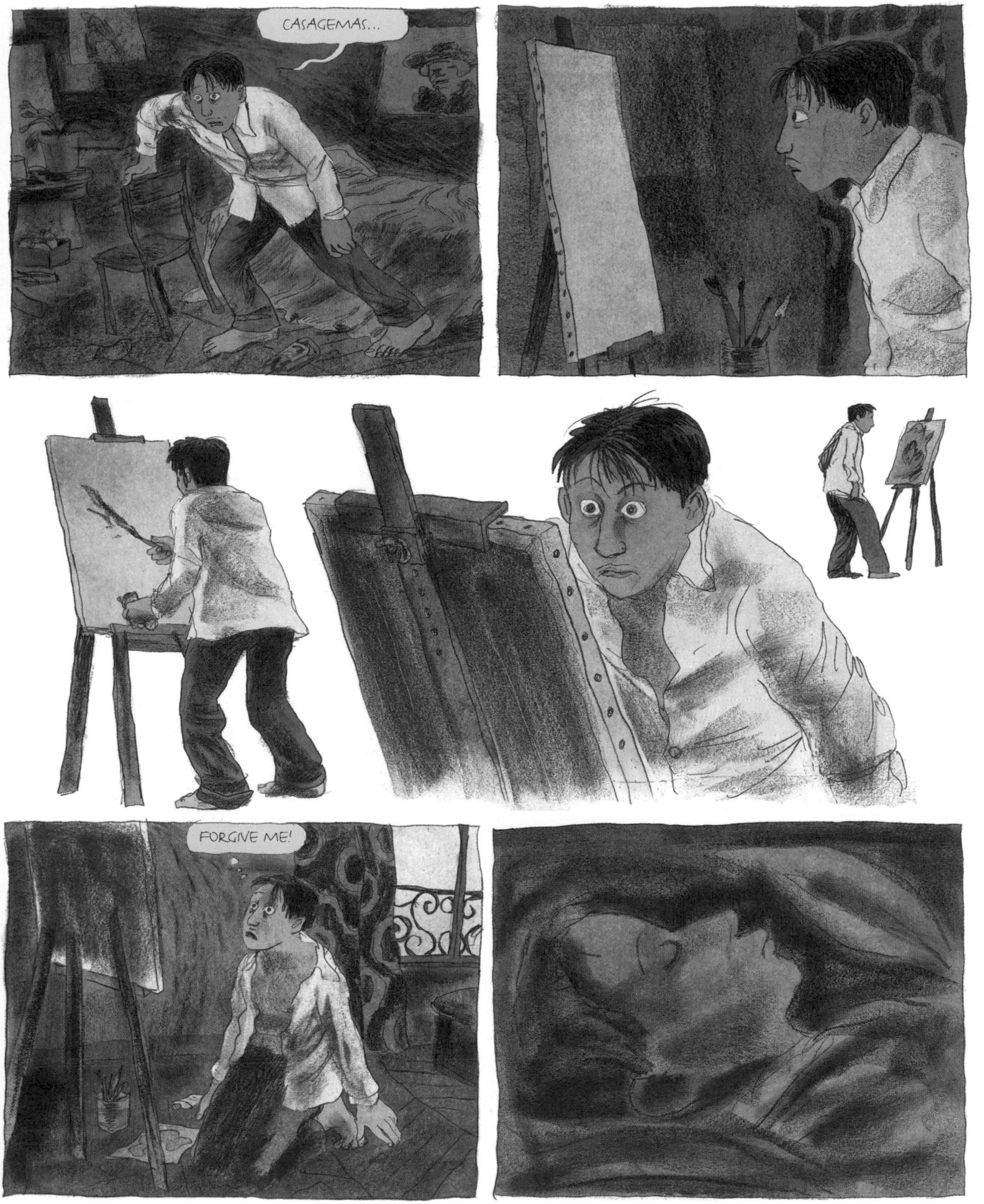
CASAGEMAS...
FORGIVE ME!

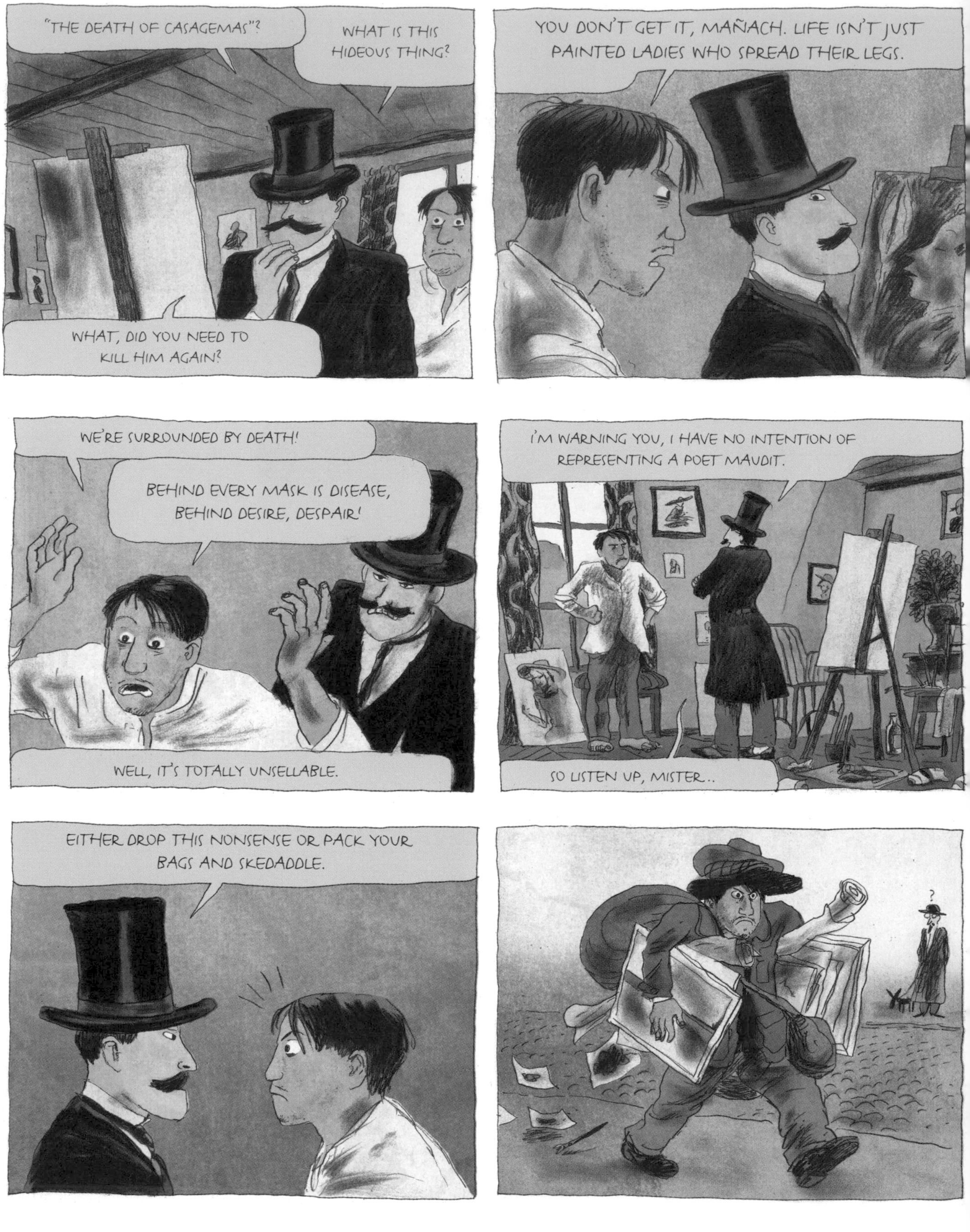
"THE DEATH OF CASAGEMAS"?
WHAT IS THIS HIDEOUS THING?
WHAT, DID YOU NEED TO KILL HIM AGAIN?
YOU DON'T GET IT, MAÑACH. LIFE ISN'T JUST PAINTED LADIES WHO SPREAD THEIR LEGS.
WE'RE SURROUNDED BY DEATH!
BEHIND EVERY MASK IS DISEASE, BEHIND DESIRE, DESPAIR!
WELL, IT'S TOTALLY UNSELLABLE.
I'M WARNING YOU, I HAVE NO INTENTION OF REPRESENTING A POET MAUDIT.
SO LISTEN UP, MISTER..
EITHER DROP THIS NONSENSE OR PACK YOUR BAGS AND SKEDADDLE.
?

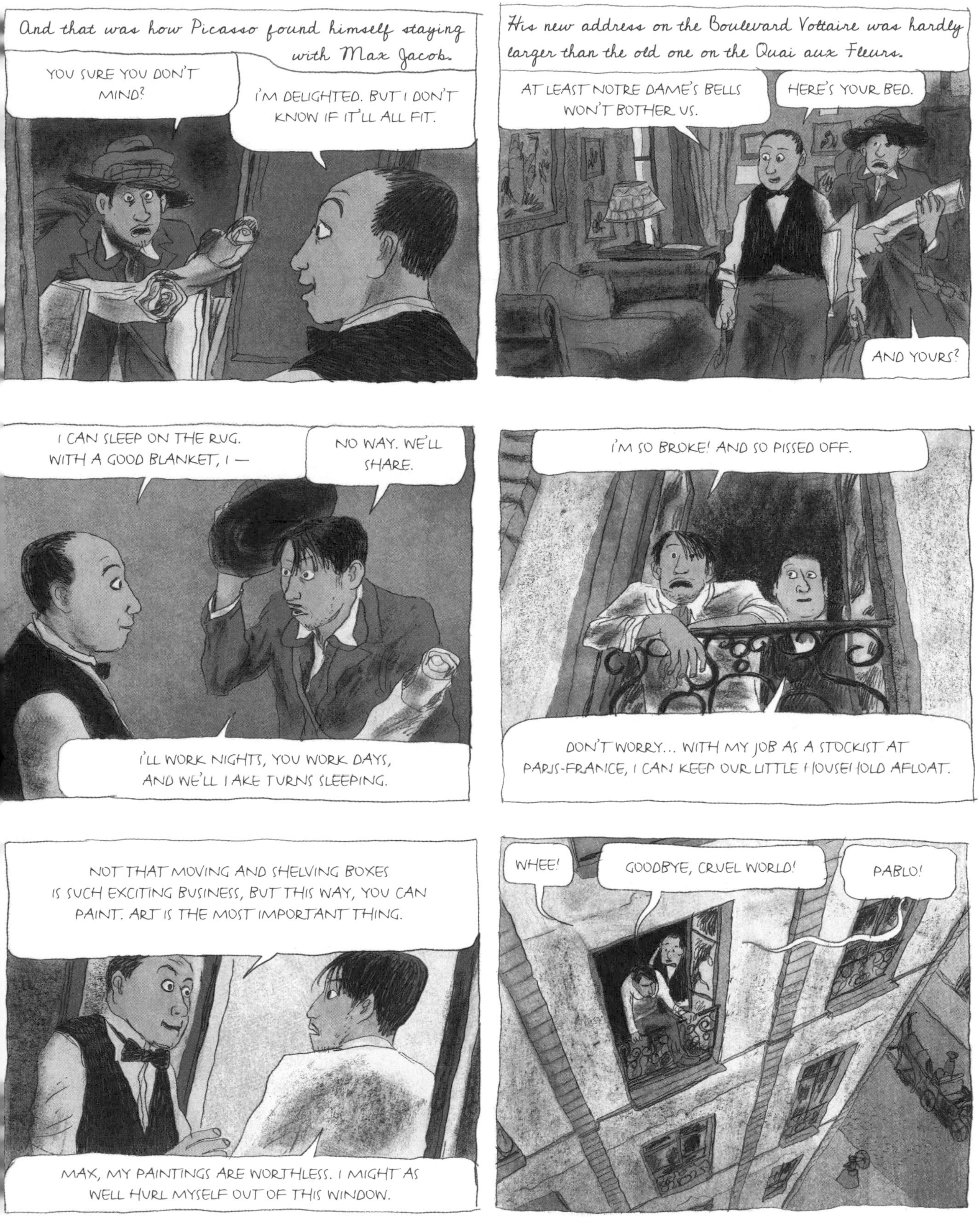

And that was how Picasso found himself staying with Max Jacob.
YOU SURE YOU DON'T MIND?
I'M DELIGHTED. BUT I DON'T KNOW IF IT'LL ALL FIT.
His new address on the Boulevard Voltaire was hardly larger than the old one on the Quai aux Fleurs.
AT LEAST NOTRE DAME'S BELLS WON'T BOTHER US.
HERE'S YOUR BED.
AND YOURS?
I CAN SLEEP ON THE RUG. WITH A GOOD BLANKET, I —
NO WAY. WE'LL SHARE.
I'LL WORK NIGHTS, YOU WORK DAYS, AND WE'LL TAKE TURNS SLEEPING.
I'M SO BROKE! AND SO PISSED OFF.
DON'T WORRY... WITH MY JOB AS A STOCKIST AT PARIS-FRANCE, I CAN KEEP OUR LITTLE HOUSEHOLD AFLOAT.
NOT THAT MOVING AND SHELVING BOXES IS SUCH EXCITING BUSINESS, BUT THIS WAY, YOU CAN PAINT. ART IS THE MOST IMPORTANT THING.
MAX, MY PAINTINGS ARE WORTHLESS. I MIGHT AS WELL HURL MYSELF OUT OF THIS WINDOW.
WHEE!
GOODBYE, CRUEL WORLD!
PABLO!

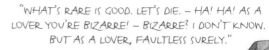

"BAH, DESPITE JEALOUS DESTINIES, LET'S DIE TOGETHER, SHALL WE? – WELL, YOUR PROPOSITION'S RARE."

"WHAT'S RARE IS GOOD. LET'S DIE. – HA! HA! AS A LOVER YOU'RE BIZARRE! – BIZARRE? I DON'T KNOW. BUT AS A LOVER, FAULTLESS SURELY."

"HENCE TONIGHT IT HAPPENED THAT DORIMENE AND TIRCIS SAT AND IRREMISSIBLY DID WRONG, POSTPONING AN EXQUISITE DEATH TOO LONG."

THAT'S NOT YOURS!   VERLAINE. "THE INDOLENT ONES."

DUMBASS!

ALRIGHT, COME ON. LET'S GO OUT TO EAT.

CELEBRATE OUR NEW LIFE.

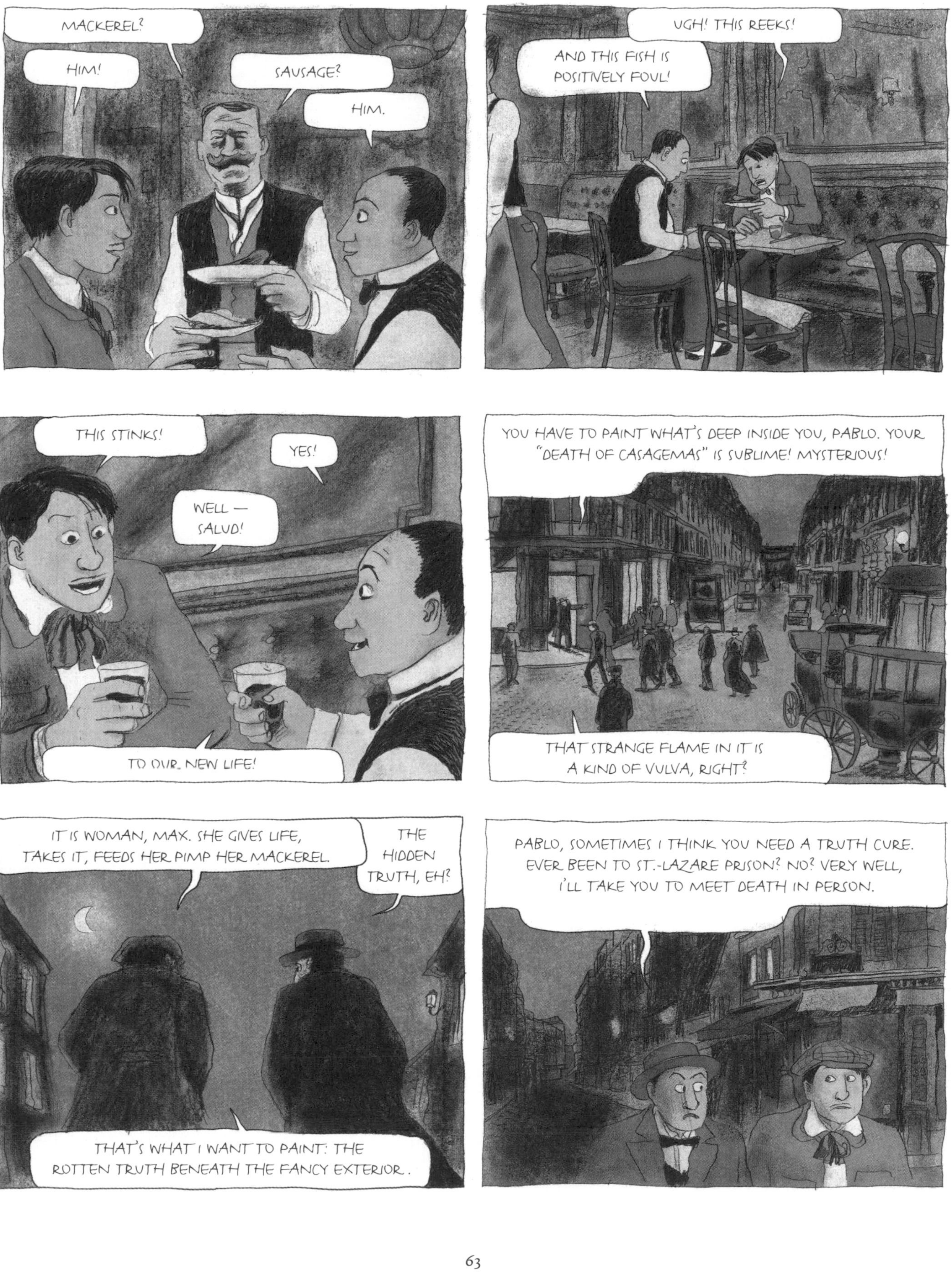
MACKEREL?
HIM!
SAUSAGE?
HIM.
UGH! THIS REEKS!
AND THIS FISH IS POSITIVELY FOUL!
THIS STINKS!
YES!
WELL — SALUD!
TO OUR NEW LIFE!
YOU HAVE TO PAINT WHAT'S DEEP INSIDE YOU, PABLO. YOUR "DEATH OF CASAGEMAS" IS SUBLIME! MYSTERIOUS!
THAT STRANGE FLAME IN IT IS A KIND OF VULVA, RIGHT?
IT IS WOMAN, MAX. SHE GIVES LIFE, TAKES IT, FEEDS HER PIMP HER MACKEREL.
THE HIDDEN TRUTH, EH?
THAT'S WHAT I WANT TO PAINT: THE ROTTEN TRUTH BENEATH THE FANCY EXTERIOR.
PABLO, SOMETIMES I THINK YOU NEED A TRUTH CURE. EVER BEEN TO ST.-LAZARE PRISON? NO? VERY WELL, I'LL TAKE YOU TO MEET DEATH IN PERSON.

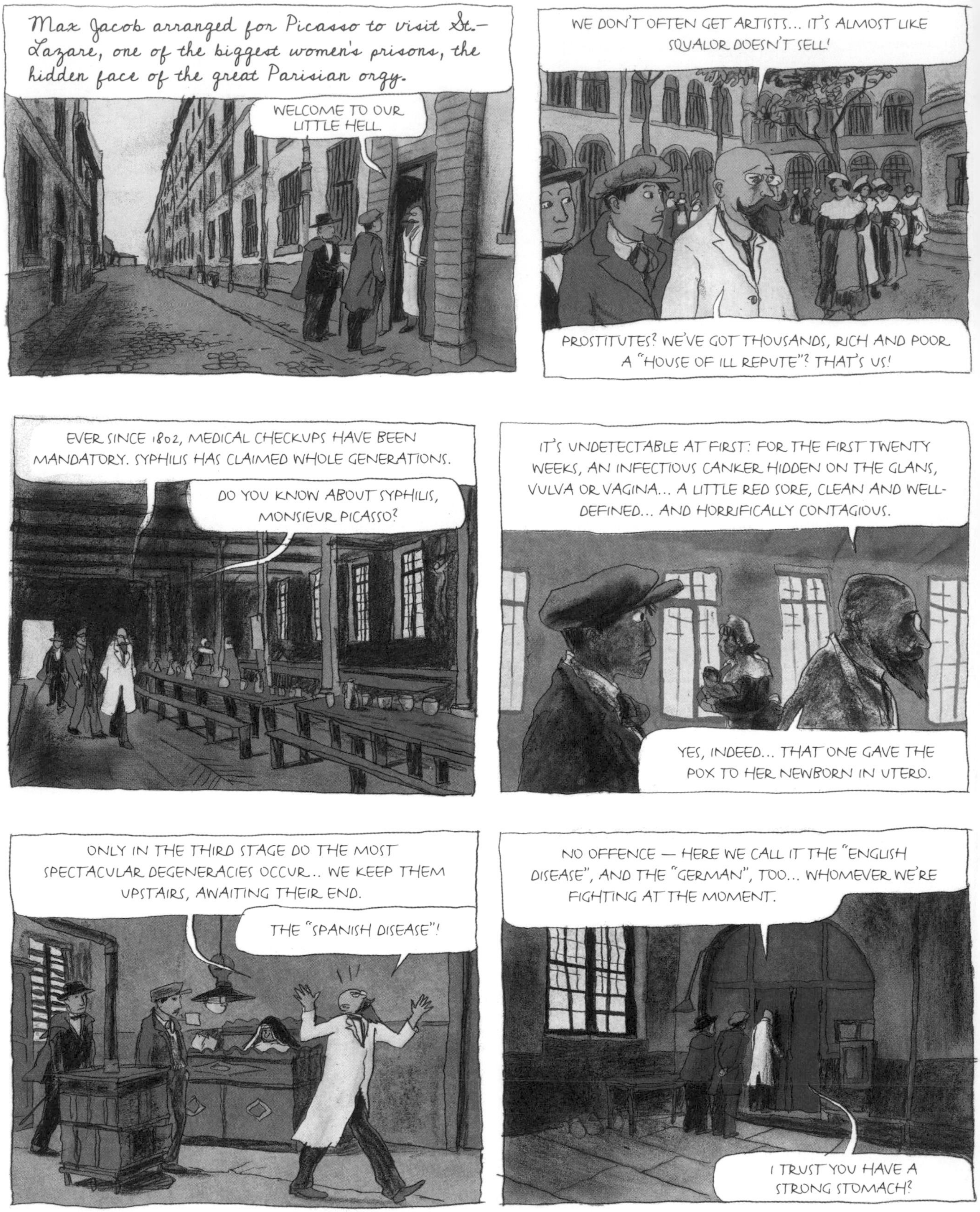
Max Jacob arranged for Picasso to visit St.-Lazare, one of the biggest women's prisons, the hidden face of the great Parisian orgy.
WELCOME TO OUR LITTLE HELL.
WE DON'T OFTEN GET ARTISTS... IT'S ALMOST LIKE SQUALOR DOESN'T SELL!
PROSTITUTES? WE'VE GOT THOUSANDS, RICH AND POOR. A "HOUSE OF ILL REPUTE"? THAT'S US!
EVER SINCE 1802, MEDICAL CHECKUPS HAVE BEEN MANDATORY. SYPHILIS HAS CLAIMED WHOLE GENERATIONS.
DO YOU KNOW ABOUT SYPHILIS, MONSIEUR PICASSO?
IT'S UNDETECTABLE AT FIRST: FOR THE FIRST TWENTY WEEKS, AN INFECTIOUS CANKER HIDDEN ON THE GLANS, VULVA OR VAGINA... A LITTLE RED SORE, CLEAN AND WELL-DEFINED... AND HORRIFICALLY CONTAGIOUS.
YES, INDEED... THAT ONE GAVE THE POX TO HER NEWBORN IN UTERO.
ONLY IN THE THIRD STAGE DO THE MOST SPECTACULAR DEGENERACIES OCCUR.. WE KEEP THEM UPSTAIRS, AWAITING THEIR END.
THE "SPANISH DISEASE"!
NO OFFENCE — HERE WE CALL IT THE "ENGLISH DISEASE", AND THE "GERMAN", TOO... WHOMEVER WE'RE FIGHTING AT THE MOMENT.
I TRUST YOU HAVE A STRONG STOMACH?

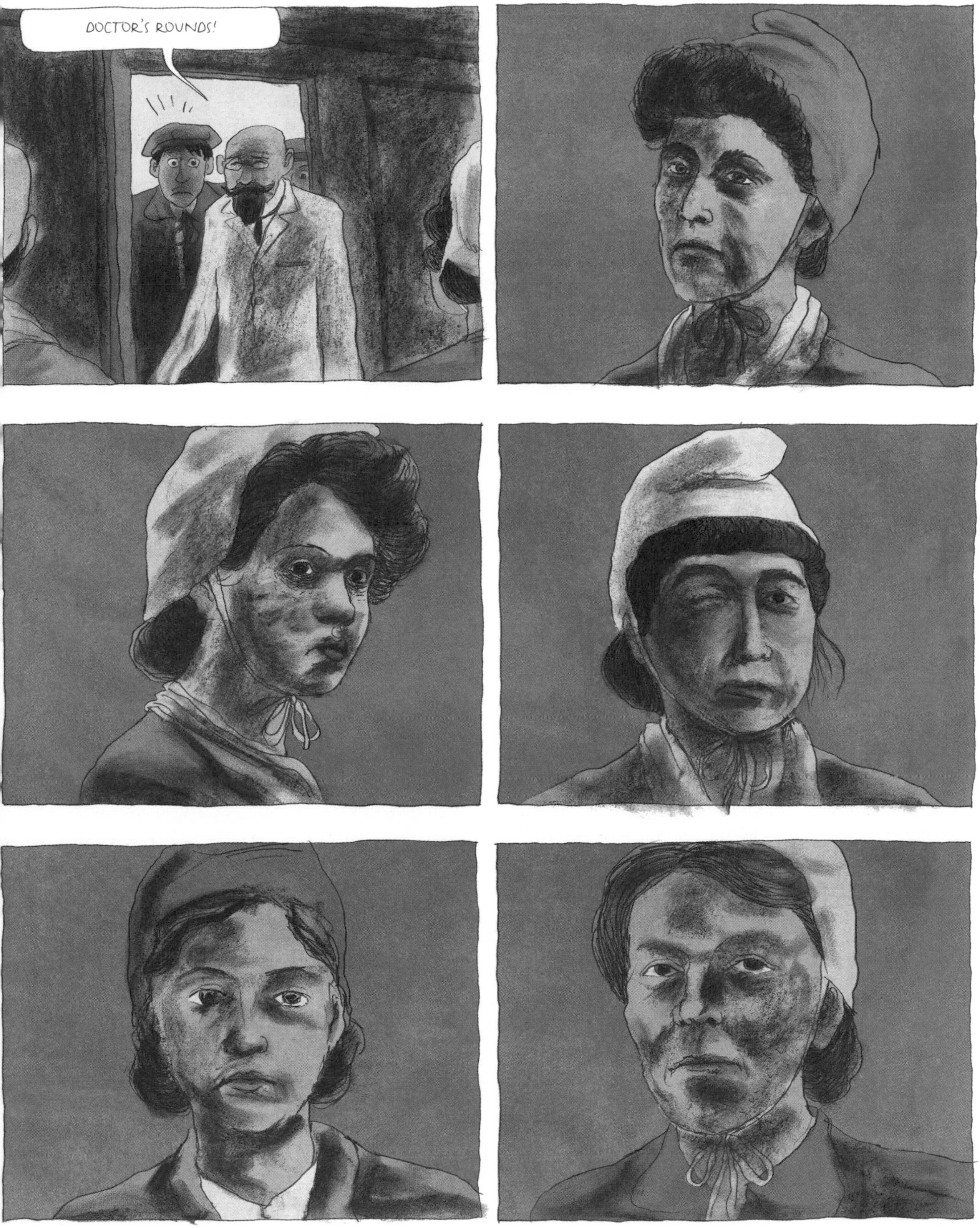
DOCTOR'S ROUNDS!

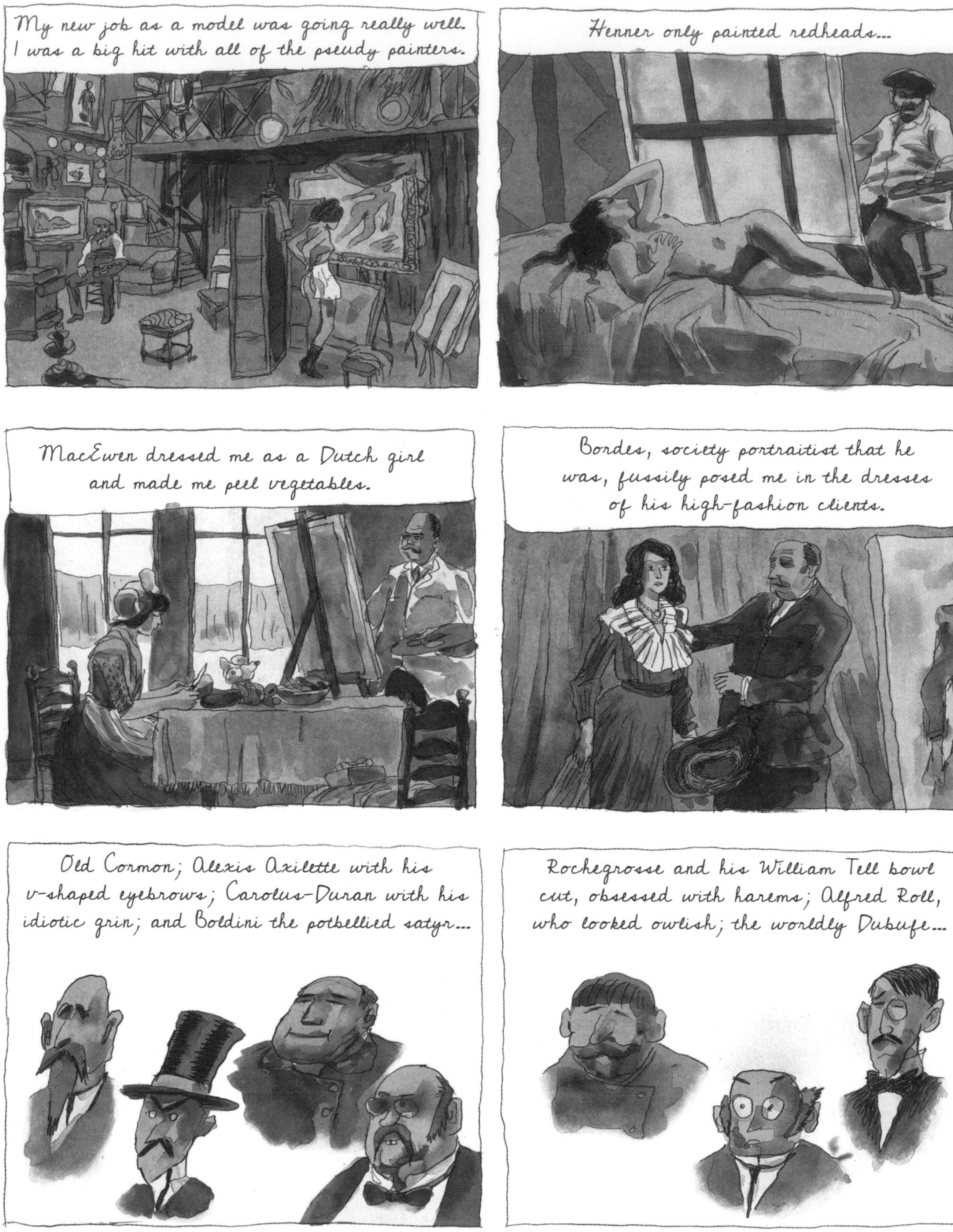
My new job as a model was going really well. I was a big hit with all of the pseudy painters.
Henner only painted redheads...
MacEwen dressed me as a Dutch girl and made me peel vegetables.
Bordes, society portraitist that he was, fussily posed me in the dresses of his high-fashion clients.
Old Cormon; Alexis Axilette with his v-shaped eyebrows; Carolus-Duran with his idiotic grin; and Boldini the potbellied satyr...
Rochegrosse and his William Tell bowl cut, obsessed with harems; Alfred Roll, who looked owlish; the worldly Dubufe...

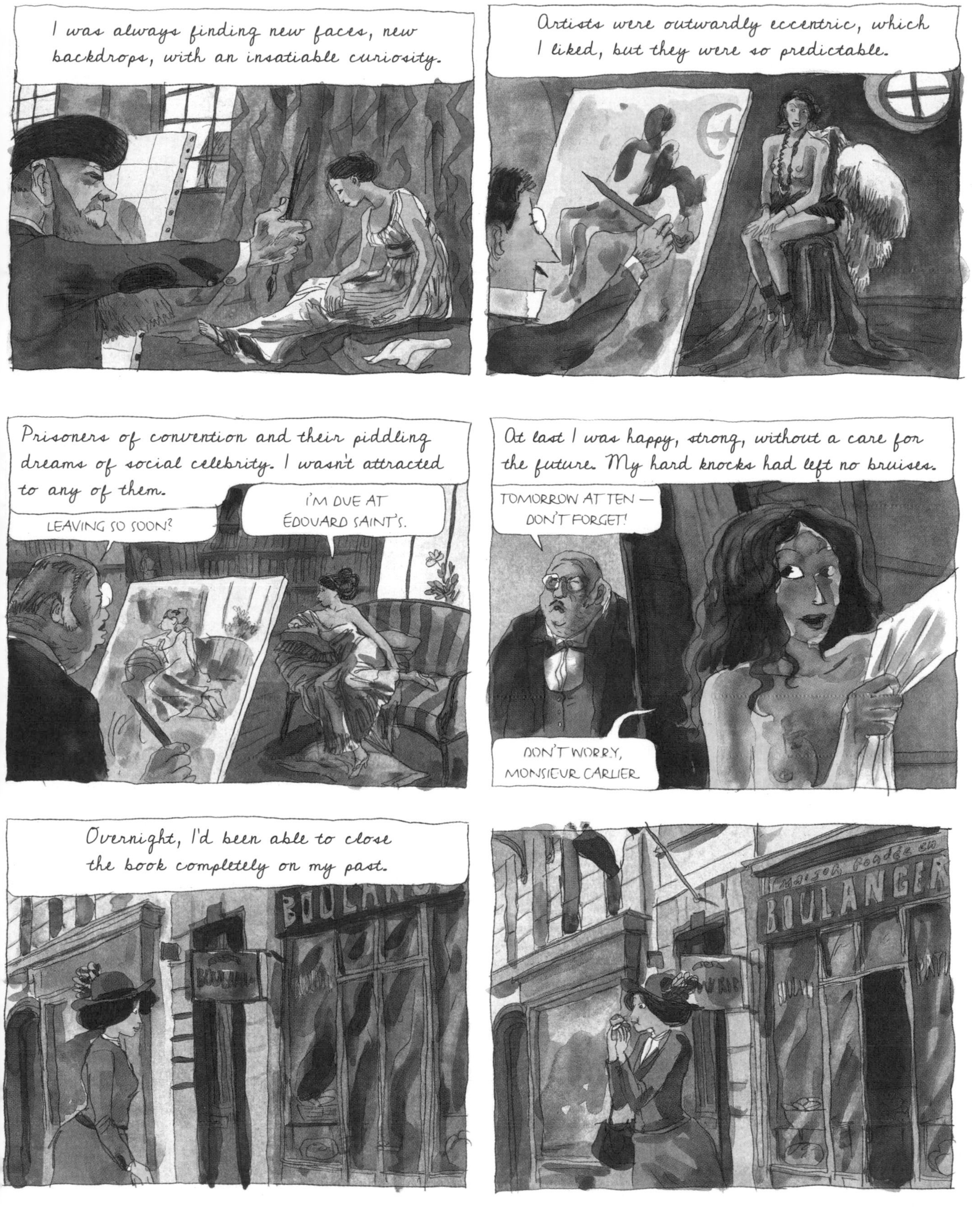
I was always finding new faces, new backdrops, with an insatiable curiosity.
Artists were outwardly eccentric, which I liked, but they were so predictable.
Prisoners of convention and their piddling dreams of social celebrity. I wasn't attracted to any of them.
LEAVING SO SOON?
I'M DUE AT ÉDOUARD SAINT'S.
At last I was happy, strong, without a care for the future. My hard knocks had left no bruises.
TOMORROW AT TEN — DON'T FORGET!
DON'T WORRY, MONSIEUR CARLIER
Overnight, I'd been able to close the book completely on my past.
BOULANGER

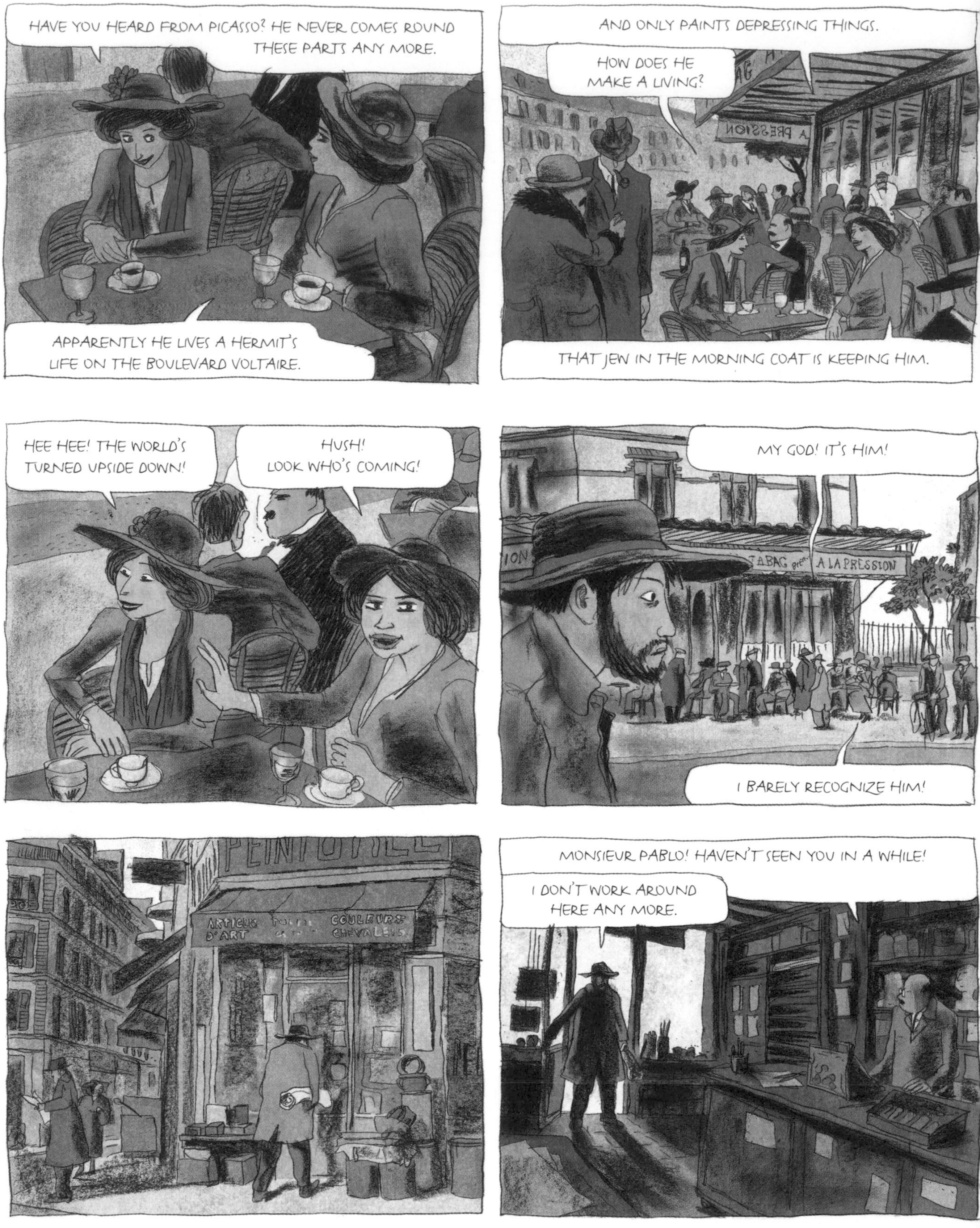
HAVE YOU HEARD FROM PICASSO? HE NEVER COMES ROUND THESE PARTS ANY MORE.
APPARENTLY HE LIVES A HERMIT'S LIFE ON THE BOULEVARD VOLTAIRE.
AND ONLY PAINTS DEPRESSING THINGS.
HOW DOES HE MAKE A LIVING?
THAT JEW IN THE MORNING COAT IS KEEPING HIM.
HEE HEE! THE WORLD'S TURNED UPSIDE DOWN!
HUSH! LOOK WHO'S COMING!
MY GOD! IT'S HIM!
A LA PRESSION
I BARELY RECOGNIZE HIM!
MONSIEUR PABLO! HAVEN'T SEEN YOU IN A WHILE!
I DON'T WORK AROUND HERE ANY MORE.

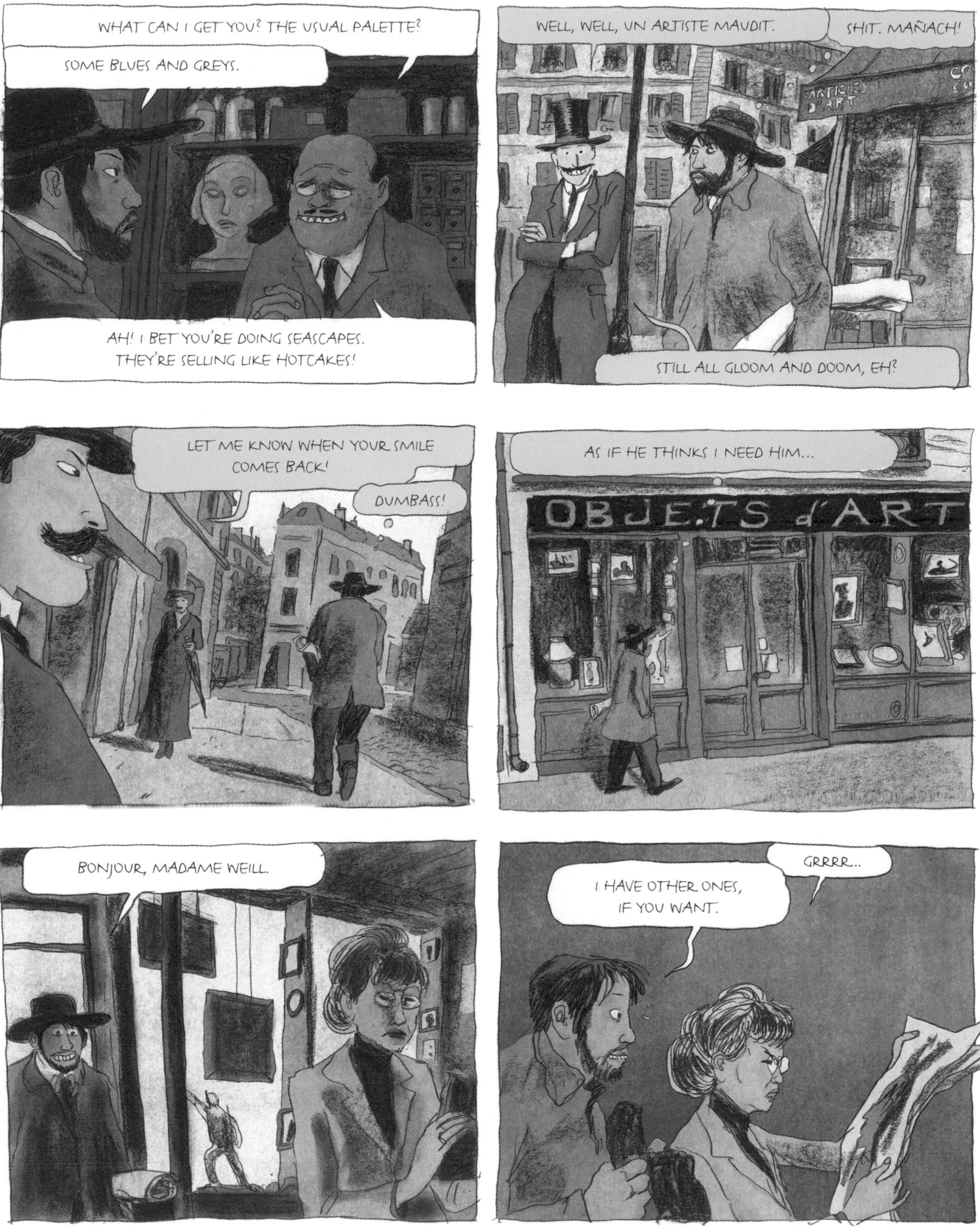
WHAT CAN I GET YOU? THE USUAL PALETTE?
SOME BLUES AND GREYS.
AH! I BET YOU'RE DOING SEASCAPES. THEY'RE SELLING LIKE HOTCAKES!
WELL, WELL, UN ARTISTE MAUDIT.
SHIT. MAÑACH!
ARTICLES D'ART
STILL ALL GLOOM AND DOOM, EH?
LET ME KNOW WHEN YOUR SMILE COMES BACK!
DUMBASS!
AS IF HE THINKS I NEED HIM...
OBJETS d'ART
BONJOUR, MADAME WEILL.
I HAVE OTHER ONES, IF YOU WANT.
GRRRR...

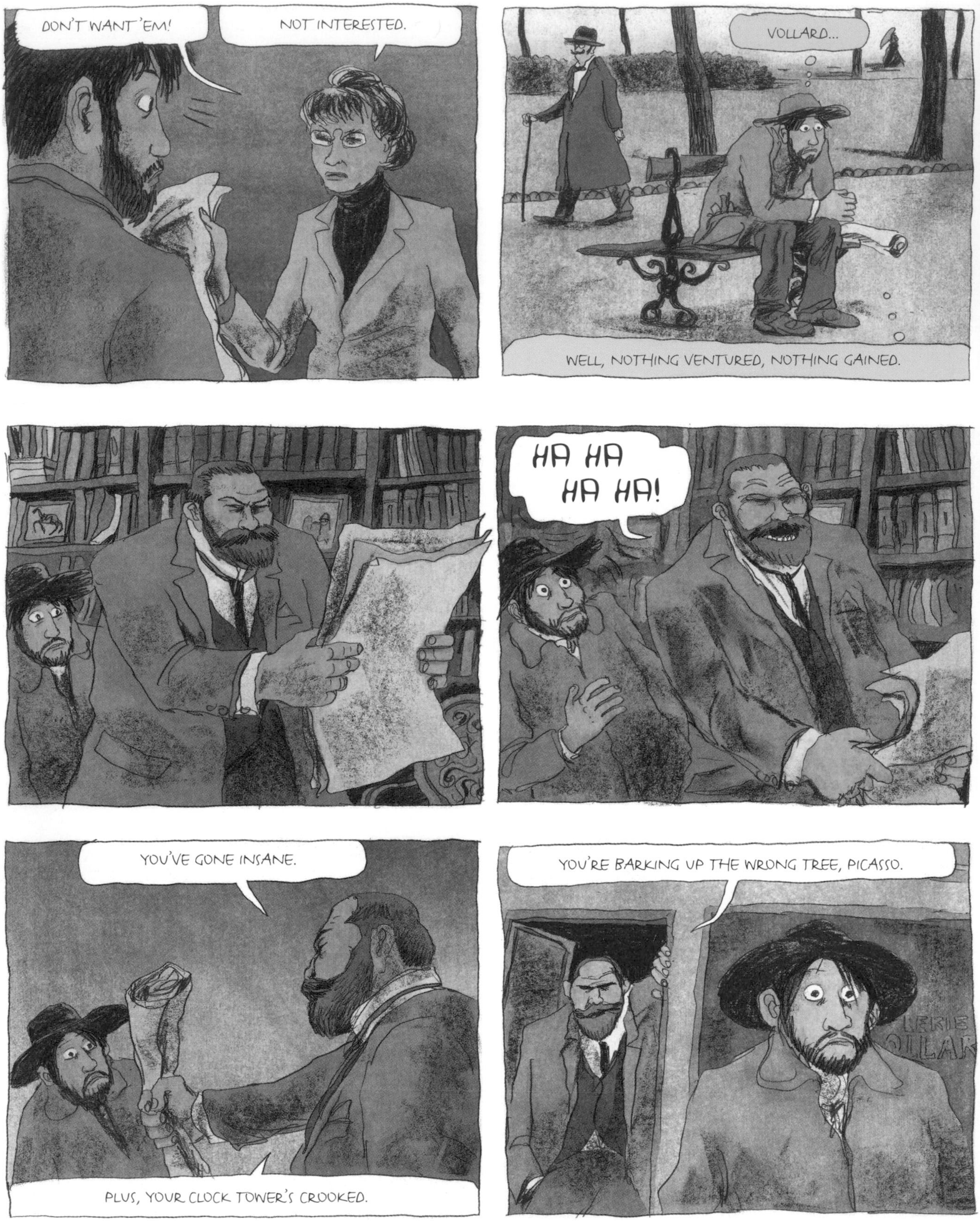
DON'T WANT 'EM!
NOT INTERESTED.
VOLLARD...
WELL, NOTHING VENTURED, NOTHING GAINED.
HA HA HA HA!
YOU'VE GONE INSANE.
PLUS, YOUR CLOCK TOWER'S CROOKED.
YOU'RE BARKING UP THE WRONG TREE, PICASSO.

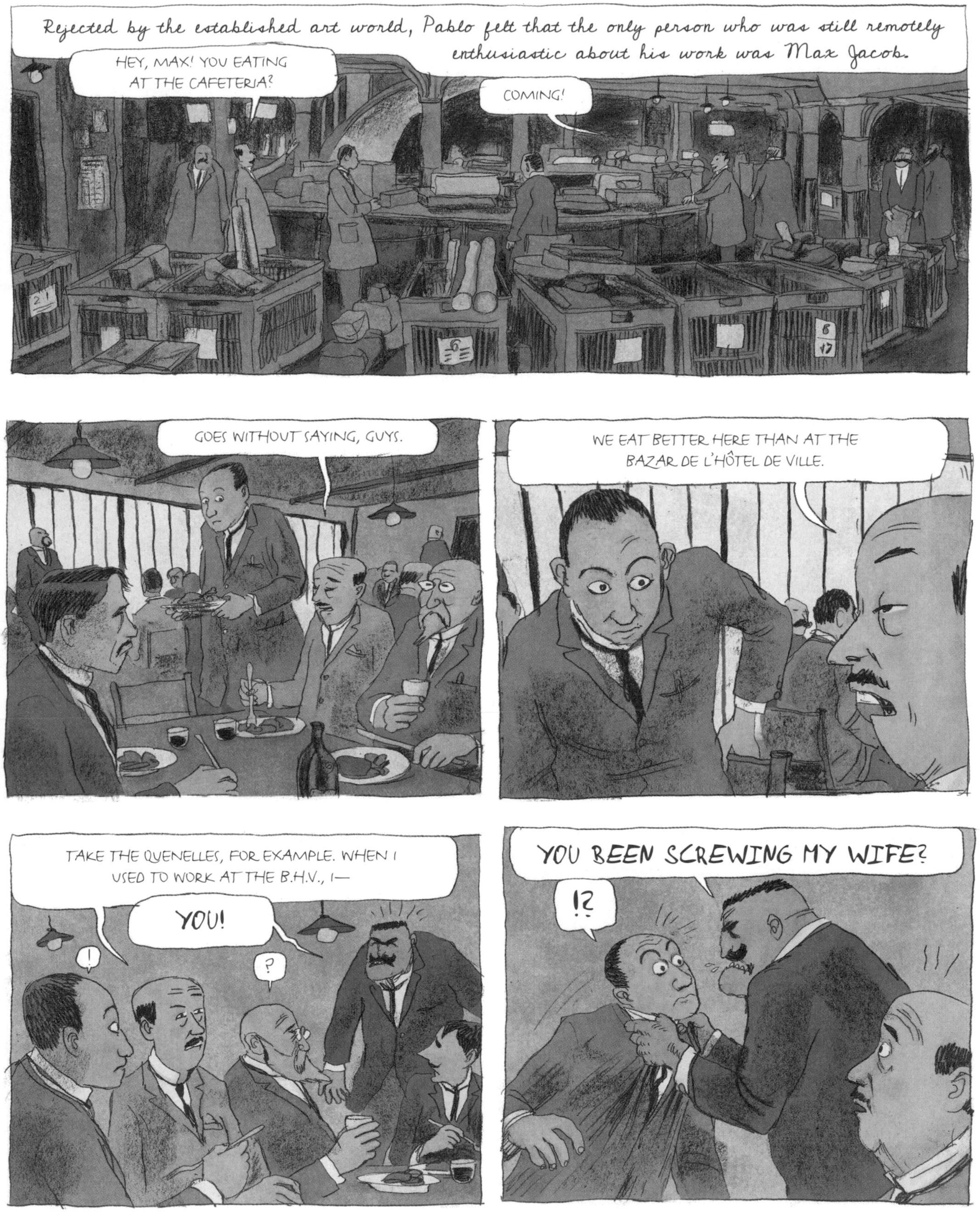
Rejected by the established art world, Pablo felt that the only person who was still remotely enthusiastic about his work was Max Jacob.
HEY, MAX! YOU EATING AT THE CAFETERIA?
COMING!
GOES WITHOUT SAYING, GUYS.
WE EAT BETTER HERE THAN AT THE BAZAR DE L'HÔTEL DE VILLE.
TAKE THE QUENELLES, FOR EXAMPLE. WHEN I USED TO WORK AT THE B.H.V., I—
YOU!
!
?
YOU BEEN SCREWING MY WIFE?
!?

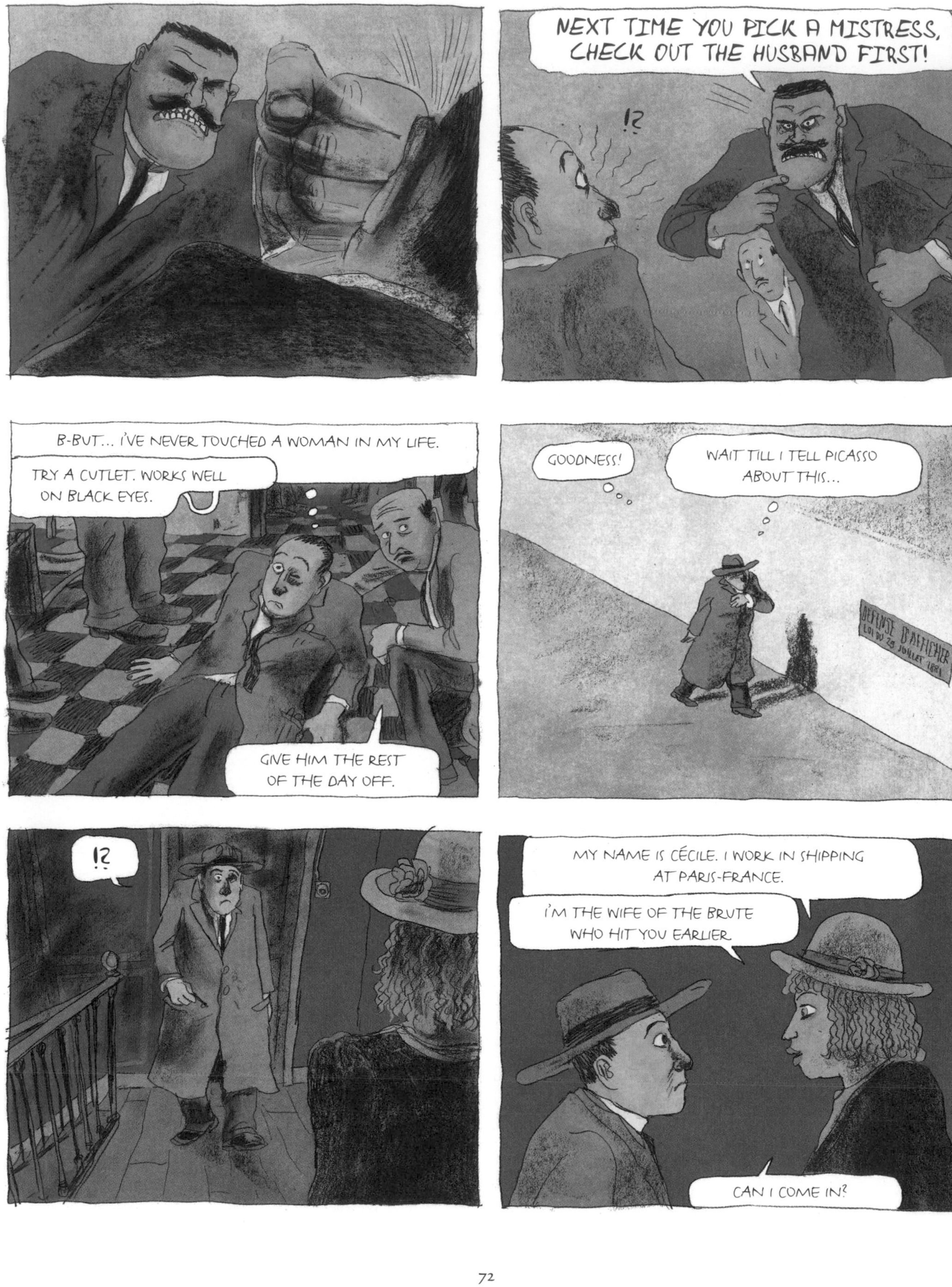
NEXT TIME YOU PICK A MISTRESS, CHECK OUT THE HUSBAND FIRST!
!?
B-BUT... I'VE NEVER TOUCHED A WOMAN IN MY LIFE.
TRY A CUTLET. WORKS WELL ON BLACK EYES.
GIVE HIM THE REST OF THE DAY OFF.
GOODNESS!
WAIT TILL I TELL PICASSO ABOUT THIS...
DEFENSE D'AFFICHER
LOI DU 29 JUILLET 1881
!?
MY NAME IS CÉCILE. I WORK IN SHIPPING AT PARIS-FRANCE.
I'M THE WIFE OF THE BRUTE WHO HIT YOU EARLIER.
CAN I COME IN?

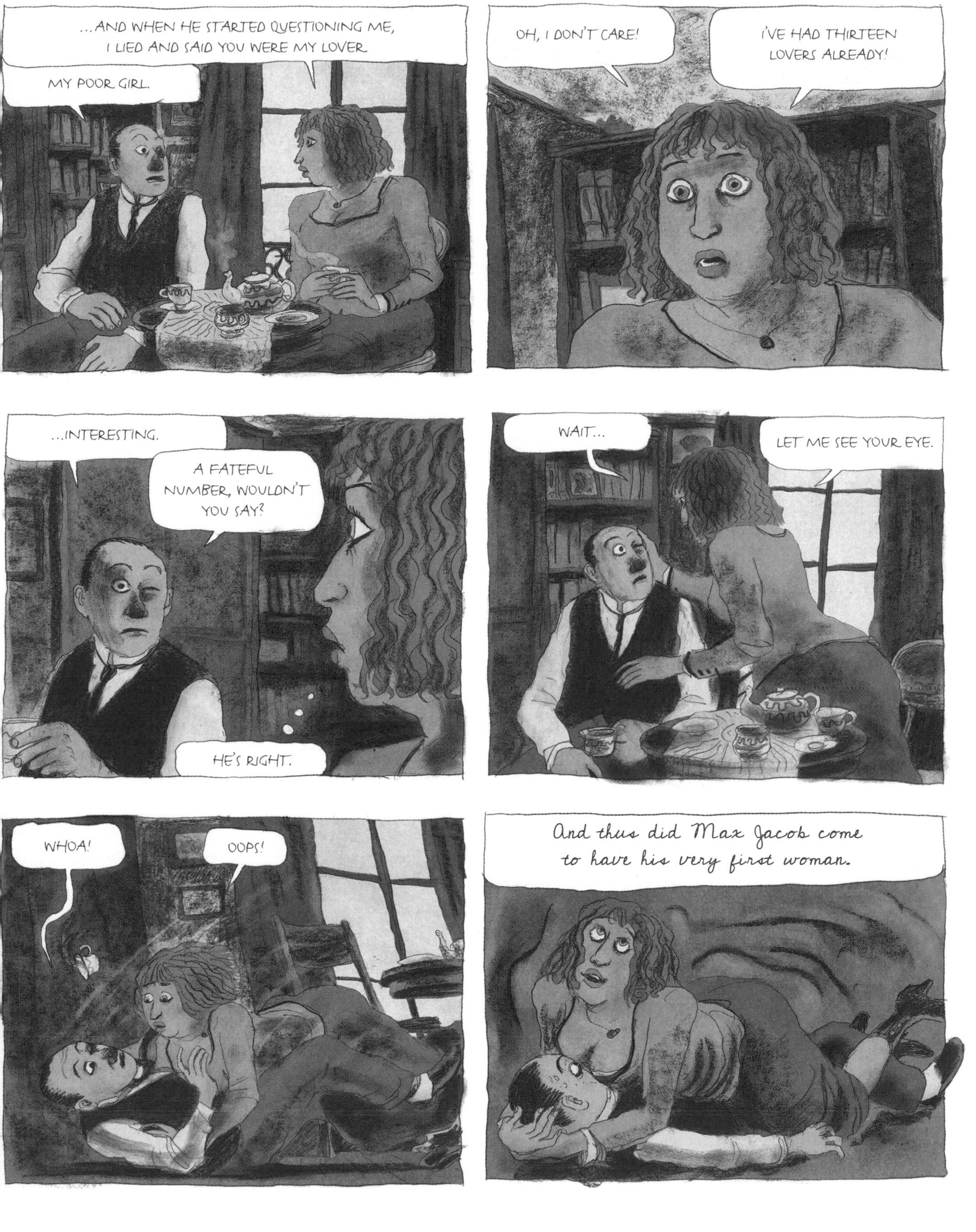
...AND WHEN HE STARTED QUESTIONING ME, I LIED AND SAID YOU WERE MY LOVER.
MY POOR GIRL.
OH, I DON'T CARE!
I'VE HAD THIRTEEN LOVERS ALREADY!
...INTERESTING.
A FATEFUL NUMBER, WOULDN'T YOU SAY?
HE'S RIGHT.
WAIT...
LET ME SEE YOUR EYE.
WHOA!
OOPS!
And thus did Max Jacob come to have his very first woman.

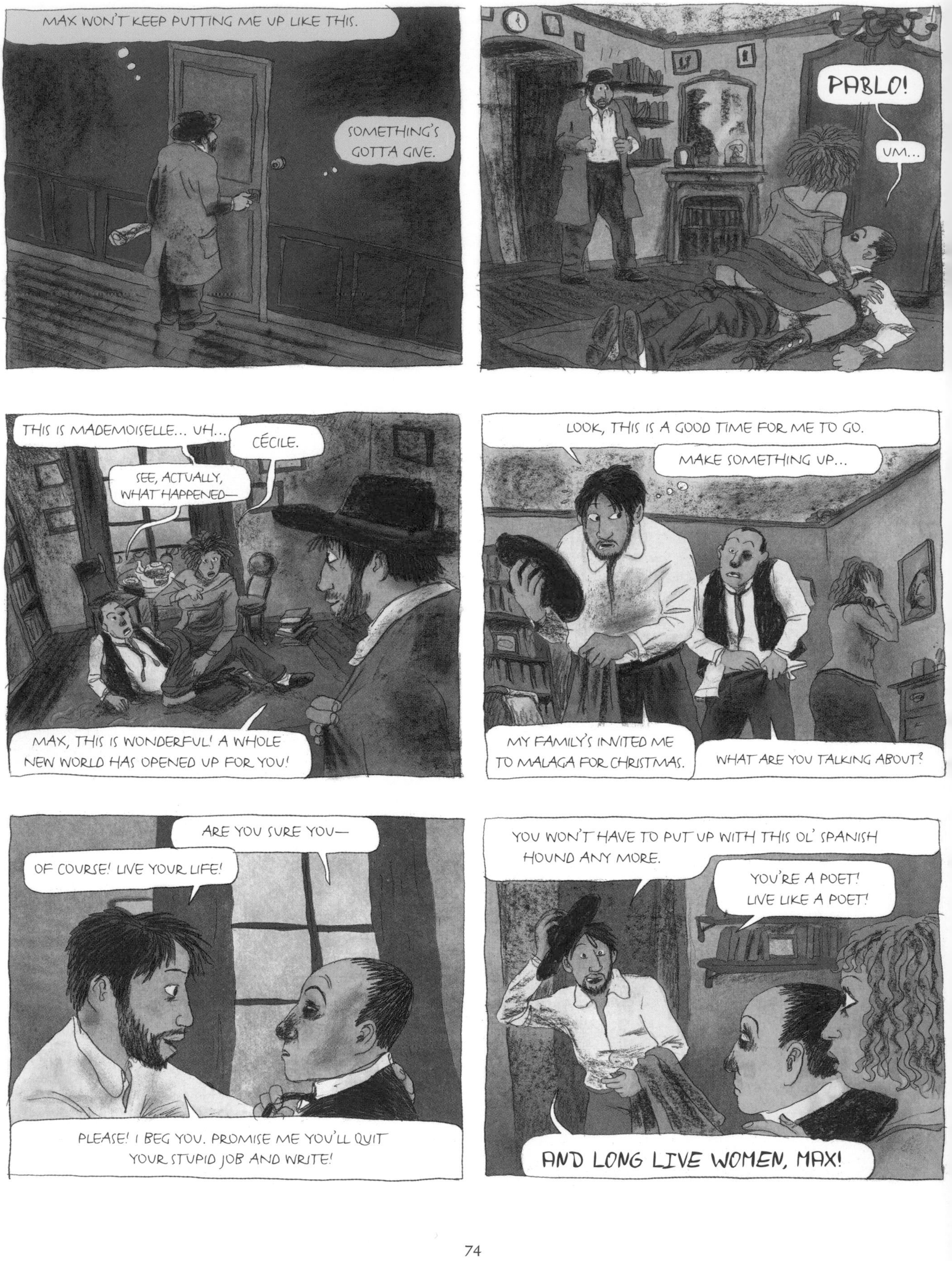
MAX WON'T KEEP PUTTING ME UP LIKE THIS.
SOMETHING'S GOTTA GIVE.
PABLO!
UM...
THIS IS MADEMOISELLE... UH...
CÉCILE.
SEE, ACTUALLY, WHAT HAPPENED—
MAX, THIS IS WONDERFUL! A WHOLE NEW WORLD HAS OPENED UP FOR YOU!
LOOK, THIS IS A GOOD TIME FOR ME TO GO.
MAKE SOMETHING UP...
MY FAMILY'S INVITED ME TO MALAGA FOR CHRISTMAS.
WHAT ARE YOU TALKING ABOUT?
ARE YOU SURE YOU—
OF COURSE! LIVE YOUR LIFE!
PLEASE! I BEG YOU. PROMISE ME YOU'LL QUIT YOUR STUPID JOB AND WRITE!
YOU WON'T HAVE TO PUT UP WITH THIS OL' SPANISH HOUND ANY MORE.
YOU'RE A POET! LIVE LIKE A POET!
AND LONG LIVE WOMEN, MAX!

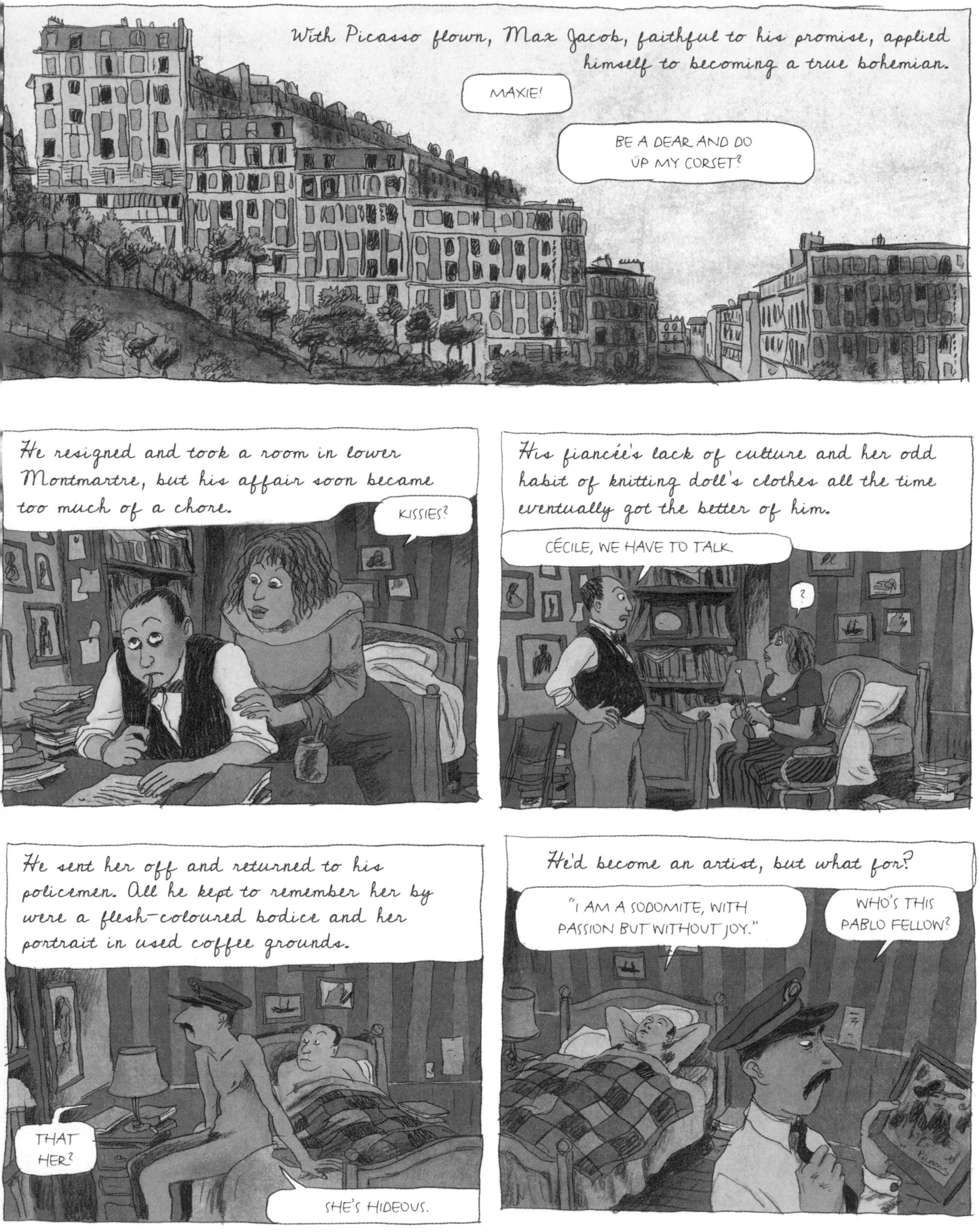
With Picasso flown, Max Jacob, faithful to his promise, applied himself to becoming a true bohemian.
MAXIE!
BE A DEAR AND DO UP MY CORSET?
He resigned and took a room in lower Montmartre, but his affair soon became too much of a chore.
KISSIES?
His fiancée's lack of culture and her odd habit of knitting doll's clothes all the time eventually got the better of him.
CÉCILE, WE HAVE TO TALK.
?
He sent her off and returned to his policemen. All he kept to remember her by were a flesh-coloured bodice and her portrait in used coffee grounds.
THAT HER?
SHE'S HIDEOUS.
He'd become an artist, but what for?
"I AM A SODOMITE, WITH PASSION BUT WITHOUT JOY."
WHO'S THIS PABLO FELLOW?

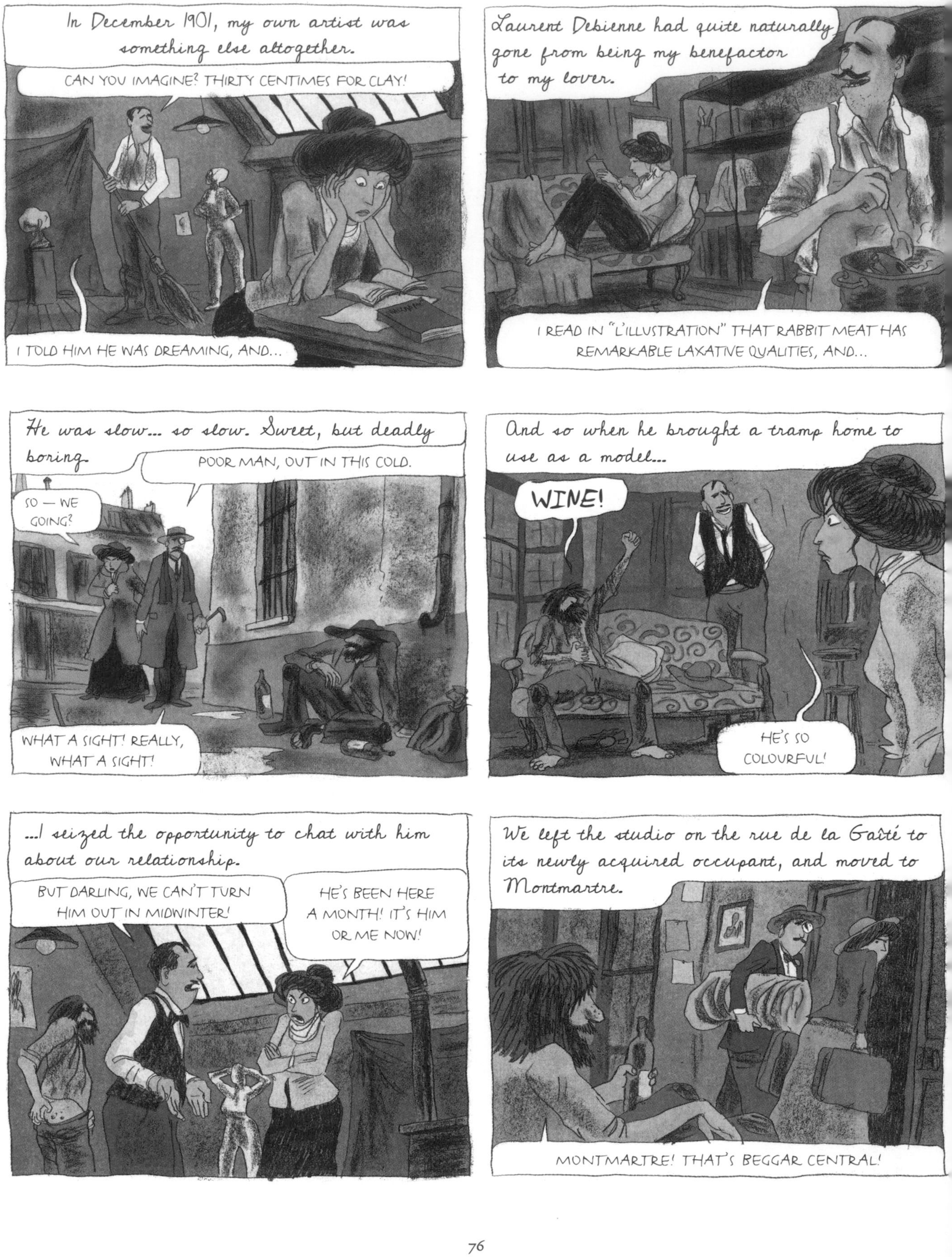
In December 1901, my own artist was something else altogether.
CAN YOU IMAGINE? THIRTY CENTIMES FOR CLAY!
I TOLD HIM HE WAS DREAMING, AND...
Laurent Debienne had quite naturally gone from being my benefactor to my lover.
I READ IN "L'ILLUSTRATION" THAT RABBIT MEAT HAS REMARKABLE LAXATIVE QUALITIES, AND...
He was slow... so slow. Sweet, but deadly boring.
POOR MAN, OUT IN THIS COLD.
SO — WE GOING?
WHAT A SIGHT! REALLY, WHAT A SIGHT!
And so when he brought a tramp home to use as a model...
WINE!
HE'S SO COLOURFUL!
...I seized the opportunity to chat with him about our relationship.
BUT DARLING, WE CAN'T TURN HIM OUT IN MIDWINTER!
HE'S BEEN HERE A MONTH! IT'S HIM OR ME NOW!
We left the studio on the rue de la Gaîté to its newly acquired occupant, and moved to Montmartre.
MONTMARTRE! THAT'S BEGGAR CENTRAL!

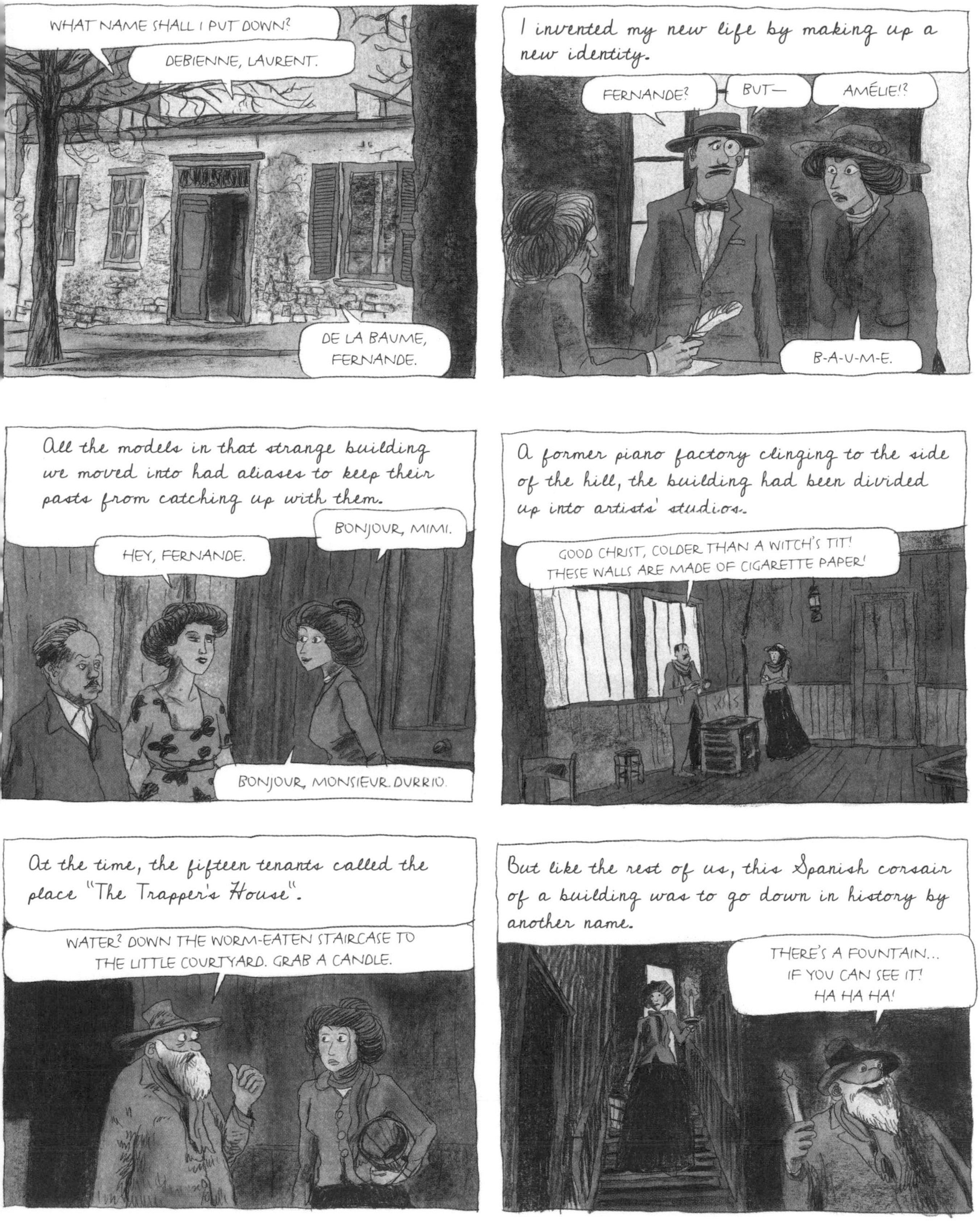
WHAT NAME SHALL I PUT DOWN?
DEBIENNE, LAURENT.
DE LA BAUME, FERNANDE.
I invented my new life by making up a new identity.
FERNANDE?
BUT—
AMÉLIE!?
B-A-U-M-E.
All the models in that strange building we moved into had aliases to keep their pasts from catching up with them.
HEY, FERNANDE.
BONJOUR, MIMI.
BONJOUR, MONSIEUR DURRIO.
A former piano factory clinging to the side of the hill, the building had been divided up into artists' studios.
GOOD CHRIST, COLDER THAN A WITCH'S TIT! THESE WALLS ARE MADE OF CIGARETTE PAPER!
At the time, the fifteen tenants called the place "The Trapper's House".
WATER? DOWN THE WORM-EATEN STAIRCASE TO THE LITTLE COURTYARD. GRAB A CANDLE.
But like the rest of us, this Spanish corsair of a building was to go down in history by another name.
THERE'S A FOUNTAIN... IF YOU CAN SEE IT! HA HA HA!

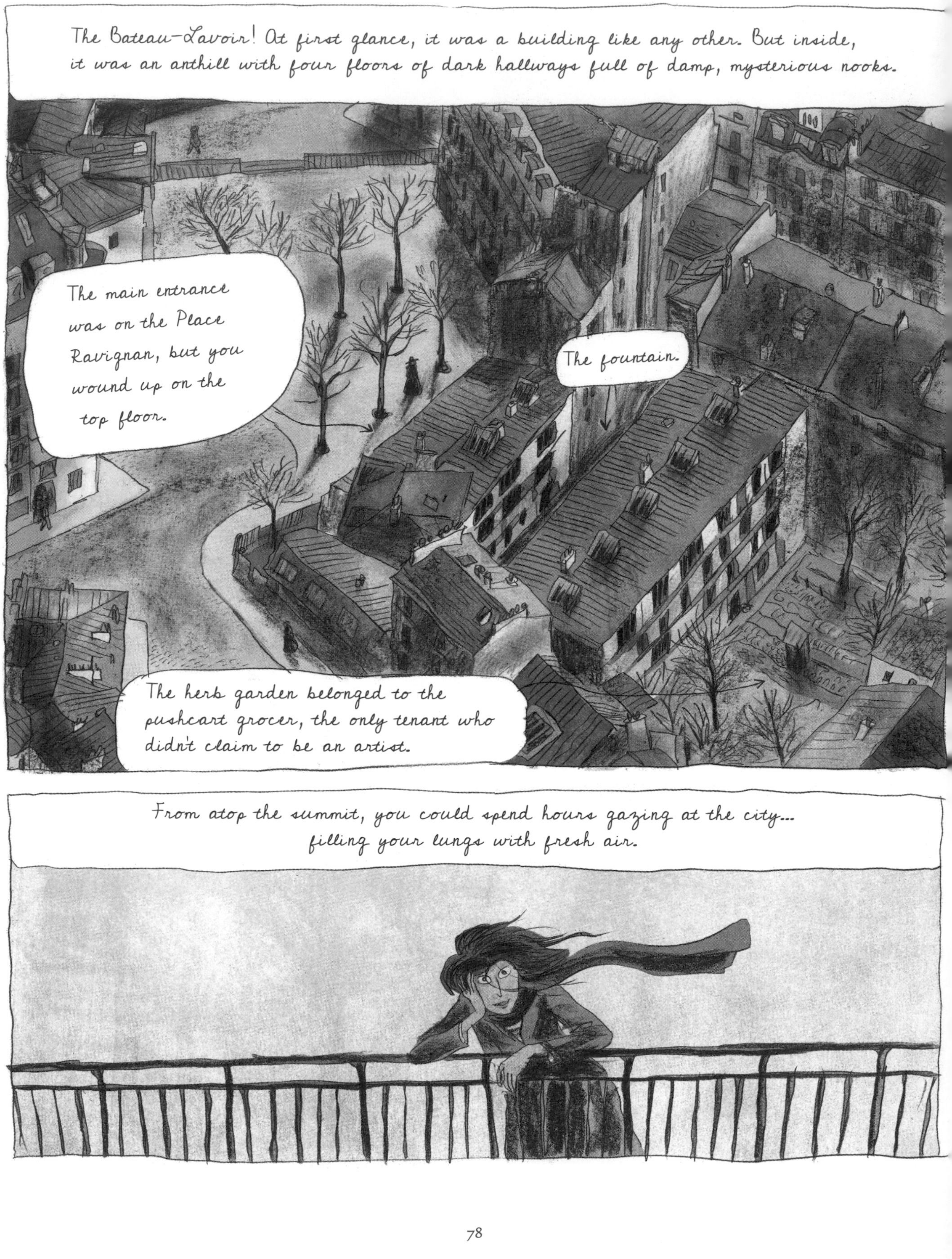
The Bateau-Lavoir! At first glance, it was a building like any other. But inside, it was an anthill with four floors of dark hallways full of damp, mysterious nooks.
The main entrance was on the Place Ravignan, but you wound up on the top floor.
The fountain.
The herb garden belonged to the pushcart grocer, the only tenant who didn't claim to be an artist.
From atop the summit, you could spend hours gazing at the city... filling your lungs with fresh air.

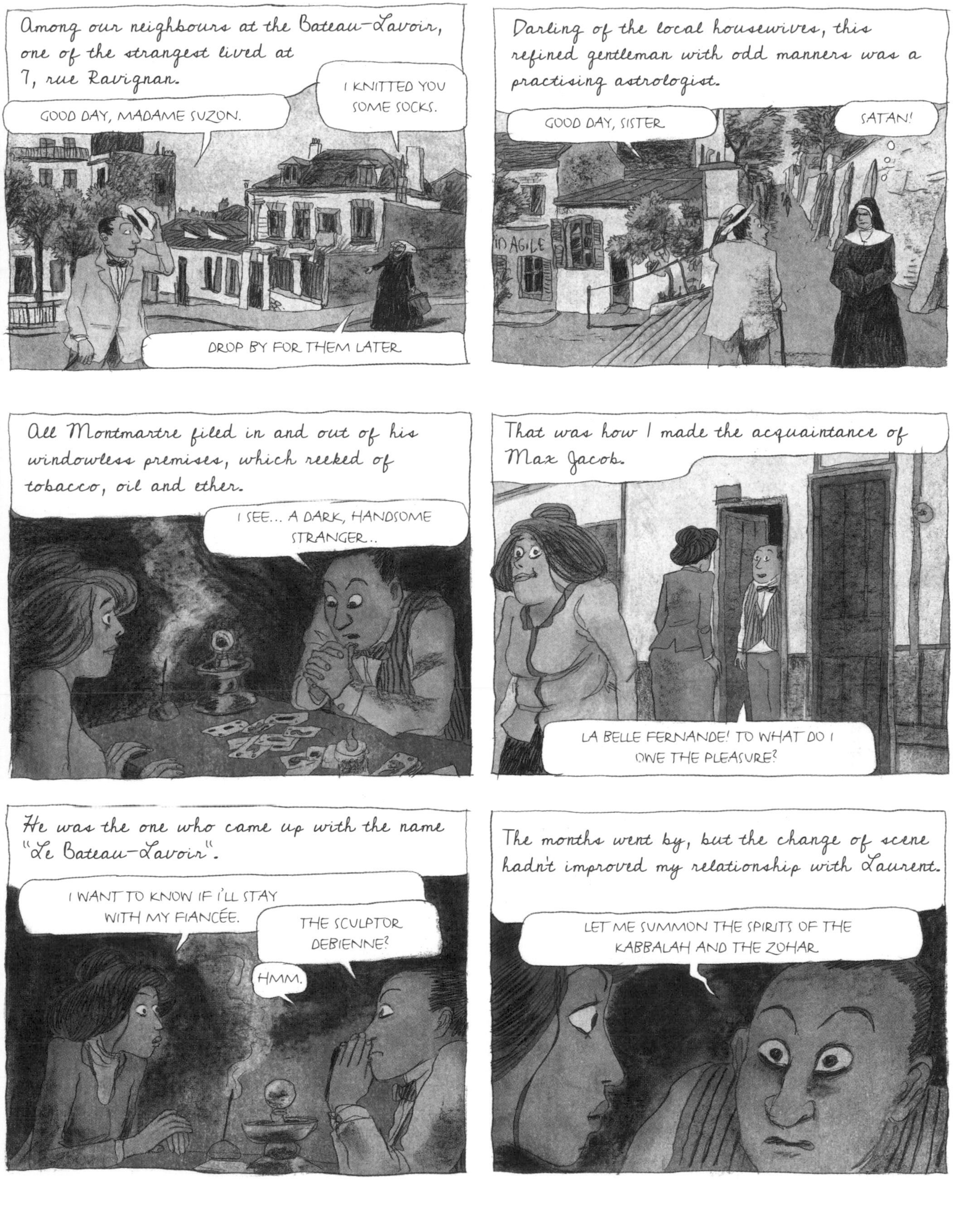
Among our neighbours at the Bateau-Lavoir, one of the strangest lived at 7, rue Ravignan.
GOOD DAY, MADAME SUZON.
I KNITTED YOU SOME SOCKS.
DROP BY FOR THEM LATER
Darling of the local housewives, this refined gentleman with odd manners was a practising astrologist.
GOOD DAY, SISTER
SATAN!
AGILE
All Montmartre filed in and out of his windowless premises, which reeked of tobacco, oil and ether.
I SEE... A DARK, HANDSOME STRANGER..
That was how I made the acquaintance of Max Jacob.
LA BELLE FERNANDE! TO WHAT DO I OWE THE PLEASURE?
He was the one who came up with the name "Le Bateau-Lavoir".
I WANT TO KNOW IF I'LL STAY WITH MY FIANCÉE.
THE SCULPTOR DEBIENNE?
HMM.
The months went by, but the change of scene hadn't improved my relationship with Laurent.
LET ME SUMMON THE SPIRITS OF THE KABBALAH AND THE ZOHAR

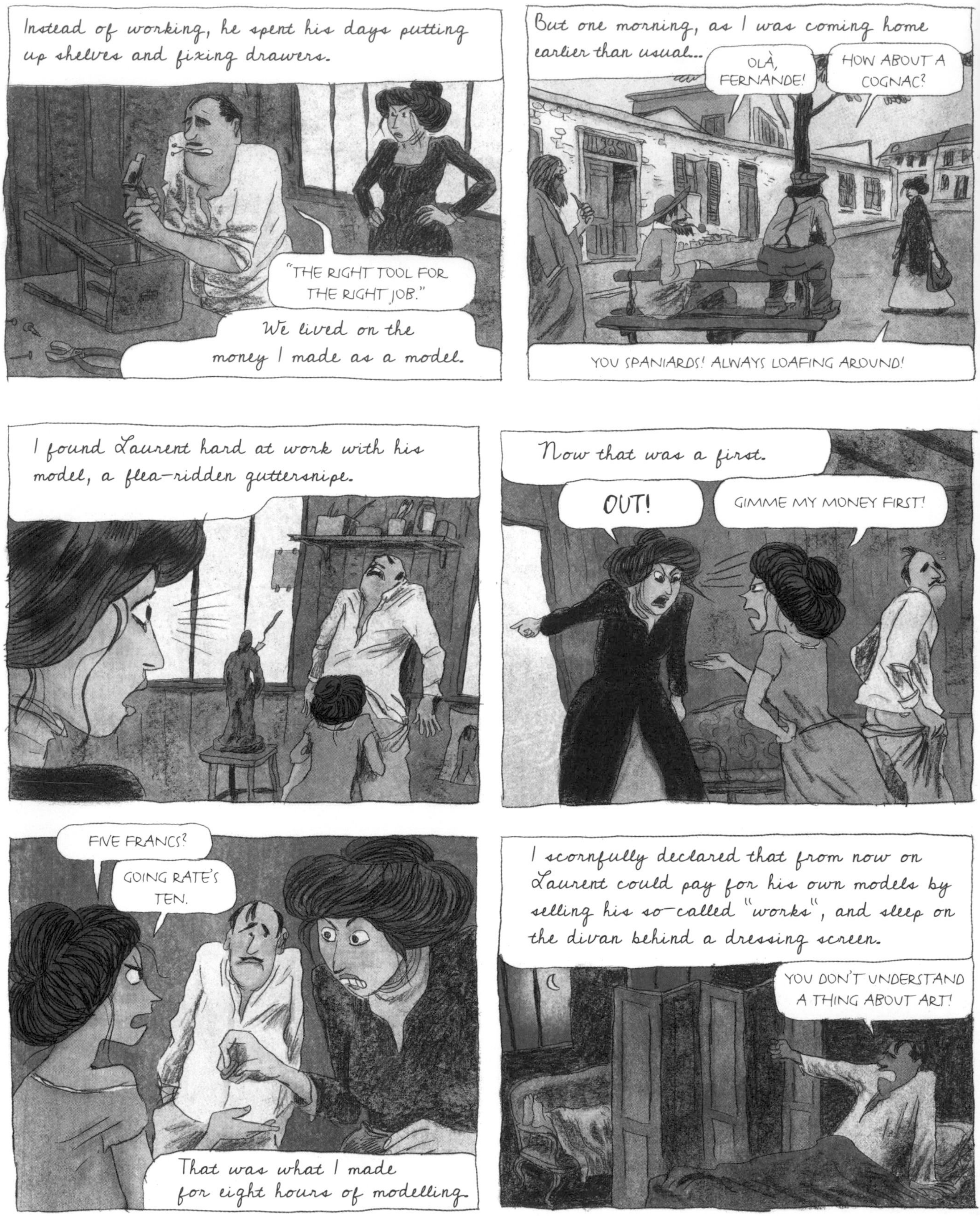
Instead of working, he spent his days putting up shelves and fixing drawers.
"THE RIGHT TOOL FOR THE RIGHT JOB."
We lived on the money I made as a model.
But one morning, as I was coming home earlier than usual...
OLÀ, FERNANDE!
HOW ABOUT A COGNAC?
YOU SPANIARDS! ALWAYS LOAFING AROUND!
I found Laurent hard at work with his model, a flea-ridden guttersnipe.
Now that was a first.
OUT!
GIMME MY MONEY FIRST!
FIVE FRANCS?
GOING RATE'S TEN.
That was what I made for eight hours of modelling.
I scornfully declared that from now on Laurent could pay for his own models by selling his so-called "works", and sleep on the divan behind a dressing screen.
YOU DON'T UNDERSTAND A THING ABOUT ART!

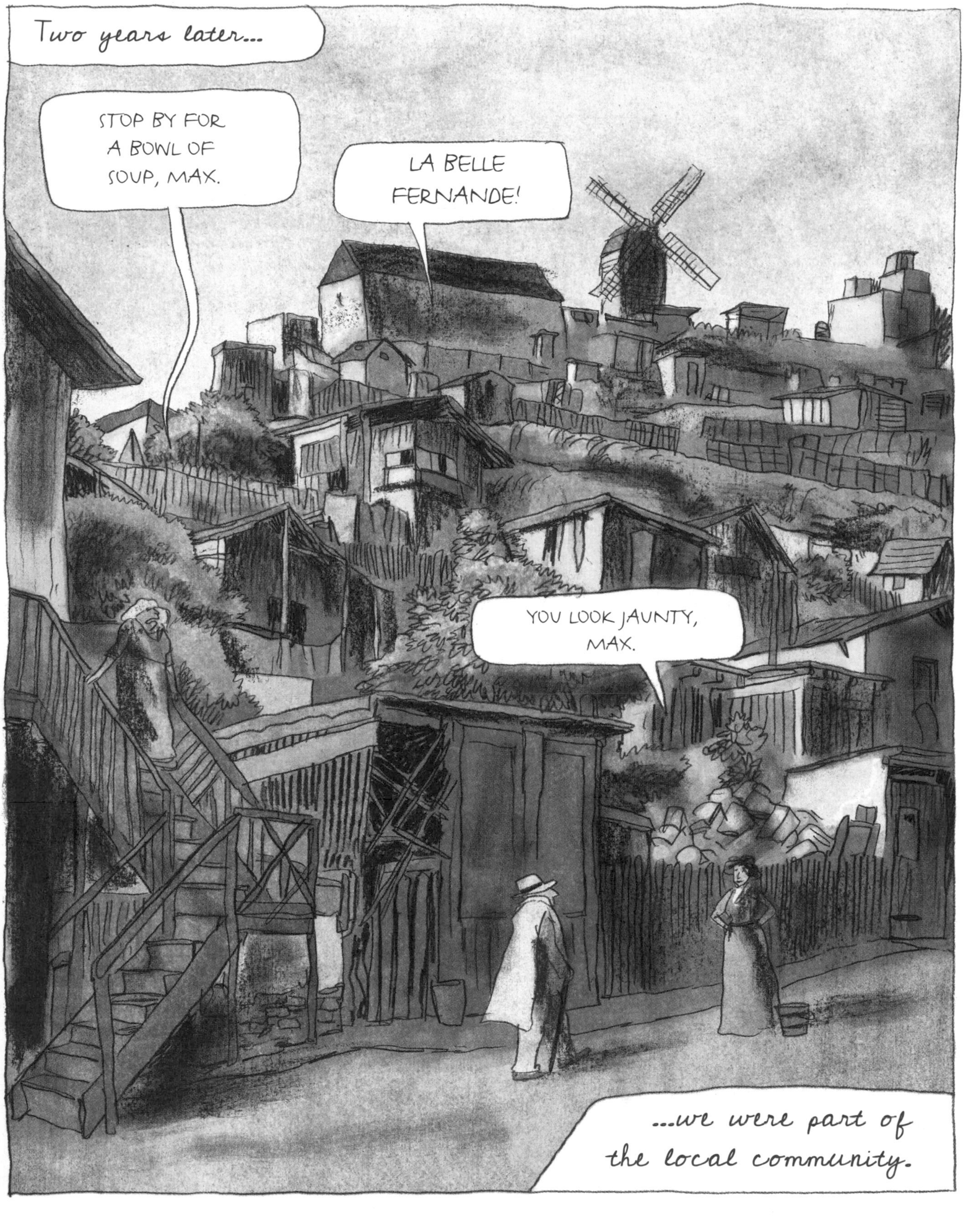
Two years later...
STOP BY FOR A BOWL OF SOUP, MAX.
LA BELLE FERNANDE!
YOU LOOK JAUNTY, MAX.
...we were part of the local community.

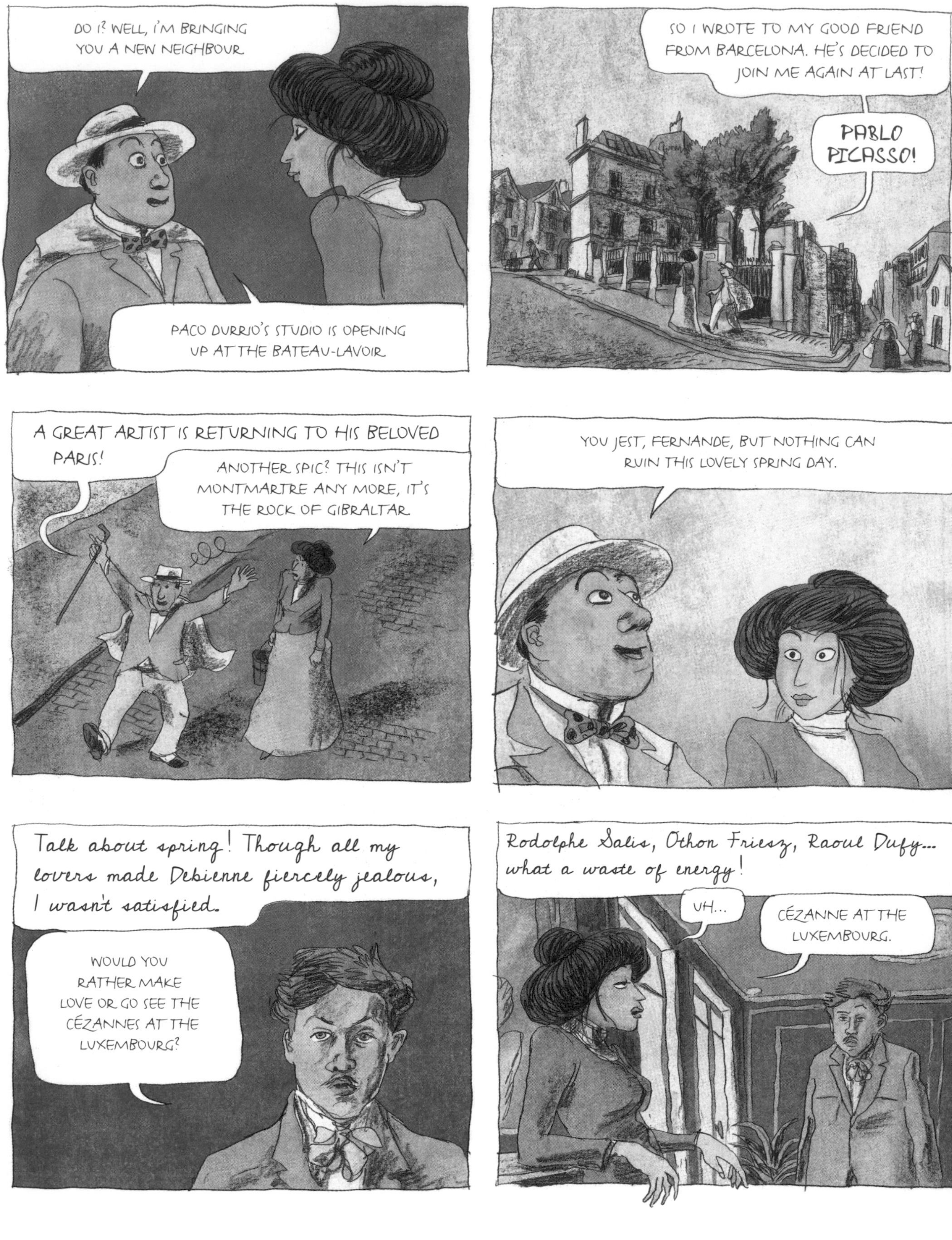
DO I? WELL, I'M BRINGING YOU A NEW NEIGHBOUR
PACO DURRIO'S STUDIO IS OPENING UP AT THE BATEAU-LAVOIR
SO I WROTE TO MY GOOD FRIEND FROM BARCELONA. HE'S DECIDED TO JOIN ME AGAIN AT LAST!
PABLO PICASSO!
A GREAT ARTIST IS RETURNING TO HIS BELOVED PARIS!
ANOTHER SPIC? THIS ISN'T MONTMARTRE ANY MORE, IT'S THE ROCK OF GIBRALTAR
YOU JEST, FERNANDE, BUT NOTHING CAN RUIN THIS LOVELY SPRING DAY.
Talk about spring! Though all my lovers made Debienne fiercely jealous, I wasn't satisfied.
WOULD YOU RATHER MAKE LOVE OR GO SEE THE CÉZANNES AT THE LUXEMBOURG?
Rodolphe Salis, Othon Friesz, Raoul Dufy... what a waste of energy!
UH...
CÉZANNE AT THE LUXEMBOURG.

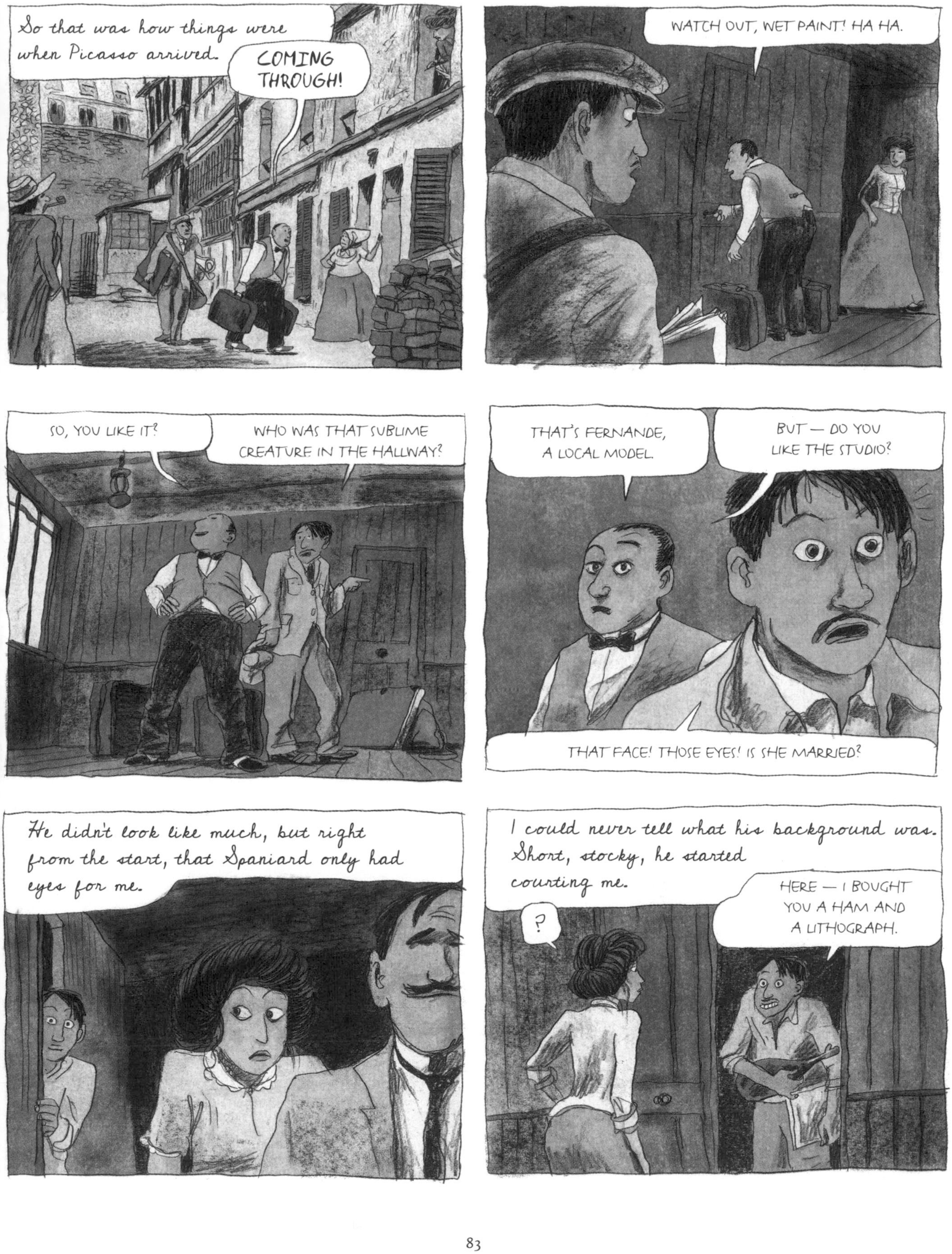
So that was how things were when Picasso arrived.
COMING THROUGH!
WATCH OUT, WET PAINT! HA HA.
SO, YOU LIKE IT?
WHO WAS THAT SUBLIME CREATURE IN THE HALLWAY?
THAT'S FERNANDE, A LOCAL MODEL.
BUT — DO YOU LIKE THE STUDIO?
THAT FACE! THOSE EYES! IS SHE MARRIED?
He didn't look like much, but right from the start, that Spaniard only had eyes for me.
I could never tell what his background was. Short, stocky, he started courting me.
?
HERE — I BOUGHT YOU A HAM AND A LITHOGRAPH.

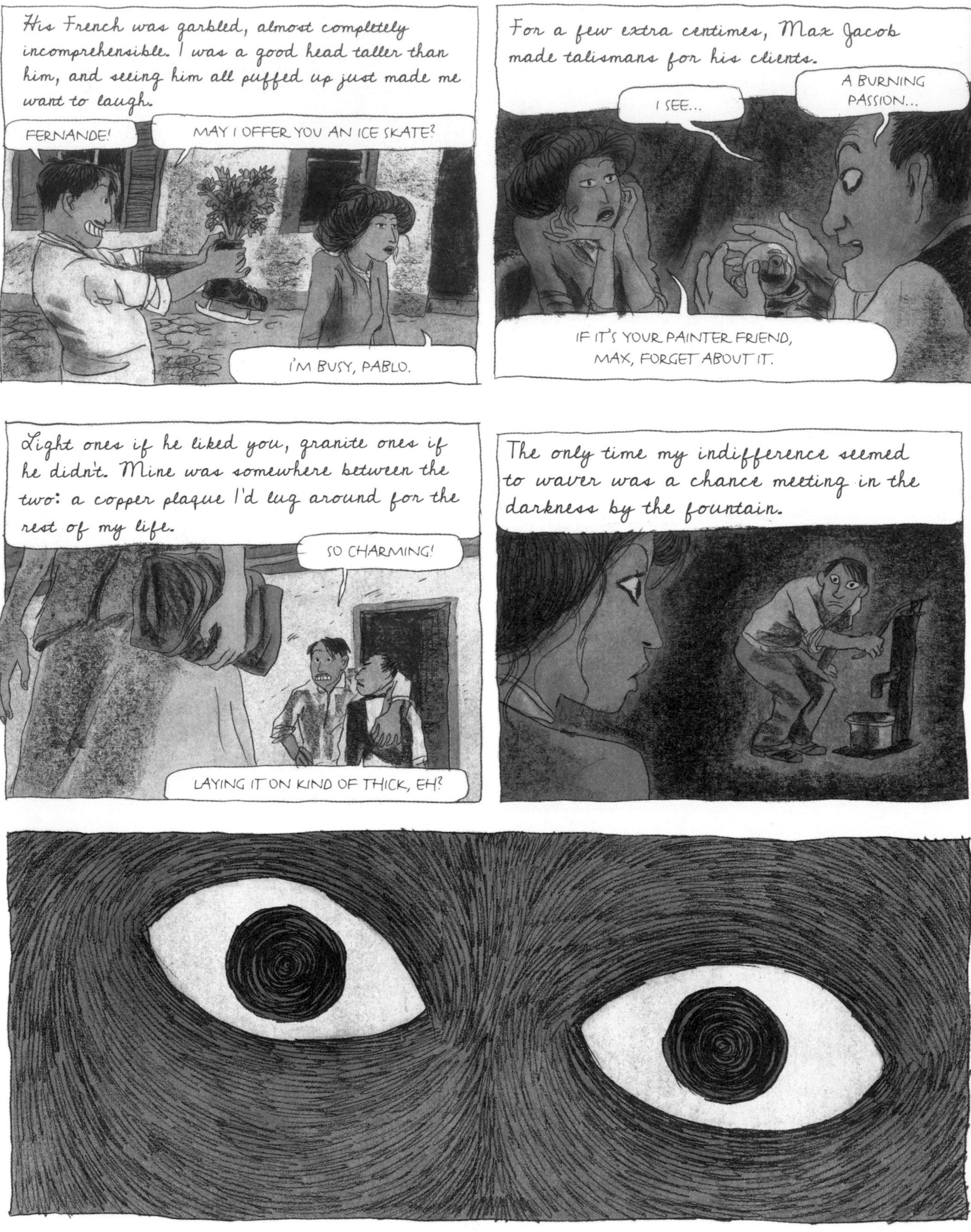
His French was garbled, almost completly incomprehensible. I was a good head taller than him, and seeing him all puffed up just made me want to laugh.
FERNANDE!
MAY I OFFER YOU AN ICE SKATE?
I'M BUSY, PABLO.
For a few extra centimes, Max Jacob made talismans for his clients.
I SEE...
A BURNING PASSION...
IF IT'S YOUR PAINTER FRIEND, MAX, FORGET ABOUT IT.
Light ones if he liked you, granite ones if he didn't. Mine was somewhere between the two: a copper plaque I'd lug around for the rest of my life.
SO CHARMING!
LAYING IT ON KIND OF THICK, EH?
The only time my indifference seemed to waver was a chance meeting in the darkness by the fountain.

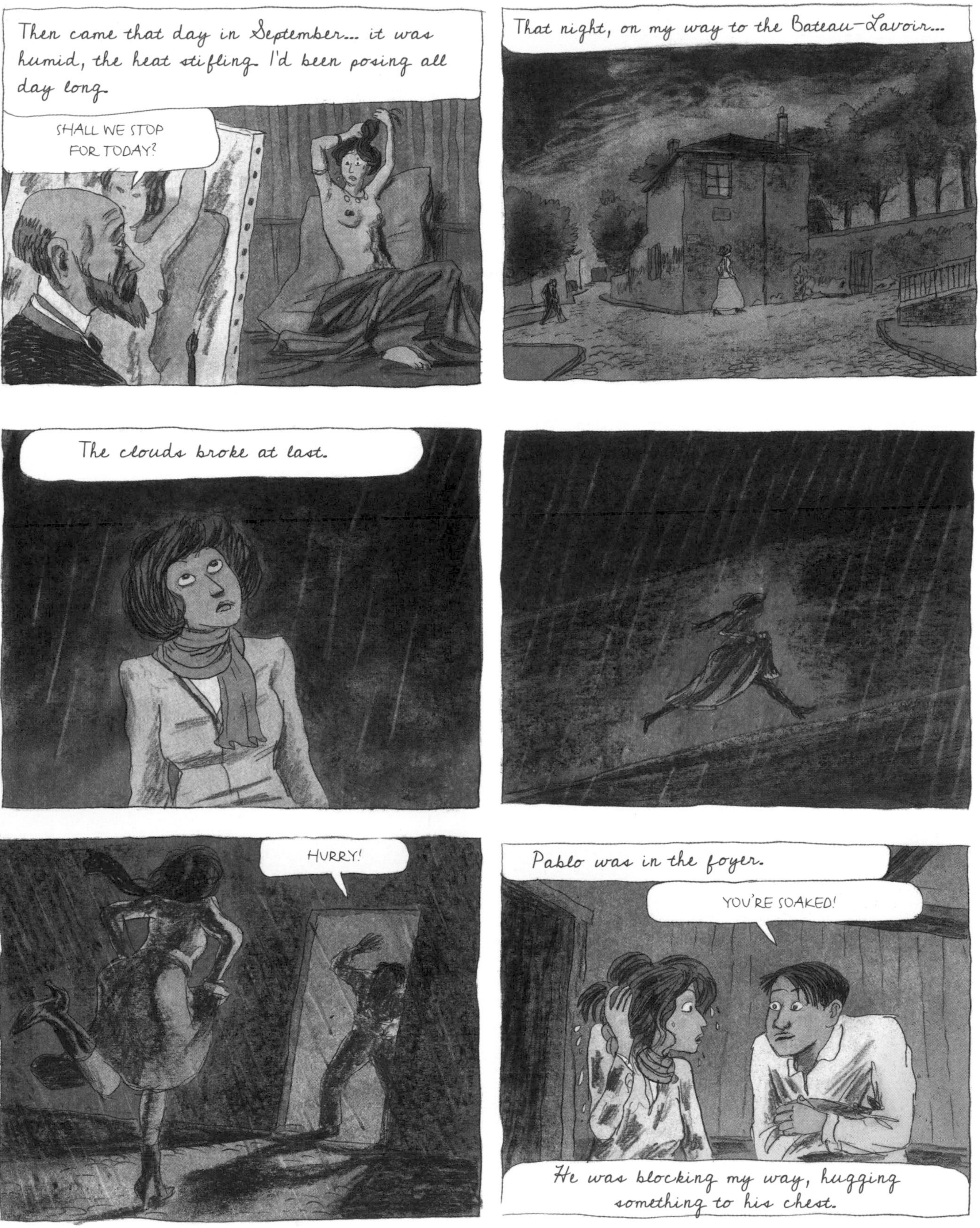
Then came that day in September... it was humid, the heat stifling. I'd been posing all day long.
SHALL WE STOP FOR TODAY?
That night, on my way to the Bateau-Lavoir...
The clouds broke at last.
HURRY!
Pablo was in the foyer.
YOU'RE SOAKED!
He was blocking my way, hugging something to his chest.

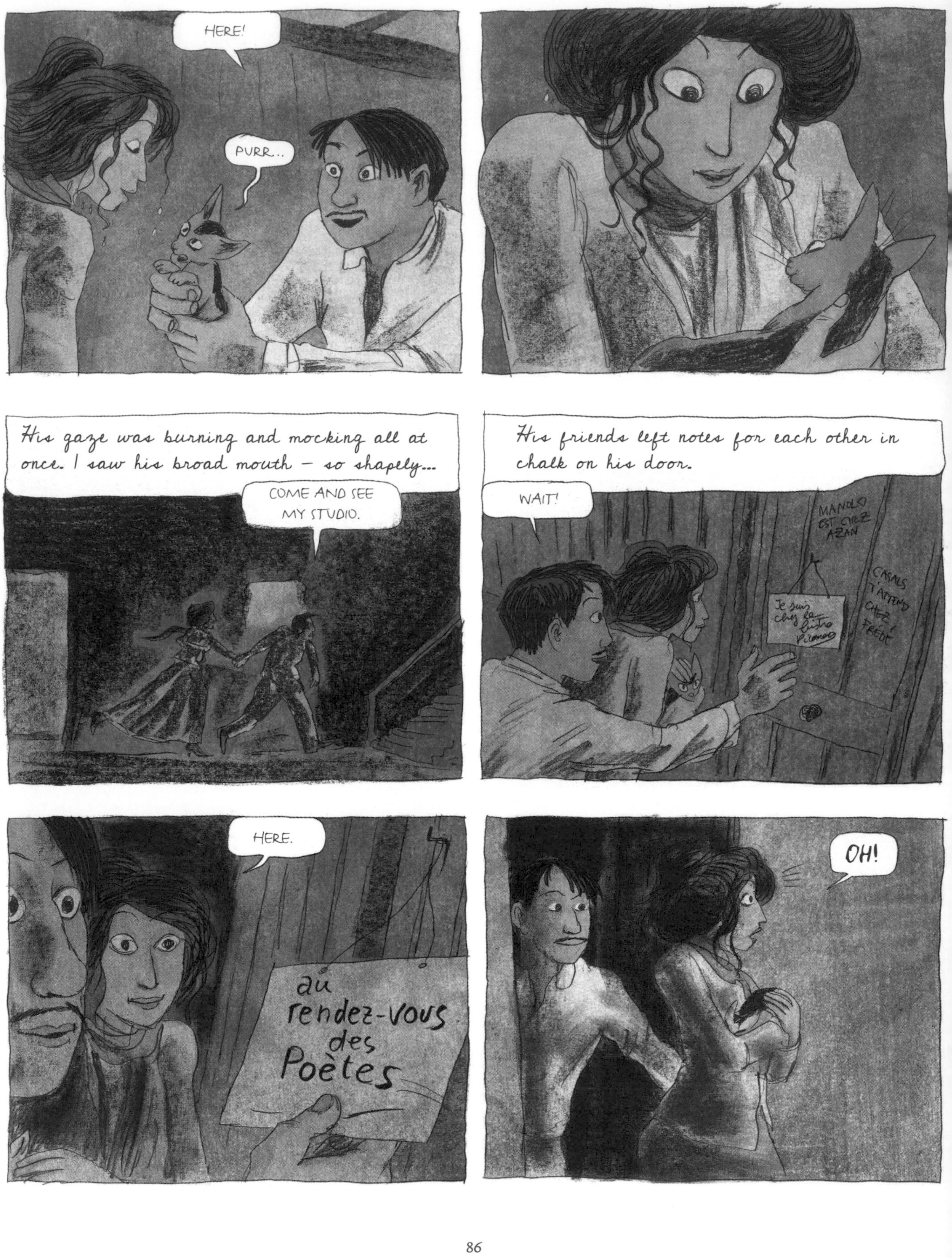
HERE!
PURR..
His gaze was burning and mocking all at once. I saw his broad mouth – so shapely...
COME AND SEE MY STUDIO.
His friends left notes for each other in chalk on his door.
WAIT!
MANOLO EST CHEZ AZAN
CASALS T'ATTEND CHEZ FRÉDÉ!
HERE.
au rendez-vous des Poètes
OH!

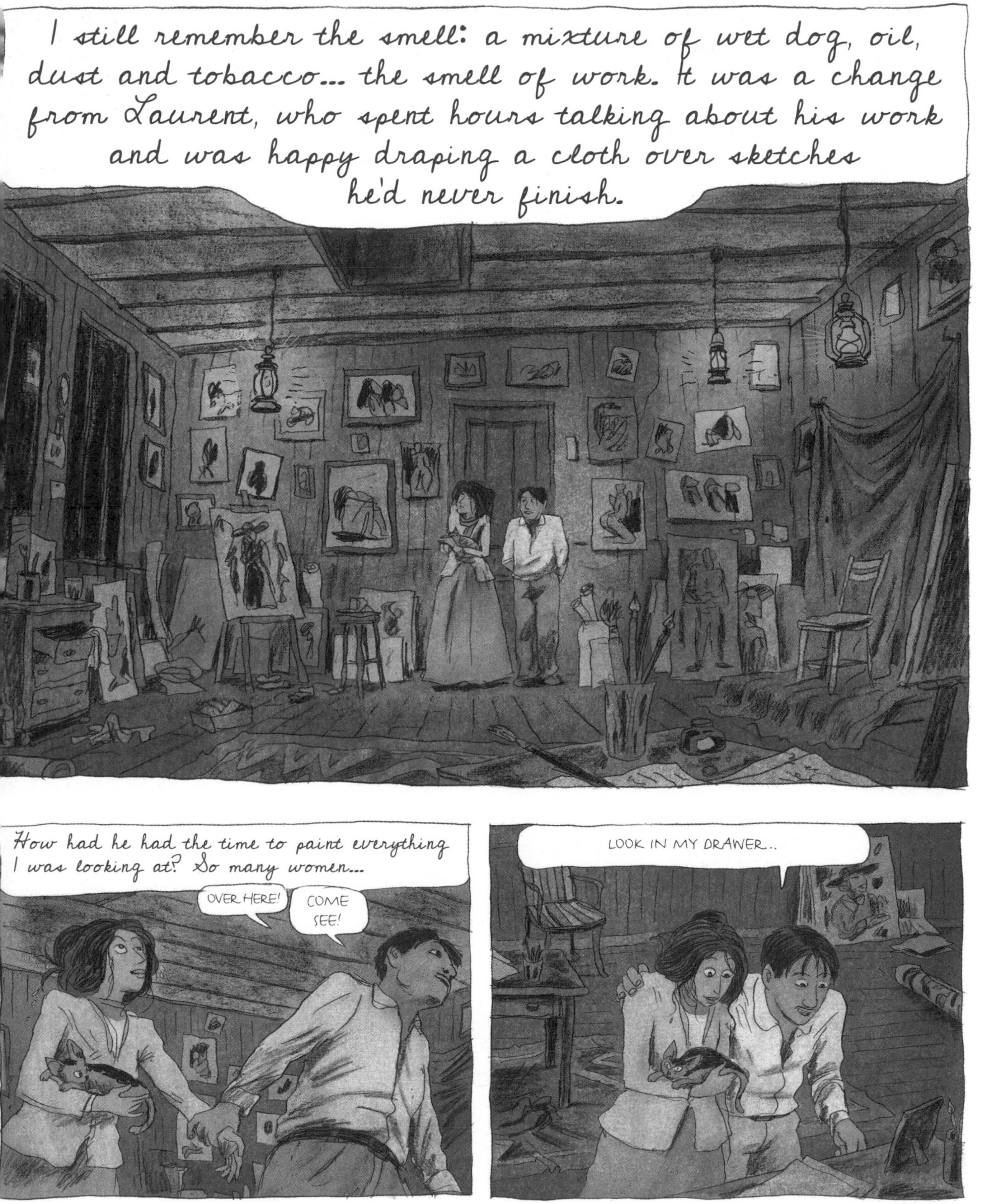
I still remember the smell: a mixture of wet dog, oil, dust and tobacco... the smell of work. It was a change from Laurent, who spent hours talking about his work and was happy draping a cloth over sketches he'd never finish.
How had he had the time to paint everything I was looking at? So many women...
OVER HERE!
COME SEE!
LOOK IN MY DRAWER..

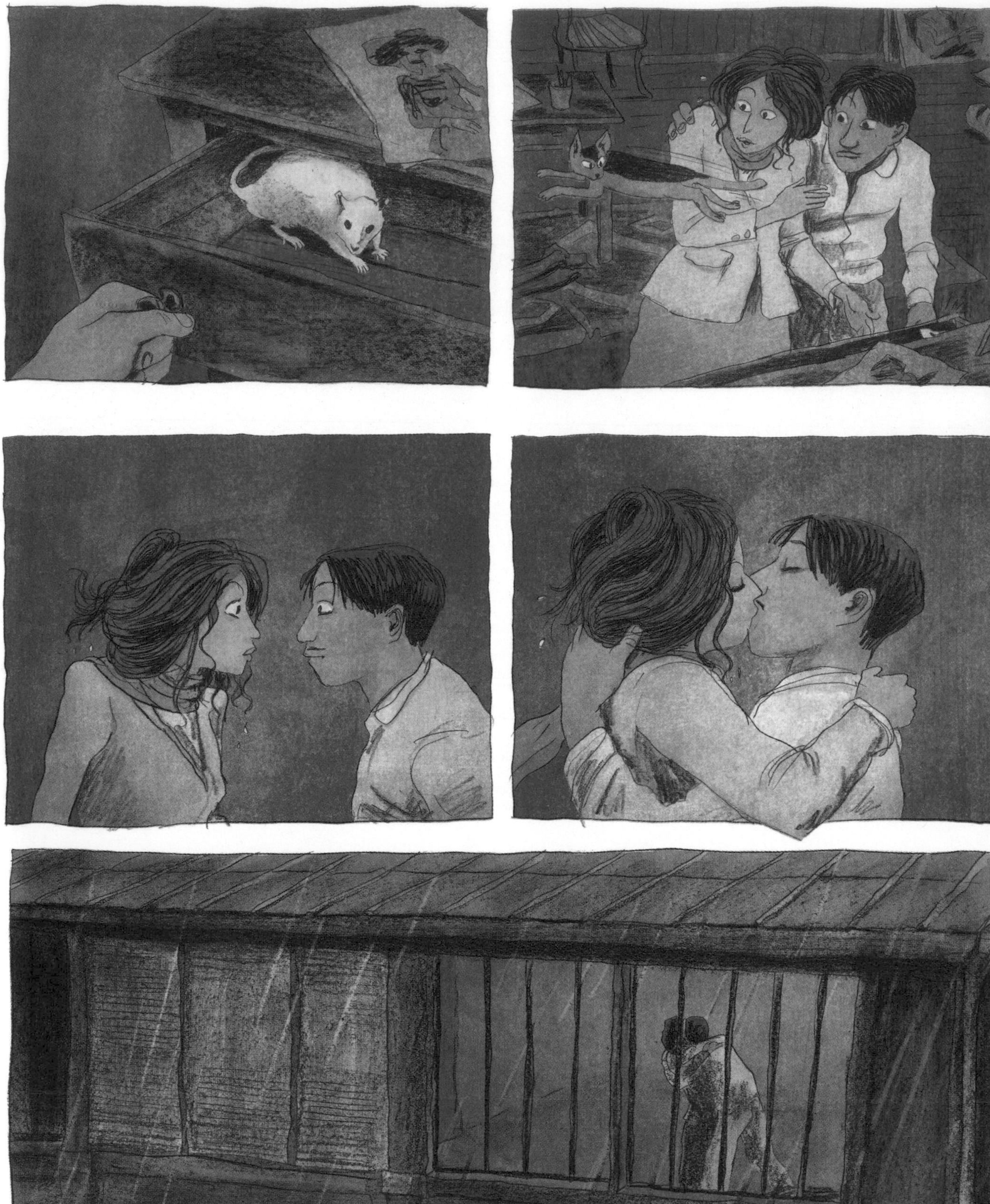

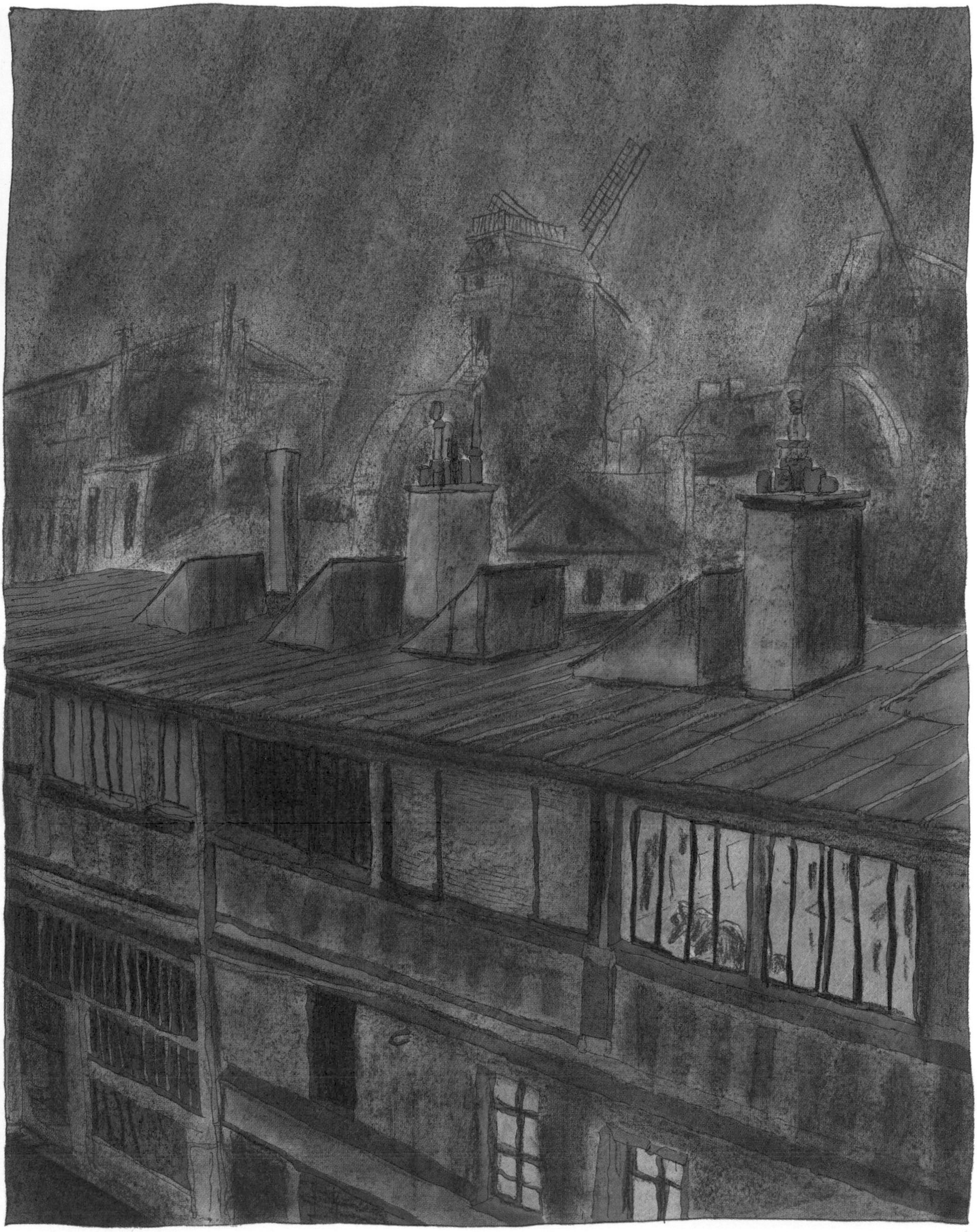

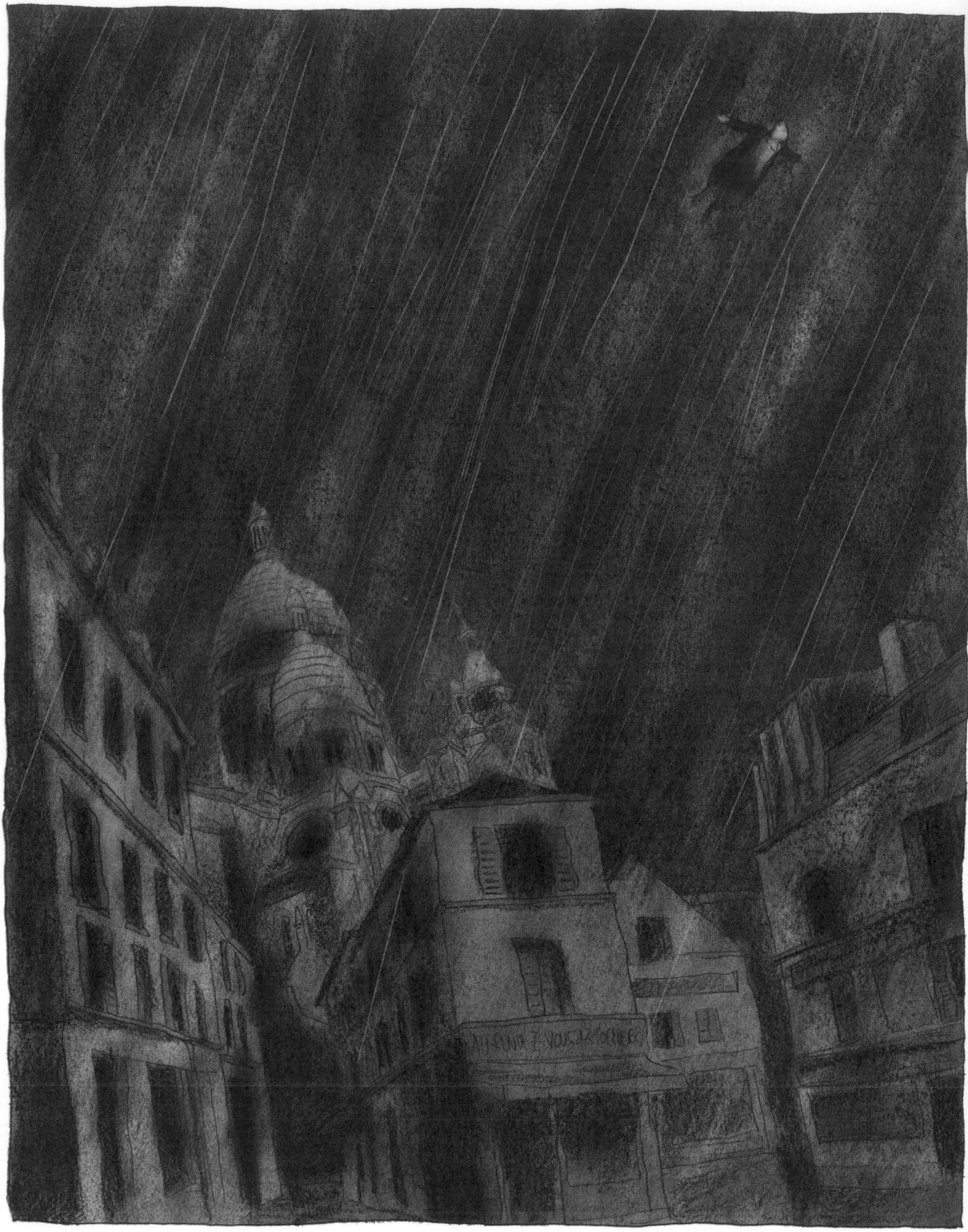

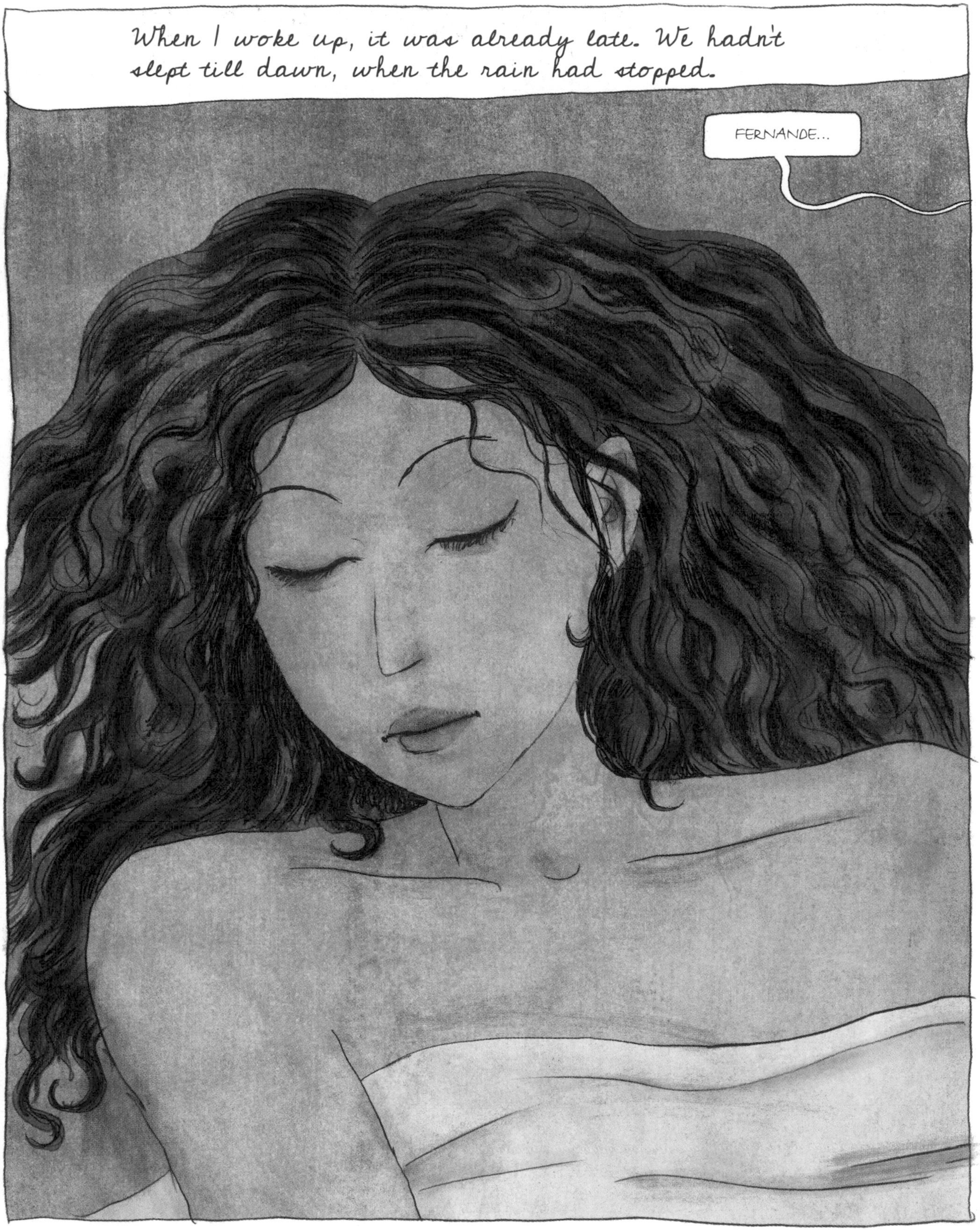
When I woke up, it was already late. We hadn't slept till dawn, when the rain had stopped.
FERNANDE...

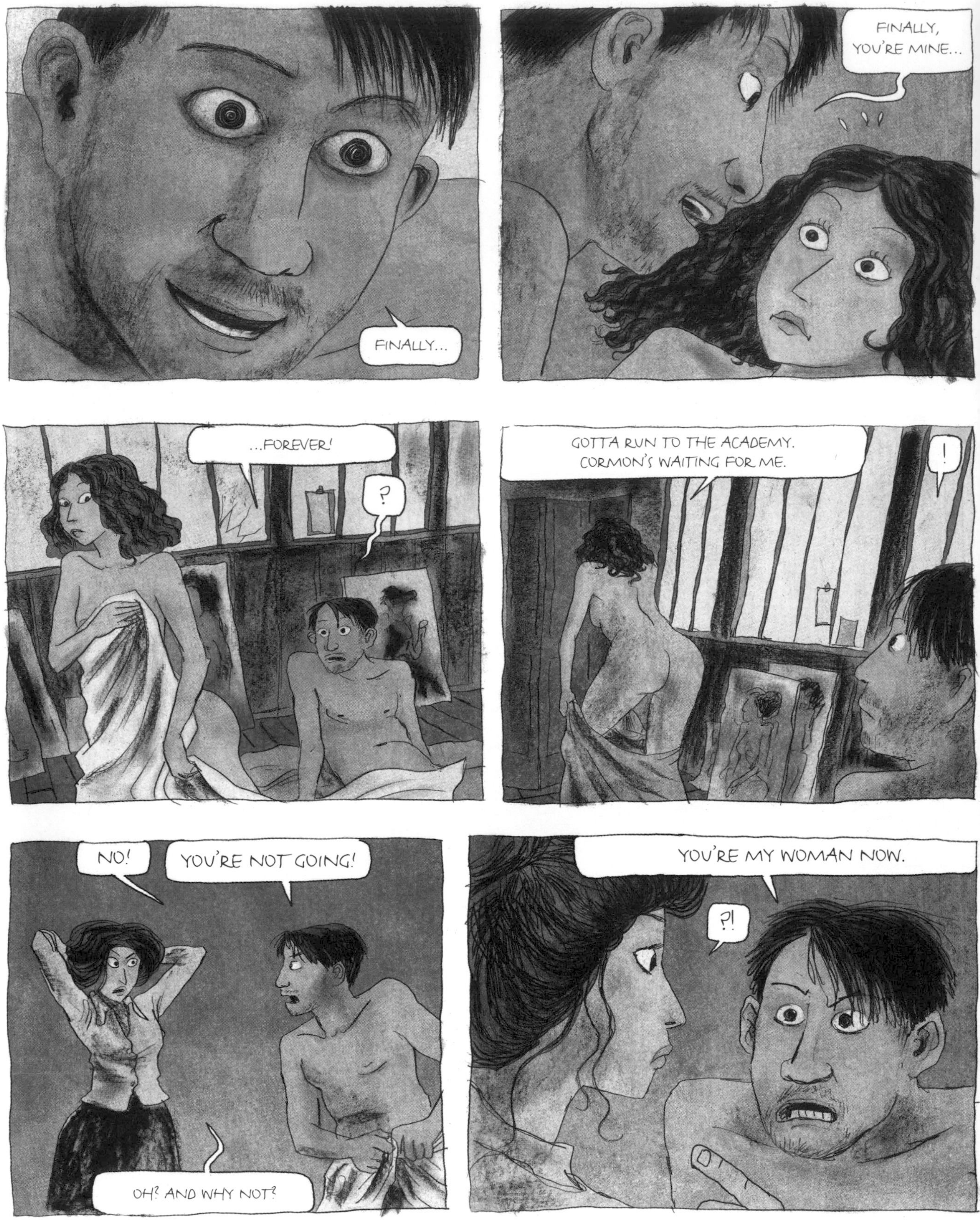

FINALLY...
FINALLY, YOU'RE MINE...
...FOREVER!
?
GOTTA RUN TO THE ACADEMY. CORMON'S WAITING FOR ME.
!
NO!
YOU'RE NOT GOING!
OH? AND WHY NOT?
YOU'RE MY WOMAN NOW.
?!

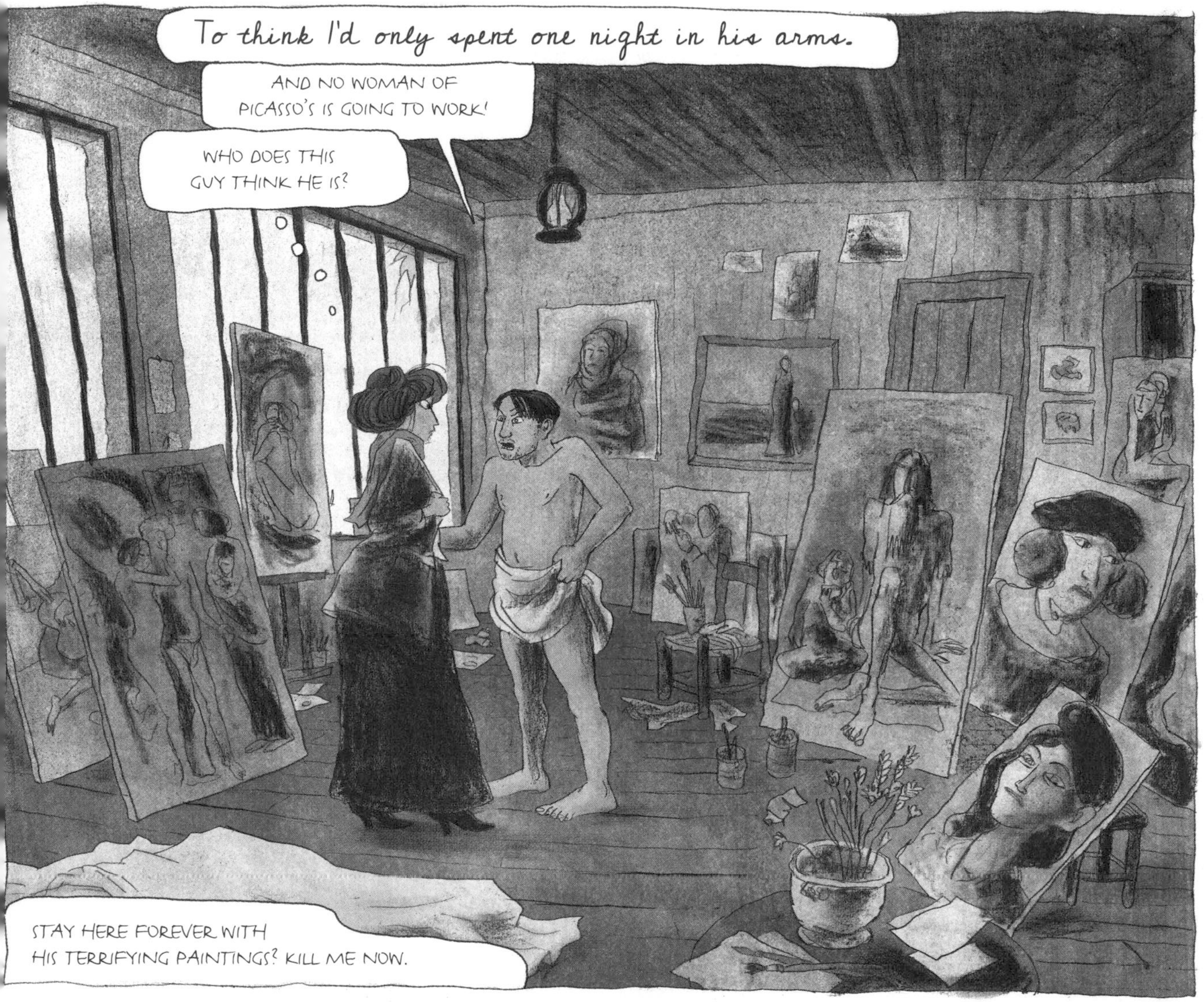
To think I'd only spent one night in his arms.
AND NO WOMAN OF PICASSO'S IS GOING TO WORK!
WHO DOES THIS GUY THINK HE IS?
STAY HERE FOREVER WITH HIS TERRIFYING PAINTINGS? KILL ME NOW.

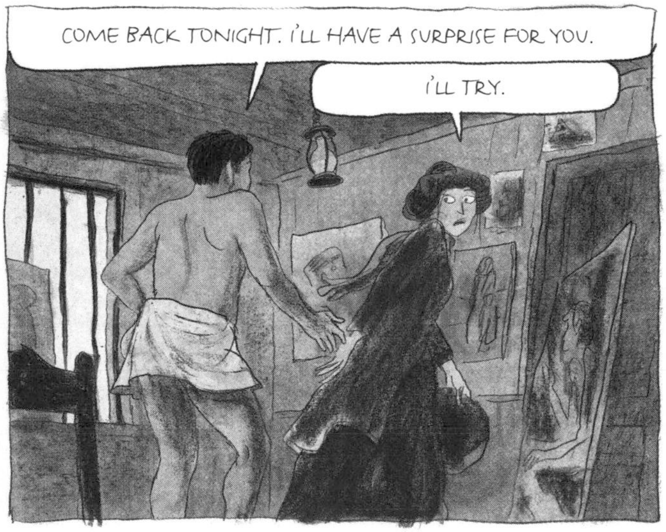
COME BACK TONIGHT. I'LL HAVE A SURPRISE FOR YOU.
I'LL TRY.

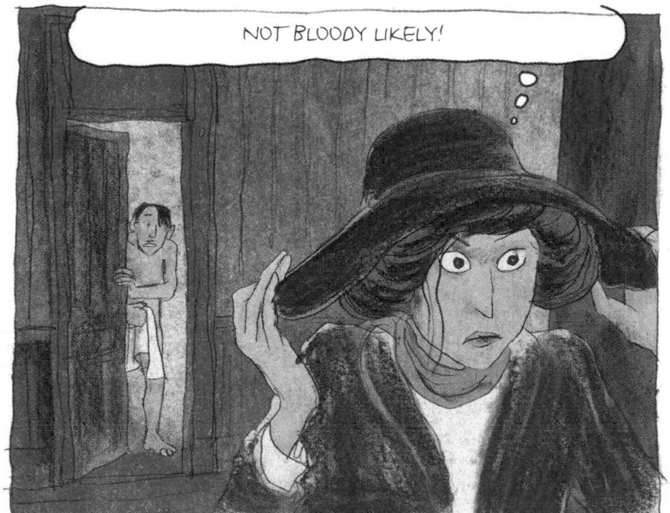
NOT BLOODY LIKELY!

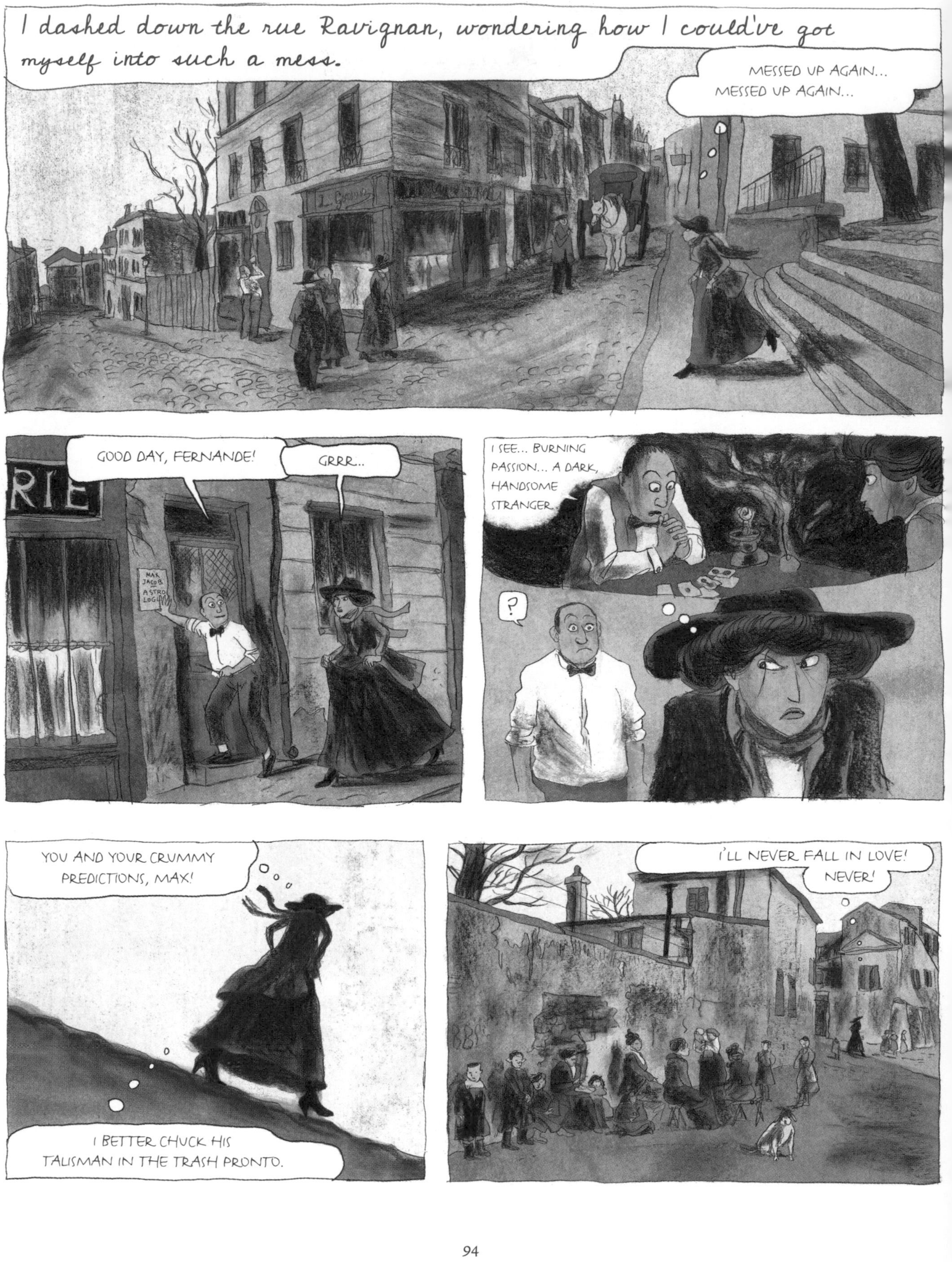
I dashed down the rue Ravignan, wondering how I could've got myself into such a mess.
MESSED UP AGAIN... MESSED UP AGAIN...
GOOD DAY, FERNANDE!
GRRR...
MAX JACOB ASTROLOG
I SEE... BURNING PASSION... A DARK, HANDSOME STRANGER.
?
YOU AND YOUR CRUMMY PREDICTIONS, MAX!
I BETTER CHUCK HIS TALISMAN IN THE TRASH PRONTO.
I'LL NEVER FALL IN LOVE! NEVER!

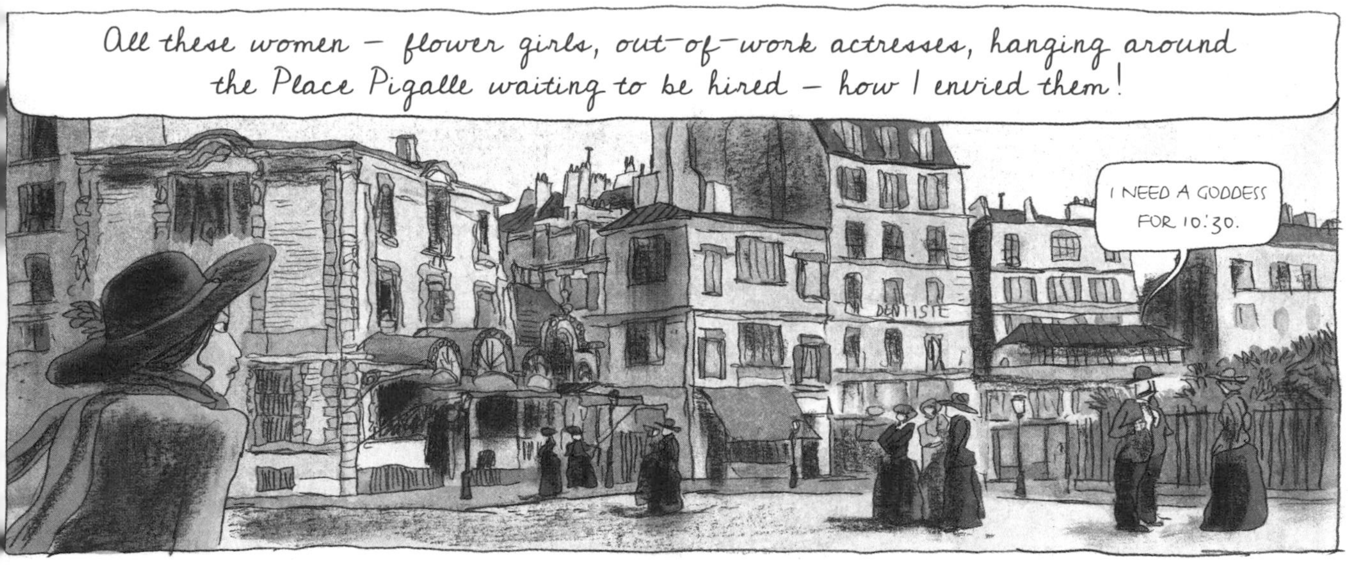
All these women – flower girls, out-of-work actresses, hanging around the Place Pigalle waiting to be hired – how I envied them!
I NEED A GODDESS FOR 10:30.
DENTISTE

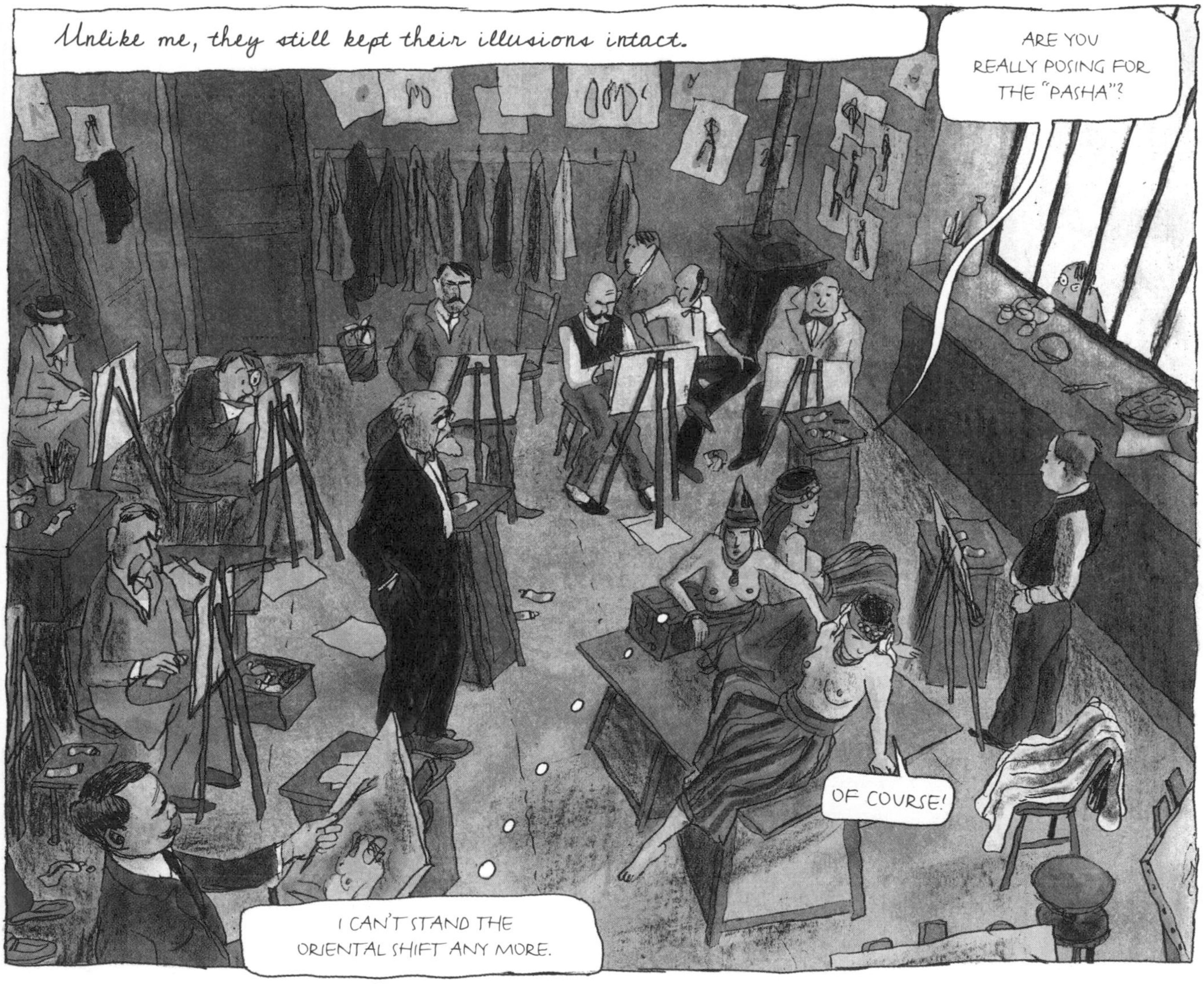
Unlike me, they still kept their illusions intact.
ARE YOU REALLY POSING FOR THE "PASHA"?
OF COURSE!
I CAN'T STAND THE ORIENTAL SHIFT ANY MORE.

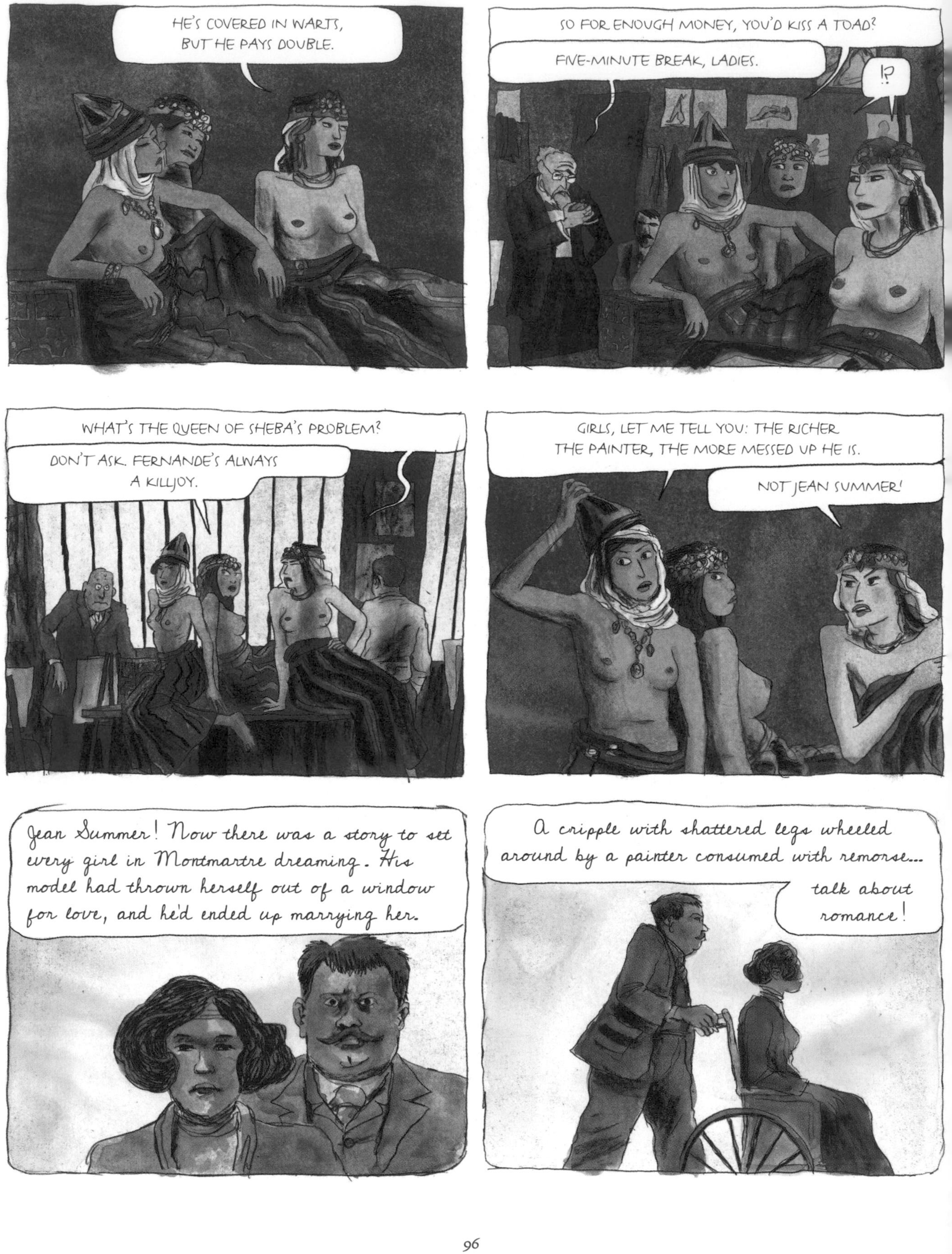
HE'S COVERED IN WARTS, BUT HE PAYS DOUBLE.
SO FOR ENOUGH MONEY, YOU'D KISS A TOAD?
FIVE-MINUTE BREAK, LADIES.
!?
WHAT'S THE QUEEN OF SHEBA'S PROBLEM?
DON'T ASK. FERNANDE'S ALWAYS A KILLJOY.
GIRLS, LET ME TELL YOU: THE RICHER THE PAINTER, THE MORE MESSED UP HE IS.
NOT JEAN SUMMER!
Jean Summer! Now there was a story to set every girl in Montmartre dreaming. His model had thrown herself out of a window for love, and he'd ended up marrying her.
A cripple with shattered legs wheeled around by a painter consumed with remorse...
talk about romance!

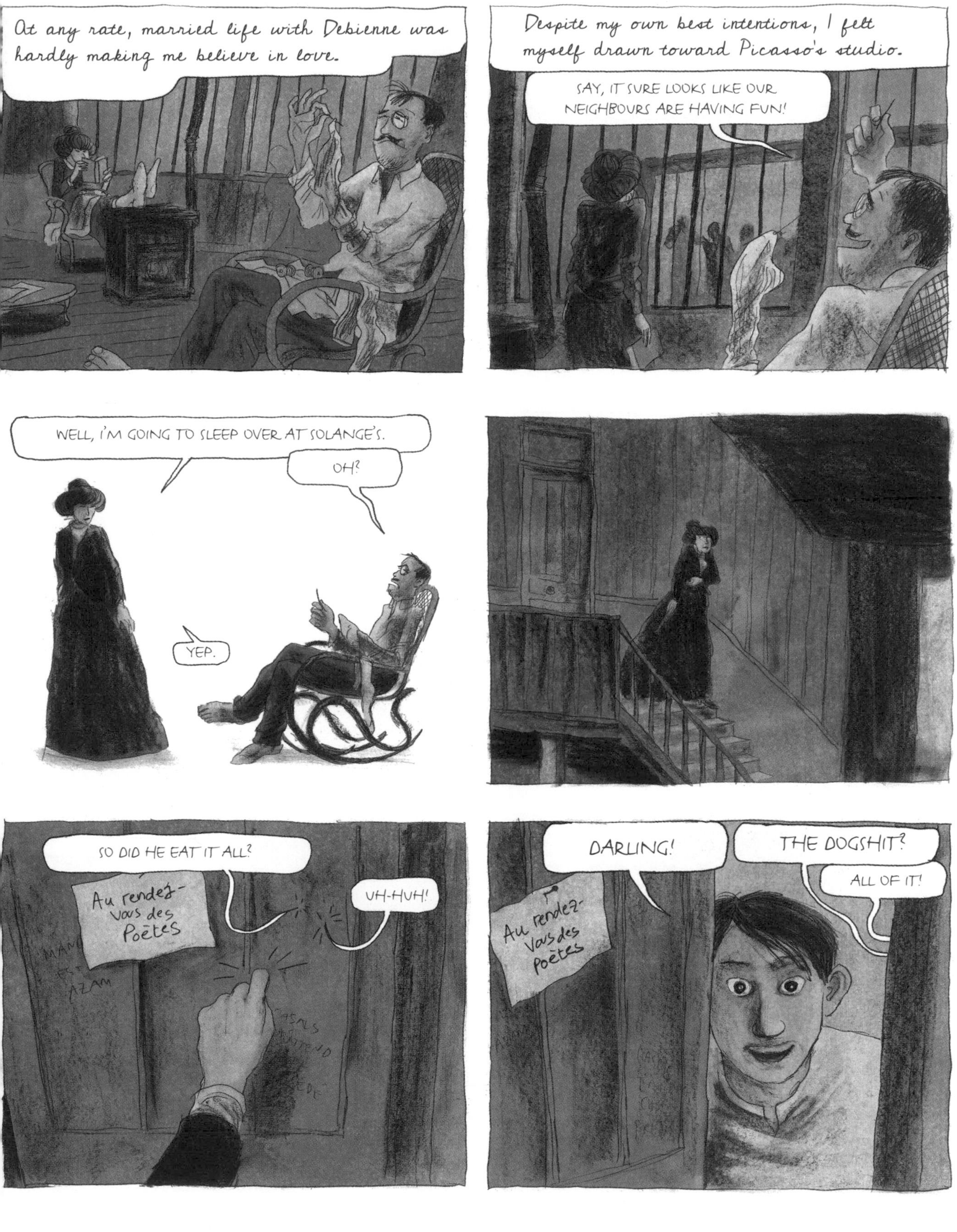
At any rate, married life with Debienne was hardly making me believe in love.
Despite my own best intentions, I felt myself drawn toward Picasso's studio.
SAY, IT SURE LOOKS LIKE OUR NEIGHBOURS ARE HAVING FUN!
WELL, I'M GOING TO SLEEP OVER AT SOLANGE'S.
OH?
YEP.
SO DID HE EAT IT ALL?
Au rendez-vous des Poètes
UH-HUH!
DARLING!
THE DOGSHIT?
ALL OF IT!
Au rendez-vous des poètes

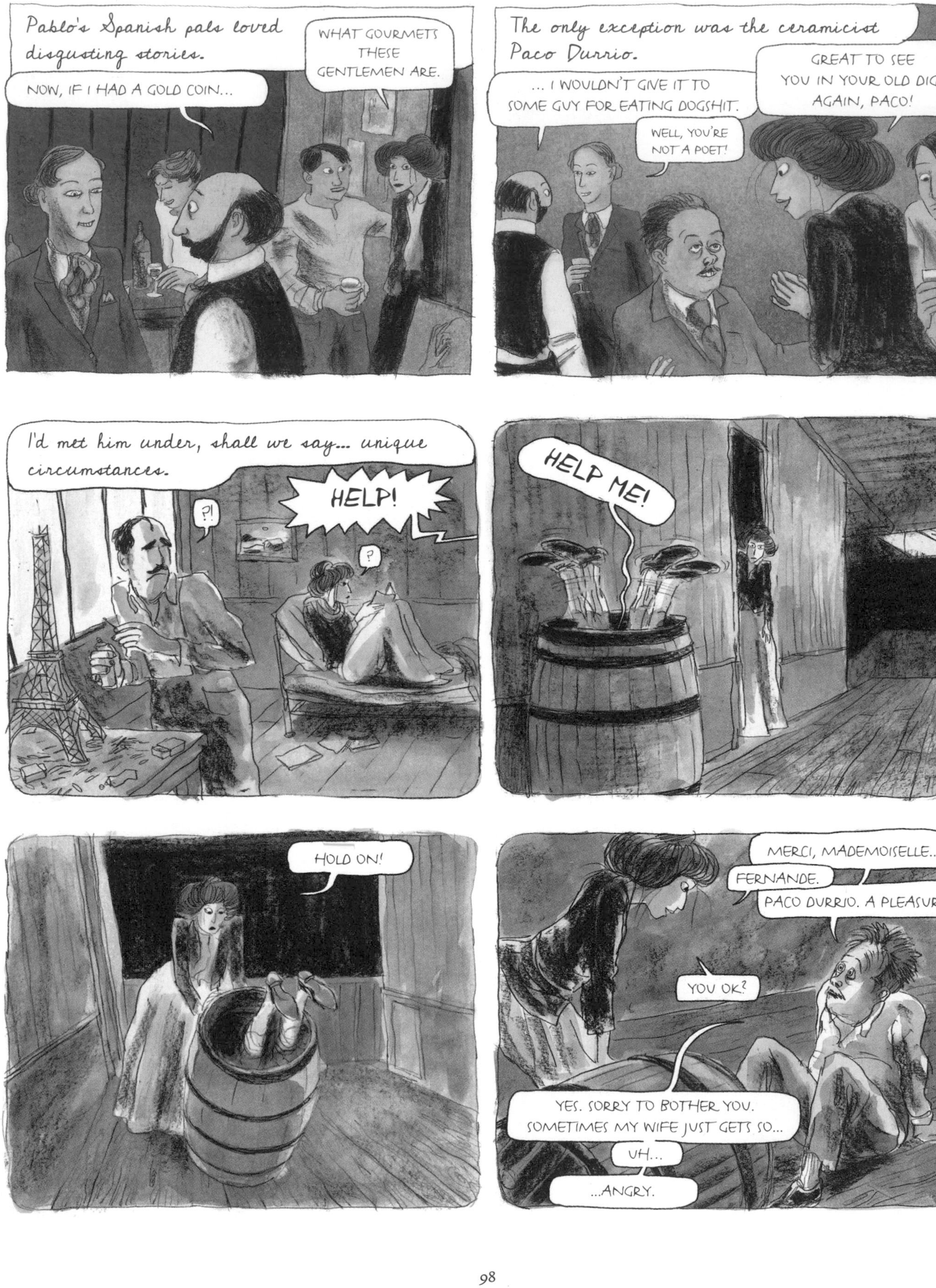
Pablo's Spanish pals loved disgusting stories.
WHAT GOURMETS THESE GENTLEMEN ARE.
NOW, IF I HAD A GOLD COIN...
The only exception was the ceramicist Paco Durrio.
... I WOULDN'T GIVE IT TO SOME GUY FOR EATING DOGSHIT.
WELL, YOU'RE NOT A POET!
GREAT TO SEE YOU IN YOUR OLD DIGS AGAIN, PACO!
I'd met him under, shall we say... unique circumstances.
HELP!
?!
?
HELP ME!
HOLD ON!
MERCI, MADEMOISELLE...
FERNANDE.
PACO DURRIO. A PLEASURE.
YOU OK?
YES. SORRY TO BOTHER YOU. SOMETIMES MY WIFE JUST GETS SO...
UH...
...ANGRY.

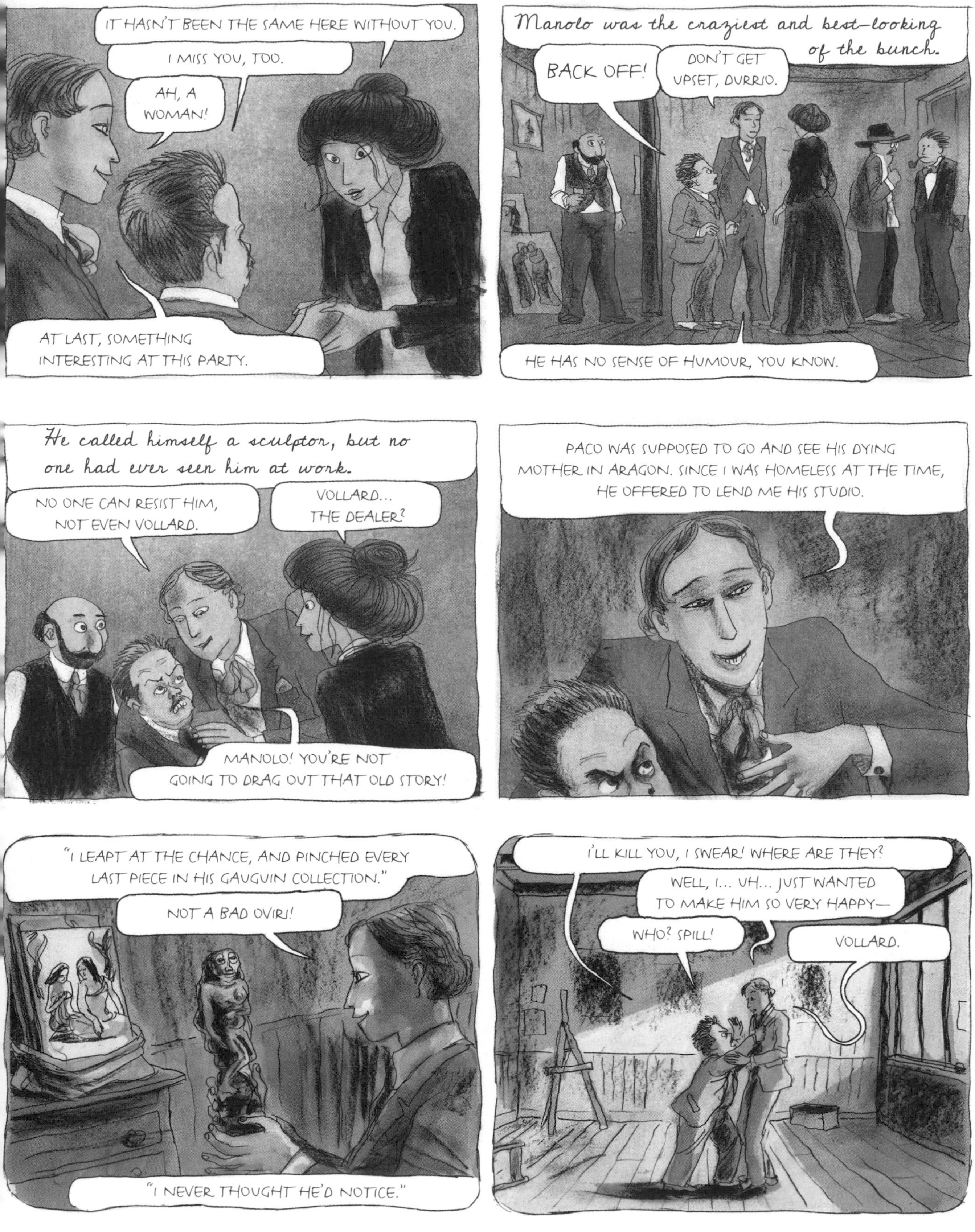
IT HASN'T BEEN THE SAME HERE WITHOUT YOU.
I MISS YOU, TOO.
AH, A WOMAN!
AT LAST, SOMETHING INTERESTING AT THIS PARTY.
Manolo was the craziest and best-looking of the bunch.
BACK OFF!
DON'T GET UPSET, DURRIO.
HE HAS NO SENSE OF HUMOUR, YOU KNOW.
He called himself a sculptor, but no one had ever seen him at work.
NO ONE CAN RESIST HIM, NOT EVEN VOLLARD.
VOLLARD... THE DEALER?
MANOLO! YOU'RE NOT GOING TO DRAG OUT THAT OLD STORY!
PACO WAS SUPPOSED TO GO AND SEE HIS DYING MOTHER IN ARAGON. SINCE I WAS HOMELESS AT THE TIME, HE OFFERED TO LEND ME HIS STUDIO.
"I LEAPT AT THE CHANCE, AND PINCHED EVERY LAST PIECE IN HIS GAUGUIN COLLECTION."
NOT A BAD OVIRI!
"I NEVER THOUGHT HE'D NOTICE."
I'LL KILL YOU, I SWEAR! WHERE ARE THEY?
WELL, I... UH... JUST WANTED TO MAKE HIM SO VERY HAPPY—
WHO? SPILL!
VOLLARD.

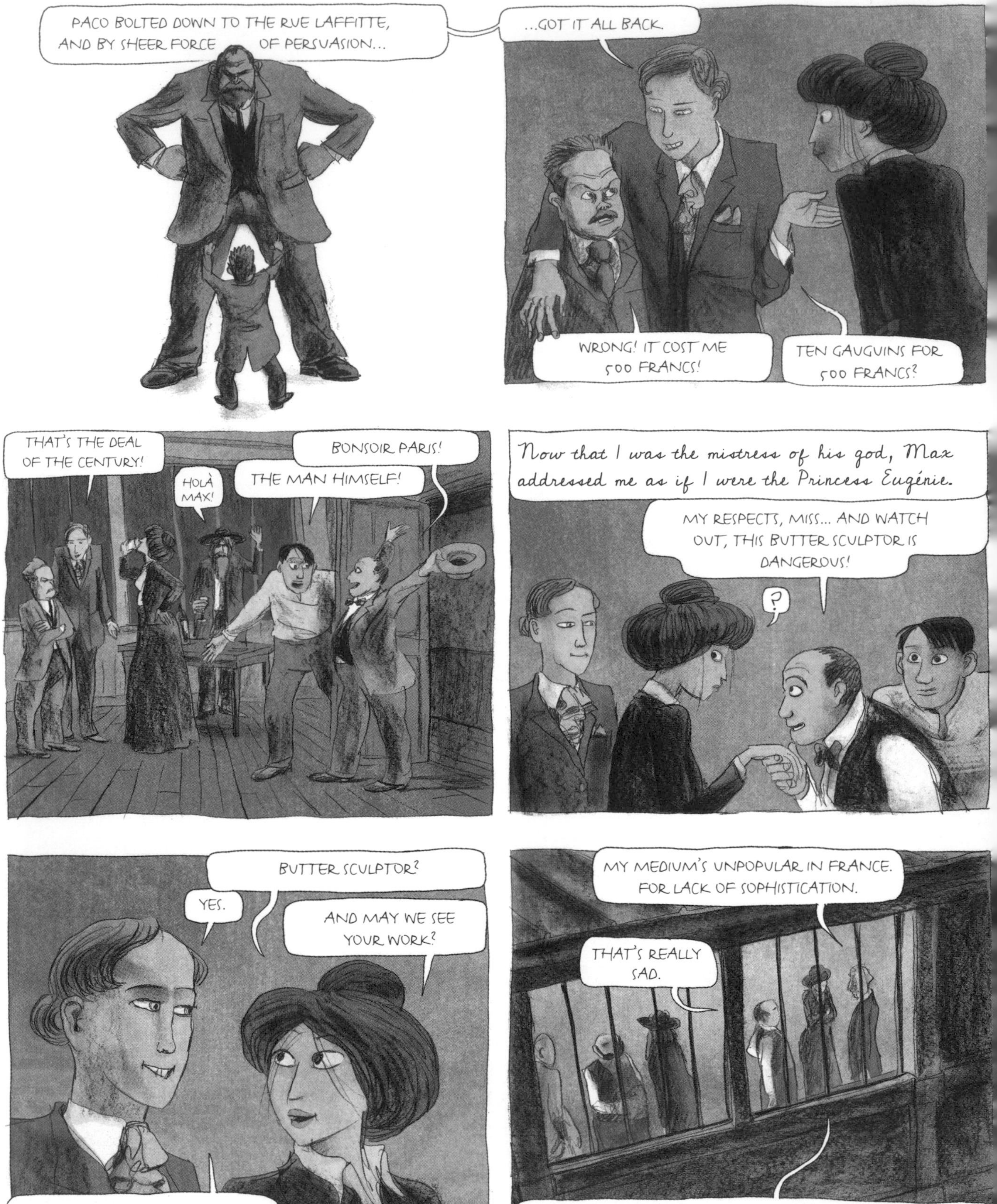
PACO BOLTED DOWN TO THE RUE LAFFITTE, AND BY SHEER FORCE OF PERSUASION...
...GOT IT ALL BACK.
WRONG! IT COST ME 500 FRANCS!
TEN GAUGUINS FOR 500 FRANCS?
THAT'S THE DEAL OF THE CENTURY!
HOLÀ MAX!
THE MAN HIMSELF!
BONSOIR PARIS!
Now that I was the mistress of his god, Max addressed me as if I were the Princess Eugénie.
MY RESPECTS, MISS... AND WATCH OUT, THIS BUTTER SCULPTOR IS DANGEROUS!
?
BUTTER SCULPTOR?
YES.
AND MAY WE SEE YOUR WORK?
UNFORTUNATELY, NO.
MY MEDIUM'S UNPOPULAR IN FRANCE. FOR LACK OF SOPHISTICATION.
THAT'S REALLY SAD.
AND HOW DID YOU EVER ARRIVE AT THIS... IDEA?

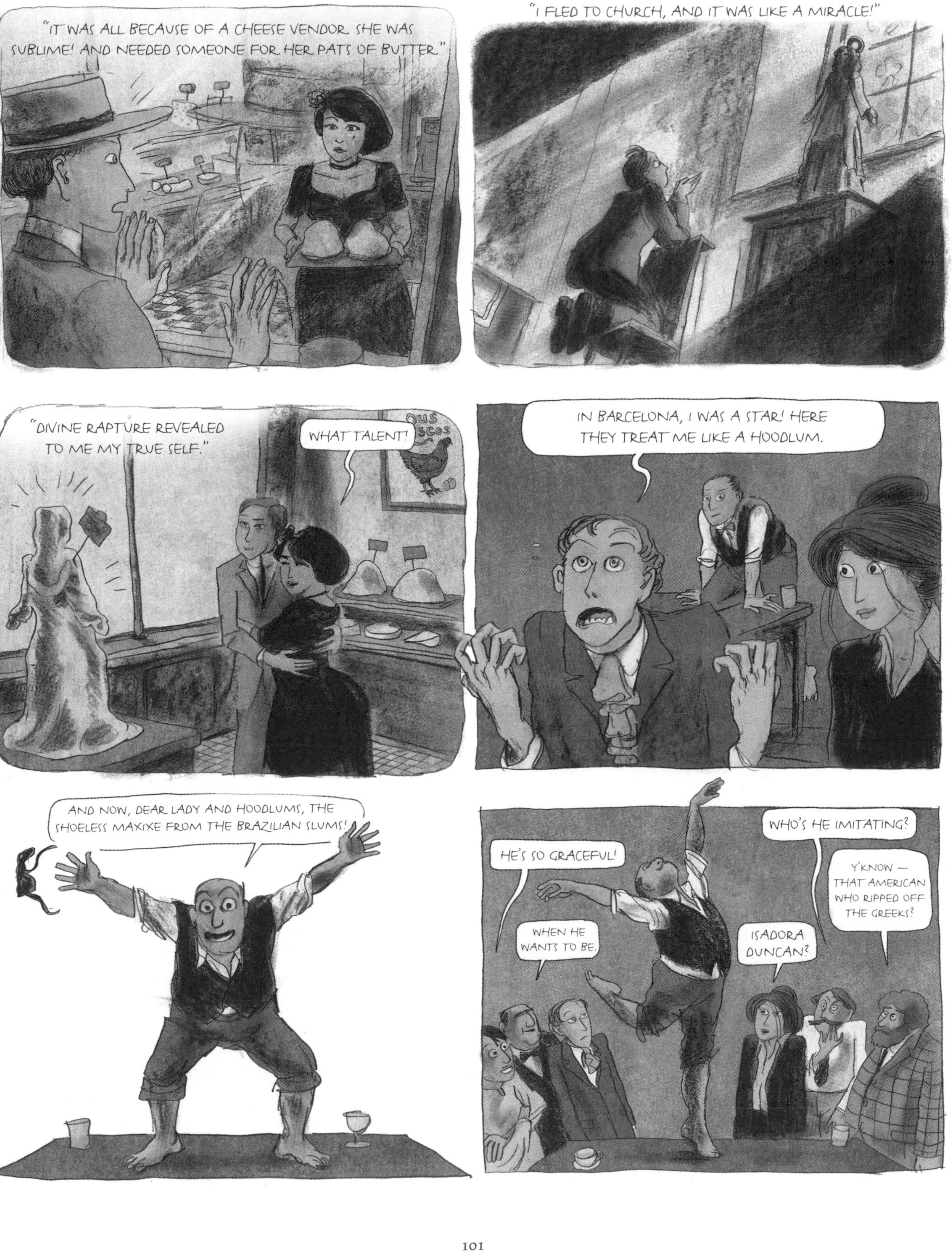
"IT WAS ALL BECAUSE OF A CHEESE VENDOR. SHE WAS SUBLIME! AND NEEDED SOMEONE FOR HER PATS OF BUTTER."
"I FLED TO CHURCH, AND IT WAS LIKE A MIRACLE!"
"DIVINE RAPTURE REVEALED TO ME MY TRUE SELF."
WHAT TALENT!
IN BARCELONA, I WAS A STAR! HERE THEY TREAT ME LIKE A HOODLUM.
AND NOW, DEAR LADY AND HOODLUMS, THE SHOELESS MAXIXE FROM THE BRAZILIAN SLUMS!
HE'S SO GRACEFUL!
WHEN HE WANTS TO BE.
WHO'S HE IMITATING?
ISADORA DUNCAN?
Y'KNOW — THAT AMERICAN WHO RIPPED OFF THE GREEKS?

Max was a born actor – the stuttering clown from the Medrano...

COME, M-M-MY H-HEN, COME, M-M-MY H-HEN.

Degas and his racist tirades...

MONTMARTRE? A SYNAGOGUE!

INVADED BY YID PAINTERS!

The grocer lady of the rue Lepic refusing to take credit...

DO I LOOK LIKE THE BANK OF FRANCE?

HERE.

OPEN IT!

FOR ME?

ANOTHER SEASHELL ASHTRAY?

♪ OH, I LOVE YOU SO, BUT IF YOU STILL SAY NO, THEN DARLING I TELL YOU, I JUST DON'T KNOW WHAT I'LL DO...

OH!

♪ ALAS, POOR WOMEN, WE LOVE MEN, MONSTERS THOUGH THEY BE, OUR PASSIONS THEY SPURN AND NEVER RETURN!

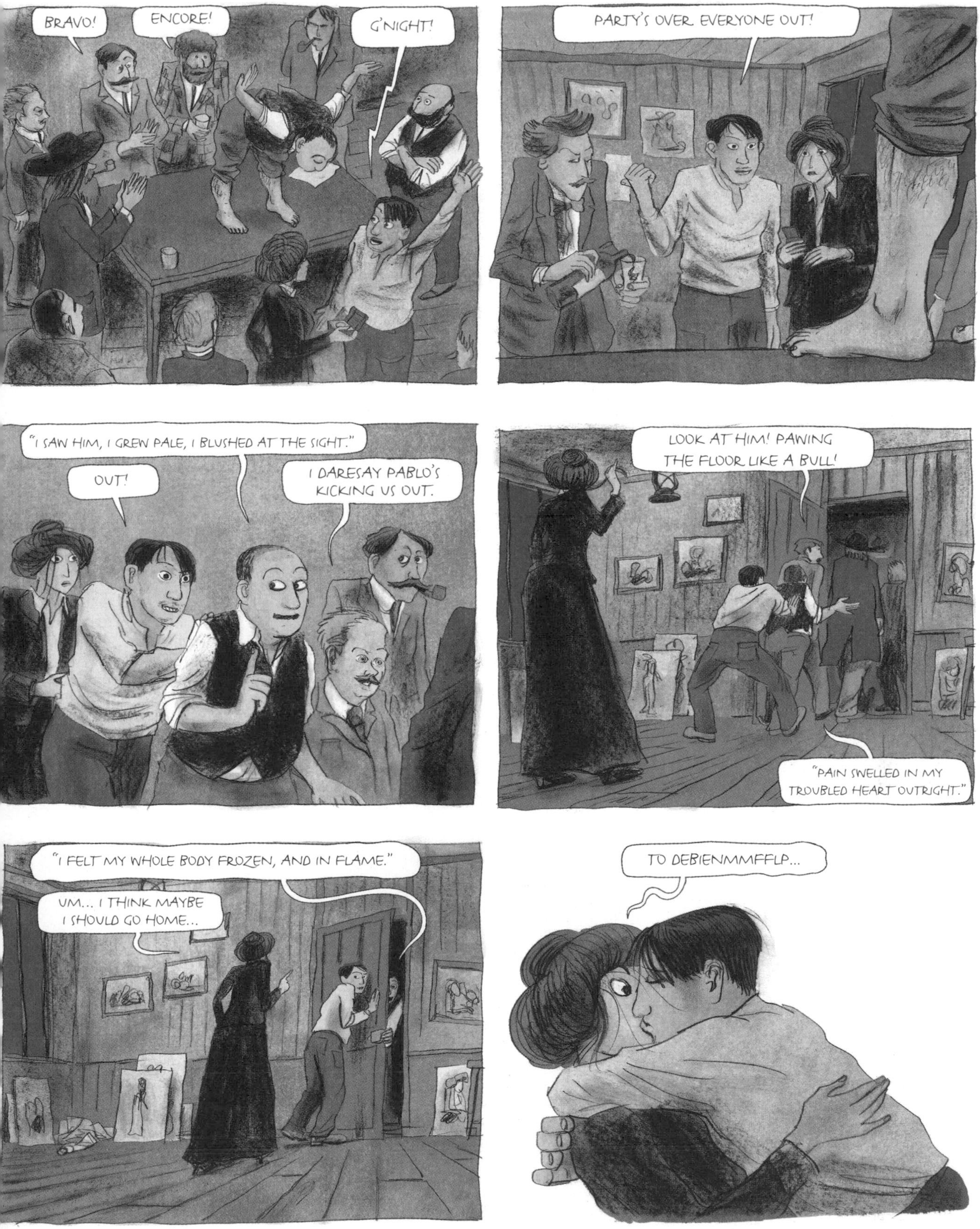
BRAVO!
ENCORE!
G'NIGHT!
PARTY'S OVER. EVERYONE OUT!
"I SAW HIM, I GREW PALE, I BLUSHED AT THE SIGHT."
OUT!
I DARESAY PABLO'S KICKING US OUT.
LOOK AT HIM! PAWING THE FLOOR LIKE A BULL!
"PAIN SWELLED IN MY TROUBLED HEART OUTRIGHT."
"I FELT MY WHOLE BODY FROZEN, AND IN FLAME."
UM... I THINK MAYBE I SHOULD GO HOME...
TO DEBIENMMFFLP...

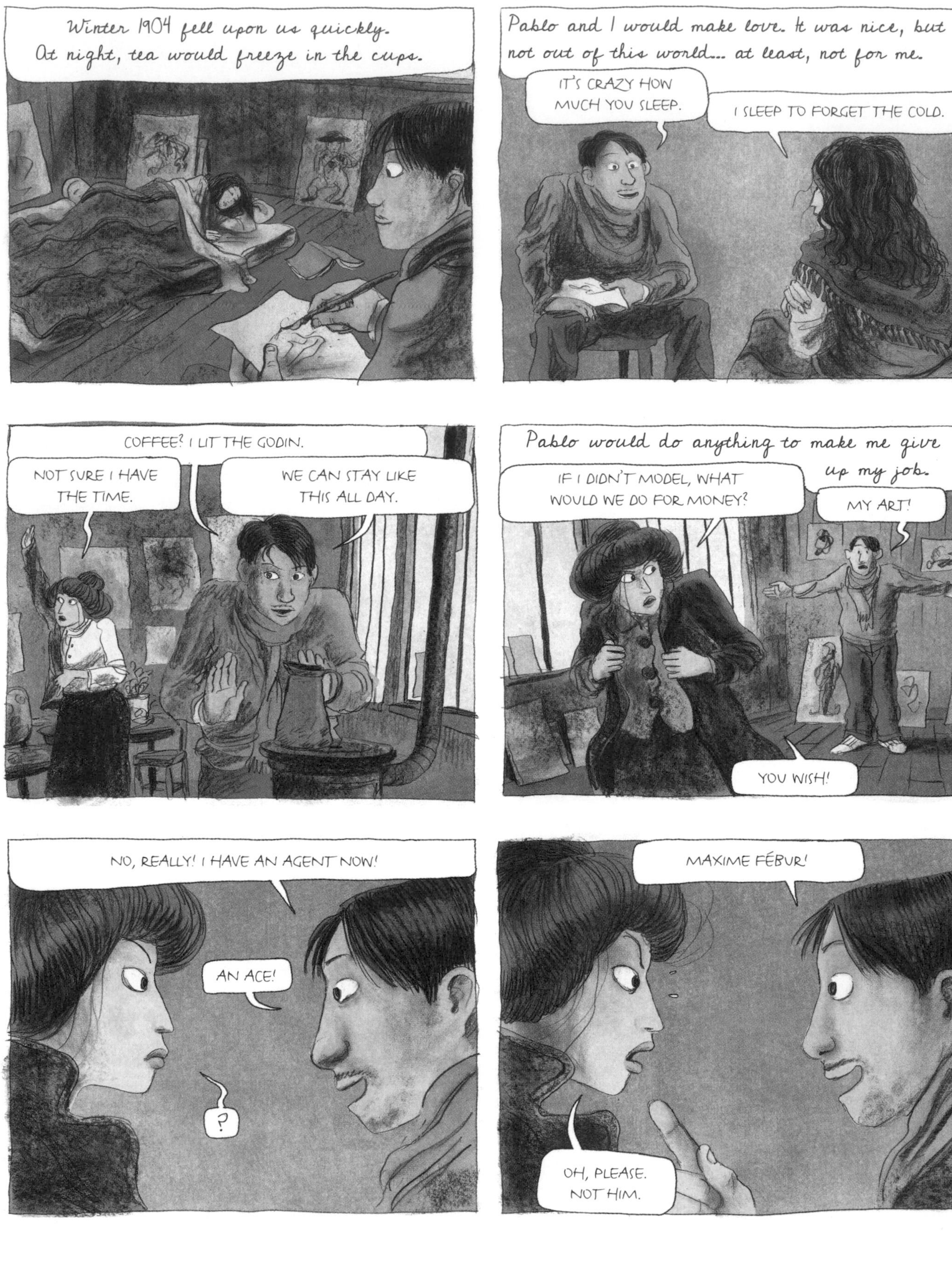
Winter 1904 fell upon us quickly. At night, tea would freeze in the cups.
Pablo and I would make love. It was nice, but not out of this world... at least, not for me.
IT'S CRAZY HOW MUCH YOU SLEEP.
I SLEEP TO FORGET THE COLD.
COFFEE? I LIT THE GODIN.
NOT SURE I HAVE THE TIME.
WE CAN STAY LIKE THIS ALL DAY.
Pablo would do anything to make me give up my job.
IF I DIDN'T MODEL, WHAT WOULD WE DO FOR MONEY?
MY ART!
YOU WISH!
NO, REALLY! I HAVE AN AGENT NOW!
AN ACE!
?
MAXIME FÉBUR!
OH, PLEASE. NOT HIM.

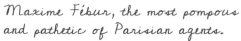

Maxime Fébur, the most pompous and pathetic of Parisian agents.

PLEASE TELL MONSIEUR DURAND-RUEL THAT MONSIEUR FÉBUR WOULD LIKE TO SPEAK WITH HIM.

OF COURSE, MONSIEUR

MONSIEUR?

I SEEK WORKS BY THE MOST EXTRAORDINARY ARTIST OF THE CENTURY...

THE A-M-AAAA-ZING PABLO PICASSO!

?

WHO?

SURELY YOU'RE JOKING.

POOR MAN, DON'T YOU KNOW **ANYTHING** ABOUT PAINTING?

SCANDALOUS!

YOU'D BEST CHANGE YOUR LINE OF WORK.

?!

Maxime Fébur, a.k.a....

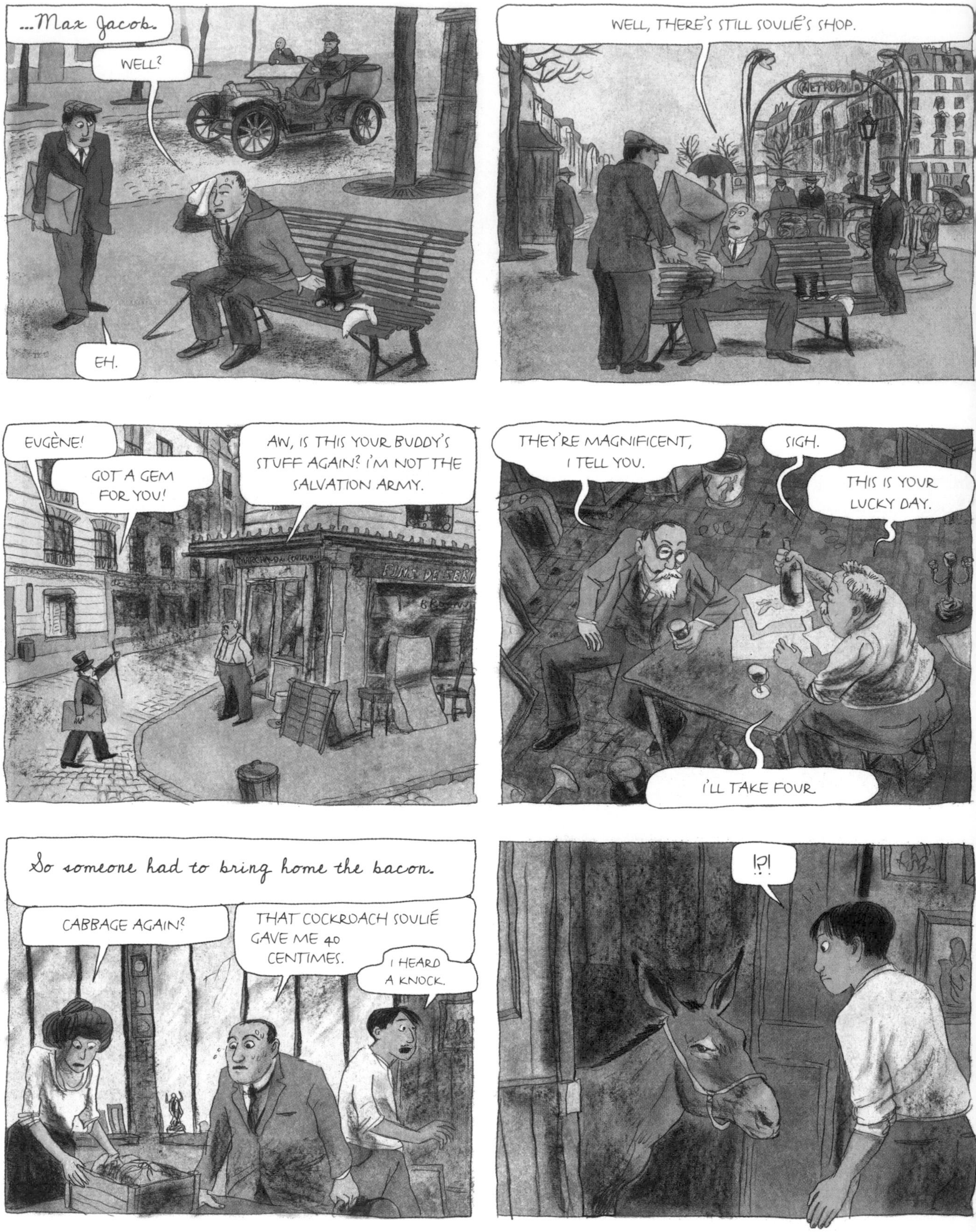
...Max Jacob.
WELL?
EH.
WELL, THERE'S STILL SOULIÉ'S SHOP.
EUGÈNE!
GOT A GEM FOR YOU!
AW, IS THIS YOUR BUDDY'S STUFF AGAIN? I'M NOT THE SALVATION ARMY.
THEY'RE MAGNIFICENT, I TELL YOU.
SIGH.
THIS IS YOUR LUCKY DAY.
I'LL TAKE FOUR
So someone had to bring home the bacon.
CABBAGE AGAIN?
THAT COCKROACH SOULIÉ GAVE ME 40 CENTIMES.
I HEARD A KNOCK.
!?!

Luckily, Frédé, the owner of the Lapin Agile, also supported us.

WINE! SALAMI!

DOES THIS FELLA COOK IN THAT HOLE YOU CALL A BAR?

LOLO? NAW, HE SINGS.

YOU'VE GOT COMPETITION, MAX.

It was no good. We were broke.

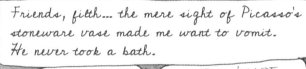

Friends, filth... the mere sight of Picasso's stoneware vase made me want to vomit. He never took a bath.

ALONE AT LAST!

PABLO... I'M NOT STAYING OVER TONIGHT.

OR ANY OTHER NIGHT.

WE CAN BE FRIENDS, IF YOU WANT.

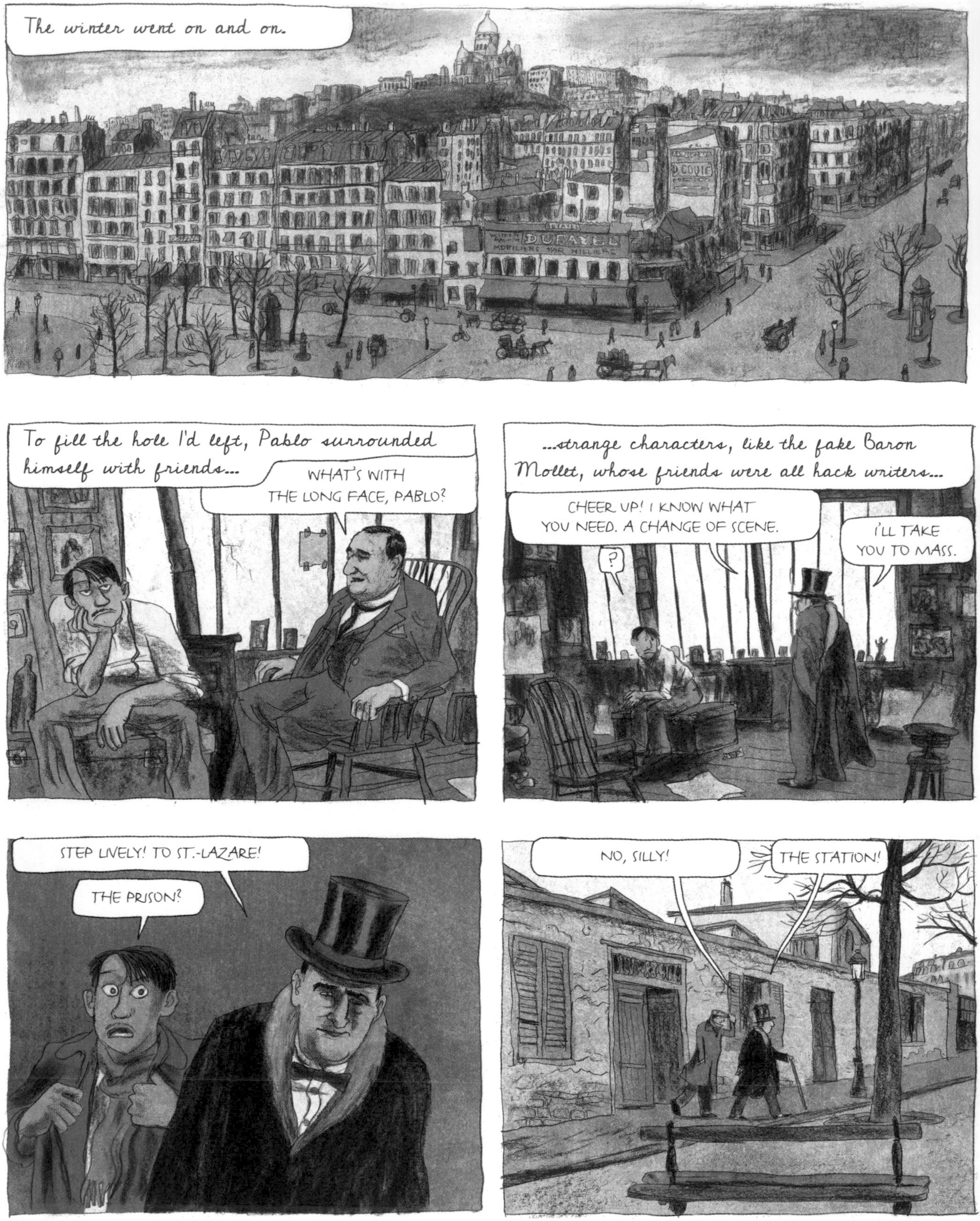
The winter went on and on.
To fill the hole I'd left, Pablo surrounded himself with friends...
WHAT'S WITH THE LONG FACE, PABLO?
...strange characters, like the fake Baron Mollet, whose friends were all hack writers...
CHEER UP! I KNOW WHAT YOU NEED. A CHANGE OF SCENE.
?
I'LL TAKE YOU TO MASS.
STEP LIVELY! TO ST.-LAZARE!
THE PRISON?
NO, SILLY!
THE STATION!

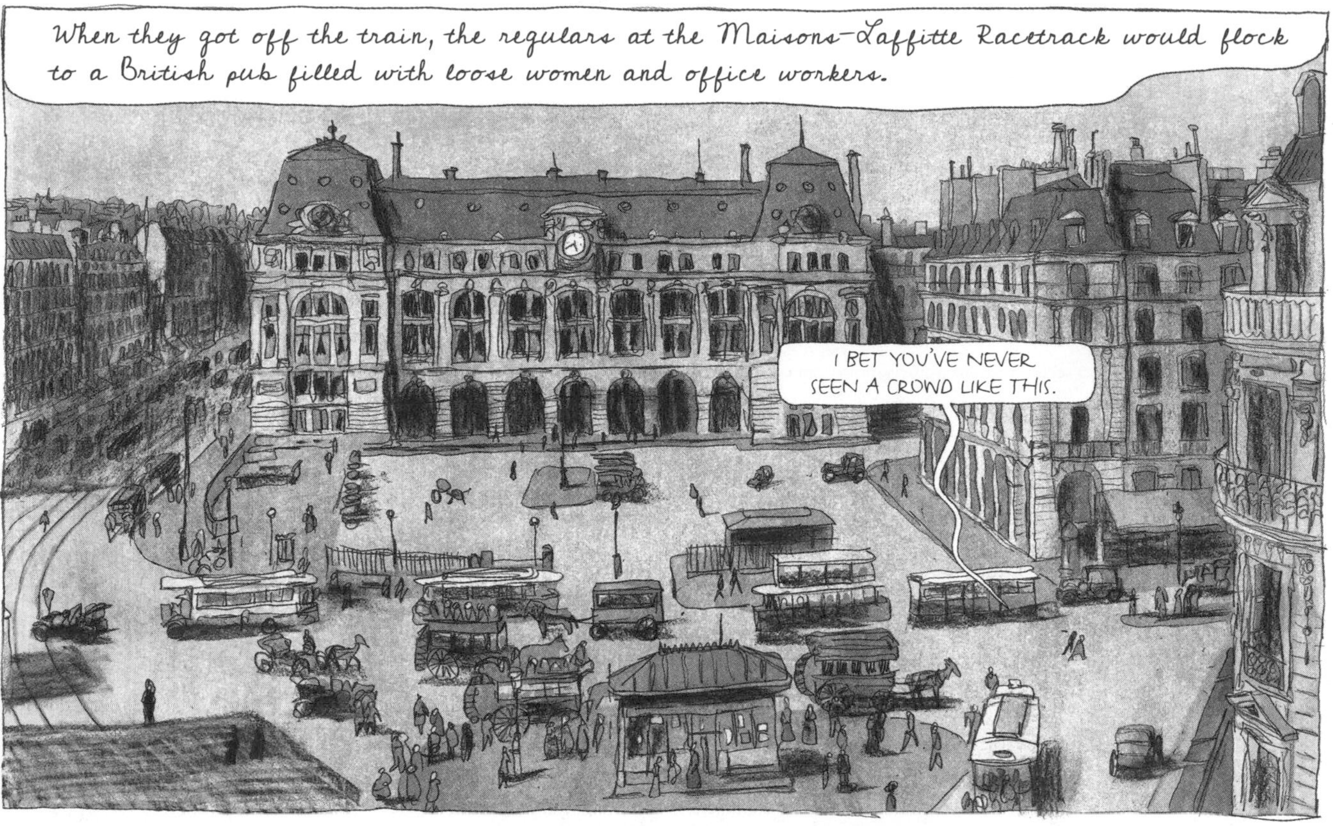
When they got off the train, the regulars at the Maisons-Laffitte Racetrack would flock to a British pub filled with loose women and office workers.
I BET YOU'VE NEVER SEEN A CROWD LIKE THIS.

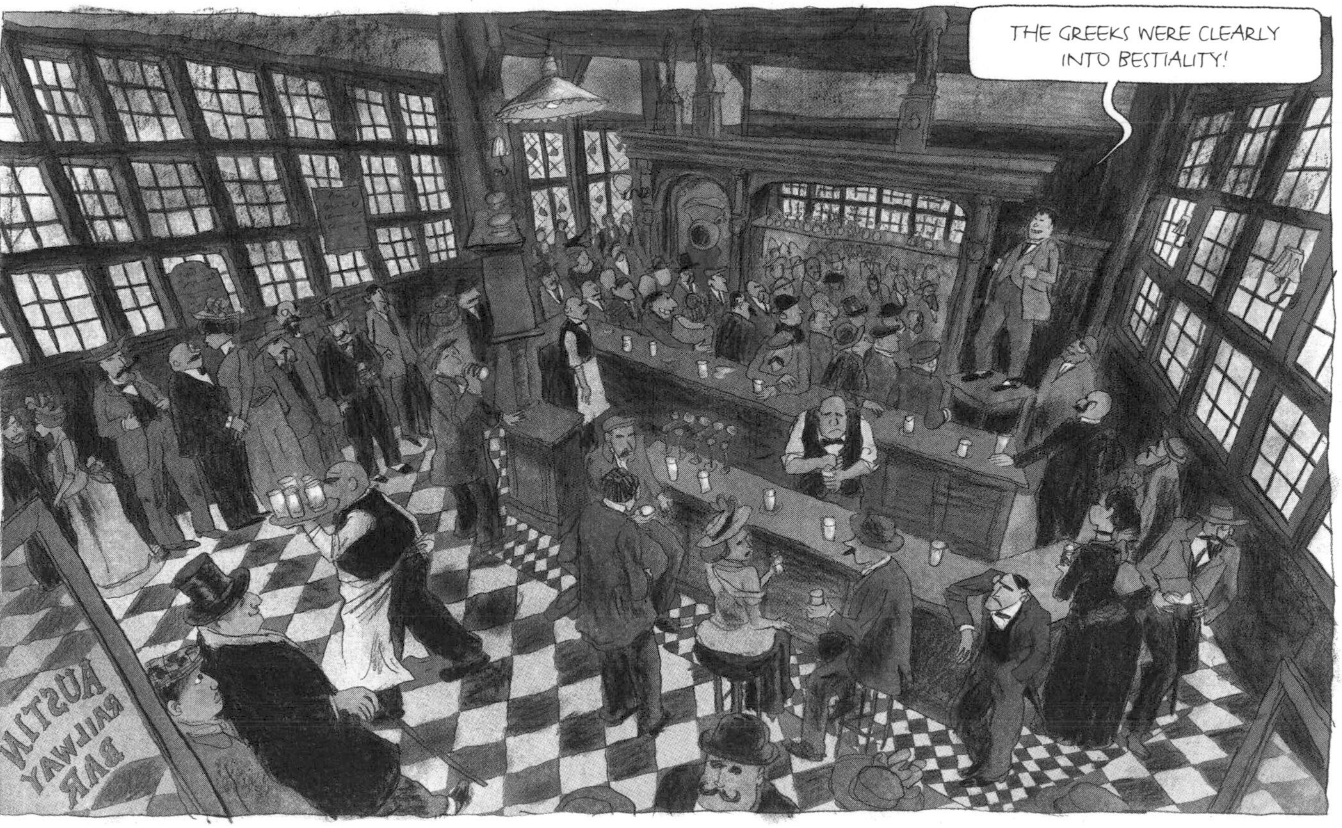
THE GREEKS WERE CLEARLY INTO BESTIALITY!
AUSTIN RAILWAY BAR

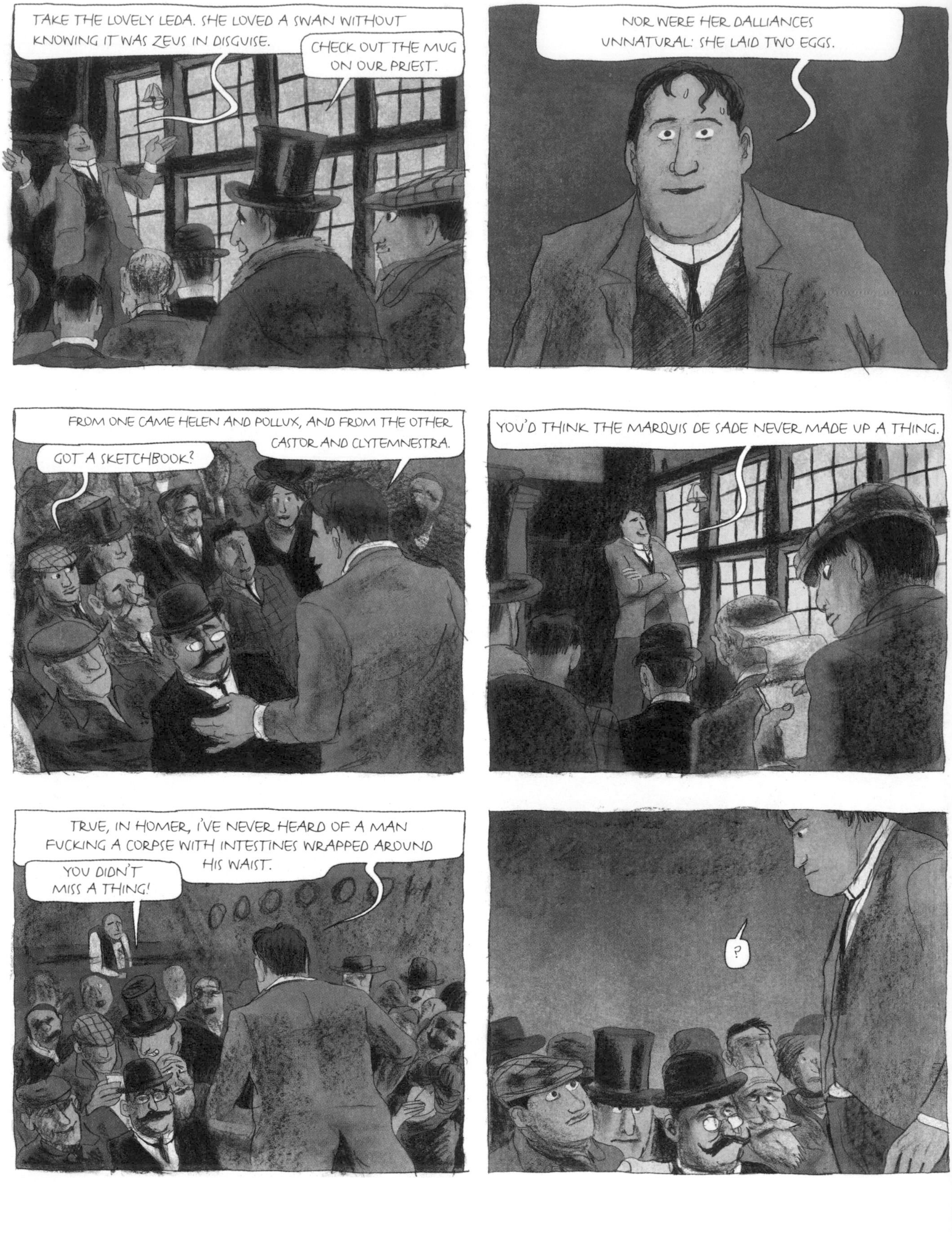
TAKE THE LOVELY LEDA. SHE LOVED A SWAN WITHOUT KNOWING IT WAS ZEUS IN DISGUISE.
CHECK OUT THE MUG ON OUR PRIEST.
NOR WERE HER DALLIANCES UNNATURAL: SHE LAID TWO EGGS.
FROM ONE CAME HELEN AND POLLUX, AND FROM THE OTHER CASTOR AND CLYTEMNESTRA.
GOT A SKETCHBOOK?
YOU'D THINK THE MARQUIS DE SADE NEVER MADE UP A THING.
TRUE, IN HOMER, I'VE NEVER HEARD OF A MAN FUCKING A CORPSE WITH INTESTINES WRAPPED AROUND HIS WAIST.
YOU DIDN'T MISS A THING!
?

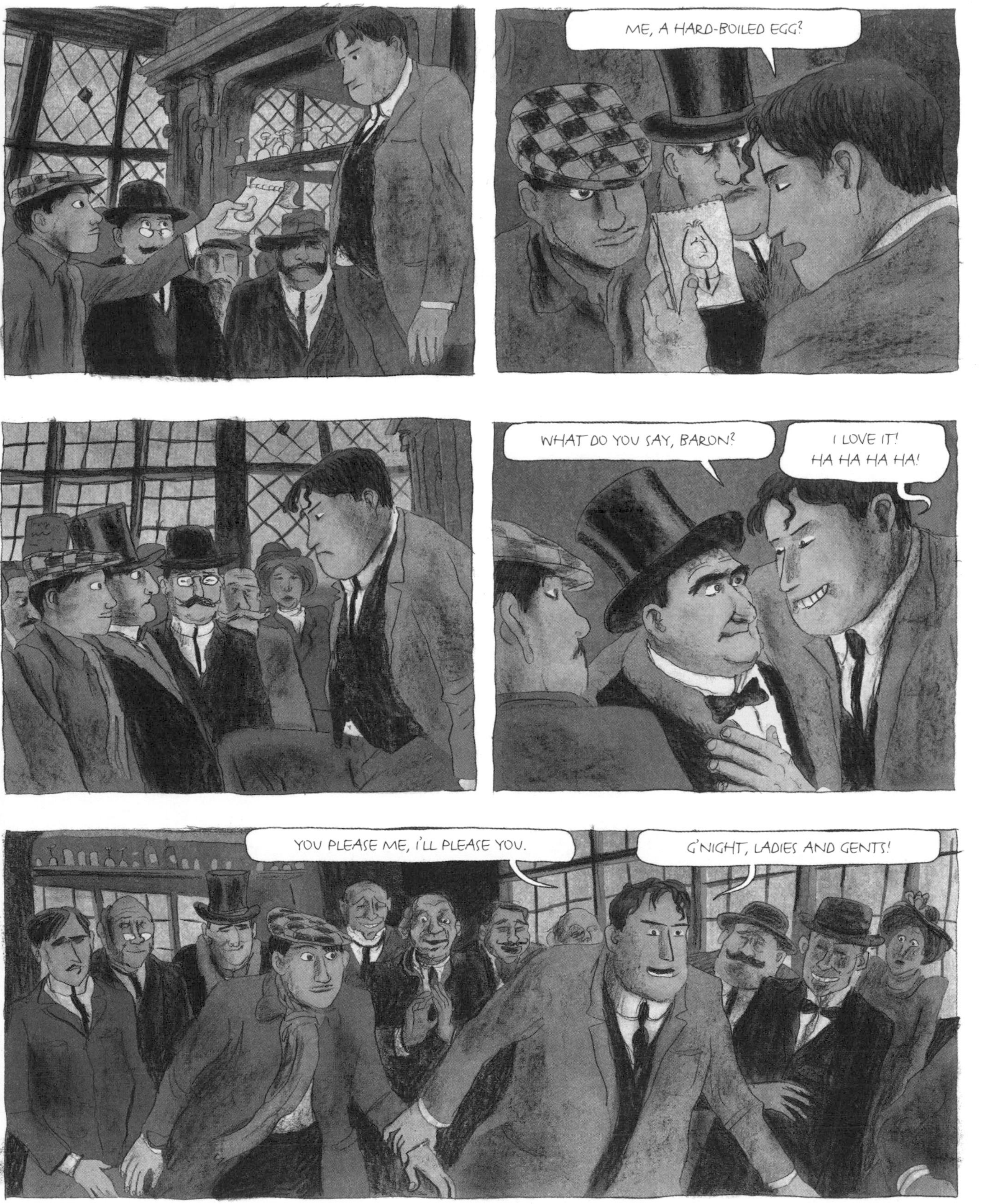

ME, A HARD-BOILED EGG?
WHAT DO YOU SAY, BARON?
I LOVE IT! HA HA HA HA!
YOU PLEASE ME, I'LL PLEASE YOU.
G'NIGHT, LADIES AND GENTS!

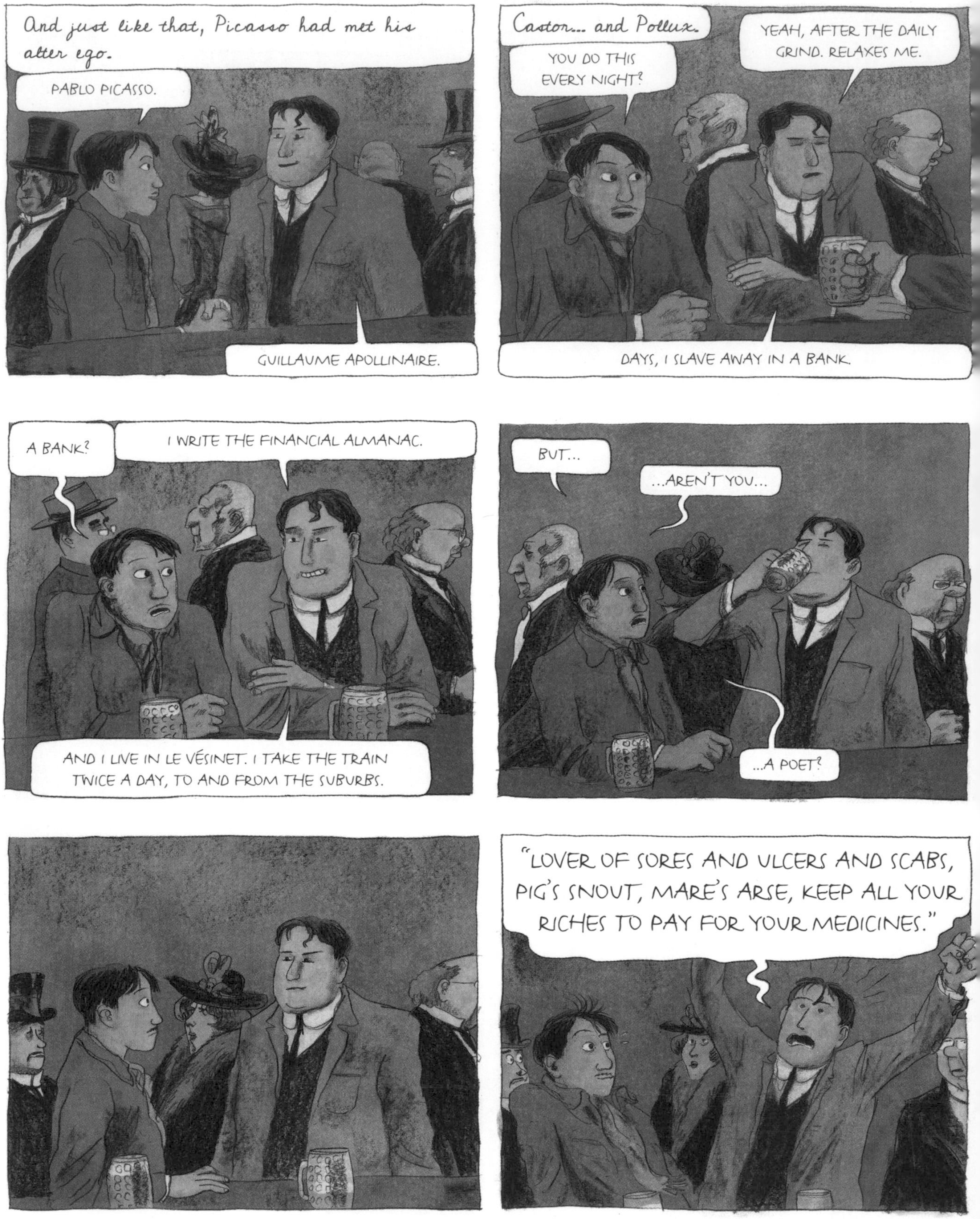
And just like that, Picasso had met his alter ego.
PABLO PICASSO.
GUILLAUME APOLLINAIRE.
Castor... and Pollux.
YOU DO THIS EVERY NIGHT?
YEAH, AFTER THE DAILY GRIND. RELAXES ME.
DAYS, I SLAVE AWAY IN A BANK.
A BANK?
I WRITE THE FINANCIAL ALMANAC.
AND I LIVE IN LE VÉSINET. I TAKE THE TRAIN TWICE A DAY, TO AND FROM THE SUBURBS.
BUT...
...AREN'T YOU...
...A POET?
"LOVER OF SORES AND ULCERS AND SCABS, PIG'S SNOUT, MARE'S ARSE, KEEP ALL YOUR RICHES TO PAY FOR YOUR MEDICINES."

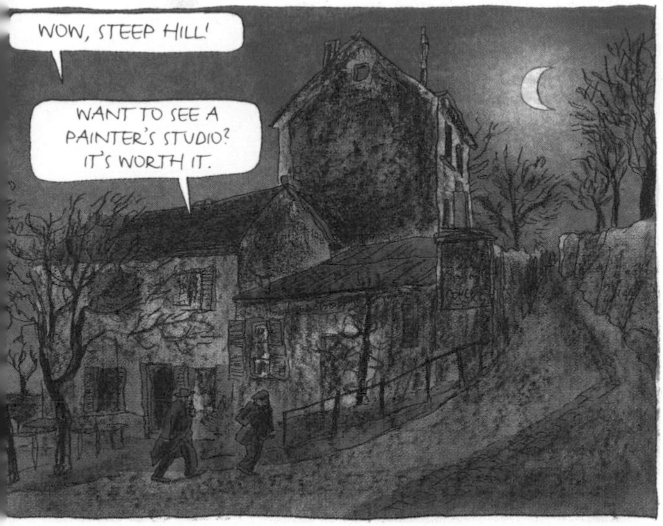
WOW, STEEP HILL!
WANT TO SEE A PAINTER'S STUDIO? IT'S WORTH IT.

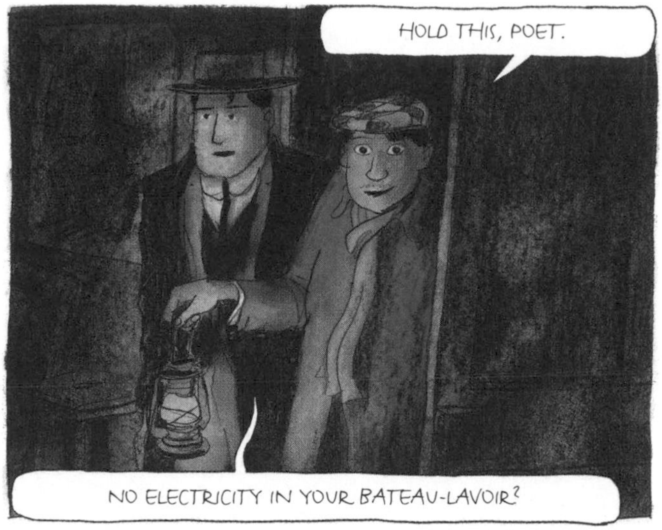
HOLD THIS, POET.
NO ELECTRICITY IN YOUR BATEAU-LAVOIR?

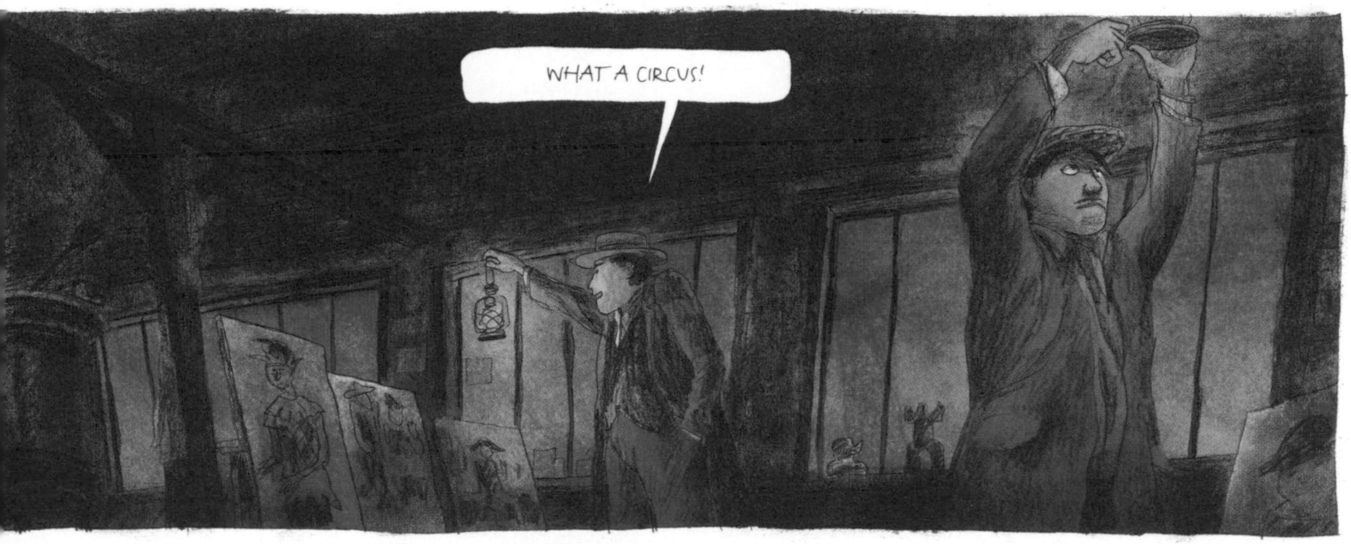
WHAT A CIRCUS!

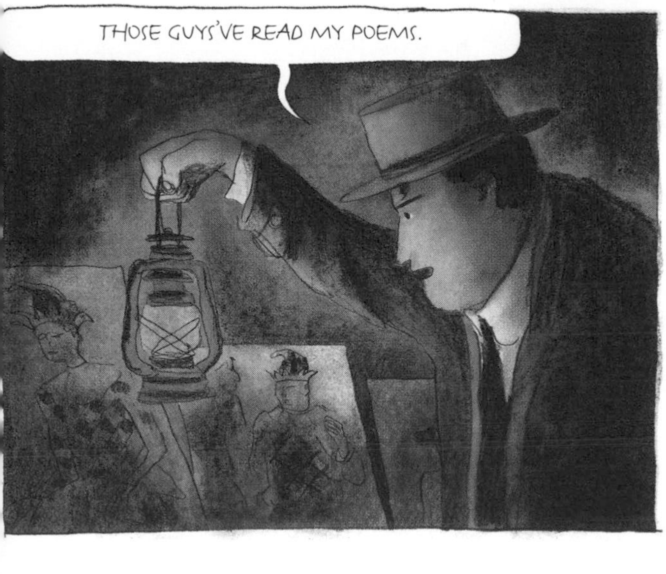
THOSE GUYS'VE READ MY POEMS.

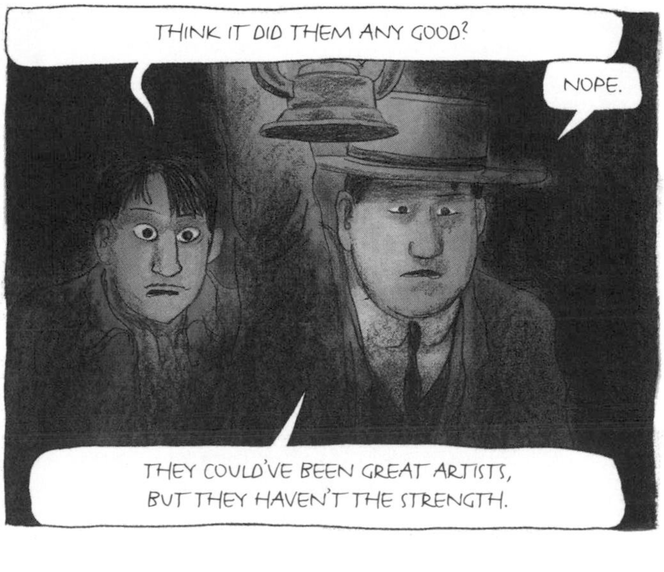
THINK IT DID THEM ANY GOOD?
NOPE.
THEY COULD'VE BEEN GREAT ARTISTS, BUT THEY HAVEN'T THE STRENGTH.

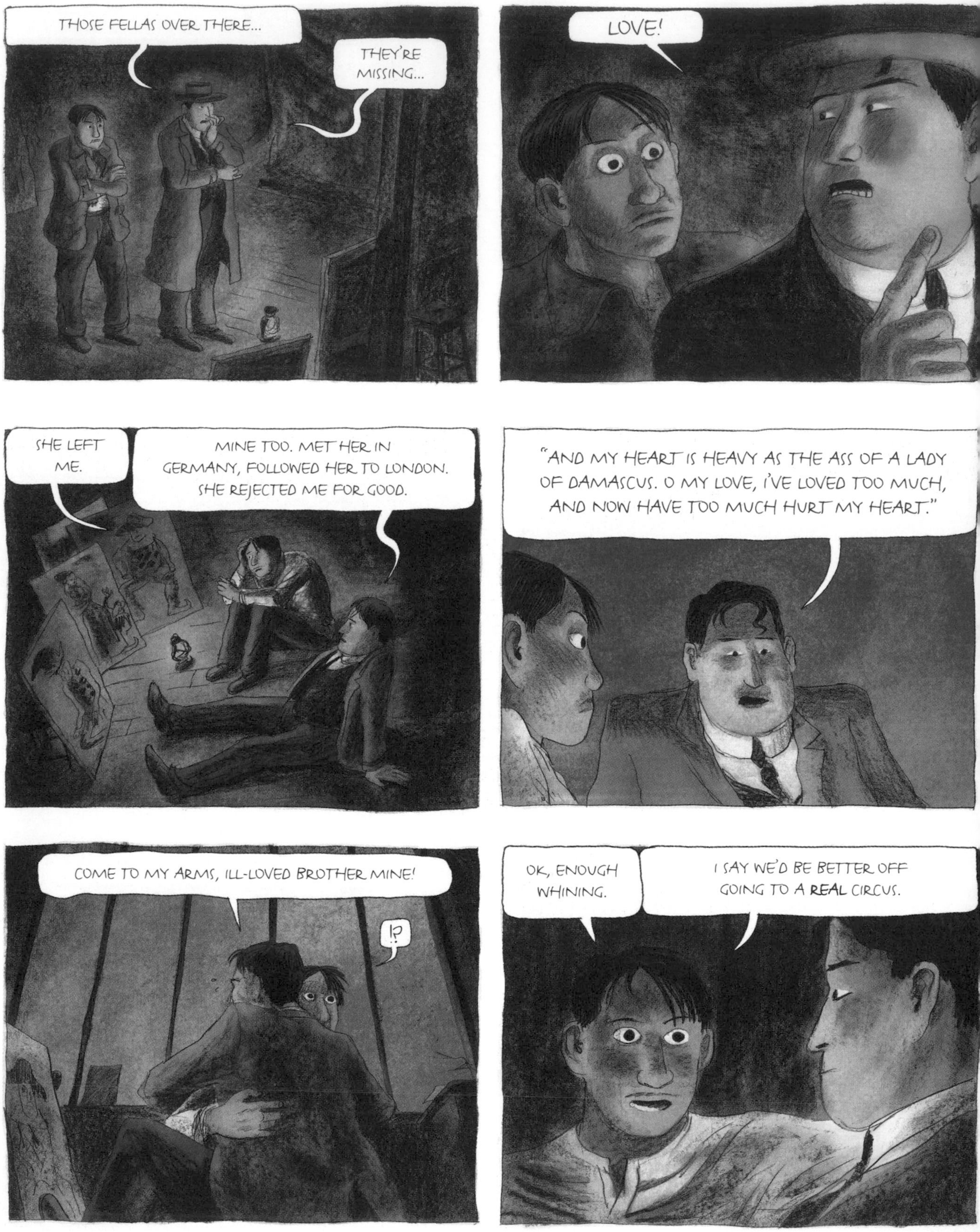
THOSE FELLAS OVER THERE...
THEY'RE MISSING...
LOVE!
SHE LEFT ME.
MINE TOO. MET HER IN GERMANY, FOLLOWED HER TO LONDON. SHE REJECTED ME FOR GOOD.
"AND MY HEART IS HEAVY AS THE ASS OF A LADY OF DAMASCUS. O MY LOVE, I'VE LOVED TOO MUCH, AND NOW HAVE TOO MUCH HURT MY HEART."
COME TO MY ARMS, ILL-LOVED BROTHER MINE!
!?
OK, ENOUGH WHINING.
I SAY WE'D BE BETTER OFF GOING TO A **REAL** CIRCUS.

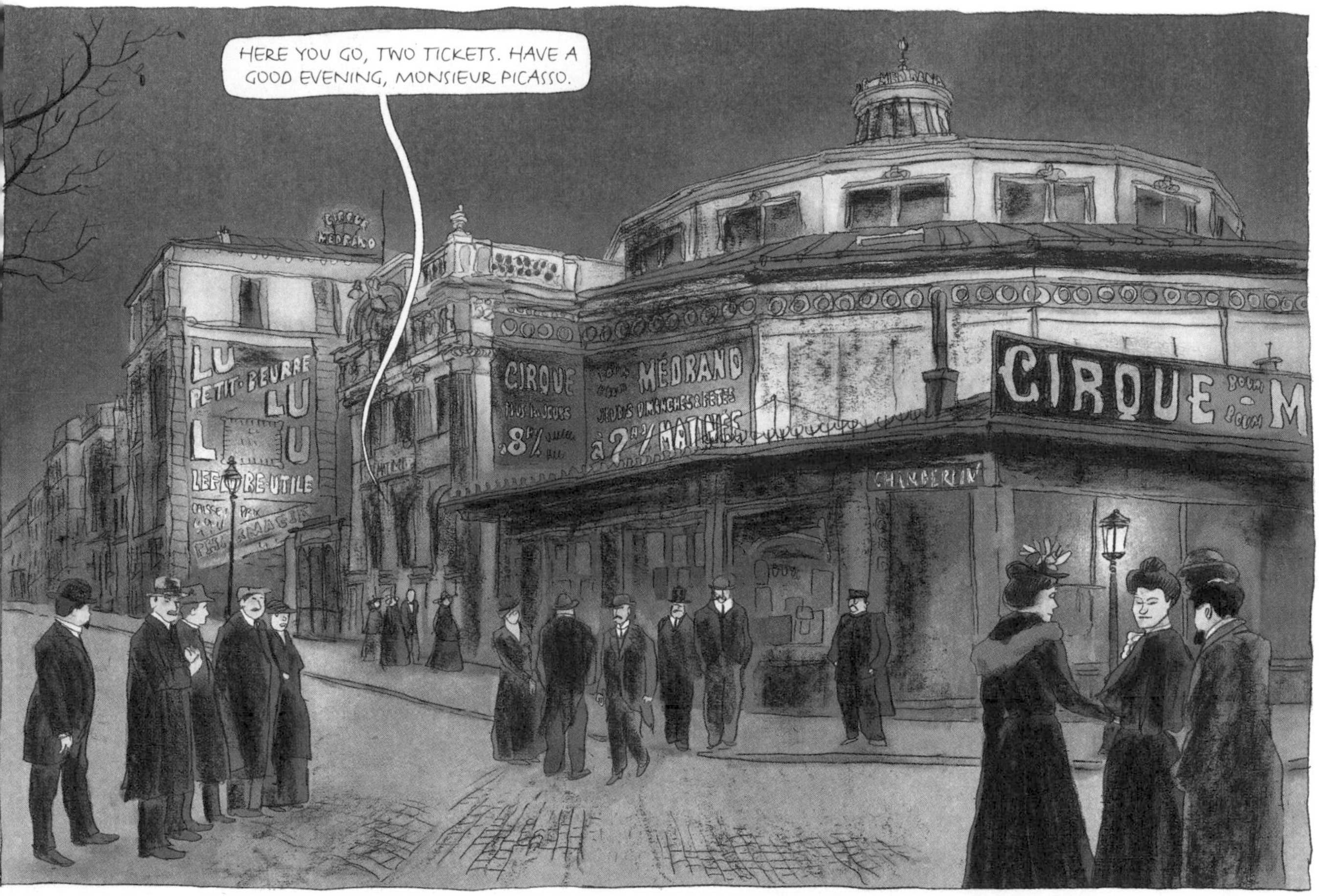
HERE YOU GO, TWO TICKETS. HAVE A GOOD EVENING, MONSIEUR PICASSO.
LU
PETIT-BEURRE
CIRQUE
MÉDRANO
CIRQUE

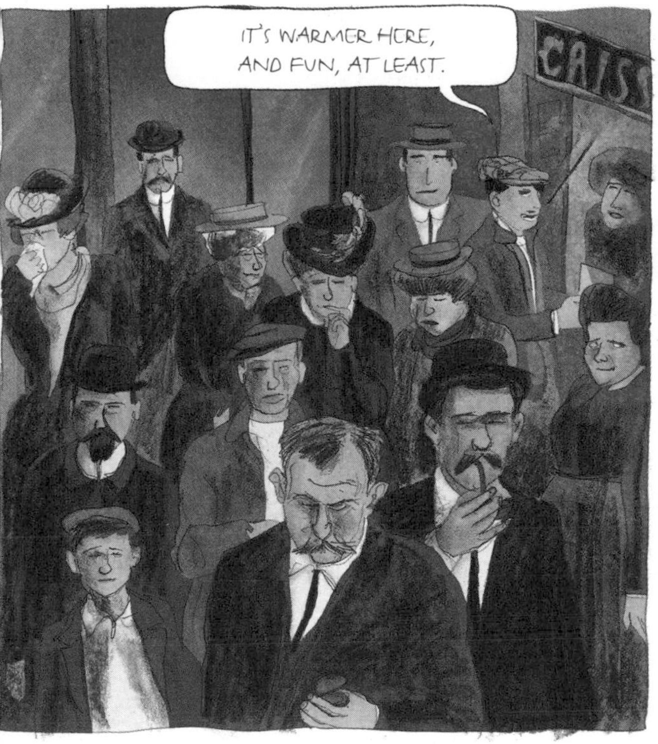
IT'S WARMER HERE, AND FUN, AT LEAST.

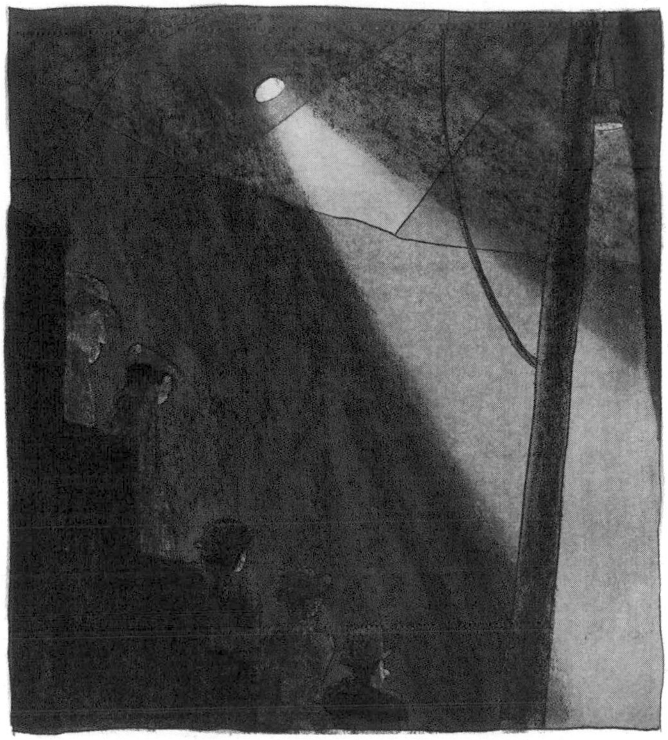

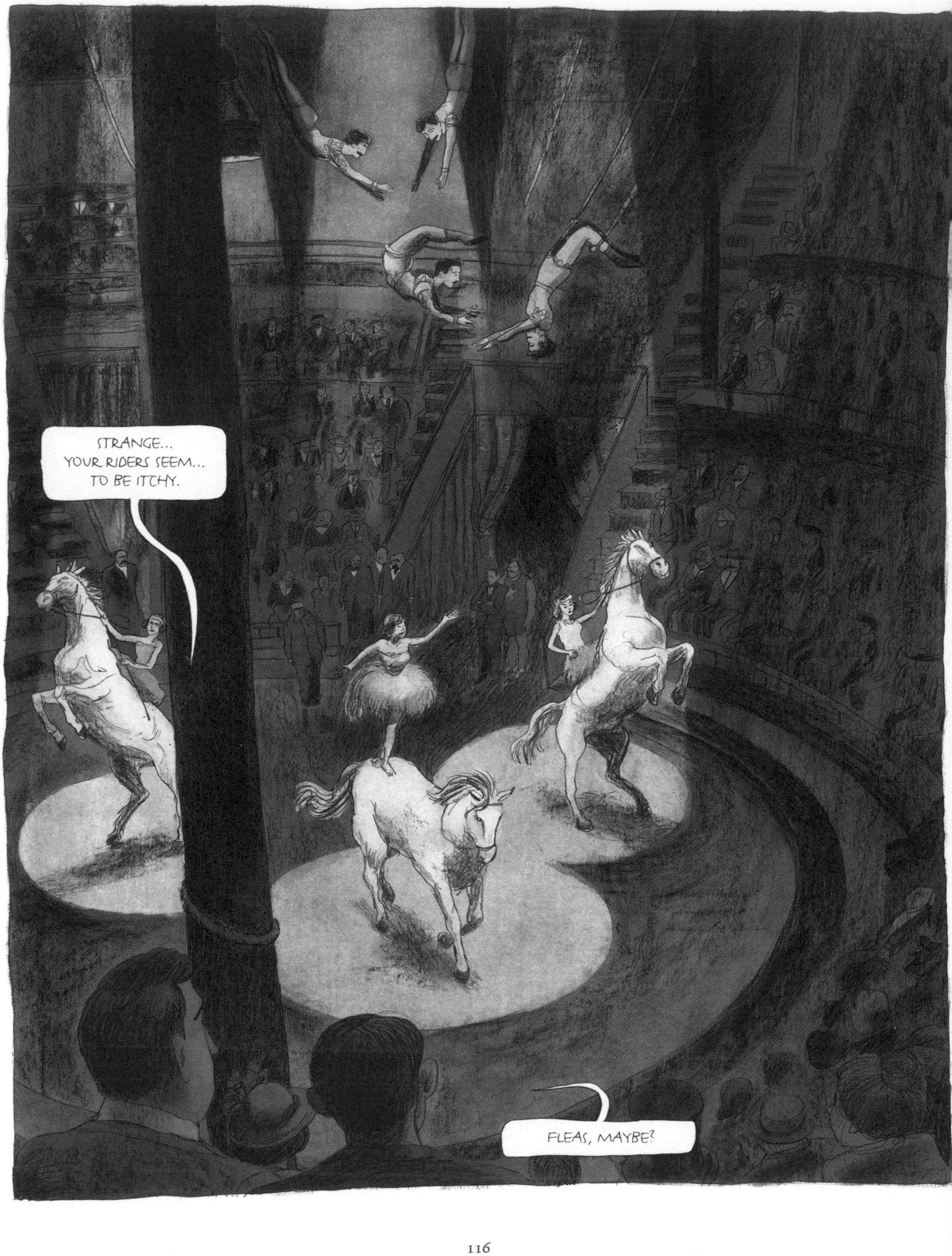
STRANGE... YOUR RIDERS SEEM... TO BE ITCHY.
FLEAS, MAYBE?

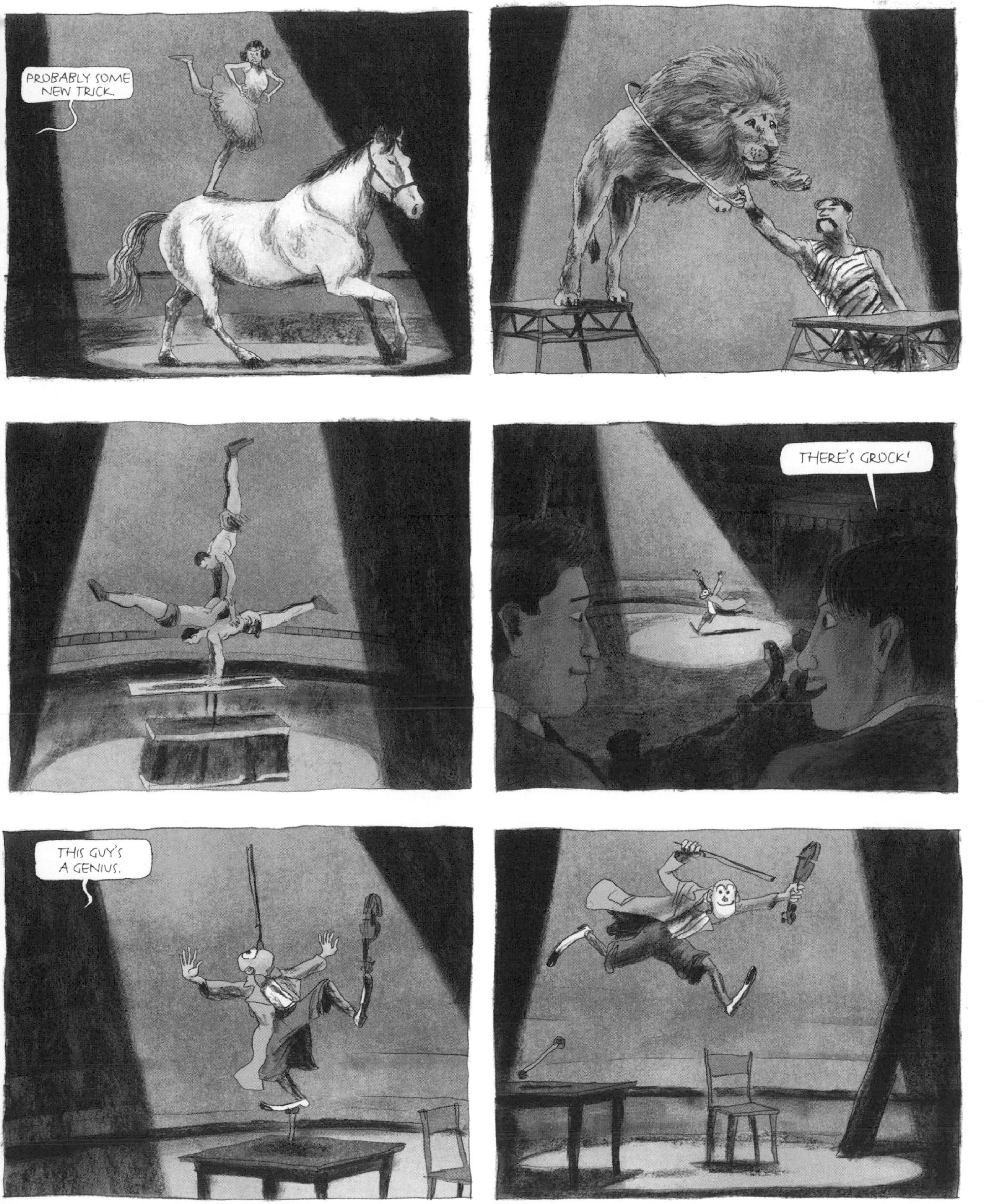
PROBABLY SOME NEW TRICK.
THERE'S GROCK!
THIS GUY'S A GENIUS.

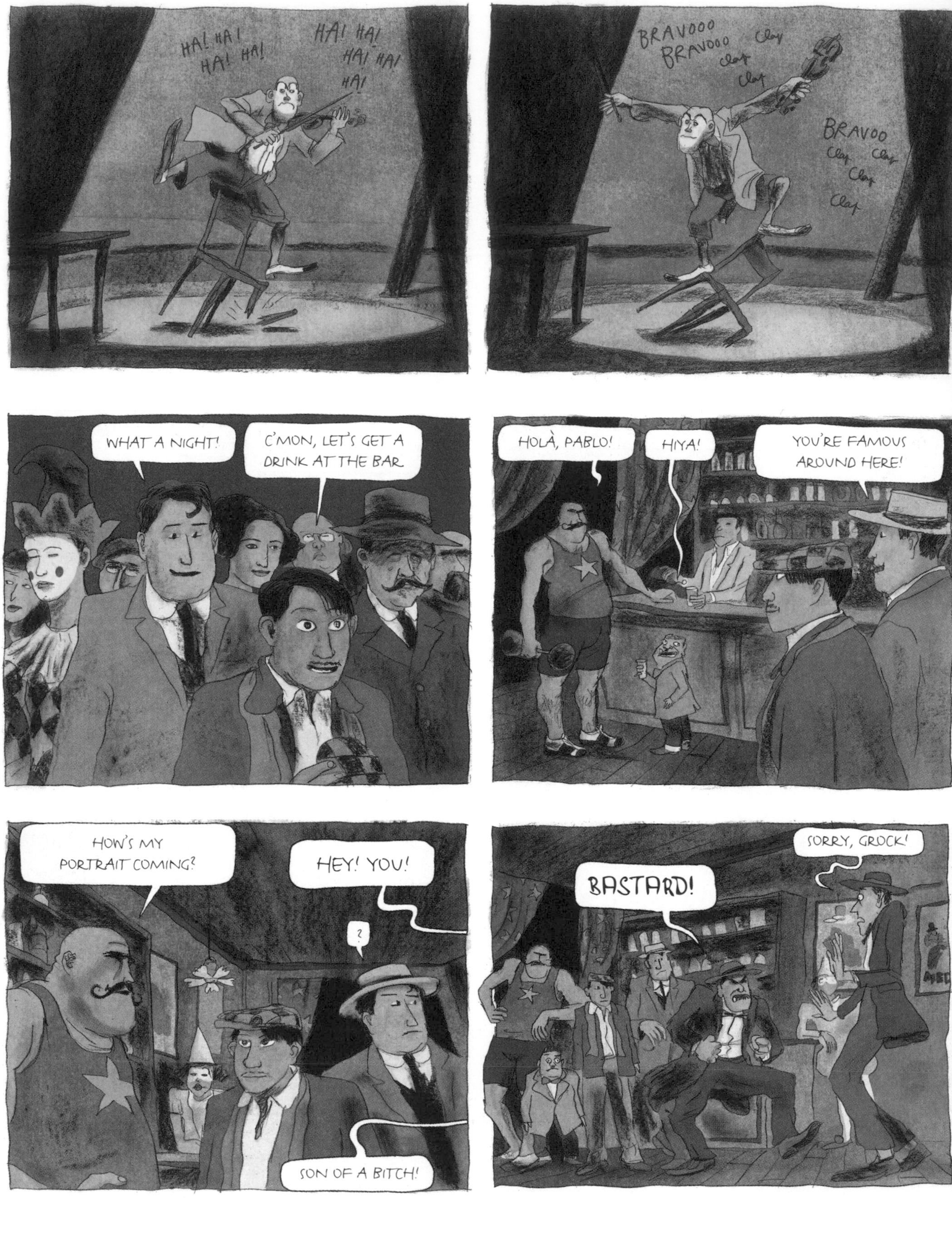
HA! HA! HA! HA!
HA! HA! HA! HA! HA!
BRAVOOO BRAVOOO
Clap Clap Clap
BRAVOO
Clap Clap Clap Clap
WHAT A NIGHT!
C'MON, LET'S GET A DRINK AT THE BAR
HOLÀ, PABLO!
HIYA!
YOU'RE FAMOUS AROUND HERE!
HOW'S MY PORTRAIT COMING?
HEY! YOU!
?
SON OF A BITCH!
BASTARD!
SORRY, GROCK!

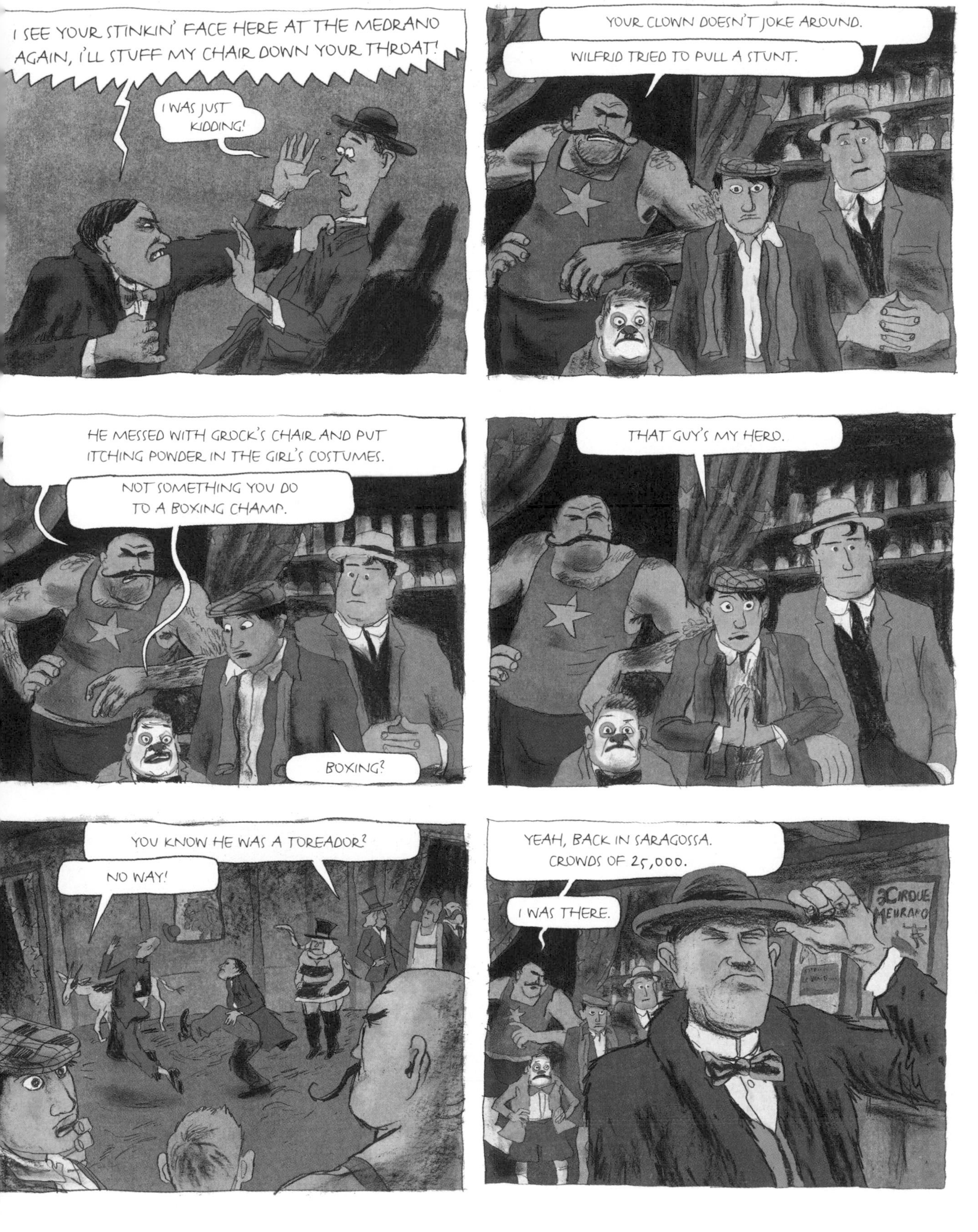
I SEE YOUR STINKIN' FACE HERE AT THE MEDRANO AGAIN, I'LL STUFF MY CHAIR DOWN YOUR THROAT!
I WAS JUST KIDDING!
YOUR CLOWN DOESN'T JOKE AROUND.
WILFRID TRIED TO PULL A STUNT.
HE MESSED WITH GROCK'S CHAIR AND PUT ITCHING POWDER IN THE GIRL'S COSTUMES.
NOT SOMETHING YOU DO TO A BOXING CHAMP.
BOXING?
THAT GUY'S MY HERO.
YOU KNOW HE WAS A TOREADOR?
NO WAY!
YEAH, BACK IN SARAGOSSA. CROWDS OF 25,000.
I WAS THERE.
CIRQUE MEDRANO

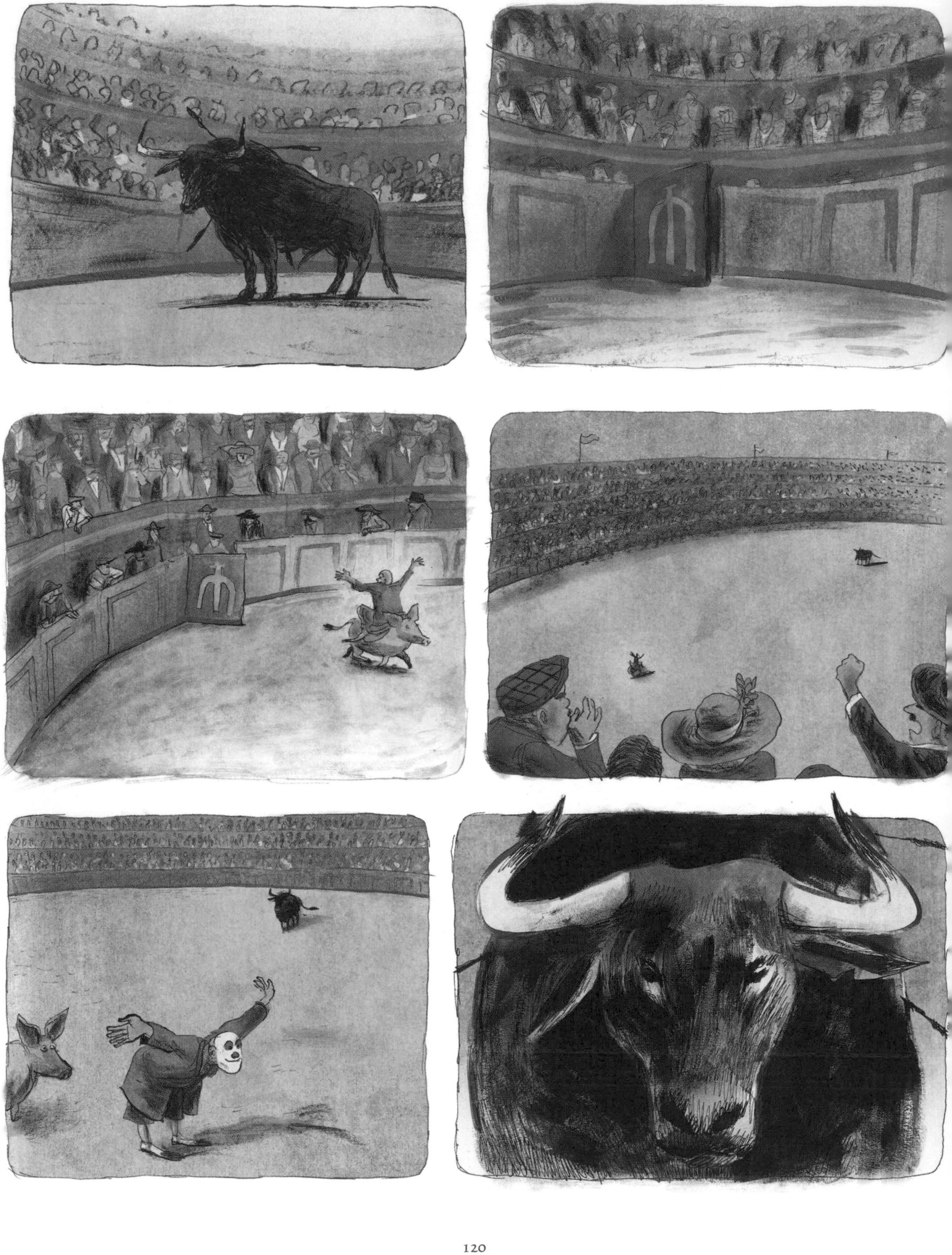

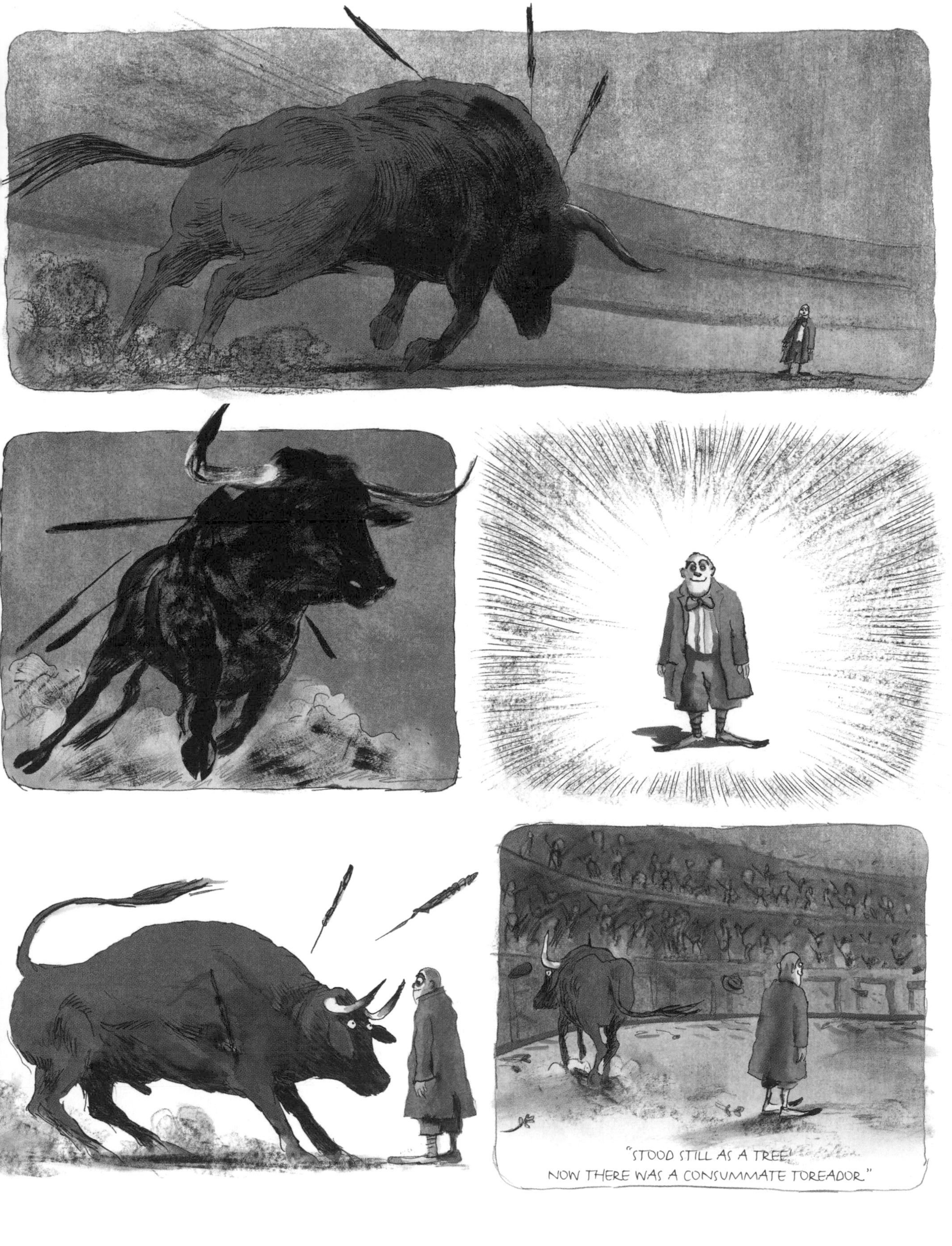
"STOOD STILL AS A TREE!
NOW THERE WAS A CONSUMMATE TOREADOR"

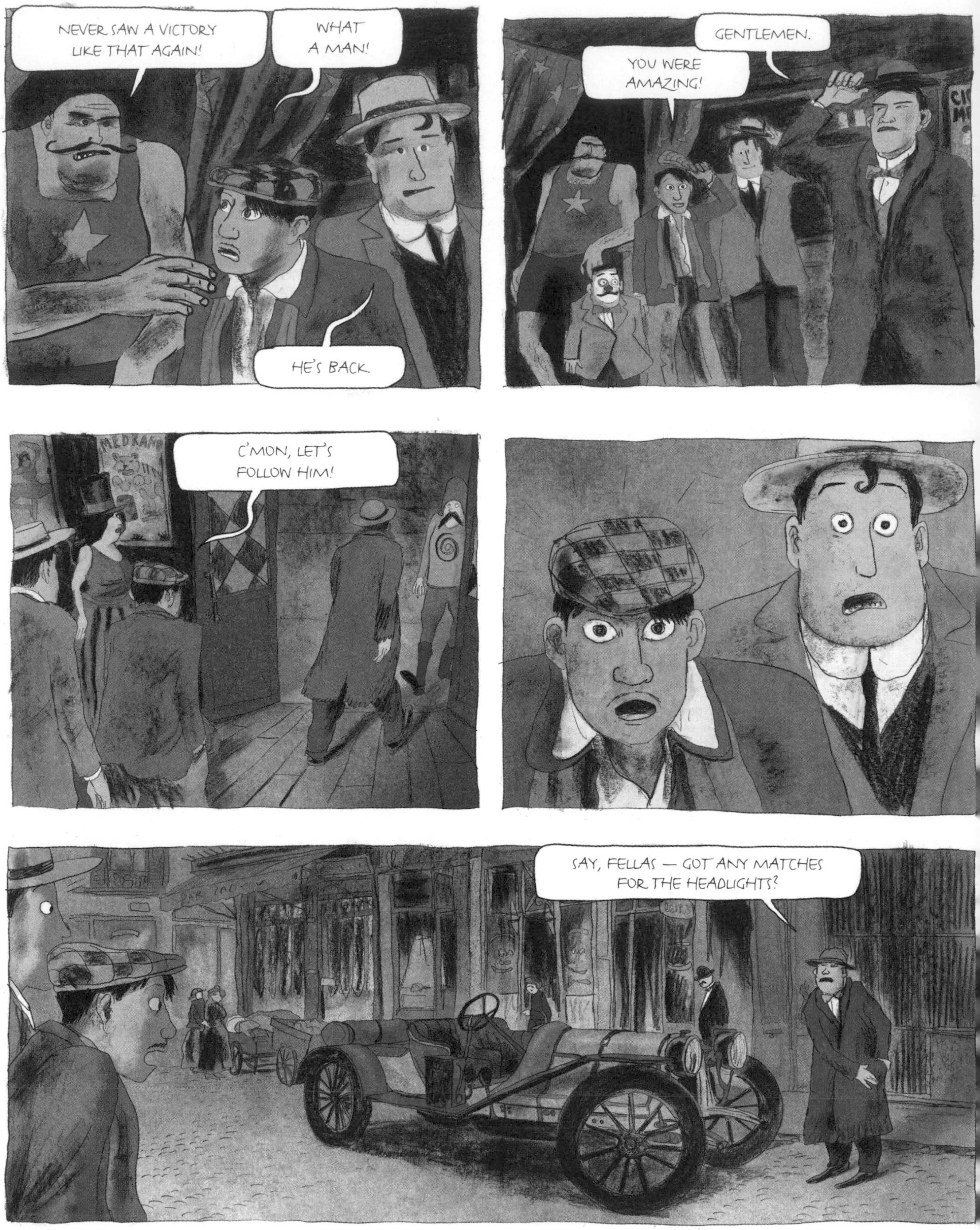
NEVER SAW A VICTORY LIKE THAT AGAIN!
WHAT A MAN!
HE'S BACK.
GENTLEMEN.
YOU WERE AMAZING!
C'MON, LET'S FOLLOW HIM!
SAY, FELLAS — GOT ANY MATCHES FOR THE HEADLIGHTS?

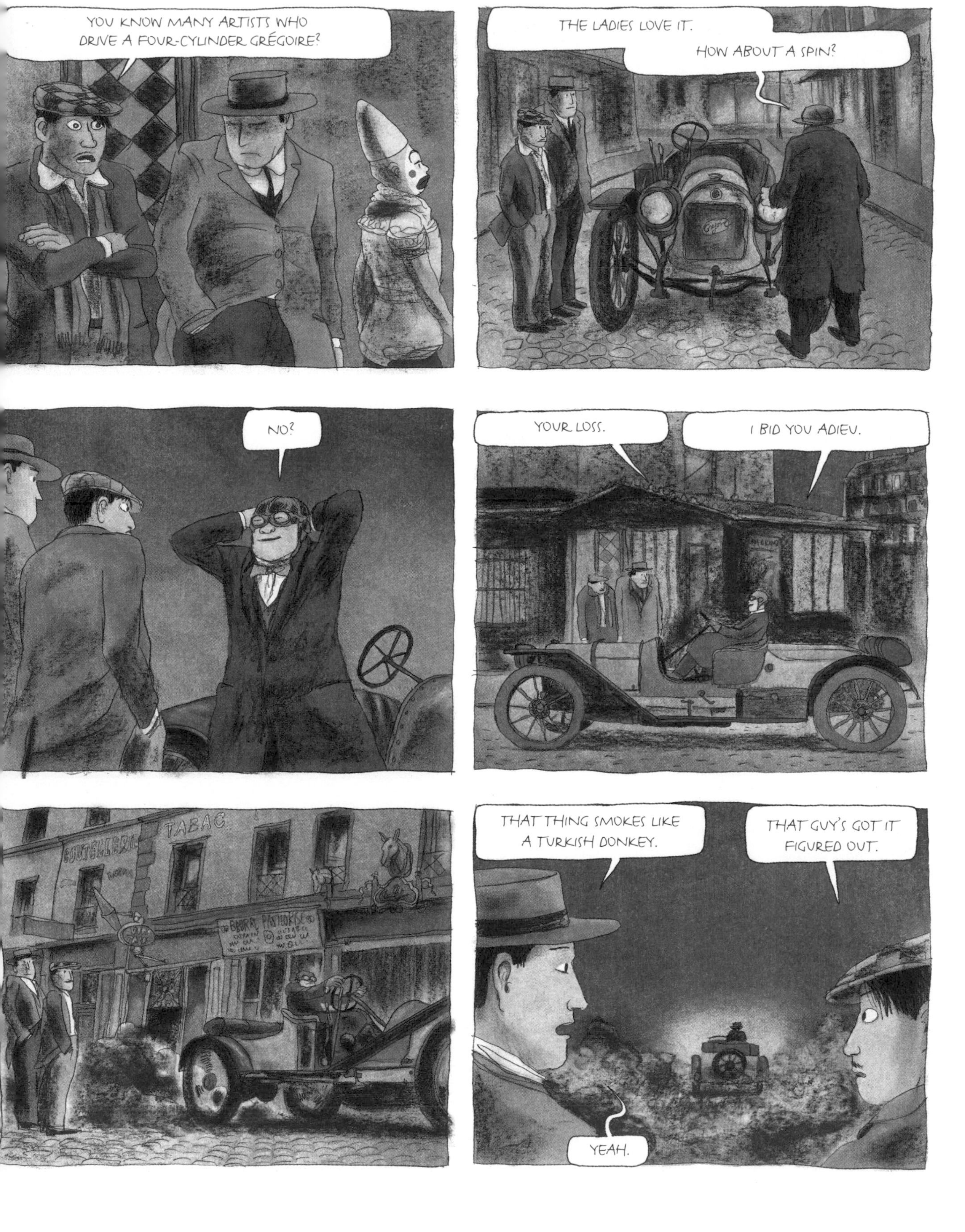
YOU KNOW MANY ARTISTS WHO DRIVE A FOUR-CYLINDER GRÉGOIRE?
THE LADIES LOVE IT.
HOW ABOUT A SPIN?
NO?
YOUR LOSS.
I BID YOU ADIEU.
TABAC
THAT THING SMOKES LIKE A TURKISH DONKEY.
THAT GUY'S GOT IT FIGURED OUT.
YEAH.

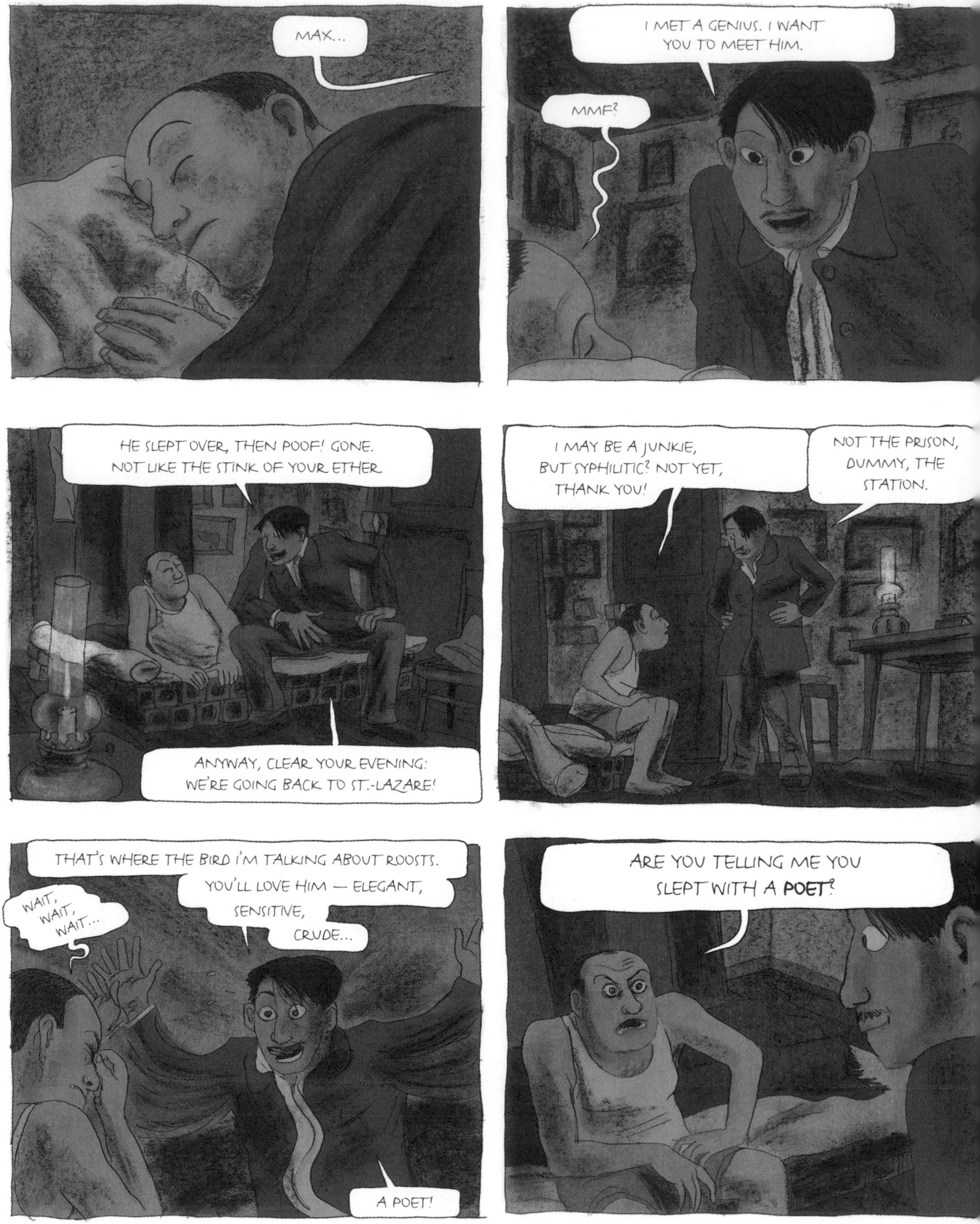
MAX...
I MET A GENIUS. I WANT YOU TO MEET HIM.
MMF?
HE SLEPT OVER, THEN POOF! GONE. NOT LIKE THE STINK OF YOUR ETHER
ANYWAY, CLEAR YOUR EVENING: WE'RE GOING BACK TO ST.-LAZARE!
I MAY BE A JUNKIE, BUT SYPHILITIC? NOT YET, THANK YOU!
NOT THE PRISON, DUMMY, THE STATION.
THAT'S WHERE THE BIRD I'M TALKING ABOUT ROOSTS.
YOU'LL LOVE HIM — ELEGANT,
SENSITIVE,
CRUDE...
WAIT, WAIT, WAIT...
A POET!
ARE YOU TELLING ME YOU SLEPT WITH A **POET**?

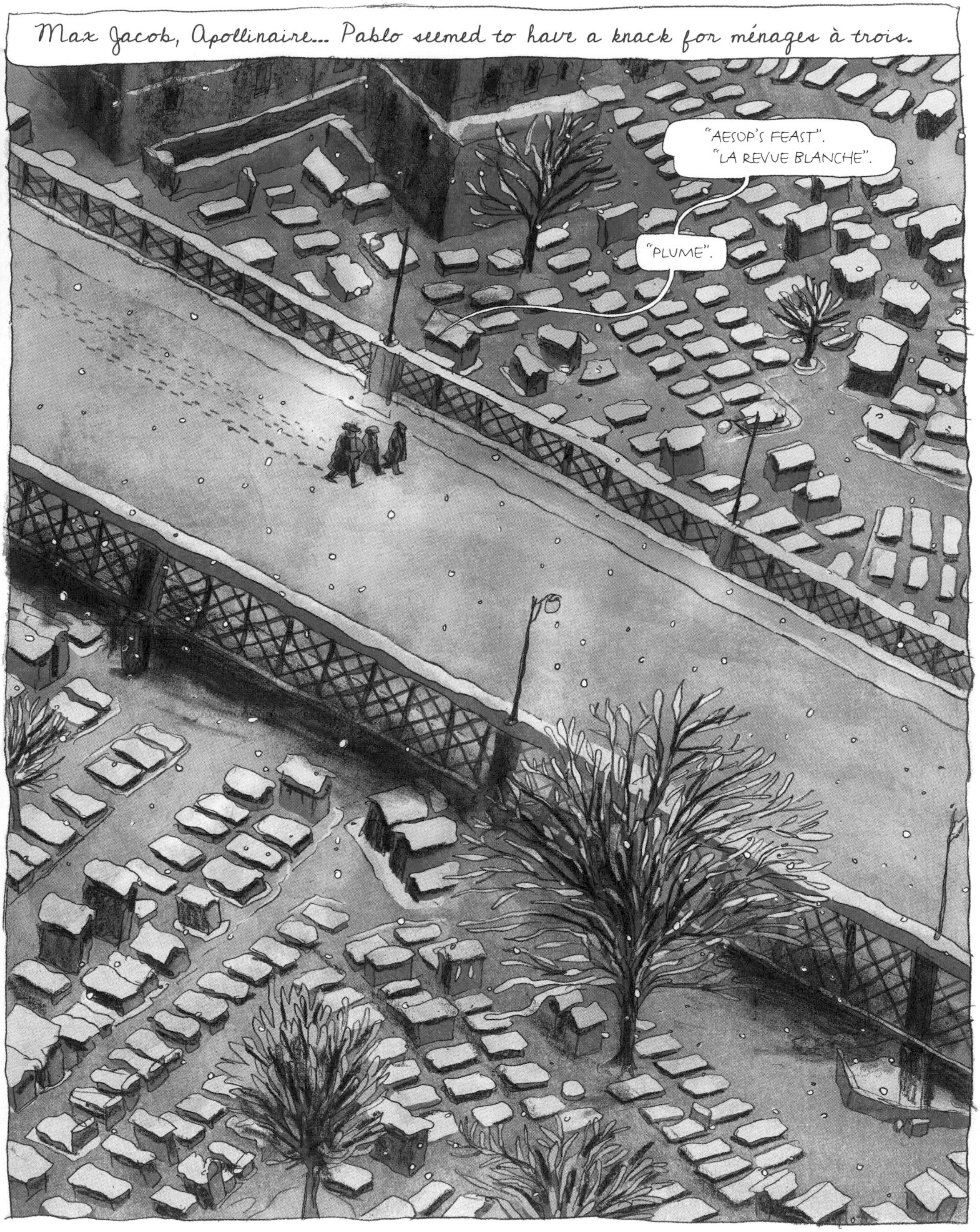
Max Jacob, Apollinaire... Pablo seemed to have a knack for ménages à trois.
"PLUME".
"AESOP'S FEAST". "LA REVUE BLANCHE".

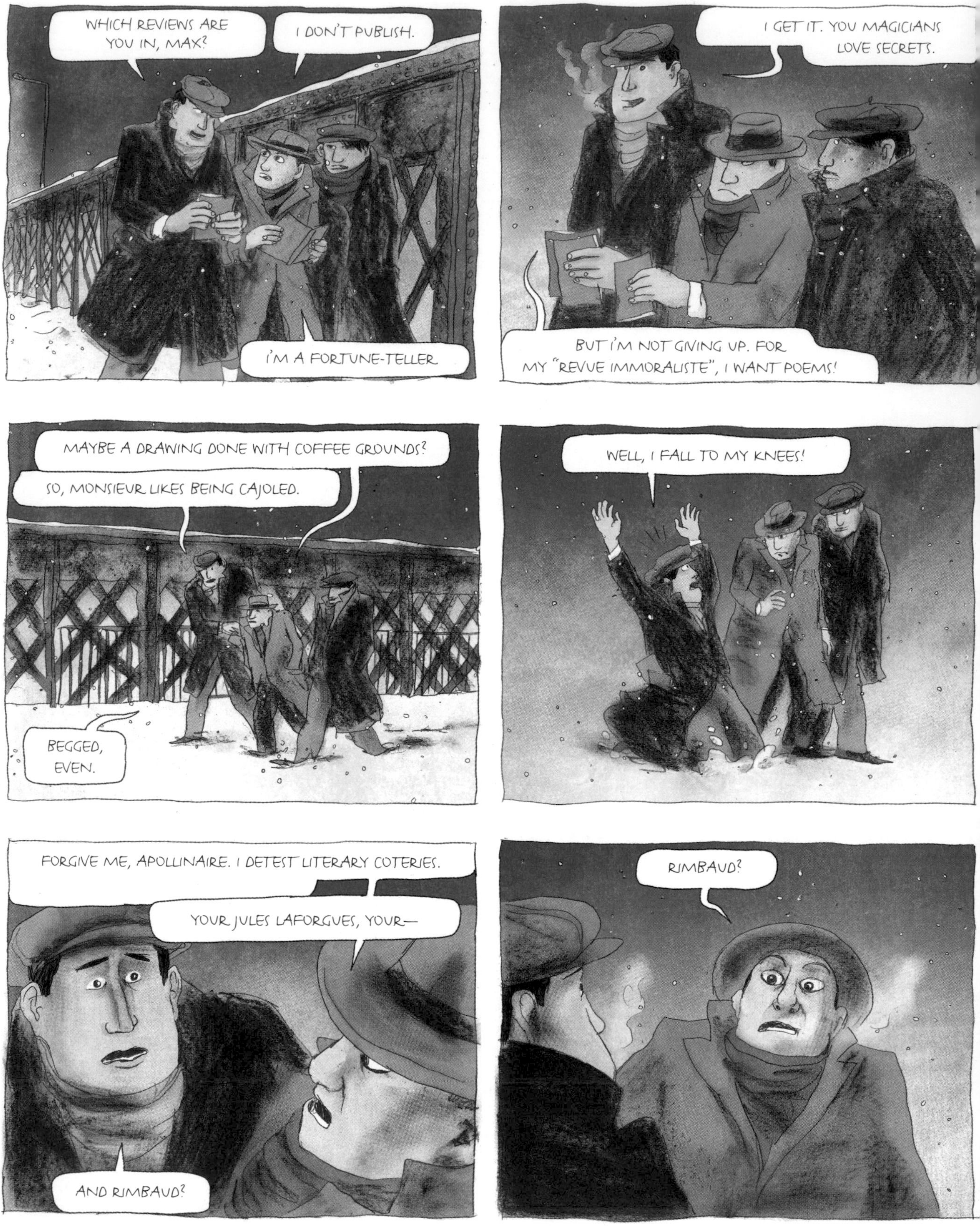
WHICH REVIEWS ARE YOU IN, MAX?
I DON'T PUBLISH.
I'M A FORTUNE-TELLER
I GET IT. YOU MAGICIANS LOVE SECRETS.
BUT I'M NOT GIVING UP. FOR MY "REVUE IMMORALISTE", I WANT POEMS!
MAYBE A DRAWING DONE WITH COFFEE GROUNDS?
SO, MONSIEUR LIKES BEING CAJOLED.
BEGGED, EVEN.
WELL, I FALL TO MY KNEES!
FORGIVE ME, APOLLINAIRE. I DETEST LITERARY COTERIES.
YOUR JULES LAFORGUES, YOUR—
AND RIMBAUD?
RIMBAUD?

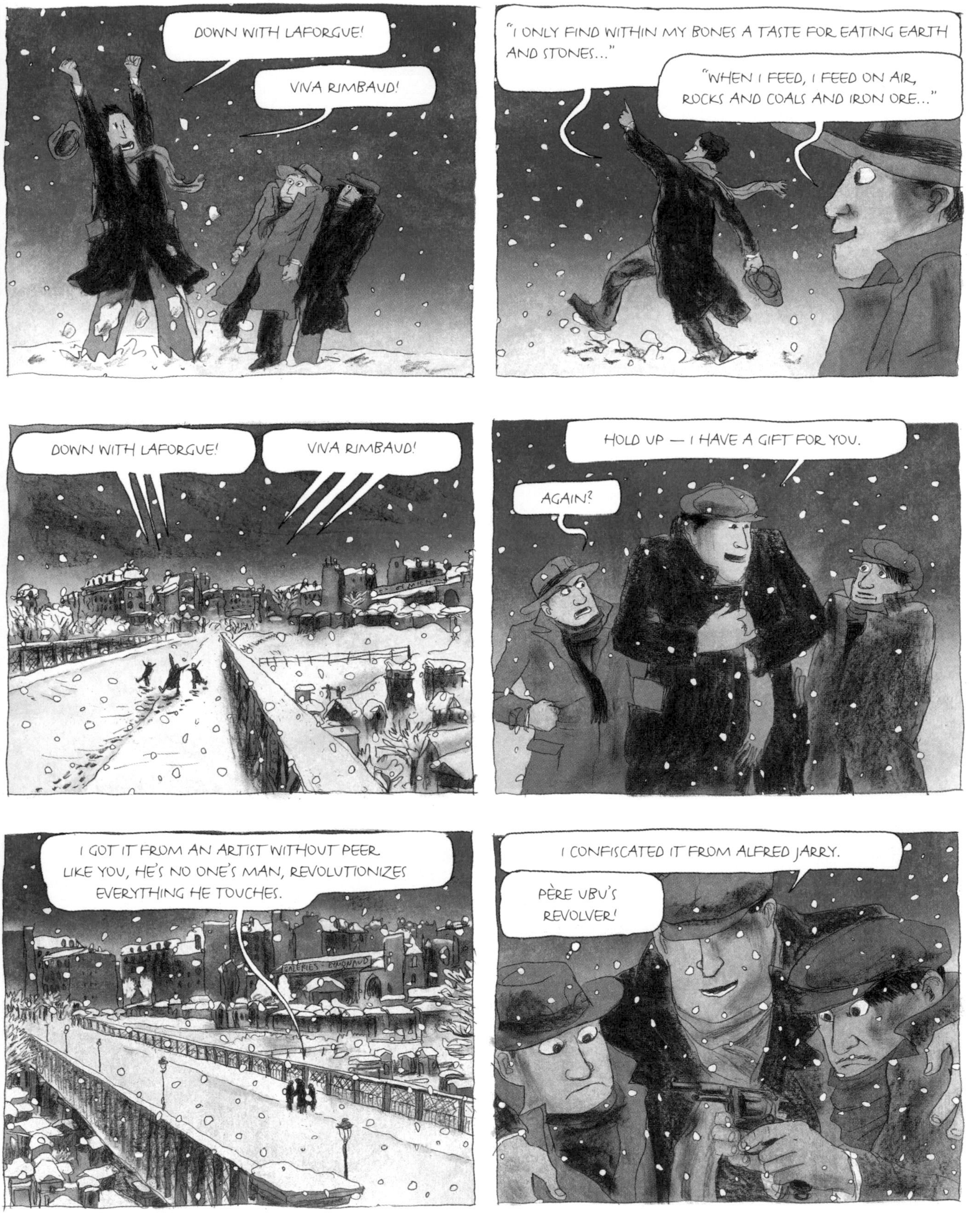
DOWN WITH LAFORGUE!
VIVA RIMBAUD!
"I ONLY FIND WITHIN MY BONES A TASTE FOR EATING EARTH AND STONES..."
"WHEN I FEED, I FEED ON AIR, ROCKS AND COALS AND IRON ORE..."
DOWN WITH LAFORGUE!
VIVA RIMBAUD!
HOLD UP — I HAVE A GIFT FOR YOU.
AGAIN?
I GOT IT FROM AN ARTIST WITHOUT PEER LIKE YOU, HE'S NO ONE'S MAN, REVOLUTIONIZES EVERYTHING HE TOUCHES.
GALERIES - EYMONAUD
I CONFISCATED IT FROM ALFRED JARRY.
PÈRE UBU'S REVOLVER!

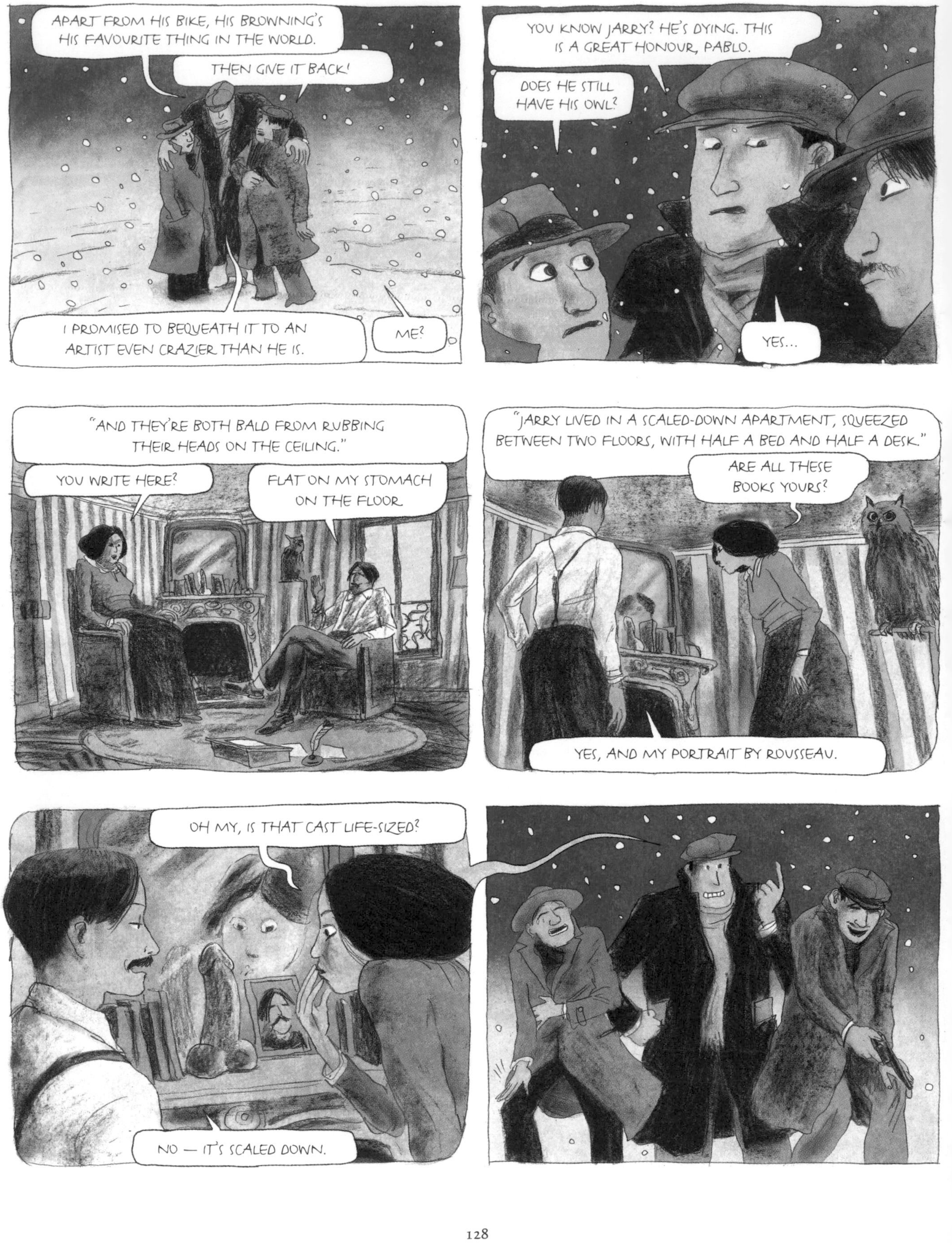
APART FROM HIS BIKE, HIS BROWNING'S HIS FAVOURITE THING IN THE WORLD.
THEN GIVE IT BACK!
I PROMISED TO BEQUEATH IT TO AN ARTIST EVEN CRAZIER THAN HE IS.
ME?
YOU KNOW JARRY? HE'S DYING. THIS IS A GREAT HONOUR, PABLO.
DOES HE STILL HAVE HIS OWL?
YES...
"AND THEY'RE BOTH BALD FROM RUBBING THEIR HEADS ON THE CEILING."
YOU WRITE HERE?
FLAT ON MY STOMACH ON THE FLOOR.
"JARRY LIVED IN A SCALED-DOWN APARTMENT, SQUEEZED BETWEEN TWO FLOORS, WITH HALF A BED AND HALF A DESK."
ARE ALL THESE BOOKS YOURS?
YES, AND MY PORTRAIT BY ROUSSEAU.
OH MY, IS THAT CAST LIFE-SIZED?
NO — IT'S SCALED DOWN.

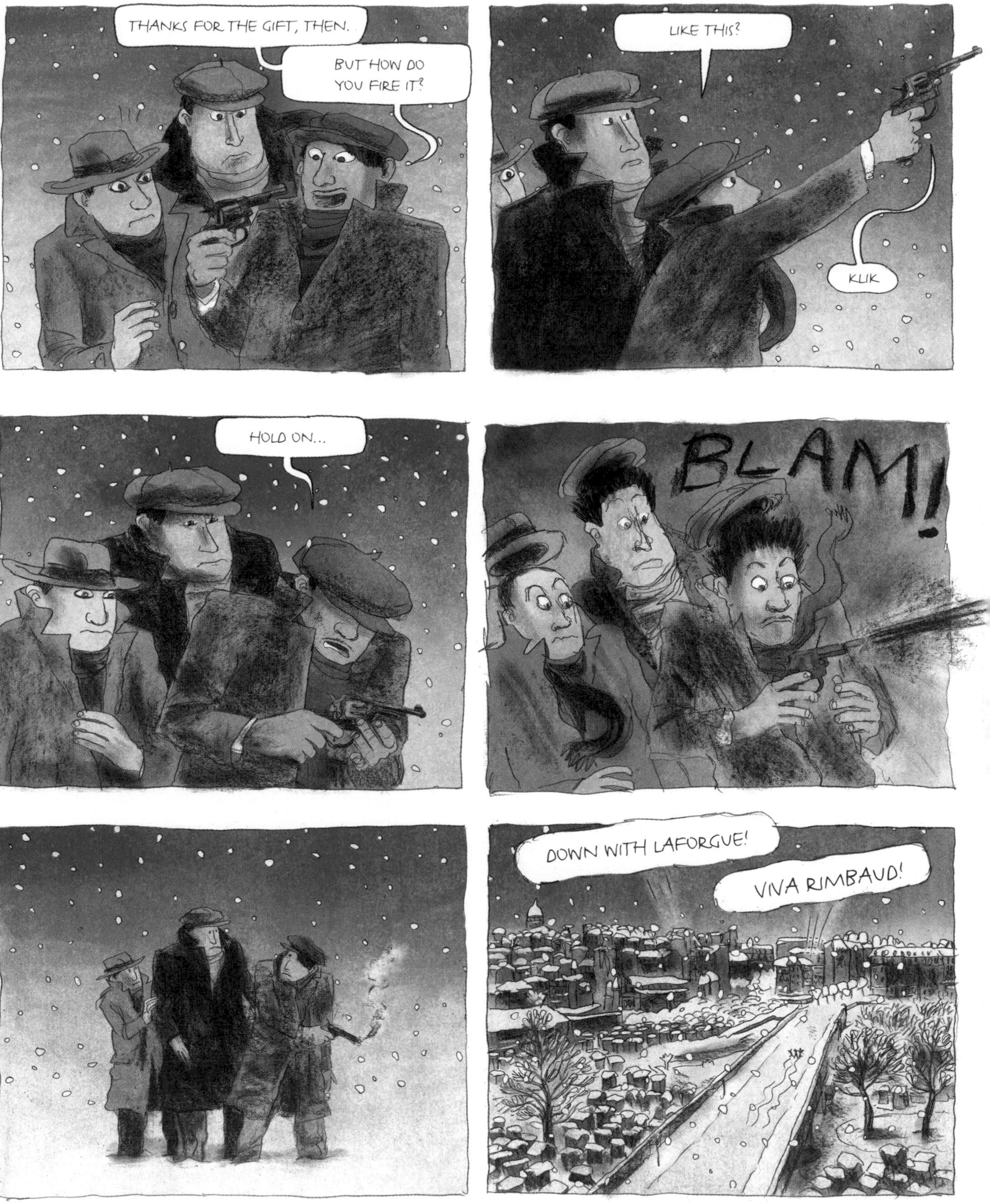
THANKS FOR THE GIFT, THEN.
BUT HOW DO YOU FIRE IT?
LIKE THIS?
KLIK
HOLD ON...
BLAM!!
DOWN WITH LAFORGUE!
VIVA RIMBAUD!

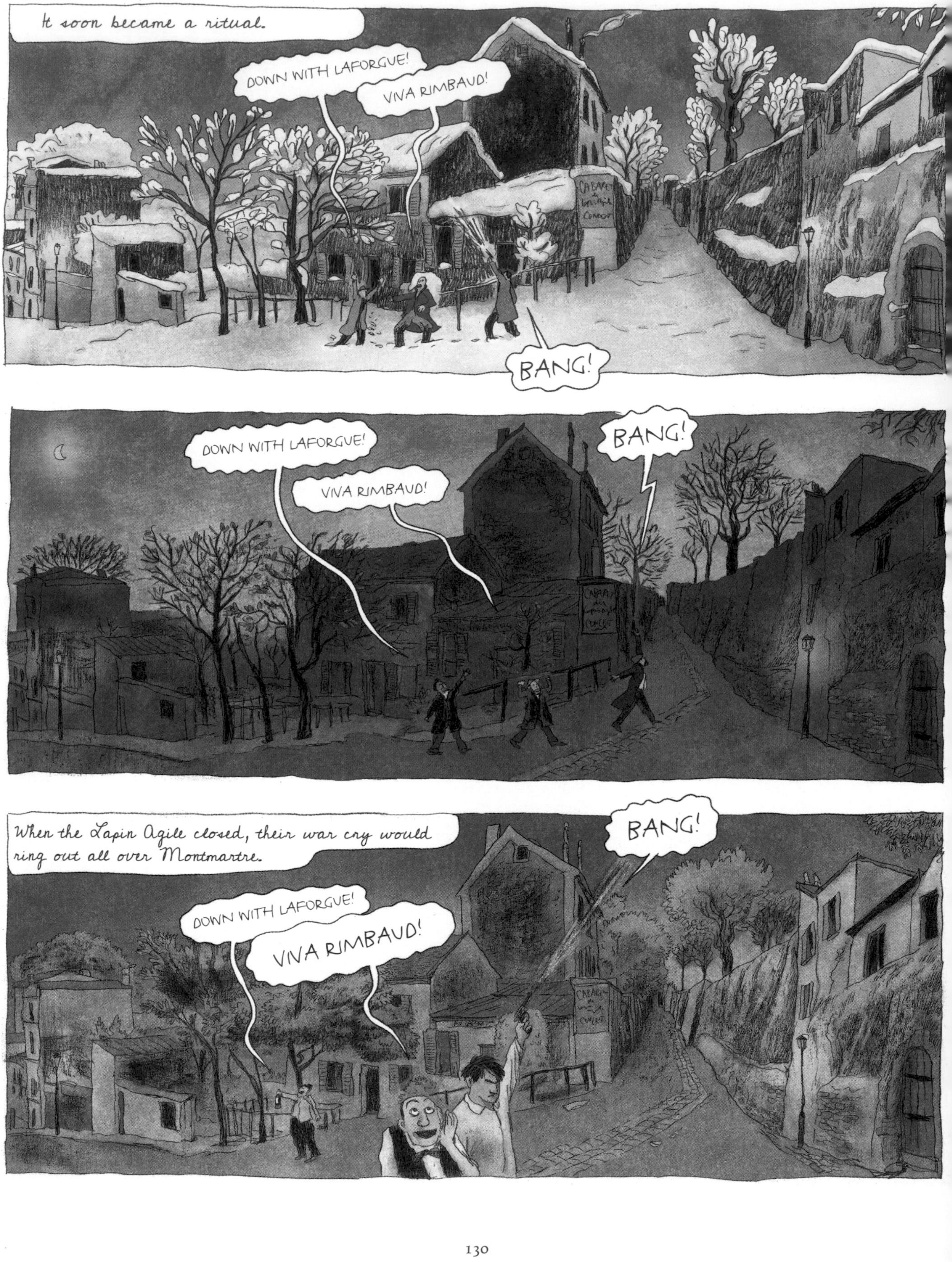
It soon became a ritual.
DOWN WITH LAFORGUE!
VIVA RIMBAUD!
BANG!
DOWN WITH LAFORGUE!
VIVA RIMBAUD!
BANG!
When the Lapin Agile closed, their war cry would ring out all over Montmartre.
BANG!
DOWN WITH LAFORGUE!
VIVA RIMBAUD!

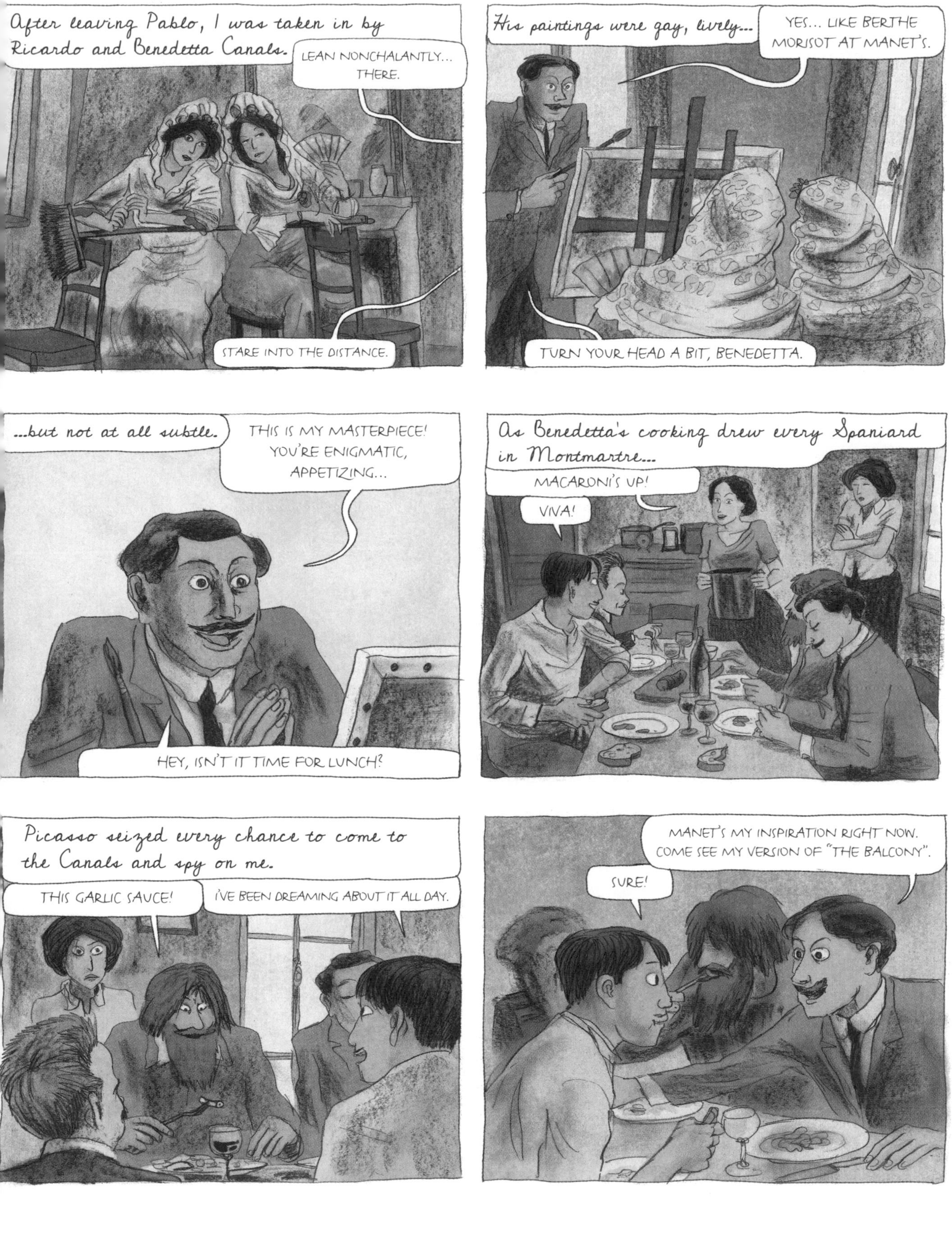
After leaving Pablo, I was taken in by Ricardo and Benedetta Canals.
LEAN NONCHALANTLY... THERE.
STARE INTO THE DISTANCE.
His paintings were gay, lively...
YES... LIKE BERTHE MORISOT AT MANET'S.
TURN YOUR HEAD A BIT, BENEDETTA.
...but not at all subtle.
THIS IS MY MASTERPIECE! YOU'RE ENIGMATIC, APPETIZING...
HEY, ISN'T IT TIME FOR LUNCH?
As Benedetta's cooking drew every Spaniard in Montmartre...
MACARONI'S UP!
VIVA!
Picasso seized every chance to come to the Canals and spy on me.
THIS GARLIC SAUCE!
I'VE BEEN DREAMING ABOUT IT ALL DAY.
MANET'S MY INSPIRATION RIGHT NOW. COME SEE MY VERSION OF "THE BALCONY".
SURE!

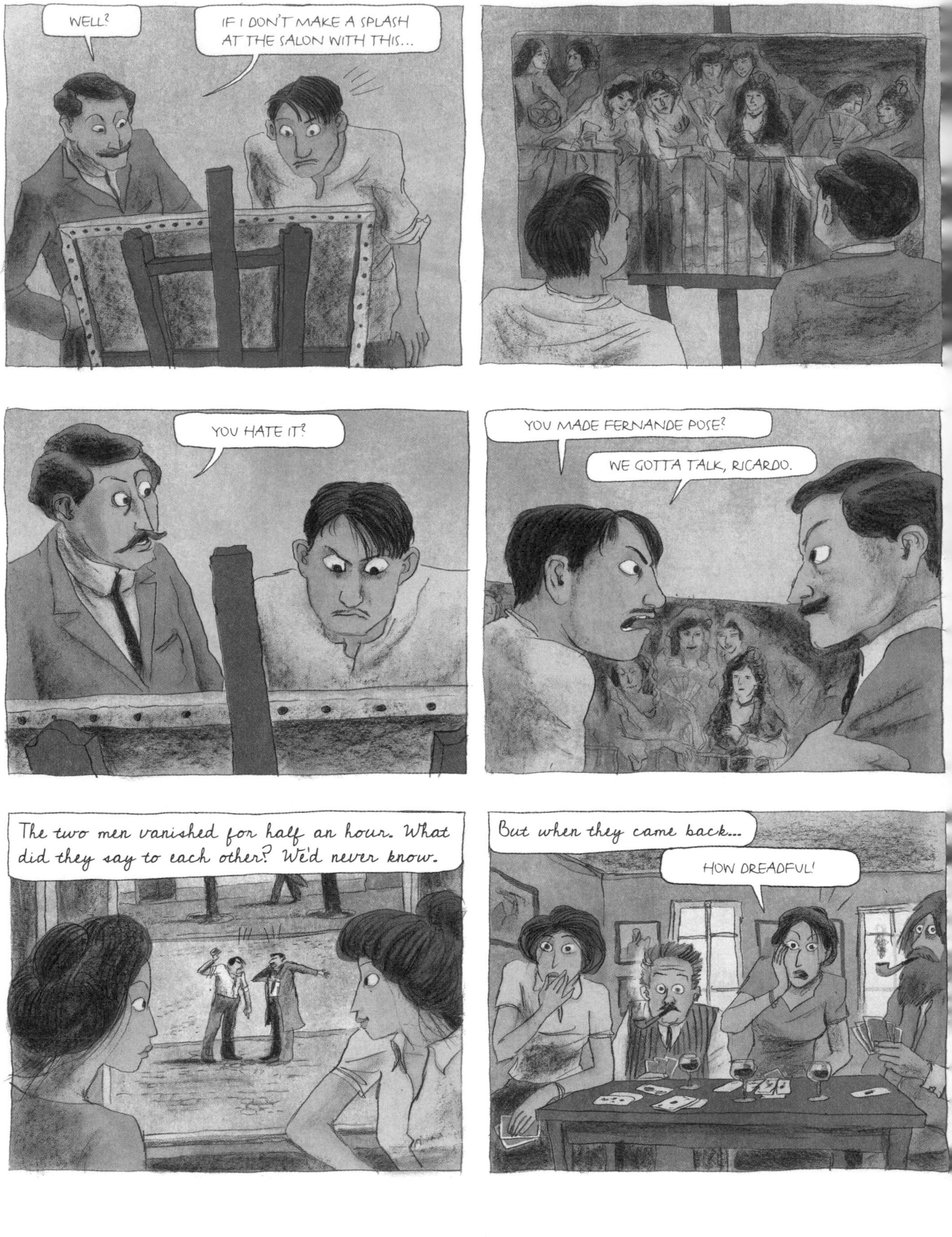
WELL?
IF I DON'T MAKE A SPLASH AT THE SALON WITH THIS...
YOU HATE IT?
YOU MADE FERNANDE POSE?
WE GOTTA TALK, RICARDO.
The two men vanished for half an hour. What did they say to each other? We'd never know.
But when they came back...
HOW DREADFUL!

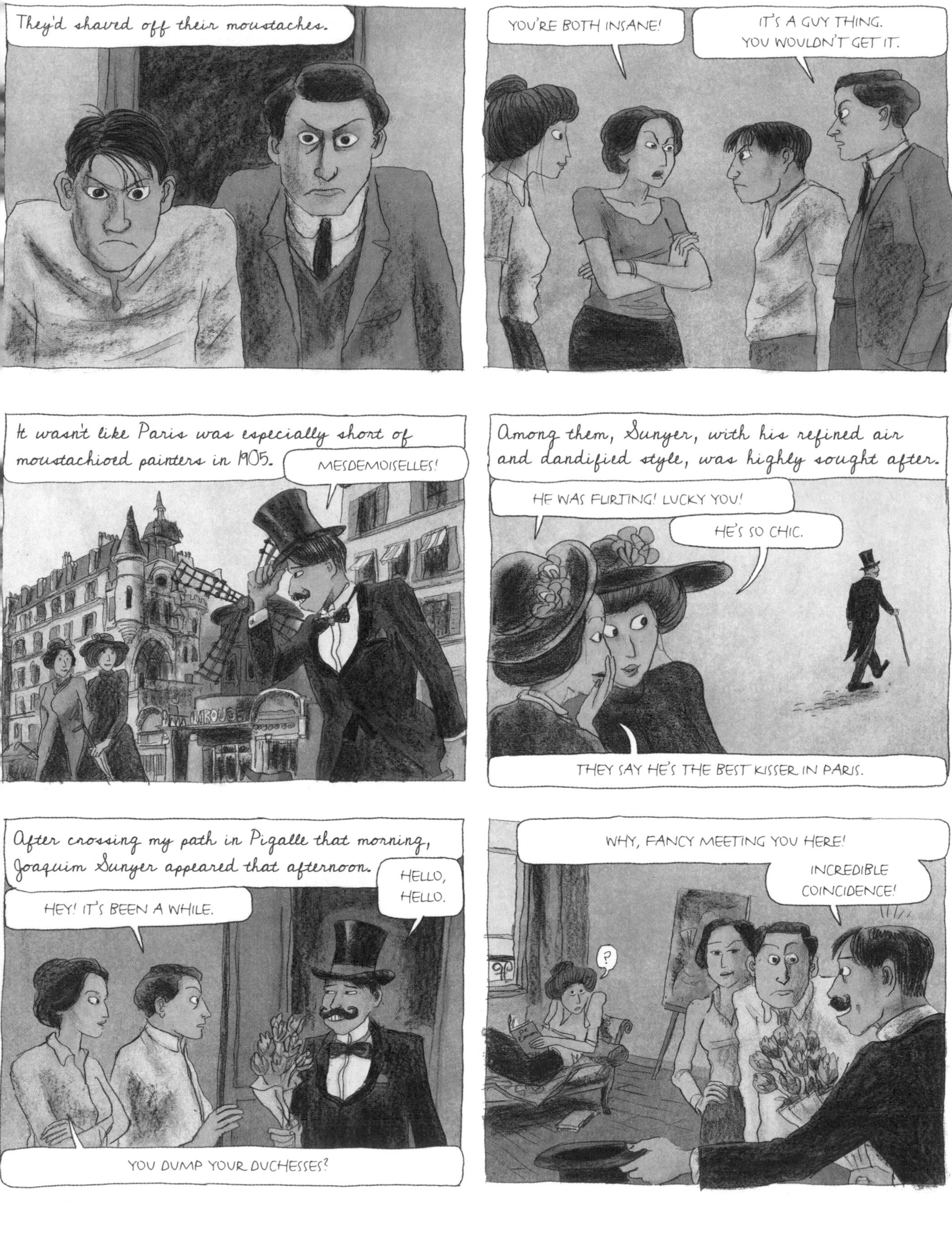
They'd shaved off their moustaches.
YOU'RE BOTH INSANE!
IT'S A GUY THING. YOU WOULDN'T GET IT.
It wasn't like Paris was especially short of moustachioed painters in 1905.
MESDEMOISELLES!
Among them, Sunyer, with his refined air and dandified style, was highly sought after.
HE WAS FLIRTING! LUCKY YOU!
HE'S SO CHIC.
THEY SAY HE'S THE BEST KISSER IN PARIS.
After crossing my path in Pigalle that morning, Joaquim Sunyer appeared that afternoon.
HELLO, HELLO.
HEY! IT'S BEEN A WHILE.
YOU DUMP YOUR DUCHESSES?
WHY, FANCY MEETING YOU HERE!
INCREDIBLE COINCIDENCE!
?

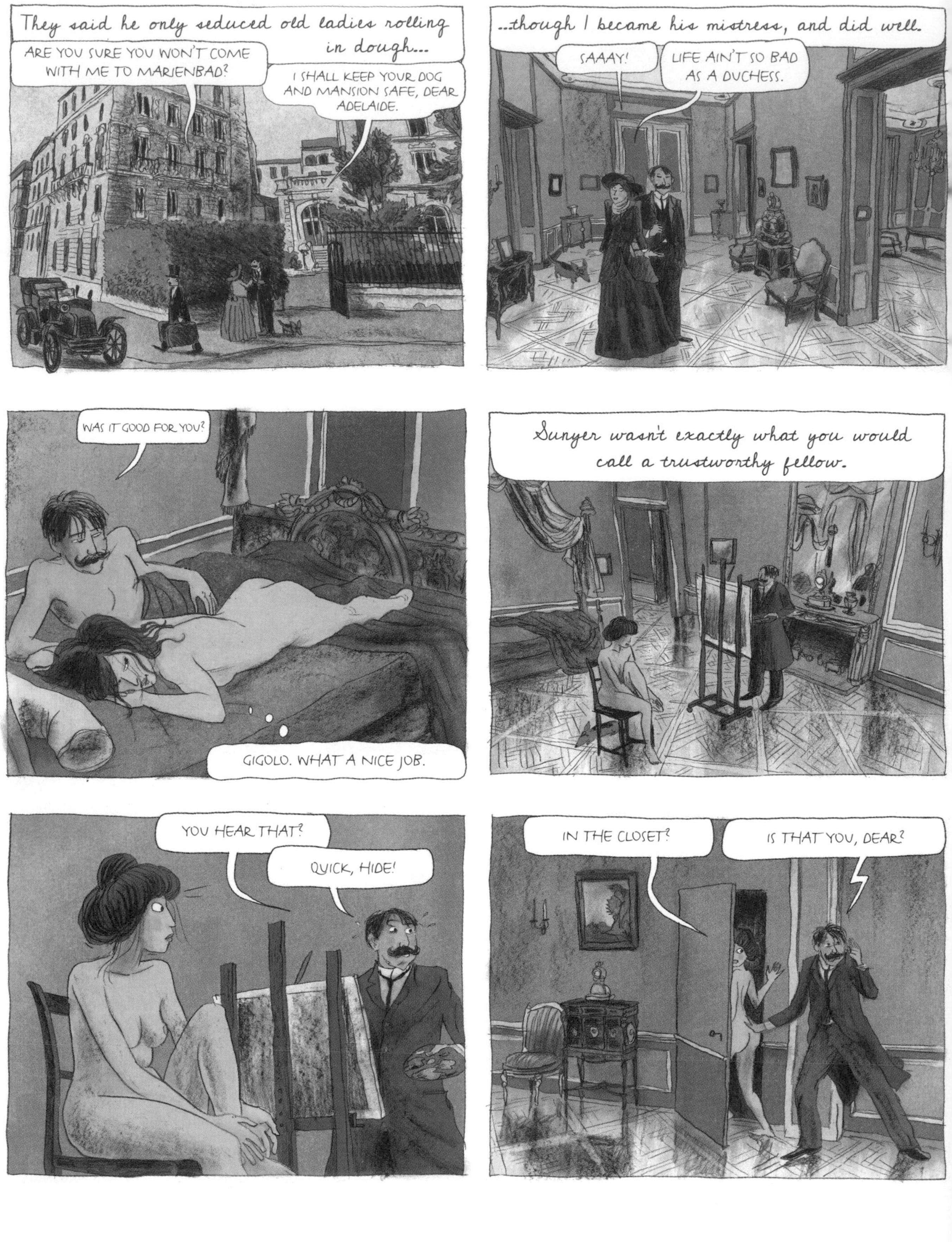
They said he only seduced old ladies rolling in dough...
ARE YOU SURE YOU WON'T COME WITH ME TO MARIENBAD?
I SHALL KEEP YOUR DOG AND MANSION SAFE, DEAR ADELAIDE.
...though I became his mistress, and did well.
SAAAY!
LIFE AIN'T SO BAD AS A DUCHESS.
WAS IT GOOD FOR YOU?
GIGOLO. WHAT A NICE JOB.
Sunyer wasn't exactly what you would call a trustworthy fellow.
YOU HEAR THAT?
QUICK, HIDE!
IN THE CLOSET?
IS THAT YOU, DEAR?

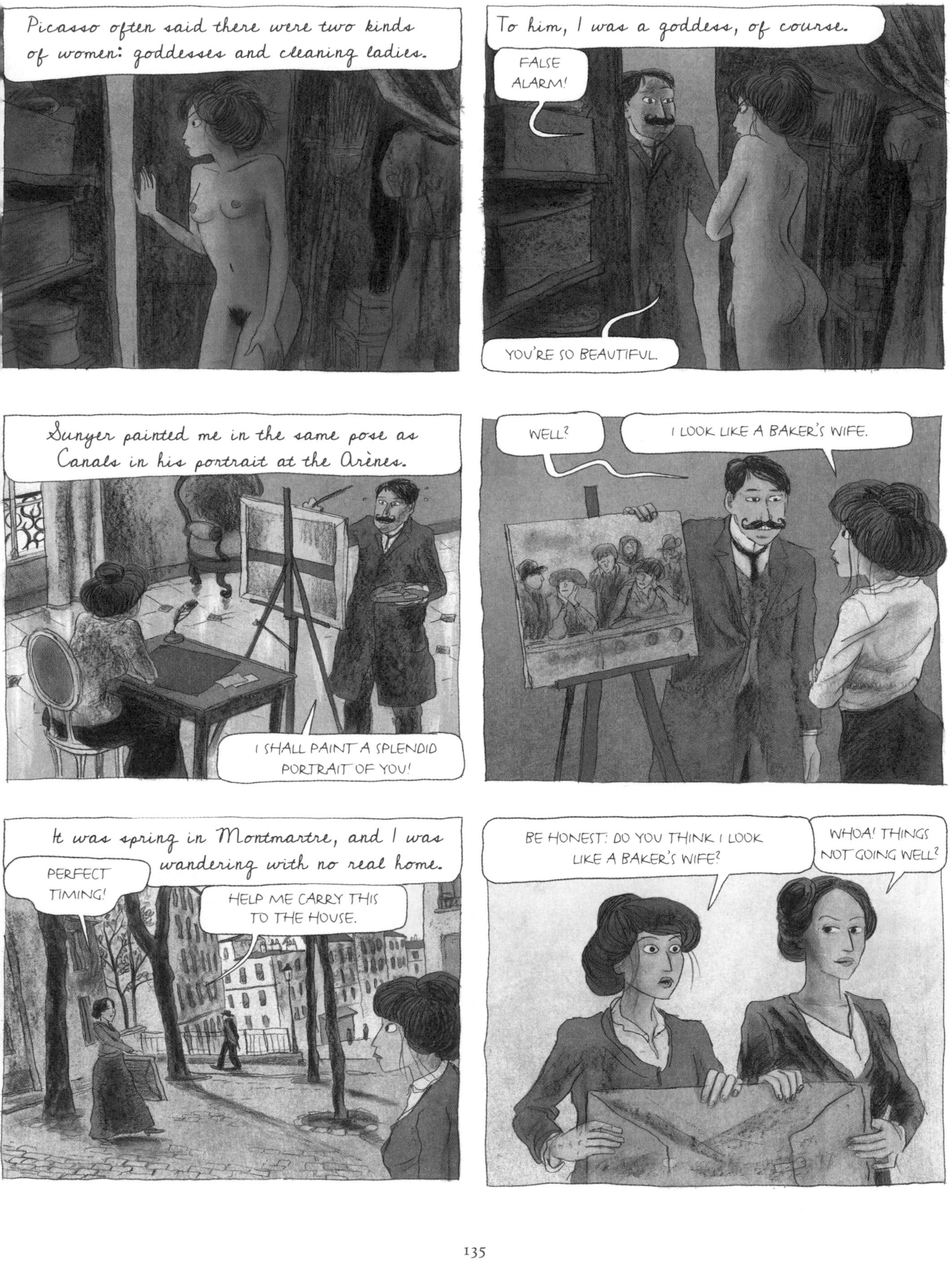

Picasso often said there were two kinds of women: goddesses and cleaning ladies.
To him, I was a goddess, of course.
FALSE ALARM!
YOU'RE SO BEAUTIFUL.
Sunyer painted me in the same pose as Canals in his portrait at the Arènes.
I SHALL PAINT A SPLENDID PORTRAIT OF YOU!
WELL?
I LOOK LIKE A BAKER'S WIFE.
It was spring in Montmartre, and I was wandering with no real home.
PERFECT TIMING!
HELP ME CARRY THIS TO THE HOUSE.
BE HONEST: DO YOU THINK I LOOK LIKE A BAKER'S WIFE?
WHOA! THINGS NOT GOING WELL?

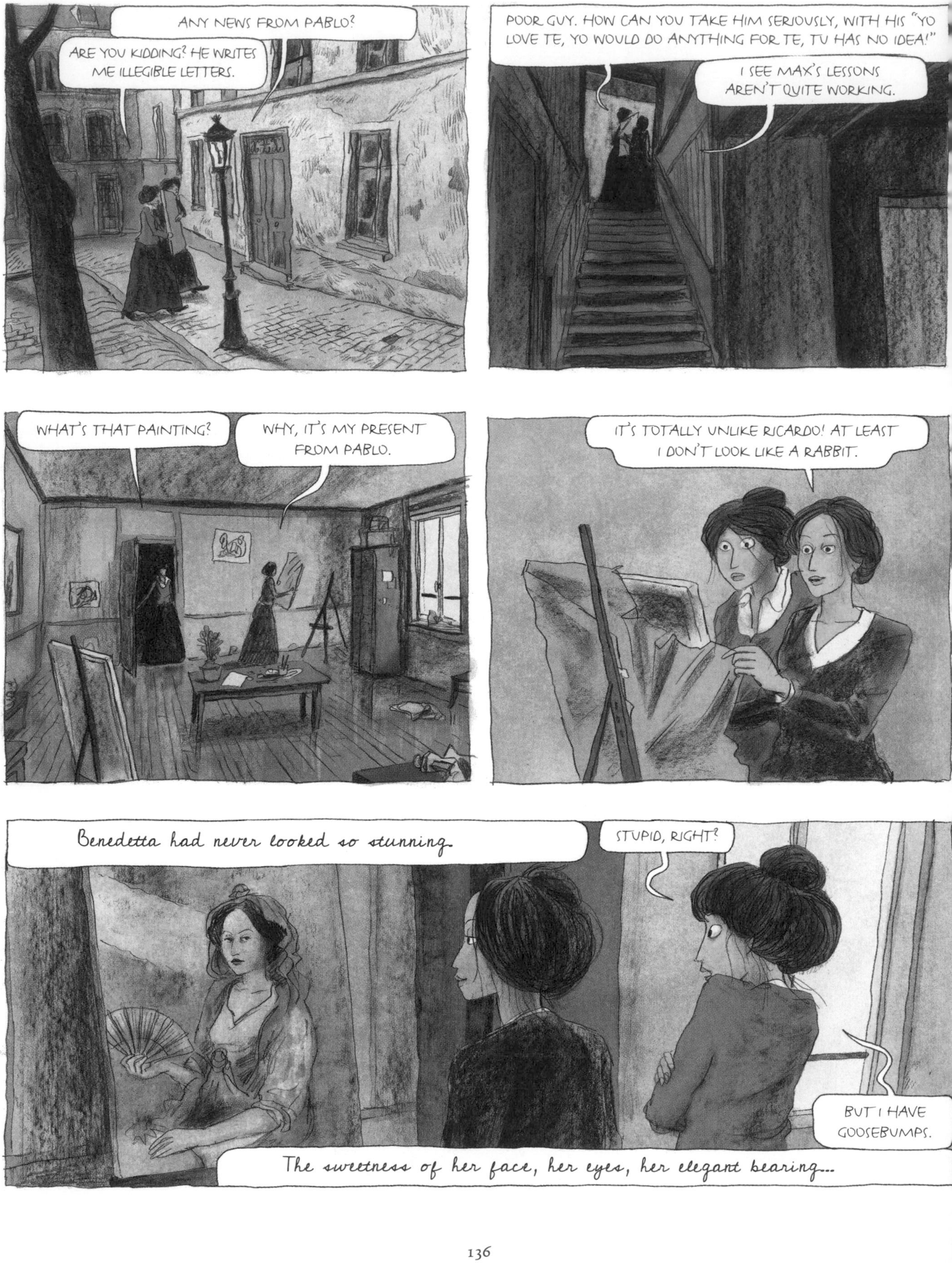
ANY NEWS FROM PABLO?
ARE YOU KIDDING? HE WRITES ME ILLEGIBLE LETTERS.
POOR GUY. HOW CAN YOU TAKE HIM SERIOUSLY, WITH HIS "YO LOVE TE, YO WOULD DO ANYTHING FOR TE, TU HAS NO IDEA!"
I SEE MAX'S LESSONS AREN'T QUITE WORKING.
WHAT'S THAT PAINTING?
WHY, IT'S MY PRESENT FROM PABLO.
IT'S TOTALLY UNLIKE RICARDO! AT LEAST I DON'T LOOK LIKE A RABBIT.
Benedetta had never looked so stunning.
STUPID, RIGHT?
BUT I HAVE GOOSEBUMPS.
The sweetness of her face, her eyes, her elegant bearing...

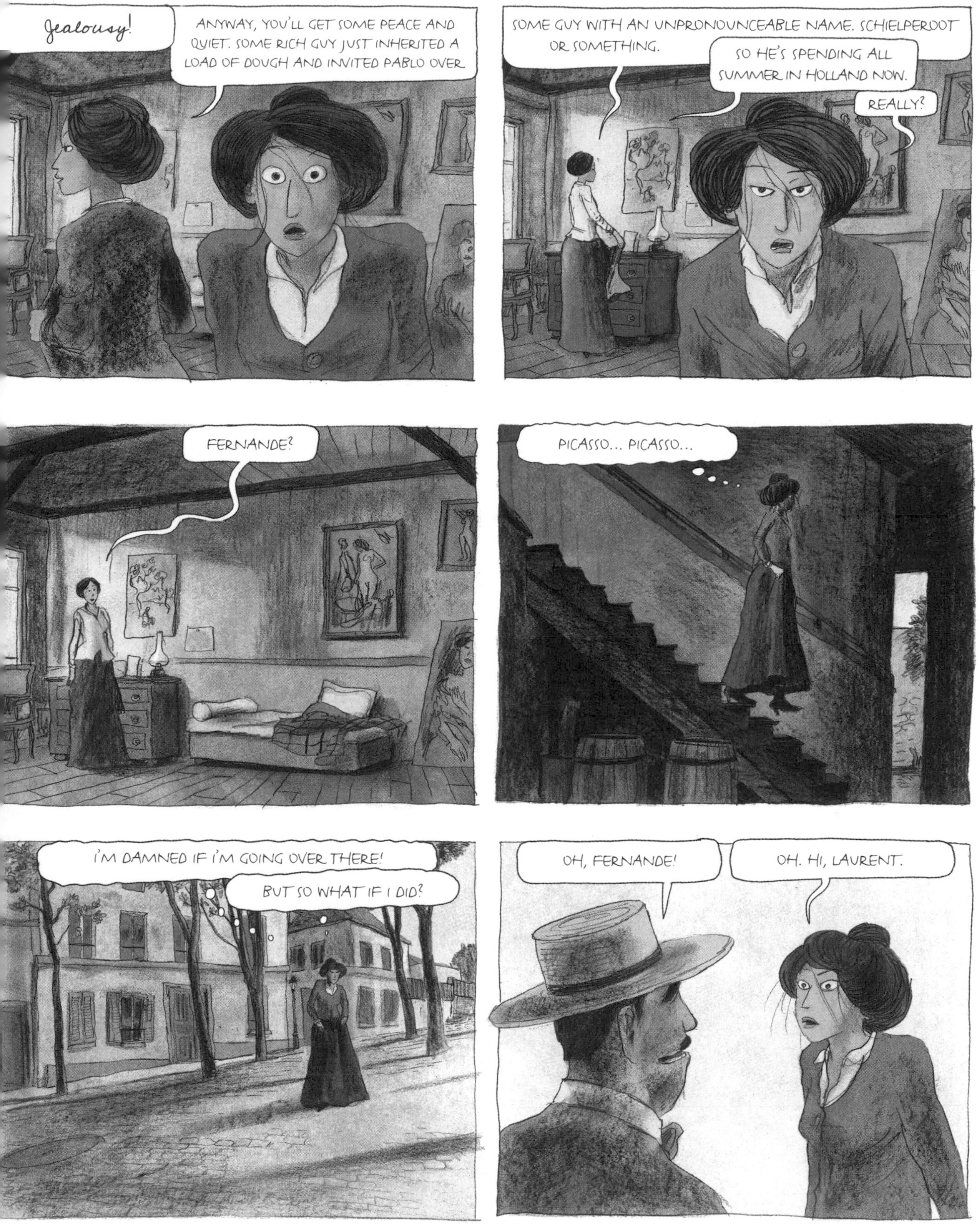
Jealousy!
ANYWAY, YOU'LL GET SOME PEACE AND QUIET. SOME RICH GUY JUST INHERITED A LOAD OF DOUGH AND INVITED PABLO OVER
SOME GUY WITH AN UNPRONOUNCEABLE NAME. SCHIELPEROOT OR SOMETHING.
SO HE'S SPENDING ALL SUMMER IN HOLLAND NOW.
REALLY?
FERNANDE?
PICASSO... PICASSO...
I'M DAMNED IF I'M GOING OVER THERE!
BUT SO WHAT IF I DID?
OH, FERNANDE!
OH. HI, LAURENT.

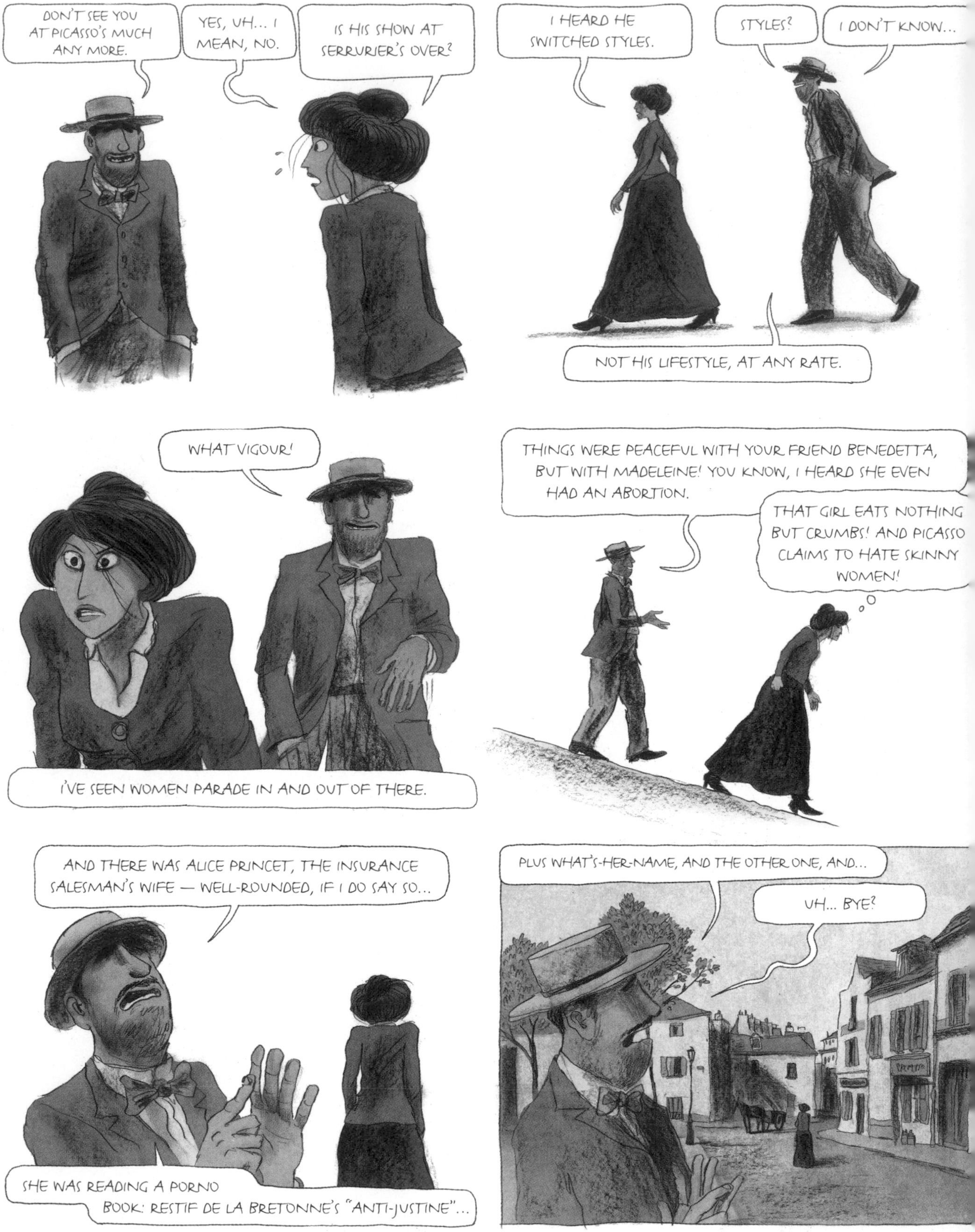
DON'T SEE YOU AT PICASSO'S MUCH ANY MORE.
YES, UH... I MEAN, NO.
IS HIS SHOW AT SERRURIER'S OVER?
I HEARD HE SWITCHED STYLES.
STYLES?
I DON'T KNOW...
NOT HIS LIFESTYLE, AT ANY RATE.
WHAT VIGOUR!
I'VE SEEN WOMEN PARADE IN AND OUT OF THERE.
THINGS WERE PEACEFUL WITH YOUR FRIEND BENEDETTA, BUT WITH MADELEINE! YOU KNOW, I HEARD SHE EVEN HAD AN ABORTION.
THAT GIRL EATS NOTHING BUT CRUMBS! AND PICASSO CLAIMS TO HATE SKINNY WOMEN!
AND THERE WAS ALICE PRINCET, THE INSURANCE SALESMAN'S WIFE — WELL-ROUNDED, IF I DO SAY SO...
SHE WAS READING A PORNO BOOK: RESTIF DE LA BRETONNE'S "ANTI-JUSTINE"...
PLUS WHAT'S-HER-NAME, AND THE OTHER ONE, AND...
UH... BYE?

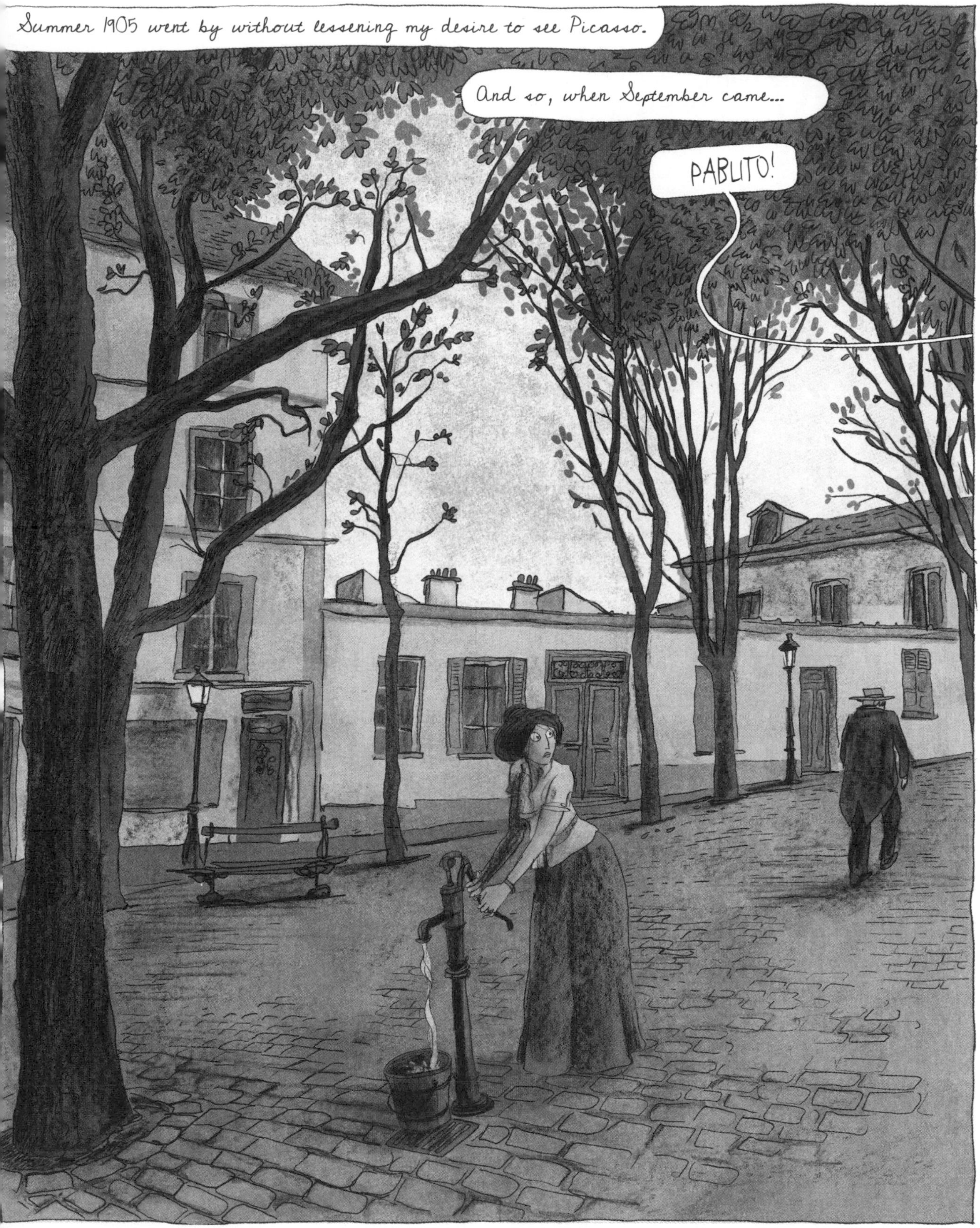
Summer 1905 went by without lessening my desire to see Picasso.
And so, when September came...
PABLITO!

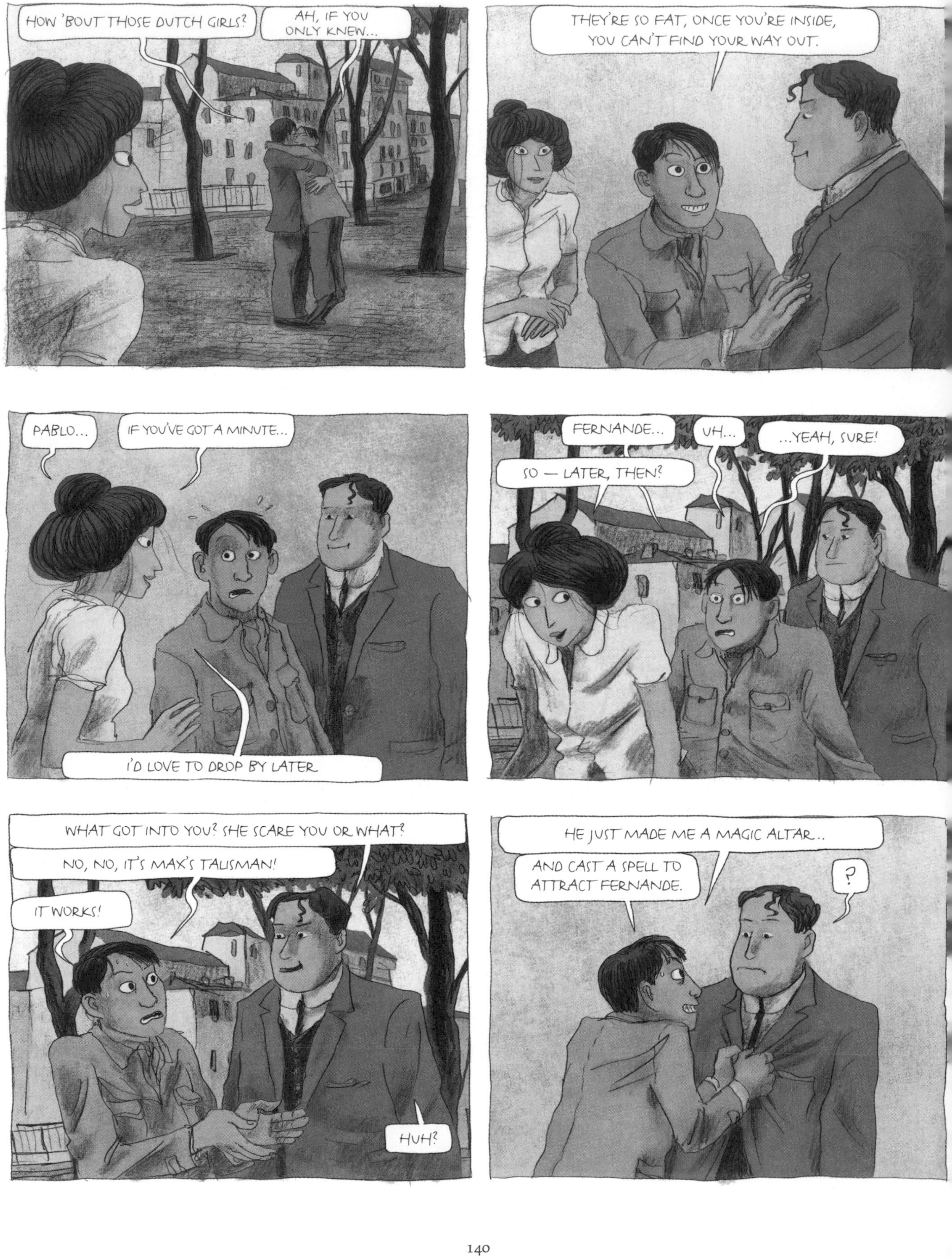

HOW 'BOUT THOSE DUTCH GIRLS?
AH, IF YOU ONLY KNEW...
THEY'RE SO FAT, ONCE YOU'RE INSIDE, YOU CAN'T FIND YOUR WAY OUT.
PABLO...
IF YOU'VE GOT A MINUTE...
I'D LOVE TO DROP BY LATER
FERNANDE...
SO — LATER, THEN?
UH...
...YEAH, SURE!
WHAT GOT INTO YOU? SHE SCARE YOU OR WHAT?
NO, NO, IT'S MAX'S TALISMAN!
IT WORKS!
HUH?
HE JUST MADE ME A MAGIC ALTAR..
AND CAST A SPELL TO ATTRACT FERNANDE.
?

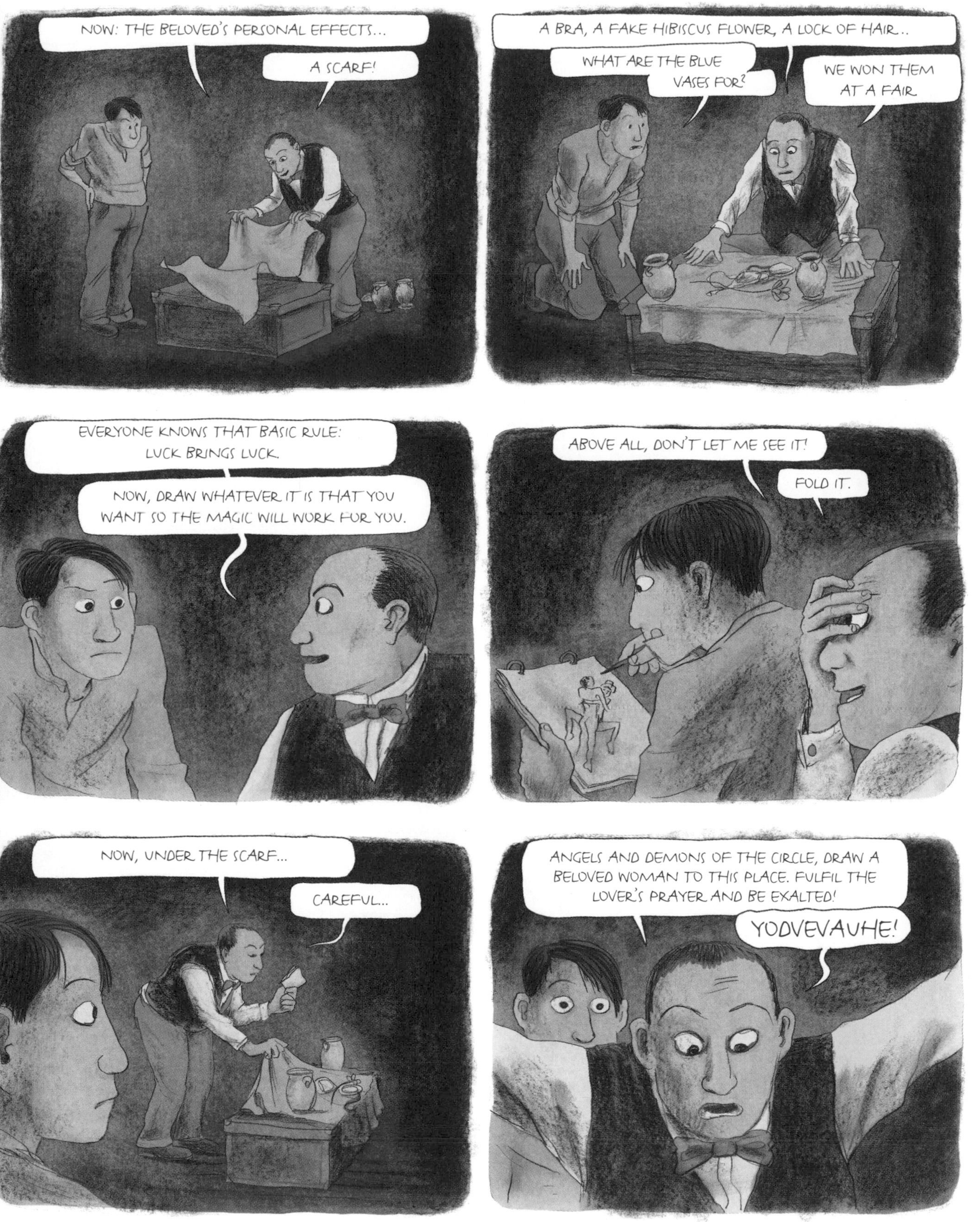
NOW: THE BELOVED'S PERSONAL EFFECTS...
A SCARF!
A BRA, A FAKE HIBISCUS FLOWER, A LOCK OF HAIR..
WHAT ARE THE BLUE VASES FOR?
WE WON THEM AT A FAIR.
EVERYONE KNOWS THAT BASIC RULE: LUCK BRINGS LUCK.
NOW, DRAW WHATEVER IT IS THAT YOU WANT SO THE MAGIC WILL WORK FOR YOU.
ABOVE ALL, DON'T LET ME SEE IT!
FOLD IT.
NOW, UNDER THE SCARF...
CAREFUL...
ANGELS AND DEMONS OF THE CIRCLE, DRAW A BELOVED WOMAN TO THIS PLACE. FULFIL THE LOVER'S PRAYER AND BE EXALTED!
YODVEVAUHE!

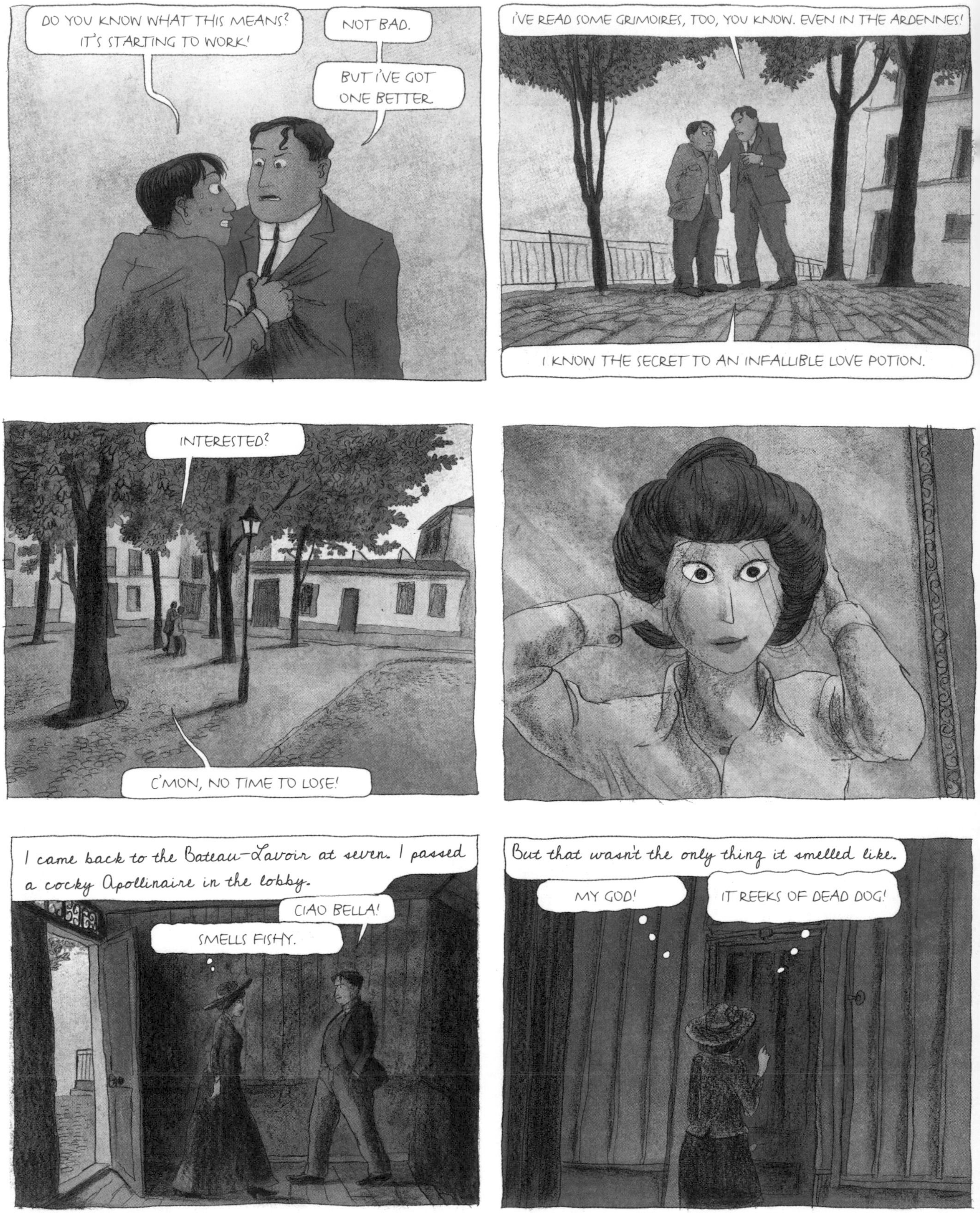
DO YOU KNOW WHAT THIS MEANS? IT'S STARTING TO WORK!
NOT BAD.
BUT I'VE GOT ONE BETTER
I'VE READ SOME GRIMOIRES, TOO, YOU KNOW. EVEN IN THE ARDENNES!
I KNOW THE SECRET TO AN INFALLIBLE LOVE POTION.
INTERESTED?
C'MON, NO TIME TO LOSE!
I came back to the Bateau-Lavoir at seven. I passed a cocky Apollinaire in the lobby.
CIAO BELLA!
SMELLS FISHY.
But that wasn't the only thing it smelled like.
MY GOD!
IT REEKS OF DEAD DOG!

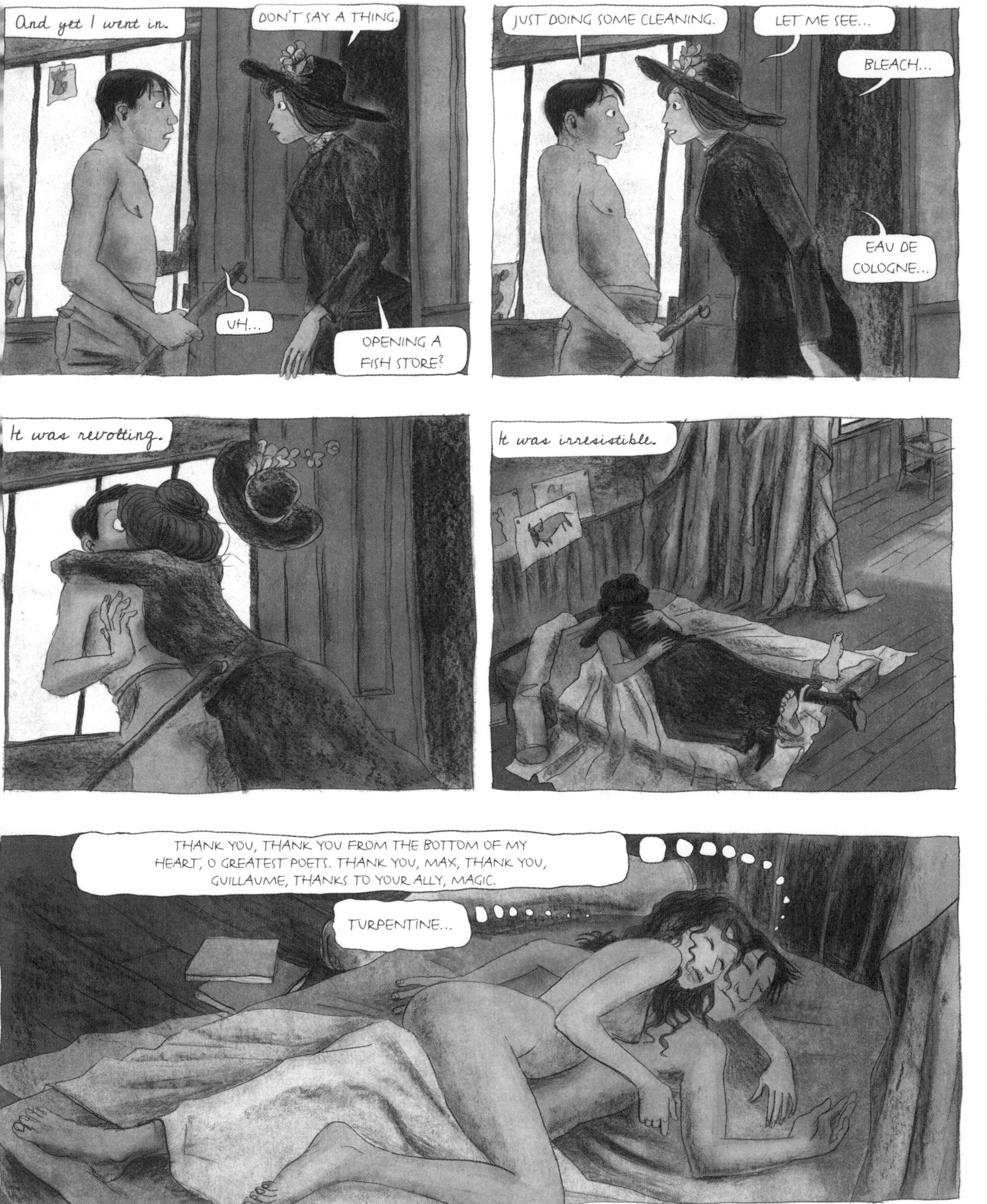
And yet I went in.
DON'T SAY A THING.
UH...
OPENING A FISH STORE?
JUST DOING SOME CLEANING.
LET ME SEE...
BLEACH...
EAU DE COLOGNE...
It was revolting.
It was irresistible.
THANK YOU, THANK YOU FROM THE BOTTOM OF MY HEART, O GREATEST POETS. THANK YOU, MAX, THANK YOU, GUILLAUME, THANKS TO YOUR ALLY, MAGIC.
TURPENTINE...

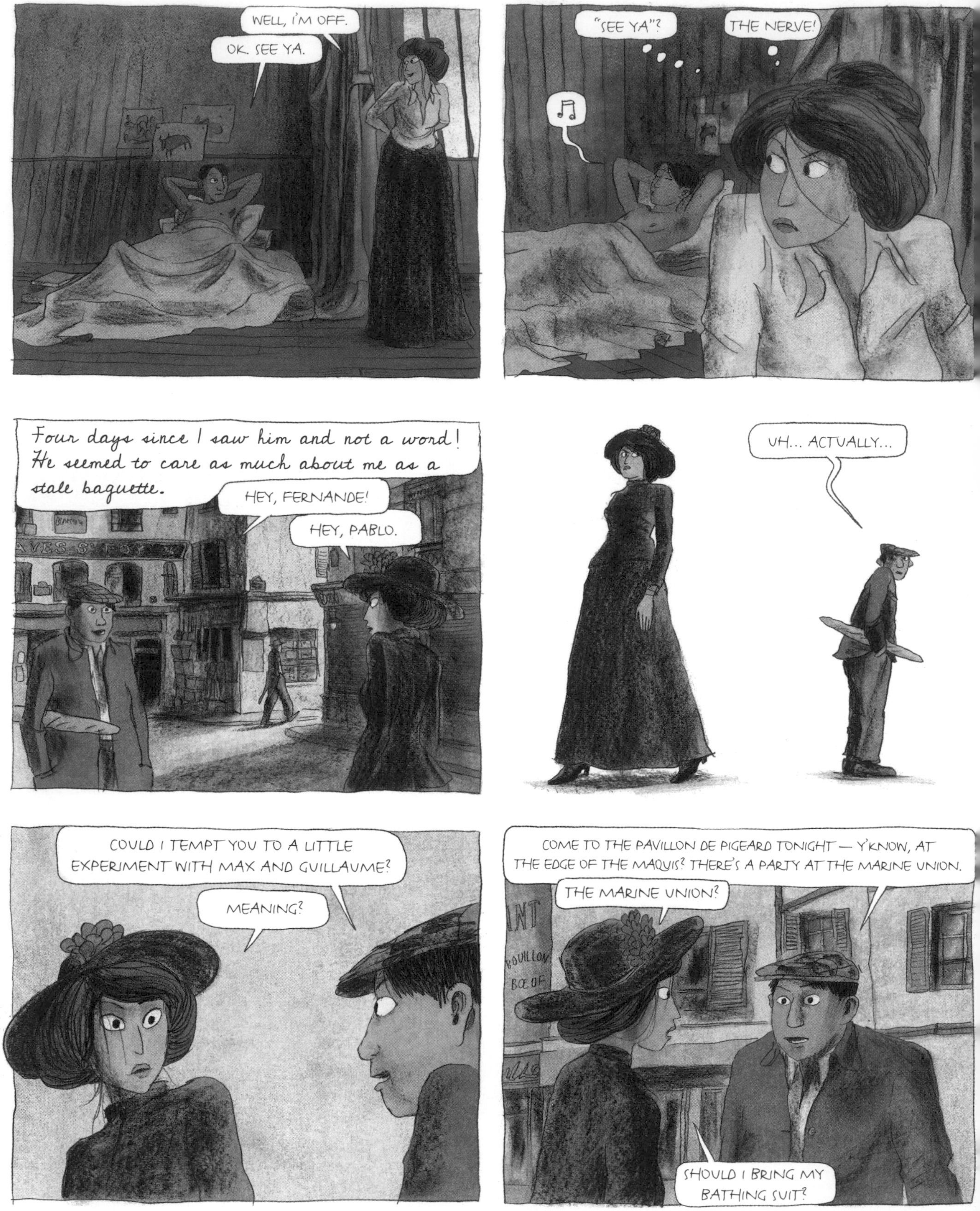
WELL, I'M OFF.
OK. SEE YA.
"SEE YA"?
THE NERVE!
Four days since I saw him and not a word! He seemed to care as much about me as a stale baguette.
HEY, FERNANDE!
HEY, PABLO.
UH... ACTUALLY...
COULD I TEMPT YOU TO A LITTLE EXPERIMENT WITH MAX AND GUILLAUME?
MEANING?
COME TO THE PAVILLON DE PIGEARD TONIGHT — Y'KNOW, AT THE EDGE OF THE MAQUIS? THERE'S A PARTY AT THE MARINE UNION.
THE MARINE UNION?
SHOULD I BRING MY BATHING SUIT?

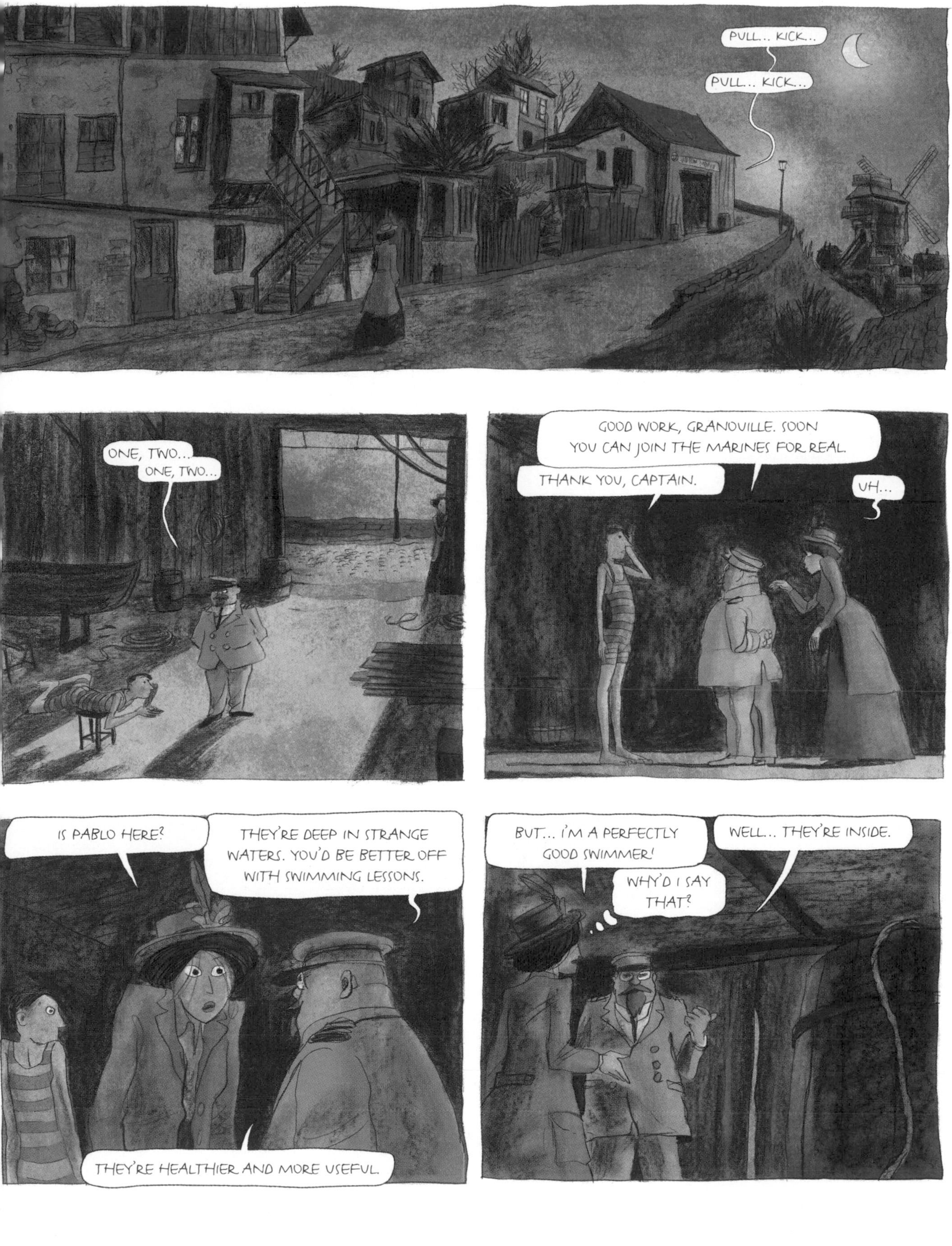
PULL... KICK...
PULL... KICK...
ONE, TWO...
ONE, TWO...
GOOD WORK, GRANOUVILLE. SOON YOU CAN JOIN THE MARINES FOR REAL.
THANK YOU, CAPTAIN.
UH...
IS PABLO HERE?
THEY'RE DEEP IN STRANGE WATERS. YOU'D BE BETTER OFF WITH SWIMMING LESSONS.
THEY'RE HEALTHIER AND MORE USEFUL.
BUT... I'M A PERFECTLY GOOD SWIMMER!
WHY'D I SAY THAT?
WELL... THEY'RE INSIDE.

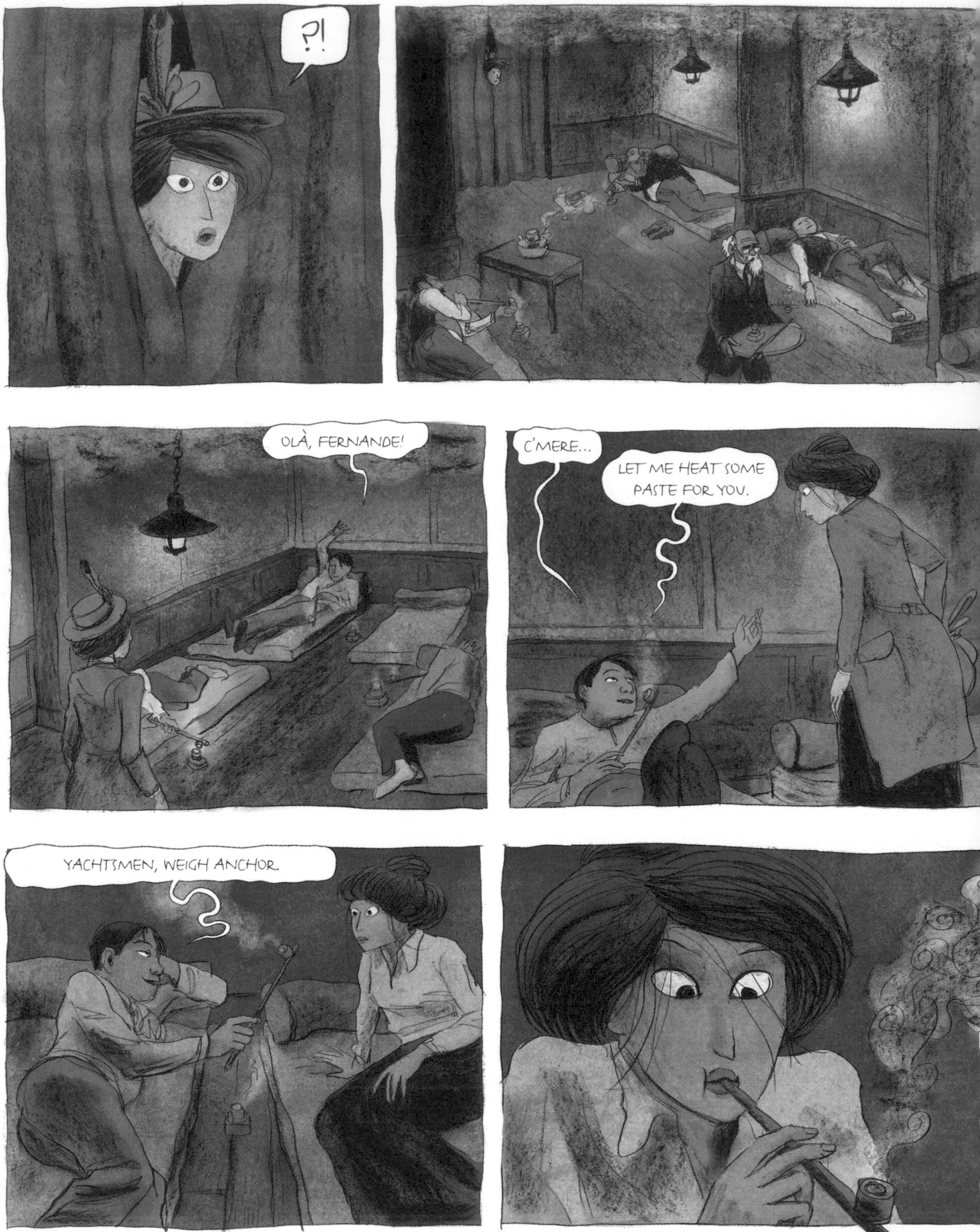
?!
OLÀ, FERNANDE!
C'MERE...
LET ME HEAT SOME PASTE FOR YOU.
YACHTSMEN, WEIGH ANCHOR

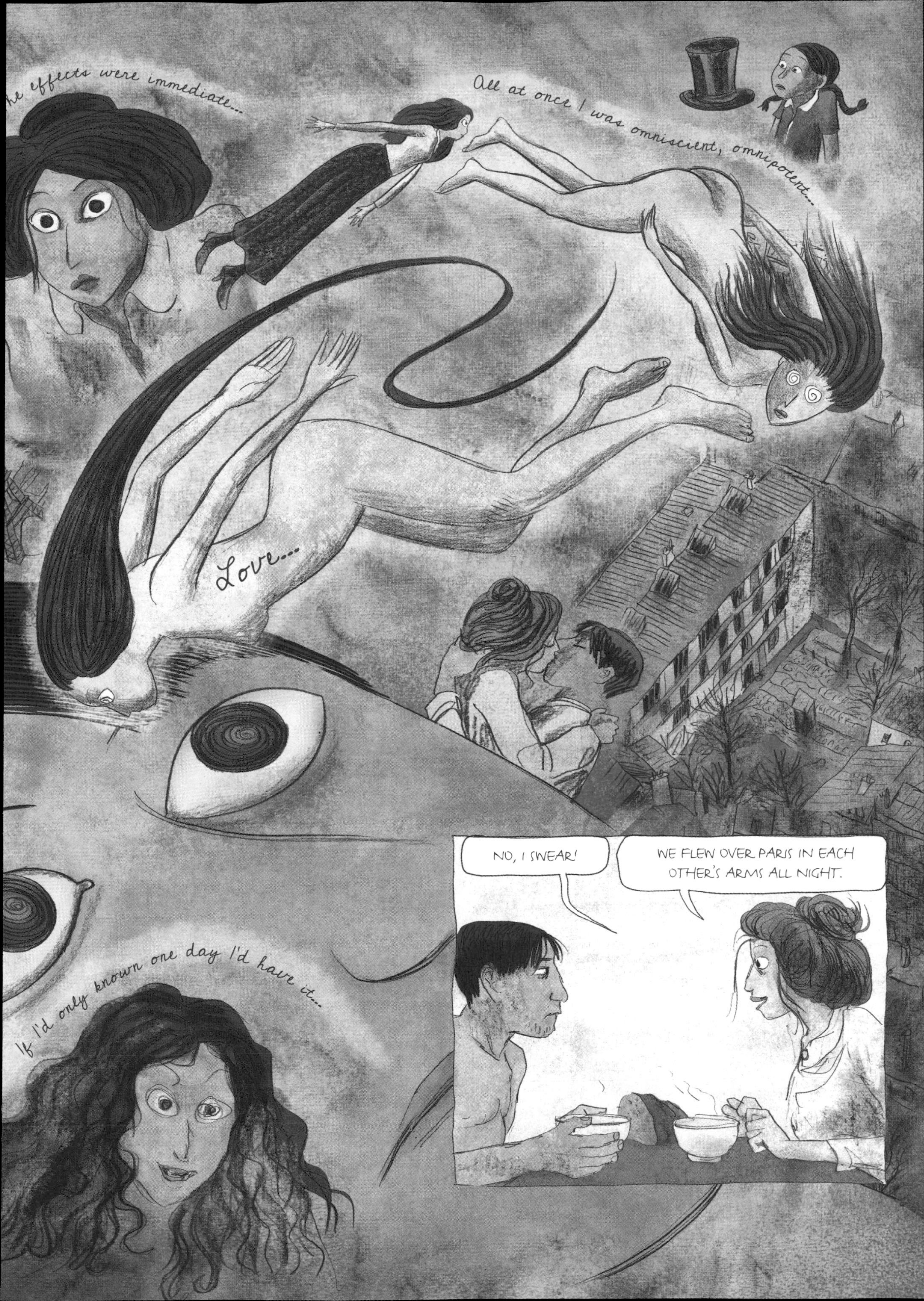
he effects were immediate...
All at once I was omniscient, omnipotent...
Love...
If I'd only known one day I'd have it...
NO, I SWEAR!
WE FLEW OVER PARIS IN EACH OTHER'S ARMS ALL NIGHT.

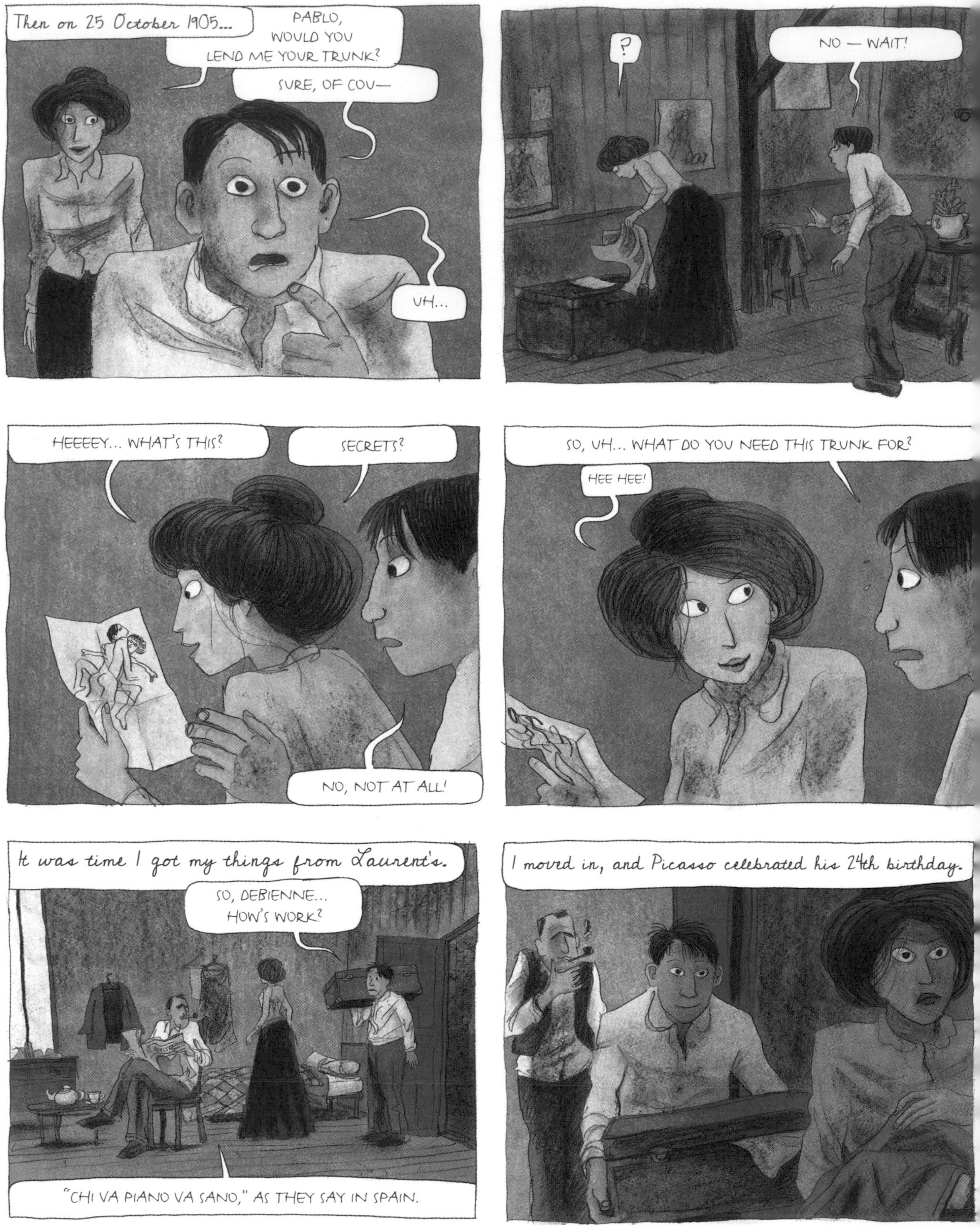
Then on 25 October 1905...
PABLO, WOULD YOU LEND ME YOUR TRUNK?
SURE, OF COU—
UH...
?
NO — WAIT!
HEEEEY... WHAT'S THIS?
SECRETS?
NO, NOT AT ALL!
SO, UH... WHAT DO YOU NEED THIS TRUNK FOR?
HEE HEE!
It was time I got my things from Laurent's.
SO, DEBIENNE... HOW'S WORK?
"CHI VA PIANO VA SANO," AS THEY SAY IN SPAIN.
I moved in, and Picasso celebrated his 24th birthday.

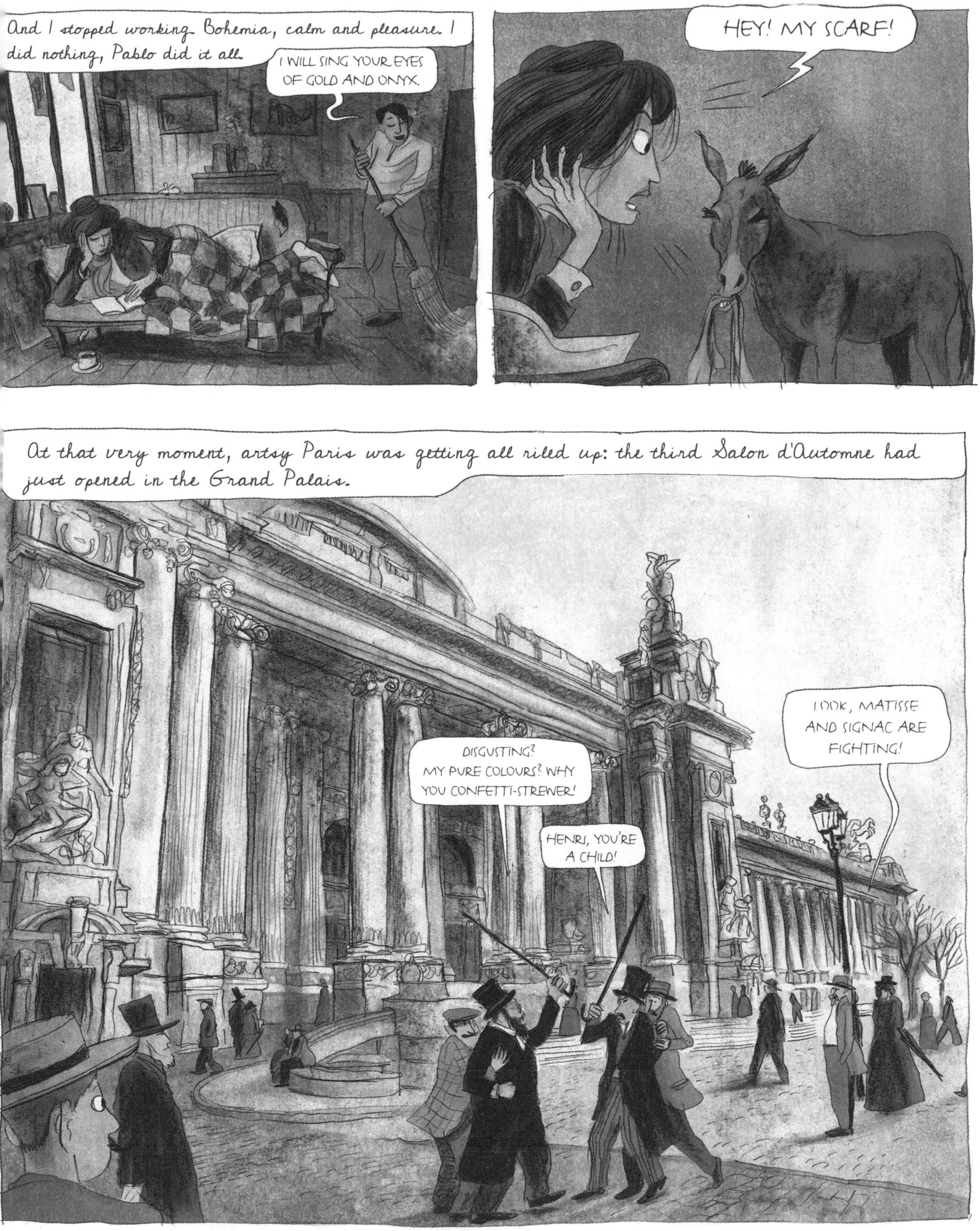
And I stopped working. Bohemia, calm and pleasure. I did nothing, Pablo did it all.
I WILL SING YOUR EYES OF GOLD AND ONYX.
HEY! MY SCARF!
At that very moment, artsy Paris was getting all riled up: the third Salon d'Automne had just opened in the Grand Palais.
DISGUSTING? MY PURE COLOURS? WHY YOU CONFETTI-STREWER!
HENRI, YOU'RE A CHILD!
LOOK, MATISSE AND SIGNAC ARE FIGHTING!

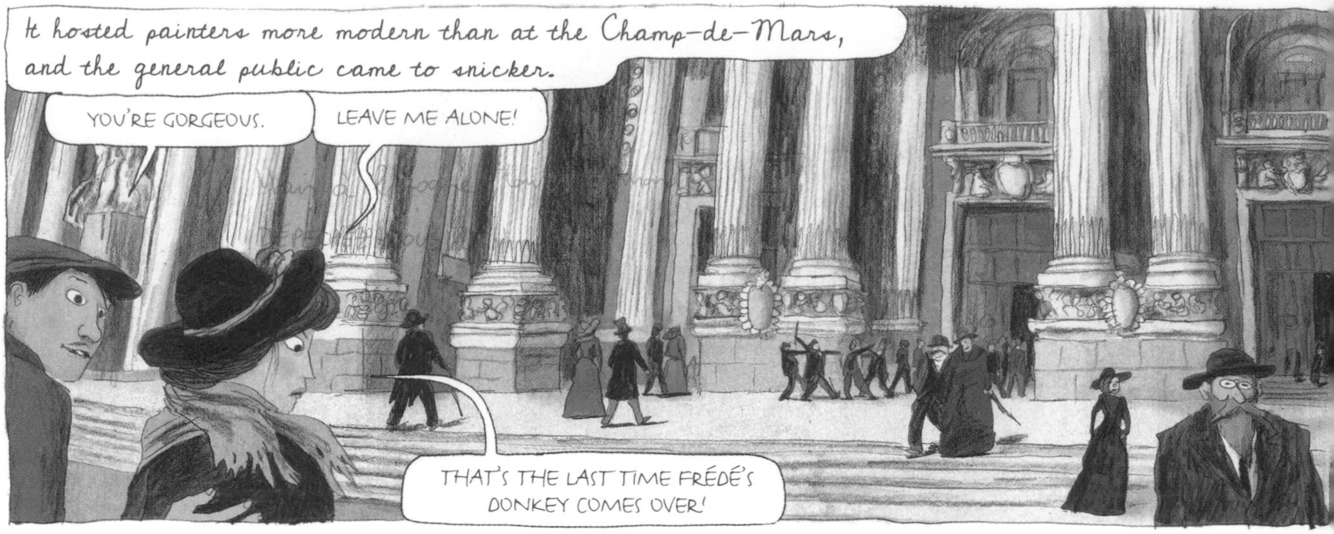
It hosted painters more modern than at the Champ-de-Mars, and the general public came to snicker.
YOU'RE GORGEOUS.
LEAVE ME ALONE!
THAT'S THE LAST TIME FRÉDÉ'S DONKEY COMES OVER!

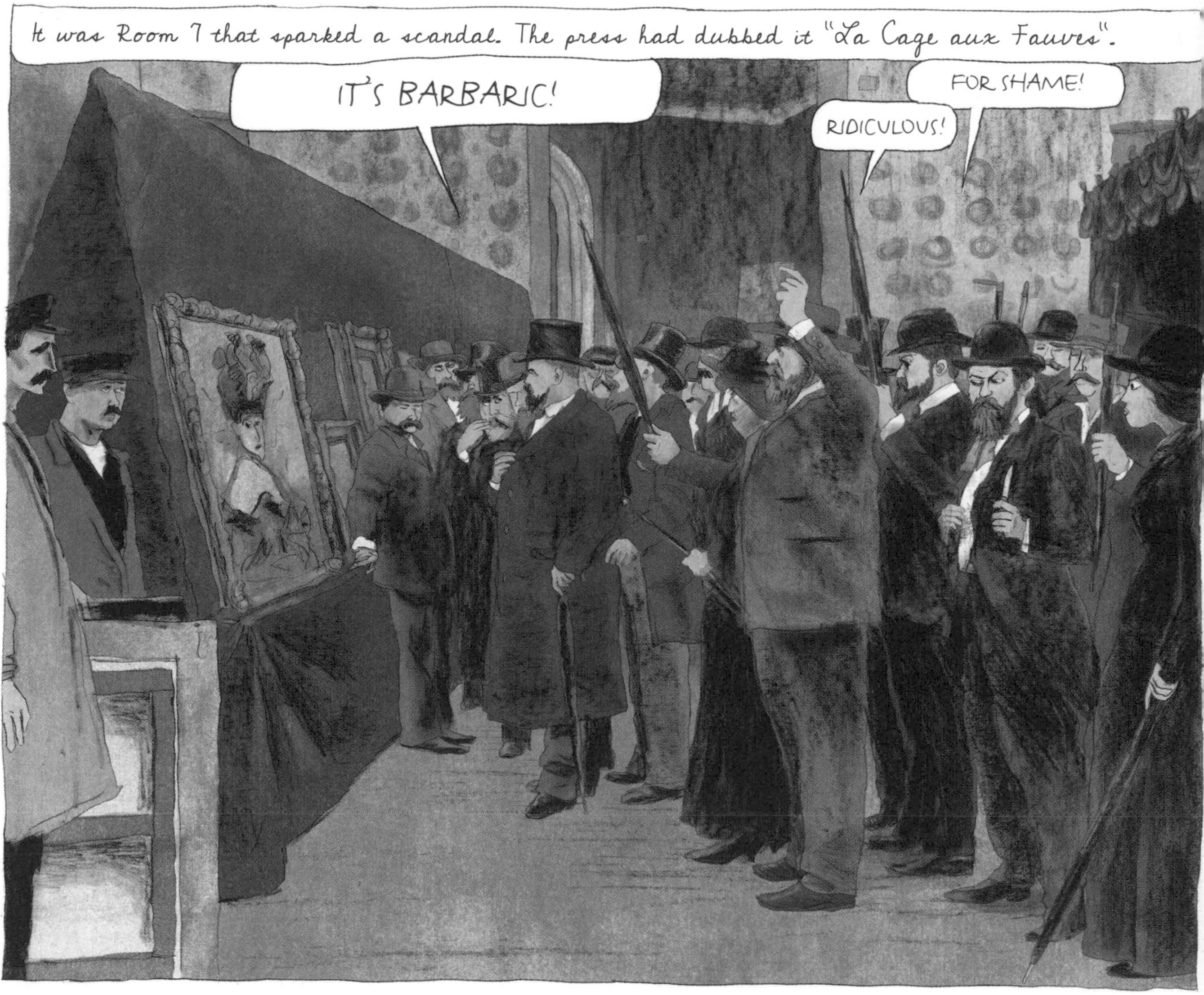
It was Room 7 that sparked a scandal. The press had dubbed it "La Cage aux Fauves".
IT'S BARBARIC!
RIDICULOUS!
FOR SHAME!

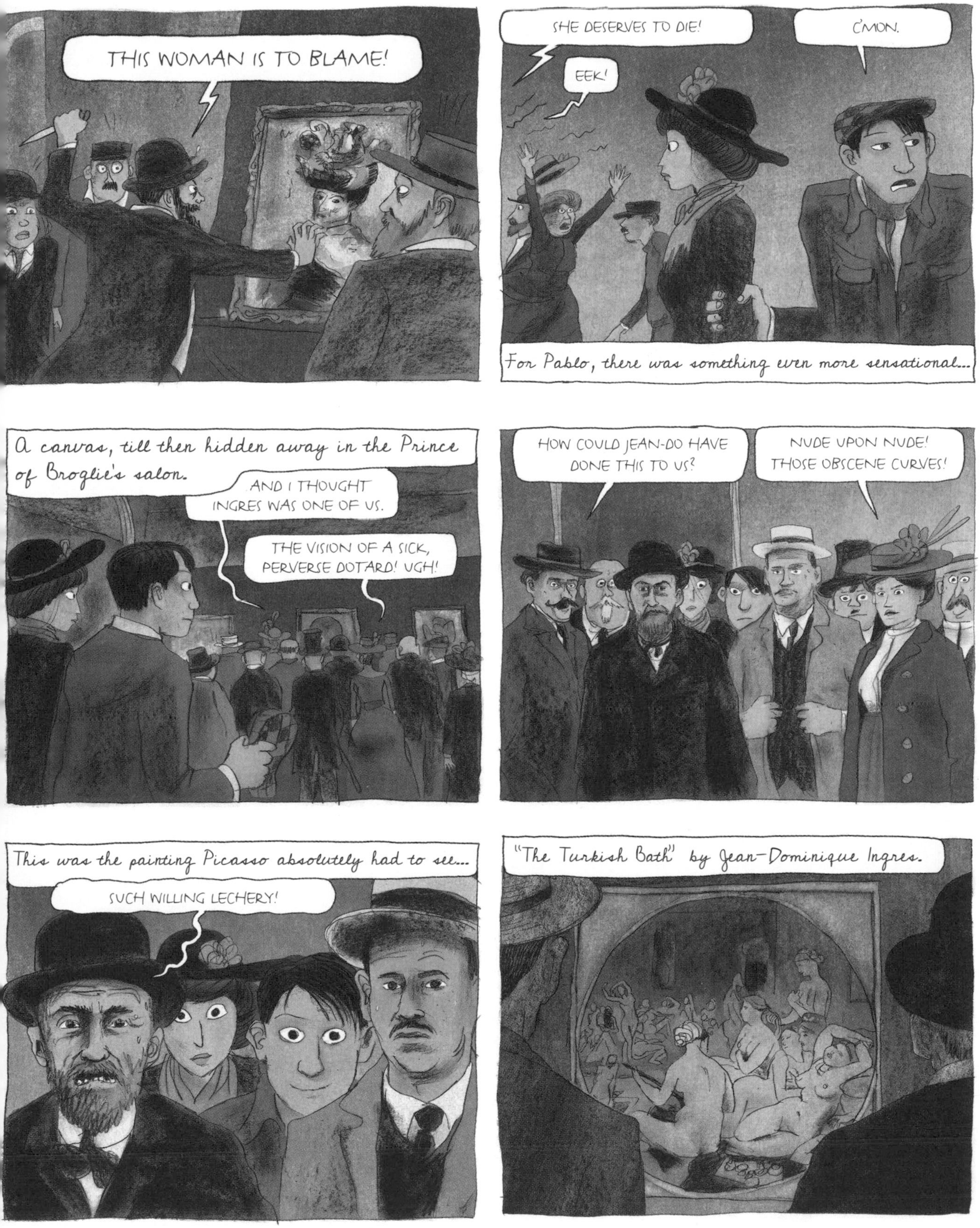
THIS WOMAN IS TO BLAME!
SHE DESERVES TO DIE!
EEK!
C'MON.
For Pablo, there was something even more sensational...
A canvas, till then hidden away in the Prince of Broglie's salon.
AND I THOUGHT INGRES WAS ONE OF US.
THE VISION OF A SICK, PERVERSE DOTARD! UGH!
HOW COULD JEAN-DO HAVE DONE THIS TO US?
NUDE UPON NUDE! THOSE OBSCENE CURVES!
This was the painting Picasso absolutely had to see...
SUCH WILLING LECHERY!
"The Turkish Bath" by Jean-Dominique Ingres.

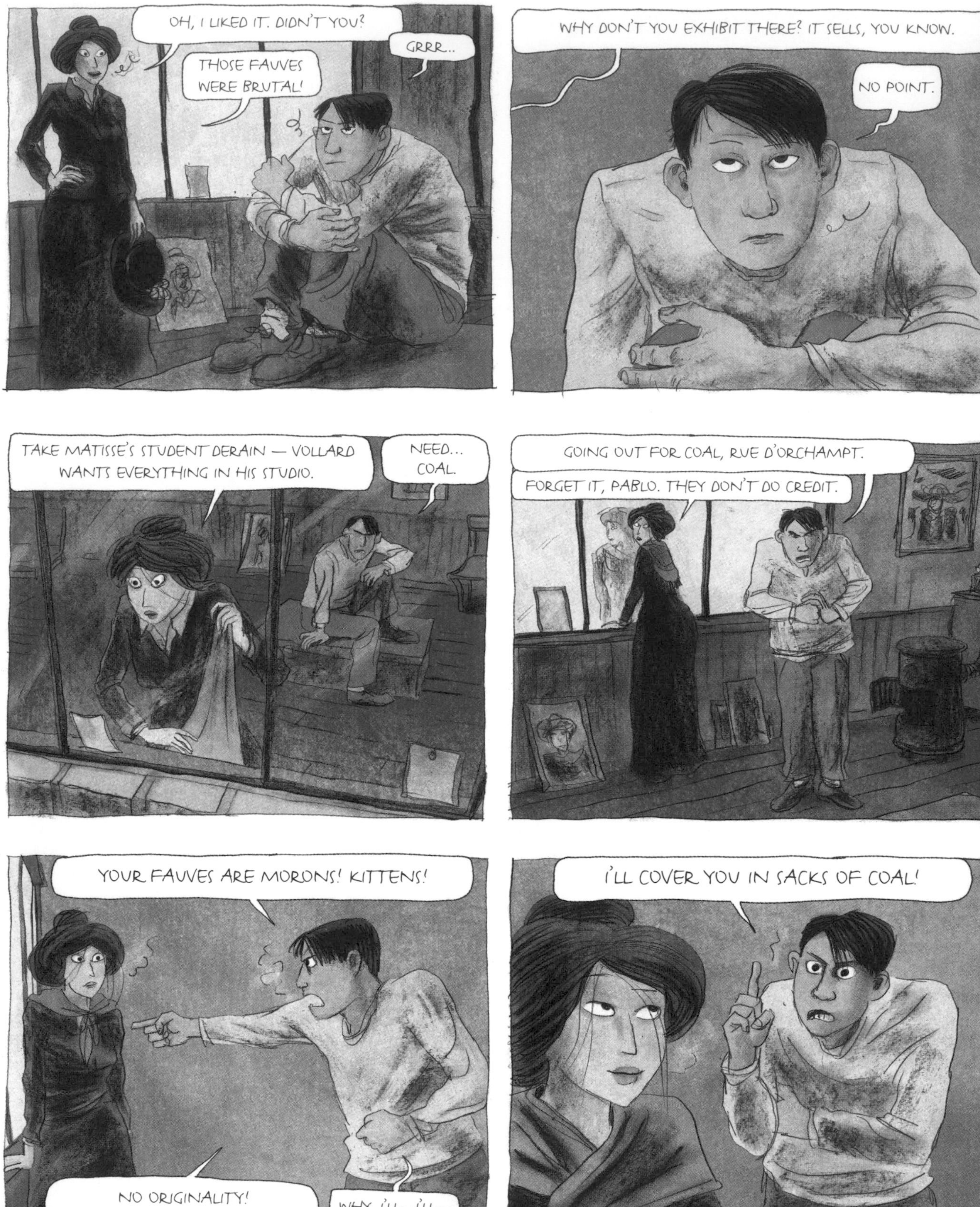
OH, I LIKED IT. DIDN'T YOU?
THOSE FAUVES WERE BRUTAL!
GRRR...
WHY DON'T YOU EXHIBIT THERE? IT SELLS, YOU KNOW.
NO POINT.
TAKE MATISSE'S STUDENT DERAIN — VOLLARD WANTS EVERYTHING IN HIS STUDIO.
NEED... COAL.
GOING OUT FOR COAL, RUE D'ORCHAMPT.
FORGET IT, PABLO. THEY DON'T DO CREDIT.
YOUR FAUVES ARE MORONS! KITTENS!
NO ORIGINALITY! BUT YOU'LL SEE — ME, I —
WHY, I'LL—I'LL—
I'LL COVER YOU IN SACKS OF COAL!

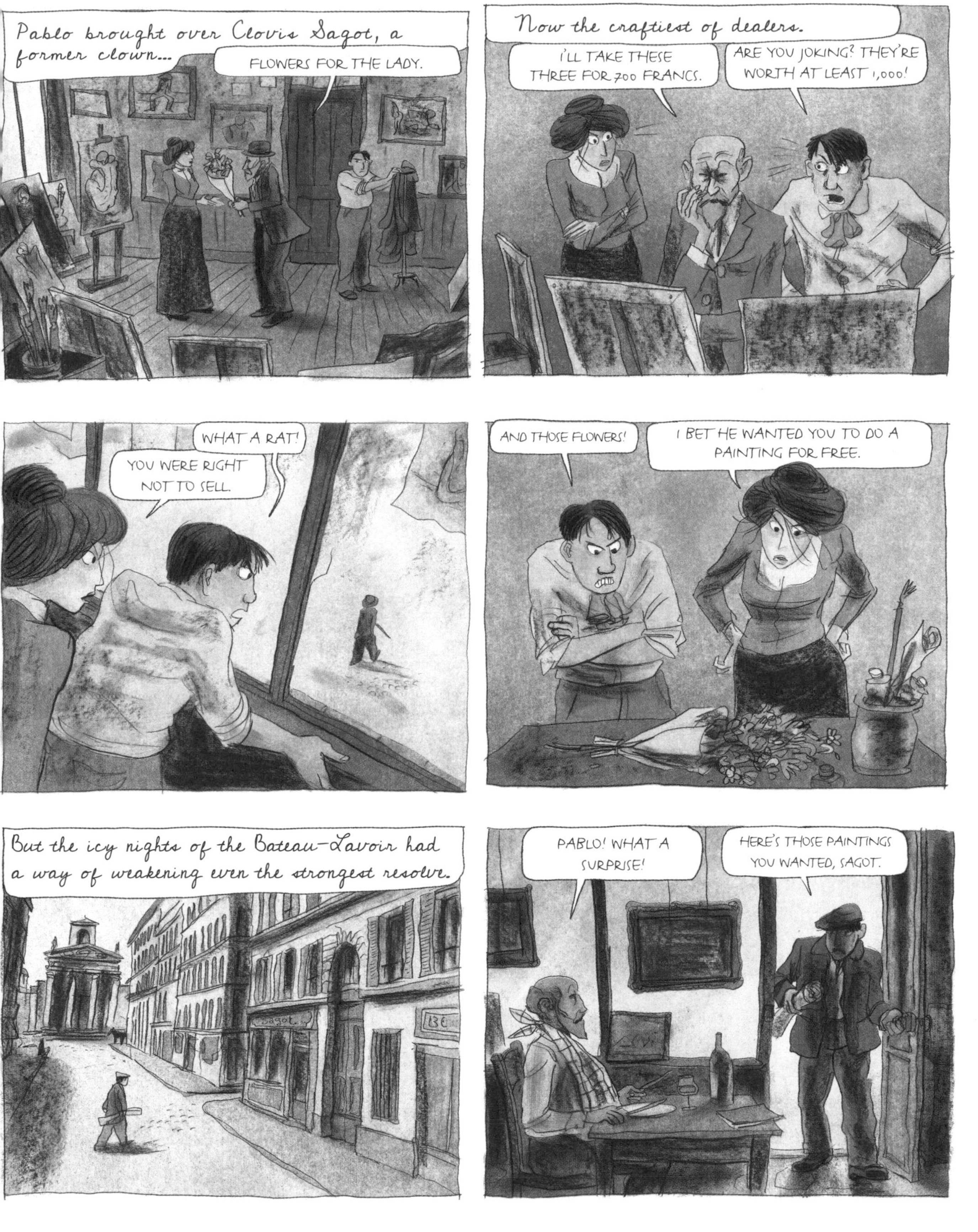
Pablo brought over Clovis Sagot, a former clown...
FLOWERS FOR THE LADY.
Now the craftiest of dealers.
I'LL TAKE THESE THREE FOR 700 FRANCS.
ARE YOU JOKING? THEY'RE WORTH AT LEAST 1,000!
WHAT A RAT!
YOU WERE RIGHT NOT TO SELL.
AND THOSE FLOWERS!
I BET HE WANTED YOU TO DO A PAINTING FOR FREE.
But the icy nights of the Bateau-Lavoir had a way of weakening even the strongest resolve.
Sagot
PABLO! WHAT A SURPRISE!
HERE'S THOSE PAINTINGS YOU WANTED, SAGOT.

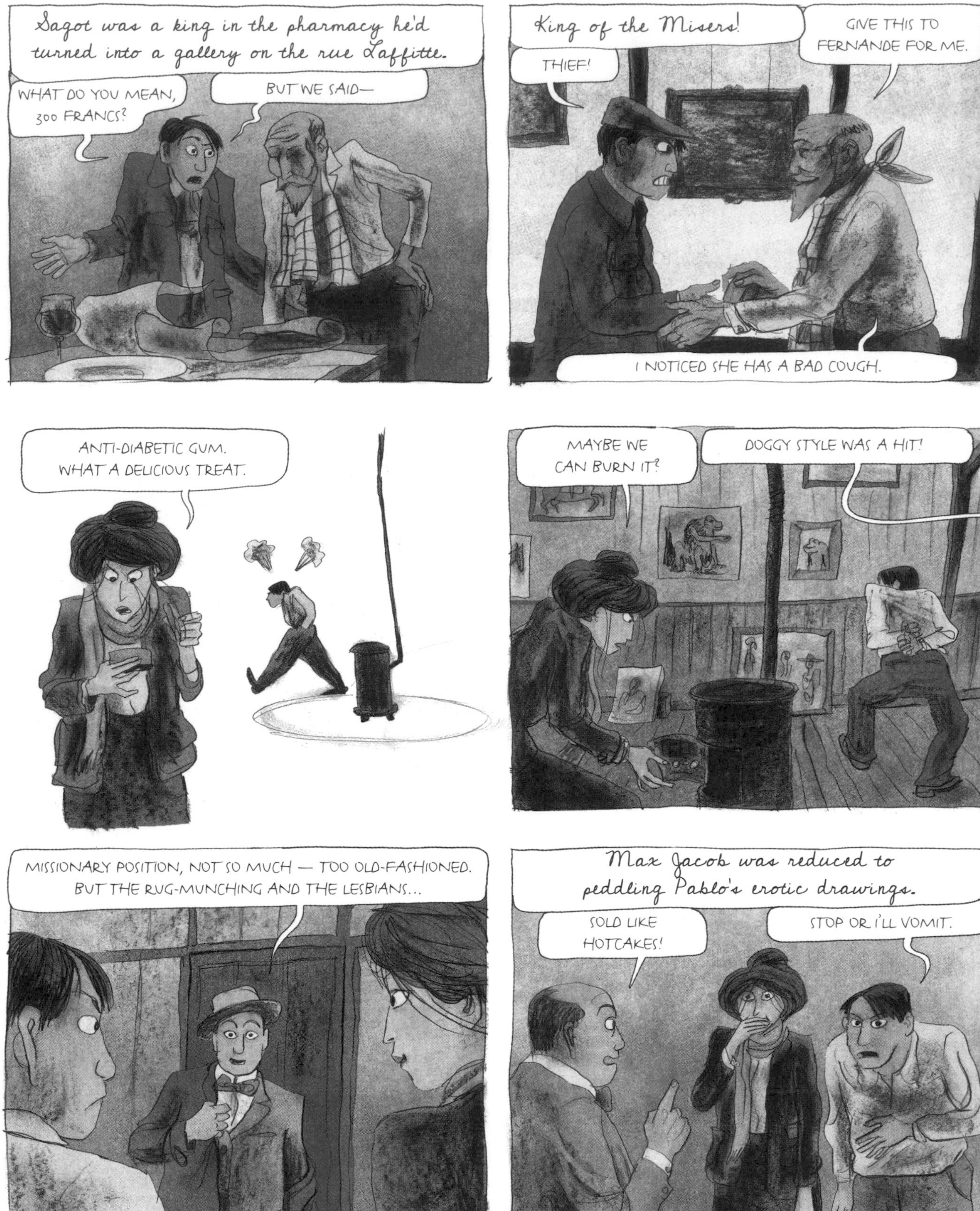
Sagot was a king in the pharmacy he'd turned into a gallery on the rue Laffitte.
WHAT DO YOU MEAN, 300 FRANCS?
BUT WE SAID—
King of the Misers!
THIEF!
GIVE THIS TO FERNANDE FOR ME.
I NOTICED SHE HAS A BAD COUGH.
ANTI-DIABETIC GUM. WHAT A DELICIOUS TREAT.
MAYBE WE CAN BURN IT?
DOGGY STYLE WAS A HIT!
MISSIONARY POSITION, NOT SO MUCH — TOO OLD-FASHIONED. BUT THE RUG-MUNCHING AND THE LESBIANS...
Max Jacob was reduced to peddling Pablo's erotic drawings.
SOLD LIKE HOTCAKES!
STOP OR I'LL VOMIT.

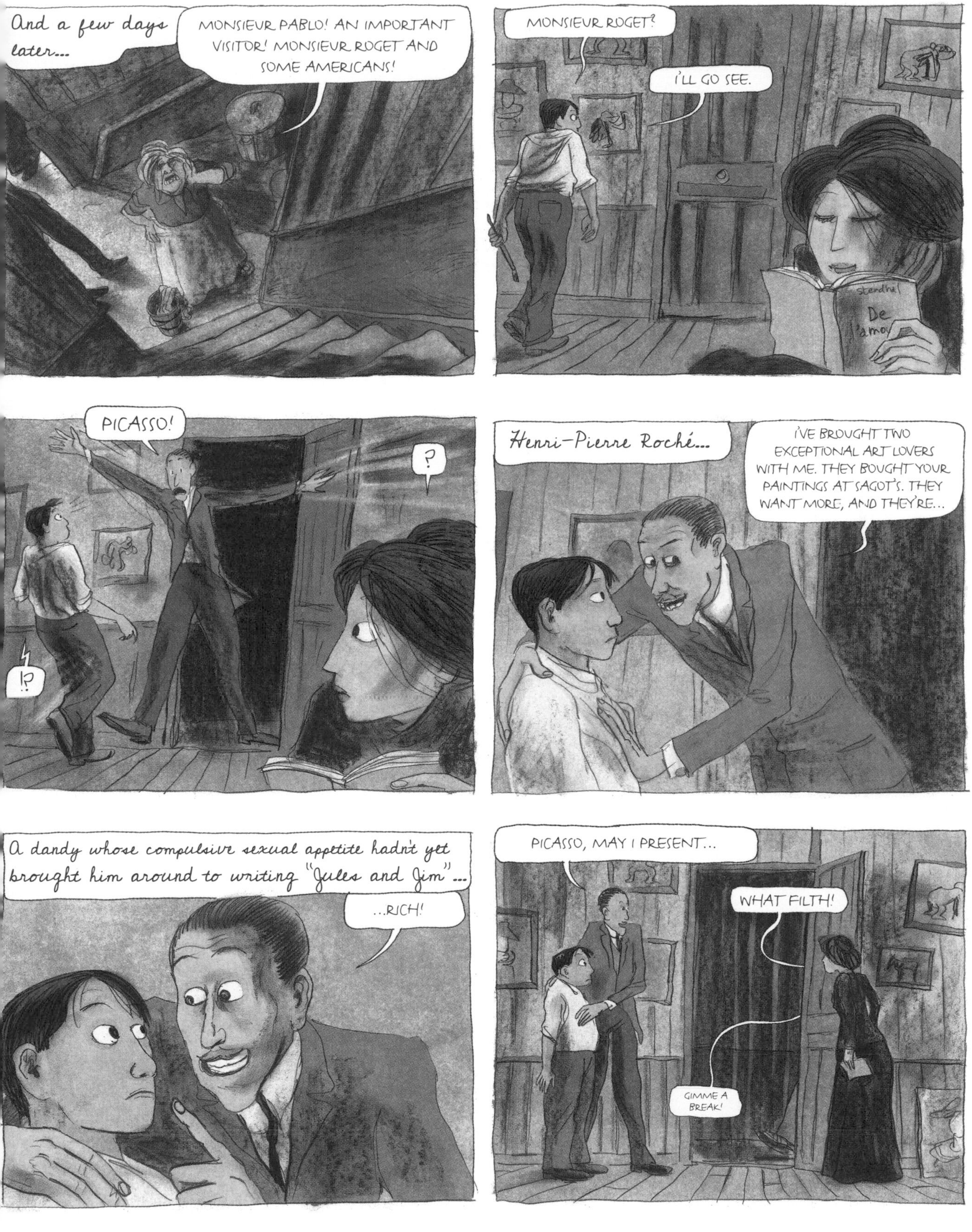
And a few days later...
MONSIEUR PABLO! AN IMPORTANT VISITOR! MONSIEUR ROGET AND SOME AMERICANS!
MONSIEUR ROGET?
I'LL GO SEE.
Stendhal
De l'amour
PICASSO!
?
!?
Henri-Pierre Roché...
I'VE BROUGHT TWO EXCEPTIONAL ART LOVERS WITH ME. THEY BOUGHT YOUR PAINTINGS AT SAGOT'S. THEY WANT MORE, AND THEY'RE...
A dandy whose compulsive sexual appetite hadn't yet brought him around to writing "Jules and Jim"...
...RICH!
PICASSO, MAY I PRESENT...
WHAT FILTH!
GIMME A BREAK!

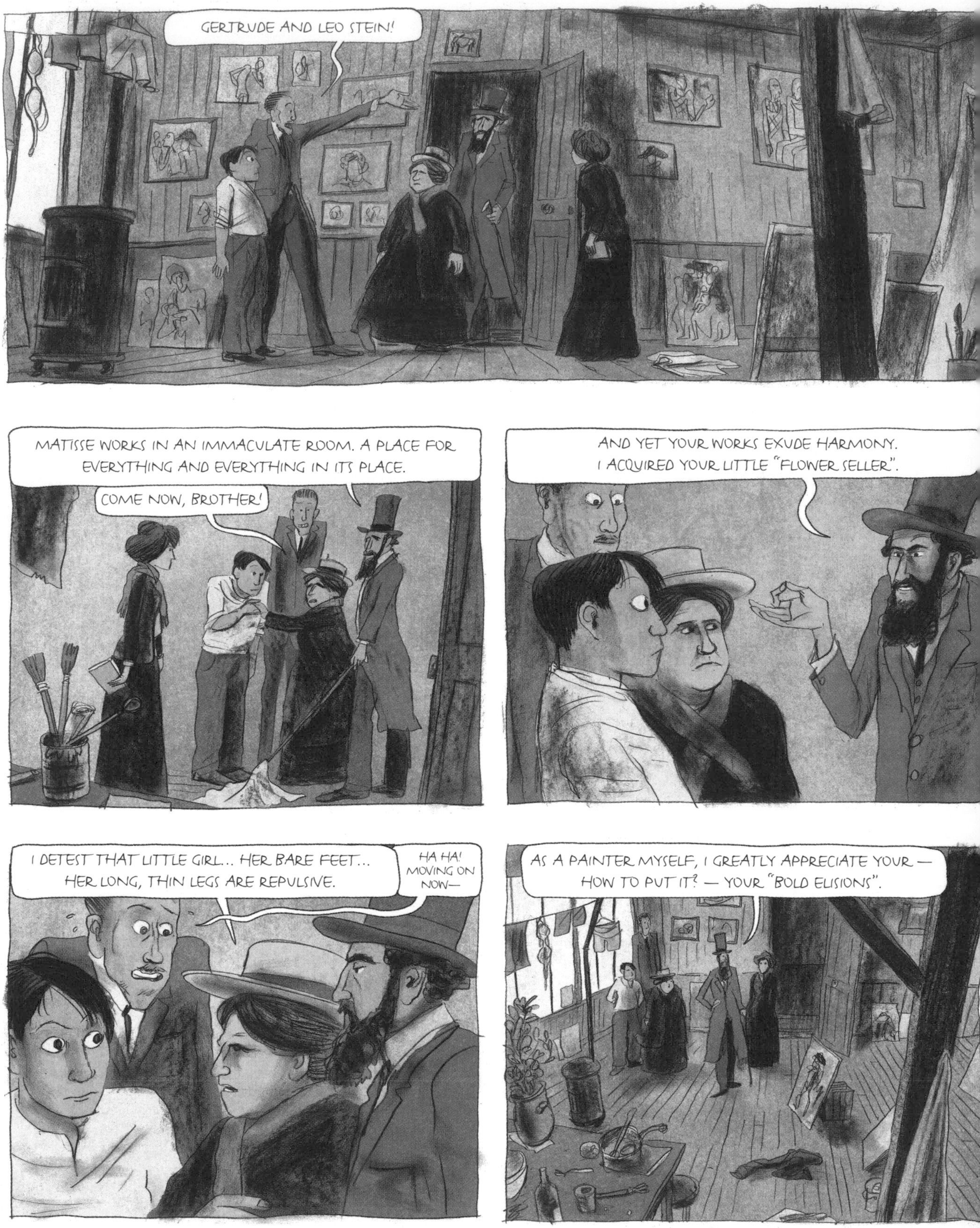
GERTRUDE AND LEO STEIN!
MATISSE WORKS IN AN IMMACULATE ROOM. A PLACE FOR EVERYTHING AND EVERYTHING IN ITS PLACE.
COME NOW, BROTHER!
AND YET YOUR WORKS EXUDE HARMONY. I ACQUIRED YOUR LITTLE "FLOWER SELLER".
I DETEST THAT LITTLE GIRL... HER BARE FEET... HER LONG, THIN LEGS ARE REPULSIVE.
HA HA! MOVING ON NOW—
AS A PAINTER MYSELF, I GREATLY APPRECIATE YOUR — HOW TO PUT IT? — YOUR "BOLD ELISIONS".

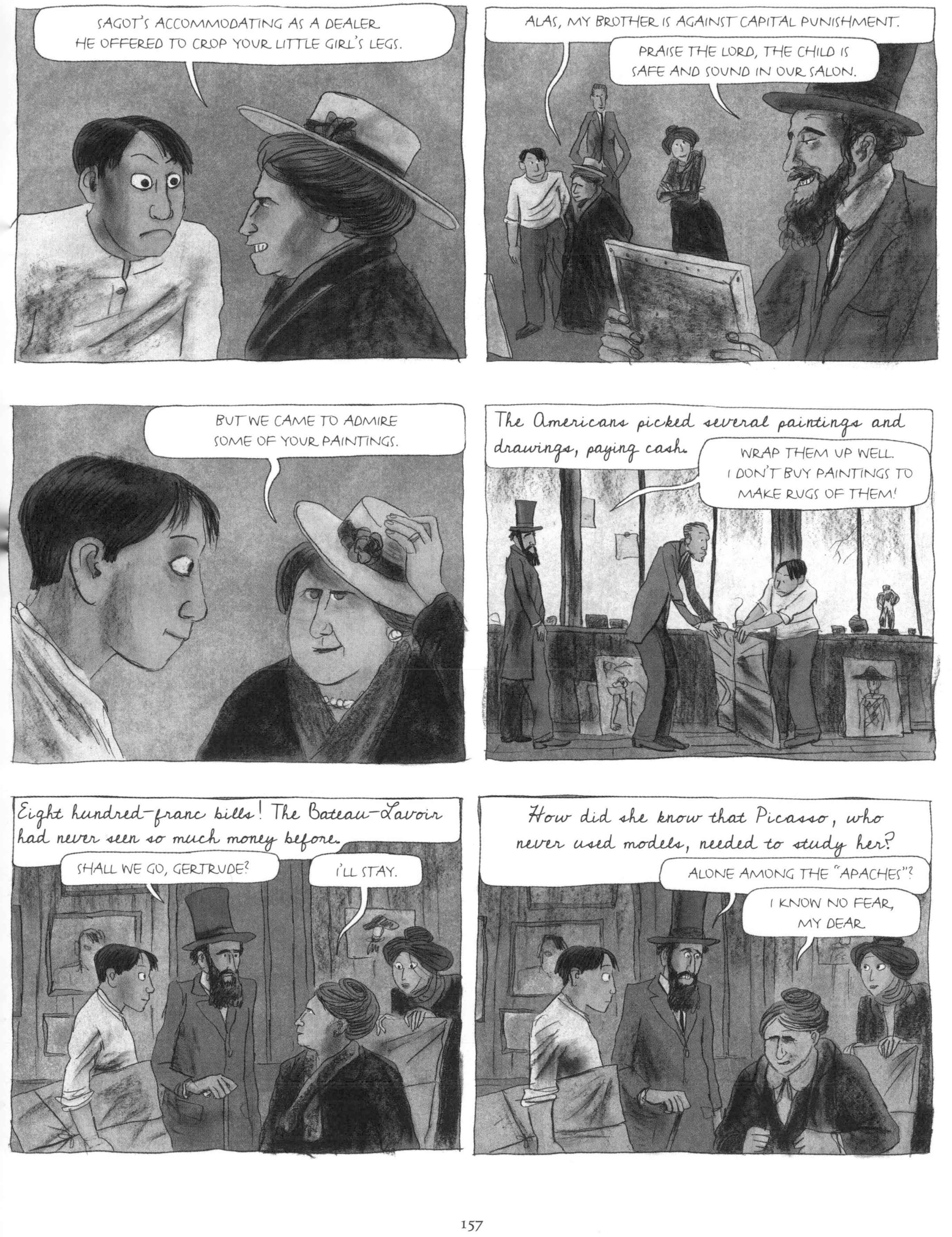
SAGOT'S ACCOMMODATING AS A DEALER
HE OFFERED TO CROP YOUR LITTLE GIRL'S LEGS.
ALAS, MY BROTHER IS AGAINST CAPITAL PUNISHMENT.
PRAISE THE LORD, THE CHILD IS SAFE AND SOUND IN OUR SALON.
BUT WE CAME TO ADMIRE SOME OF YOUR PAINTINGS.
The Americans picked several paintings and drawings, paying cash.
WRAP THEM UP WELL. I DON'T BUY PAINTINGS TO MAKE RUGS OF THEM!
Eight hundred-franc bills! The Bateau-Lavoir had never seen so much money before.
SHALL WE GO, GERTRUDE?
I'LL STAY.
How did she know that Picasso, who never used models, needed to study her?
ALONE AMONG THE "APACHES"?
I KNOW NO FEAR, MY DEAR.

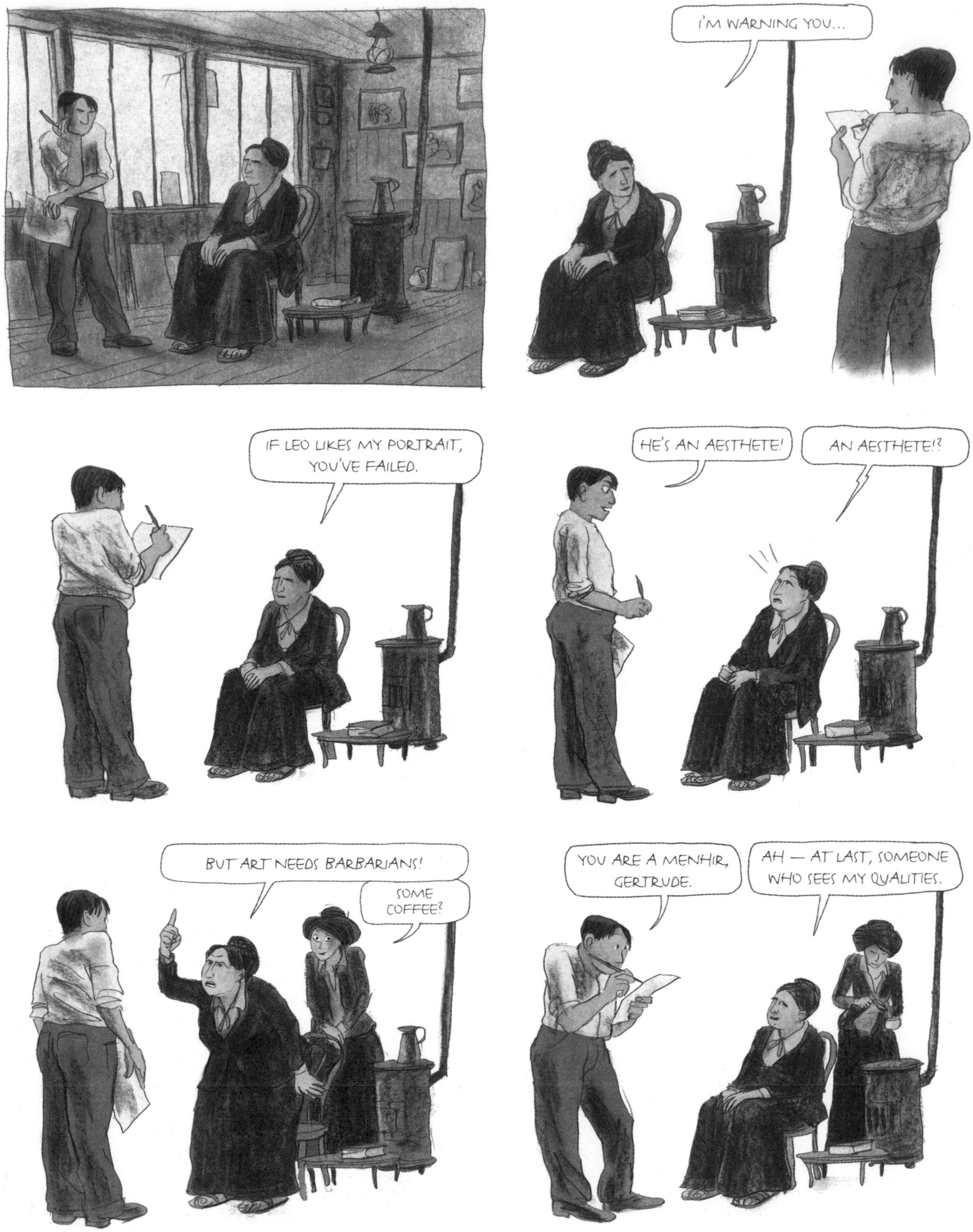
I'M WARNING YOU...
IF LEO LIKES MY PORTRAIT, YOU'VE FAILED.
HE'S AN AESTHETE!
AN AESTHETE!?
BUT ART NEEDS BARBARIANS!
SOME COFFEE?
YOU ARE A MENHIR, GERTRUDE.
AH — AT LAST, SOMEONE WHO SEES MY QUALITIES.

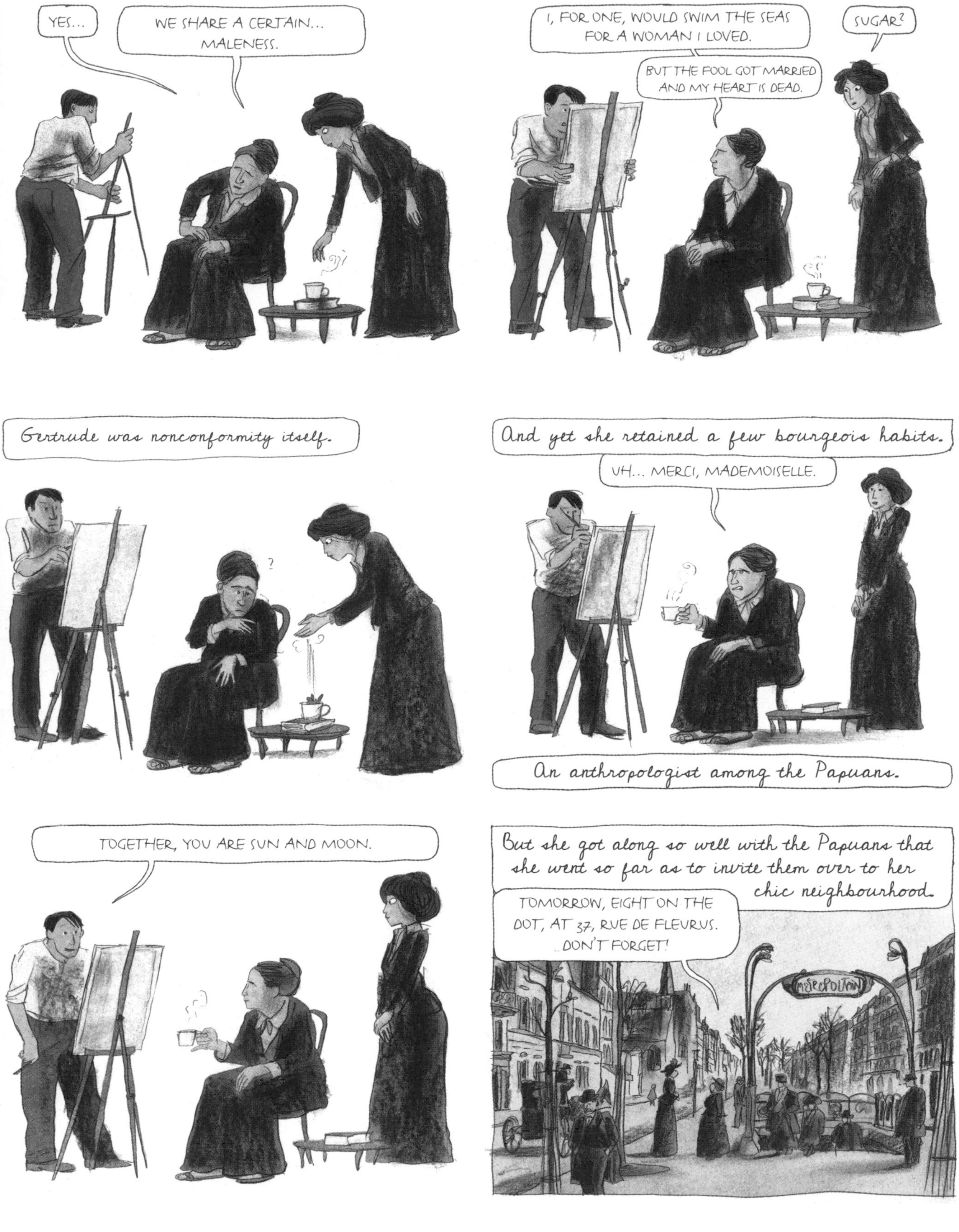
YES...
WE SHARE A CERTAIN... MALENESS.
I, FOR ONE, WOULD SWIM THE SEAS FOR A WOMAN I LOVED.
BUT THE FOOL GOT MARRIED AND MY HEART IS DEAD.
SUGAR?
Gertrude was nonconformity itself.
?
And yet she retained a few bourgeois habits.
UH... MERCI, MADEMOISELLE.
An anthropologist among the Papuans.
TOGETHER, YOU ARE SUN AND MOON.
But she got along so well with the Papuans that she went so far as to invite them over to her chic neighbourhood.
TOMORROW, EIGHT ON THE DOT, AT 37, RUE DE FLEURUS. DON'T FORGET!
METROPOLITAIN

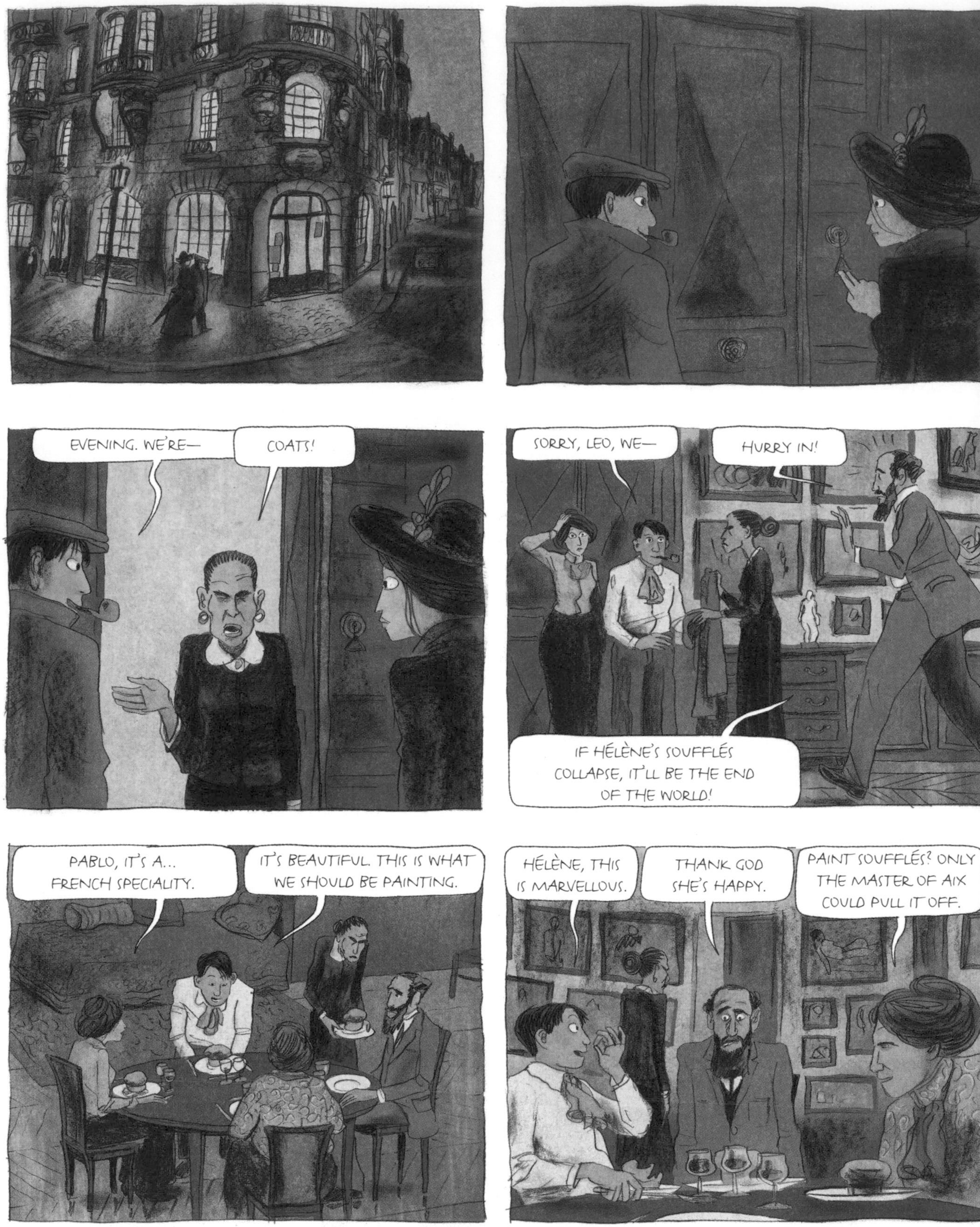
EVENING. WE'RE—
COATS!
SORRY, LEO, WE—
HURRY IN!
IF HÉLÈNE'S SOUFFLÉS COLLAPSE, IT'LL BE THE END OF THE WORLD!
PABLO, IT'S A... FRENCH SPECIALITY.
IT'S BEAUTIFUL. THIS IS WHAT WE SHOULD BE PAINTING.
HÉLÈNE, THIS IS MARVELLOUS.
THANK GOD SHE'S HAPPY.
PAINT SOUFFLÉS? ONLY THE MASTER OF AIX COULD PULL IT OFF.

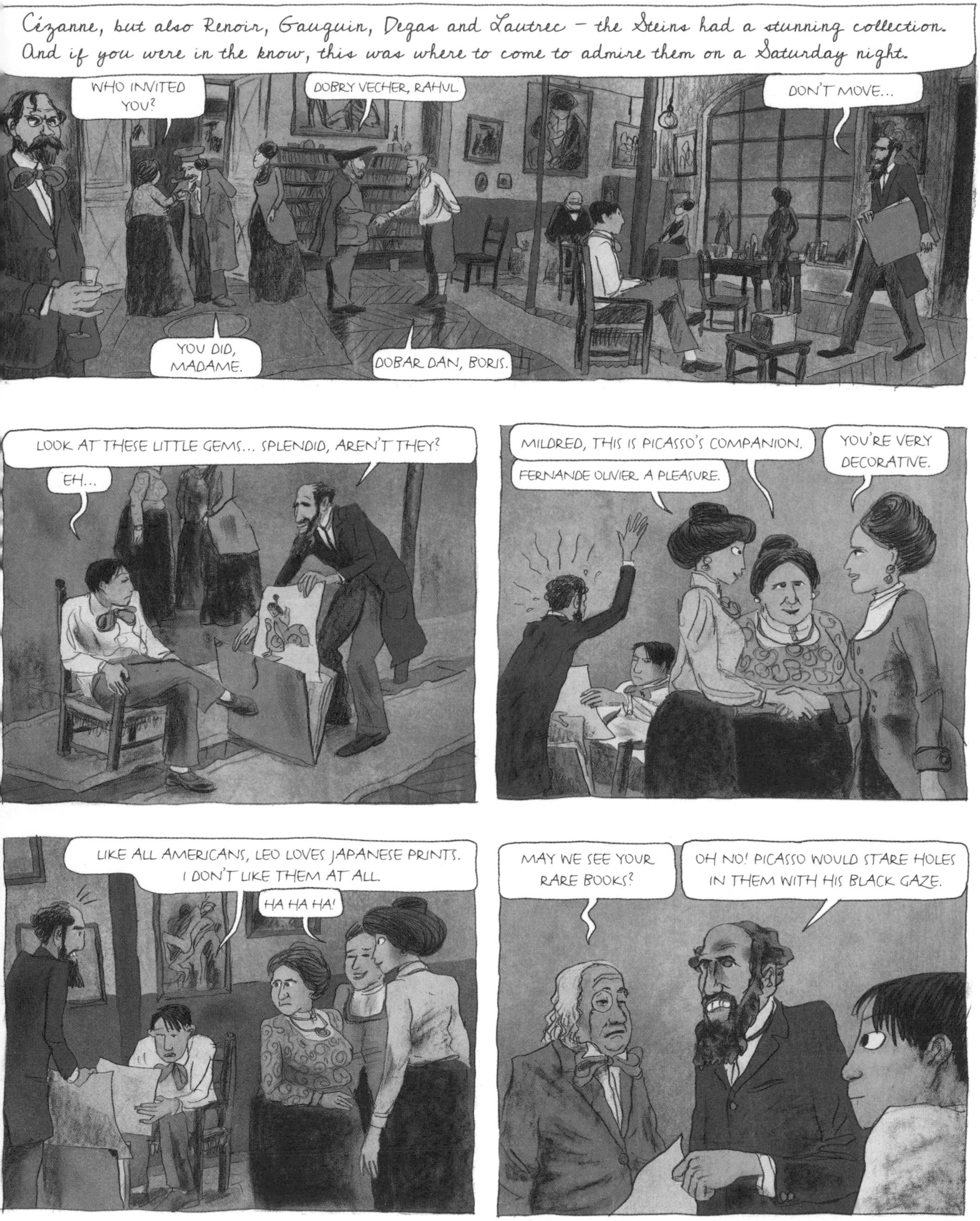
Cézanne, but also Renoir, Gauguin, Degas and Lautrec – the Steins had a stunning collection.
And if you were in the know, this was where to come to admire them on a Saturday night.
WHO INVITED YOU?
YOU DID, MADAME.
DOBRY VECHER, RAHUL.
DOBAR DAN, BORIS.
DON'T MOVE...
LOOK AT THESE LITTLE GEMS... SPLENDID, AREN'T THEY?
EH...
MILDRED, THIS IS PICASSO'S COMPANION.
FERNANDE OLIVIER. A PLEASURE.
YOU'RE VERY DECORATIVE.
LIKE ALL AMERICANS, LEO LOVES JAPANESE PRINTS. I DON'T LIKE THEM AT ALL.
HA HA HA!
MAY WE SEE YOUR RARE BOOKS?
OH NO! PICASSO WOULD STARE HOLES IN THEM WITH HIS BLACK GAZE.

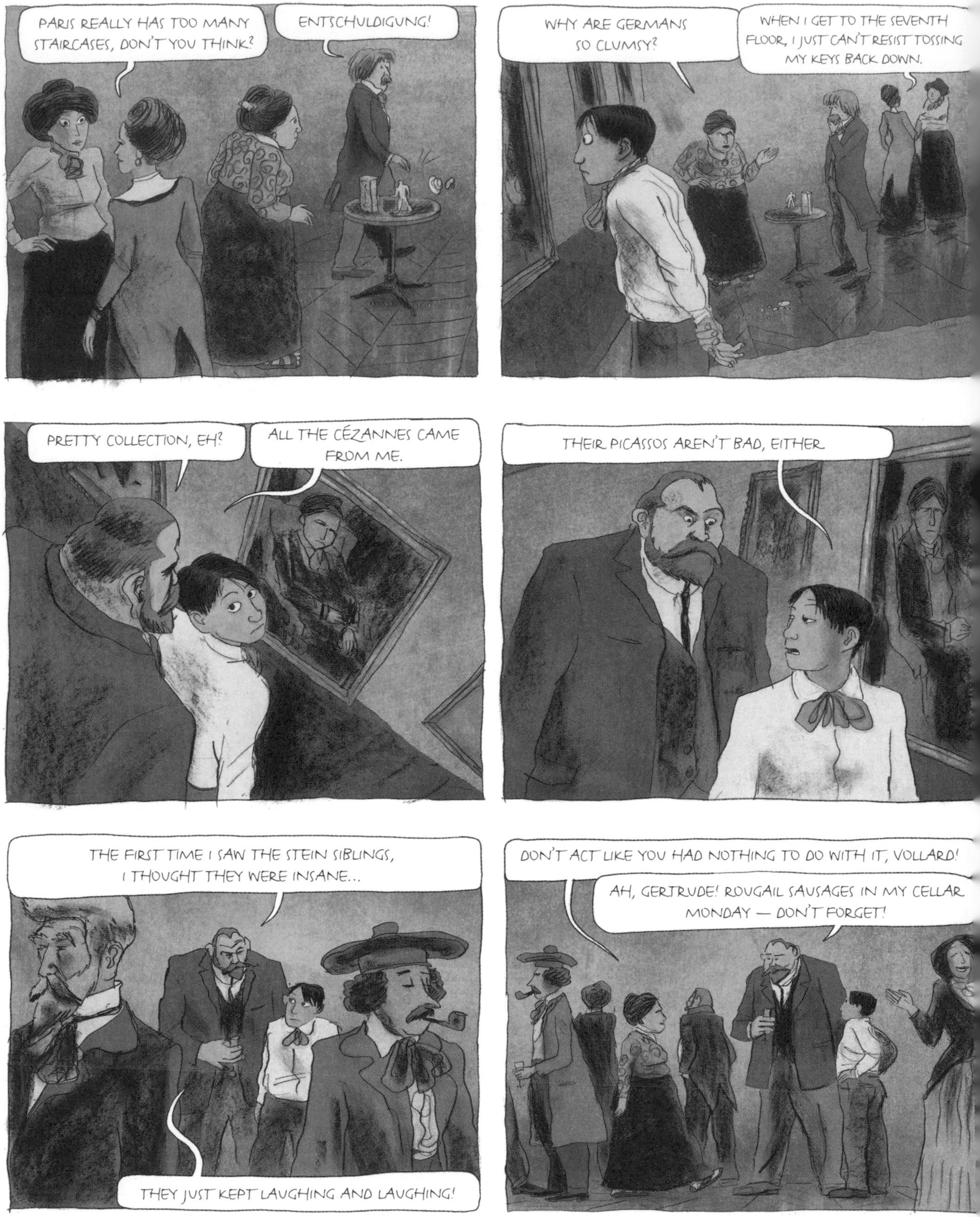
PARIS REALLY HAS TOO MANY STAIRCASES, DON'T YOU THINK?
ENTSCHULDIGUNG!
WHY ARE GERMANS SO CLUMSY?
WHEN I GET TO THE SEVENTH FLOOR, I JUST CAN'T RESIST TOSSING MY KEYS BACK DOWN.
PRETTY COLLECTION, EH?
ALL THE CÉZANNES CAME FROM ME.
THEIR PICASSOS AREN'T BAD, EITHER
THE FIRST TIME I SAW THE STEIN SIBLINGS, I THOUGHT THEY WERE INSANE...
THEY JUST KEPT LAUGHING AND LAUGHING!
DON'T ACT LIKE YOU HAD NOTHING TO DO WITH IT, VOLLARD!
AH, GERTRUDE! ROUGAIL SAUSAGES IN MY CELLAR MONDAY — DON'T FORGET!

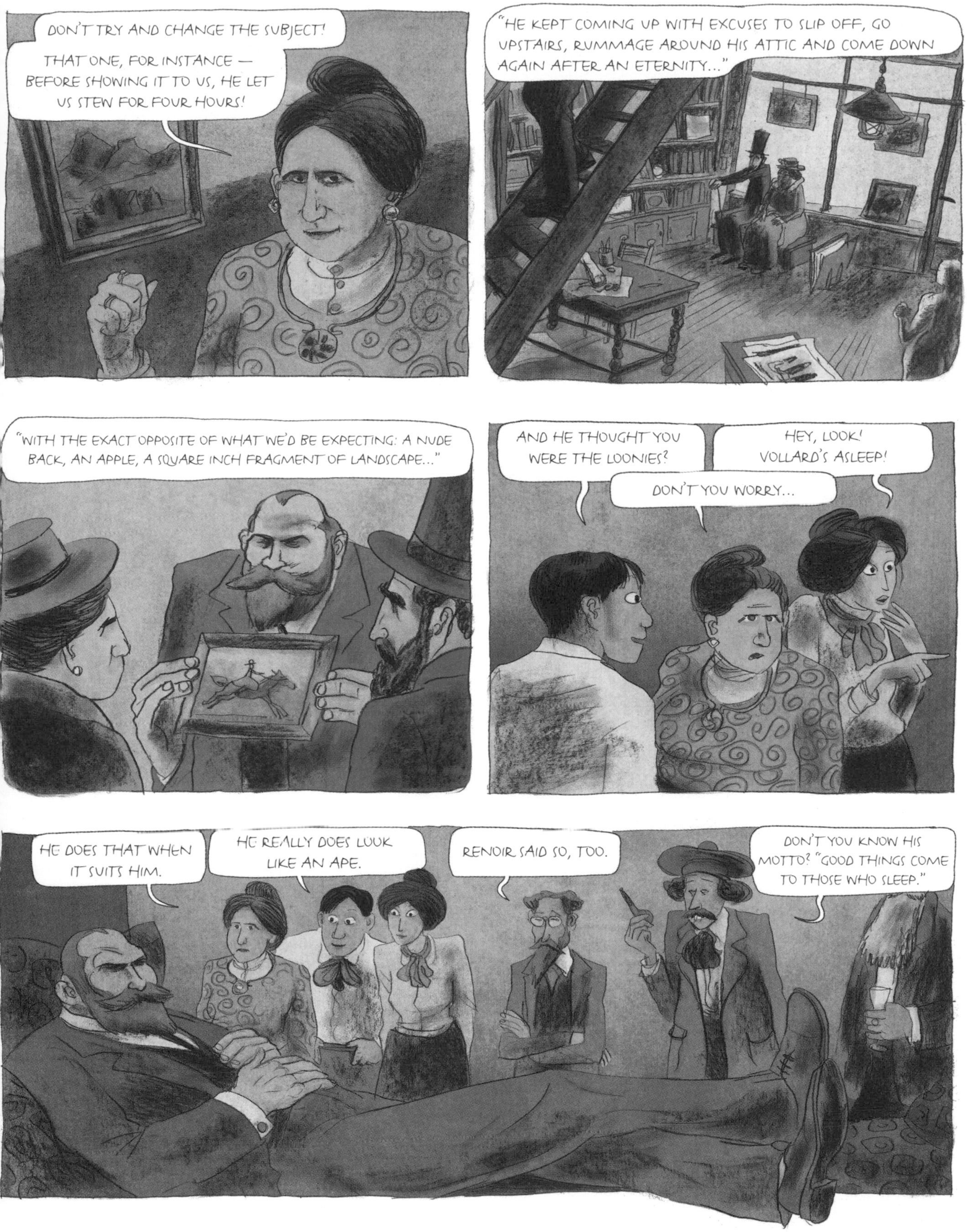
DON'T TRY AND CHANGE THE SUBJECT!
THAT ONE, FOR INSTANCE — BEFORE SHOWING IT TO US, HE LET US STEW FOR FOUR HOURS!
"HE KEPT COMING UP WITH EXCUSES TO SLIP OFF, GO UPSTAIRS, RUMMAGE AROUND HIS ATTIC AND COME DOWN AGAIN AFTER AN ETERNITY..."
"WITH THE EXACT OPPOSITE OF WHAT WE'D BE EXPECTING: A NUDE BACK, AN APPLE, A SQUARE INCH FRAGMENT OF LANDSCAPE..."
AND HE THOUGHT YOU WERE THE LOONIES?
DON'T YOU WORRY...
HEY, LOOK! VOLLARD'S ASLEEP!
HE DOES THAT WHEN IT SUITS HIM.
HE REALLY DOES LOOK LIKE AN APE.
RENOIR SAID SO, TOO.
DON'T YOU KNOW HIS MOTTO? "GOOD THINGS COME TO THOSE WHO SLEEP."

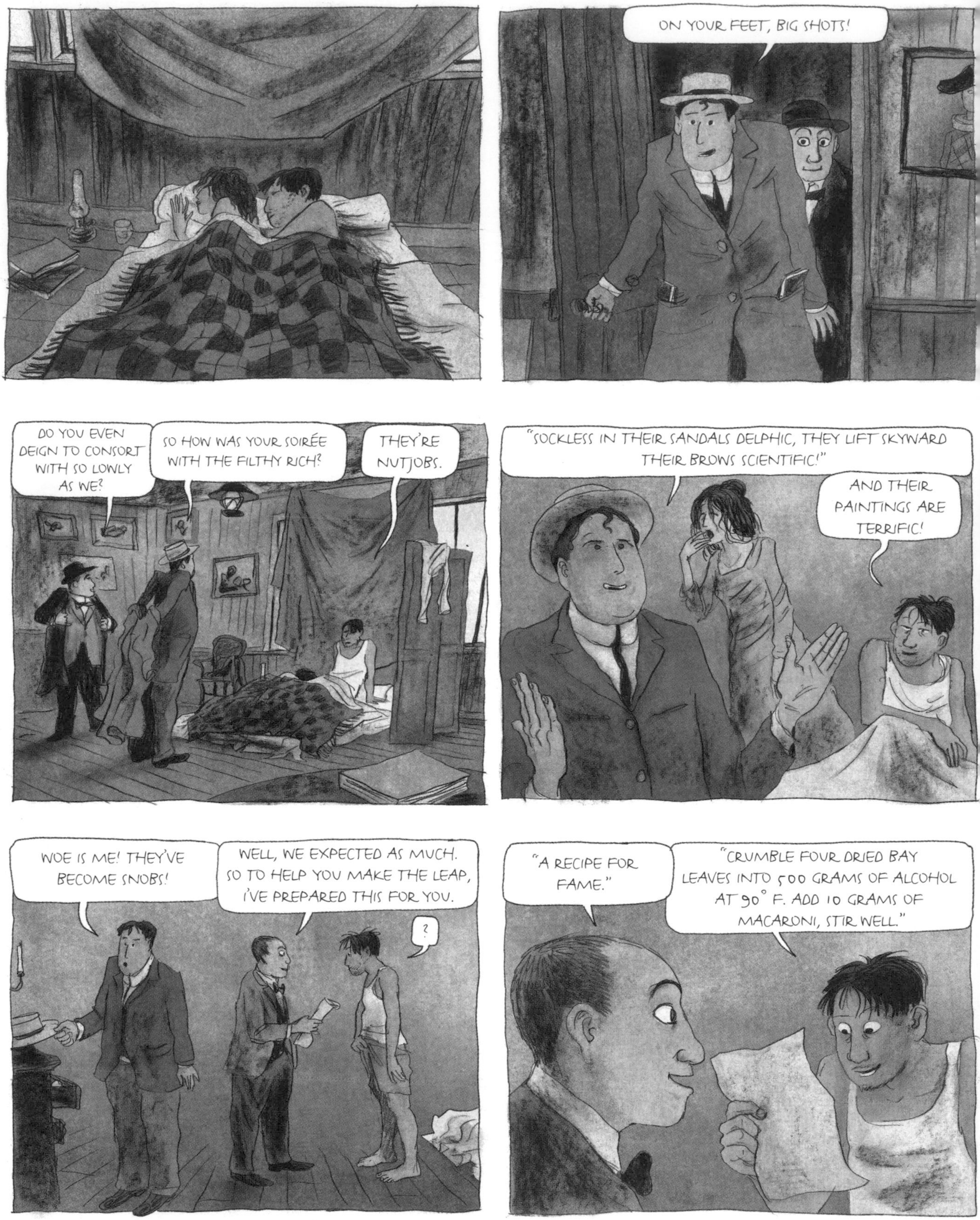
ON YOUR FEET, BIG SHOTS!
DO YOU EVEN DEIGN TO CONSORT WITH SO LOWLY AS WE?
SO HOW WAS YOUR SOIRÉE WITH THE FILTHY RICH?
THEY'RE NUTJOBS.
"SOCKLESS IN THEIR SANDALS DELPHIC, THEY LIFT SKYWARD THEIR BROWS SCIENTIFIC!"
AND THEIR PAINTINGS ARE TERRIFIC!
WOE IS ME! THEY'VE BECOME SNOBS!
WELL, WE EXPECTED AS MUCH. SO TO HELP YOU MAKE THE LEAP, I'VE PREPARED THIS FOR YOU.
?
"A RECIPE FOR FAME."
"CRUMBLE FOUR DRIED BAY LEAVES INTO 500 GRAMS OF ALCOHOL AT 90° F. ADD 10 GRAMS OF MACARONI, STIR WELL."

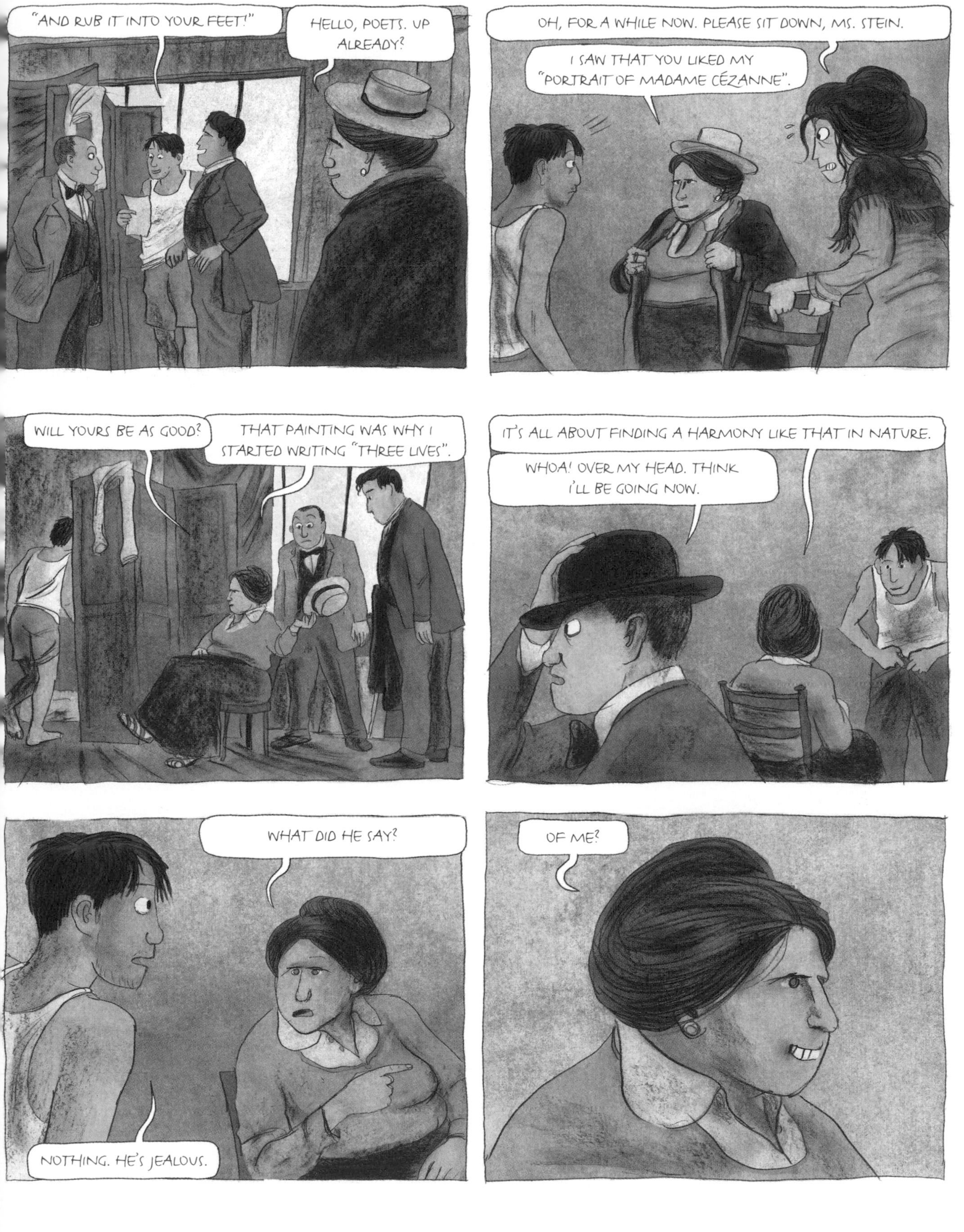
"AND RUB IT INTO YOUR FEET!"
HELLO, POETS. UP ALREADY?
OH, FOR A WHILE NOW. PLEASE SIT DOWN, MS. STEIN.
I SAW THAT YOU LIKED MY "PORTRAIT OF MADAME CÉZANNE".
WILL YOURS BE AS GOOD?
THAT PAINTING WAS WHY I STARTED WRITING "THREE LIVES".
IT'S ALL ABOUT FINDING A HARMONY LIKE THAT IN NATURE.
WHOA! OVER MY HEAD. THINK I'LL BE GOING NOW.
WHAT DID HE SAY?
NOTHING. HE'S JEALOUS.
OF ME?

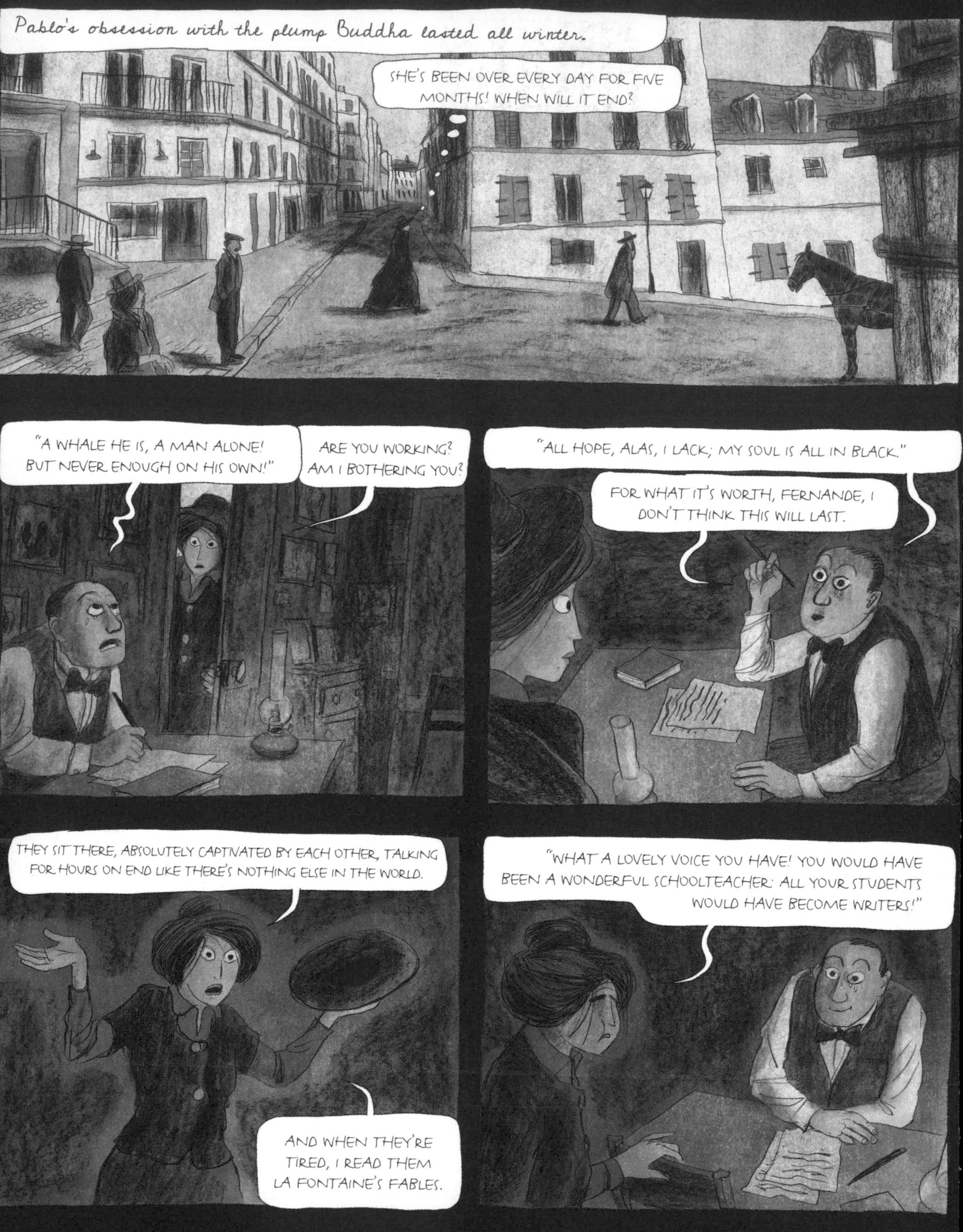
Pablo's obsession with the plump Buddha lasted all winter.
SHE'S BEEN OVER EVERY DAY FOR FIVE MONTHS! WHEN WILL IT END?
"A WHALE HE IS, A MAN ALONE! BUT NEVER ENOUGH ON HIS OWN!"
ARE YOU WORKING? AM I BOTHERING YOU?
"ALL HOPE, ALAS, I LACK; MY SOUL IS ALL IN BLACK."
FOR WHAT IT'S WORTH, FERNANDE, I DON'T THINK THIS WILL LAST.
THEY SIT THERE, ABSOLUTELY CAPTIVATED BY EACH OTHER, TALKING FOR HOURS ON END LIKE THERE'S NOTHING ELSE IN THE WORLD.
AND WHEN THEY'RE TIRED, I READ THEM LA FONTAINE'S FABLES.
"WHAT A LOVELY VOICE YOU HAVE! YOU WOULD HAVE BEEN A WONDERFUL SCHOOLTEACHER: ALL YOUR STUDENTS WOULD HAVE BECOME WRITERS!"

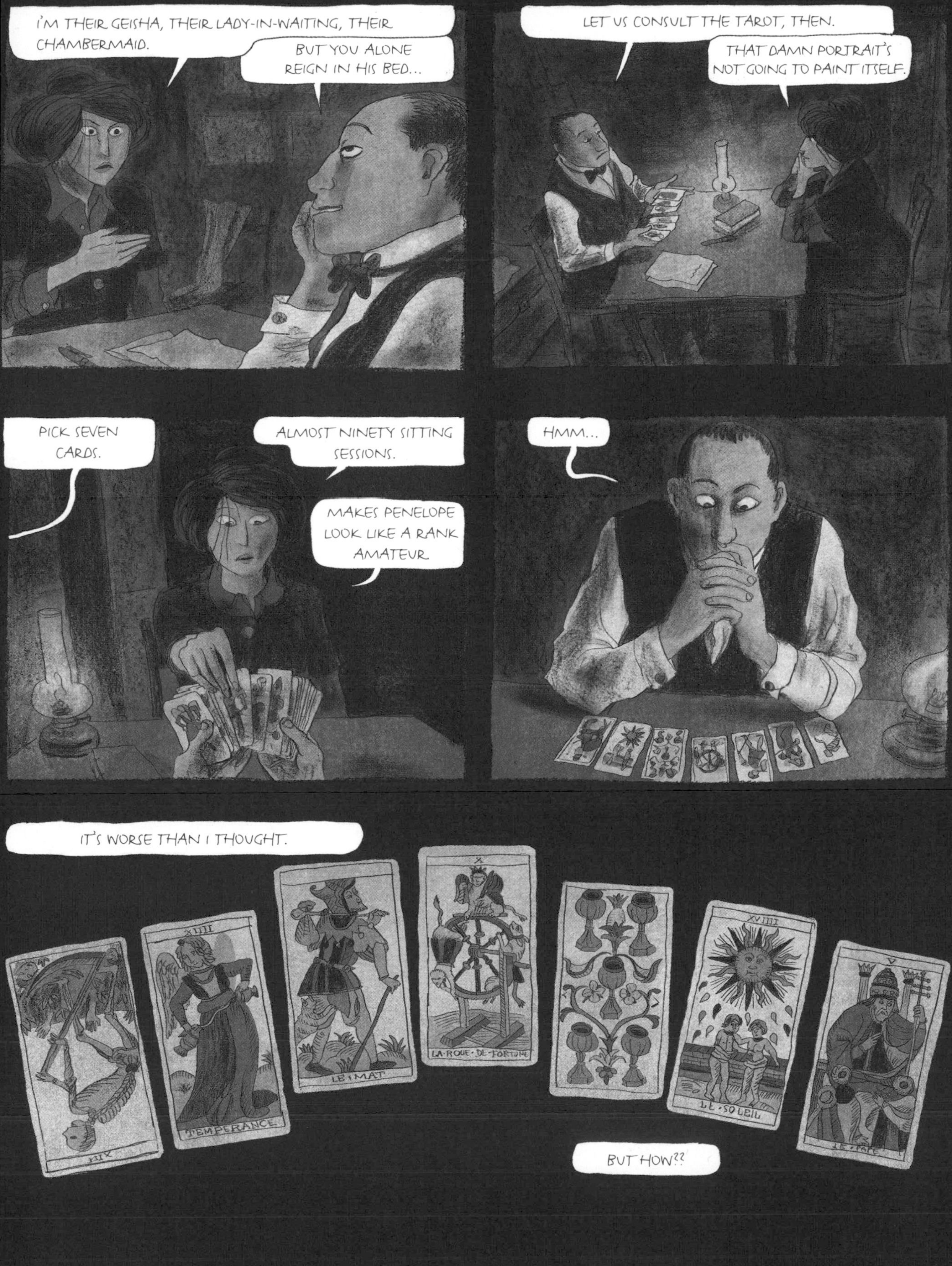
I'M THEIR GEISHA, THEIR LADY-IN-WAITING, THEIR CHAMBERMAID.
BUT YOU ALONE REIGN IN HIS BED...
LET US CONSULT THE TAROT, THEN.
THAT DAMN PORTRAIT'S NOT GOING TO PAINT ITSELF.
PICK SEVEN CARDS.
ALMOST NINETY SITTING SESSIONS.
MAKES PENELOPE LOOK LIKE A RANK AMATEUR
HMM...
IT'S WORSE THAN I THOUGHT.
XIIII
TEMPERANCE
LE MAT
X
LA ROUE DE FORTUNE
XVIIII
LE SOLEIL
V
LE PAPE
BUT HOW??

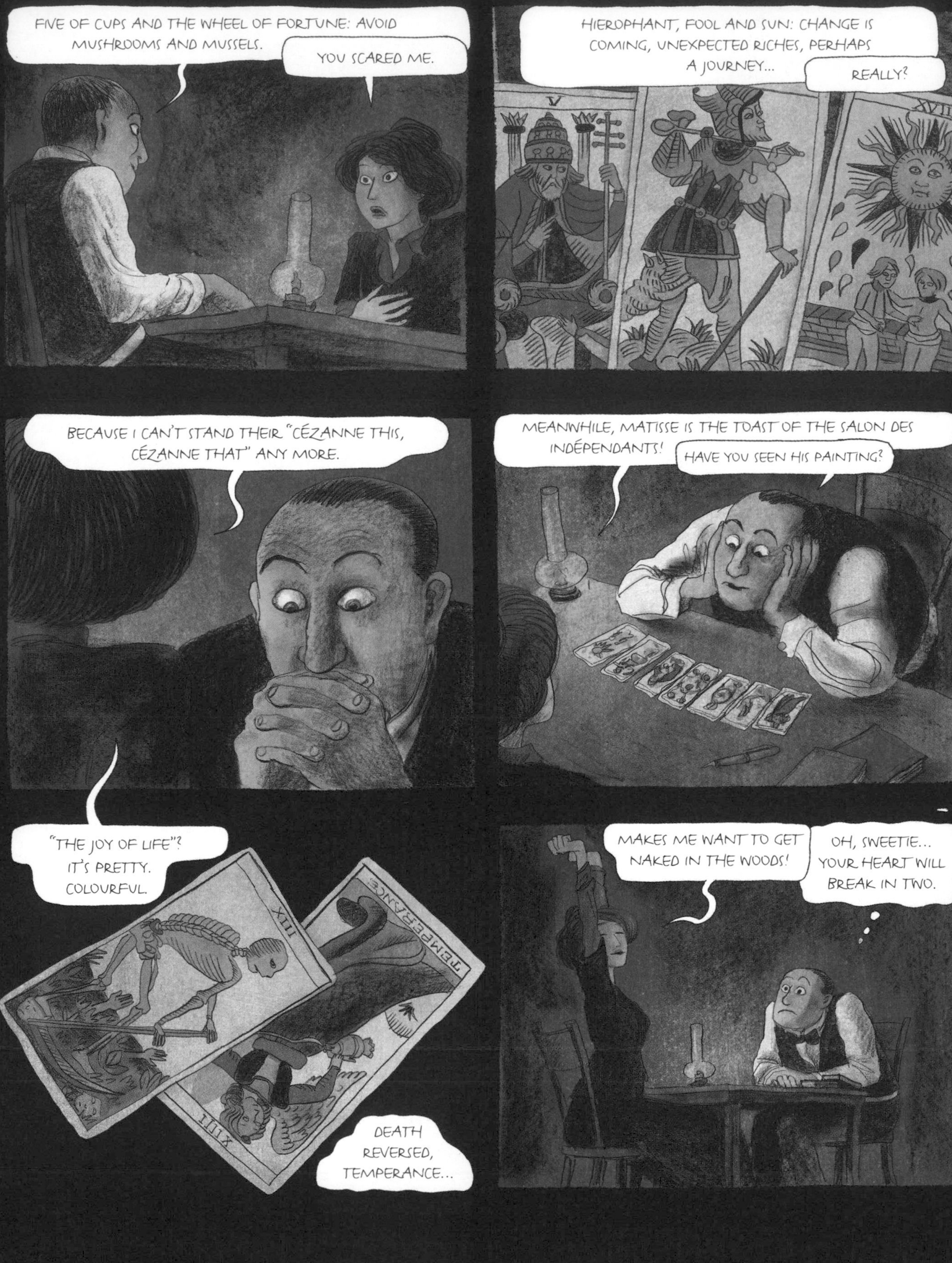
FIVE OF CUPS AND THE WHEEL OF FORTUNE: AVOID MUSHROOMS AND MUSSELS.
YOU SCARED ME.
HIEROPHANT, FOOL AND SUN: CHANGE IS COMING, UNEXPECTED RICHES, PERHAPS A JOURNEY...
REALLY?
BECAUSE I CAN'T STAND THEIR "CÉZANNE THIS, CÉZANNE THAT" ANY MORE.
MEANWHILE, MATISSE IS THE TOAST OF THE SALON DES INDÉPENDANTS!
HAVE YOU SEEN HIS PAINTING?
"THE JOY OF LIFE"? IT'S PRETTY. COLOURFUL.
XIII
TEMPERANCE
XIIII
DEATH REVERSED, TEMPERANCE...
MAKES ME WANT TO GET NAKED IN THE WOODS!
OH, SWEETIE... YOUR HEART WILL BREAK IN TWO.

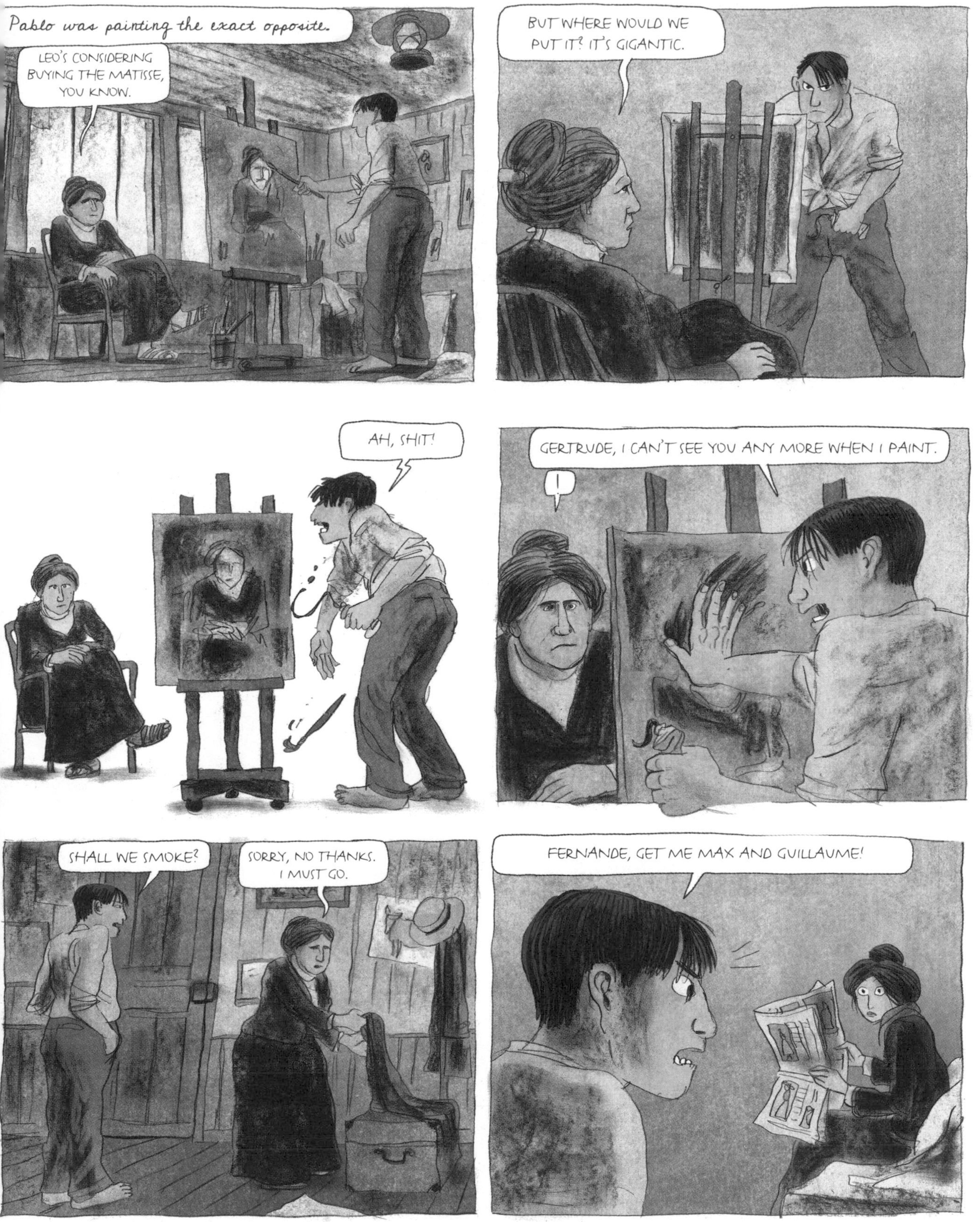
Pablo was painting the exact opposite.
LEO'S CONSIDERING BUYING THE MATISSE, YOU KNOW.
BUT WHERE WOULD WE PUT IT? IT'S GIGANTIC.
AH, SHIT!
GERTRUDE, I CAN'T SEE YOU ANY MORE WHEN I PAINT.
!
SHALL WE SMOKE?
SORRY, NO THANKS. I MUST GO.
FERNANDE, GET ME MAX AND GUILLAUME!

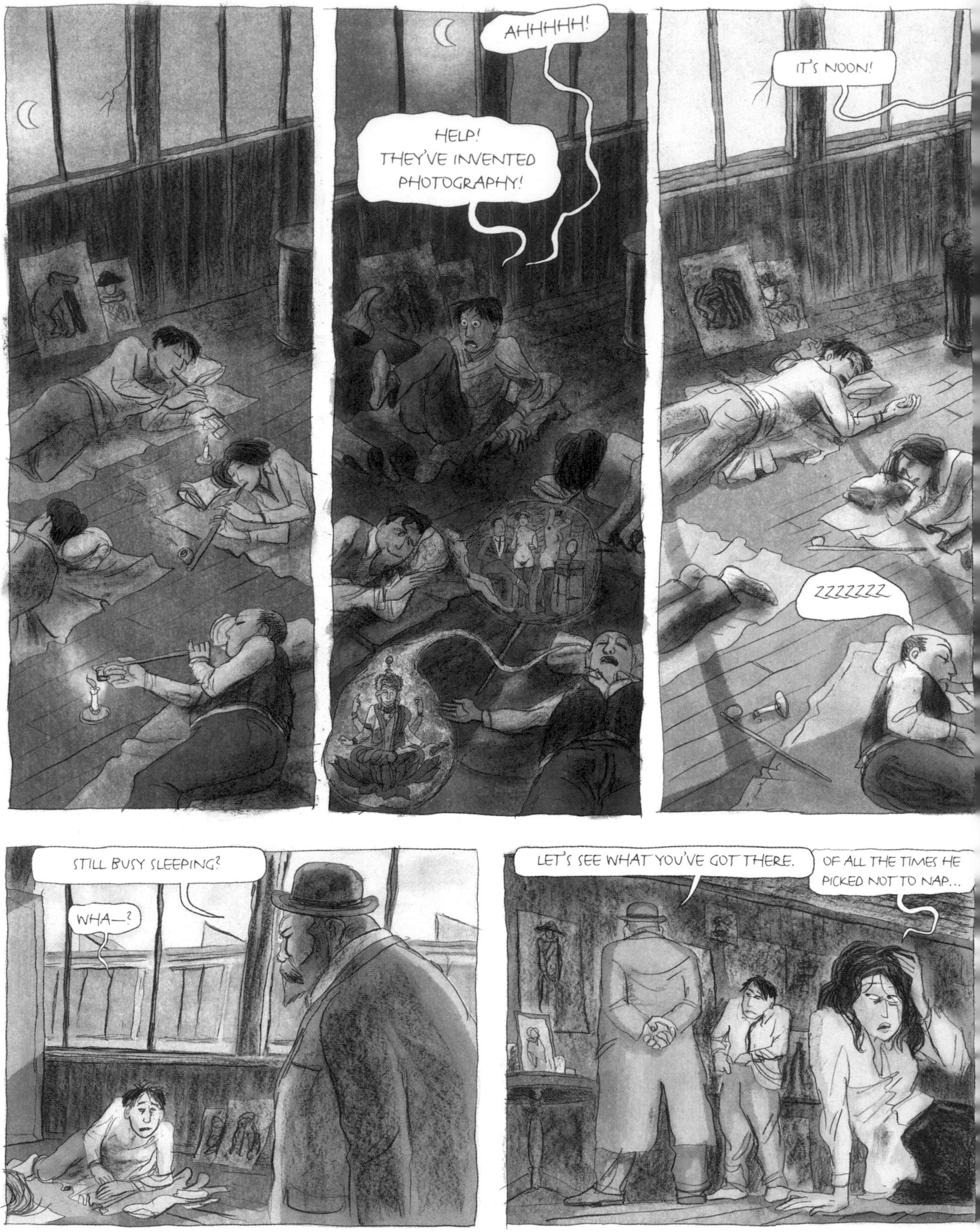
AHHHHH!
HELP! THEY'VE INVENTED PHOTOGRAPHY!
IT'S NOON!
ZZZZZZZ
STILL BUSY SLEEPING?
WHA—?
LET'S SEE WHAT YOU'VE GOT THERE.
OF ALL THE TIMES HE PICKED NOT TO NAP...

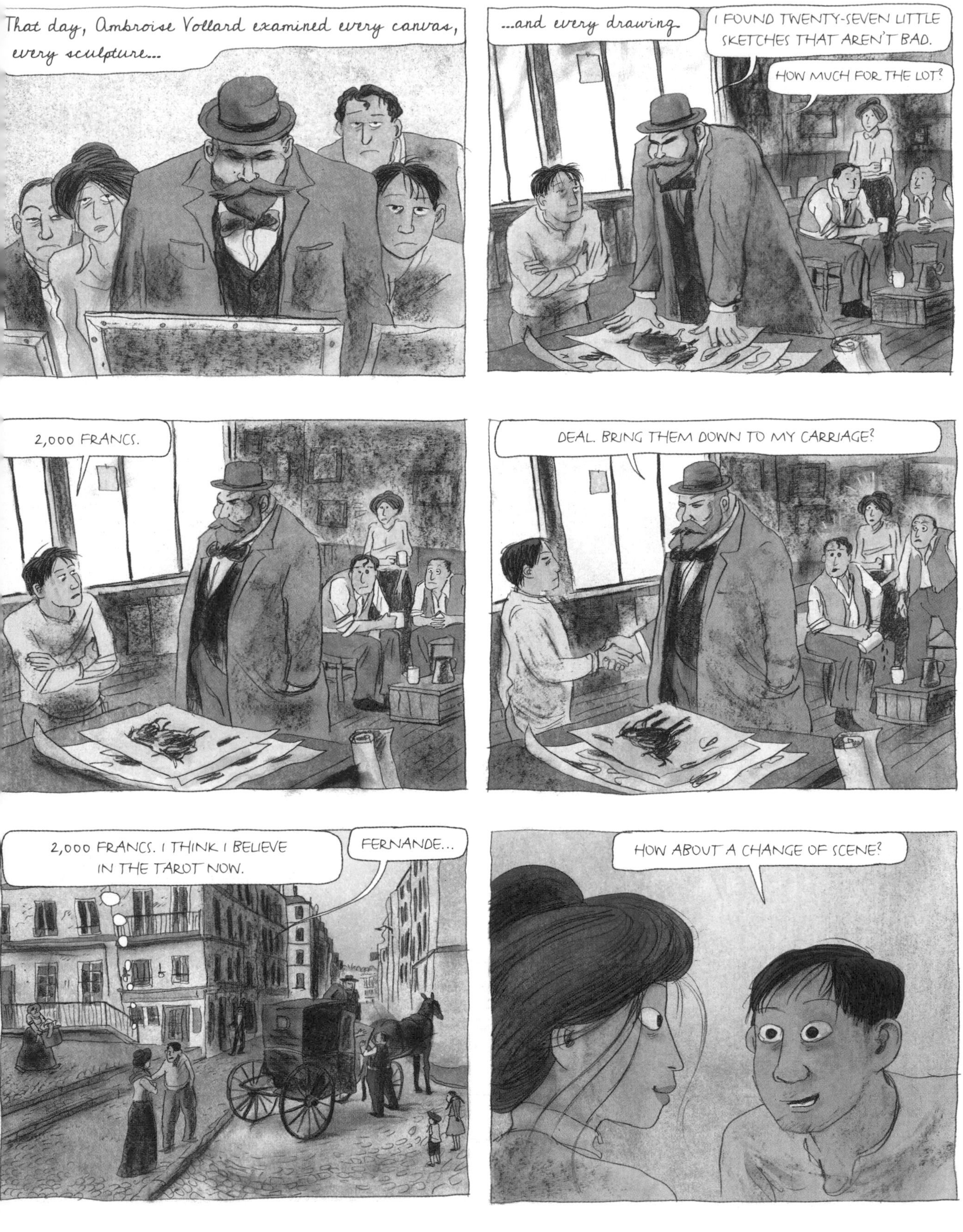

That day, Ambroise Vollard examined every canvas, every sculpture...
...and every drawing.
I FOUND TWENTY-SEVEN LITTLE SKETCHES THAT AREN'T BAD.
HOW MUCH FOR THE LOT?
2,000 FRANCS.
DEAL. BRING THEM DOWN TO MY CARRIAGE?
2,000 FRANCS. I THINK I BELIEVE IN THE TAROT NOW.
FERNANDE...
HOW ABOUT A CHANGE OF SCENE?

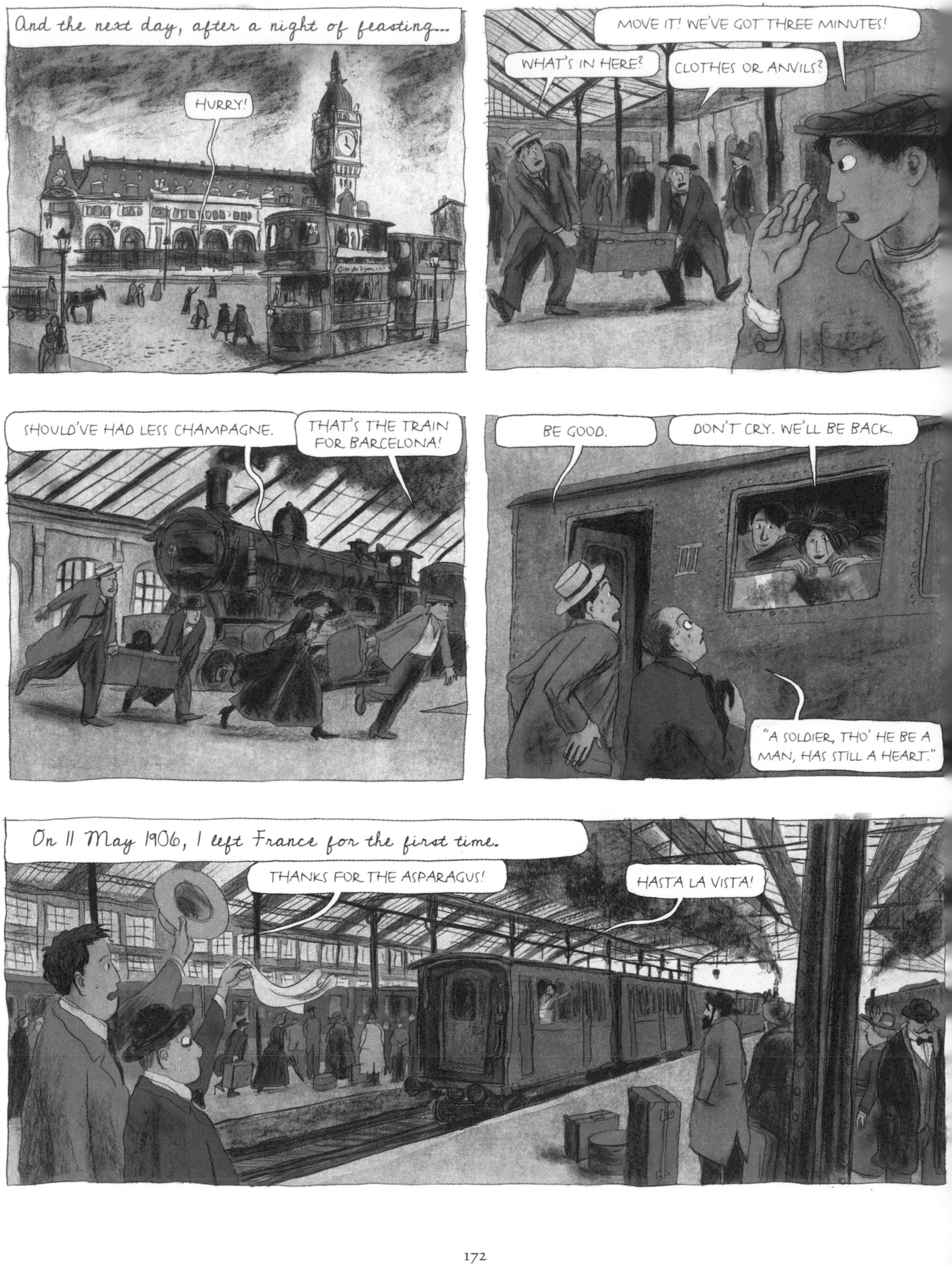
And the next day, after a night of feasting...
HURRY!
MOVE IT! WE'VE GOT THREE MINUTES!
WHAT'S IN HERE?
CLOTHES OR ANVILS?
SHOULD'VE HAD LESS CHAMPAGNE.
THAT'S THE TRAIN FOR BARCELONA!
BE GOOD.
DON'T CRY. WE'LL BE BACK.
"A SOLDIER, THO' HE BE A MAN, HAS STILL A HEART."
On 11 May 1906, I left France for the first time.
THANKS FOR THE ASPARAGUS!
HASTA LA VISTA!

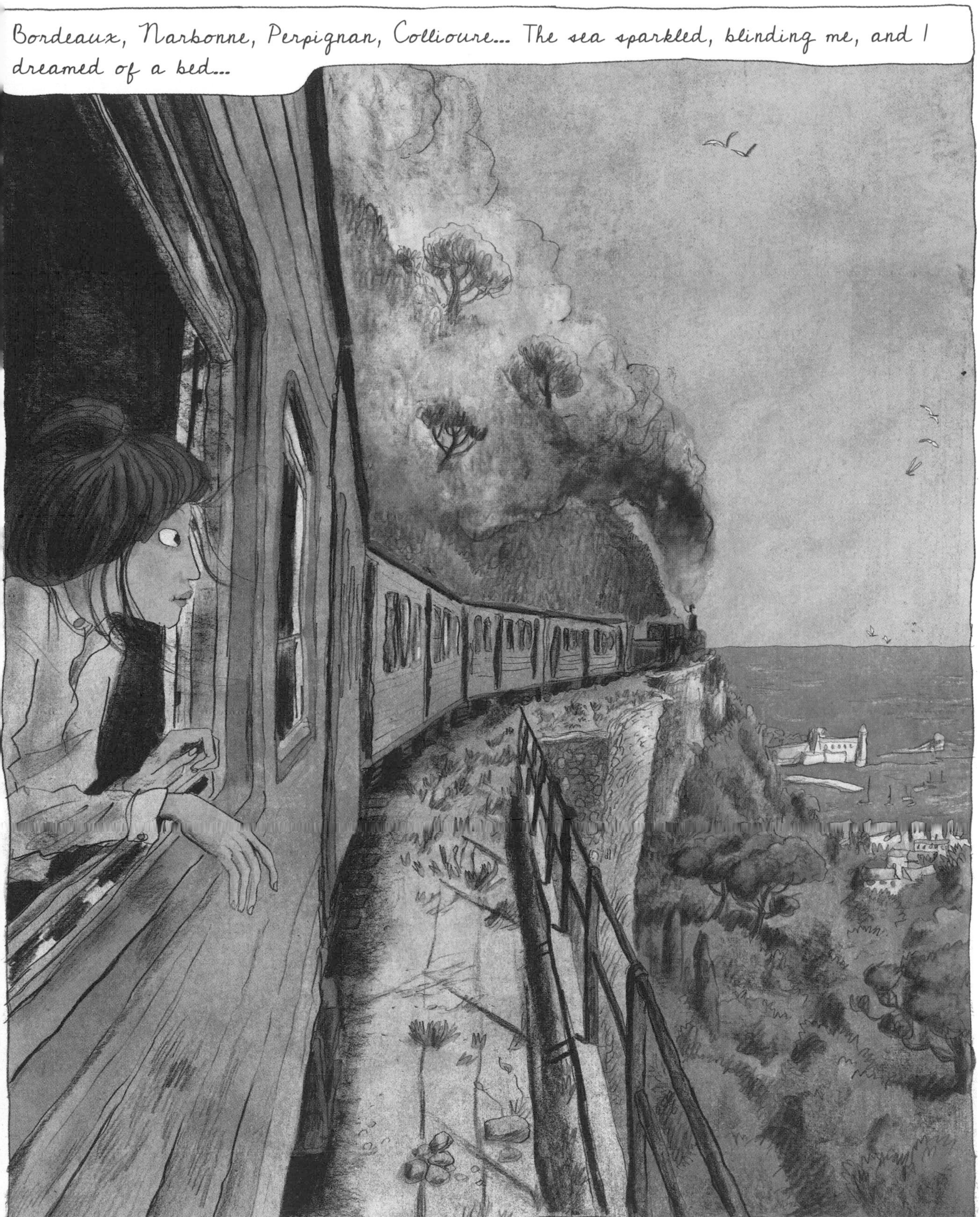
Bordeaux, Narbonne, Perpignan, Collioure... The sea sparkled, blinding me, and I dreamed of a bed...

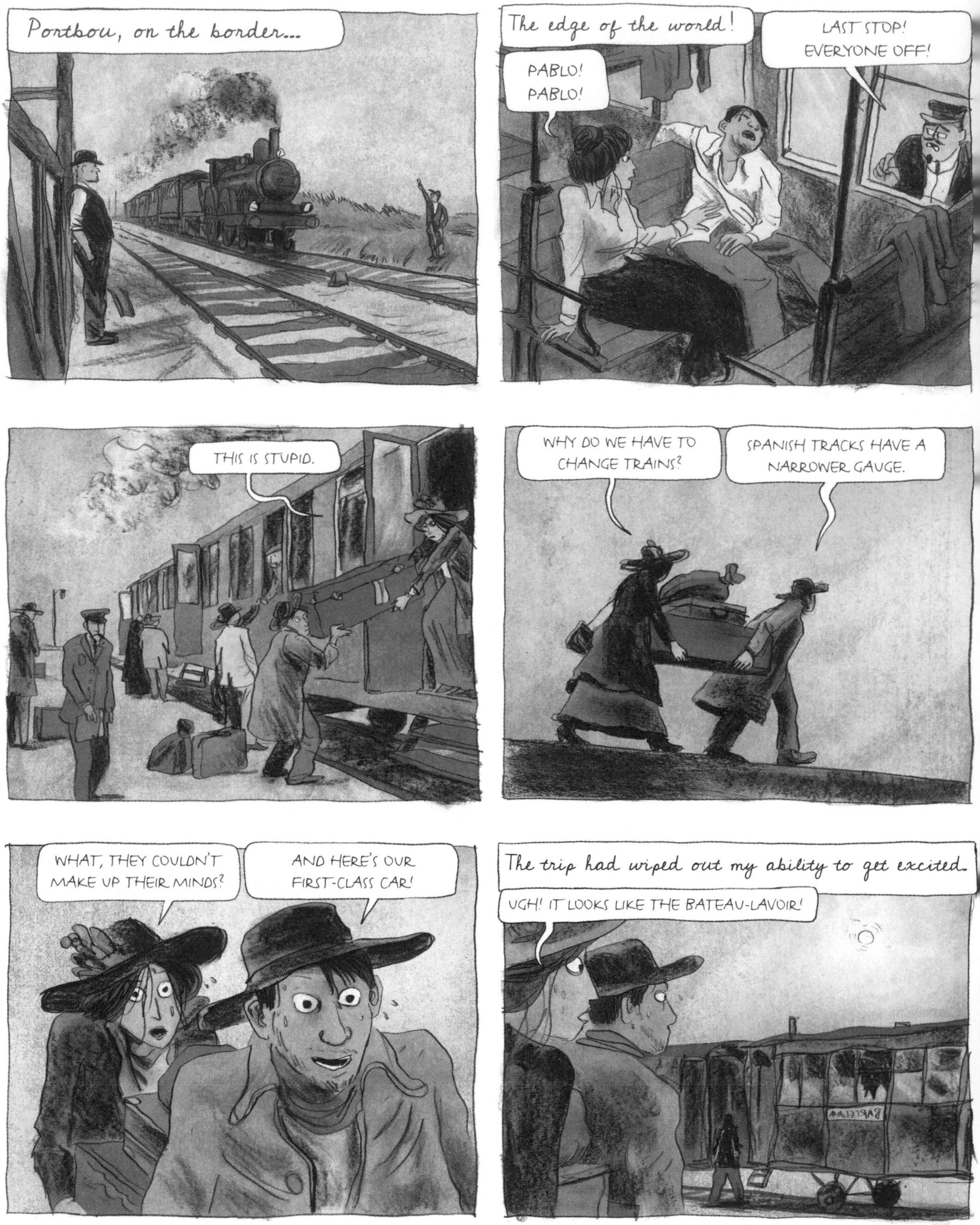
Portbou, on the border...
The edge of the world!
PABLO! PABLO!
LAST STOP! EVERYONE OFF!
THIS IS STUPID.
WHY DO WE HAVE TO CHANGE TRAINS?
SPANISH TRACKS HAVE A NARROWER GAUGE.
WHAT, THEY COULDN'T MAKE UP THEIR MINDS?
AND HERE'S OUR FIRST-CLASS CAR!
The trip had wiped out my ability to get excited.
UGH! IT LOOKS LIKE THE BATEAU-LAVOIR!

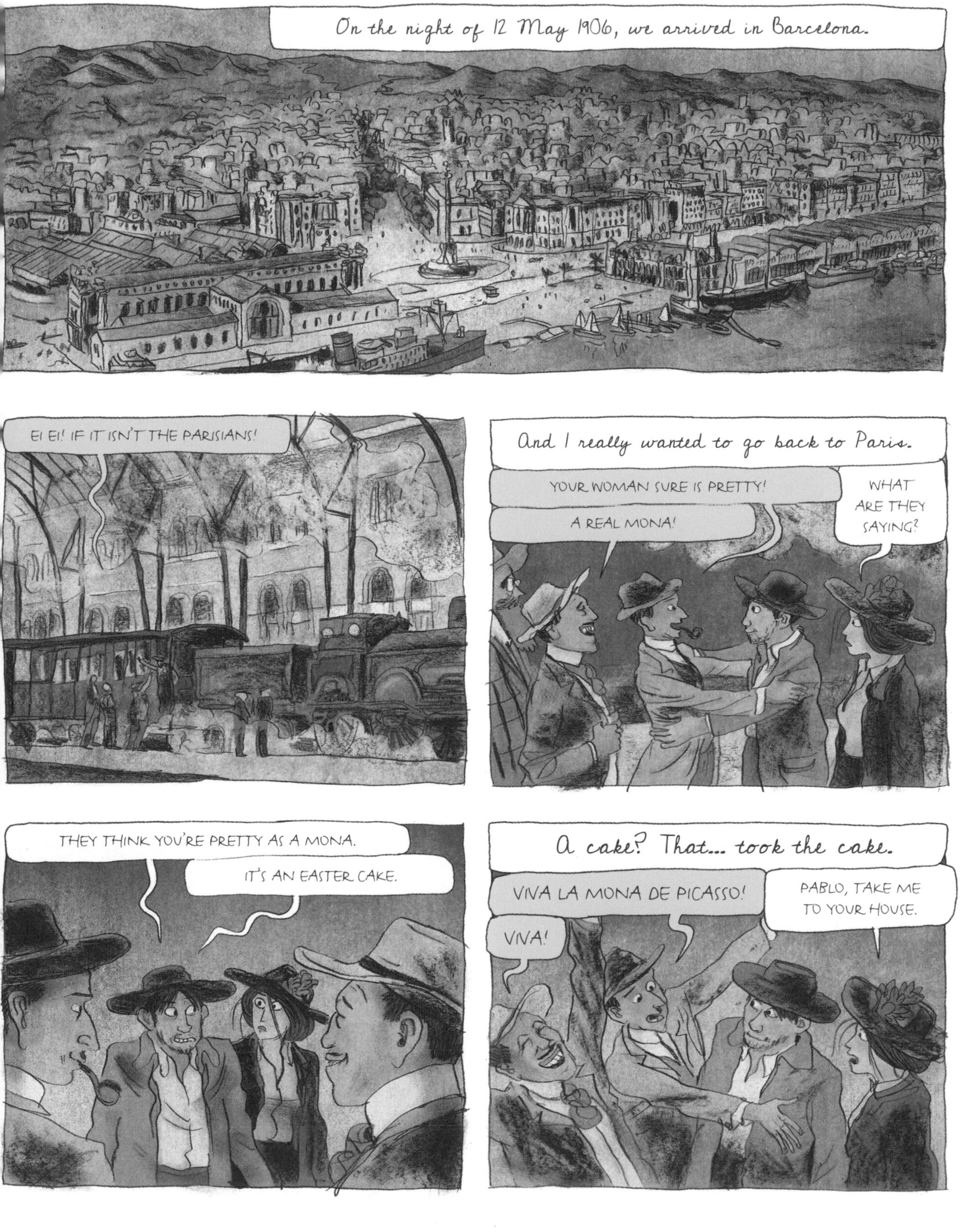
On the night of 12 May 1906, we arrived in Barcelona.
EI EI! IF IT ISN'T THE PARISIANS!
And I really wanted to go back to Paris.
YOUR WOMAN SURE IS PRETTY!
A REAL MONA!
WHAT ARE THEY SAYING?
THEY THINK YOU'RE PRETTY AS A MONA.
IT'S AN EASTER CAKE.
A cake? That... took the cake.
VIVA LA MONA DE PICASSO!
VIVA!
PABLO, TAKE ME TO YOUR HOUSE.

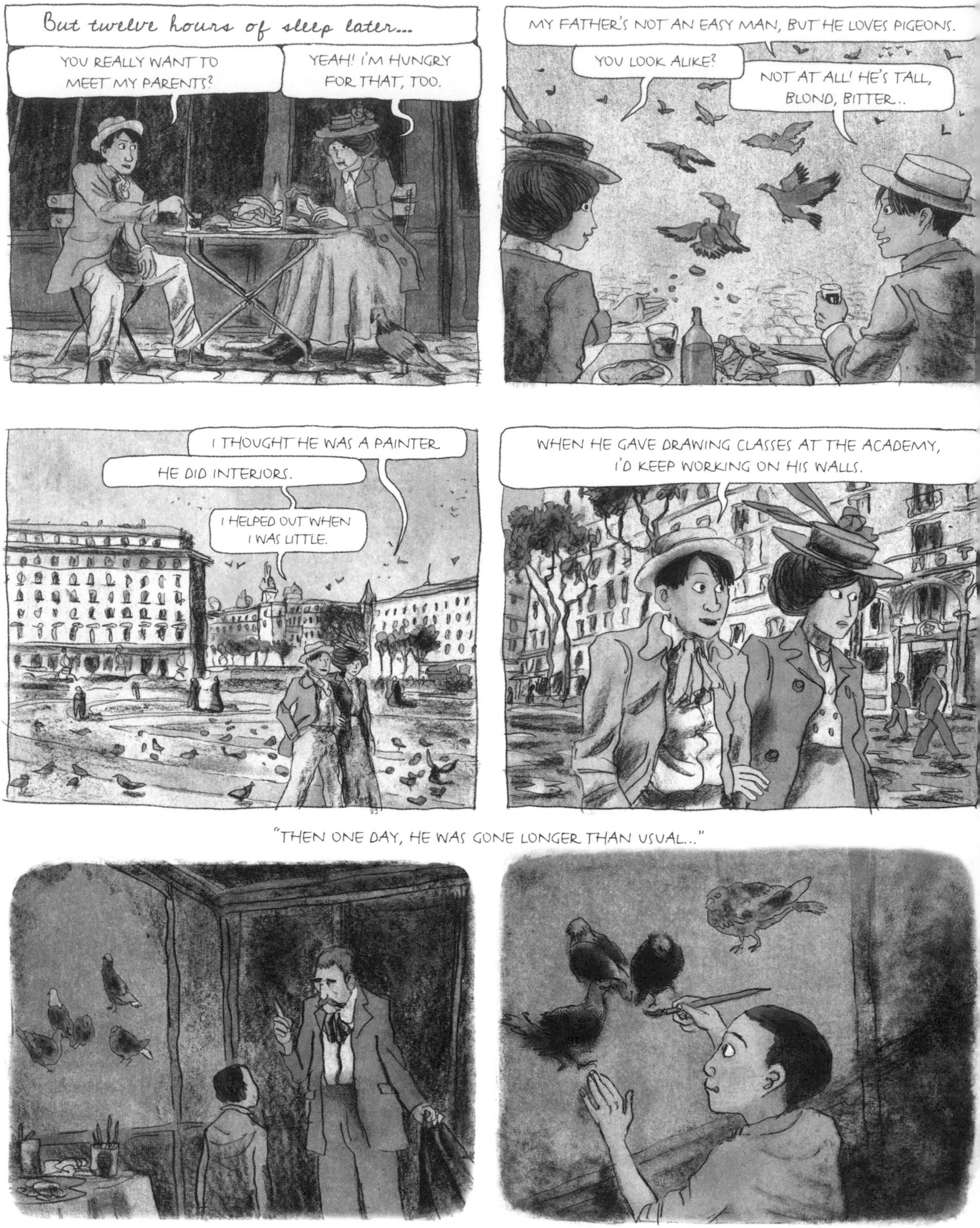
But twelve hours of sleep later...
YOU REALLY WANT TO MEET MY PARENTS?
YEAH! I'M HUNGRY FOR THAT, TOO.
MY FATHER'S NOT AN EASY MAN, BUT HE LOVES PIGEONS.
YOU LOOK ALIKE?
NOT AT ALL! HE'S TALL, BLOND, BITTER..
I THOUGHT HE WAS A PAINTER
HE DID INTERIORS.
I HELPED OUT WHEN I WAS LITTLE.
WHEN HE GAVE DRAWING CLASSES AT THE ACADEMY, I'D KEEP WORKING ON HIS WALLS.
"THEN ONE DAY, HE WAS GONE LONGER THAN USUAL..."

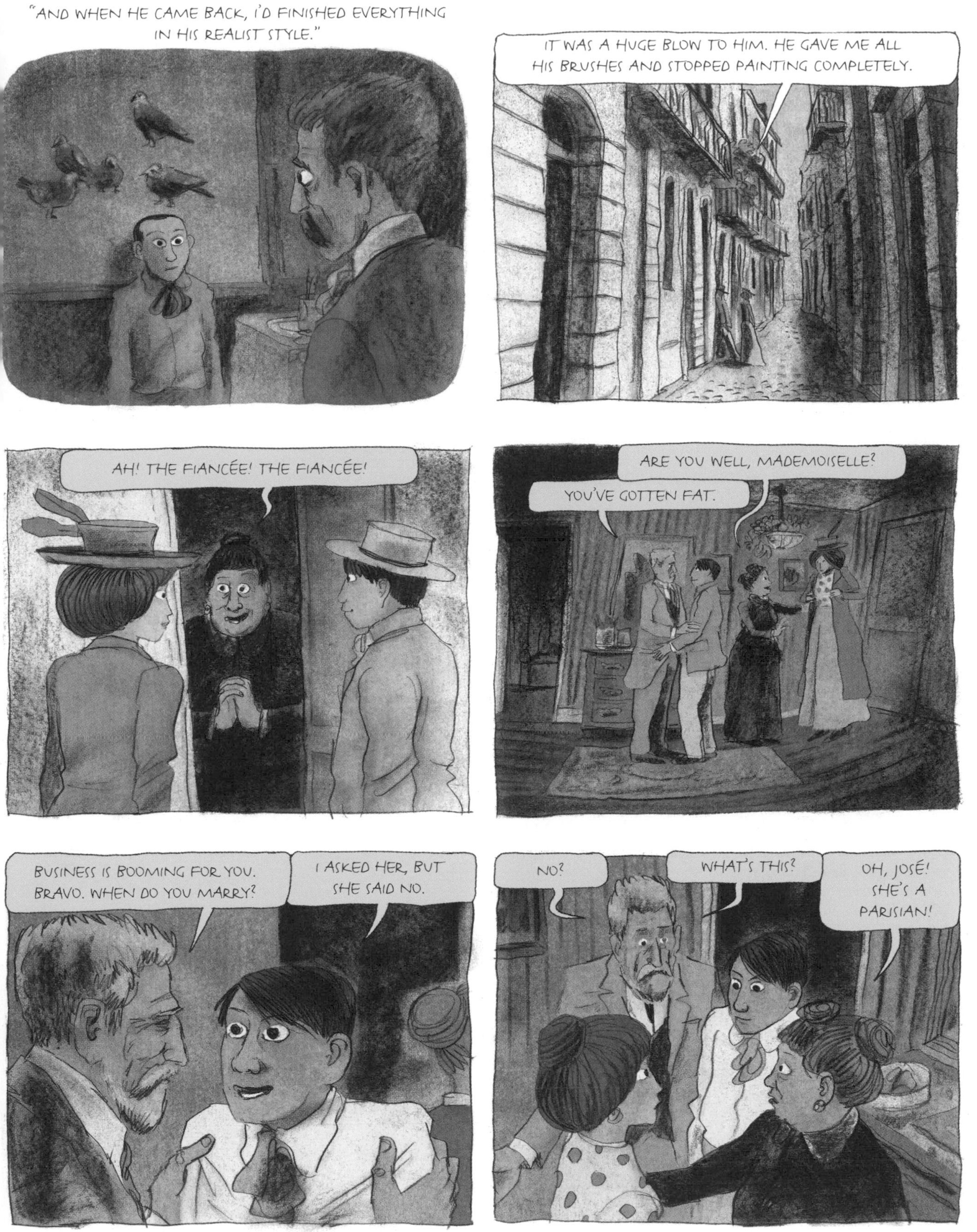
"AND WHEN HE CAME BACK, I'D FINISHED EVERYTHING IN HIS REALIST STYLE."
IT WAS A HUGE BLOW TO HIM. HE GAVE ME ALL HIS BRUSHES AND STOPPED PAINTING COMPLETELY.
AH! THE FIANCÉE! THE FIANCÉE!
ARE YOU WELL, MADEMOISELLE?
YOU'VE GOTTEN FAT.
BUSINESS IS BOOMING FOR YOU. BRAVO. WHEN DO YOU MARRY?
I ASKED HER, BUT SHE SAID NO.
NO?
WHAT'S THIS?
OH, JOSÉ! SHE'S A PARISIAN!

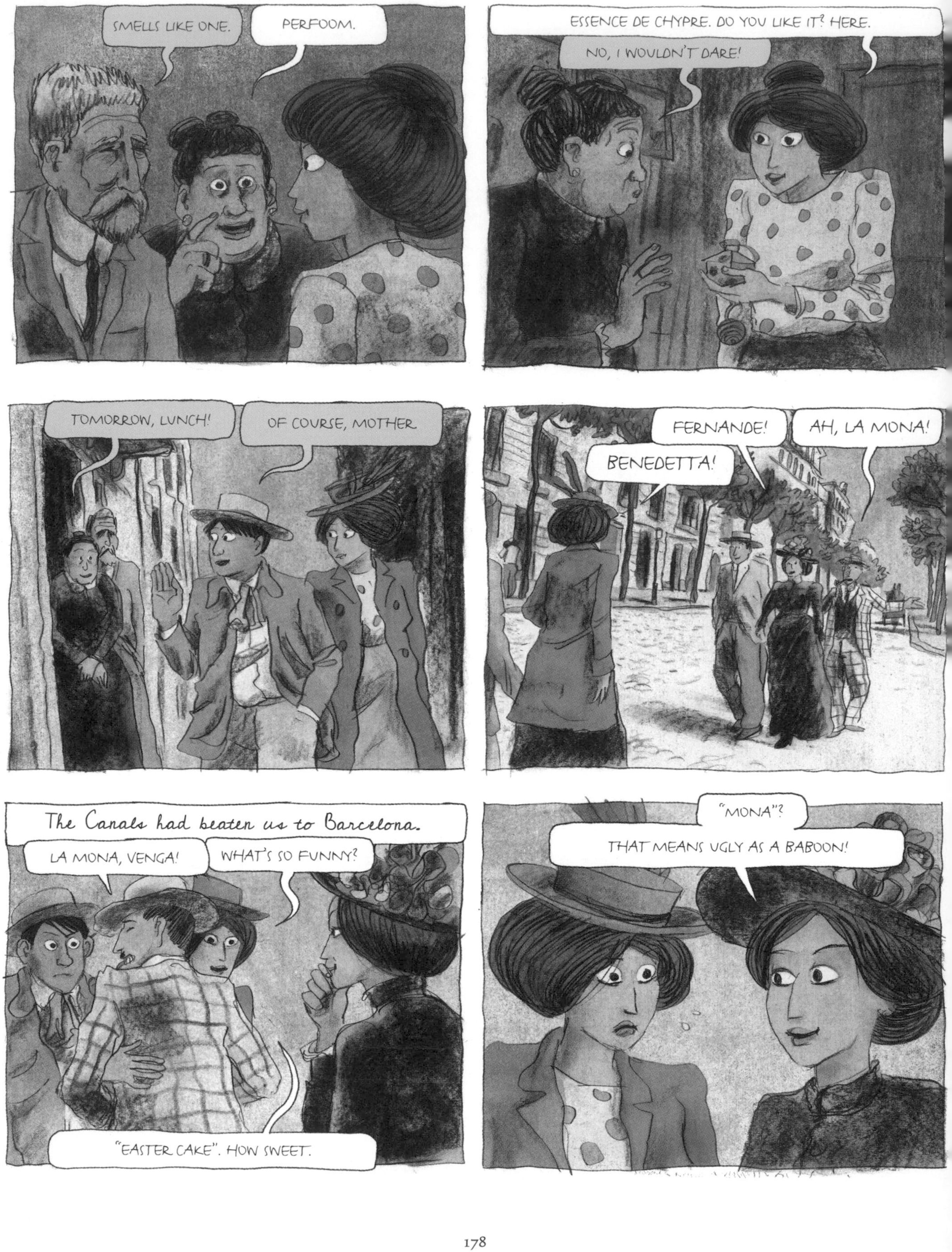
SMELLS LIKE ONE.
PERFOOM.
ESSENCE DE CHYPRE. DO YOU LIKE IT? HERE.
NO, I WOULDN'T DARE!
TOMORROW, LUNCH!
OF COURSE, MOTHER
FERNANDE!
AH, LA MONA!
BENEDETTA!
The Canals had beaten us to Barcelona.
LA MONA, VENGA!
WHAT'S SO FUNNY?
"EASTER CAKE". HOW SWEET.
"MONA"?
THAT MEANS UGLY AS A BABOON!

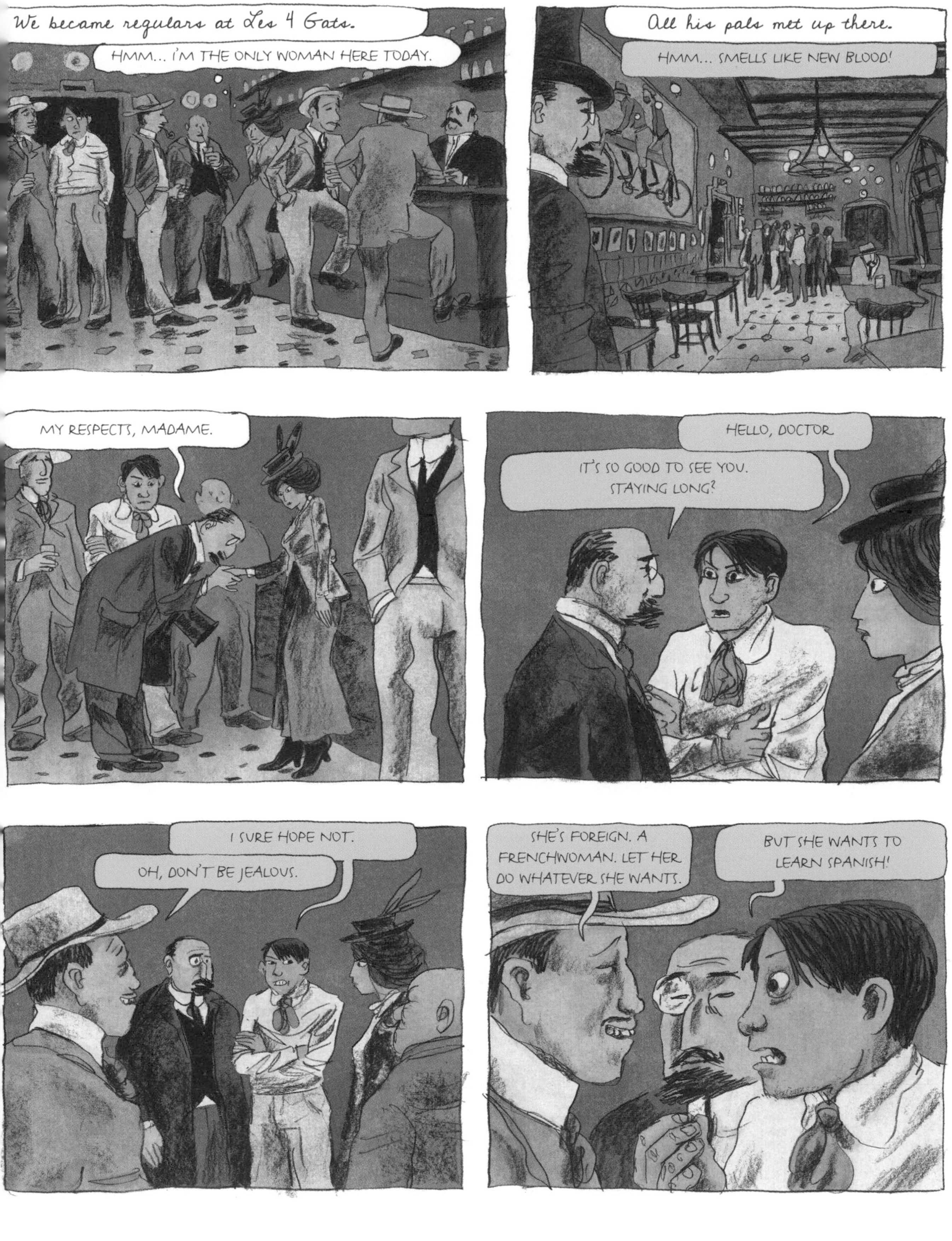
We became regulars at Les 4 Gats.
HMM... I'M THE ONLY WOMAN HERE TODAY.
All his pals met up there.
HMM... SMELLS LIKE NEW BLOOD!
MY RESPECTS, MADAME.
HELLO, DOCTOR
IT'S SO GOOD TO SEE YOU. STAYING LONG?
I SURE HOPE NOT.
OH, DON'T BE JEALOUS.
SHE'S FOREIGN. A FRENCHWOMAN. LET HER DO WHATEVER SHE WANTS.
BUT SHE WANTS TO LEARN SPANISH!

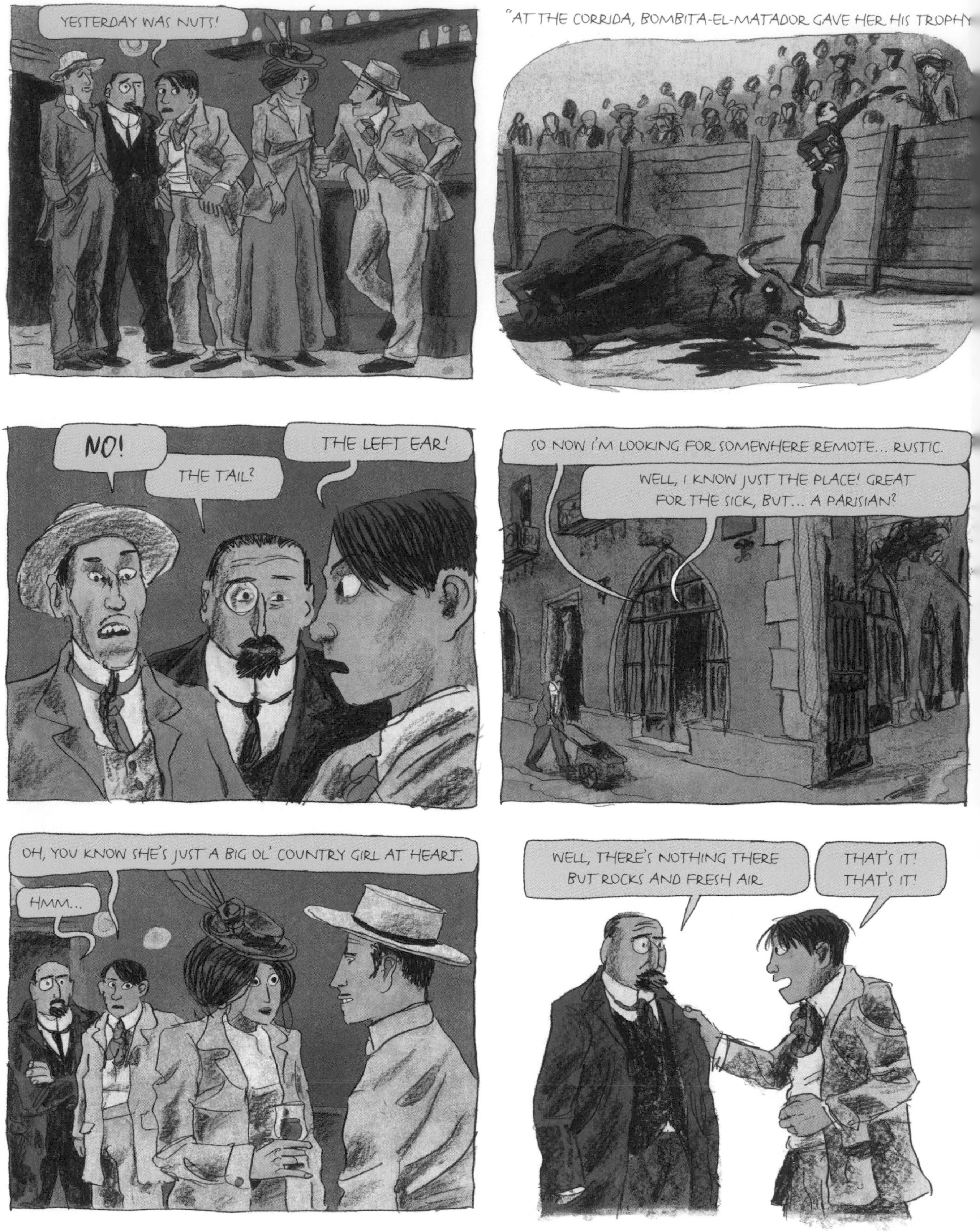
YESTERDAY WAS NUTS!
"AT THE CORRIDA, BOMBITA-EL-MATADOR GAVE HER HIS TROPHY
NO!
THE TAIL?
THE LEFT EAR!
SO NOW I'M LOOKING FOR SOMEWHERE REMOTE... RUSTIC.
WELL, I KNOW JUST THE PLACE! GREAT FOR THE SICK, BUT... A PARISIAN?
OH, YOU KNOW SHE'S JUST A BIG OL' COUNTRY GIRL AT HEART.
HMM...
WELL, THERE'S NOTHING THERE BUT ROCKS AND FRESH AIR.
THAT'S IT! THAT'S IT!

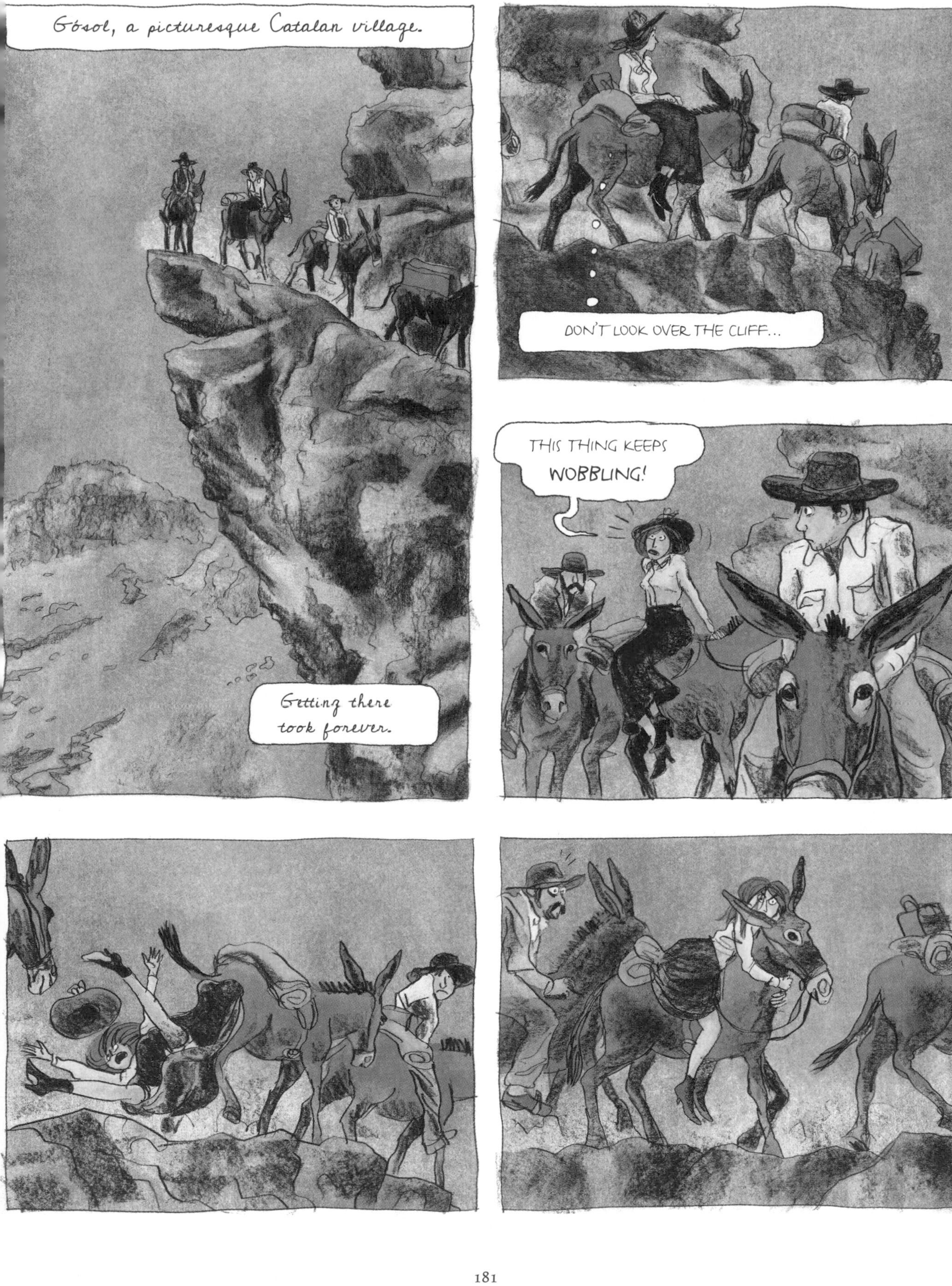
Gósol, a picturesque Catalan village.
Getting there took forever.
DON'T LOOK OVER THE CLIFF...
THIS THING KEEPS WOBBLING!

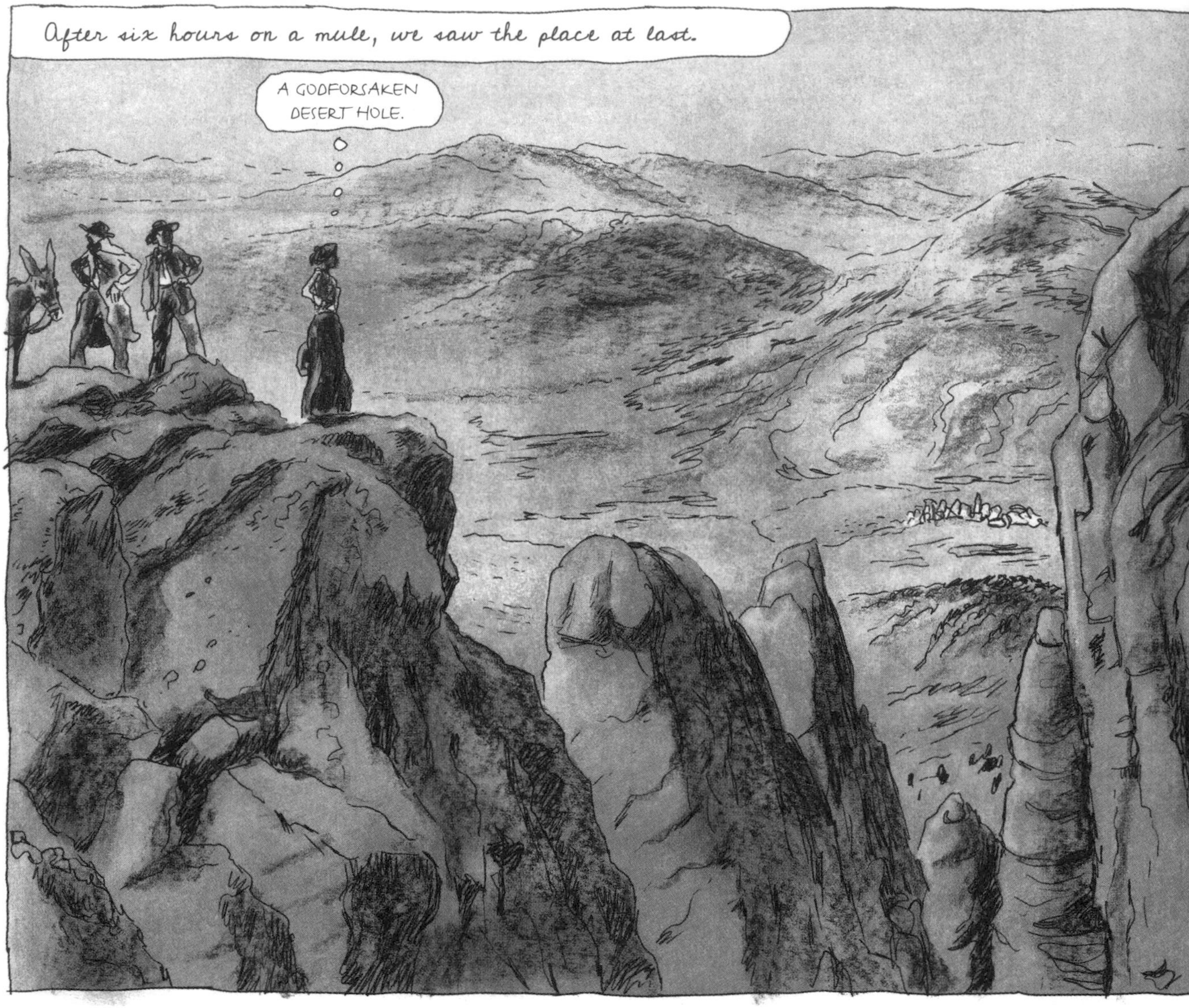
After six hours on a mule, we saw the place at last.
A GODFORSAKEN DESERT HOLE.

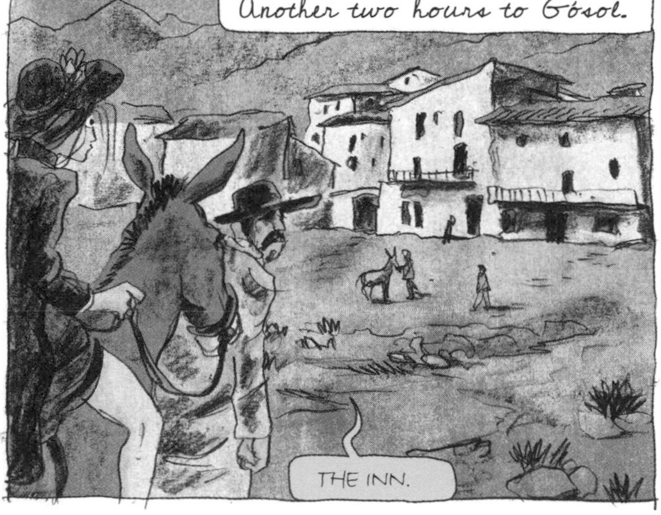
Another two hours to Gósol.
THE INN.

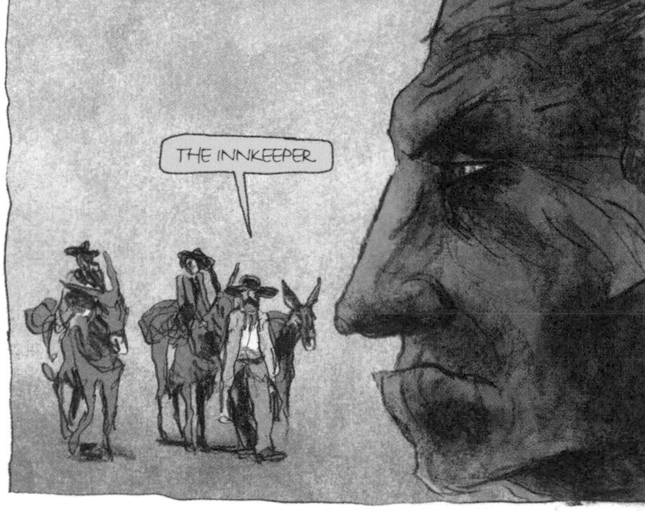
THE INNKEEPER

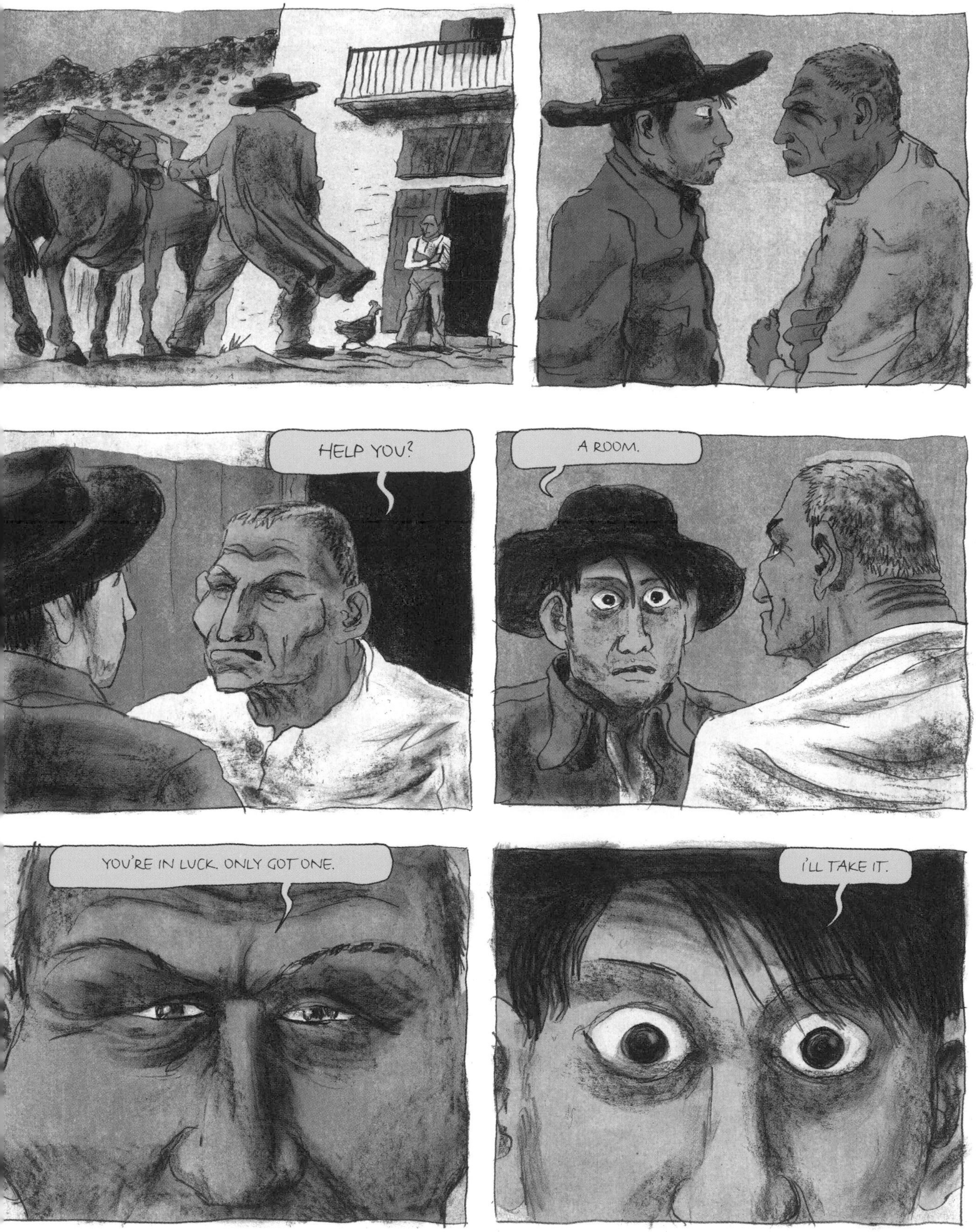
HELP YOU?
A ROOM.
YOU'RE IN LUCK. ONLY GOT ONE.
I'LL TAKE IT.

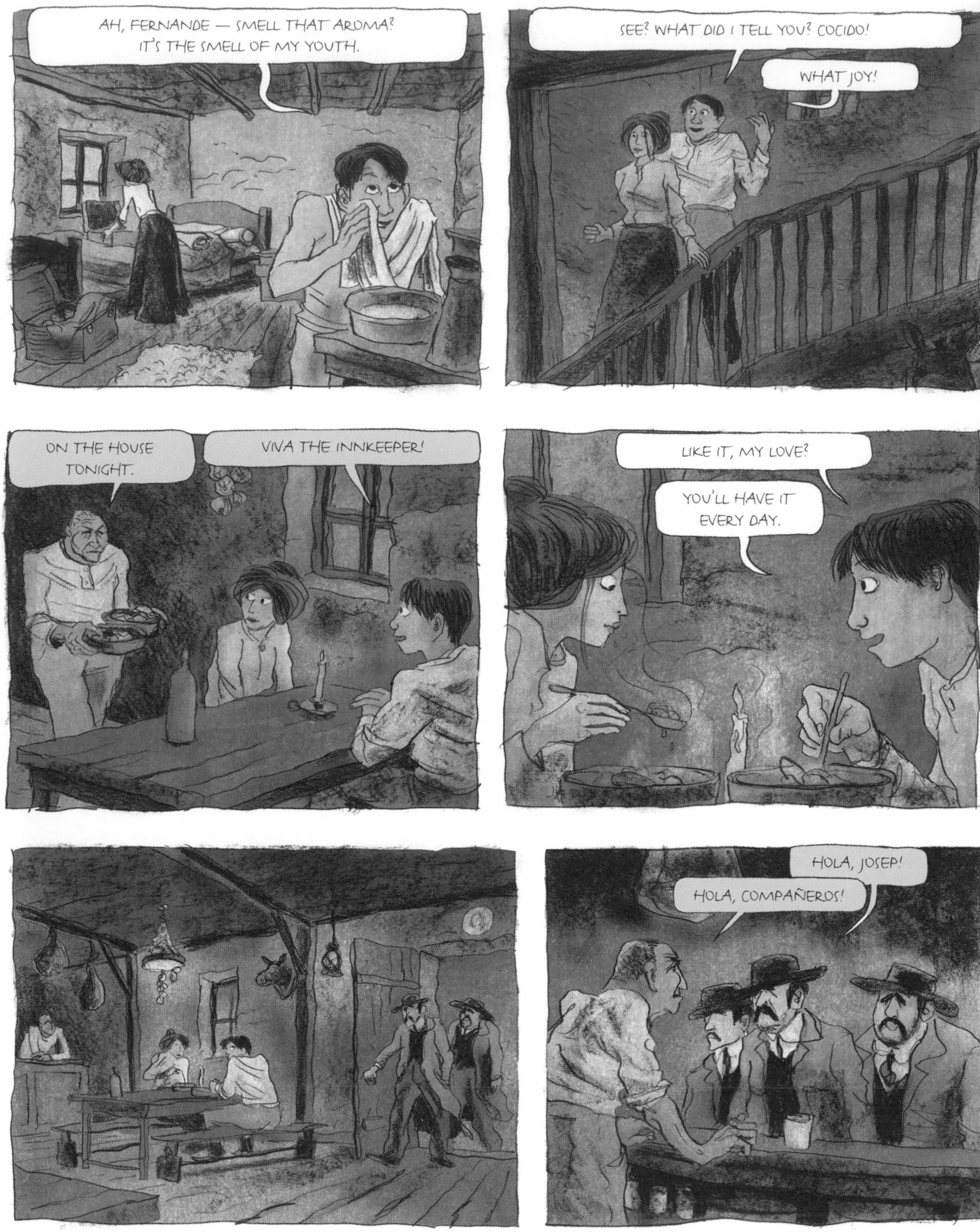
AH, FERNANDE — SMELL THAT AROMA? IT'S THE SMELL OF MY YOUTH.
SEE? WHAT DID I TELL YOU? COCIDO!
WHAT JOY!
ON THE HOUSE TONIGHT.
VIVA THE INNKEEPER!
LIKE IT, MY LOVE?
YOU'LL HAVE IT EVERY DAY.
HOLA, JOSEP!
HOLA, COMPAÑEROS!

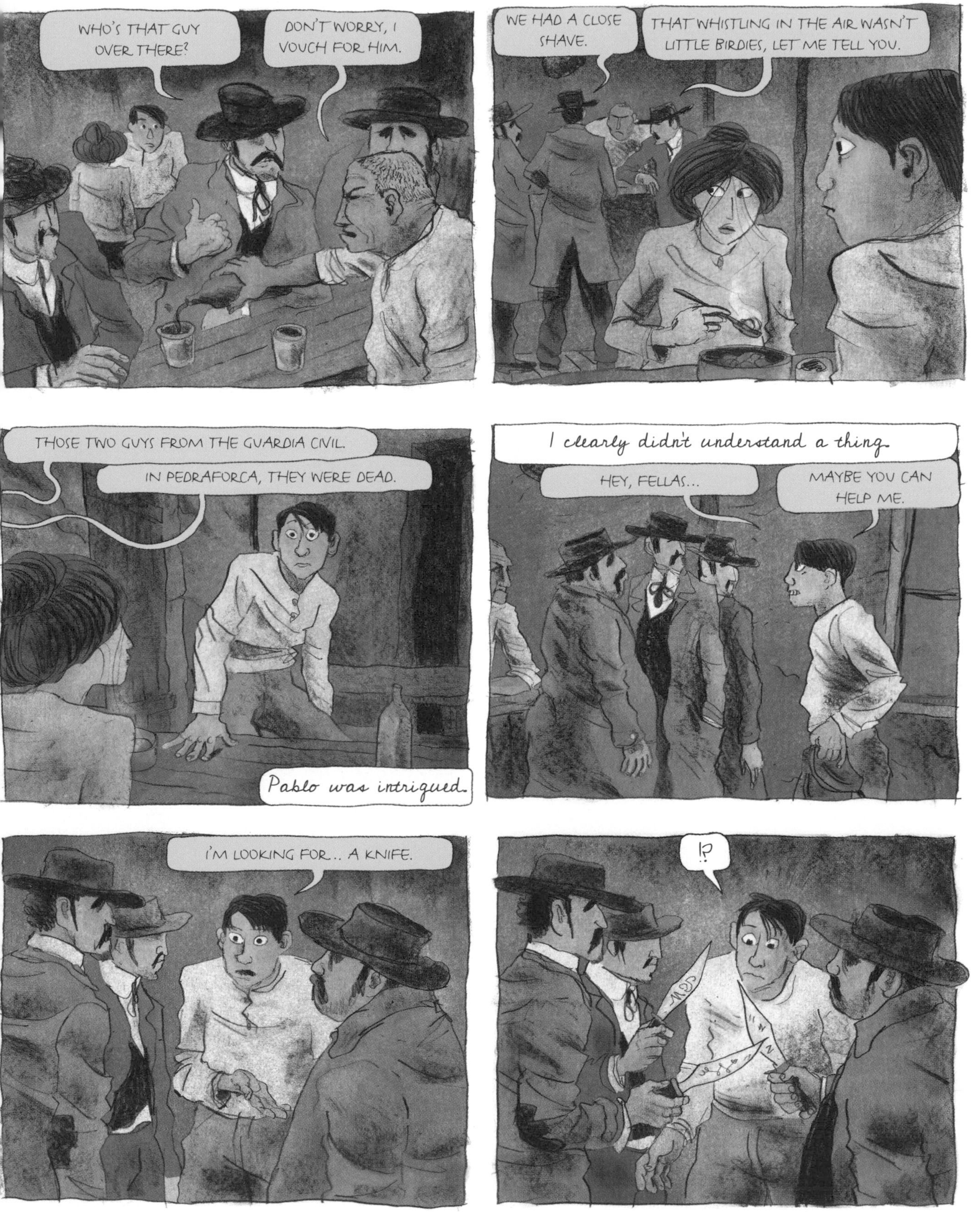
WHO'S THAT GUY OVER THERE?
DON'T WORRY, I VOUCH FOR HIM.
WE HAD A CLOSE SHAVE.
THAT WHISTLING IN THE AIR WASN'T LITTLE BIRDIES, LET ME TELL YOU.
THOSE TWO GUYS FROM THE GUARDIA CIVIL.
IN PEDRAFORCA, THEY WERE DEAD.
Pablo was intrigued.
I clearly didn't understand a thing.
HEY, FELLAS...
MAYBE YOU CAN HELP ME.
I'M LOOKING FOR... A KNIFE.
!?

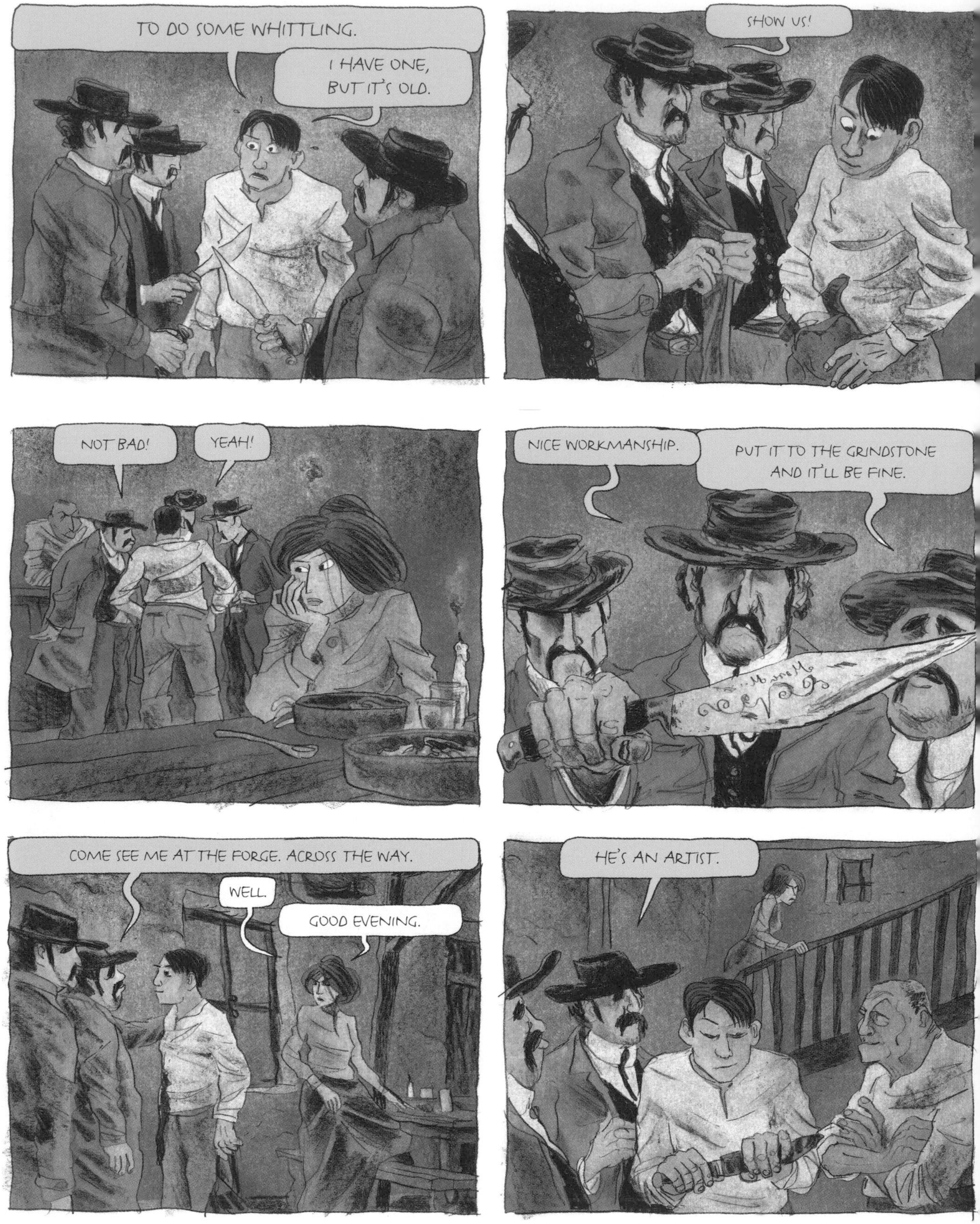

TO DO SOME WHITTLING.
I HAVE ONE, BUT IT'S OLD.
SHOW US!
NOT BAD!
YEAH!
NICE WORKMANSHIP.
PUT IT TO THE GRINDSTONE AND IT'LL BE FINE.
COME SEE ME AT THE FORGE. ACROSS THE WAY.
WELL.
GOOD EVENING.
HE'S AN ARTIST.

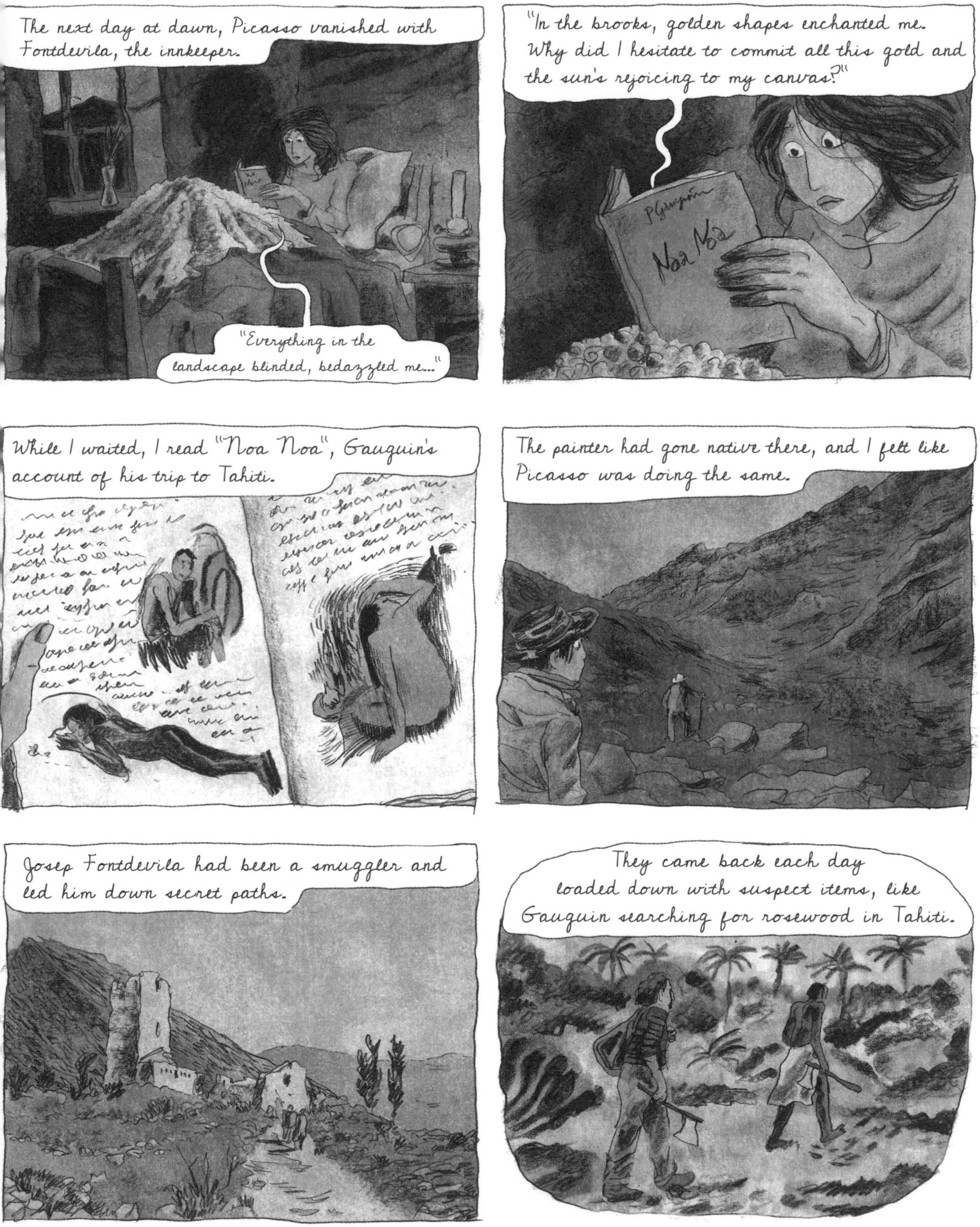
The next day at dawn, Picasso vanished with Fontdevila, the innkeeper.
"Everything in the landscape blinded, bedazzled me..."
"In the brooks, golden shapes enchanted me. Why did I hesitate to commit all this gold and the sun's rejoicing to my canvas?"
Noa Noa
While I waited, I read "Noa Noa", Gauguin's account of his trip to Tahiti.
The painter had gone native there, and I felt like Picasso was doing the same.
Josep Fontdevila had been a smuggler and led him down secret paths.
They came back each day loaded down with suspect items, like Gauguin searching for rosewood in Tahiti.

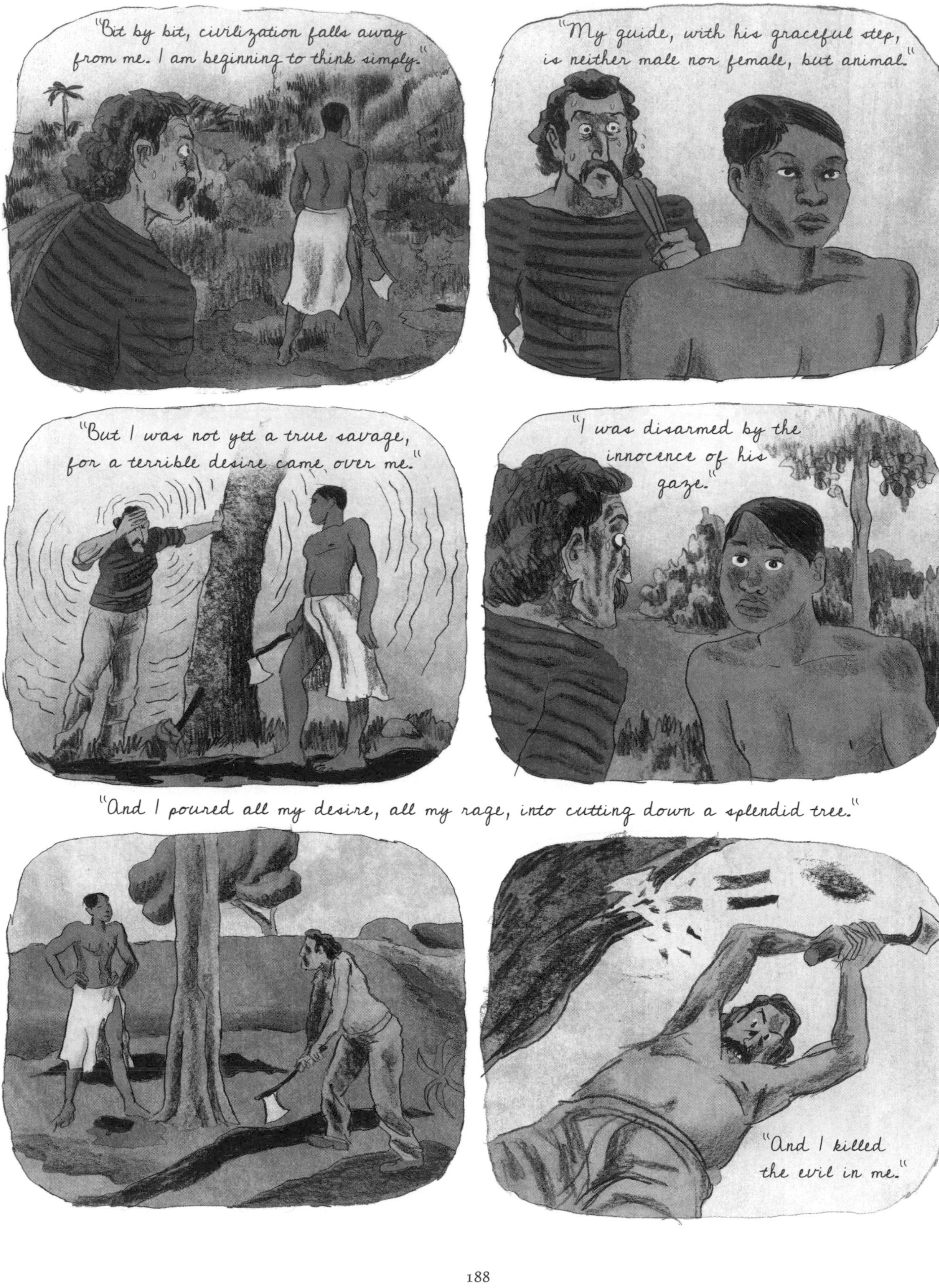
"Bit by bit, civilization falls away from me. I am beginning to think simply."
"My guide, with his graceful step, is neither male nor female, but animal."
"But I was not yet a true savage, for a terrible desire came over me."
"I was disarmed by the innocence of his gaze."
"And I poured all my desire, all my rage, into cutting down a splendid tree."
"And I killed the evil in me."

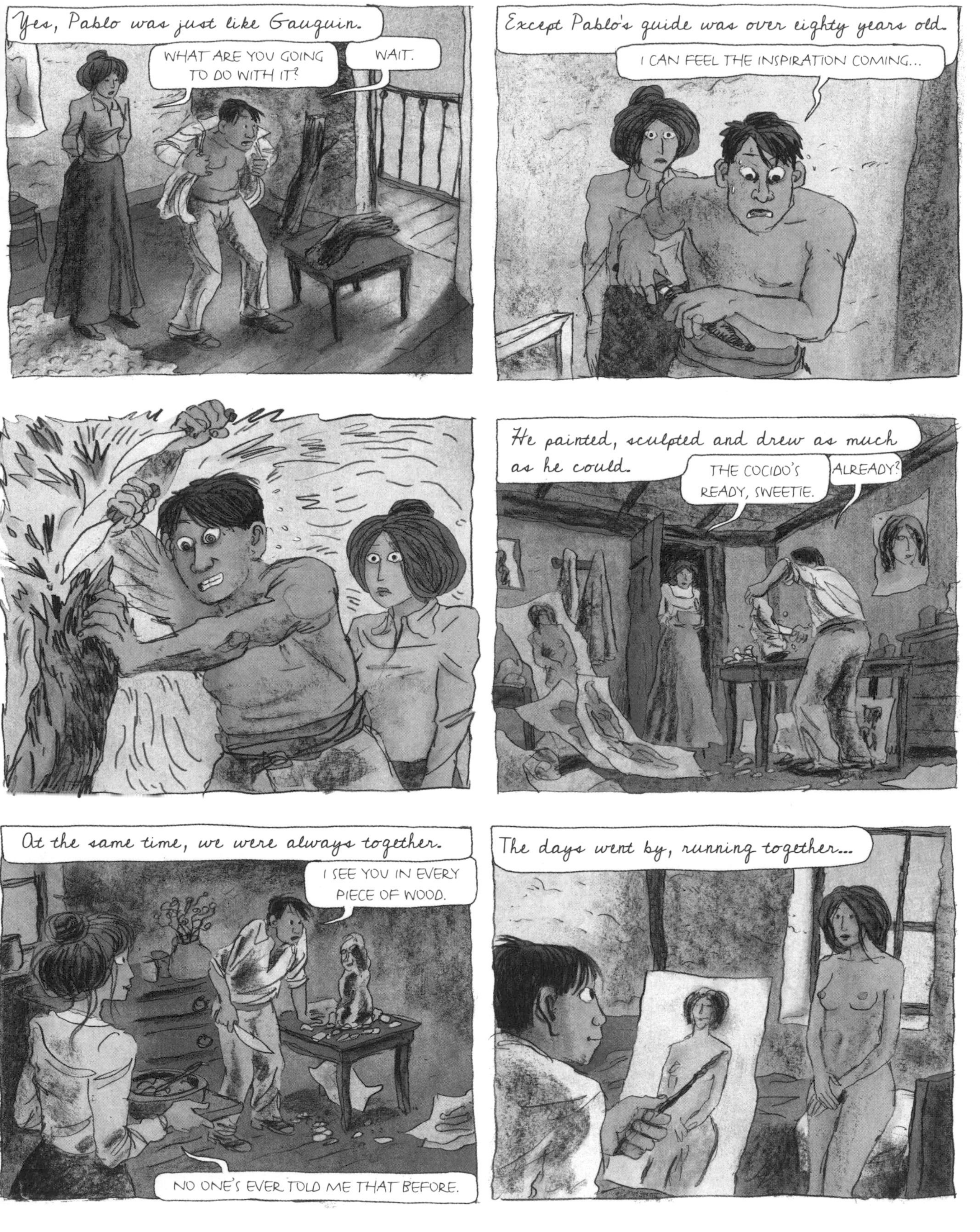
Yes, Pablo was just like Gauguin.
WHAT ARE YOU GOING TO DO WITH IT?
WAIT.
Except Pablo's guide was over eighty years old.
I CAN FEEL THE INSPIRATION COMING...
He painted, sculpted and drew as much as he could.
THE COCIDO'S READY, SWEETIE.
ALREADY?
At the same time, we were always together.
I SEE YOU IN EVERY PIECE OF WOOD.
NO ONE'S EVER TOLD ME THAT BEFORE.
The days went by, running together...

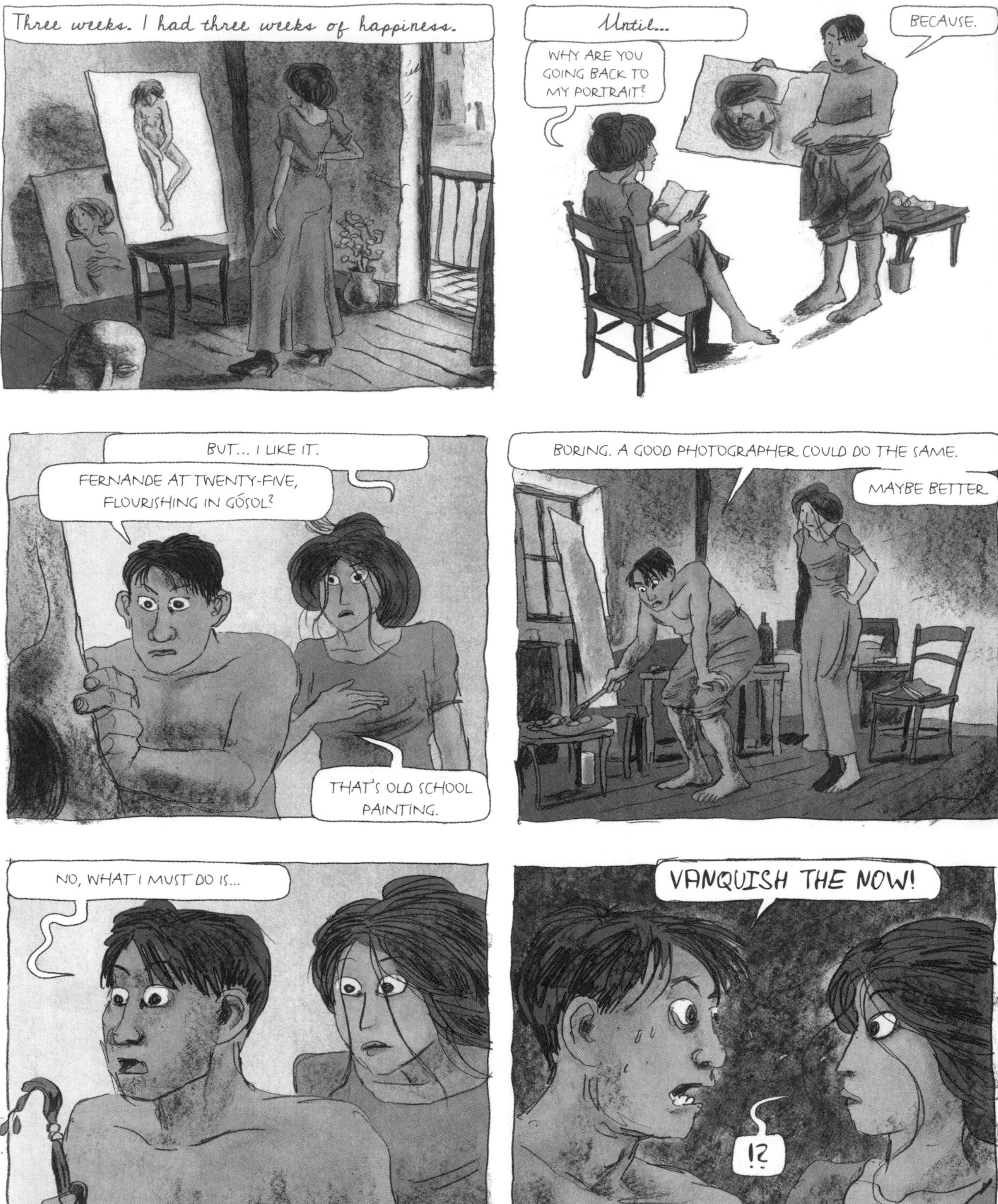

Three weeks. I had three weeks of happiness.
Until...
WHY ARE YOU GOING BACK TO MY PORTRAIT?
BECAUSE.
BUT... I LIKE IT.
FERNANDE AT TWENTY-FIVE, FLOURISHING IN GÓSOL?
THAT'S OLD SCHOOL PAINTING.
BORING. A GOOD PHOTOGRAPHER COULD DO THE SAME.
MAYBE BETTER.
NO, WHAT I MUST DO IS...
VANQUISH THE NOW!
!?

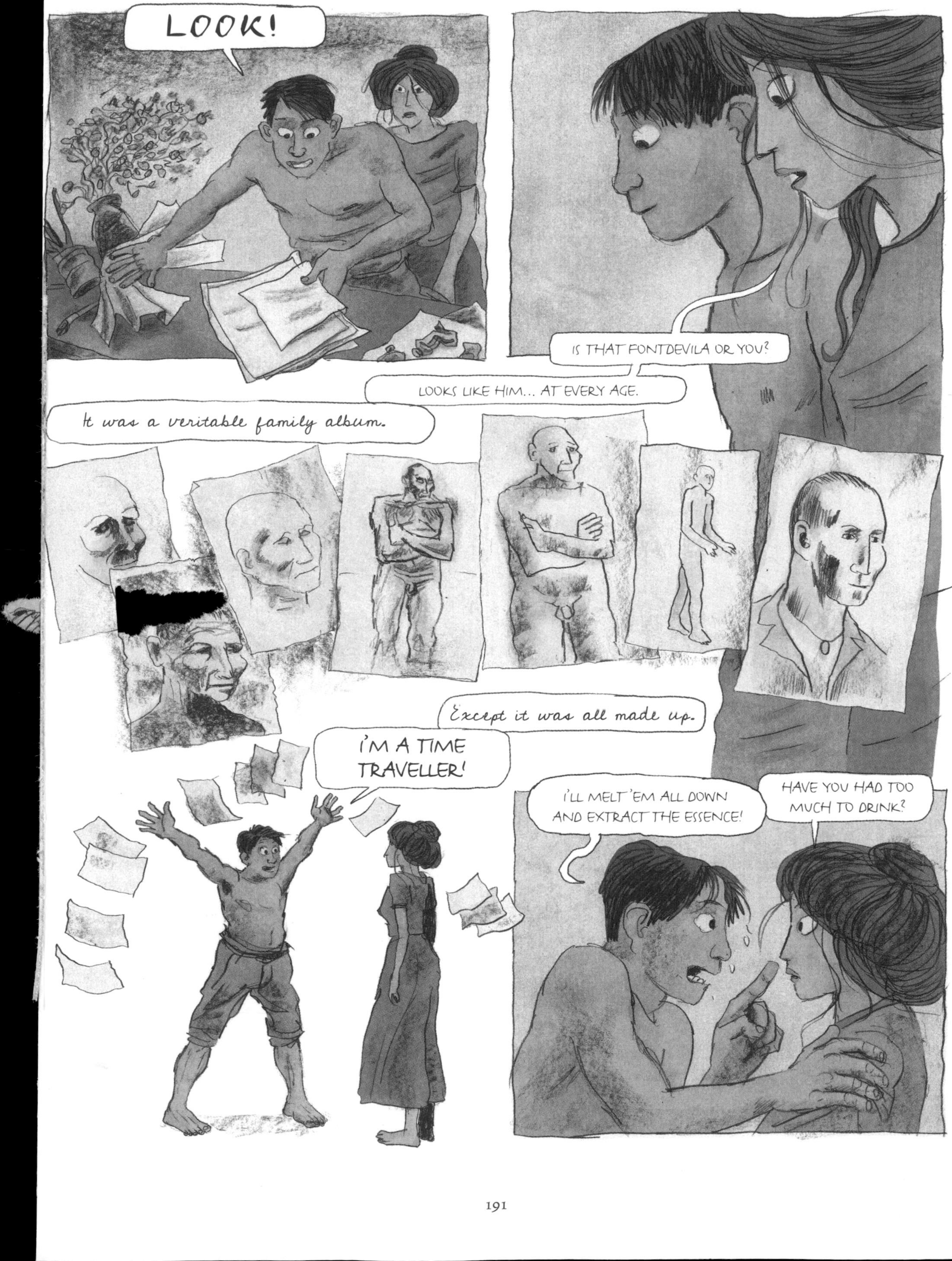
LOOK!
IS THAT FONTDEVILA OR YOU?
LOOKS LIKE HIM... AT EVERY AGE.
It was a veritable family album.
Except it was all made up.
I'M A TIME TRAVELLER!
I'LL MELT 'EM ALL DOWN AND EXTRACT THE ESSENCE!
HAVE YOU HAD TOO MUCH TO DRINK?

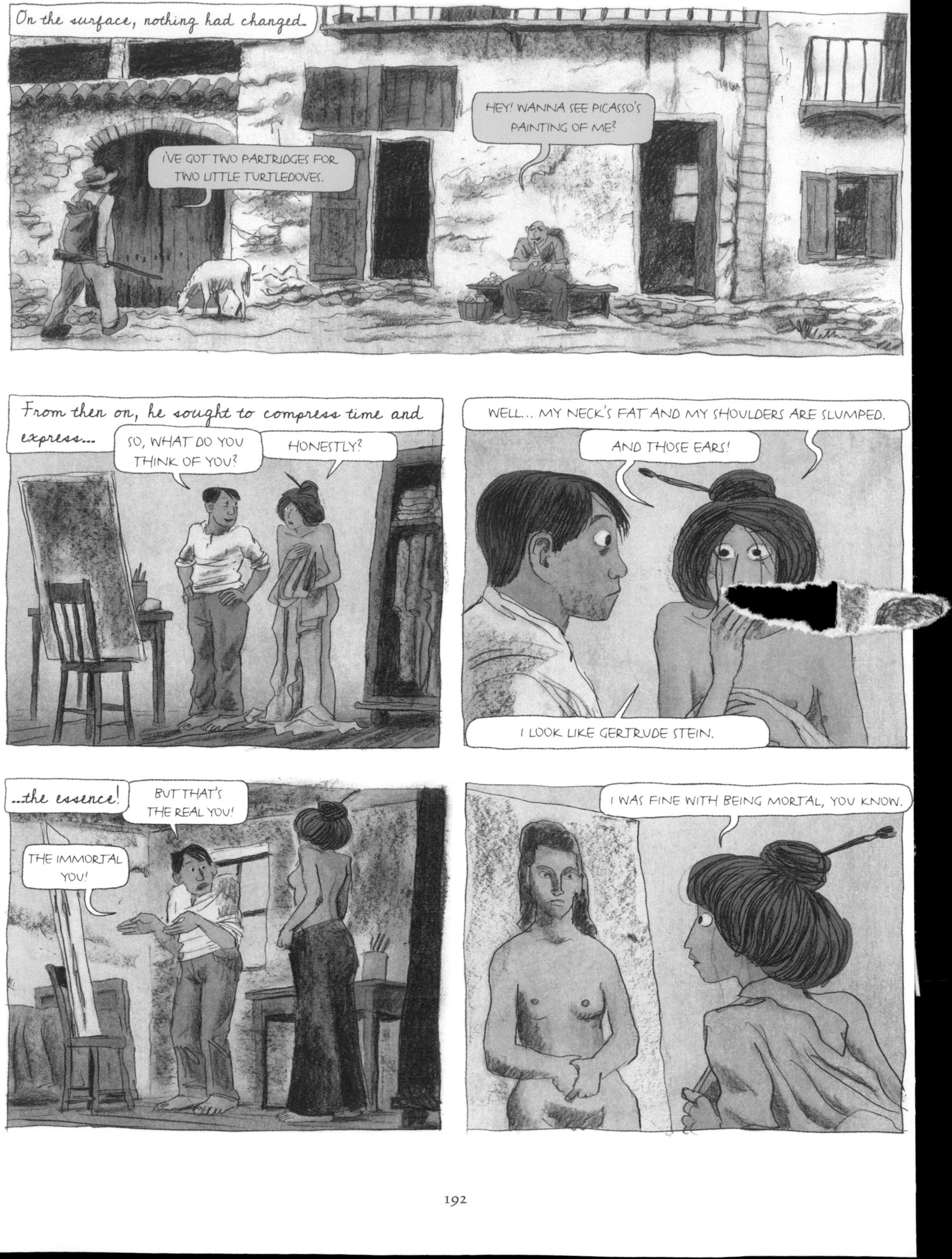
On the surface, nothing had changed.
I'VE GOT TWO PARTRIDGES FOR TWO LITTLE TURTLEDOVES.
HEY! WANNA SEE PICASSO'S PAINTING OF ME?
From then on, he sought to compress time and express...
SO, WHAT DO YOU THINK OF YOU?
HONESTLY?
WELL... MY NECK'S FAT AND MY SHOULDERS ARE SLUMPED.
AND THOSE EARS!
I LOOK LIKE GERTRUDE STEIN.
...the essence!
BUT THAT'S THE REAL YOU!
THE IMMORTAL YOU!
I WAS FINE WITH BEING MORTAL, YOU KNOW.

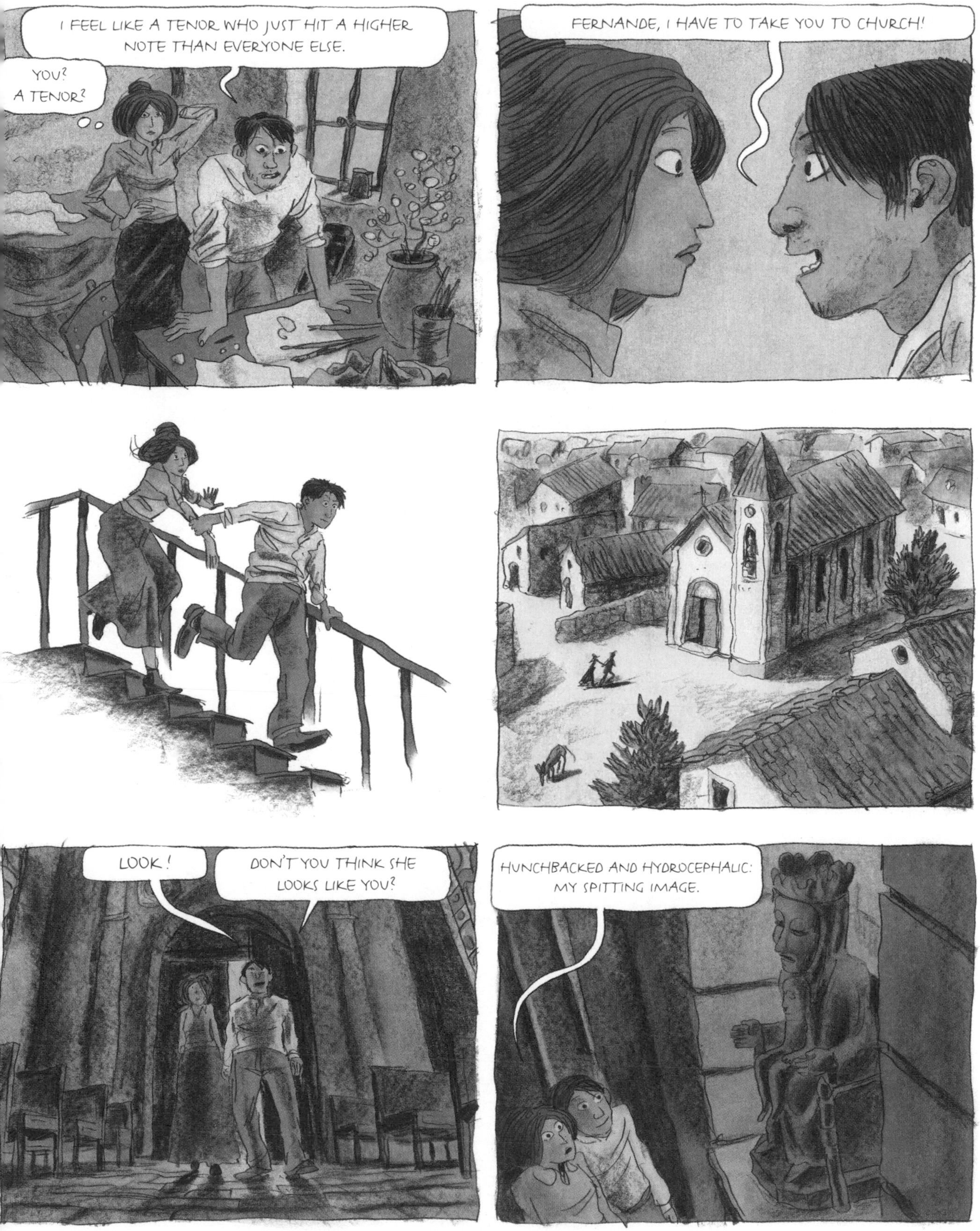
I FEEL LIKE A TENOR WHO JUST HIT A HIGHER NOTE THAN EVERYONE ELSE.
YOU? A TENOR?
FERNANDE, I HAVE TO TAKE YOU TO CHURCH!
LOOK!
DON'T YOU THINK SHE LOOKS LIKE YOU?
HUNCHBACKED AND HYDROCEPHALIC: MY SPITTING IMAGE.

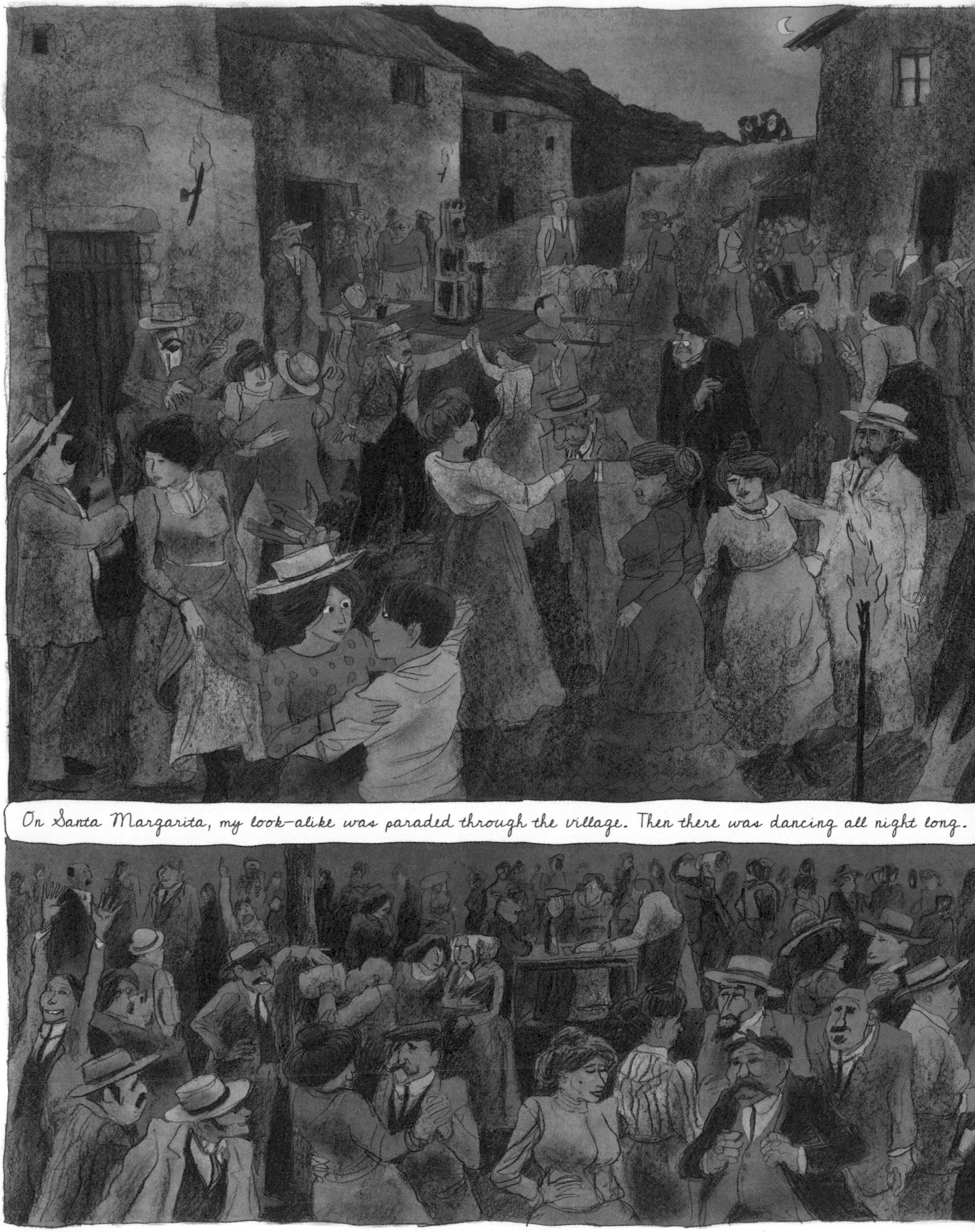
On Santa Margarita, my look-alike was paraded through the village. Then there was dancing all night long.

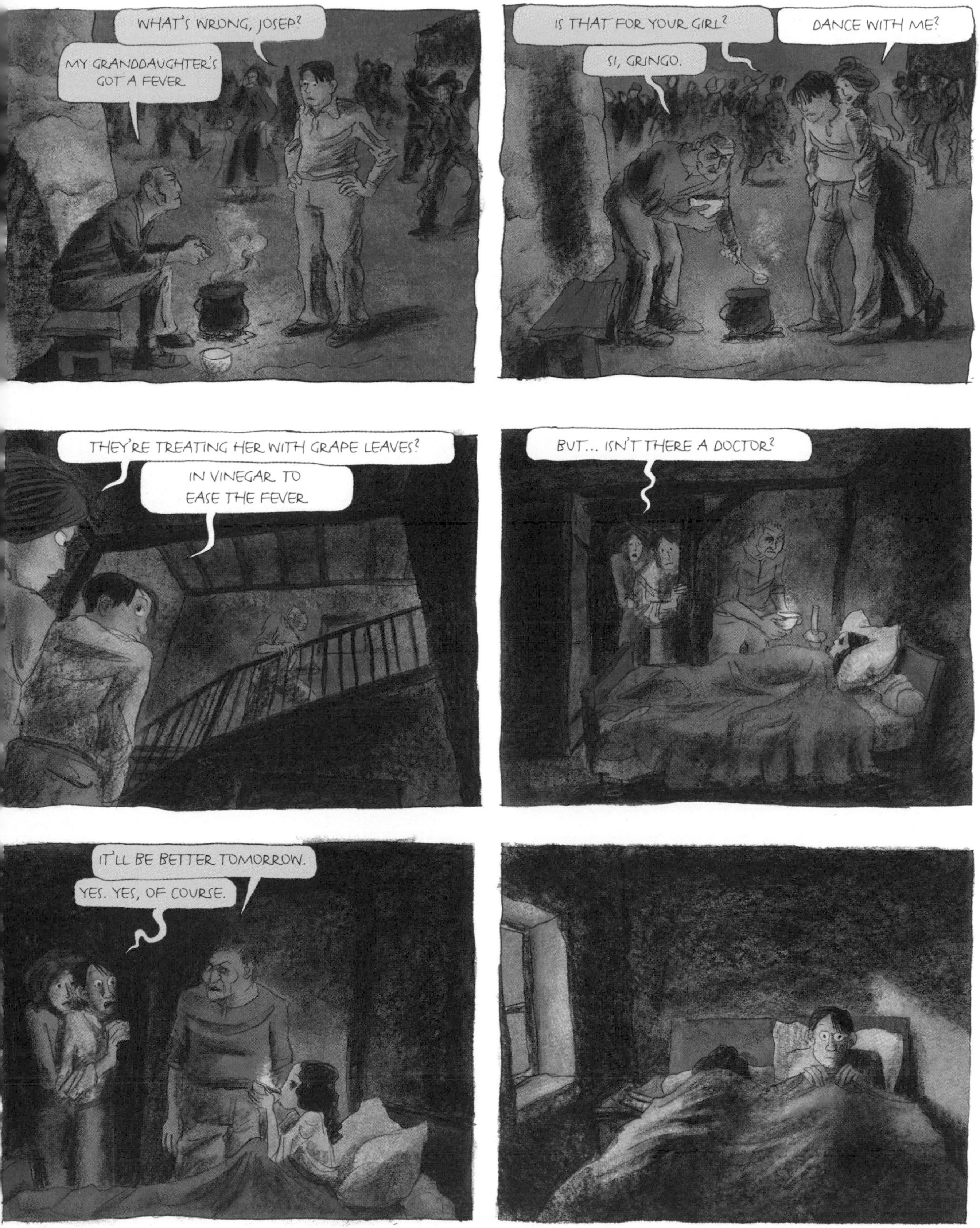
WHAT'S WRONG, JOSEP?
MY GRANDDAUGHTER'S GOT A FEVER
IS THAT FOR YOUR GIRL?
SI, GRINGO.
DANCE WITH ME?
THEY'RE TREATING HER WITH GRAPE LEAVES?
IN VINEGAR TO EASE THE FEVER
BUT... ISN'T THERE A DOCTOR?
IT'LL BE BETTER TOMORROW.
YES. YES, OF COURSE.

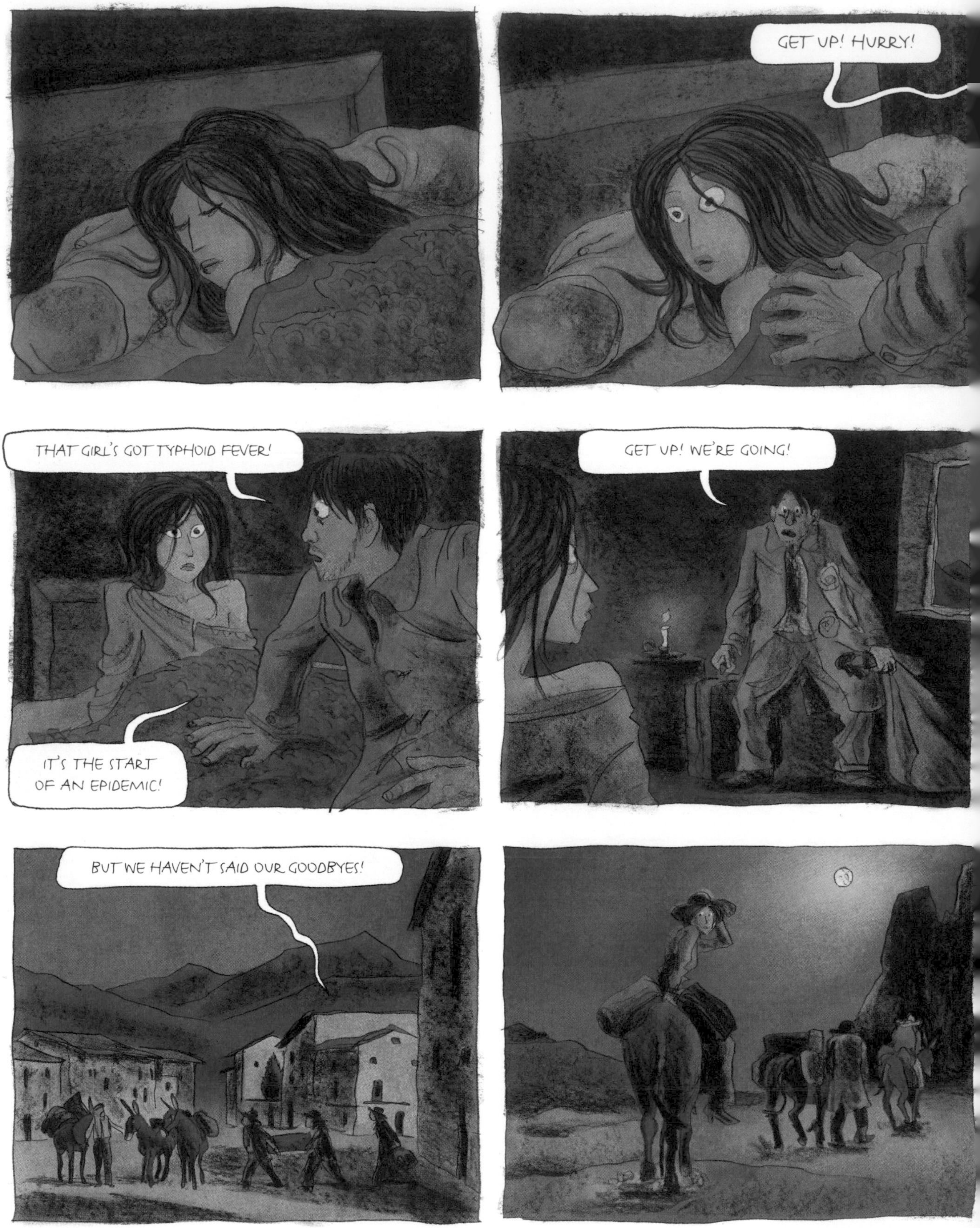
GET UP! HURRY!
THAT GIRL'S GOT TYPHOID FEVER!
IT'S THE START OF AN EPIDEMIC!
GET UP! WE'RE GOING!
BUT WE HAVEN'T SAID OUR GOODBYES!

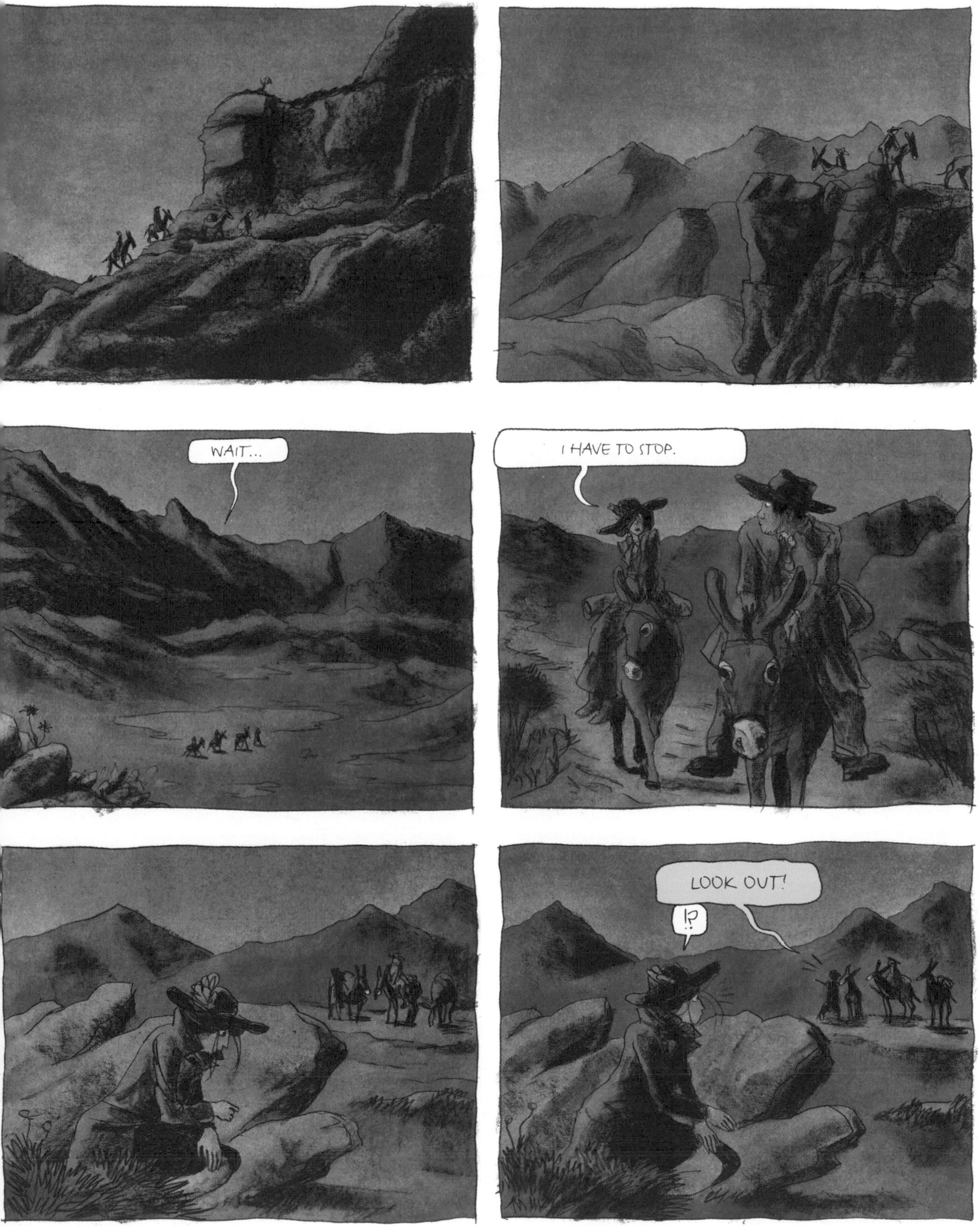
WAIT...
I HAVE TO STOP.
!?
LOOK OUT!

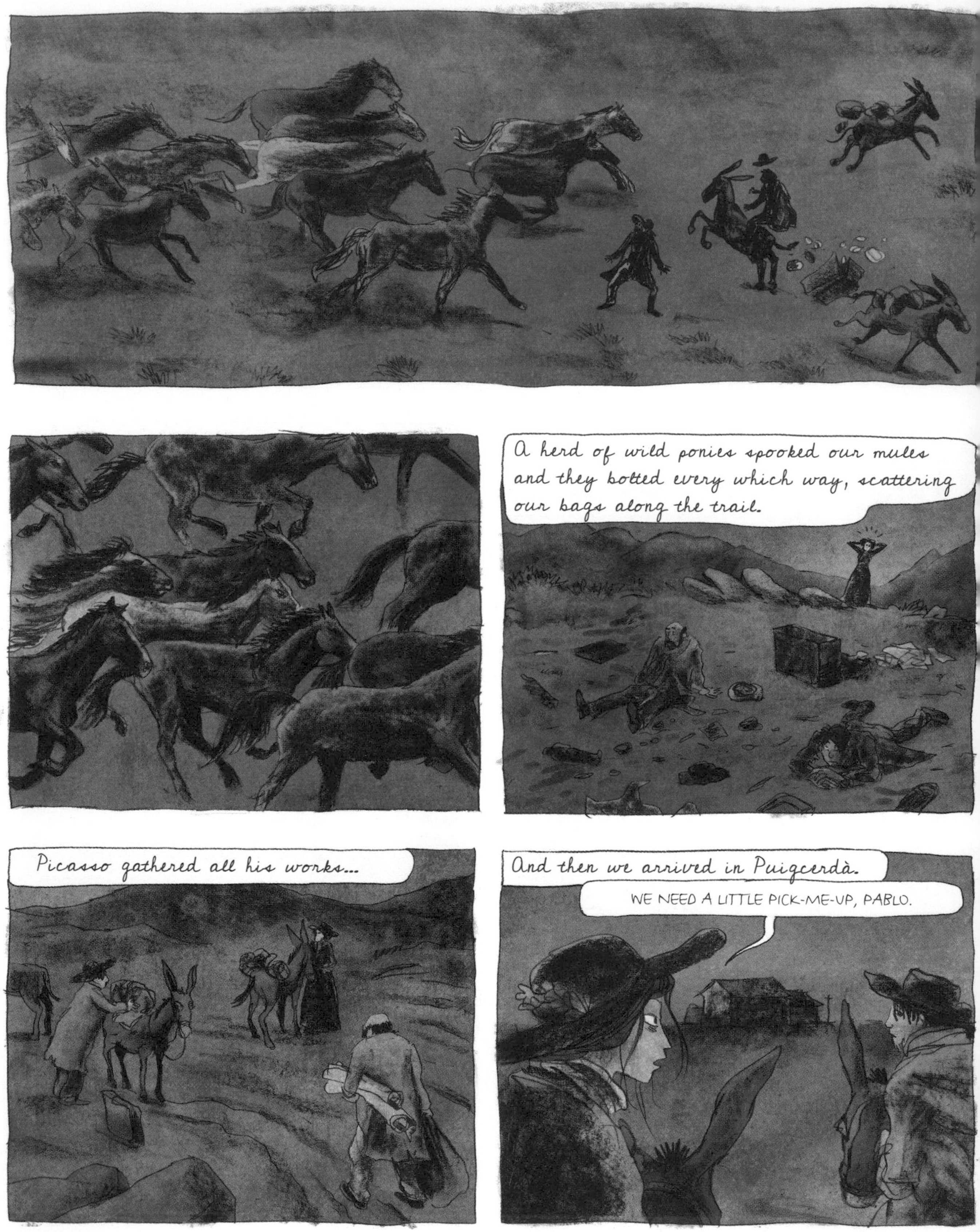
A herd of wild ponies spooked our mules and they bolted every which way, scattering our bags along the trail.
Picasso gathered all his works...
And then we arrived in Puigcerdà.
WE NEED A LITTLE PICK-ME-UP, PABLO.

After the white wine at the station restaurant, I had a devil of a time climbing into the train.

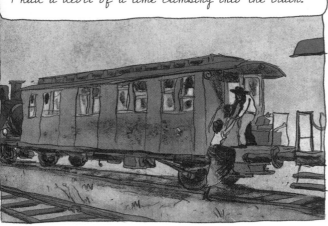

WE MADE IT!

!?

GOD WAS AGAINST US, EH? BUT WE PULLED THE EVIL OUT BY ITS ROOTS!

IF I'D STAYED, SHE WOULD'VE DIED. GOD ALWAYS PUNISHES ME LIKE THAT.

YOU THINK I'M CRAZY?

OH, I'M NOT CRAZY, FERNANDE...

"WHEN I WAS THIRTEEN, MY LITTLE SISTER GOT DIPHTHERIA."

HOW'S SHE LOOKING, DOCTOR?

PALE, VERY PALE...

OH GOD... MAKE HER BETTER AND I'LL STOP PAINTING.

"I MEANT IT, BUT I DIDN'T KNOW WHAT I WAS SAYING."

CONCHITA IS DEAD.

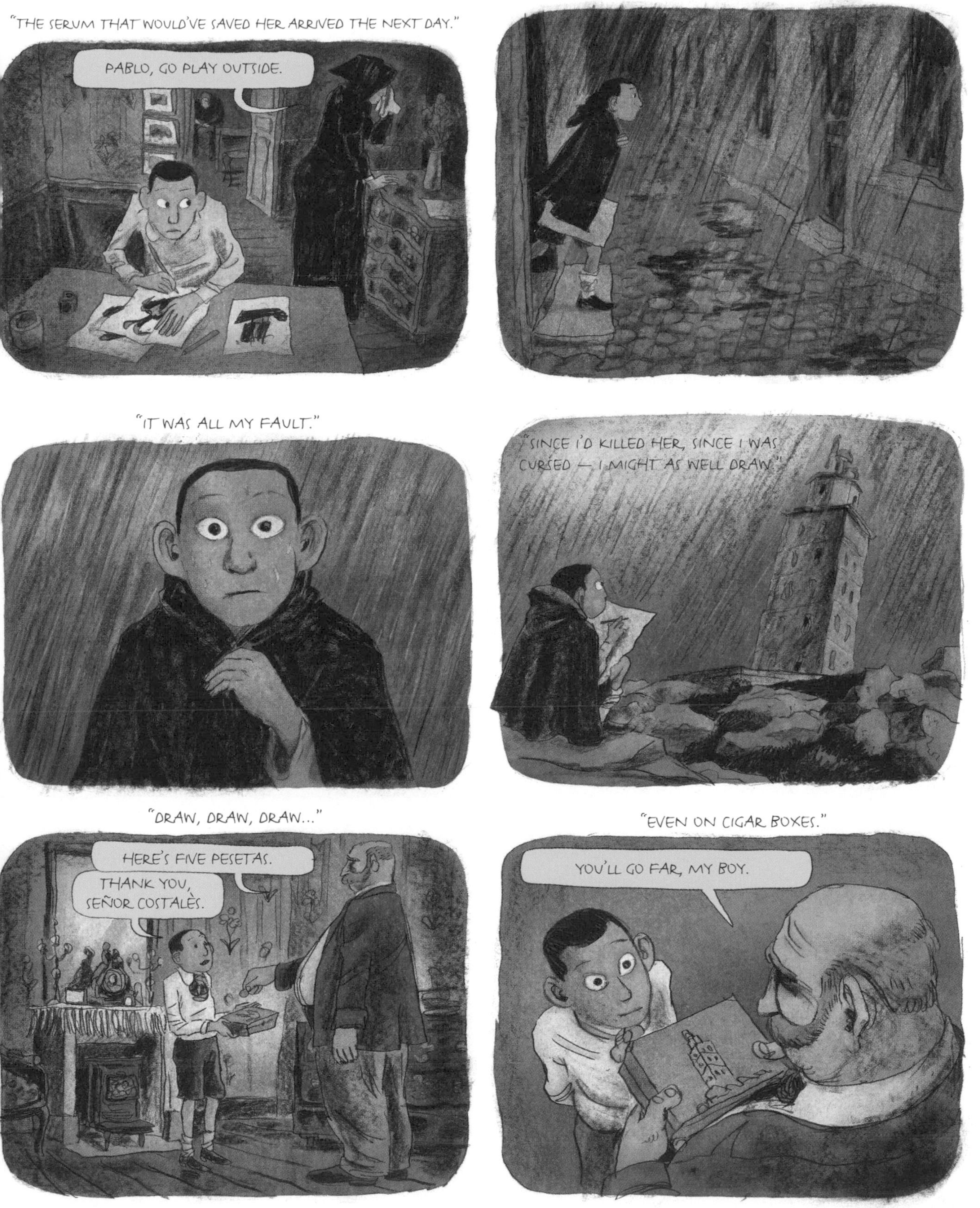
"THE SERUM THAT WOULD'VE SAVED HER ARRIVED THE NEXT DAY."
PABLO, GO PLAY OUTSIDE.
"IT WAS ALL MY FAULT."
"SINCE I'D KILLED HER, SINCE I WAS CURSED — I MIGHT AS WELL DRAW."
"DRAW, DRAW, DRAW..."
HERE'S FIVE PESETAS.
THANK YOU, SEÑOR COSTALÈS.
"EVEN ON CIGAR BOXES."
YOU'LL GO FAR, MY BOY.

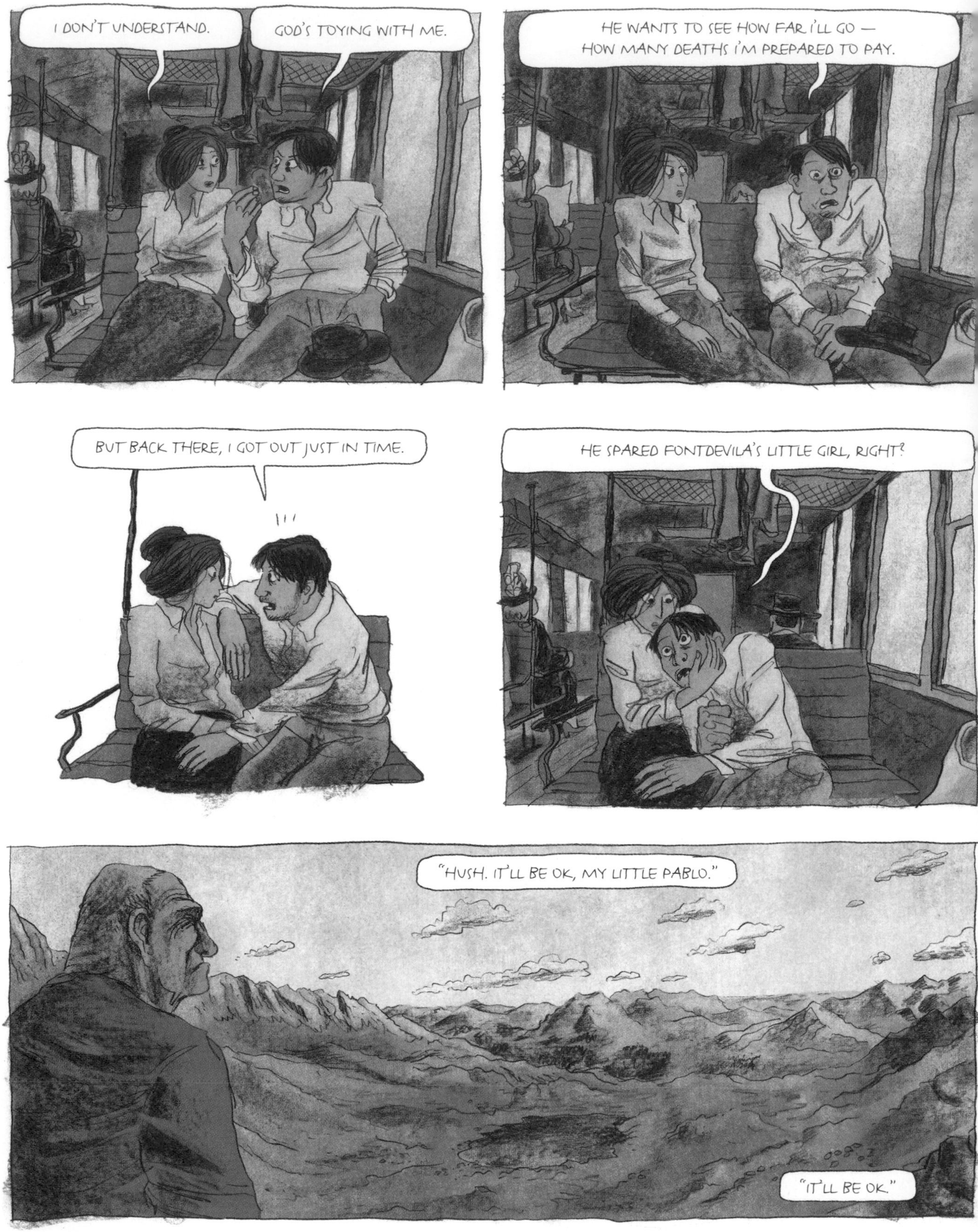
I DON'T UNDERSTAND.
GOD'S TOYING WITH ME.
HE WANTS TO SEE HOW FAR I'LL GO — HOW MANY DEATHS I'M PREPARED TO PAY.
BUT BACK THERE, I GOT OUT JUST IN TIME.
HE SPARED FONTDEVILA'S LITTLE GIRL, RIGHT?
"HUSH. IT'LL BE OK, MY LITTLE PABLO."
"IT'LL BE OK."

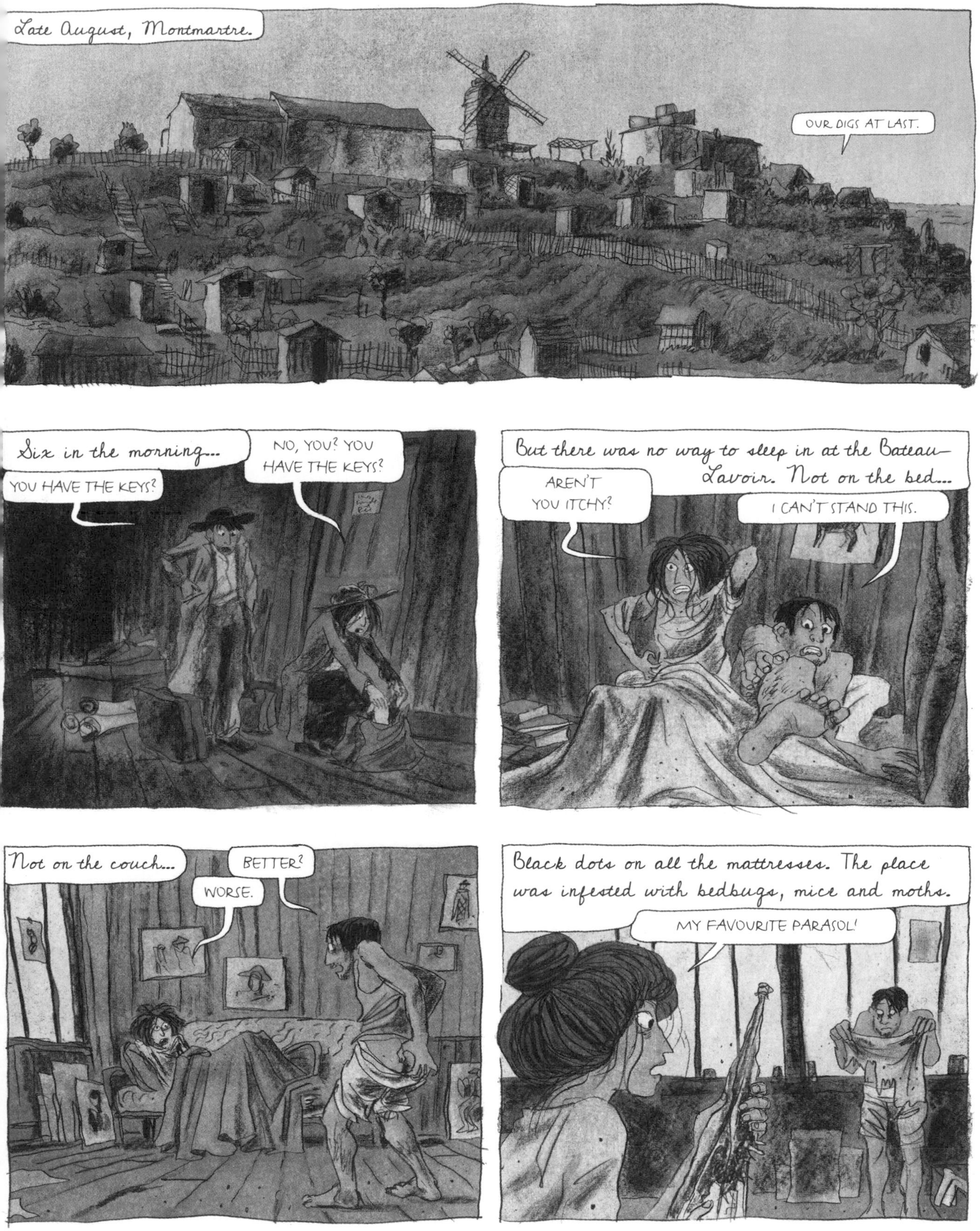
Late August, Montmartre.
OUR DIGS AT LAST.
Six in the morning...
YOU HAVE THE KEYS?
NO, YOU? YOU HAVE THE KEYS?
But there was no way to sleep in at the Bateau-Lavoir. Not on the bed...
AREN'T YOU ITCHY?
I CAN'T STAND THIS.
Not on the couch...
BETTER?
WORSE.
Black dots on all the mattresses. The place was infested with bedbugs, mice and moths.
MY FAVOURITE PARASOL!

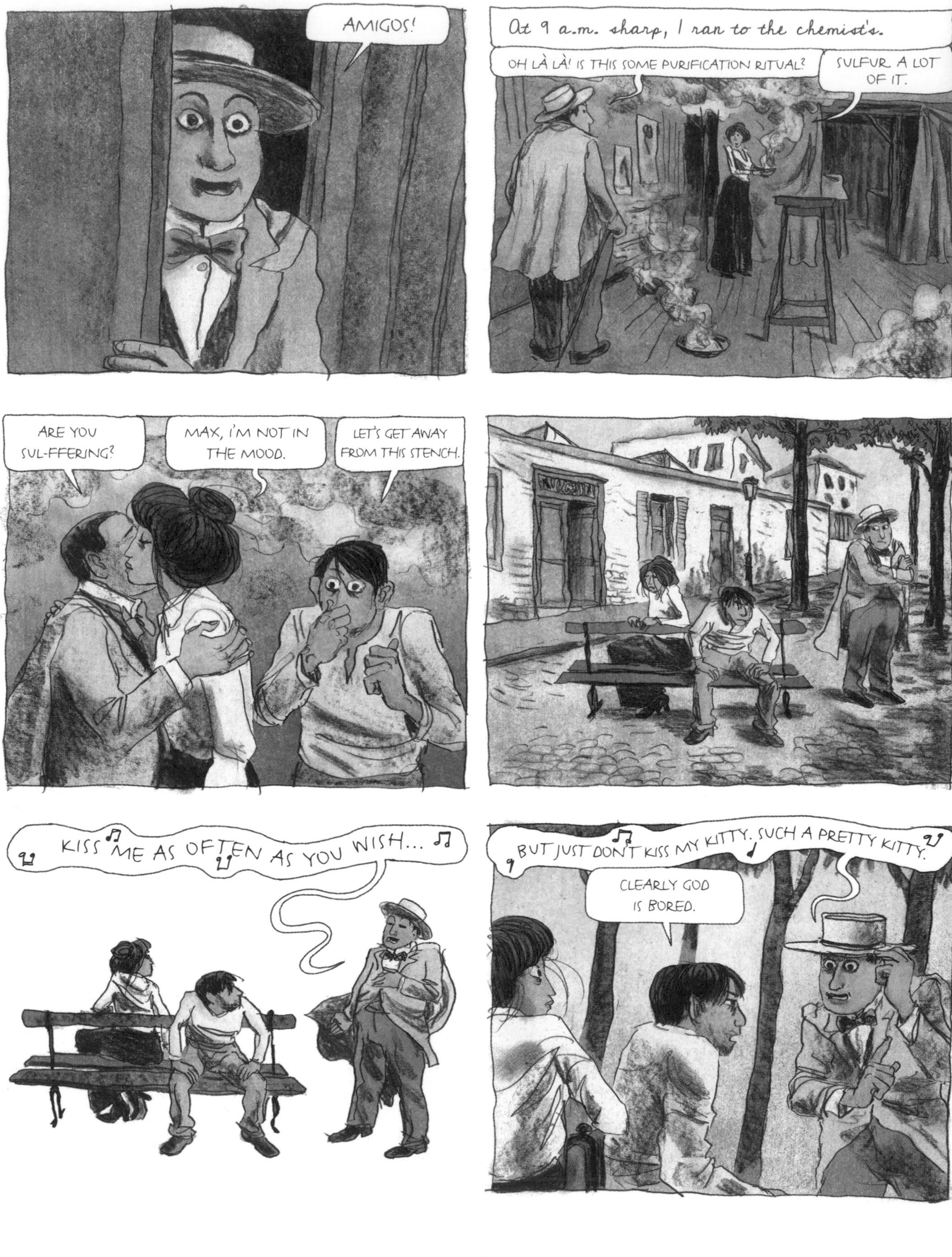
AMIGOS!
At 9 a.m. sharp, I ran to the chemist's.
OH LÀ LÀ! IS THIS SOME PURIFICATION RITUAL?
SULFUR. A LOT OF IT.
ARE YOU SUL-FFERING?
MAX, I'M NOT IN THE MOOD.
LET'S GET AWAY FROM THIS STENCH.
KISS ME AS OFTEN AS YOU WISH...
BUT JUST DON'T KISS MY KITTY. SUCH A PRETTY KITTY.
CLEARLY GOD IS BORED.

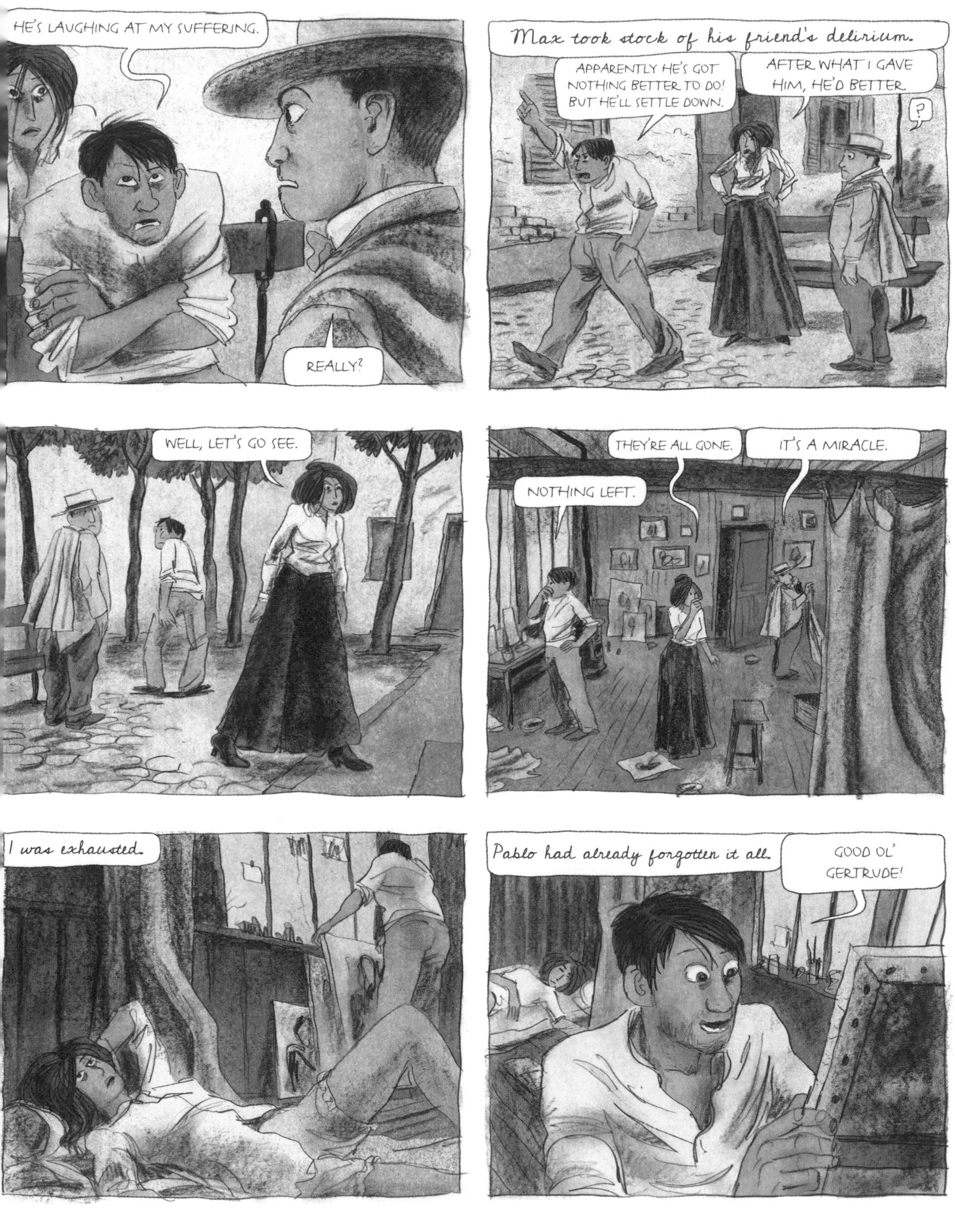
HE'S LAUGHING AT MY SUFFERING.
REALLY?
Max took stock of his friend's delirium.
APPARENTLY HE'S GOT NOTHING BETTER TO DO! BUT HE'LL SETTLE DOWN.
AFTER WHAT I GAVE HIM, HE'D BETTER.
?
WELL, LET'S GO SEE.
NOTHING LEFT.
THEY'RE ALL GONE.
IT'S A MIRACLE.
I was exhausted.
Pablo had already forgotten it all.
GOOD OL' GERTRUDE!

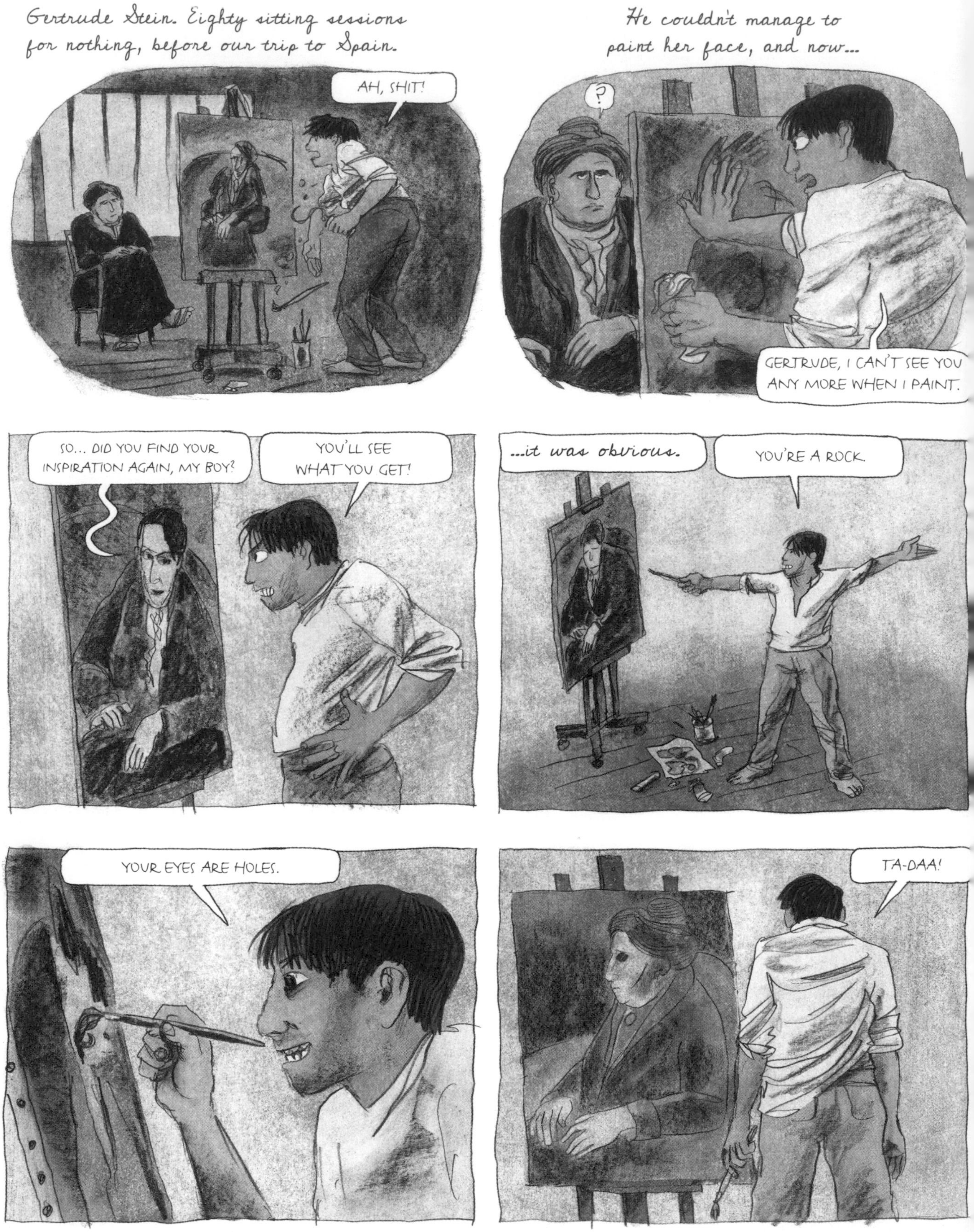
Gertrude Stein. Eighty sitting sessions for nothing, before our trip to Spain.
AH, SHIT!
He couldn't manage to paint her face, and now...
?
GERTRUDE, I CAN'T SEE YOU ANY MORE WHEN I PAINT.
SO... DID YOU FIND YOUR INSPIRATION AGAIN, MY BOY?
YOU'LL SEE WHAT YOU GET!
...it was obvious.
YOU'RE A ROCK.
YOUR EYES ARE HOLES.
TA-DAA!

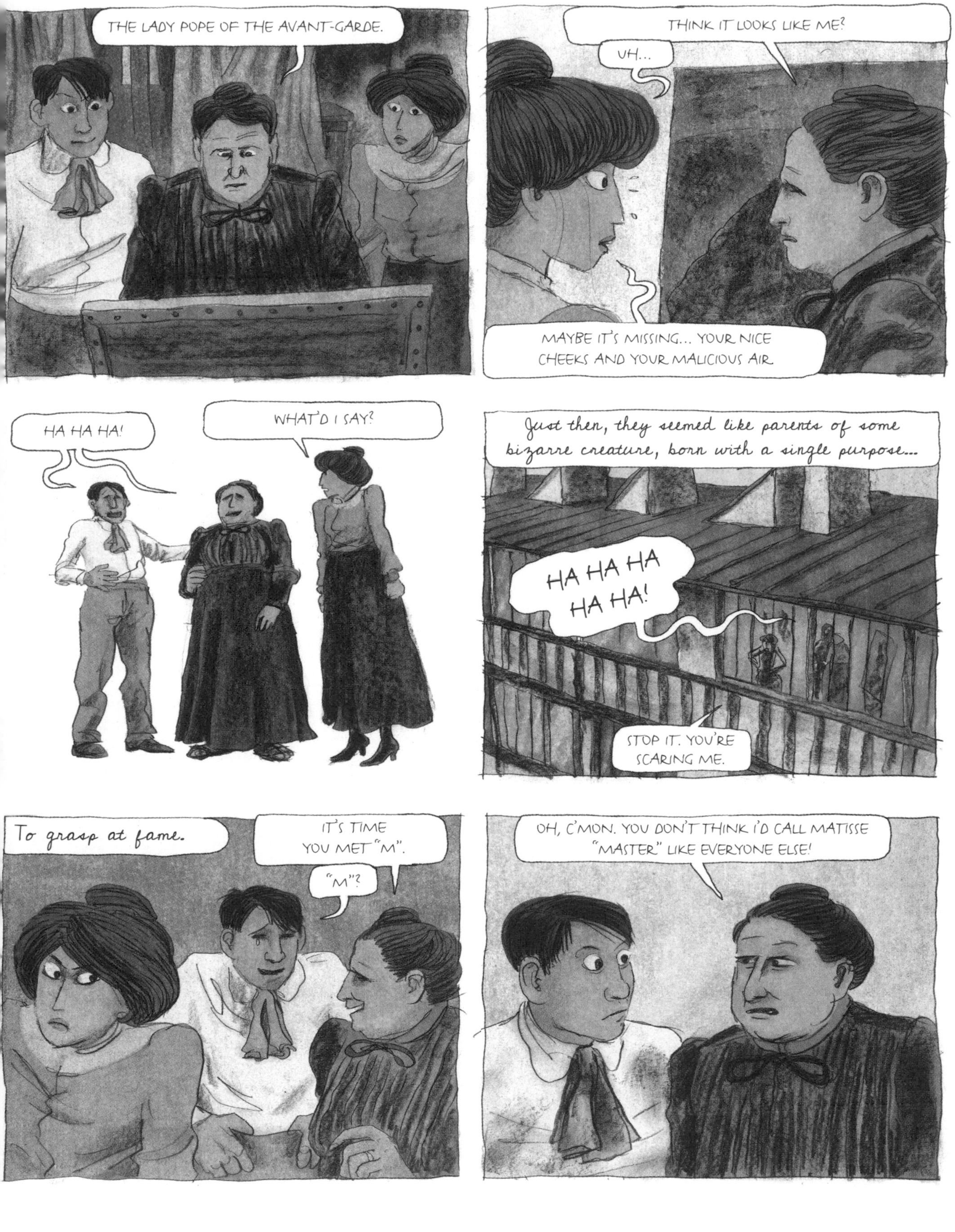
THE LADY POPE OF THE AVANT-GARDE.
THINK IT LOOKS LIKE ME?
UH...
MAYBE IT'S MISSING... YOUR NICE CHEEKS AND YOUR MALICIOUS AIR
HA HA HA!
WHAT'D I SAY?
Just then, they seemed like parents of some bizarre creature, born with a single purpose...
HA HA HA HA HA!
STOP IT. YOU'RE SCARING ME.
To grasp at fame.
IT'S TIME YOU MET "M".
"M"?
OH, C'MON. YOU DON'T THINK I'D CALL MATISSE "MASTER" LIKE EVERYONE ELSE!

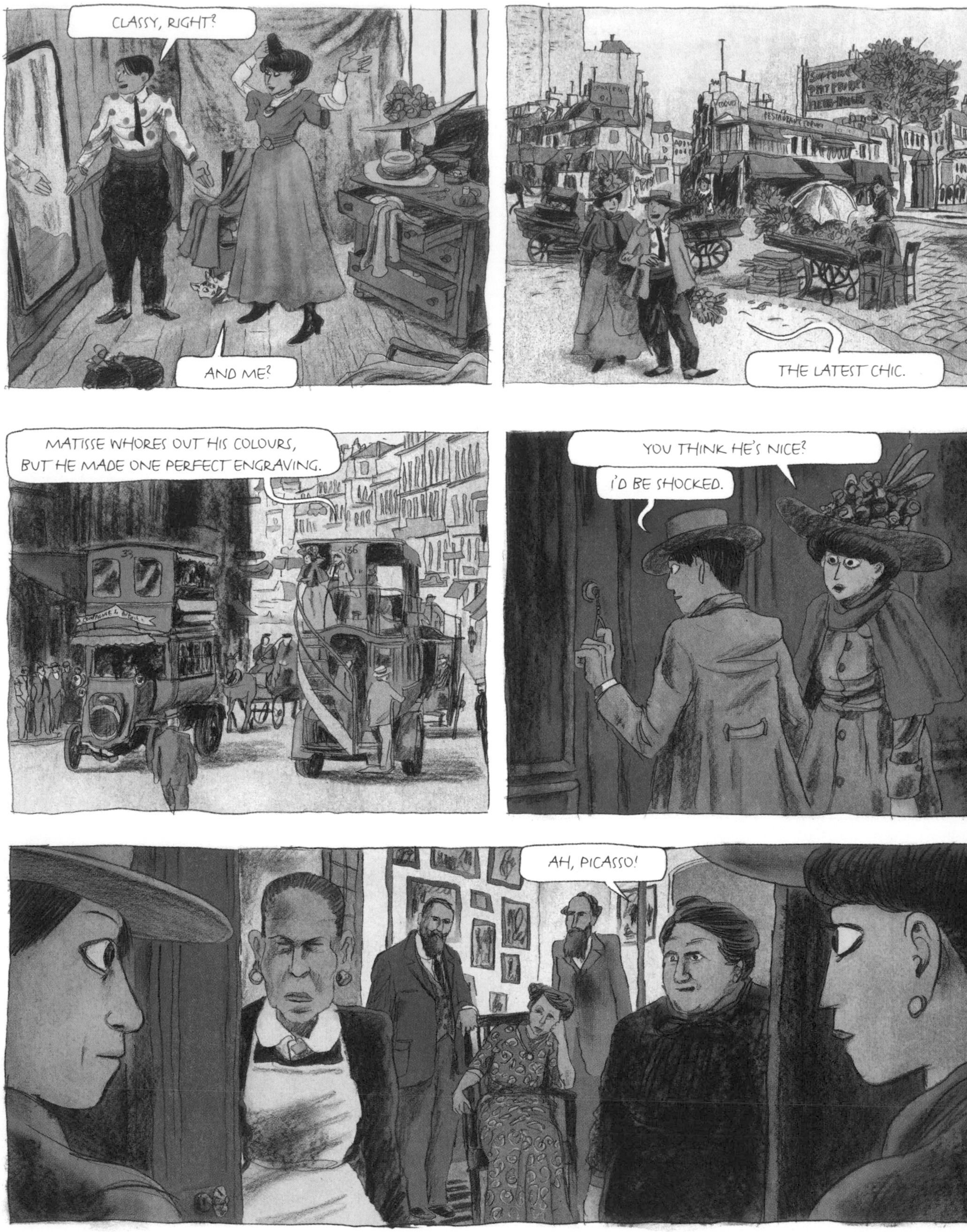
CLASSY, RIGHT?
AND ME?
THE LATEST CHIC.
MATISSE WHORES OUT HIS COLOURS, BUT HE MADE ONE PERFECT ENGRAVING.
YOU THINK HE'S NICE?
I'D BE SHOCKED.
AH, PICASSO!

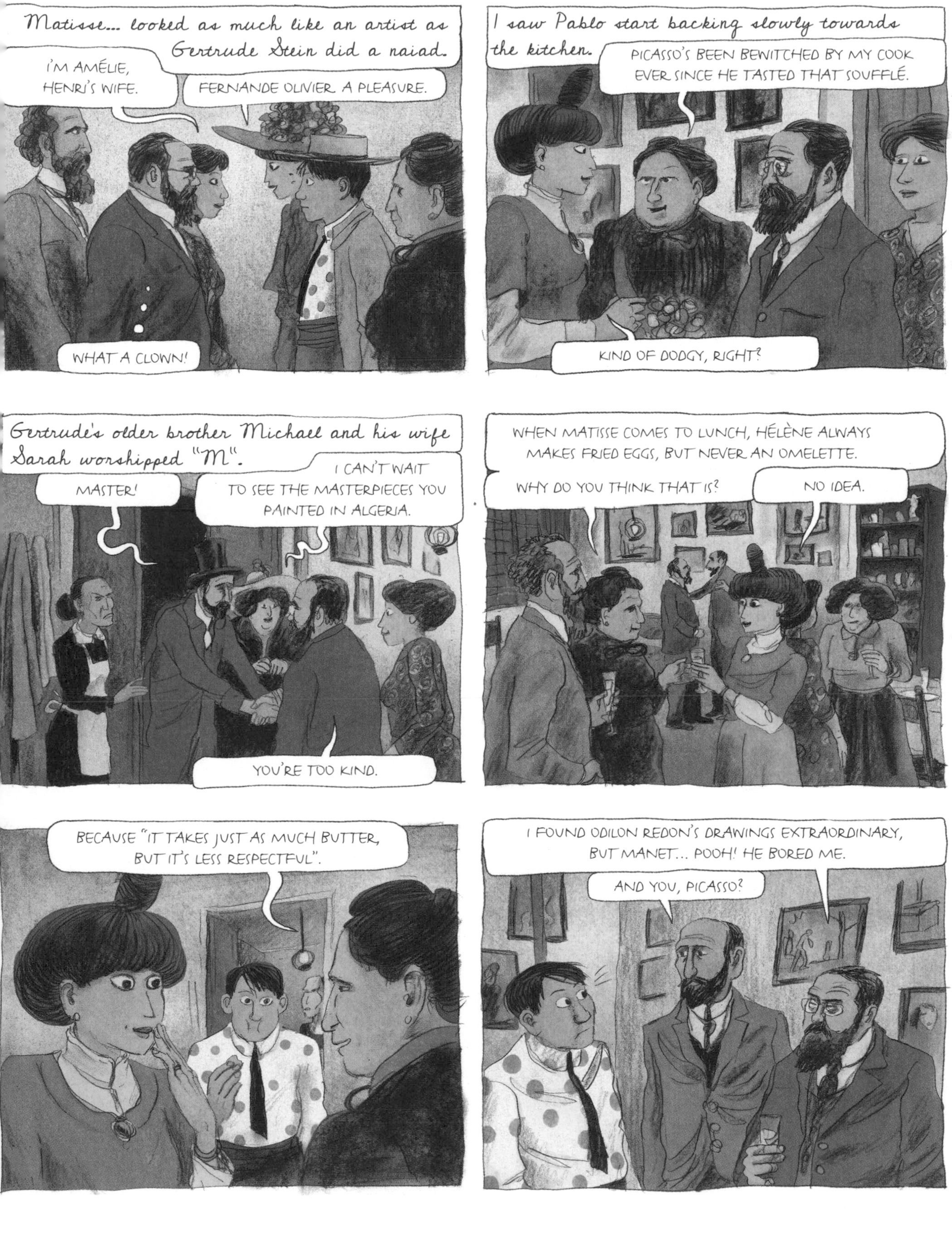

Matisse... looked as much like an artist as Gertrude Stein did a naiad.
I'M AMÉLIE, HENRI'S WIFE.
FERNANDE OLIVIER. A PLEASURE.
WHAT A CLOWN!
I saw Pablo start backing slowly towards the kitchen.
PICASSO'S BEEN BEWITCHED BY MY COOK EVER SINCE HE TASTED THAT SOUFFLÉ.
KIND OF DODGY, RIGHT?
Gertrude's older brother Michael and his wife Sarah worshipped "M".
MASTER!
I CAN'T WAIT TO SEE THE MASTERPIECES YOU PAINTED IN ALGERIA.
YOU'RE TOO KIND.
WHEN MATISSE COMES TO LUNCH, HÉLÈNE ALWAYS MAKES FRIED EGGS, BUT NEVER AN OMELETTE.
WHY DO YOU THINK THAT IS?
NO IDEA.
BECAUSE "IT TAKES JUST AS MUCH BUTTER, BUT IT'S LESS RESPECTFUL".
I FOUND ODILON REDON'S DRAWINGS EXTRAORDINARY, BUT MANET... POOH! HE BORED ME.
AND YOU, PICASSO?

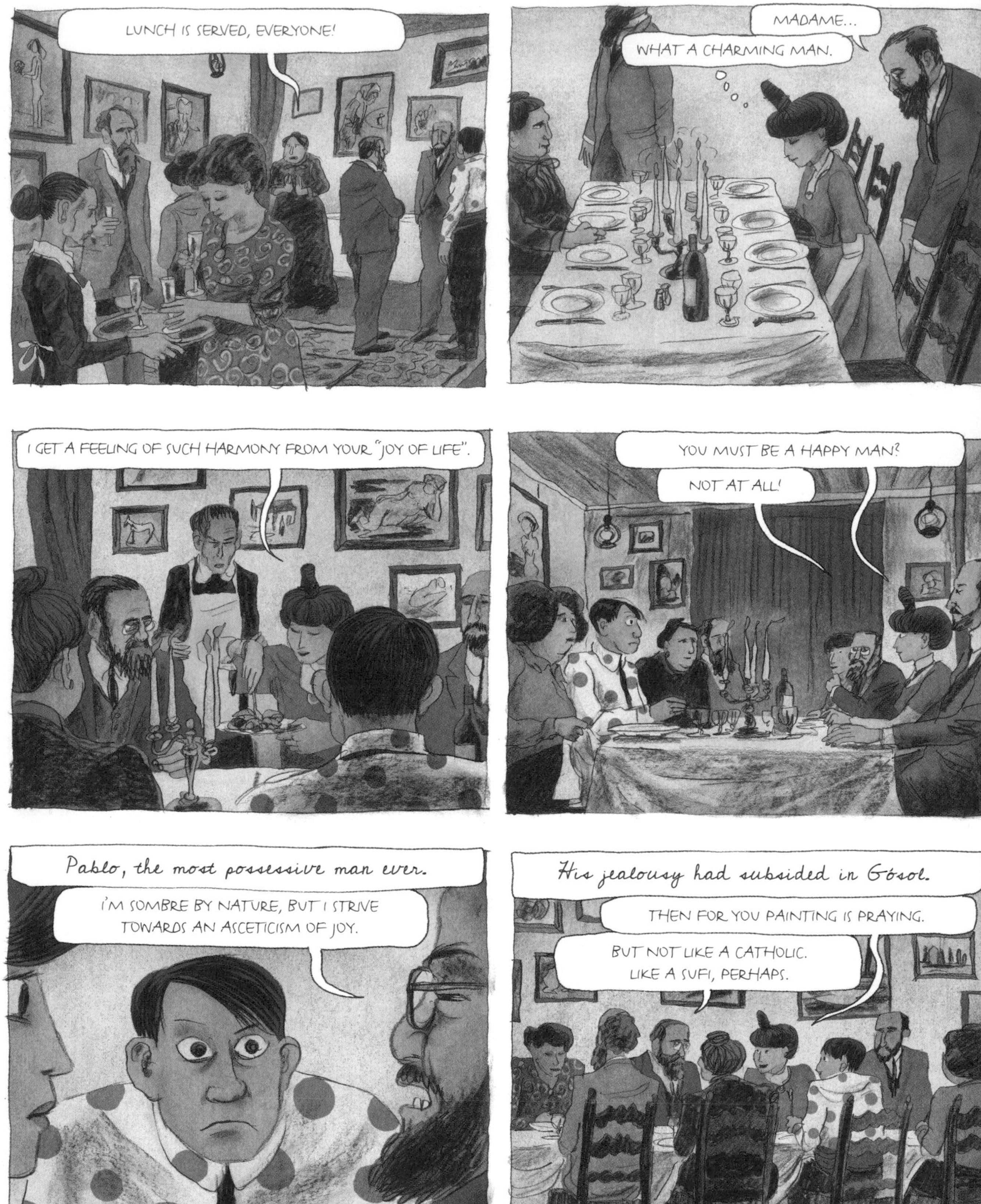
LUNCH IS SERVED, EVERYONE!
MADAME...
WHAT A CHARMING MAN.
I GET A FEELING OF SUCH HARMONY FROM YOUR "JOY OF LIFE".
YOU MUST BE A HAPPY MAN?
NOT AT ALL!
Pablo, the most possessive man ever.
I'M SOMBRE BY NATURE, BUT I STRIVE TOWARDS AN ASCETICISM OF JOY.
His jealousy had subsided in Gósol.
THEN FOR YOU PAINTING IS PRAYING.
BUT NOT LIKE A CATHOLIC. LIKE A SUFI, PERHAPS.

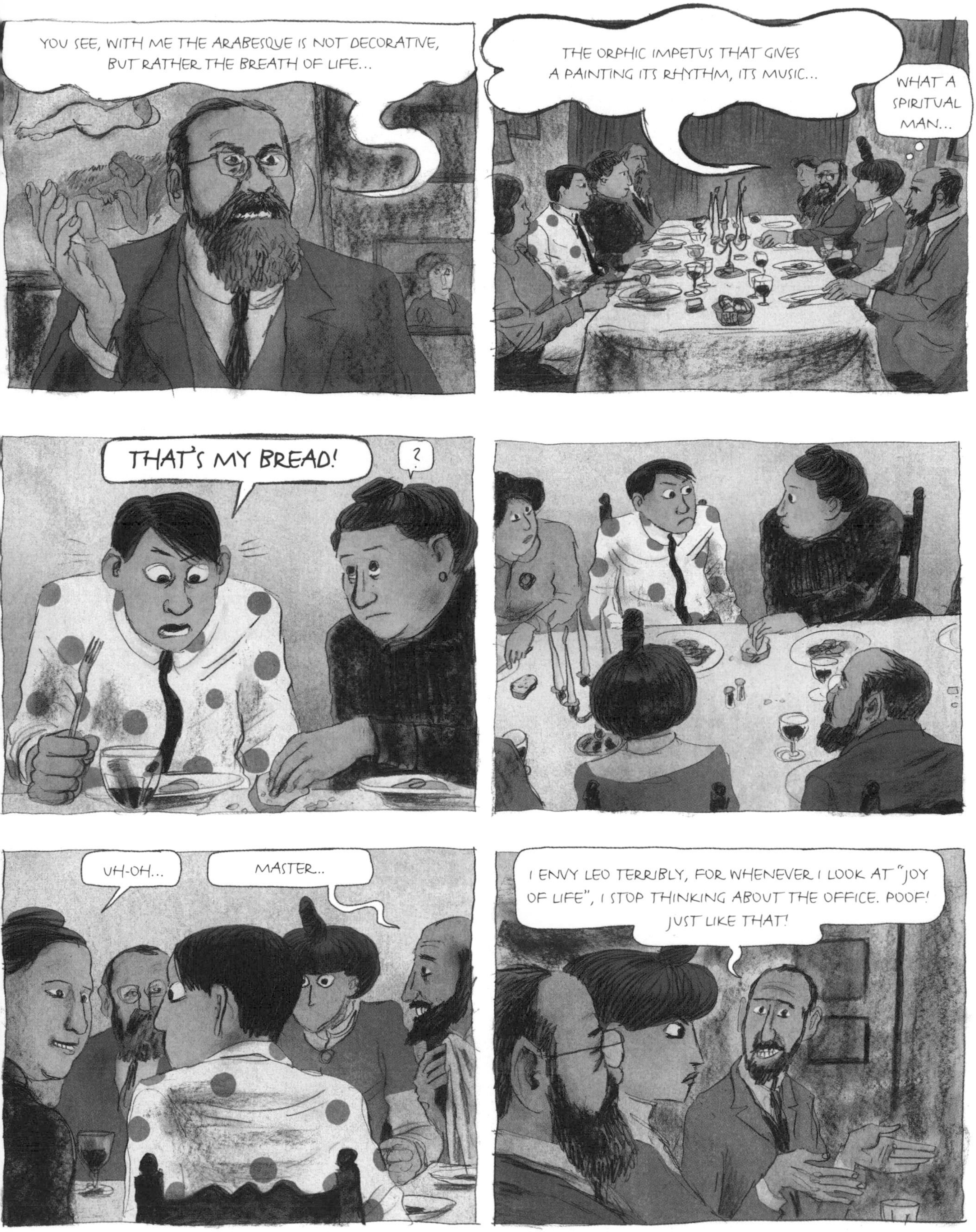
YOU SEE, WITH ME THE ARABESQUE IS NOT DECORATIVE, BUT RATHER THE BREATH OF LIFE...
THE ORPHIC IMPETUS THAT GIVES A PAINTING ITS RHYTHM, ITS MUSIC...
WHAT A SPIRITUAL MAN...
THAT'S MY BREAD!
?
UH-OH...
MASTER...
I ENVY LEO TERRIBLY, FOR WHENEVER I LOOK AT "JOY OF LIFE", I STOP THINKING ABOUT THE OFFICE. POOF! JUST LIKE THAT!

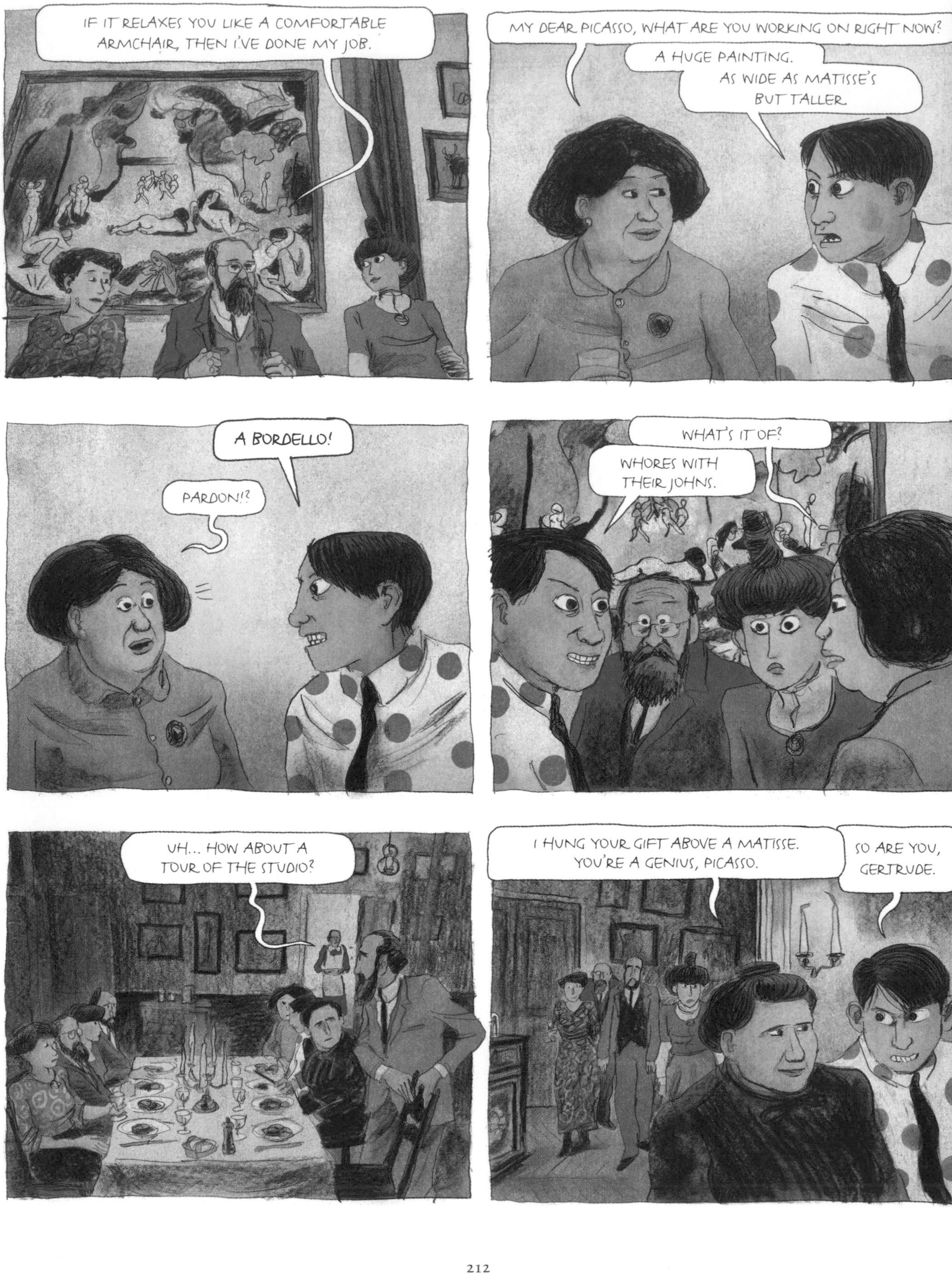

IF IT RELAXES YOU LIKE A COMFORTABLE ARMCHAIR, THEN I'VE DONE MY JOB.
MY DEAR PICASSO, WHAT ARE YOU WORKING ON RIGHT NOW?
A HUGE PAINTING.
AS WIDE AS MATISSE'S BUT TALLER.
A BORDELLO!
PARDON!?
WHAT'S IT OF?
WHORES WITH THEIR JOHNS.
UH... HOW ABOUT A TOUR OF THE STUDIO?
I HUNG YOUR GIFT ABOVE A MATISSE. YOU'RE A GENIUS, PICASSO.
SO ARE YOU, GERTRUDE.

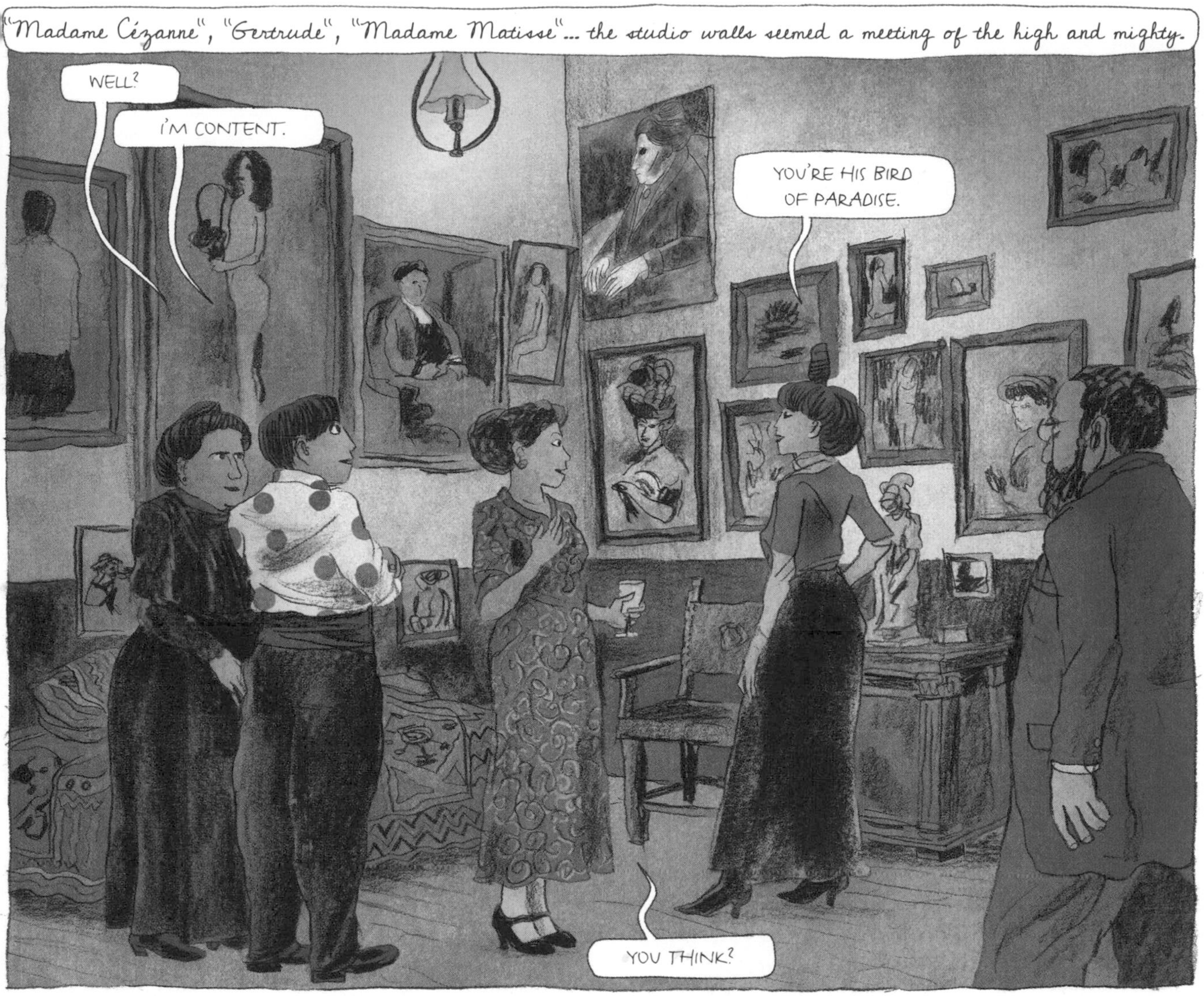
"Madame Cézanne", "Gertrude", "Madame Matisse"... the studio walls seemed a meeting of the high and mighty.
WELL?
I'M CONTENT.
YOU'RE HIS BIRD OF PARADISE.
YOU THINK?

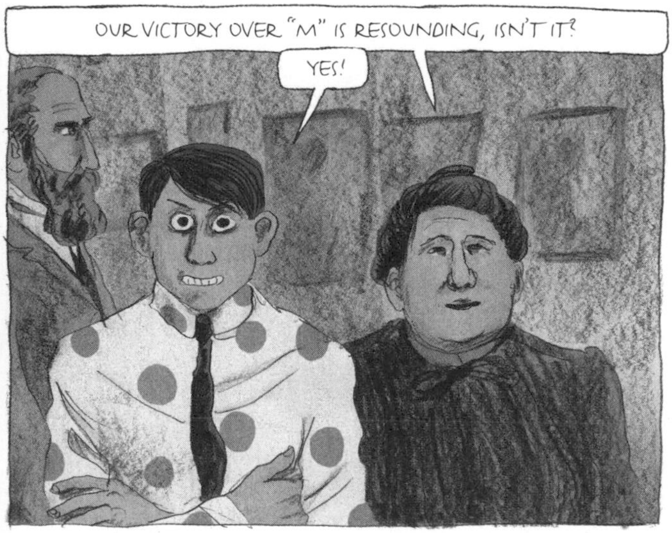
OUR VICTORY OVER "M" IS RESOUNDING, ISN'T IT?
YES!

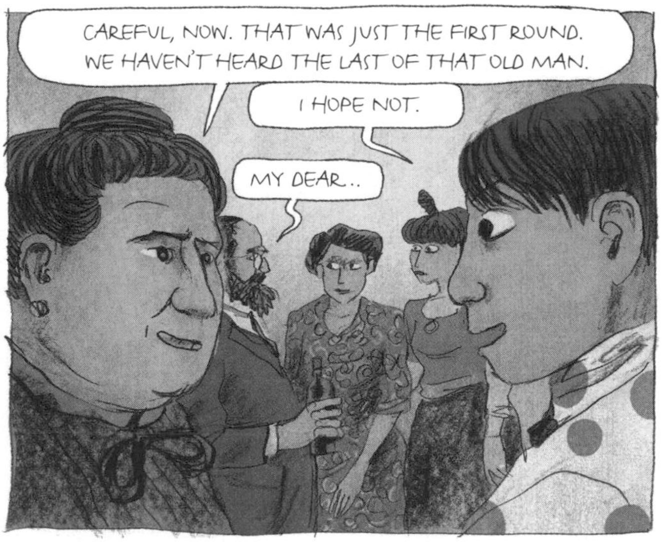
CAREFUL, NOW. THAT WAS JUST THE FIRST ROUND. WE HAVEN'T HEARD THE LAST OF THAT OLD MAN.
I HOPE NOT.
MY DEAR..

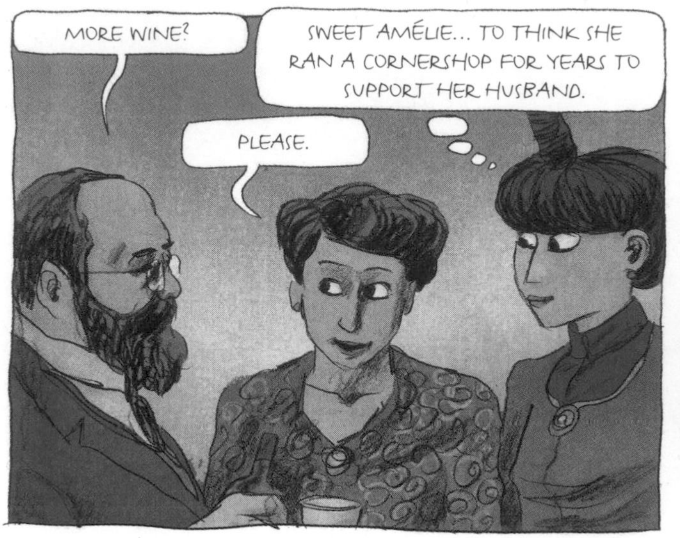
MORE WINE?
SWEET AMÉLIE... TO THINK SHE RAN A CORNERSHOP FOR YEARS TO SUPPORT HER HUSBAND.
PLEASE.

It was before their trip to Collioure with Derain...

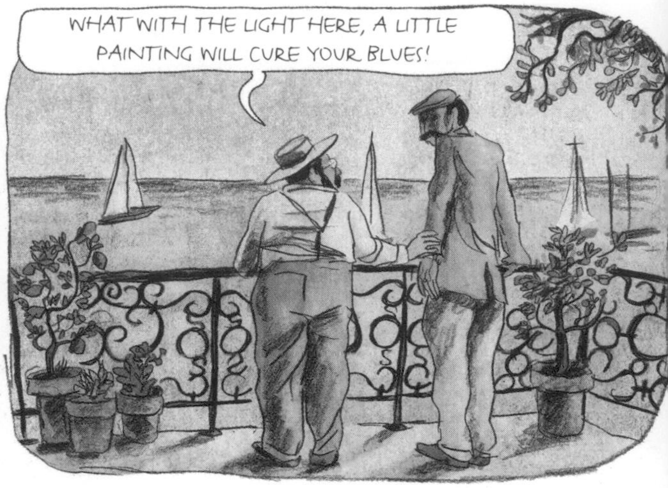
WHAT WITH THE LIGHT HERE, A LITTLE PAINTING WILL CURE YOUR BLUES!

Before Matisse rejected his venerable masters and good manners.

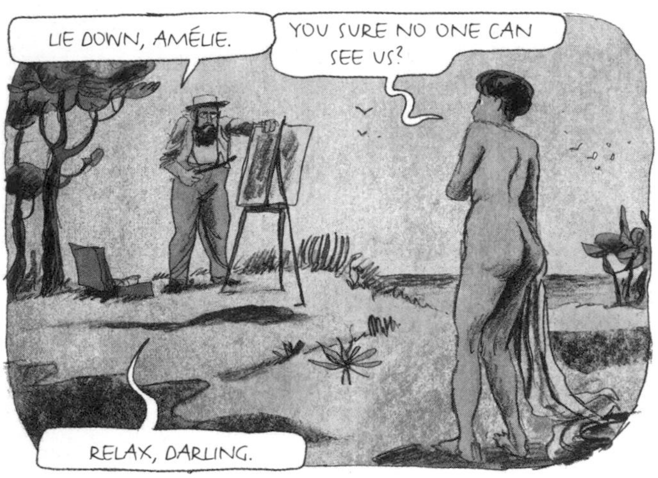
LIE DOWN, AMÉLIE.
YOU SURE NO ONE CAN SEE US?
RELAX, DARLING.

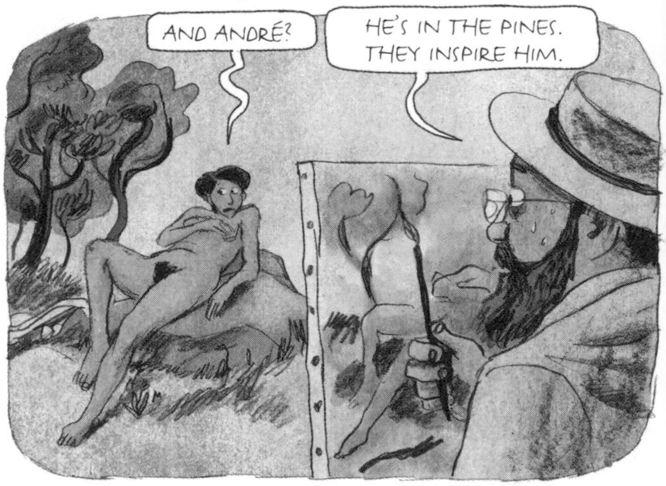
AND ANDRÉ?
HE'S IN THE PINES. THEY INSPIRE HIM.

Now that he had let himself go wild with colour, Matisse was famous, sought after...

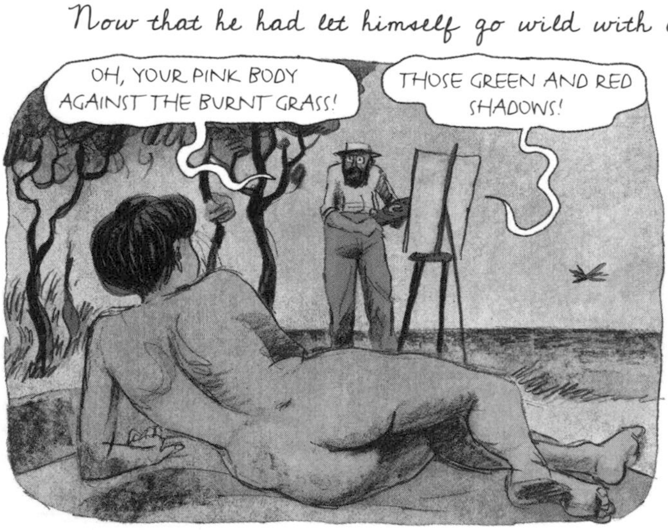
OH, YOUR PINK BODY AGAINST THE BURNT GRASS!
THOSE GREEN AND RED SHADOWS!

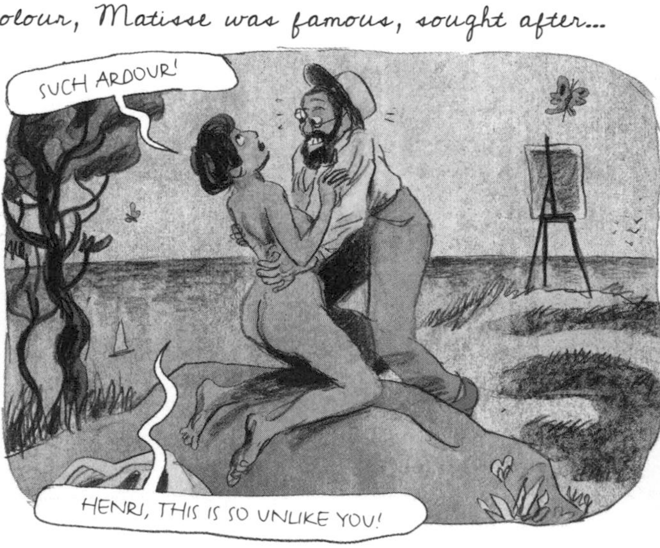
SUCH ARDOUR!
HENRI, THIS IS SO UNLIKE YOU!

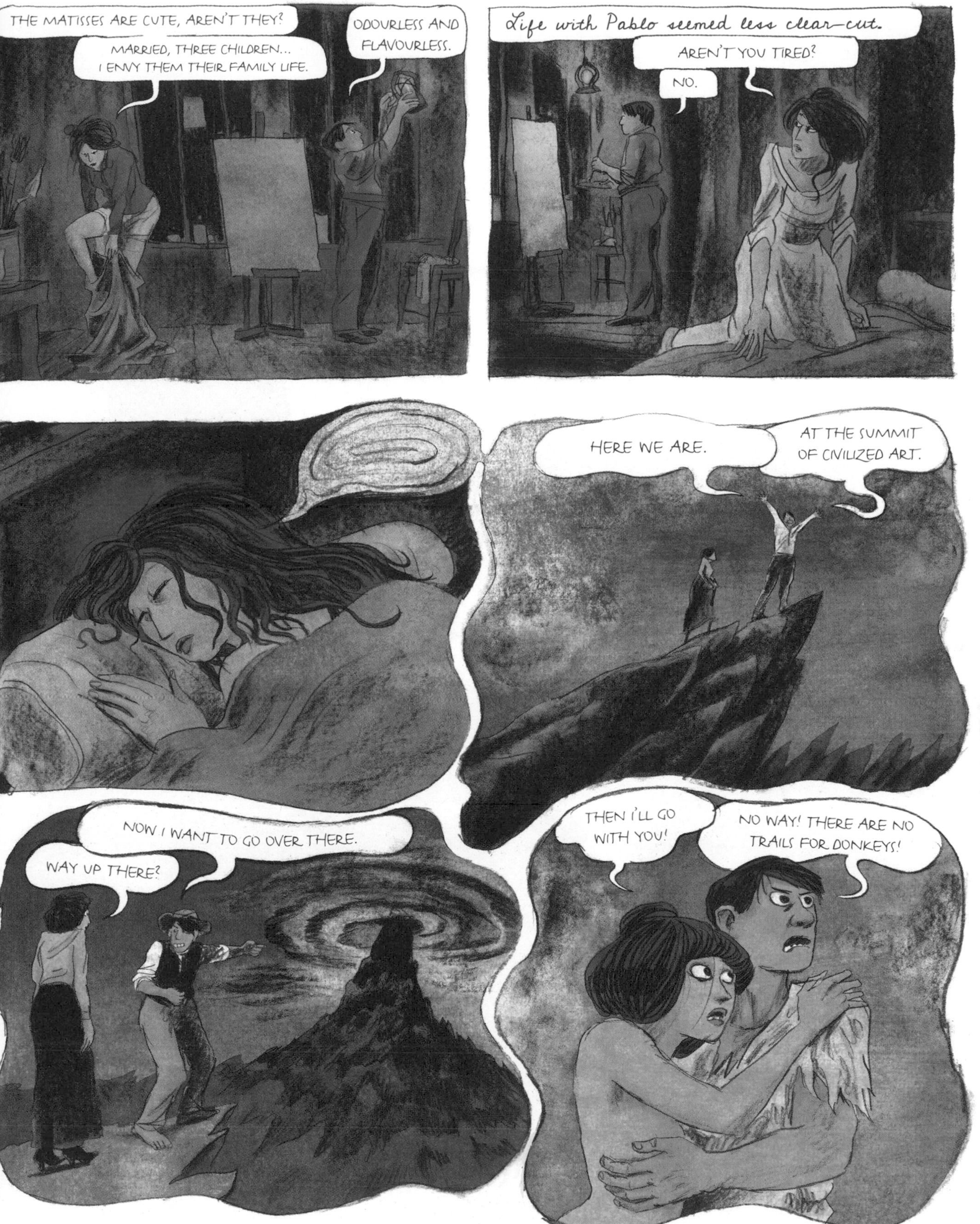
THE MATISSES ARE CUTE, AREN'T THEY?
MARRIED, THREE CHILDREN... I ENVY THEM THEIR FAMILY LIFE.
ODOURLESS AND FLAVOURLESS.
Life with Pablo seemed less clear-cut.
AREN'T YOU TIRED?
NO.
HERE WE ARE.
AT THE SUMMIT OF CIVILIZED ART.
NOW I WANT TO GO OVER THERE.
WAY UP THERE?
THEN I'LL GO WITH YOU!
NO WAY! THERE ARE NO TRAILS FOR DONKEYS!

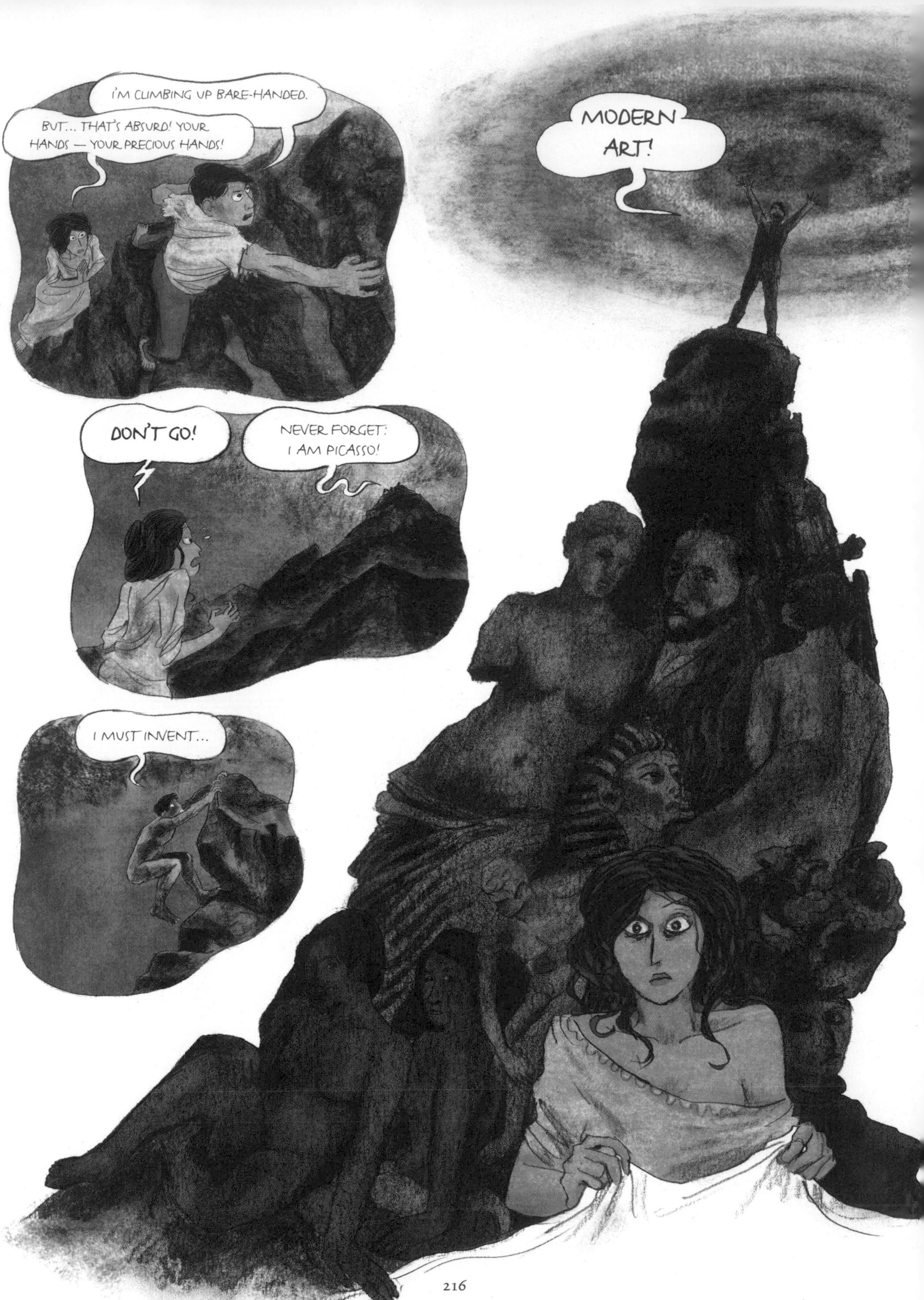
I'M CLIMBING UP BARE-HANDED.
BUT... THAT'S ABSURD! YOUR HANDS — YOUR PRECIOUS HANDS!
DON'T GO!
NEVER FORGET: I AM PICASSO!
I MUST INVENT...
MODERN ART!

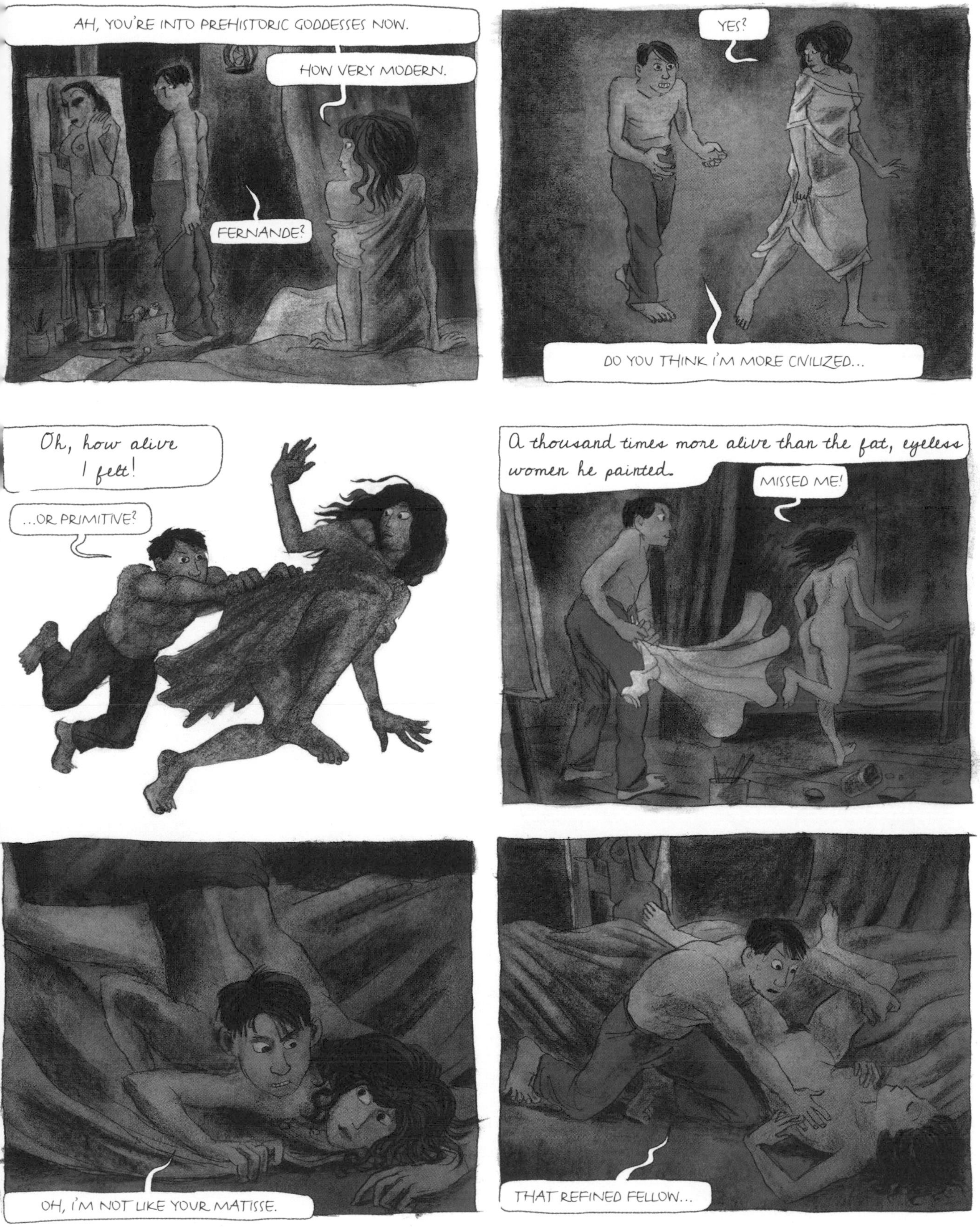
AH, YOU'RE INTO PREHISTORIC GODDESSES NOW.
HOW VERY MODERN.
FERNANDE?
YES?
DO YOU THINK I'M MORE CIVILIZED...
Oh, how alive I felt!
...OR PRIMITIVE?
A thousand times more alive than the fat, eyeless women he painted.
MISSED ME!
OH, I'M NOT LIKE YOUR MATISSE.
THAT REFINED FELLOW...

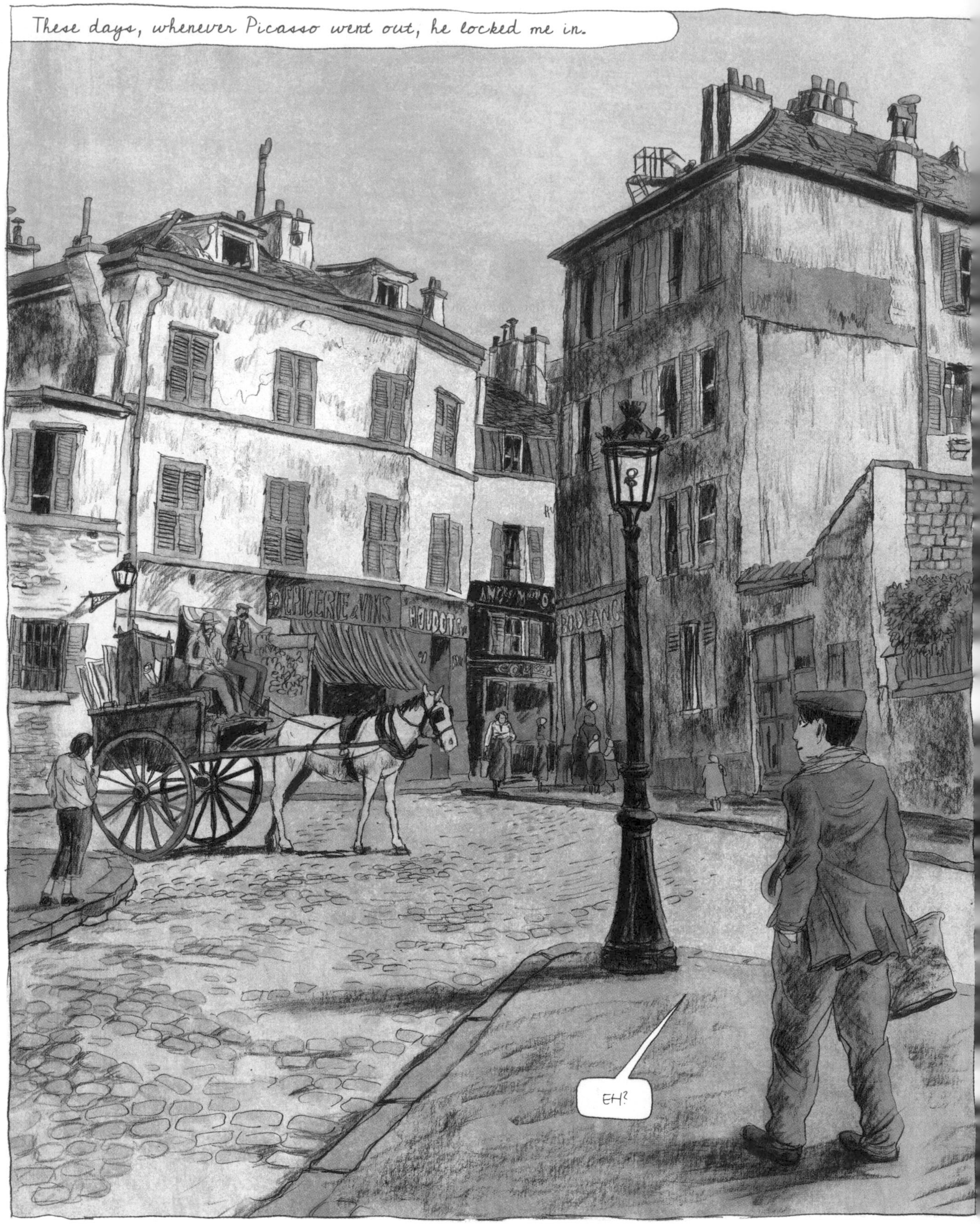
These days, whenever Picasso went out, he locked me in.
EPICERIE & VINS
HOUDOT
EH?

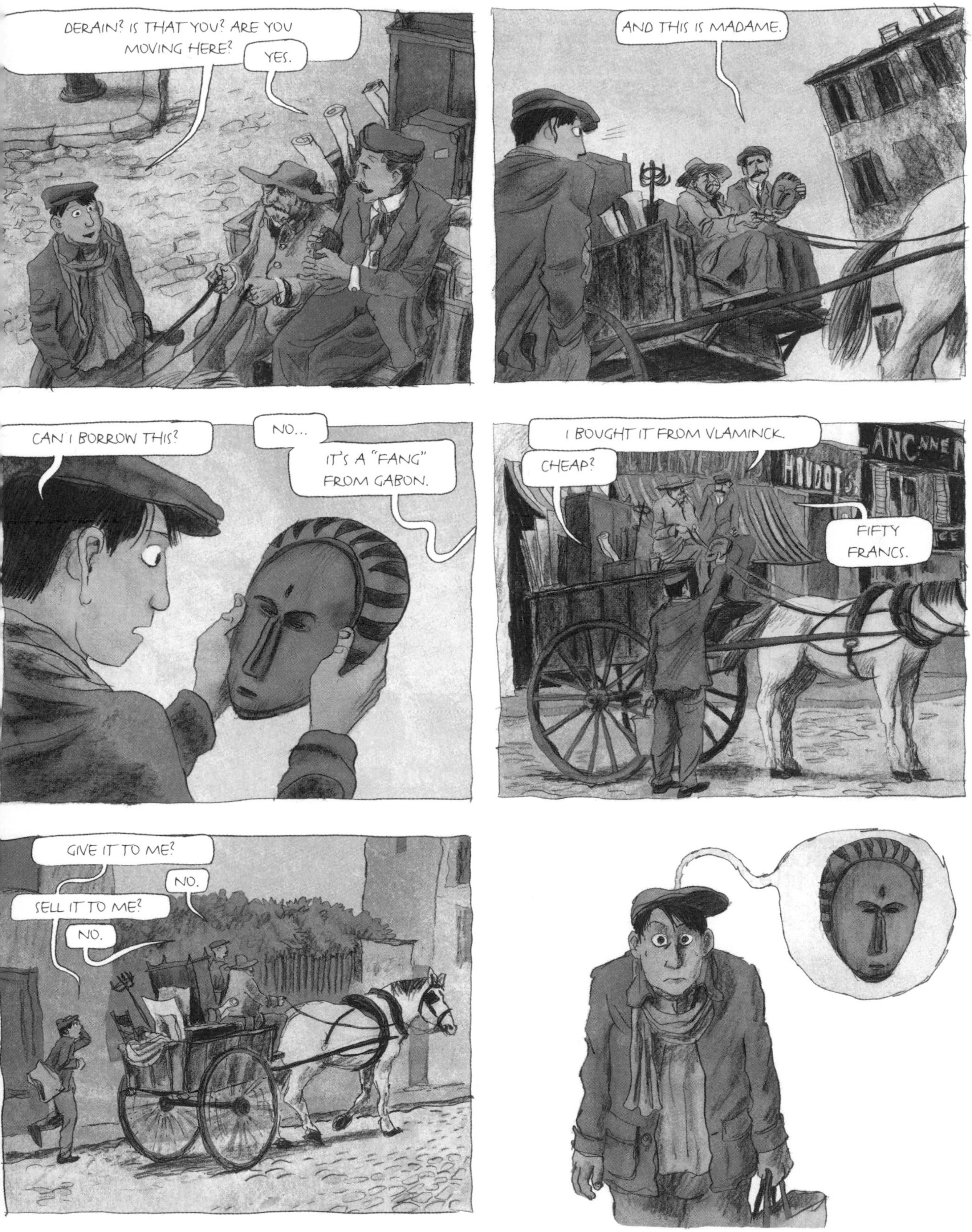
DERAIN? IS THAT YOU? ARE YOU MOVING HERE?
YES.
AND THIS IS MADAME.
CAN I BORROW THIS?
NO...
IT'S A "FANG" FROM GABON.
I BOUGHT IT FROM VLAMINCK.
CHEAP?
FIFTY FRANCS.
GIVE IT TO ME?
NO.
SELL IT TO ME?
NO.

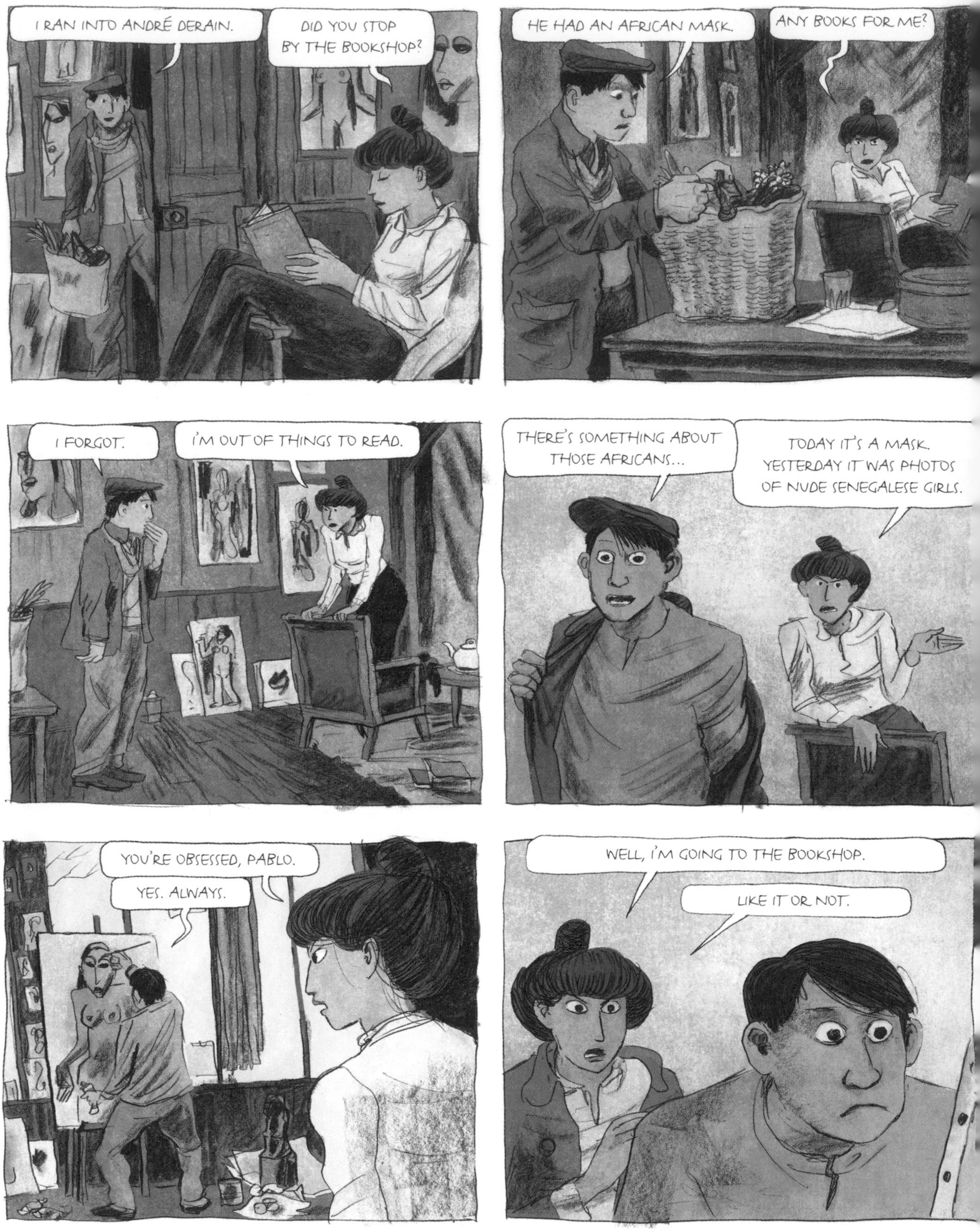
I RAN INTO ANDRÉ DERAIN.
DID YOU STOP BY THE BOOKSHOP?
HE HAD AN AFRICAN MASK.
ANY BOOKS FOR ME?
I FORGOT.
I'M OUT OF THINGS TO READ.
THERE'S SOMETHING ABOUT THOSE AFRICANS...
TODAY IT'S A MASK. YESTERDAY IT WAS PHOTOS OF NUDE SENEGALESE GIRLS.
YOU'RE OBSESSED, PABLO.
YES. ALWAYS.
WELL, I'M GOING TO THE BOOKSHOP.
LIKE IT OR NOT.

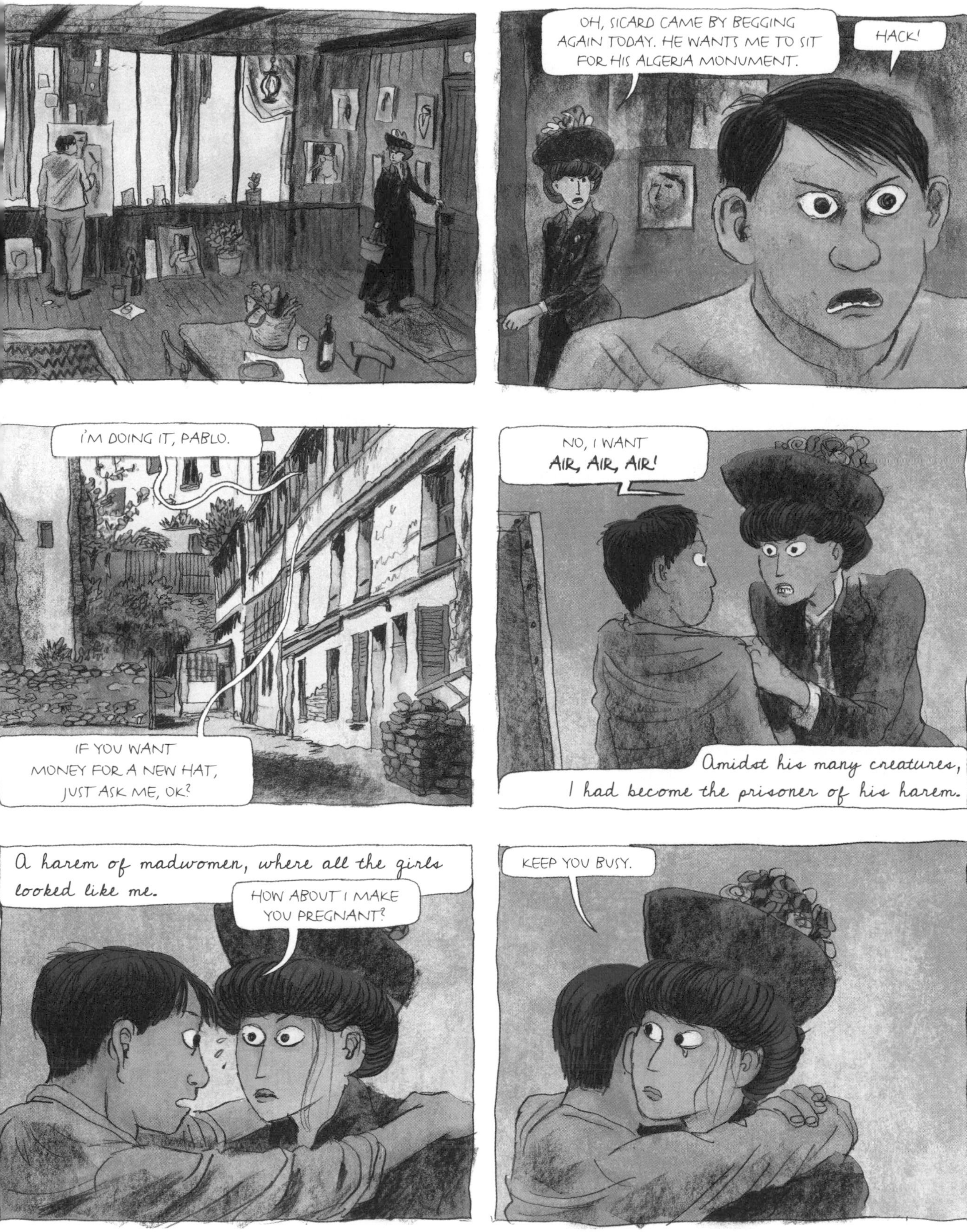
OH, SICARD CAME BY BEGGING AGAIN TODAY. HE WANTS ME TO SIT FOR HIS ALGERIA MONUMENT.
HACK!
I'M DOING IT, PABLO.
IF YOU WANT MONEY FOR A NEW HAT, JUST ASK ME, OK?
NO, I WANT AIR, AIR, AIR!
Amidst his many creatures, I had become the prisoner of his harem.
A harem of madwomen, where all the girls looked like me.
HOW ABOUT I MAKE YOU PREGNANT?
KEEP YOU BUSY.

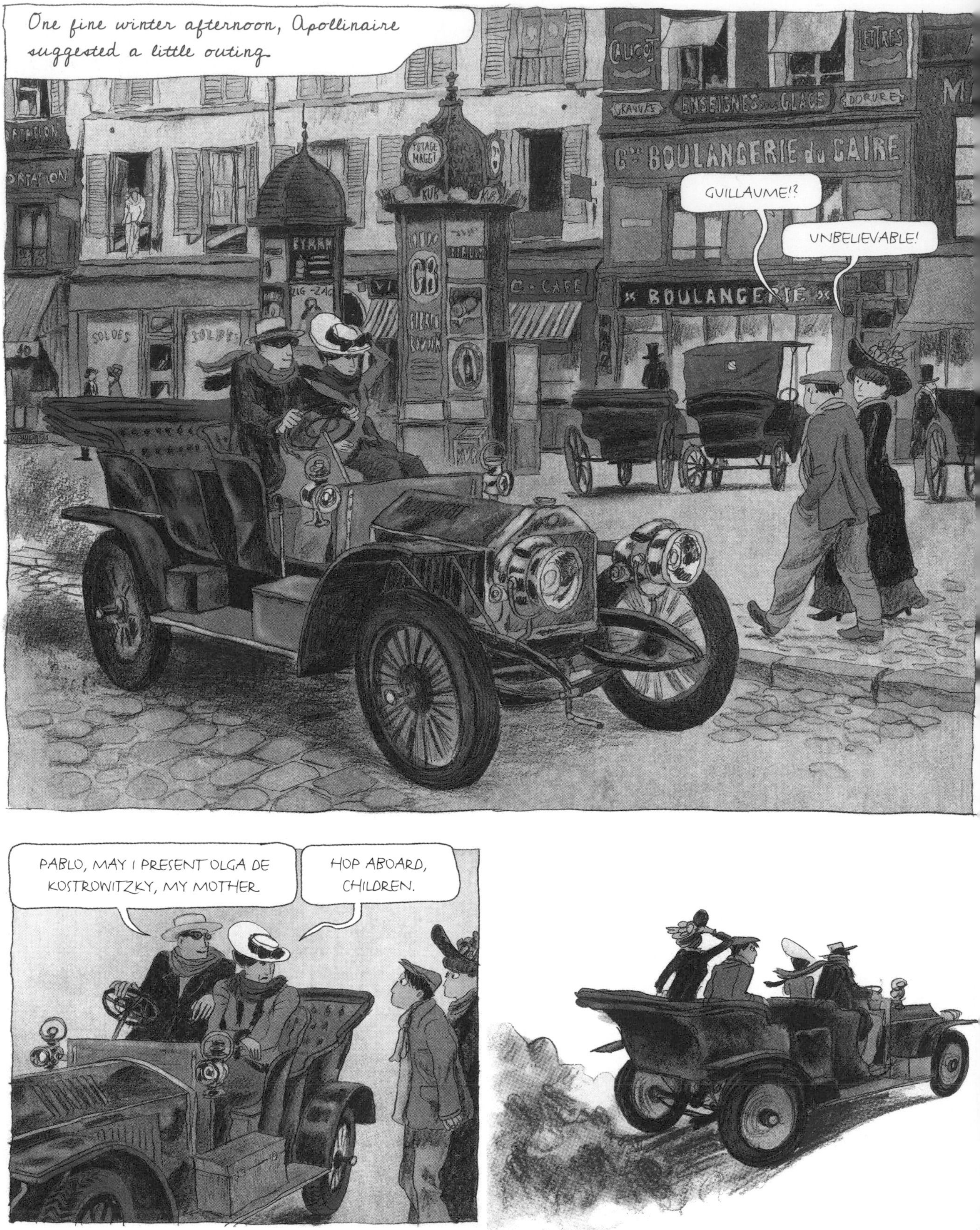
One fine winter afternoon, Apollinaire suggested a little outing.
GUILLAUME!?
UNBELIEVABLE!
BOULANGERIE du CAIRE
BOULANGERIE
PABLO, MAY I PRESENT OLGA DE KOSTROWITZKY, MY MOTHER.
HOP ABOARD, CHILDREN.

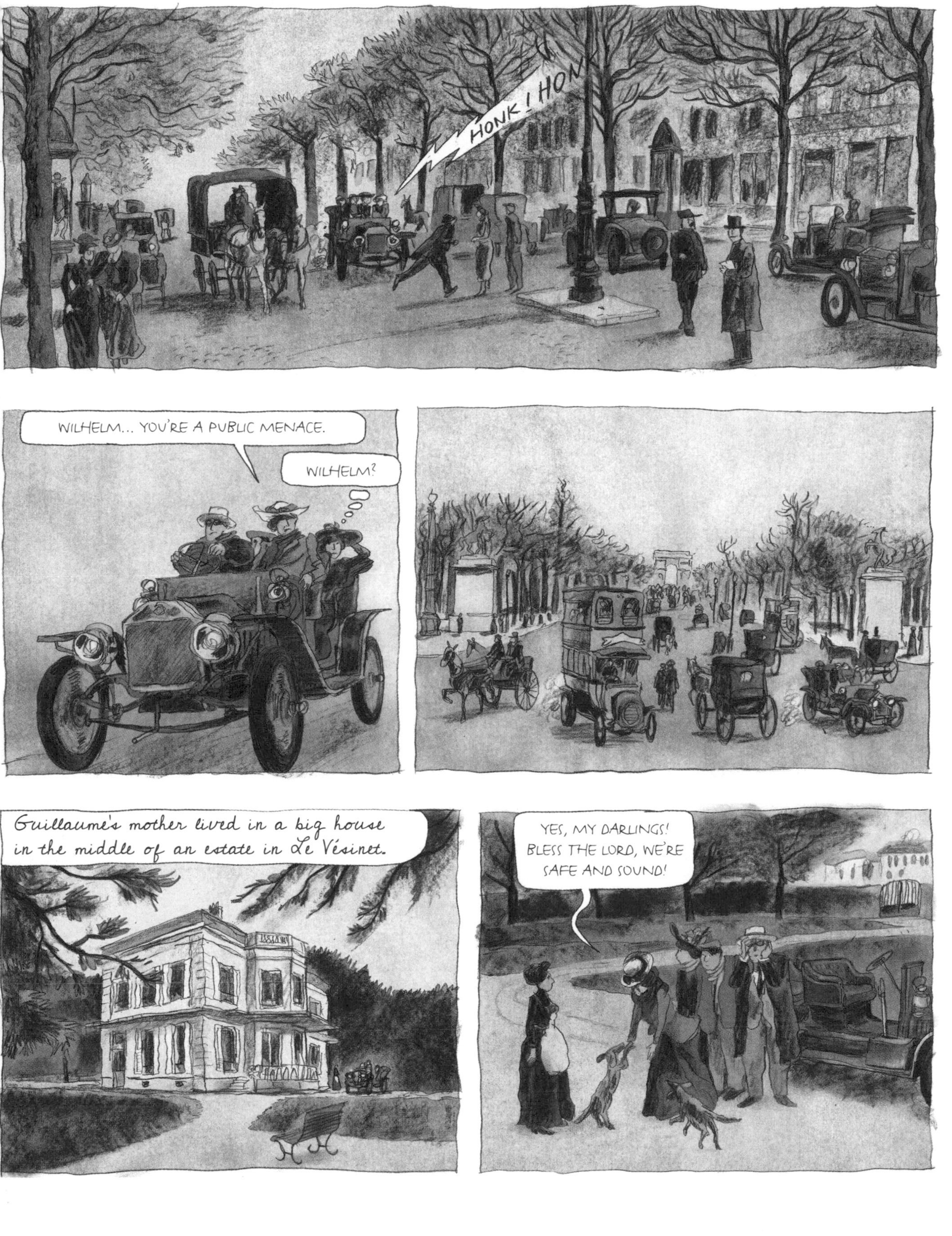
HONK! HON
WILHELM... YOU'RE A PUBLIC MENACE.
WILHELM?
Guillaume's mother lived in a big house in the middle of an estate in Le Vésinet.
YES, MY DARLINGS! BLESS THE LORD, WE'RE SAFE AND SOUND!

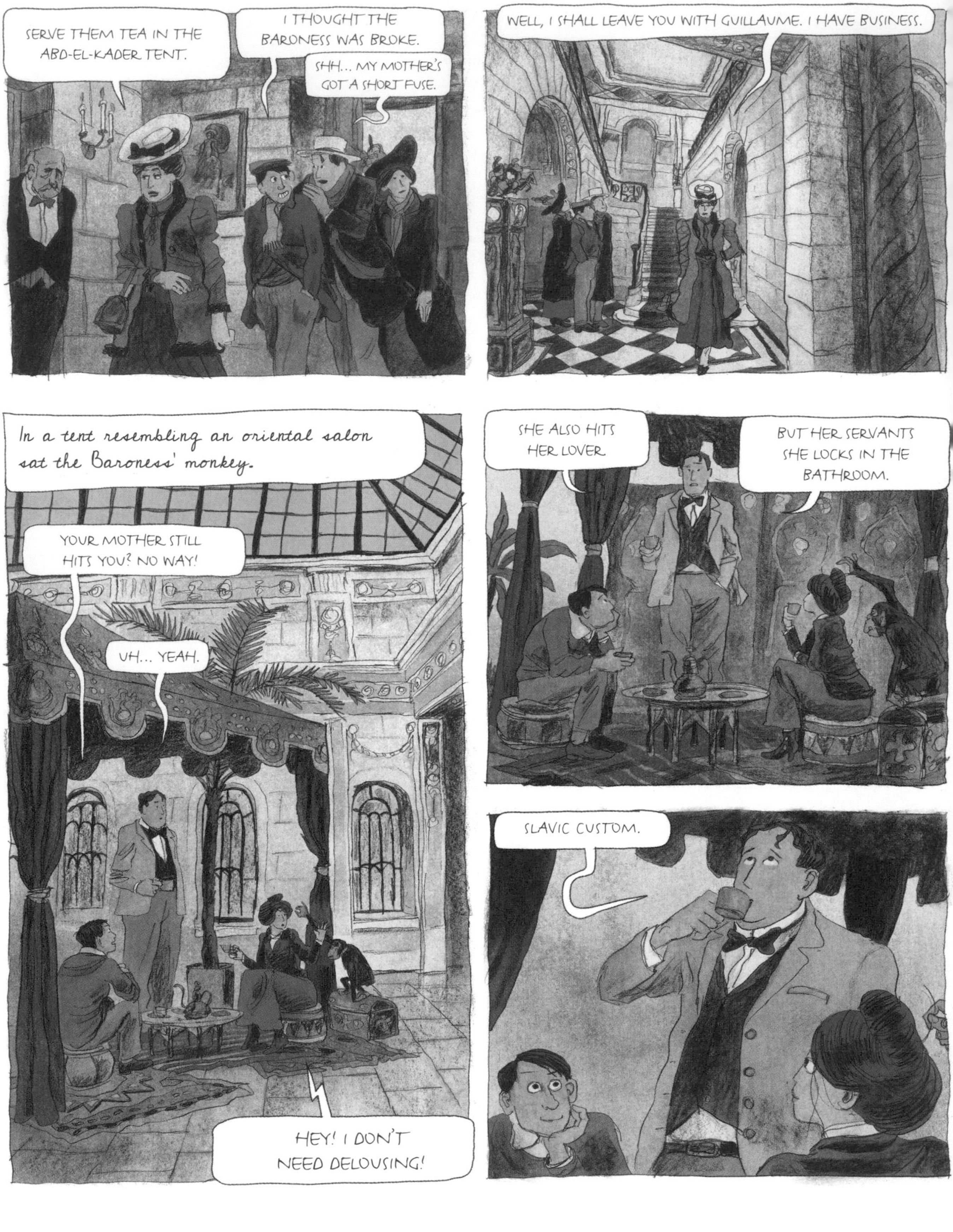
SERVE THEM TEA IN THE ABD-EL-KADER TENT.
I THOUGHT THE BARONESS WAS BROKE.
SHH... MY MOTHER'S GOT A SHORT FUSE.
WELL, I SHALL LEAVE YOU WITH GUILLAUME. I HAVE BUSINESS.
In a tent resembling an oriental salon sat the Baroness' monkey.
YOUR MOTHER STILL HITS YOU? NO WAY!
UH... YEAH.
HEY! I DON'T NEED DELOUSING!
SHE ALSO HITS HER LOVER
BUT HER SERVANTS SHE LOCKS IN THE BATHROOM.
SLAVIC CUSTOM.

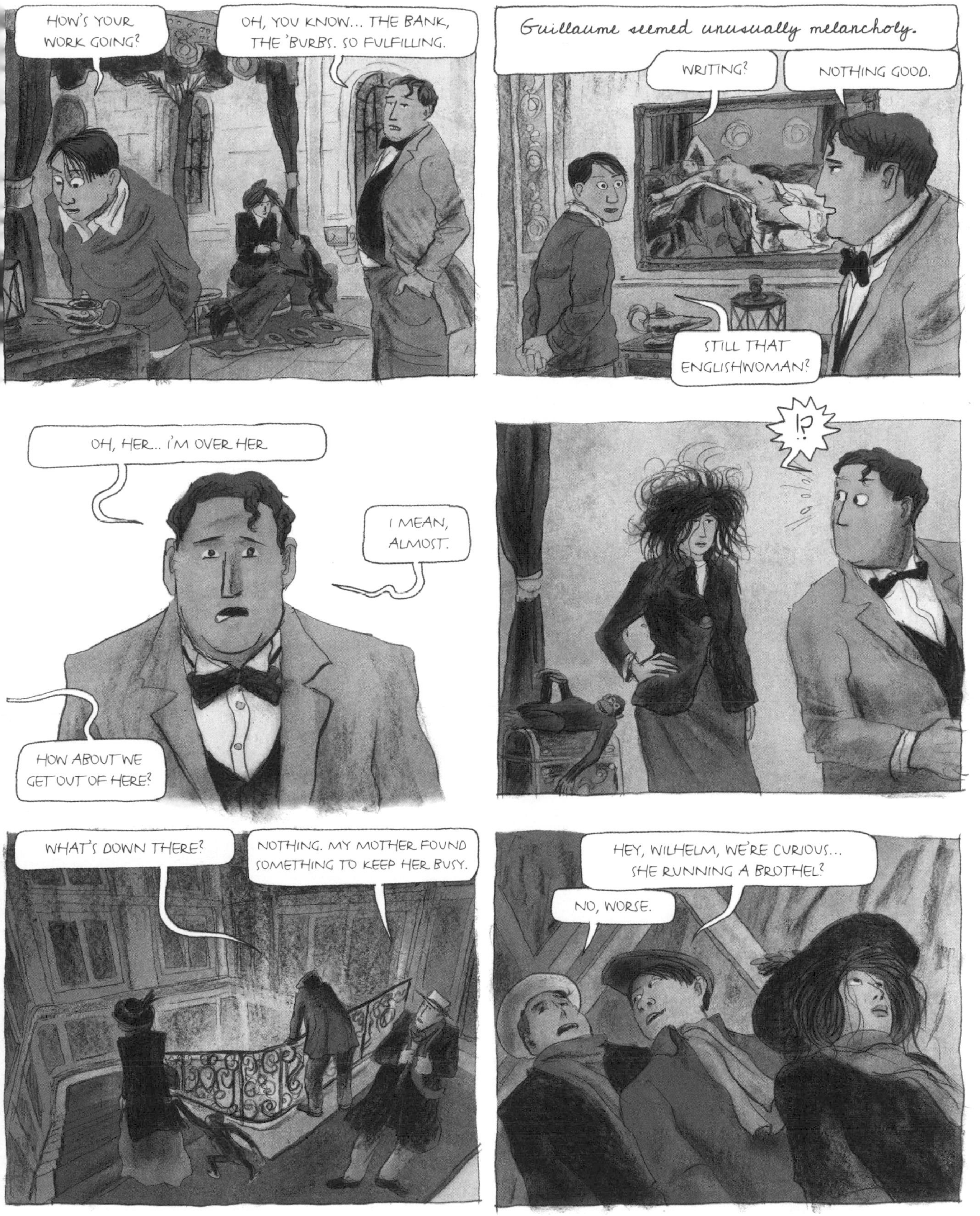
HOW'S YOUR WORK GOING?
OH, YOU KNOW... THE BANK, THE 'BURBS. SO FULFILLING.
Guillaume seemed unusually melancholy.
WRITING?
NOTHING GOOD.
STILL THAT ENGLISHWOMAN?
OH, HER... I'M OVER HER
I MEAN, ALMOST.
HOW ABOUT WE GET OUT OF HERE?
!?
WHAT'S DOWN THERE?
NOTHING. MY MOTHER FOUND SOMETHING TO KEEP HER BUSY.
HEY, WILHELM, WE'RE CURIOUS... SHE RUNNING A BROTHEL?
NO, WORSE.

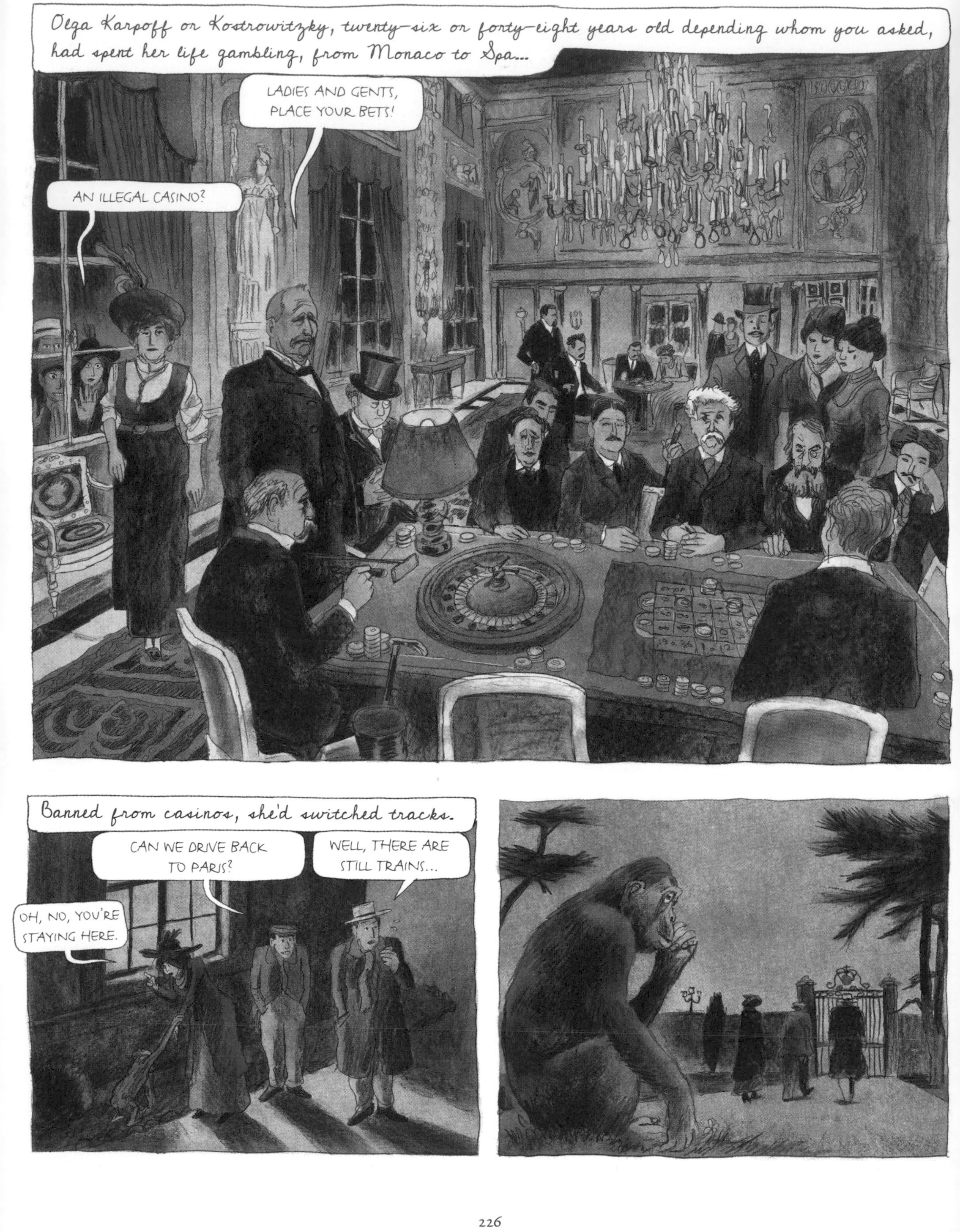
Olga Karpoff or Kostrowitzky, twenty-six or forty-eight years old depending whom you asked, had spent her life gambling, from Monaco to Spa...
AN ILLEGAL CASINO?
LADIES AND GENTS, PLACE YOUR BETS!
Banned from casinos, she'd switched tracks.
CAN WE DRIVE BACK TO PARIS?
WELL, THERE ARE STILL TRAINS...
OH, NO, YOU'RE STAYING HERE.

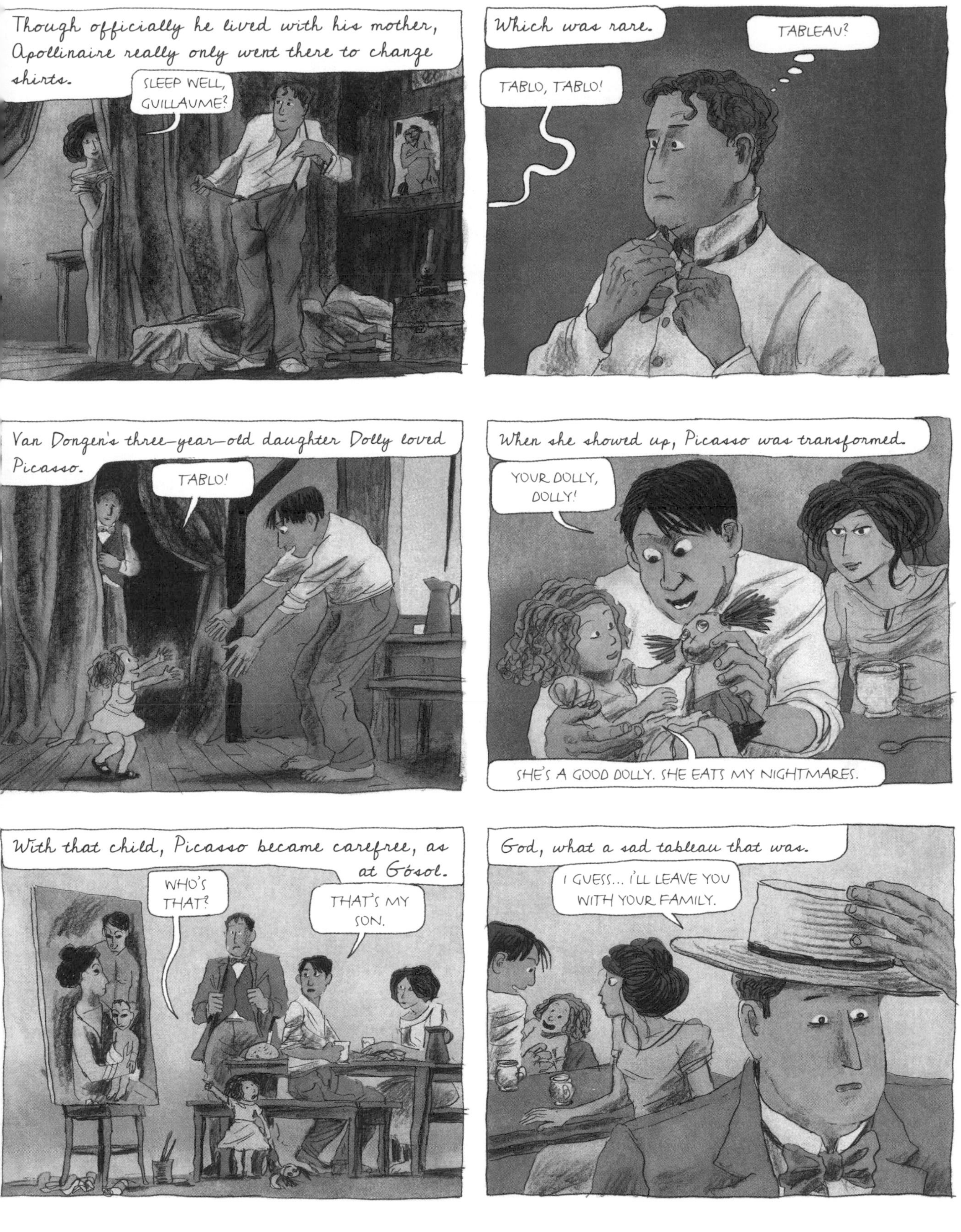
Though officially he lived with his mother, Apollinaire really only went there to change shirts.
SLEEP WELL, GUILLAUME?
Which was rare.
TABLO, TABLO!
TABLEAU?
Van Dongen's three-year-old daughter Dolly loved Picasso.
TABLO!
When she showed up, Picasso was transformed.
YOUR DOLLY, DOLLY!
SHE'S A GOOD DOLLY. SHE EATS MY NIGHTMARES.
With that child, Picasso became carefree, as at Gósol.
WHO'S THAT?
THAT'S MY SON.
God, what a sad tableau that was.
I GUESS... I'LL LEAVE YOU WITH YOUR FAMILY.

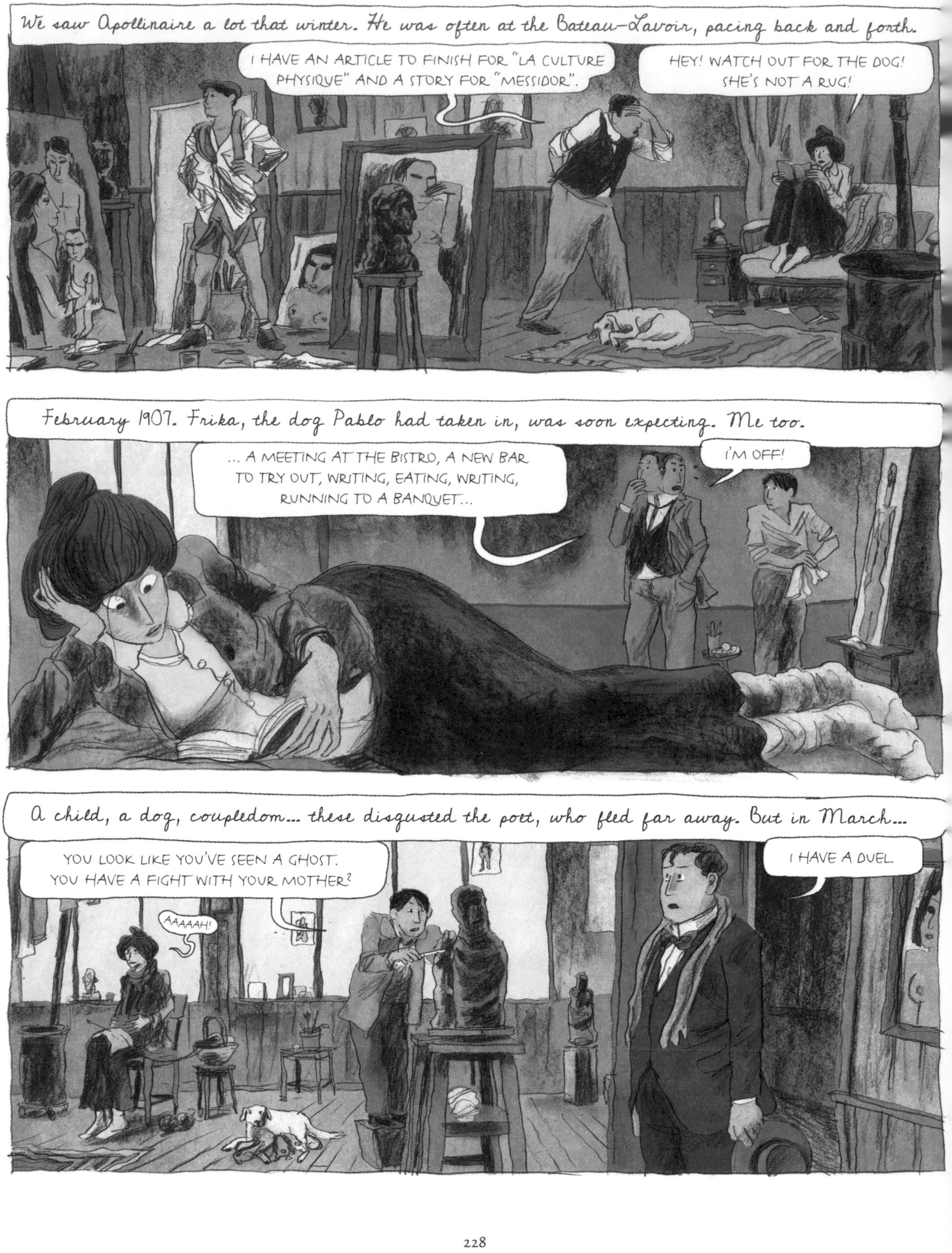
We saw Apollinaire a lot that winter. He was often at the Bateau-Lavoir, pacing back and forth.
I HAVE AN ARTICLE TO FINISH FOR "LA CULTURE PHYSIQUE" AND A STORY FOR "MESSIDOR".
HEY! WATCH OUT FOR THE DOG! SHE'S NOT A RUG!
February 1907. Frika, the dog Pablo had taken in, was soon expecting. Me too.
... A MEETING AT THE BISTRO, A NEW BAR TO TRY OUT, WRITING, EATING, WRITING, RUNNING TO A BANQUET...
I'M OFF!
A child, a dog, coupledom... these disgusted the poet, who fled far away. But in March...
YOU LOOK LIKE YOU'VE SEEN A GHOST. YOU HAVE A FIGHT WITH YOUR MOTHER?
AAAAAH!
I HAVE A DUEL.

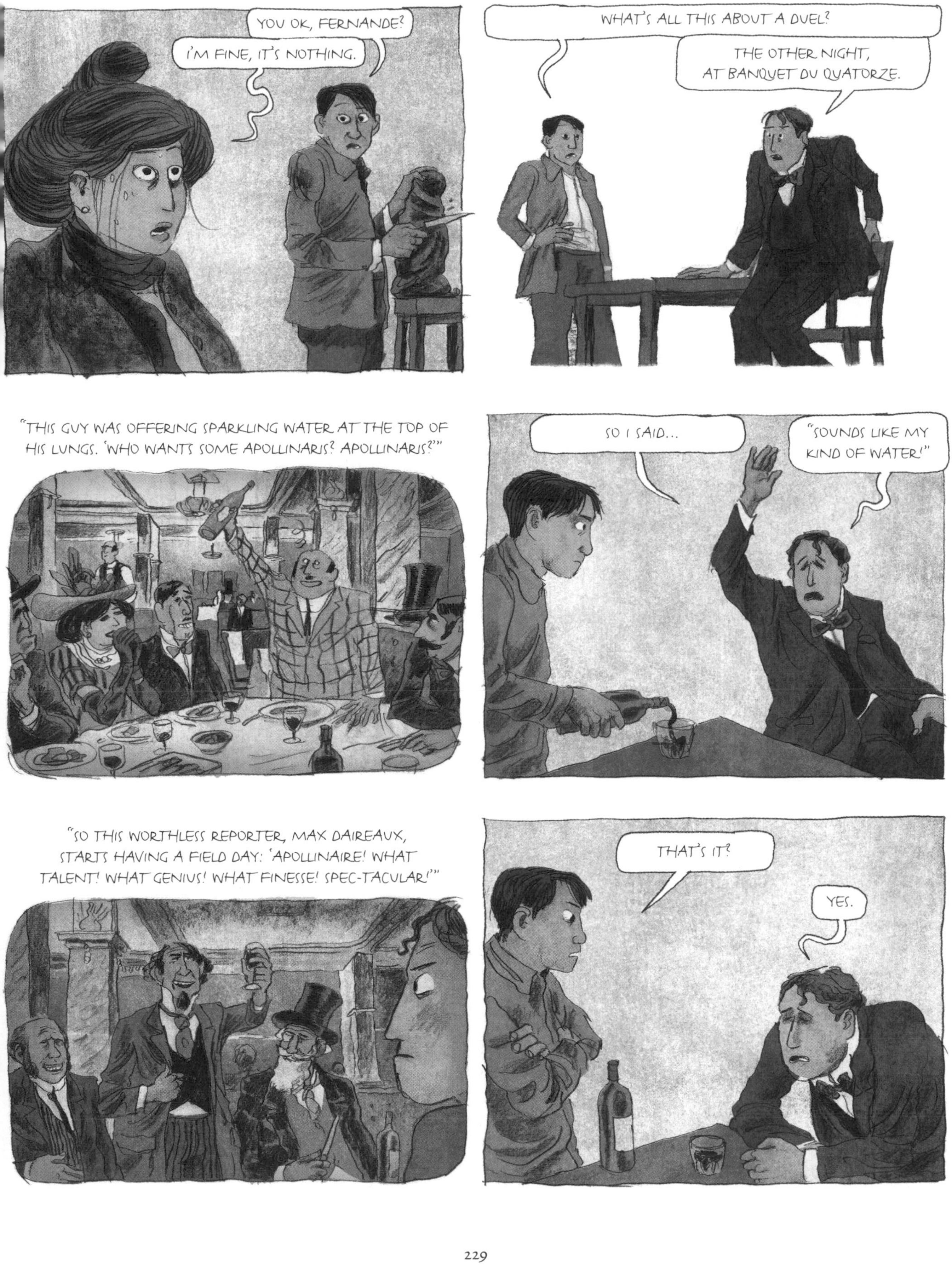
YOU OK, FERNANDE?
I'M FINE, IT'S NOTHING.
WHAT'S ALL THIS ABOUT A DUEL?
THE OTHER NIGHT, AT BANQUET DU QUATORZE.
"THIS GUY WAS OFFERING SPARKLING WATER AT THE TOP OF HIS LUNGS. 'WHO WANTS SOME APOLLINARIS? APOLLINARIS?'"
SO I SAID...
"SOUNDS LIKE MY KIND OF WATER!"
"SO THIS WORTHLESS REPORTER, MAX DAIREAUX, STARTS HAVING A FIELD DAY: 'APOLLINAIRE! WHAT TALENT! WHAT GENIUS! WHAT FINESSE! SPEC-TACULAR!'"
THAT'S IT?
YES.

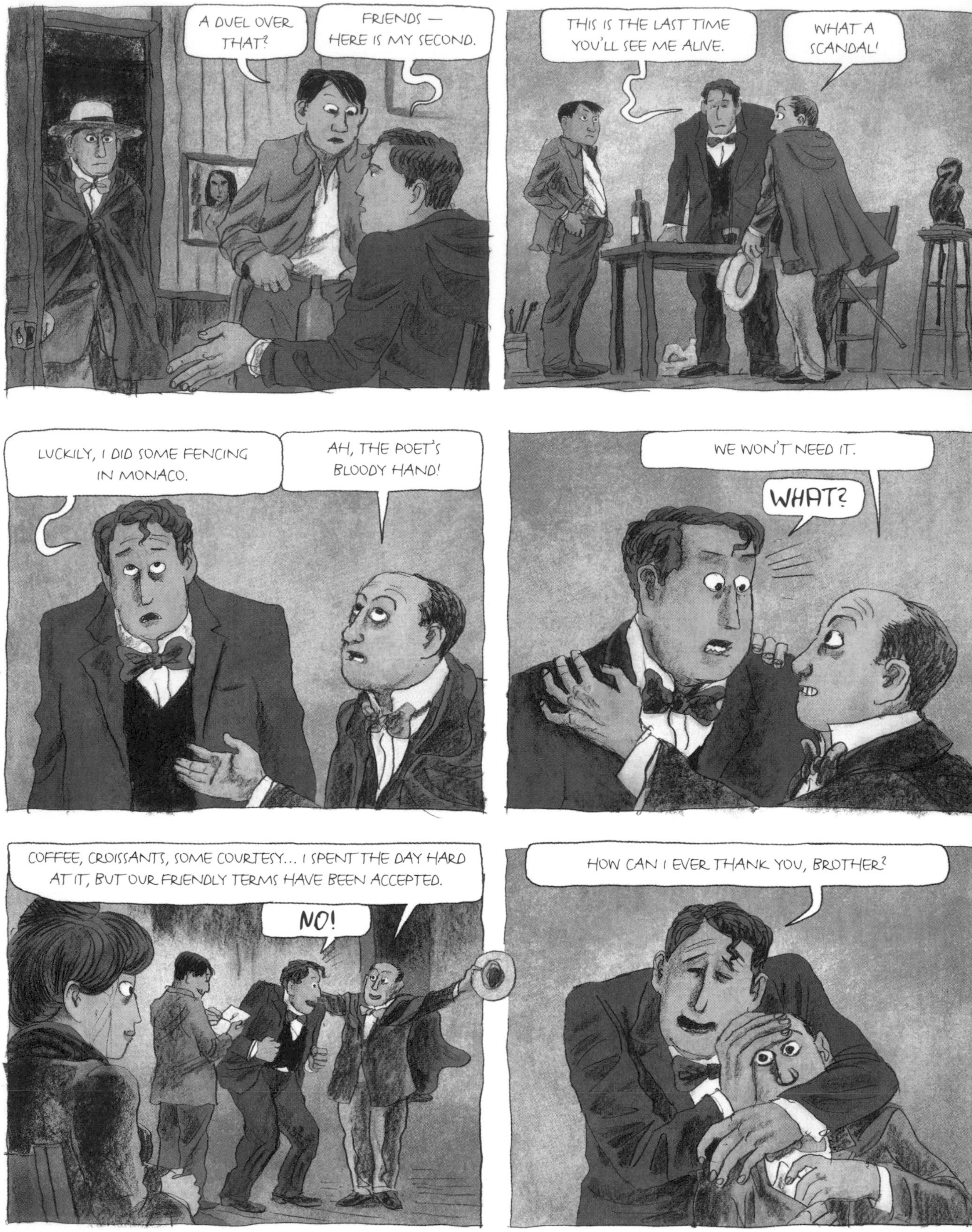

A DUEL OVER THAT?
FRIENDS — HERE IS MY SECOND.
THIS IS THE LAST TIME YOU'LL SEE ME ALIVE.
WHAT A SCANDAL!
LUCKILY, I DID SOME FENCING IN MONACO.
AH, THE POET'S BLOODY HAND!
WE WON'T NEED IT.
WHAT?
COFFEE, CROISSANTS, SOME COURTESY… I SPENT THE DAY HARD AT IT, BUT OUR FRIENDLY TERMS HAVE BEEN ACCEPTED.
NO!
HOW CAN I EVER THANK YOU, BROTHER?

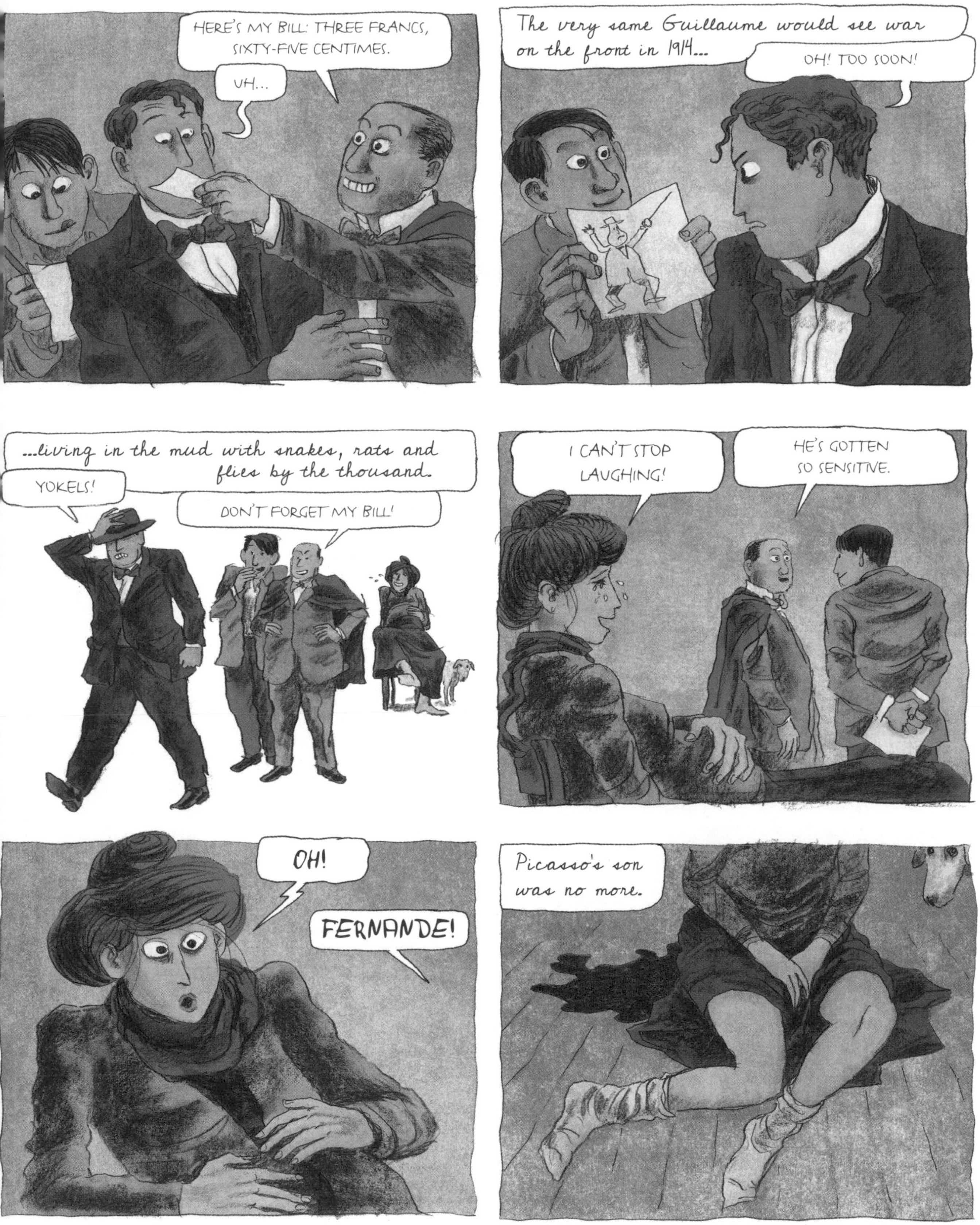

HERE'S MY BILL: THREE FRANCS, SIXTY-FIVE CENTIMES.
UH...
The very same Guillaume would see war on the front in 1914...
OH! TOO SOON!
...living in the mud with snakes, rats and flies by the thousand.
YOKELS!
DON'T FORGET MY BILL!
I CAN'T STOP LAUGHING!
HE'S GOTTEN SO SENSITIVE.
OH!
FERNANDE!
Picasso's son was no more.

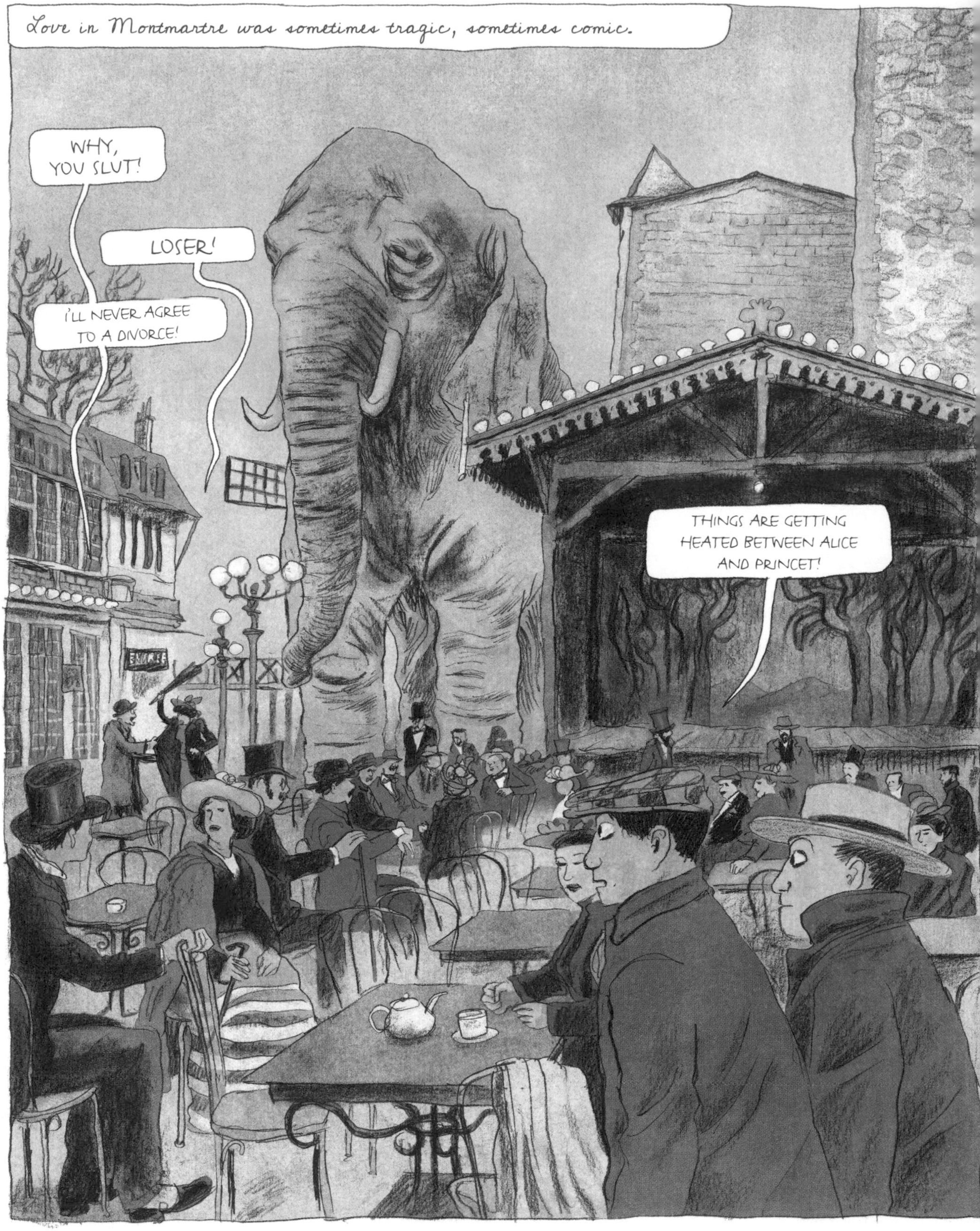
Love in Montmartre was sometimes tragic, sometimes comic.
WHY, YOU SLUT!
LOSER!
I'LL NEVER AGREE TO A DIVORCE!
THINGS ARE GETTING HEATED BETWEEN ALICE AND PRINCET!

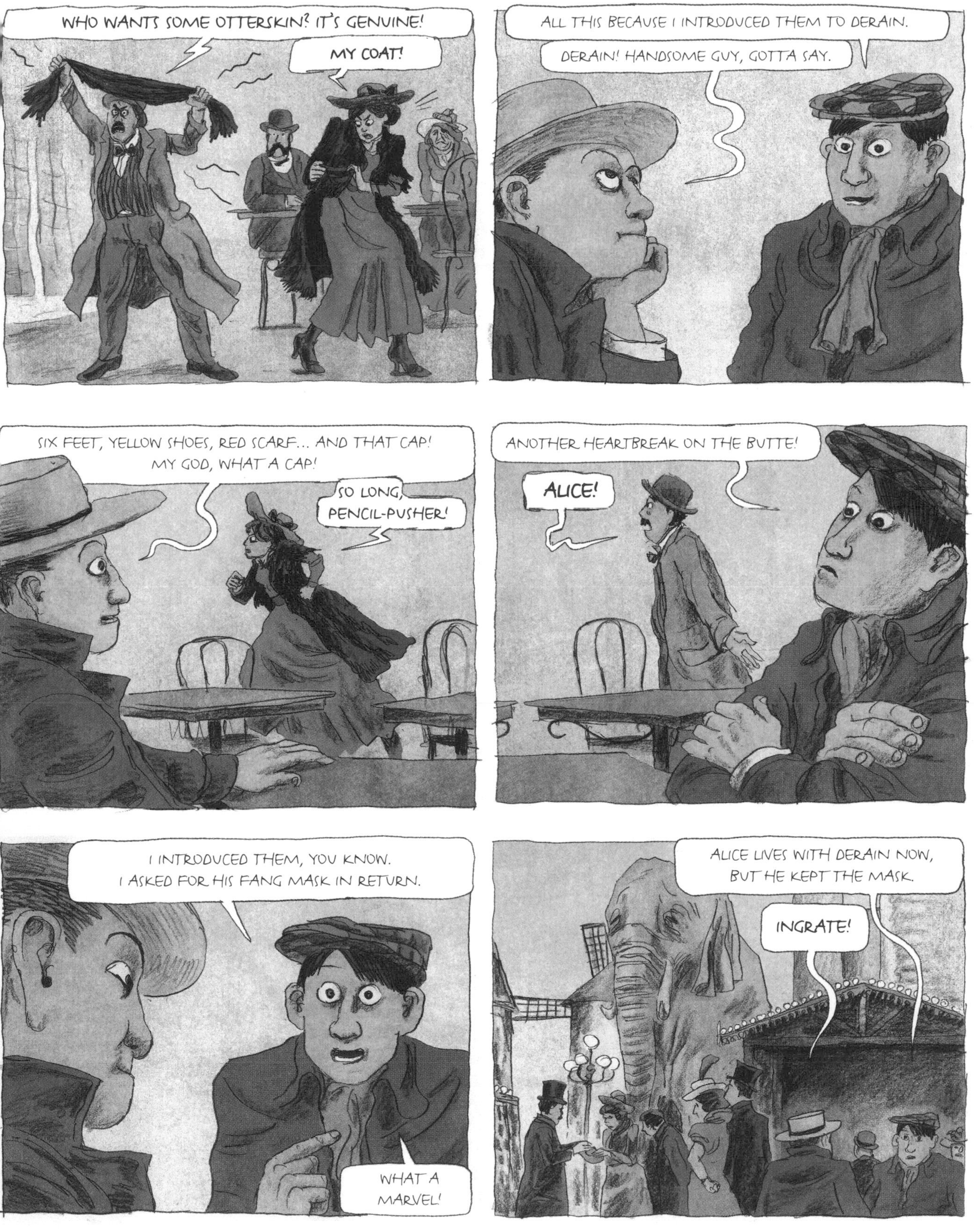
WHO WANTS SOME OTTERSKIN? IT'S GENUINE!
MY COAT!
ALL THIS BECAUSE I INTRODUCED THEM TO DERAIN.
DERAIN! HANDSOME GUY, GOTTA SAY.
SIX FEET, YELLOW SHOES, RED SCARF... AND THAT CAP! MY GOD, WHAT A CAP!
SO LONG, PENCIL-PUSHER!
ANOTHER HEARTBREAK ON THE BUTTE!
ALICE!
I INTRODUCED THEM, YOU KNOW. I ASKED FOR HIS FANG MASK IN RETURN.
WHAT A MARVEL!
ALICE LIVES WITH DERAIN NOW, BUT HE KEPT THE MASK.
INGRATE!

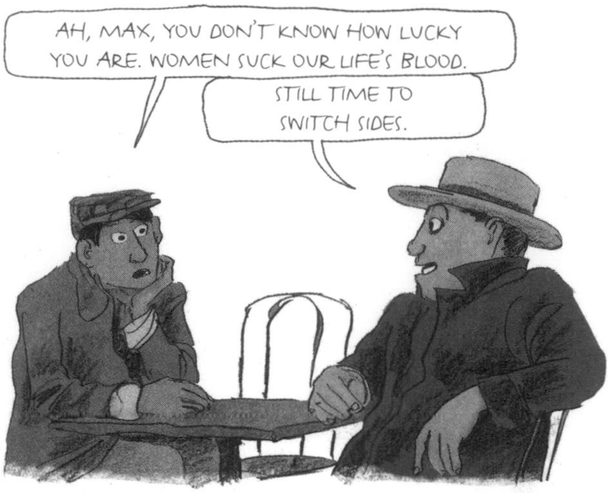
AH, MAX, YOU DON'T KNOW HOW LUCKY YOU ARE. WOMEN SUCK OUR LIFE'S BLOOD.
STILL TIME TO SWITCH SIDES.

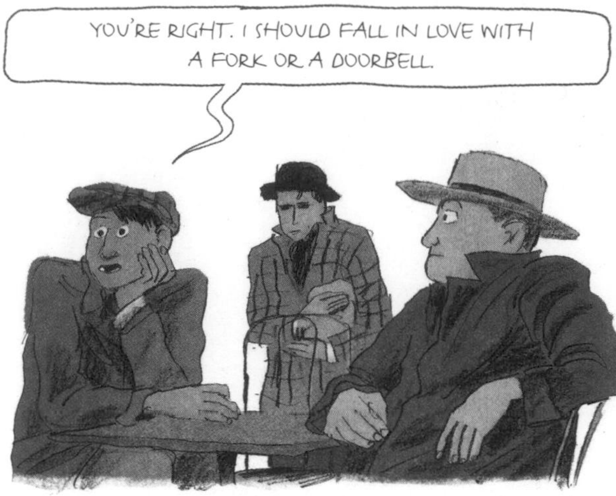
YOU'RE RIGHT. I SHOULD FALL IN LOVE WITH A FORK OR A DOORBELL.

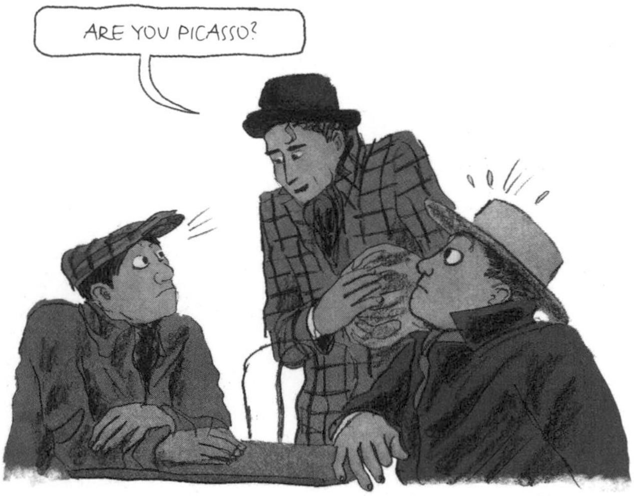
ARE YOU PICASSO?

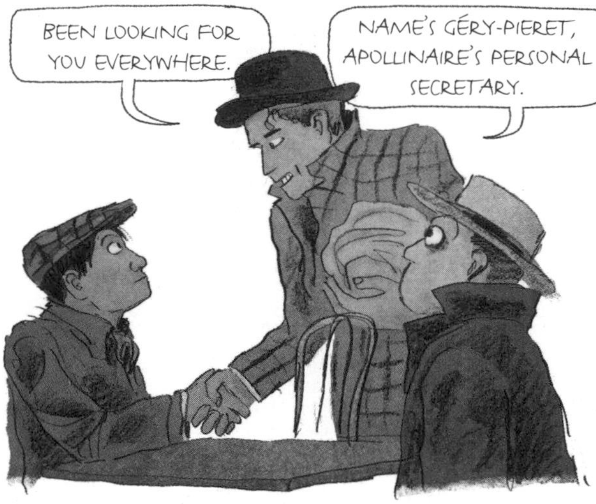
BEEN LOOKING FOR YOU EVERYWHERE.
NAME'S GÉRY-PIERET, APOLLINAIRE'S PERSONAL SECRETARY.

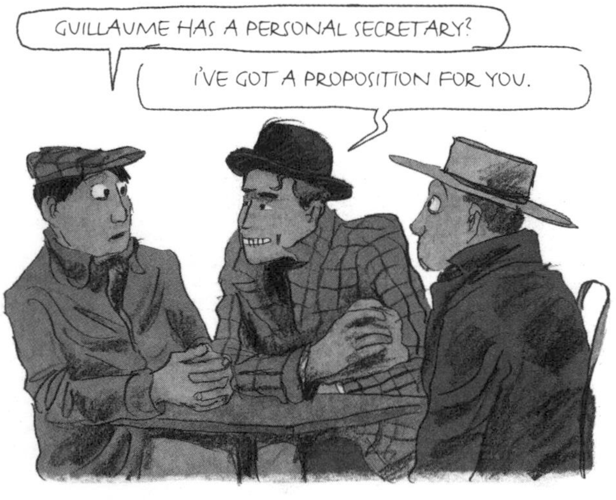
GUILLAUME HAS A PERSONAL SECRETARY?
I'VE GOT A PROPOSITION FOR YOU.

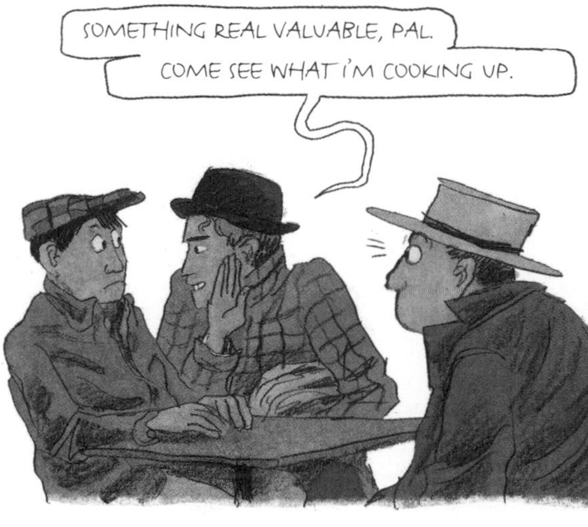
SOMETHING REAL VALUABLE, PAL.
COME SEE WHAT I'M COOKING UP.

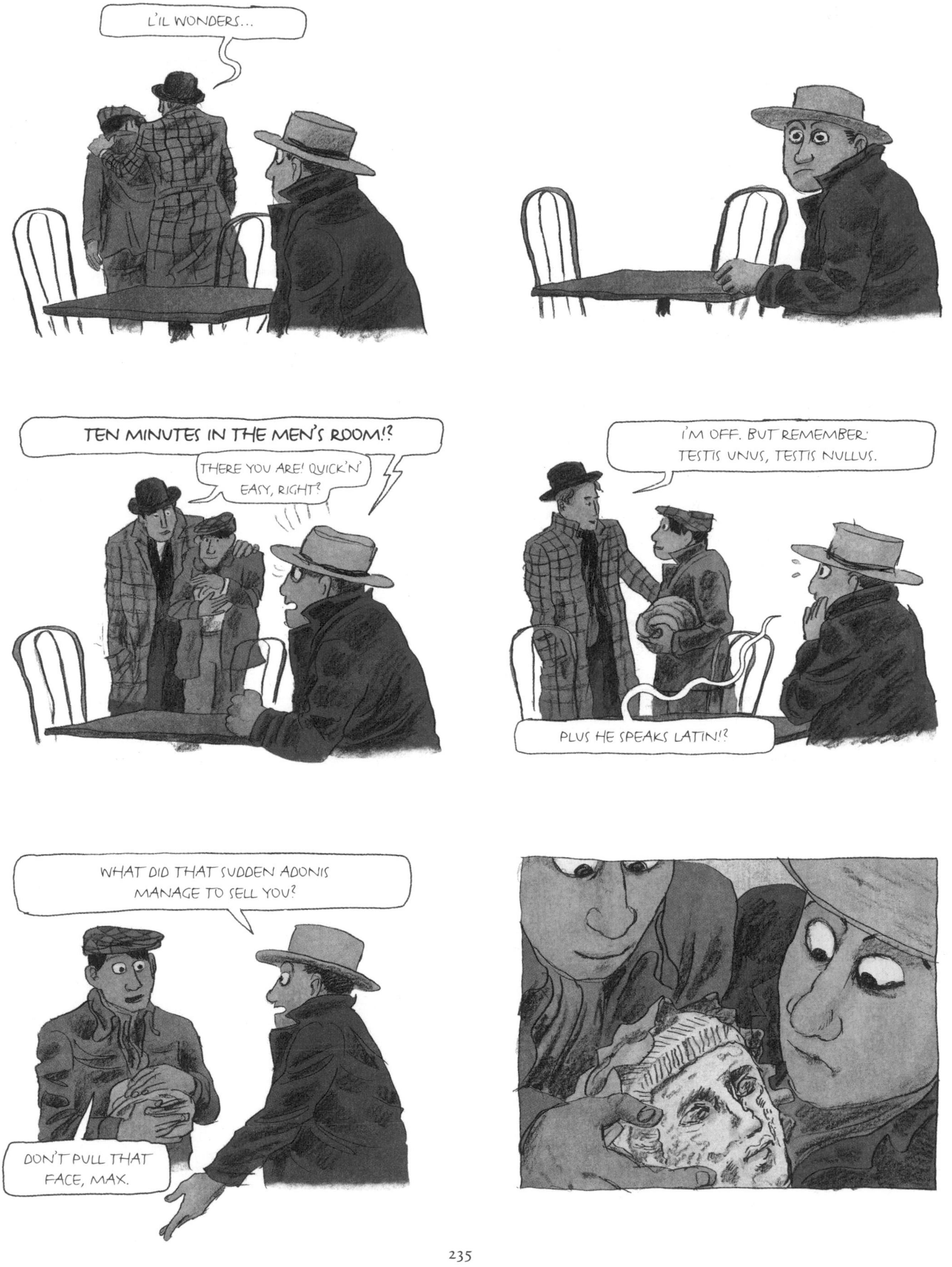
L'IL WONDERS...
TEN MINUTES IN THE MEN'S ROOM!?
THERE YOU ARE! QUICK'N' EASY, RIGHT?
I'M OFF. BUT REMEMBER: TESTIS UNUS, TESTIS NULLUS.
PLUS HE SPEAKS LATIN!?
WHAT DID THAT SUDDEN ADONIS MANAGE TO SELL YOU?
DON'T PULL THAT FACE, MAX.

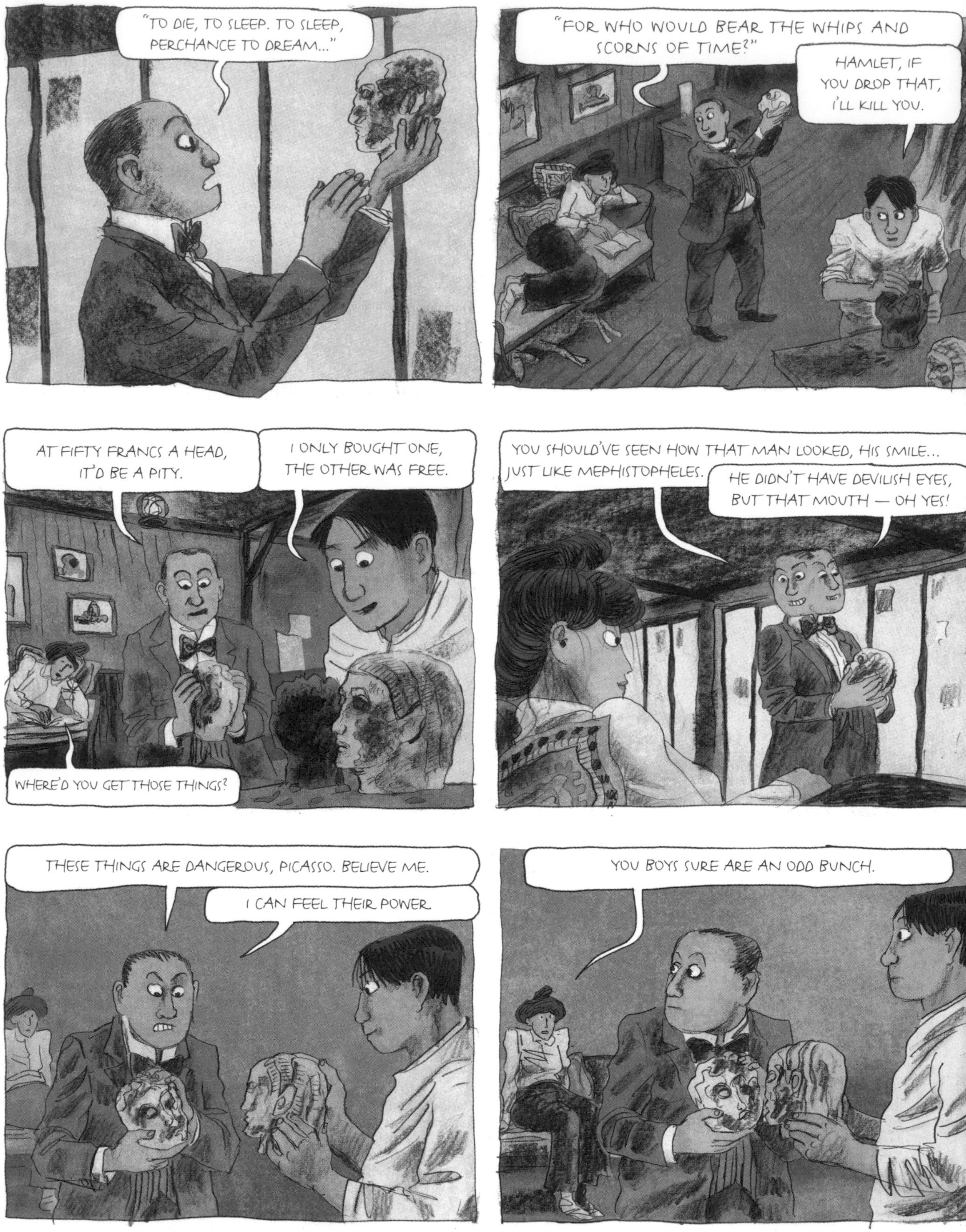
"TO DIE, TO SLEEP. TO SLEEP, PERCHANCE TO DREAM..."
"FOR WHO WOULD BEAR THE WHIPS AND SCORNS OF TIME?"
HAMLET, IF YOU DROP THAT, I'LL KILL YOU.
AT FIFTY FRANCS A HEAD, IT'D BE A PITY.
I ONLY BOUGHT ONE, THE OTHER WAS FREE.
WHERE'D YOU GET THOSE THINGS?
YOU SHOULD'VE SEEN HOW THAT MAN LOOKED, HIS SMILE... JUST LIKE MEPHISTOPHELES.
HE DIDN'T HAVE DEVILISH EYES, BUT THAT MOUTH — OH YES!
THESE THINGS ARE DANGEROUS, PICASSO. BELIEVE ME.
I CAN FEEL THEIR POWER.
YOU BOYS SURE ARE AN ODD BUNCH.

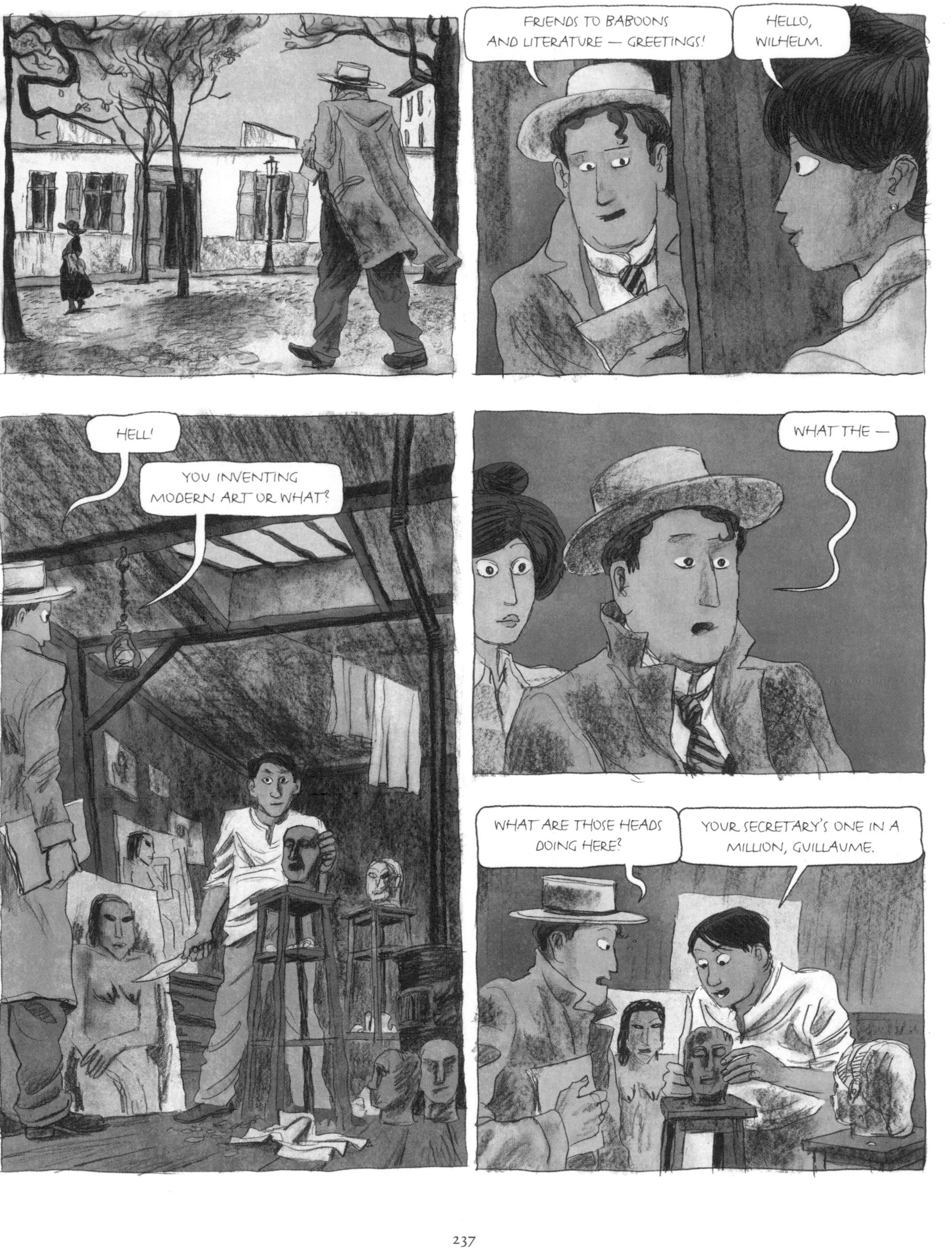
FRIENDS TO BABOONS AND LITERATURE — GREETINGS!
HELLO, WILHELM.
HELL!
YOU INVENTING MODERN ART OR WHAT?
WHAT THE —
WHAT ARE THOSE HEADS DOING HERE?
YOUR SECRETARY'S ONE IN A MILLION, GUILLAUME.

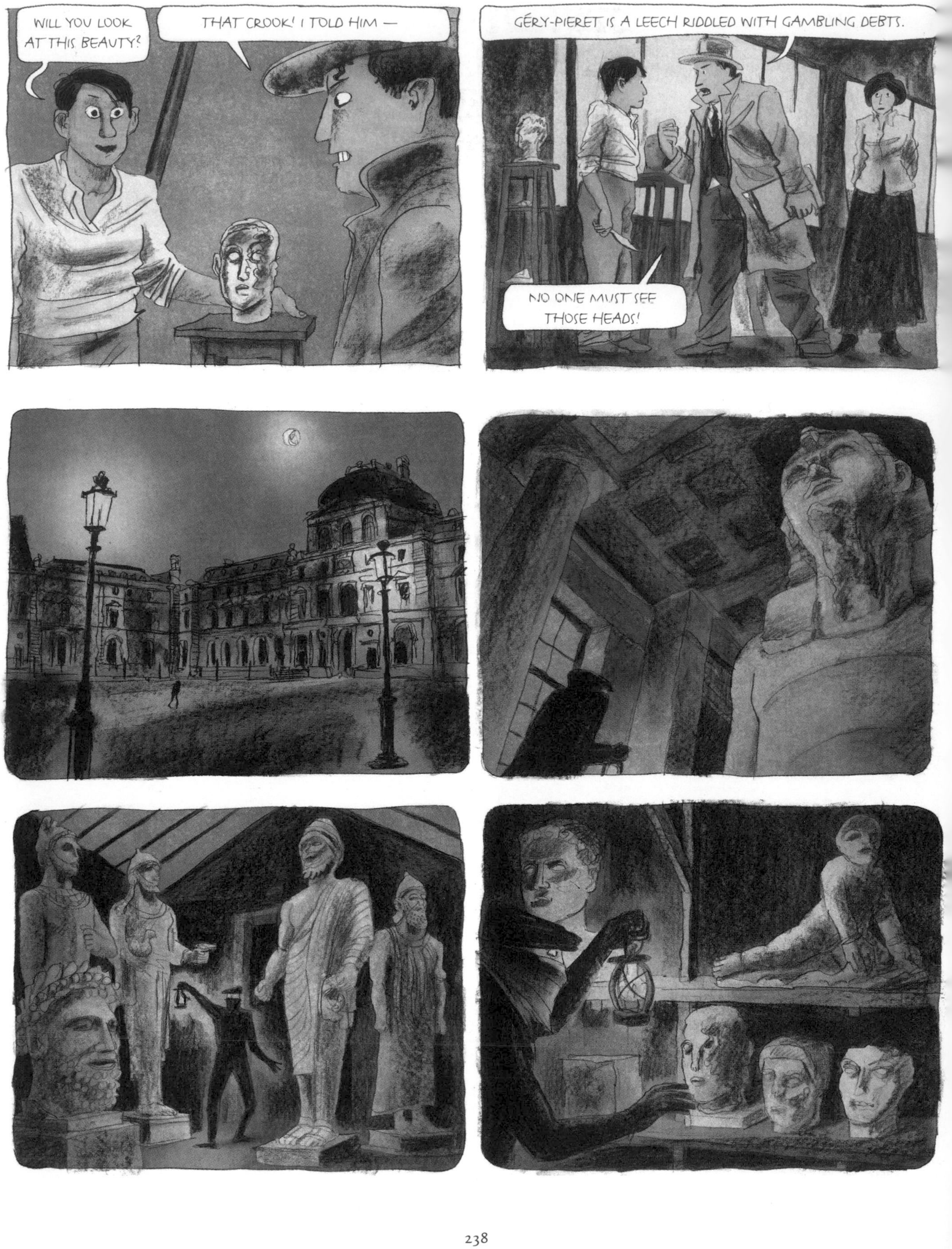
WILL YOU LOOK AT THIS BEAUTY?
THAT CROOK! I TOLD HIM —
GÉRY-PIERET IS A LEECH RIDDLED WITH GAMBLING DEBTS.
NO ONE MUST SEE THOSE HEADS!

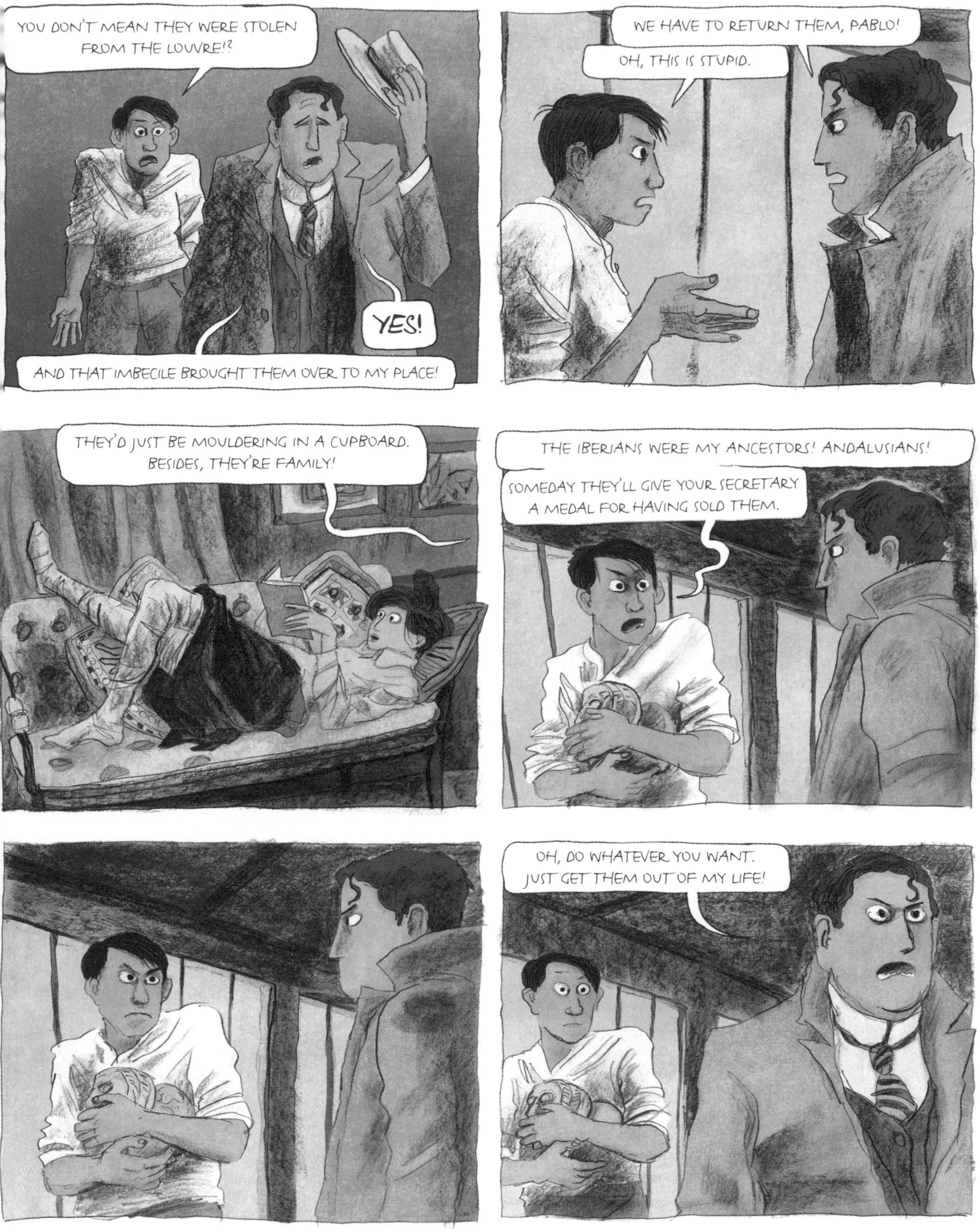
YOU DON'T MEAN THEY WERE STOLEN FROM THE LOUVRE!?
YES!
AND THAT IMBECILE BROUGHT THEM OVER TO MY PLACE!
WE HAVE TO RETURN THEM, PABLO!
OH, THIS IS STUPID.
THEY'D JUST BE MOULDERING IN A CUPBOARD. BESIDES, THEY'RE FAMILY!
THE IBERIANS WERE MY ANCESTORS! ANDALUSIANS!
SOMEDAY THEY'LL GIVE YOUR SECRETARY A MEDAL FOR HAVING SOLD THEM.
OH, DO WHATEVER YOU WANT. JUST GET THEM OUT OF MY LIFE!

HERE, COME AND LOOK AT THIS INSTEAD.

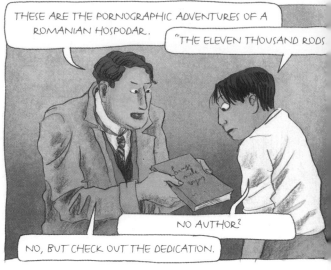

THESE ARE THE PORNOGRAPHIC ADVENTURES OF A ROMANIAN HOSPODAR.

"THE ELEVEN THOUSAND RODS

NO AUTHOR?

NO, BUT CHECK OUT THE DEDICATION.

"MONY, PRINCE OF ROMANY, COCKED HIS HEAD TOWARDS LOVE
HE PERISHED WHILE SERVING THE PEOPLE OF LOVE
A TITLE OF ENORMOUS FAME HAS HE EARNED
AT ANY MOMENT, HE CAN USE HIS WAND..."

"FLAGELLATE THE GODS ABOVE FOR MAKING HIM A MART
HIS HALO IS A ROUND, FULL MOON WE LOOK UP TO DISCOVE
O MAY PICASSO ONE DAY BE INSPIRED TO DO BETTER"

I LIKE THE END!

BUT I'VE ALREADY DONE BETTER

YOU'VE FINISHED YOUR BORDELLO PAINTING?

NO... I FOUND YOU A WIFE.

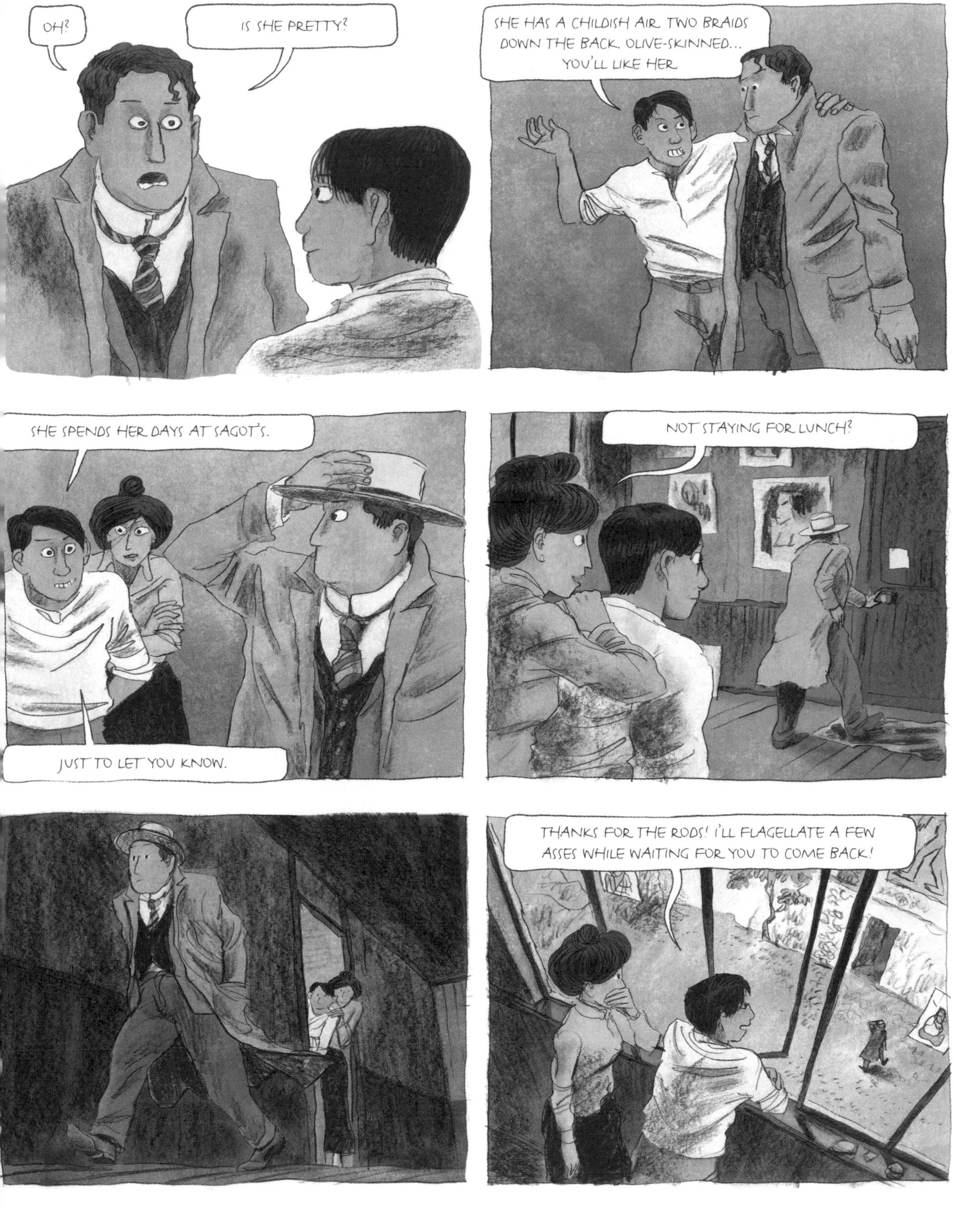
OH?
IS SHE PRETTY?
SHE HAS A CHILDISH AIR. TWO BRAIDS DOWN THE BACK. OLIVE-SKINNED... YOU'LL LIKE HER
SHE SPENDS HER DAYS AT SAGOT'S.
JUST TO LET YOU KNOW.
NOT STAYING FOR LUNCH?
THANKS FOR THE RODS! I'LL FLAGELLATE A FEW ASSES WHILE WAITING FOR YOU TO COME BACK!

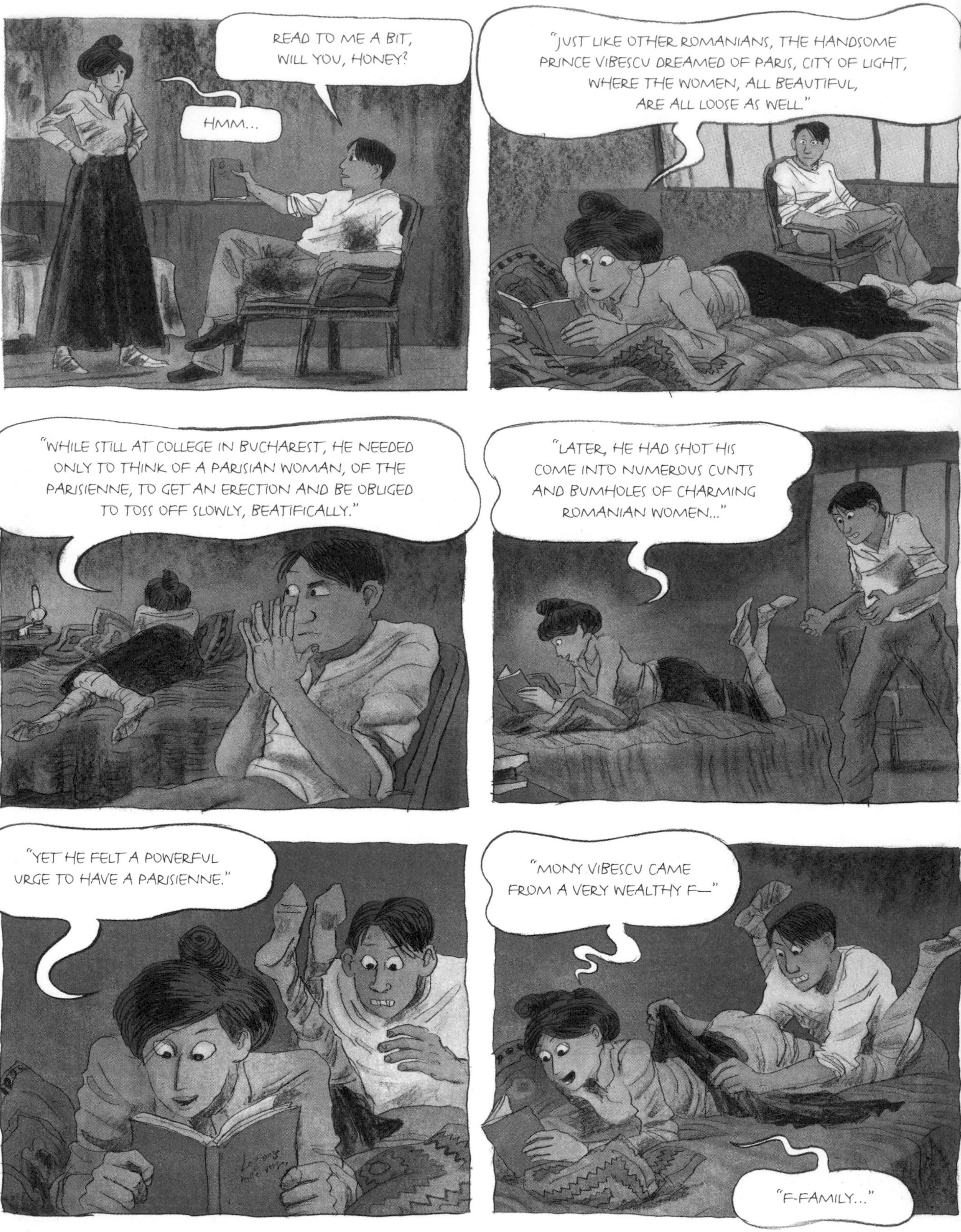

READ TO ME A BIT, WILL YOU, HONEY?
HMM...
"JUST LIKE OTHER ROMANIANS, THE HANDSOME PRINCE VIBESCU DREAMED OF PARIS, CITY OF LIGHT, WHERE THE WOMEN, ALL BEAUTIFUL, ARE ALL LOOSE AS WELL."
"WHILE STILL AT COLLEGE IN BUCHAREST, HE NEEDED ONLY TO THINK OF A PARISIAN WOMAN, OF THE PARISIENNE, TO GET AN ERECTION AND BE OBLIGED TO TOSS OFF SLOWLY, BEATIFICALLY."
"LATER, HE HAD SHOT HIS COME INTO NUMEROUS CUNTS AND BUMHOLES OF CHARMING ROMANIAN WOMEN..."
"YET HE FELT A POWERFUL URGE TO HAVE A PARISIENNE."
"MONY VIBESCU CAME FROM A VERY WEALTHY F—"
"F-FAMILY..."

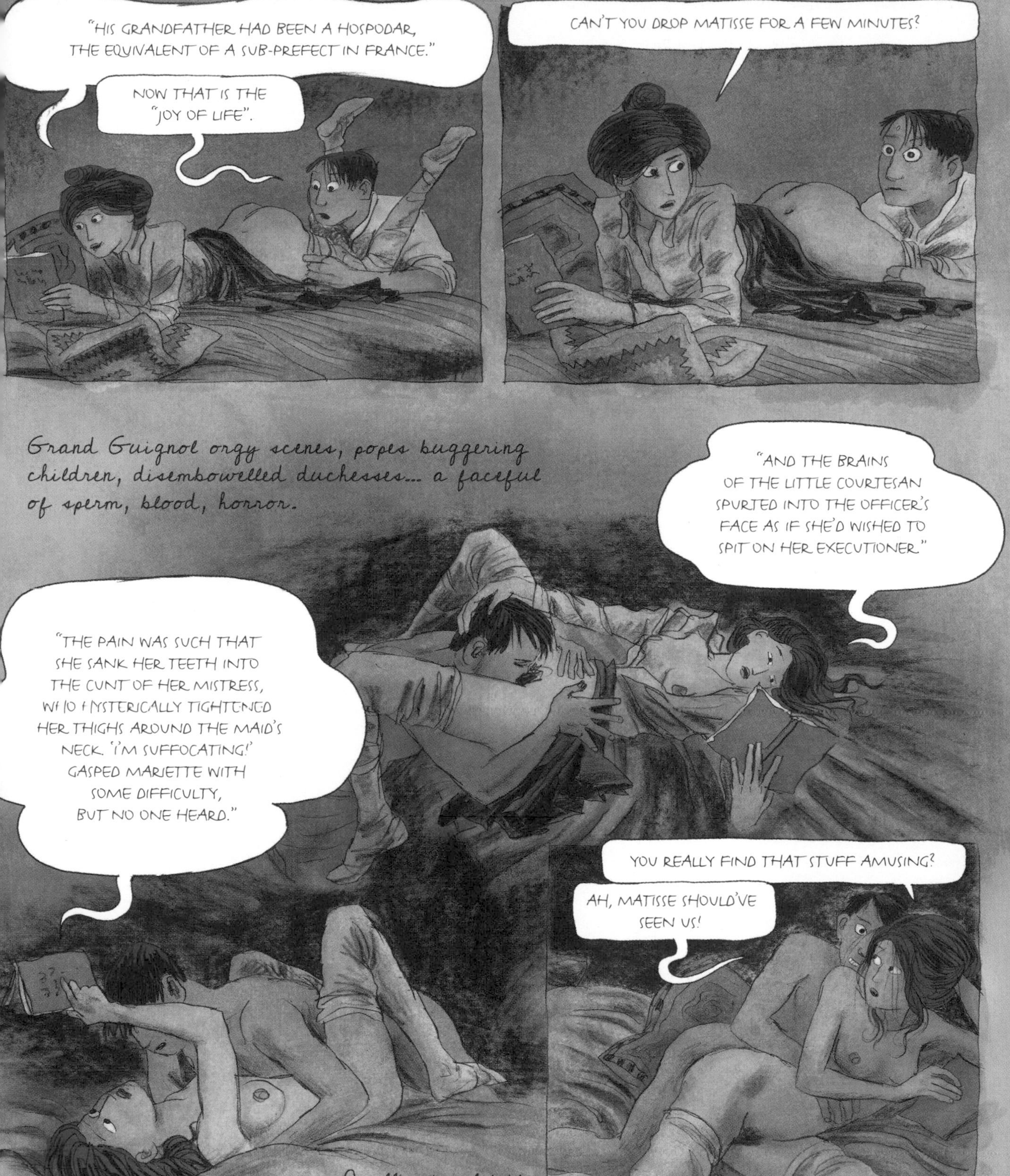
"HIS GRANDFATHER HAD BEEN A HOSPODAR, THE EQUIVALENT OF A SUB-PREFECT IN FRANCE."
NOW THAT IS THE "JOY OF LIFE".
CAN'T YOU DROP MATISSE FOR A FEW MINUTES?
Grand Guignol orgy scenes, popes buggering children, disembowelled duchesses... a faceful of sperm, blood, horror.
"AND THE BRAINS OF THE LITTLE COURTESAN SPURTED INTO THE OFFICER'S FACE AS IF SHE'D WISHED TO SPIT ON HER EXECUTIONER"
"THE PAIN WAS SUCH THAT SHE SANK HER TEETH INTO THE CUNT OF HER MISTRESS, WHO HYSTERICALLY TIGHTENED HER THIGHS AROUND THE MAID'S NECK. 'I'M SUFFOCATING!' GASPED MARIETTE WITH SOME DIFFICULTY, BUT NO ONE HEARD."
Apollinaire let it all out for 120 pages.
YOU REALLY FIND THAT STUFF AMUSING?
AH, MATISSE SHOULD'VE SEEN US!

SPEAKING OF...

WHAT'S THIS ABOUT A WIFE FOR APOLLINAIRE?

OH, I'M QUITE SERIOUS.

SHE'S IN THE PAINTING.

I WATCHED HER AT SAGOT'S. SHE AND GUILLAUME ARE MADE FOR EACH OTHER.

YOU REALLY THINK IT'LL WORK?

I KNOW IT. SHE SMELLS OF BAY LEAVES.

?

Pablo was adopting this visionary tone ever more often.

THEY'RE TWINS. PROUD, STUBBORN, THE SAME WOUNDED GLEAM IN THEIR EYES.

The rest of us poor humans were distracted by the superficial. Only he knew how to see beyond the veil of appearances.

!?

A SKINNY GIRL AND A GOURMAND — THEY'LL BE A LEGENDARY COUPLE!

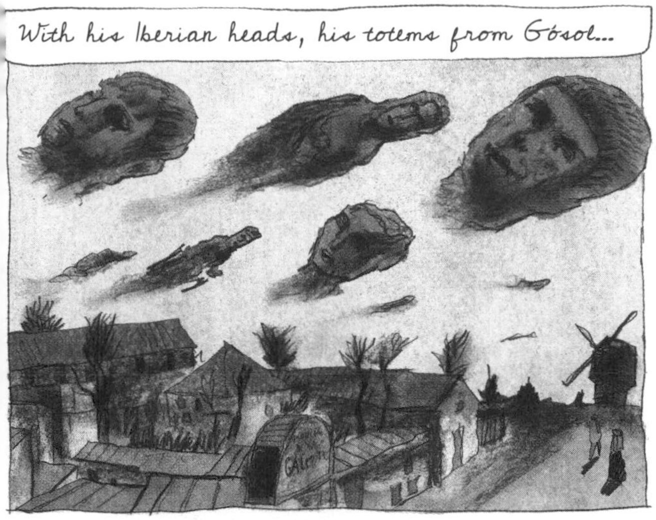
With his Iberian heads, his totems from Gósol...
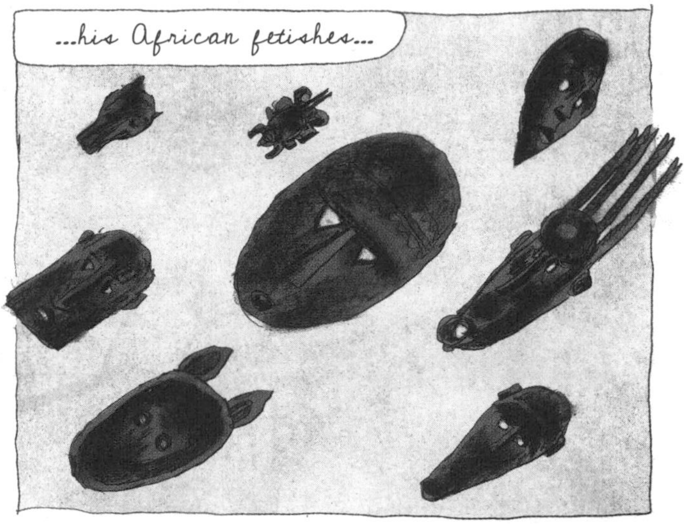
...his African fetishes...
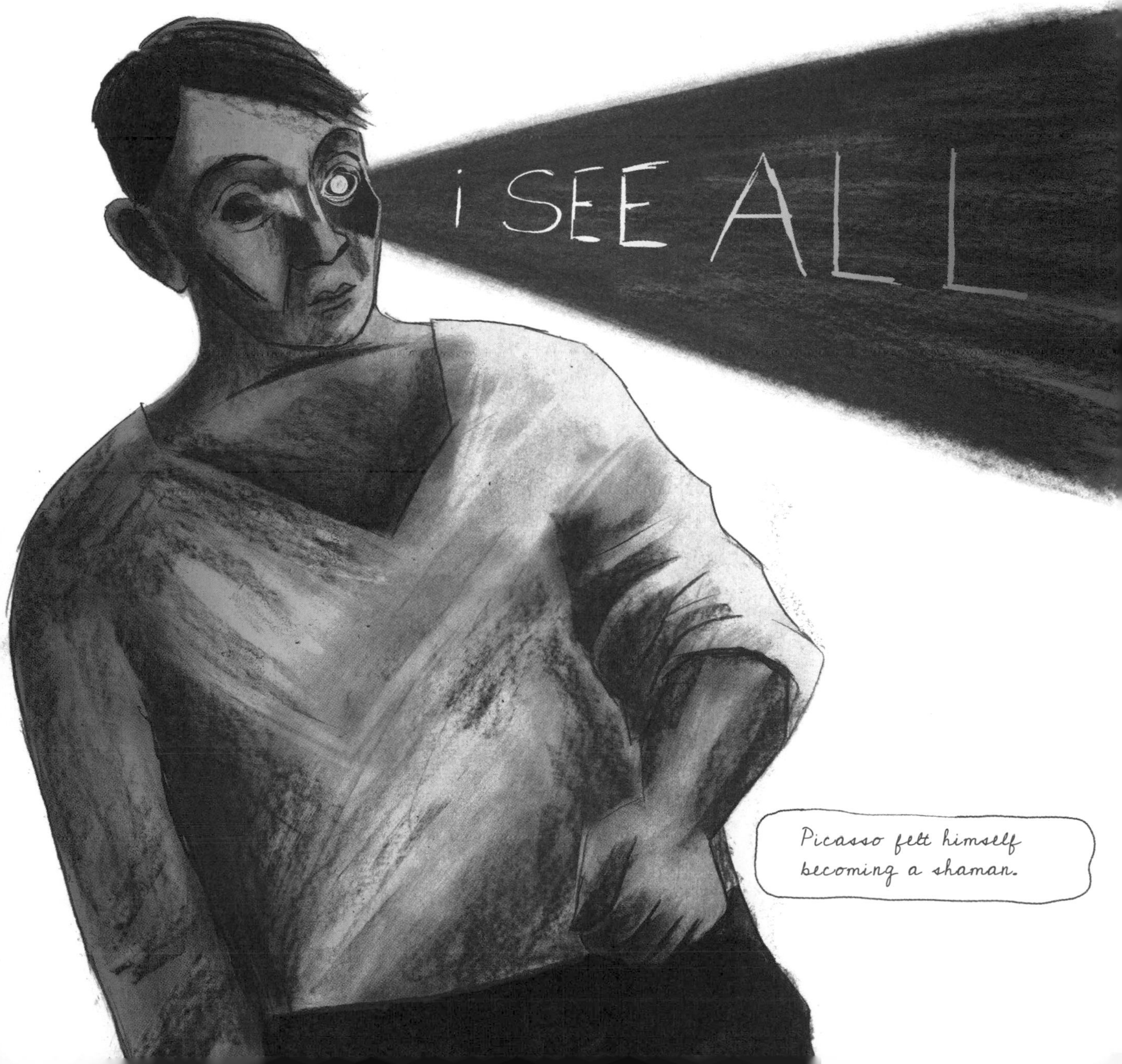
i SEE ALL
Picasso felt himself becoming a shaman.

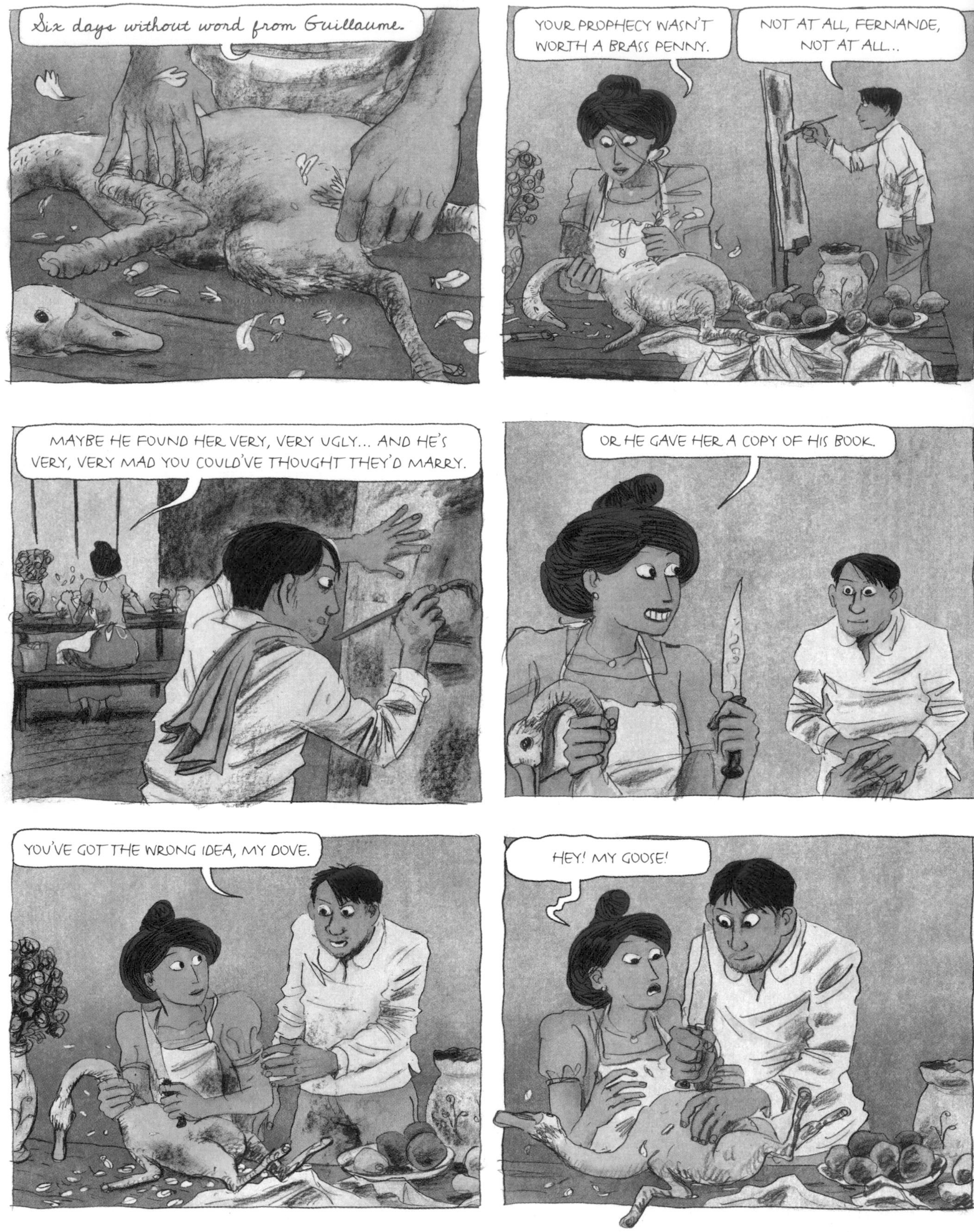
Six days without word from Guillaume.
YOUR PROPHECY WASN'T WORTH A BRASS PENNY.
NOT AT ALL, FERNANDE, NOT AT ALL...
MAYBE HE FOUND HER VERY, VERY UGLY... AND HE'S VERY, VERY MAD YOU COULD'VE THOUGHT THEY'D MARRY.
OR HE GAVE HER A COPY OF HIS BOOK.
YOU'VE GOT THE WRONG IDEA, MY DOVE.
HEY! MY GOOSE!

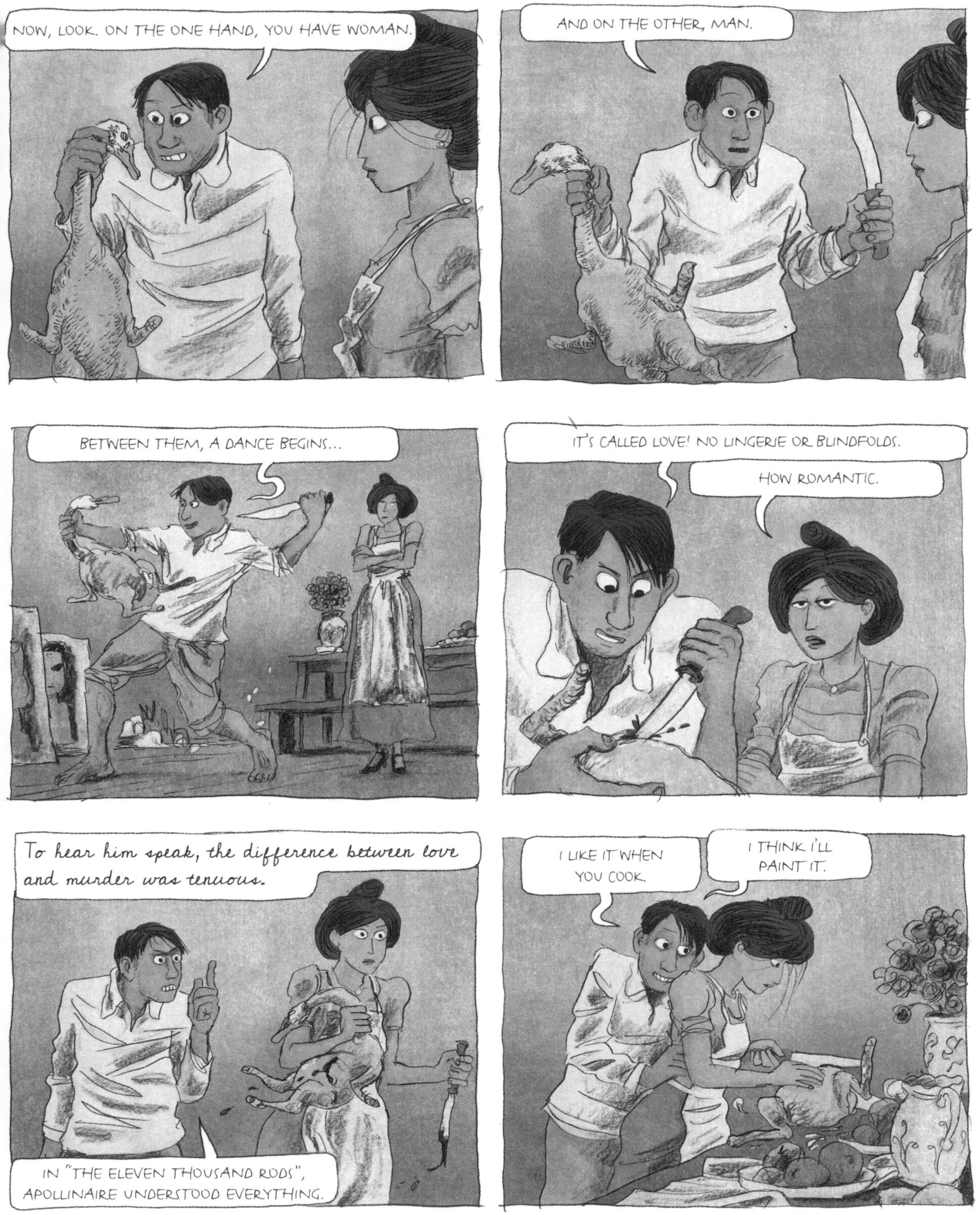
NOW, LOOK. ON THE ONE HAND, YOU HAVE WOMAN.
AND ON THE OTHER, MAN.
BETWEEN THEM, A DANCE BEGINS...
IT'S CALLED LOVE! NO LINGERIE OR BLINDFOLDS.
HOW ROMANTIC.
To hear him speak, the difference between love and murder was tenuous.
IN "THE ELEVEN THOUSAND RODS", APOLLINAIRE UNDERSTOOD EVERYTHING.
I LIKE IT WHEN YOU COOK.
I THINK I'LL PAINT IT.

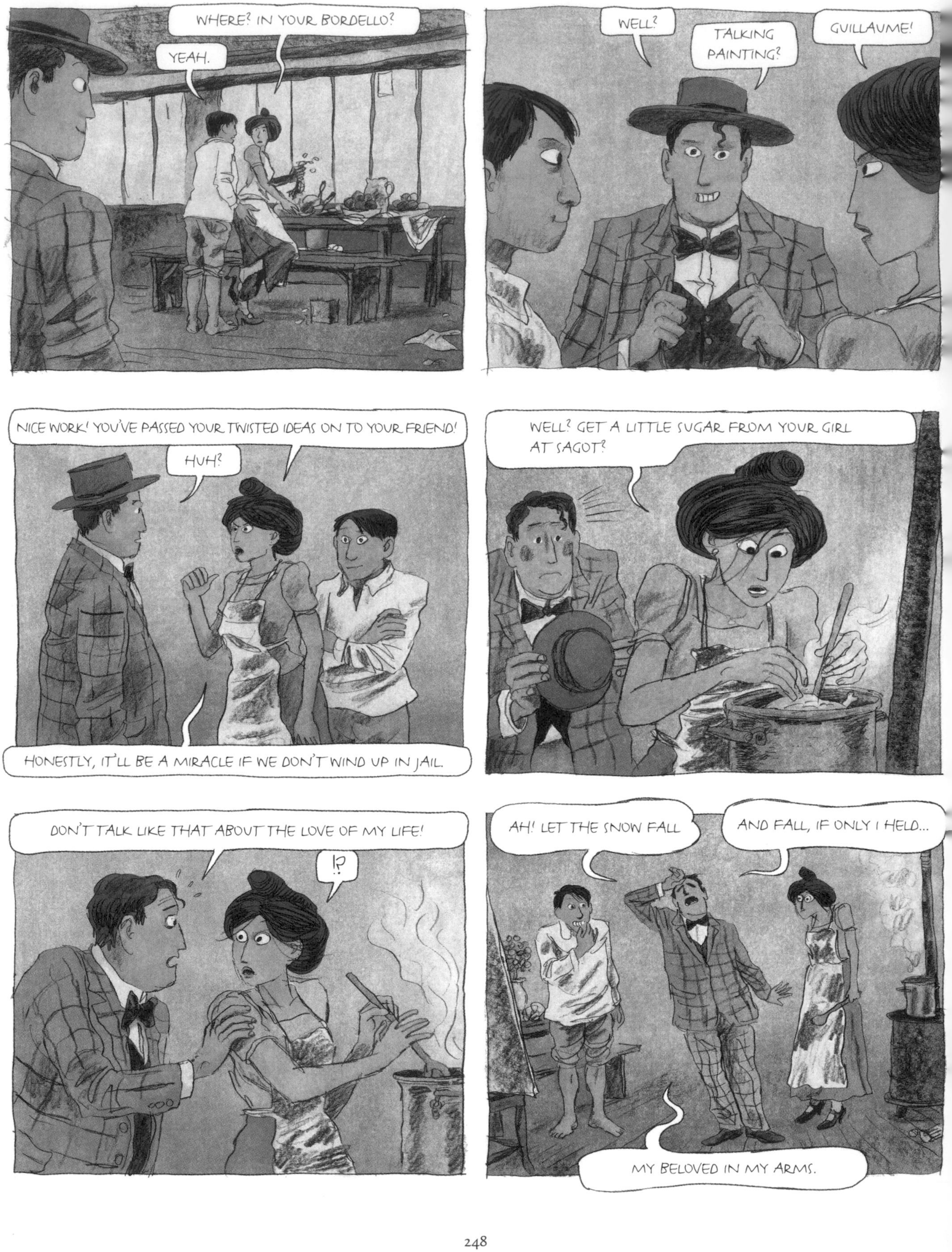
WHERE? IN YOUR BORDELLO?
YEAH.
WELL?
TALKING PAINTING?
GUILLAUME!
NICE WORK! YOU'VE PASSED YOUR TWISTED IDEAS ON TO YOUR FRIEND!
HUH?
HONESTLY, IT'LL BE A MIRACLE IF WE DON'T WIND UP IN JAIL.
WELL? GET A LITTLE SUGAR FROM YOUR GIRL AT SAGOT?
DON'T TALK LIKE THAT ABOUT THE LOVE OF MY LIFE!
!?
AH! LET THE SNOW FALL
AND FALL, IF ONLY I HELD...
MY BELOVED IN MY ARMS.

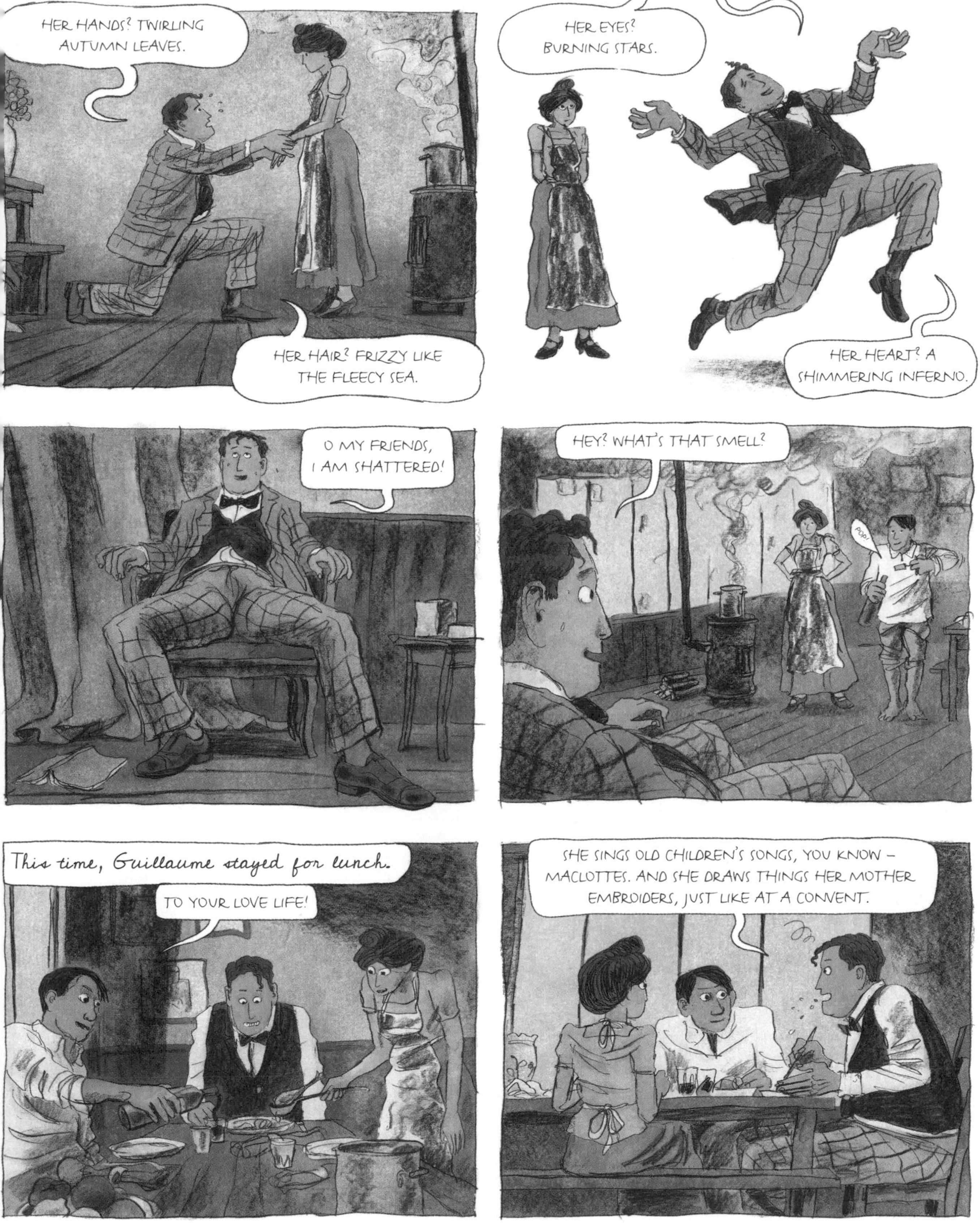
HER HANDS? TWIRLING AUTUMN LEAVES.
HER HAIR? FRIZZY LIKE THE FLEECY SEA.
HER EYES? BURNING STARS.
HER HEART? A SHIMMERING INFERNO.
O MY FRIENDS, I AM SHATTERED!
HEY? WHAT'S THAT SMELL?
POP!
This time, Guillaume stayed for lunch.
TO YOUR LOVE LIFE!
SHE SINGS OLD CHILDREN'S SONGS, YOU KNOW – MACLOTTES. AND SHE DRAWS THINGS HER MOTHER EMBROIDERS, JUST LIKE AT A CONVENT.

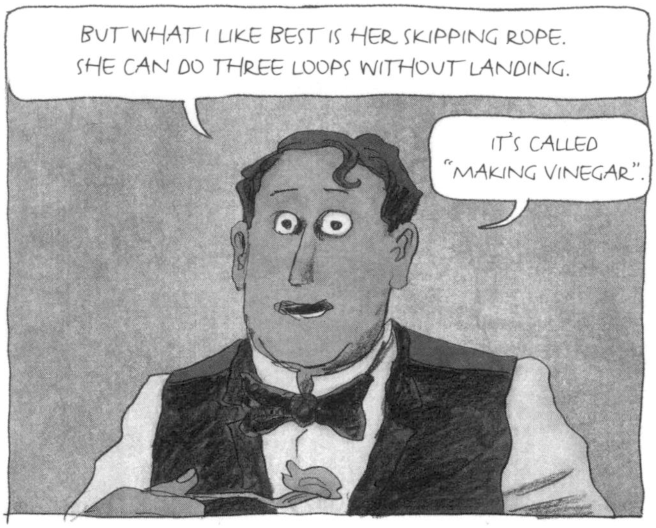
BUT WHAT I LIKE BEST IS HER SKIPPING ROPE.
SHE CAN DO THREE LOOPS WITHOUT LANDING.
IT'S CALLED "MAKING VINEGAR".

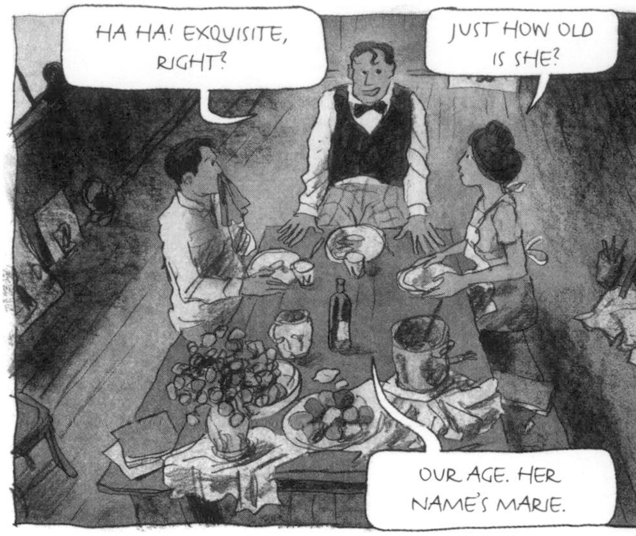
HA HA! EXQUISITE, RIGHT?
JUST HOW OLD IS SHE?
OUR AGE. HER NAME'S MARIE.

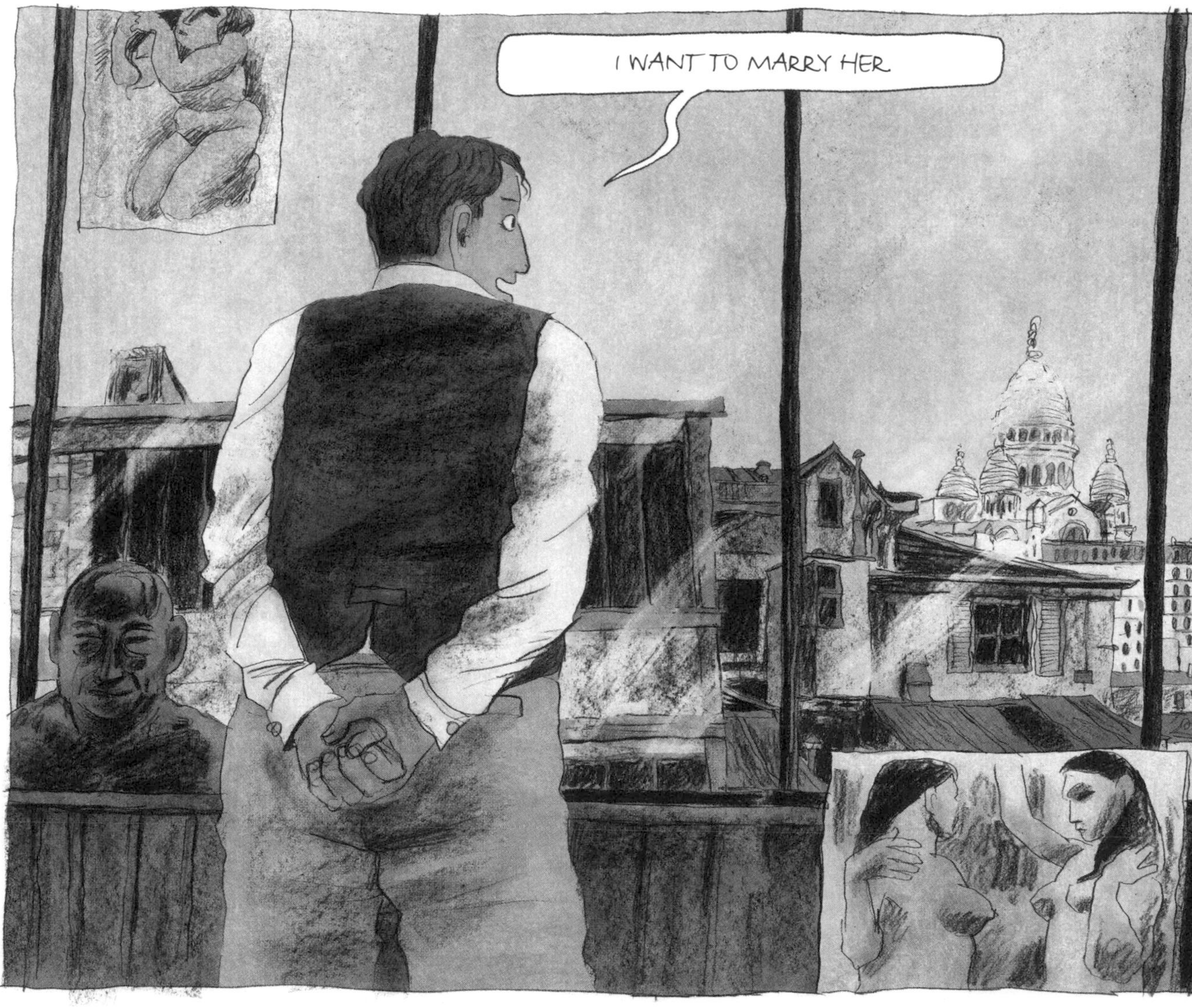
I WANT TO MARRY HER

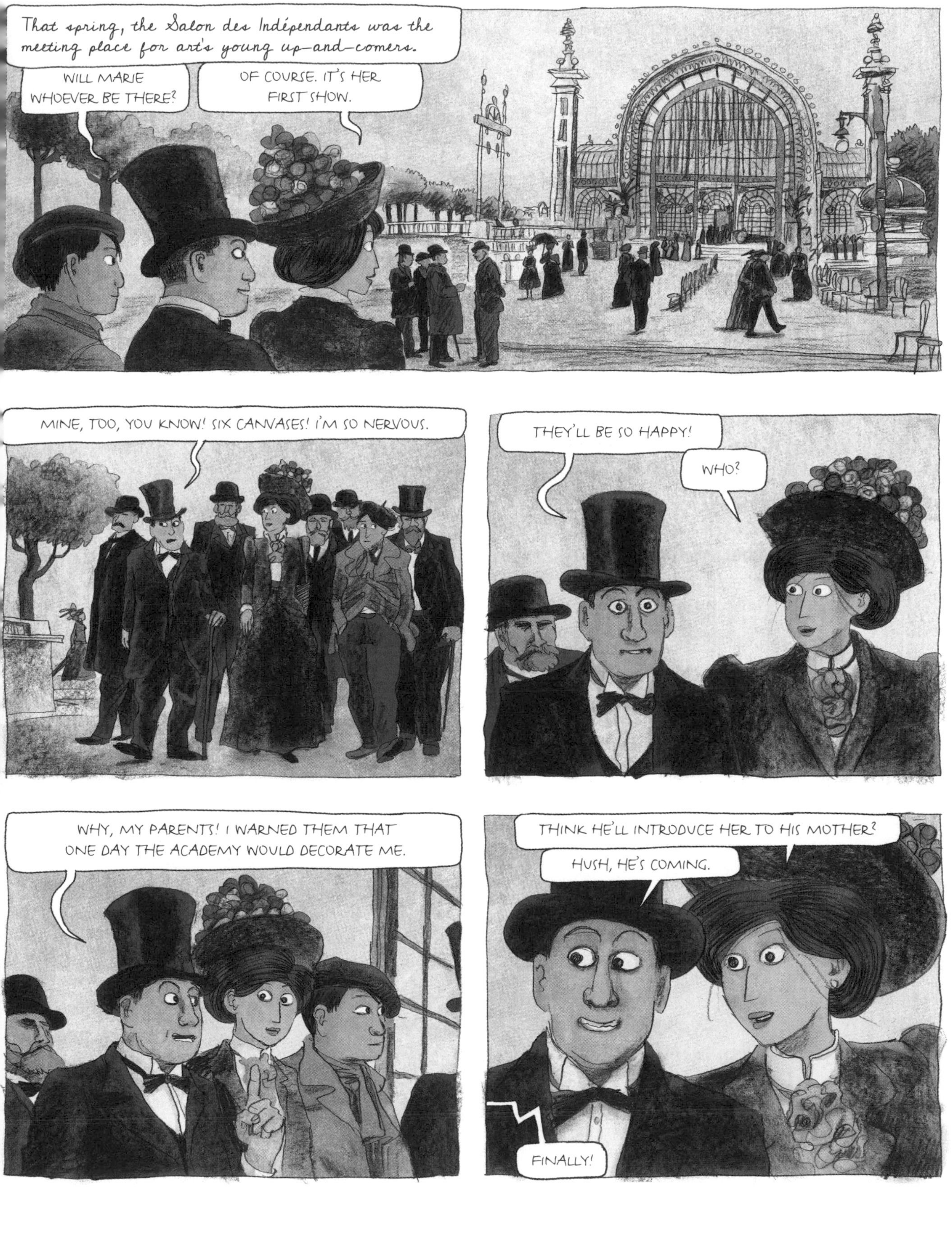
That spring, the Salon des Indépendants was the meeting place for art's young up-and-comers.
WILL MARIE WHOEVER BE THERE?
OF COURSE. IT'S HER FIRST SHOW.
MINE, TOO, YOU KNOW! SIX CANVASES! I'M SO NERVOUS.
THEY'LL BE SO HAPPY!
WHO?
WHY, MY PARENTS! I WARNED THEM THAT ONE DAY THE ACADEMY WOULD DECORATE ME.
THINK HE'LL INTRODUCE HER TO HIS MOTHER?
HUSH, HE'S COMING.
FINALLY!

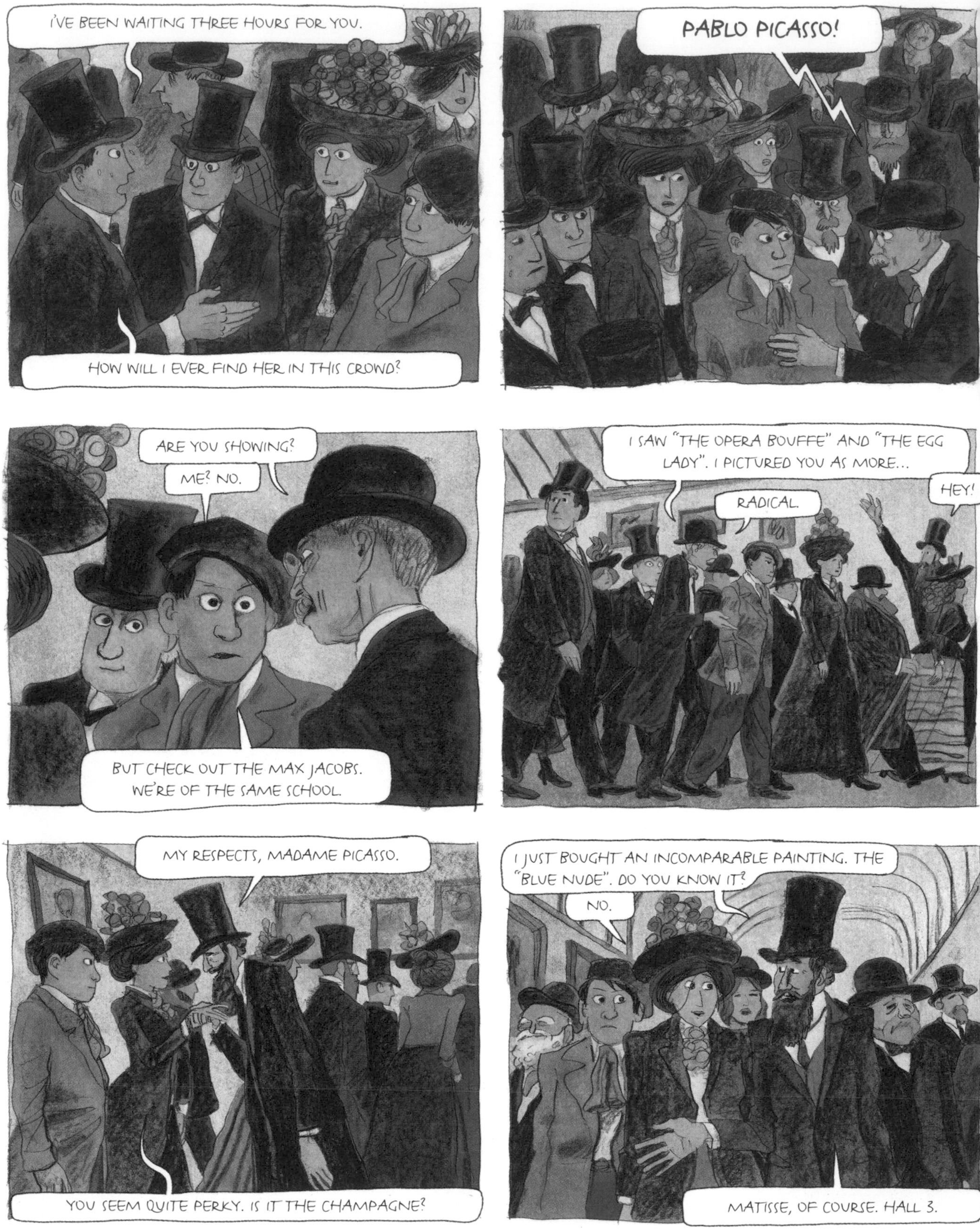
I'VE BEEN WAITING THREE HOURS FOR YOU.
HOW WILL I EVER FIND HER IN THIS CROWD?
PABLO PICASSO!
ARE YOU SHOWING?
ME? NO.
BUT CHECK OUT THE MAX JACOBS. WE'RE OF THE SAME SCHOOL.
I SAW "THE OPERA BOUFFE" AND "THE EGG LADY". I PICTURED YOU AS MORE...
RADICAL.
HEY!
MY RESPECTS, MADAME PICASSO.
YOU SEEM QUITE PERKY. IS IT THE CHAMPAGNE?
I JUST BOUGHT AN INCOMPARABLE PAINTING. THE "BLUE NUDE". DO YOU KNOW IT?
NO.
MATISSE, OF COURSE. HALL 3.

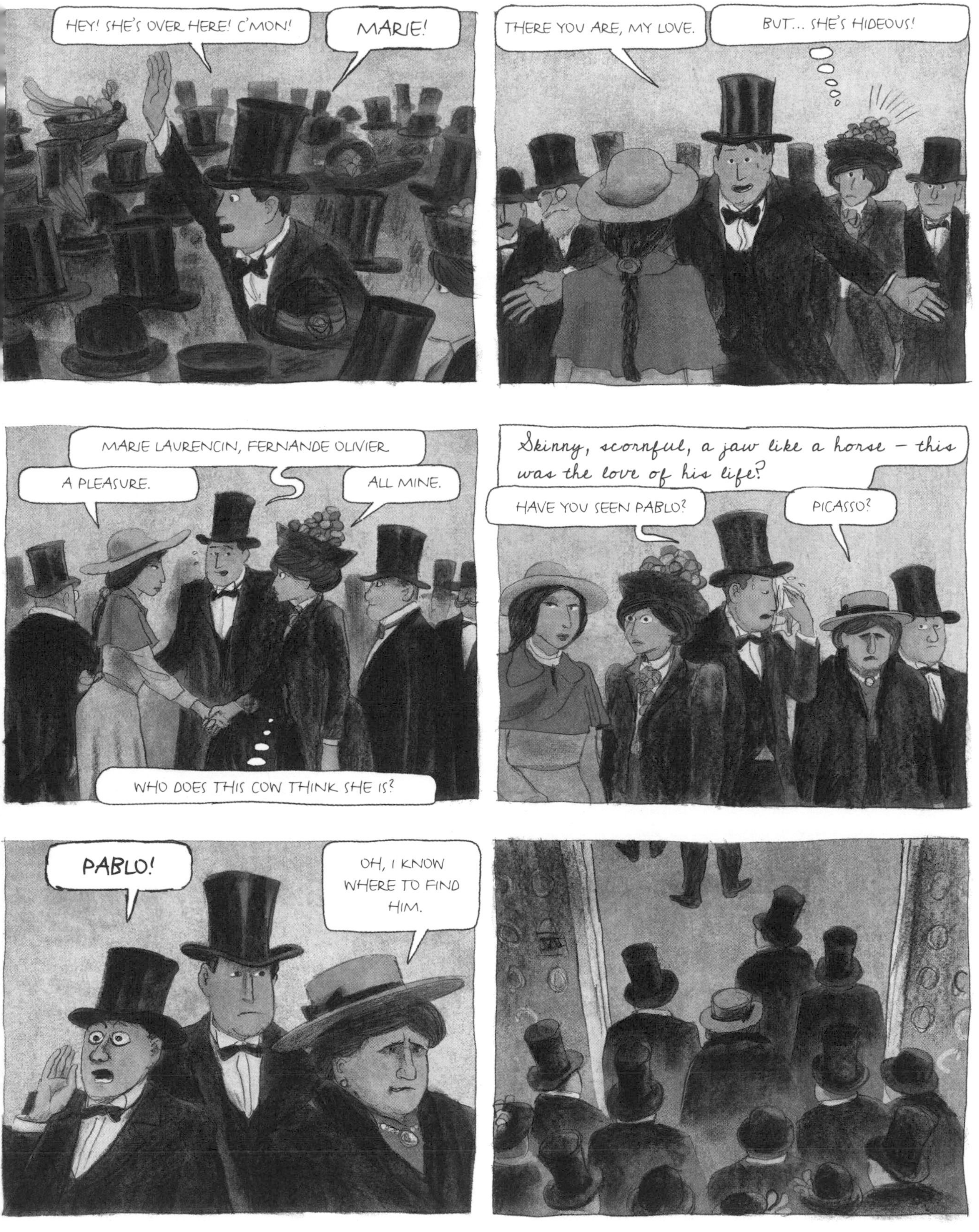
HEY! SHE'S OVER HERE! C'MON!
MARIE!
THERE YOU ARE, MY LOVE.
BUT... SHE'S HIDEOUS!
MARIE LAURENCIN, FERNANDE OLIVIER.
A PLEASURE.
ALL MINE.
WHO DOES THIS COW THINK SHE IS?
Skinny, scornful, a jaw like a horse – this was the love of his life?
HAVE YOU SEEN PABLO?
PICASSO?
PABLO!
OH, I KNOW WHERE TO FIND HIM.

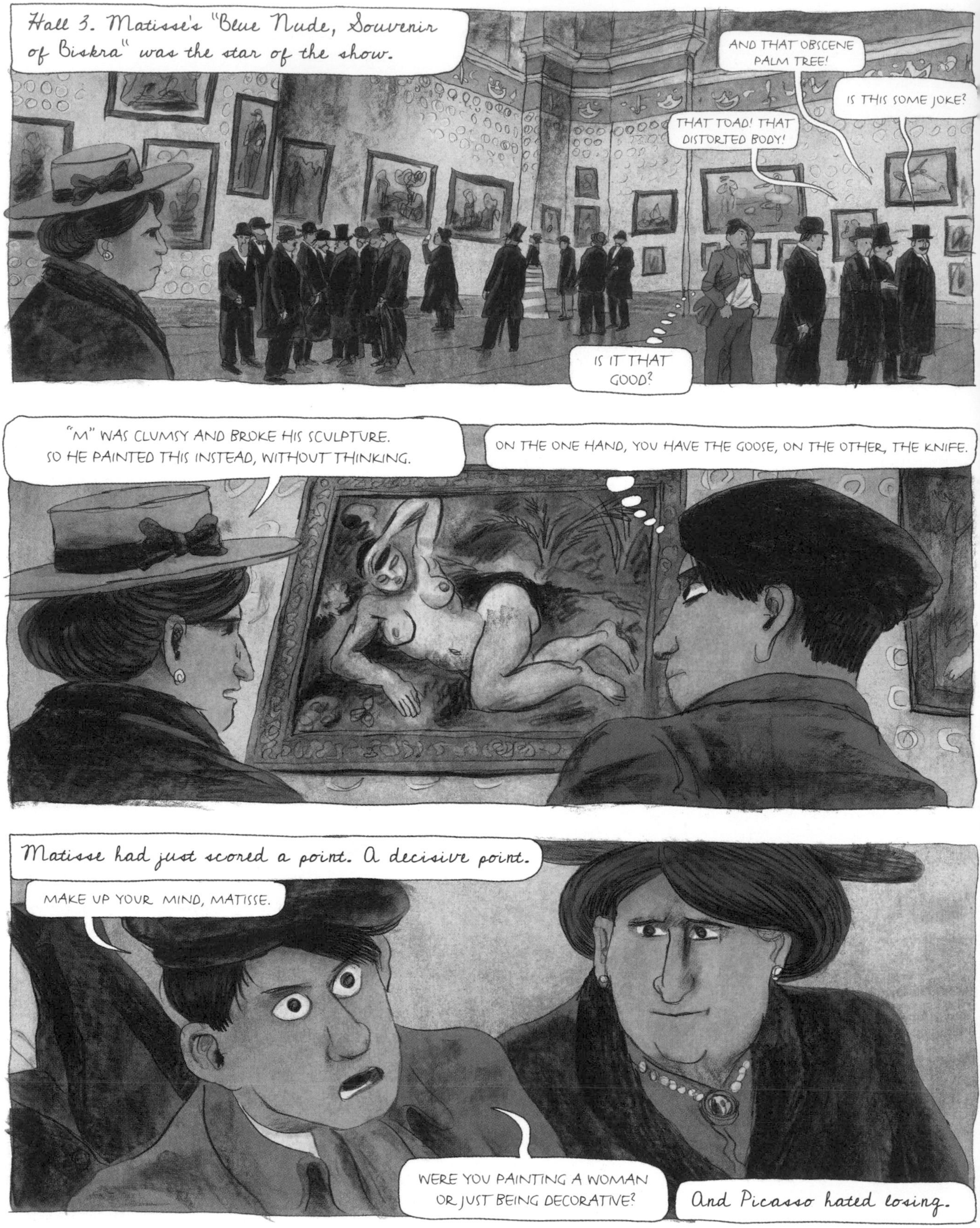
Hall 3. Matisse's "Blue Nude, Souvenir of Biskra" was the star of the show.
AND THAT OBSCENE PALM TREE!
IS THIS SOME JOKE?
THAT TOAD! THAT DISTORTED BODY!
IS IT THAT GOOD?
"M" WAS CLUMSY AND BROKE HIS SCULPTURE. SO HE PAINTED THIS INSTEAD, WITHOUT THINKING.
ON THE ONE HAND, YOU HAVE THE GOOSE, ON THE OTHER, THE KNIFE.
Matisse had just scored a point. A decisive point.
MAKE UP YOUR MIND, MATISSE.
WERE YOU PAINTING A WOMAN OR JUST BEING DECORATIVE?
And Picasso hated losing.

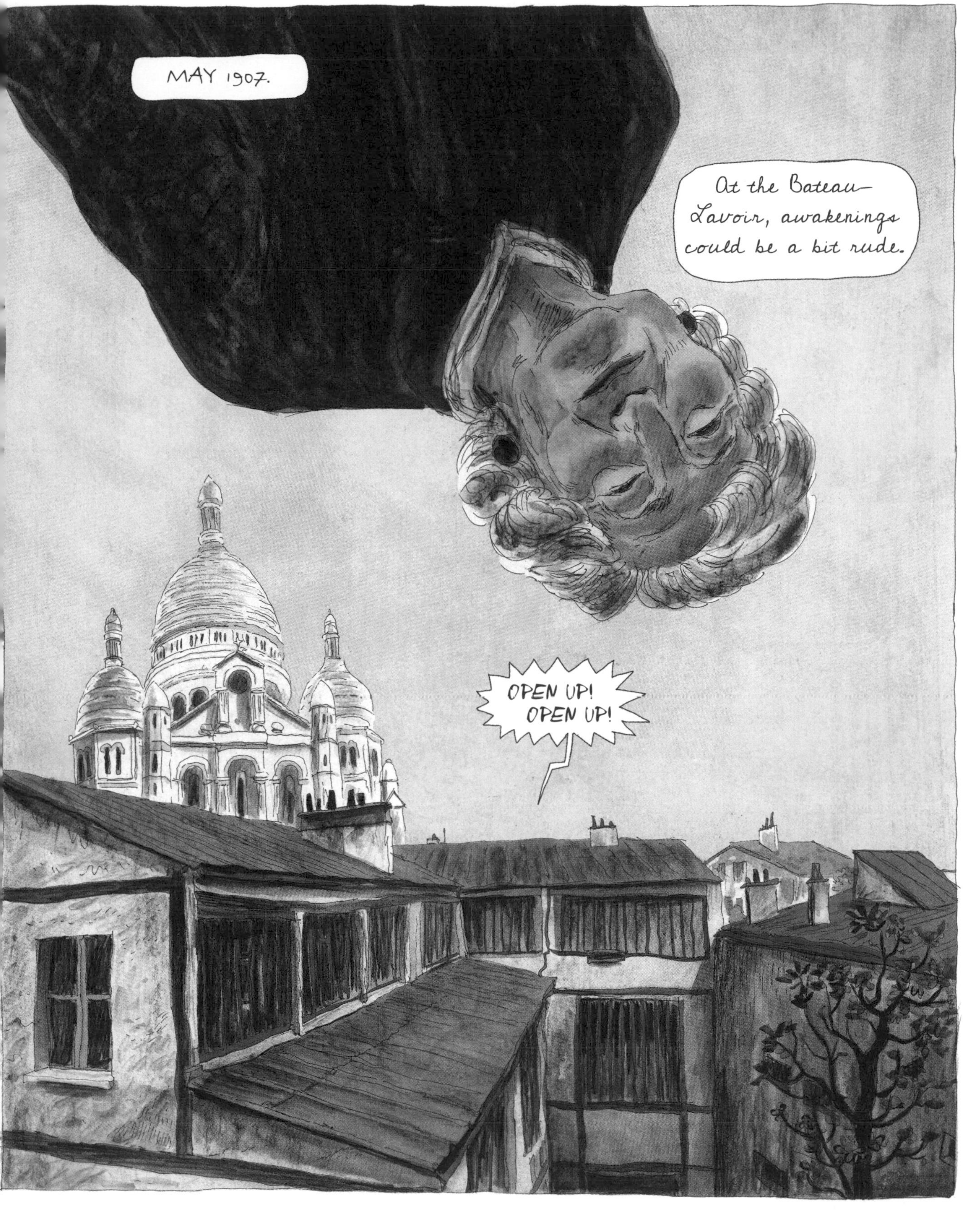
MAY 1907.
At the Bateau-Lavoir, awakenings could be a bit rude.
OPEN UP! OPEN UP!

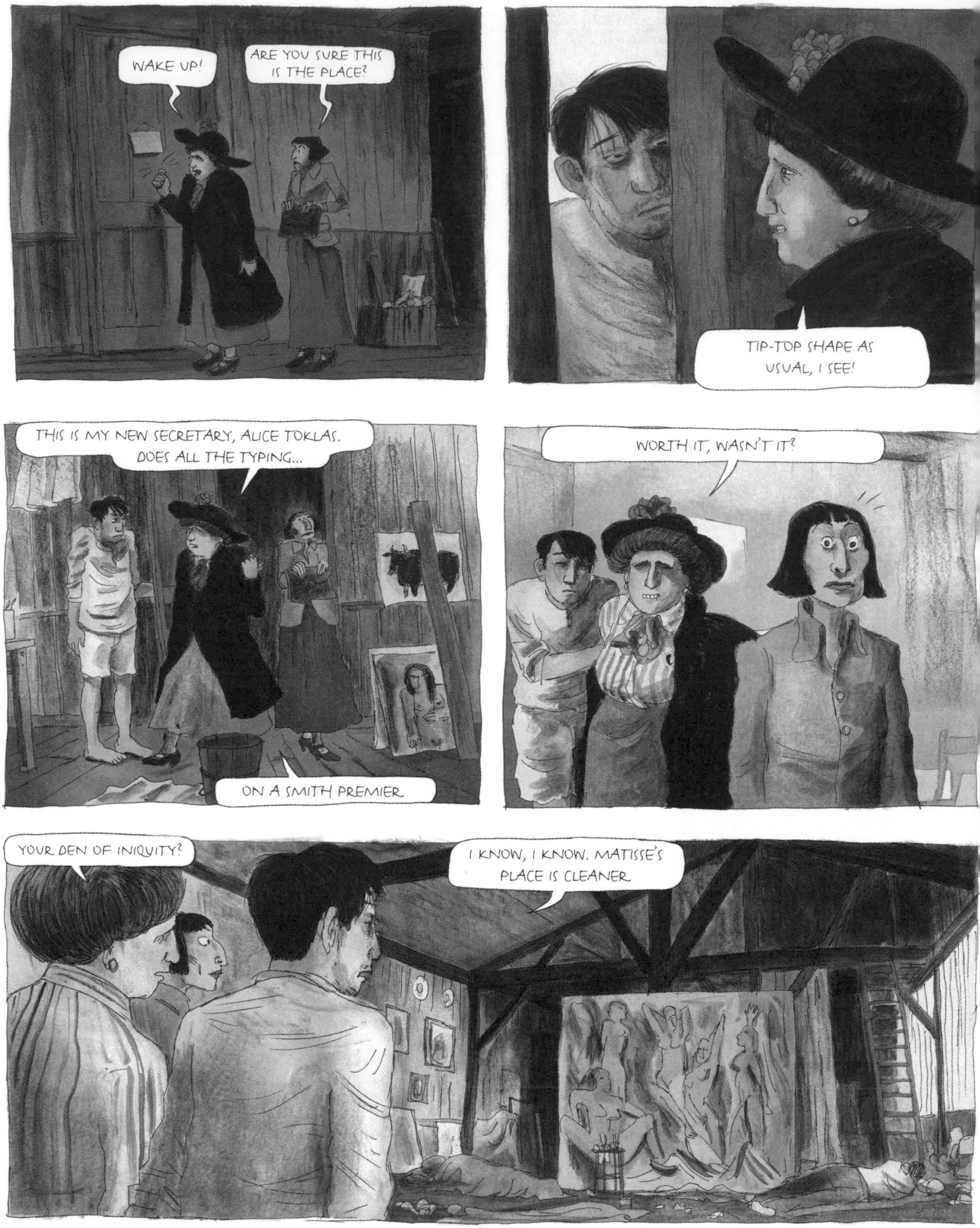
WAKE UP!
ARE YOU SURE THIS IS THE PLACE?
TIP-TOP SHAPE AS USUAL, I SEE!
THIS IS MY NEW SECRETARY, ALICE TOKLAS. DOES ALL THE TYPING...
ON A SMITH PREMIER
WORTH IT, WASN'T IT?
YOUR DEN OF INIQUITY?
I KNOW, I KNOW. MATISSE'S PLACE IS CLEANER

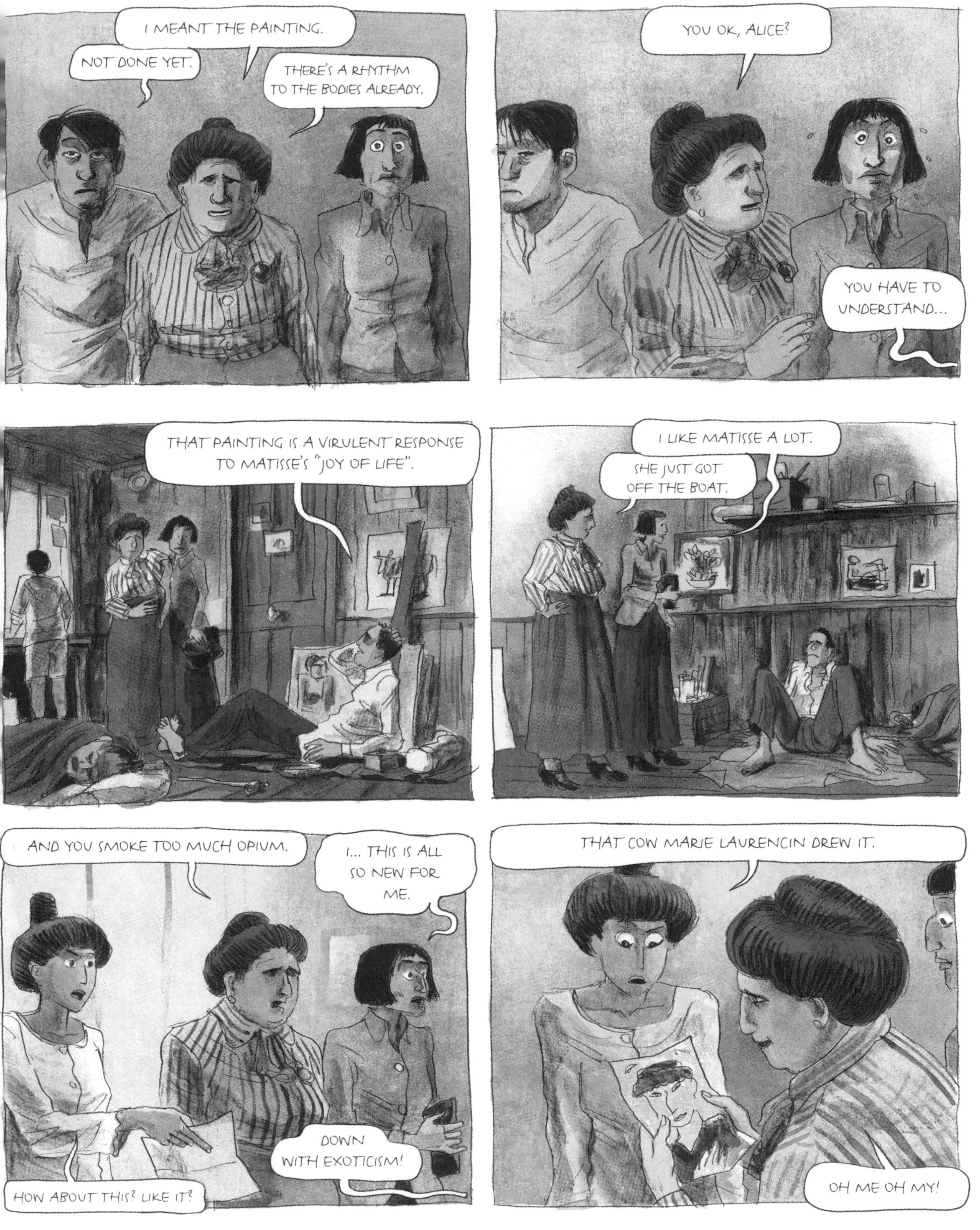
I MEANT THE PAINTING.
NOT DONE YET.
THERE'S A RHYTHM TO THE BODIES ALREADY.
YOU OK, ALICE?
YOU HAVE TO UNDERSTAND...
THAT PAINTING IS A VIRULENT RESPONSE TO MATISSE'S "JOY OF LIFE".
I LIKE MATISSE A LOT.
SHE JUST GOT OFF THE BOAT.
AND YOU SMOKE TOO MUCH OPIUM.
I... THIS IS ALL SO NEW FOR ME.
DOWN WITH EXOTICISM!
HOW ABOUT THIS? LIKE IT?
THAT COW MARIE LAURENCIN DREW IT.
OH ME OH MY!

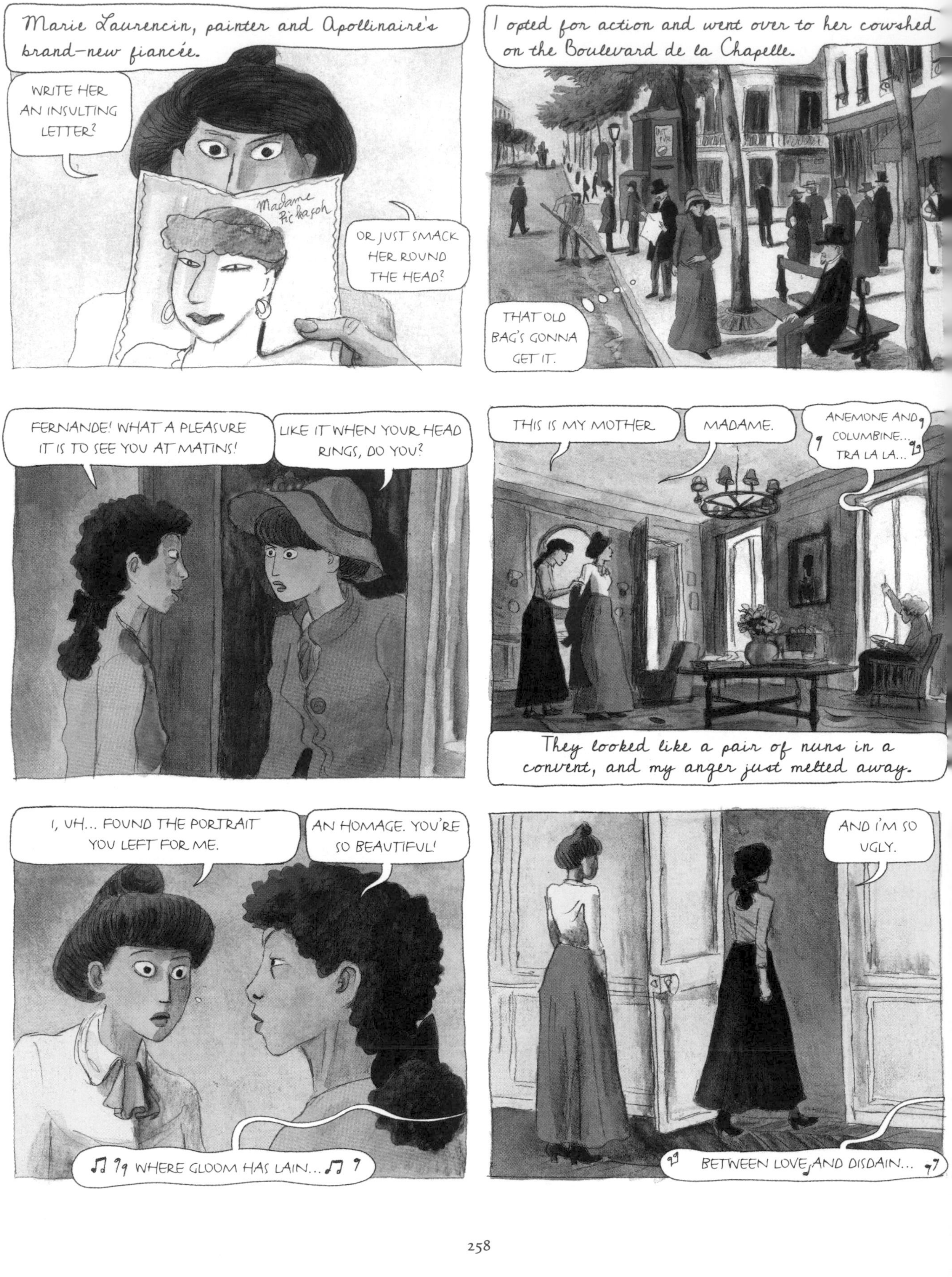

Marie Laurencin, painter and Apollinaire's brand-new fiancée.
WRITE HER AN INSULTING LETTER?
Madame Pickasoh
OR JUST SMACK HER ROUND THE HEAD?
I opted for action and went over to her cowshed on the Boulevard de la Chapelle.
THAT OLD BAG'S GONNA GET IT.
FERNANDE! WHAT A PLEASURE IT IS TO SEE YOU AT MATINS!
LIKE IT WHEN YOUR HEAD RINGS, DO YOU?
THIS IS MY MOTHER
MADAME.
ANEMONE AND COLUMBINE... TRA LA LA...
They looked like a pair of nuns in a convent, and my anger just melted away.
I, UH... FOUND THE PORTRAIT YOU LEFT FOR ME.
AN HOMAGE. YOU'RE SO BEAUTIFUL!
WHERE GLOOM HAS LAIN...
AND I'M SO UGLY.
BETWEEN LOVE AND DISDAIN...

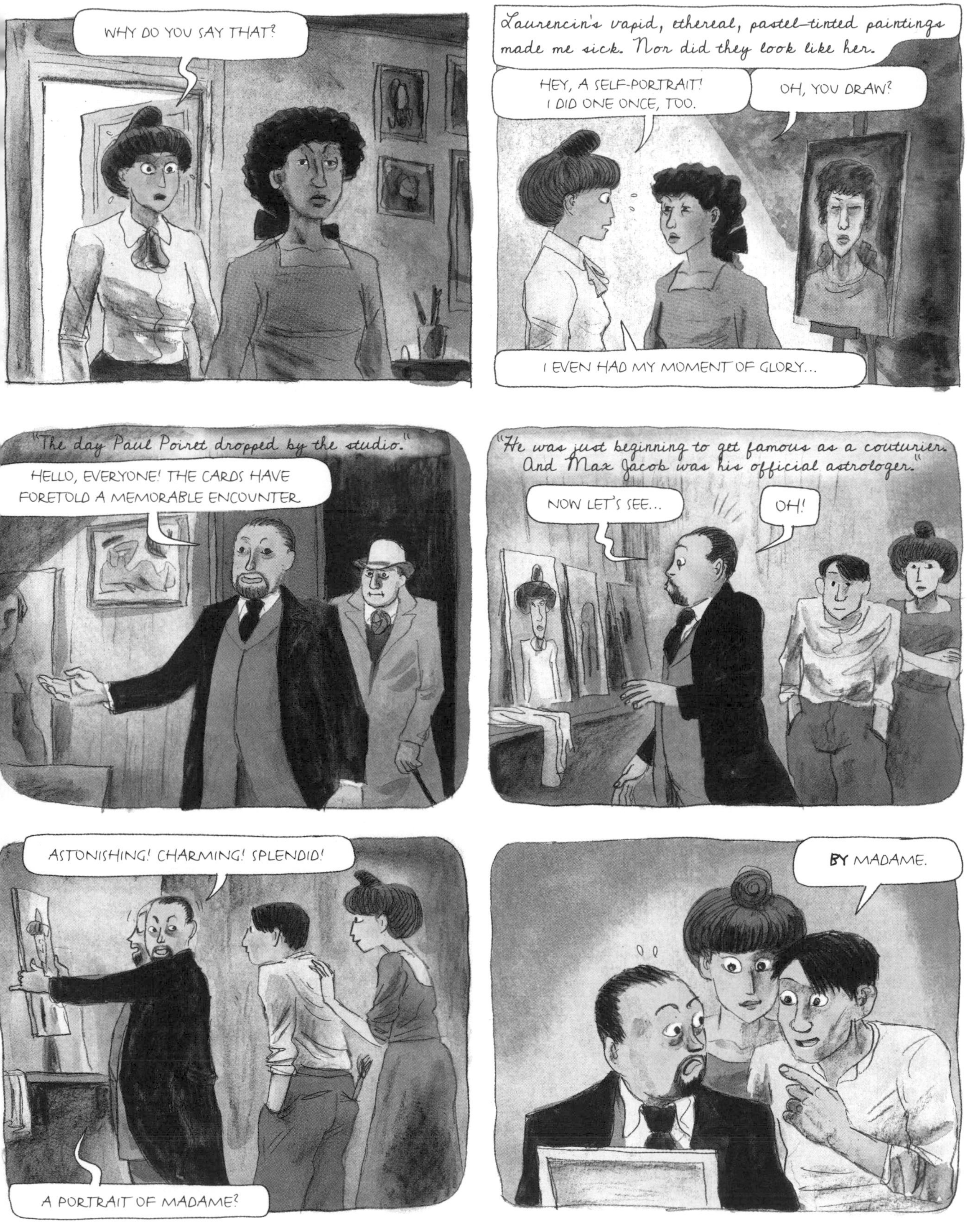
WHY DO YOU SAY THAT?
Laurencin's vapid, ethereal, pastel-tinted paintings made me sick. Nor did they look like her.
HEY, A SELF-PORTRAIT! I DID ONE ONCE, TOO.
OH, YOU DRAW?
I EVEN HAD MY MOMENT OF GLORY...
"The day Paul Poiret dropped by the studio."
HELLO, EVERYONE! THE CARDS HAVE FORETOLD A MEMORABLE ENCOUNTER
"He was just beginning to get famous as a couturier. And Max Jacob was his official astrologer."
NOW LET'S SEE...
OH!
ASTONISHING! CHARMING! SPLENDID!
A PORTRAIT OF MADAME?
BY MADAME.

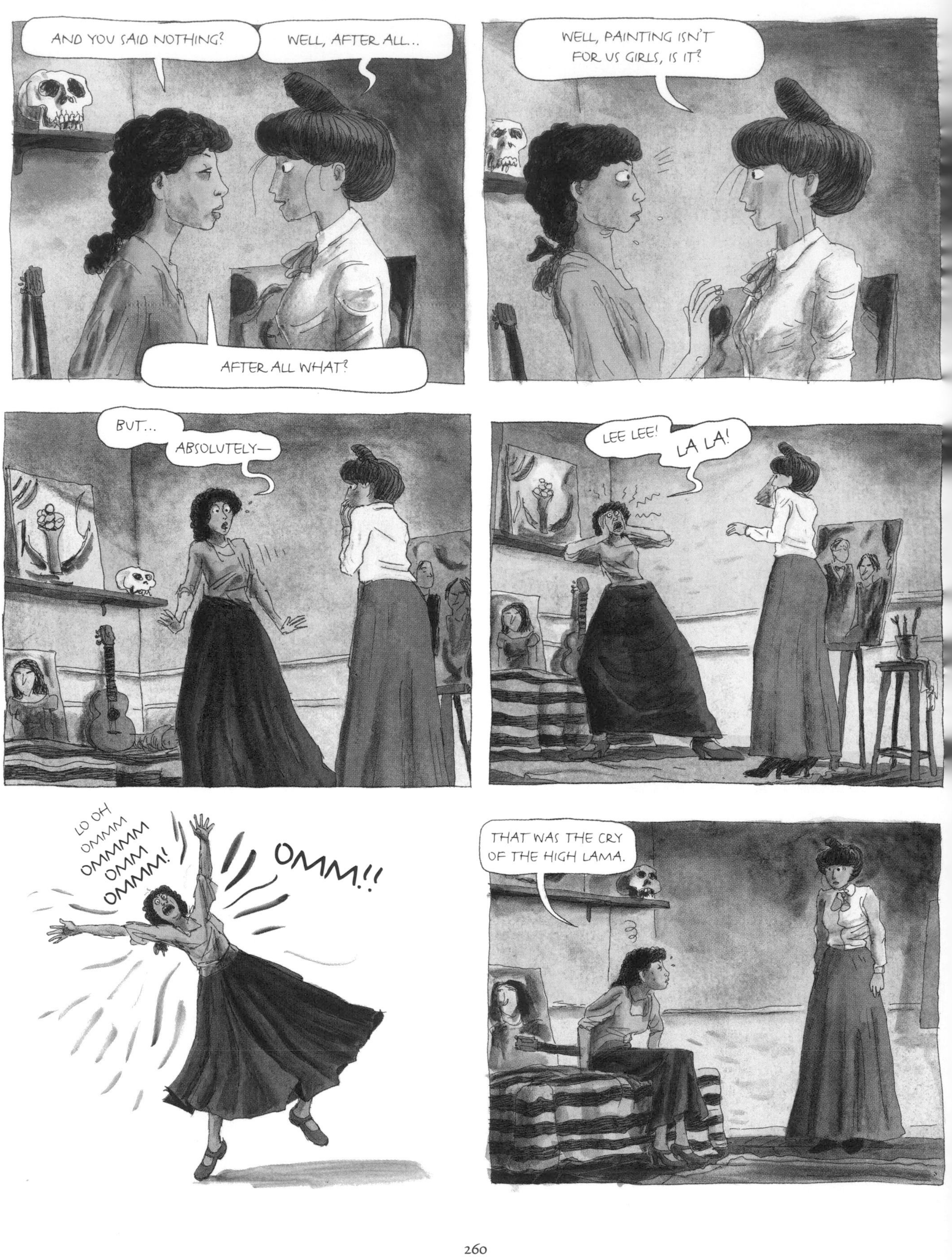
AND YOU SAID NOTHING?
WELL, AFTER ALL...
AFTER ALL WHAT?
WELL, PAINTING ISN'T FOR US GIRLS, IS IT?
BUT...
ABSOLUTELY—
LEE LEE!
LA LA!
LO OH
OMMM
OMMMM
OMM
OMMM!
OMM!!
THAT WAS THE CRY OF THE HIGH LAMA.

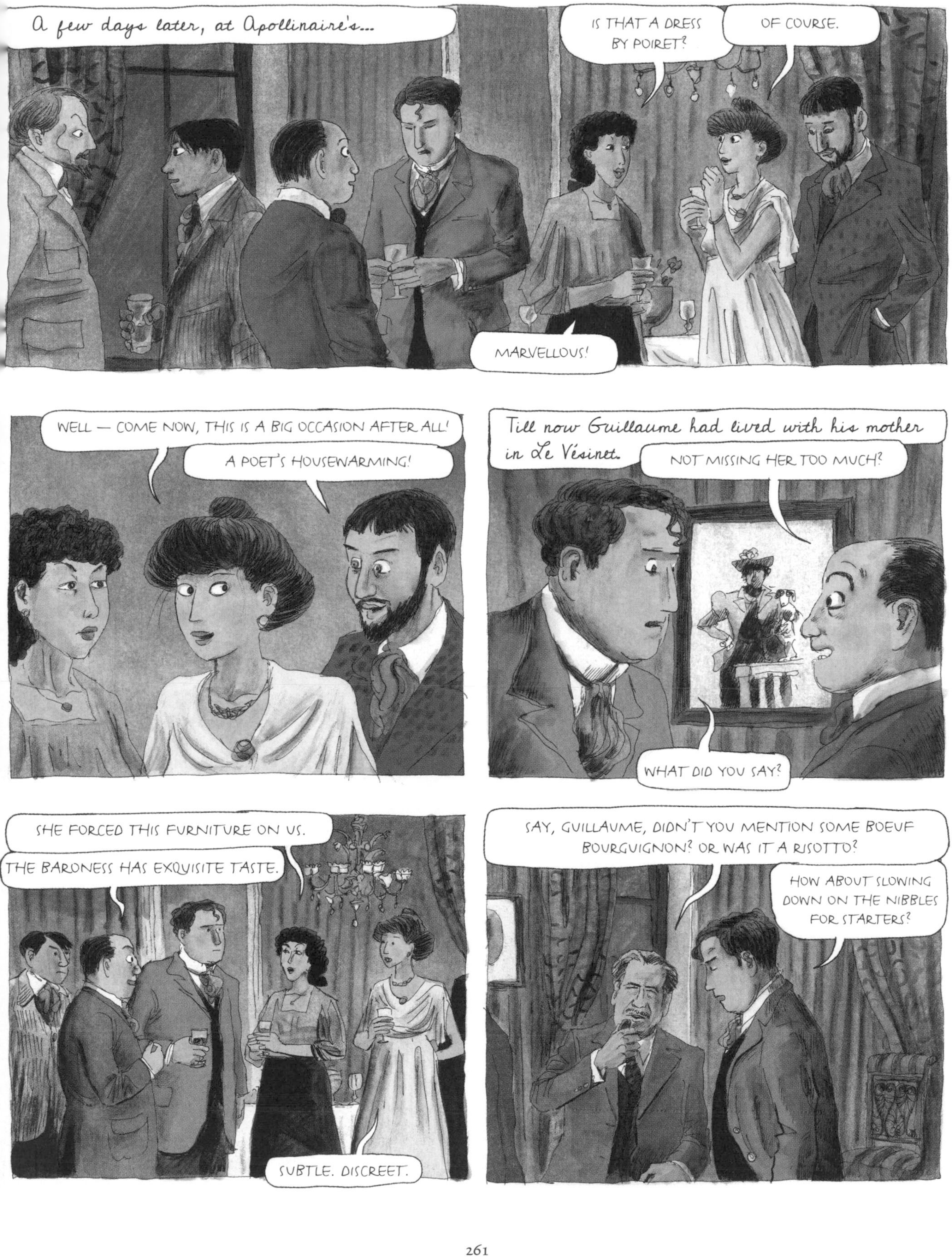
A few days later, at Apollinaire's...
IS THAT A DRESS BY POIRET?
OF COURSE.
MARVELLOUS!
WELL — COME NOW, THIS IS A BIG OCCASION AFTER ALL!
A POET'S HOUSEWARMING!
Till now Guillaume had lived with his mother in Le Vésinet.
NOT MISSING HER TOO MUCH?
WHAT DID YOU SAY?
SHE FORCED THIS FURNITURE ON US.
THE BARONESS HAS EXQUISITE TASTE.
SUBTLE. DISCREET.
SAY, GUILLAUME, DIDN'T YOU MENTION SOME BOEUF BOURGUIGNON? OR WAS IT A RISOTTO?
HOW ABOUT SLOWING DOWN ON THE NIBBLES FOR STARTERS?

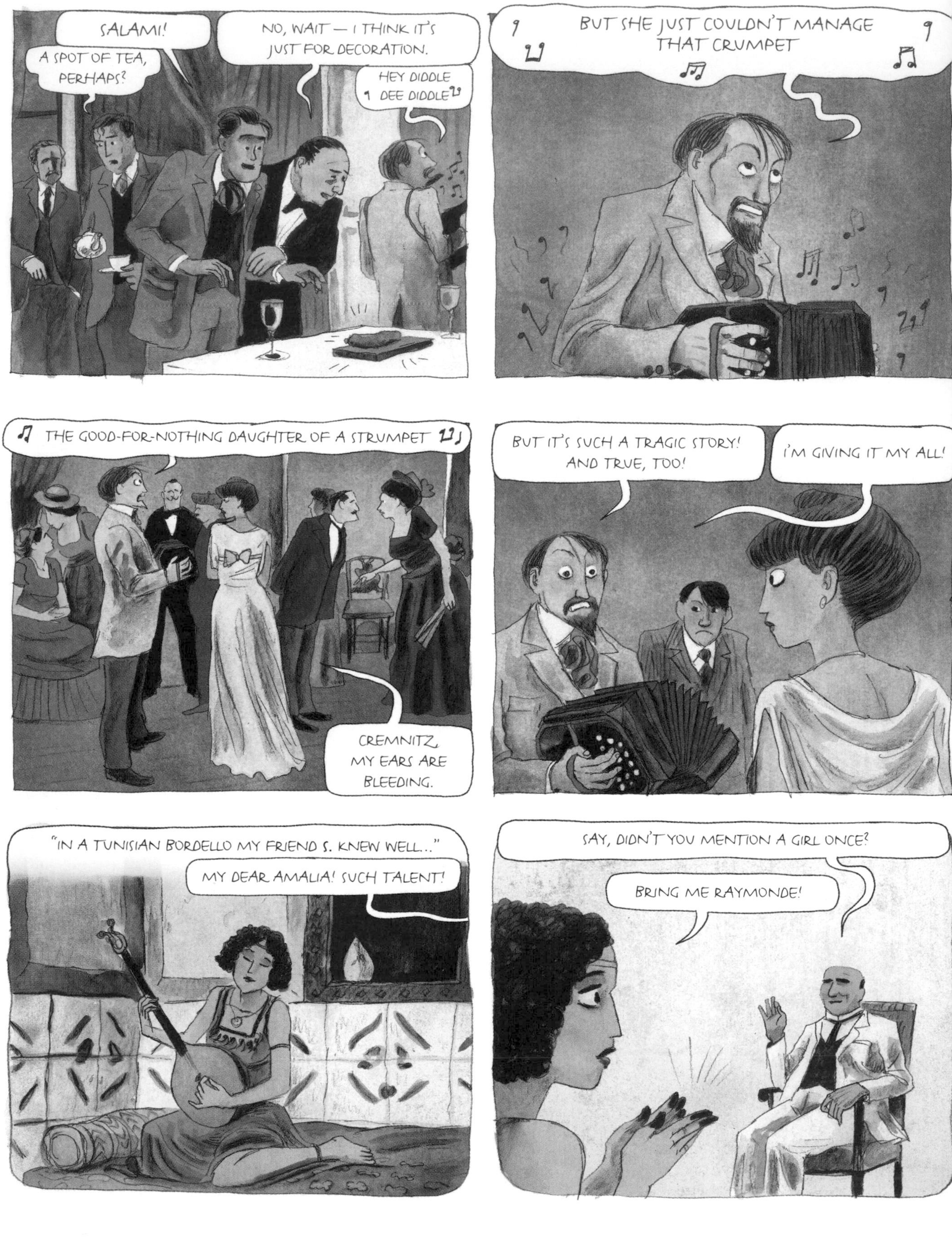
SALAMI!
A SPOT OF TEA, PERHAPS?
NO, WAIT — I THINK IT'S JUST FOR DECORATION.
HEY DIDDLE DEE DIDDLE
BUT SHE JUST COULDN'T MANAGE THAT CRUMPET
THE GOOD-FOR-NOTHING DAUGHTER OF A STRUMPET
CREMNITZ, MY EARS ARE BLEEDING.
BUT IT'S SUCH A TRAGIC STORY! AND TRUE, TOO!
I'M GIVING IT MY ALL!
"IN A TUNISIAN BORDELLO MY FRIEND S. KNEW WELL..."
MY DEAR AMALIA! SUCH TALENT!
SAY, DIDN'T YOU MENTION A GIRL ONCE?
BRING ME RAYMONDE!

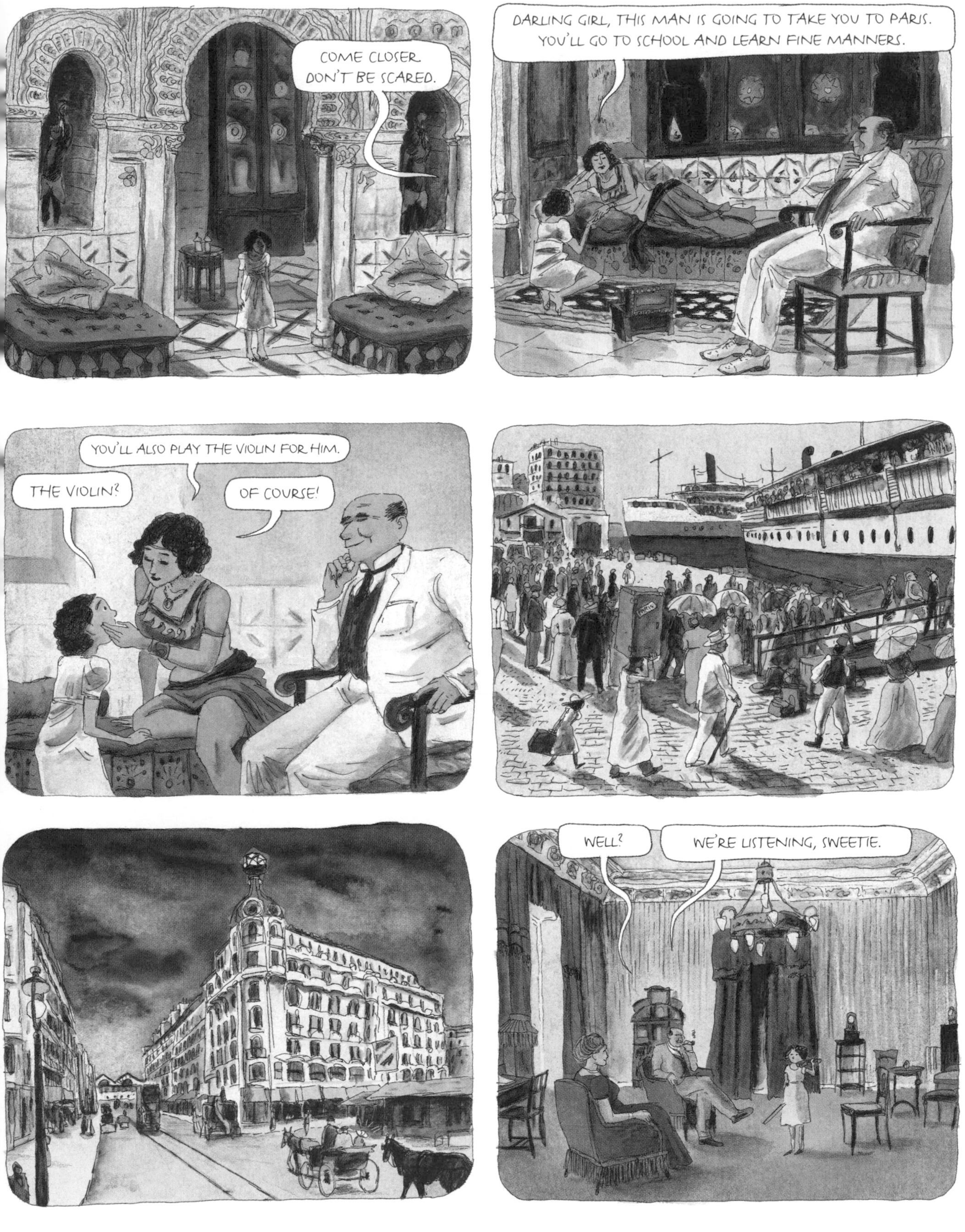
COME CLOSER
DON'T BE SCARED.
DARLING GIRL, THIS MAN IS GOING TO TAKE YOU TO PARIS. YOU'LL GO TO SCHOOL AND LEARN FINE MANNERS.
YOU'LL ALSO PLAY THE VIOLIN FOR HIM.
THE VIOLIN?
OF COURSE!
PARIS
WELL?
WE'RE LISTENING, SWEETIE.

"THE LITTLE GIRL COULDN'T PLAY THE FIRST NOTE."
SO THEY SENT HER PACKING TO AN ORPHANAGE.
HOW MOVING.
A LITTLE TOUR, PERHAPS?
YOUR ROOM'S SO CUTE!
ARE YOU GOING TO LIVE HERE?
STOP THAT! ARE YOU CRAZY!?
THAT BED IS HOLY!
?

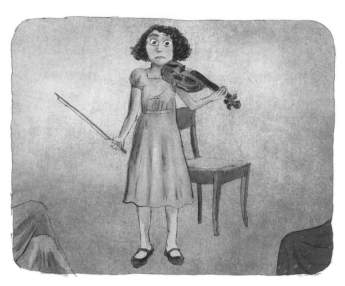

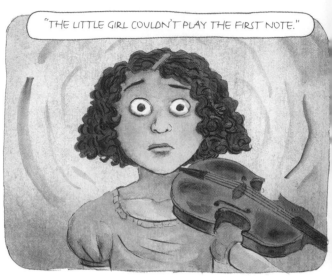

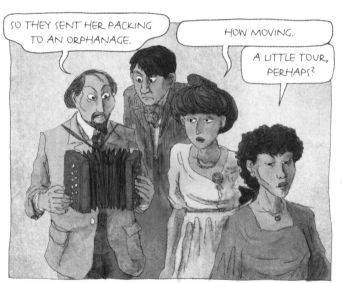

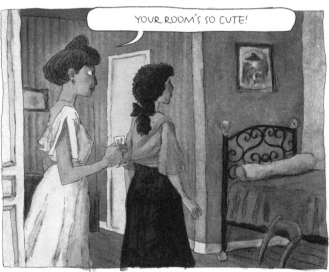

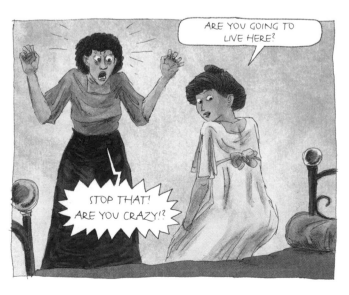

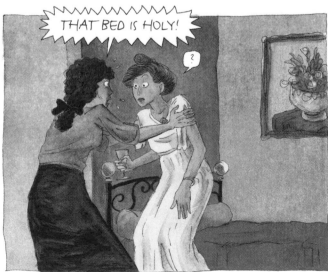

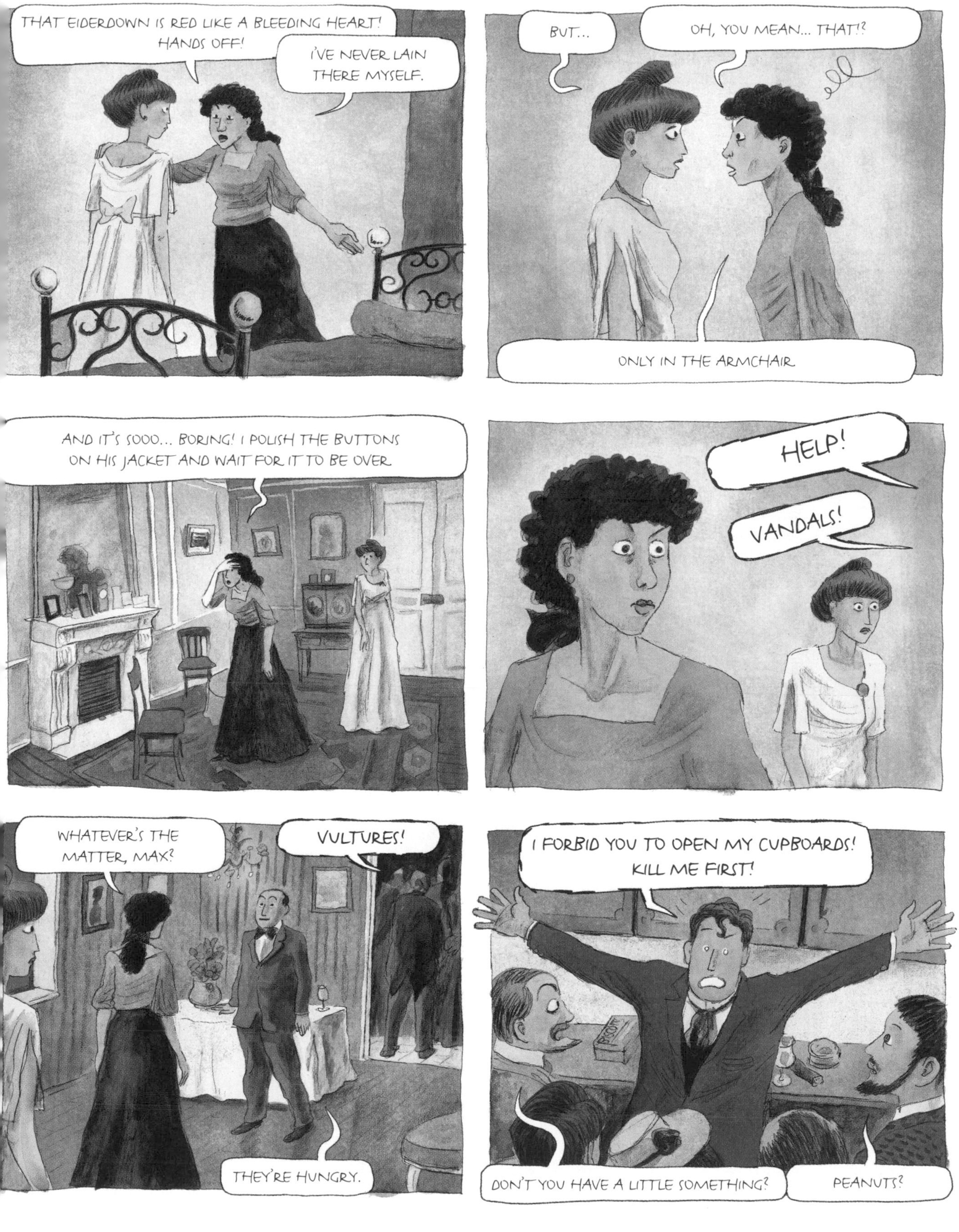
THAT EIDERDOWN IS RED LIKE A BLEEDING HEART! HANDS OFF!
I'VE NEVER LAIN THERE MYSELF.
BUT...
OH, YOU MEAN... THAT!?
ONLY IN THE ARMCHAIR
AND IT'S SOOO... BORING! I POLISH THE BUTTONS ON HIS JACKET AND WAIT FOR IT TO BE OVER
HELP!
VANDALS!
WHATEVER'S THE MATTER, MAX?
VULTURES!
THEY'RE HUNGRY.
I FORBID YOU TO OPEN MY CUPBOARDS! KILL ME FIRST!
DON'T YOU HAVE A LITTLE SOMETHING?
PEANUTS?

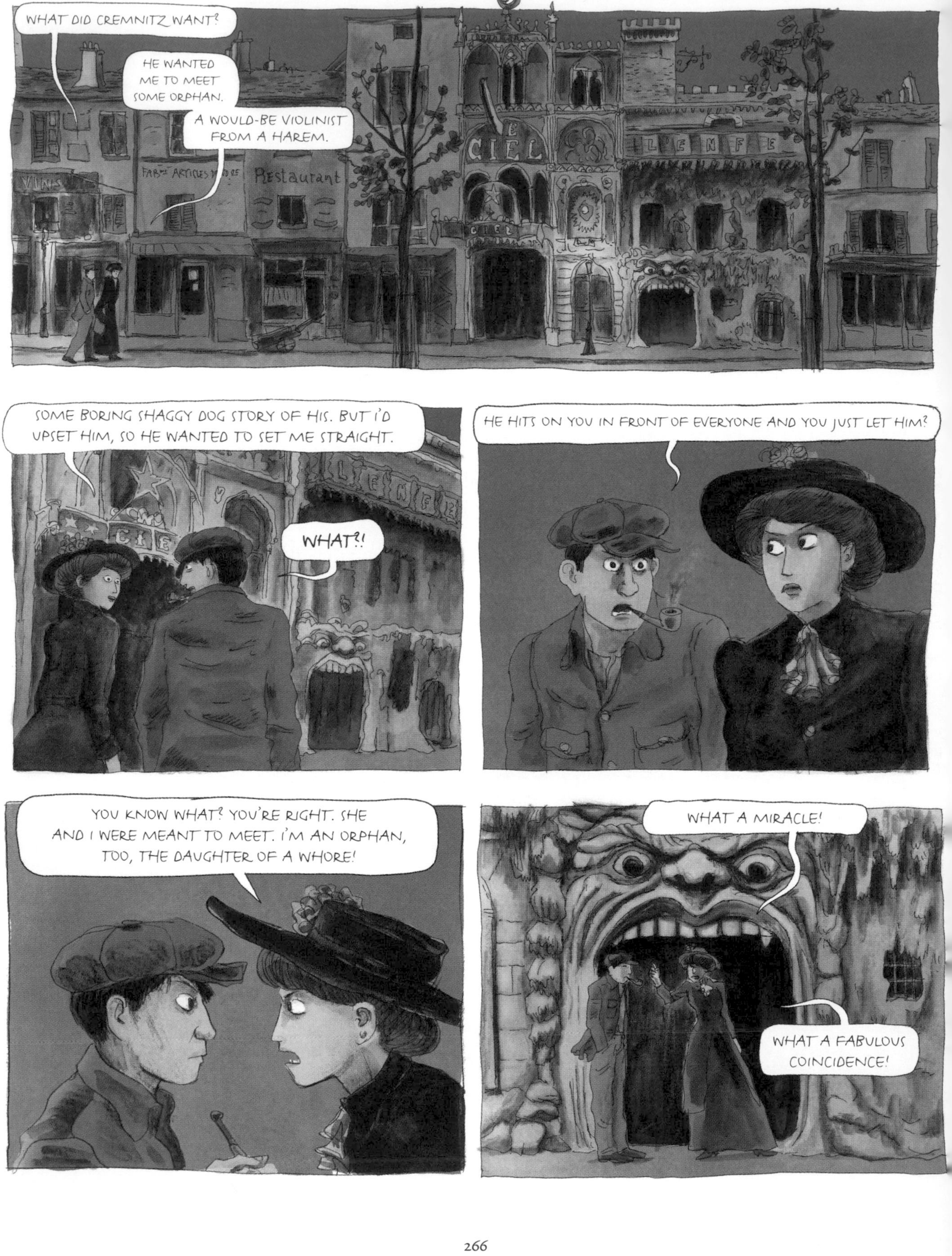

WHAT DID CREMNITZ WANT?
HE WANTED ME TO MEET SOME ORPHAN.
A WOULD-BE VIOLINIST FROM A HAREM.
SOME BORING SHAGGY DOG STORY OF HIS. BUT I'D UPSET HIM, SO HE WANTED TO SET ME STRAIGHT.
WHAT?!
HE HITS ON YOU IN FRONT OF EVERYONE AND YOU JUST LET HIM?
YOU KNOW WHAT? YOU'RE RIGHT. SHE AND I WERE MEANT TO MEET. I'M AN ORPHAN, TOO, THE DAUGHTER OF A WHORE!
WHAT A MIRACLE!
WHAT A FABULOUS COINCIDENCE!

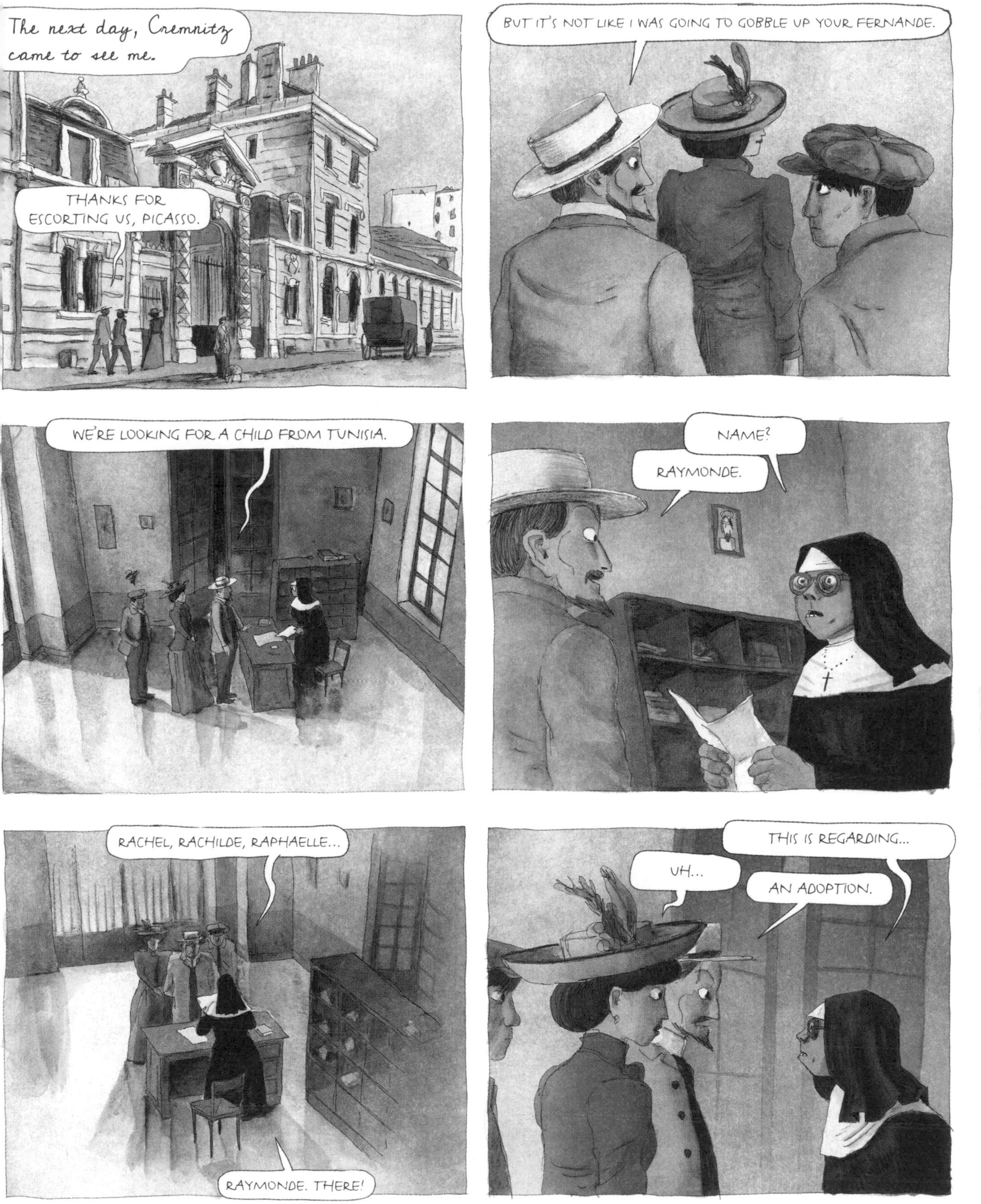
The next day, Cremnitz came to see me.
THANKS FOR ESCORTING US, PICASSO.
BUT IT'S NOT LIKE I WAS GOING TO GOBBLE UP YOUR FERNANDE.
WE'RE LOOKING FOR A CHILD FROM TUNISIA.
NAME?
RAYMONDE.
RACHEL, RACHILDE, RAPHAELLE...
RAYMONDE. THERE!
THIS IS REGARDING...
UH...
AN ADOPTION.

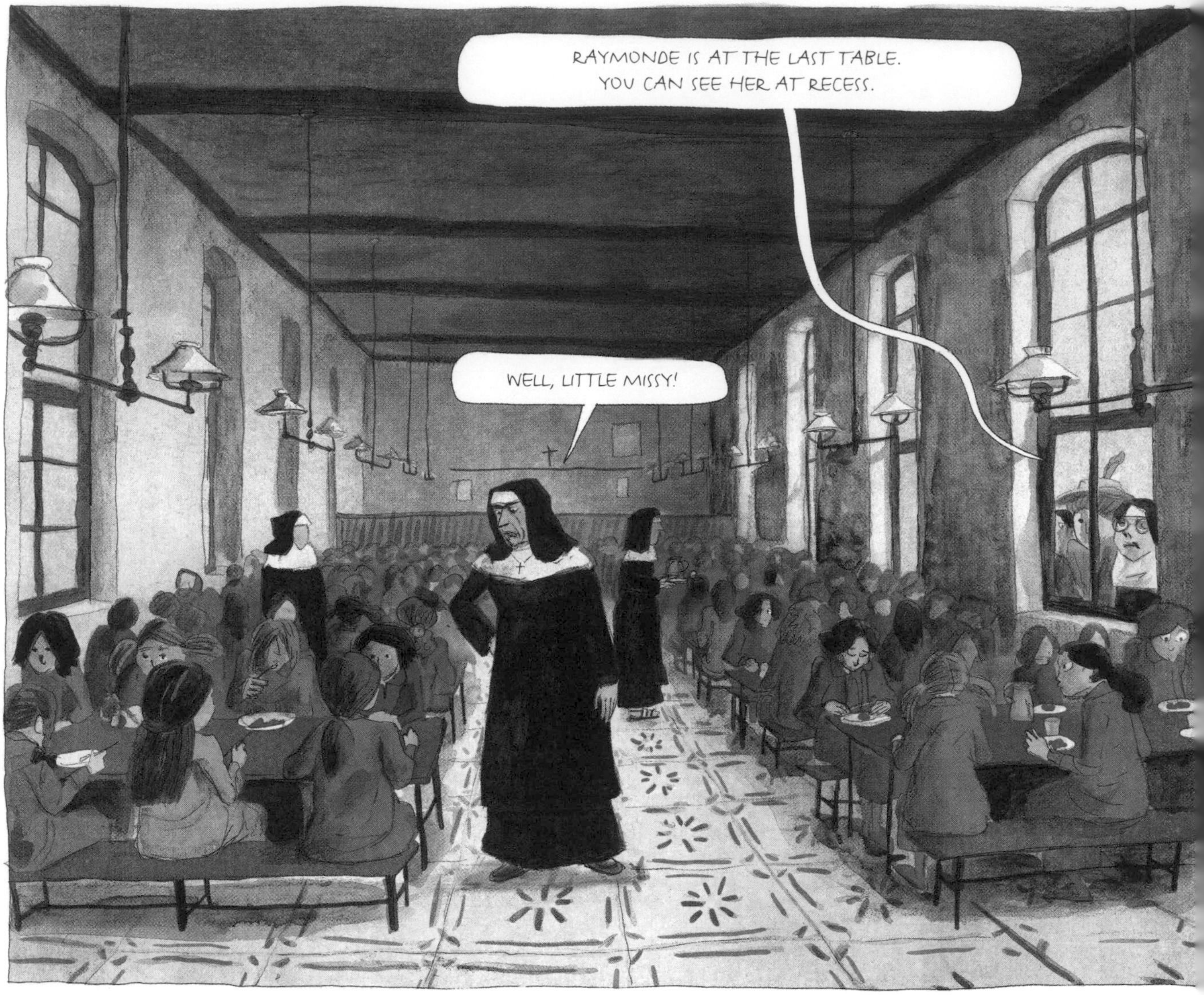
RAYMONDE IS AT THE LAST TABLE. YOU CAN SEE HER AT RECESS.
WELL, LITTLE MISSY!

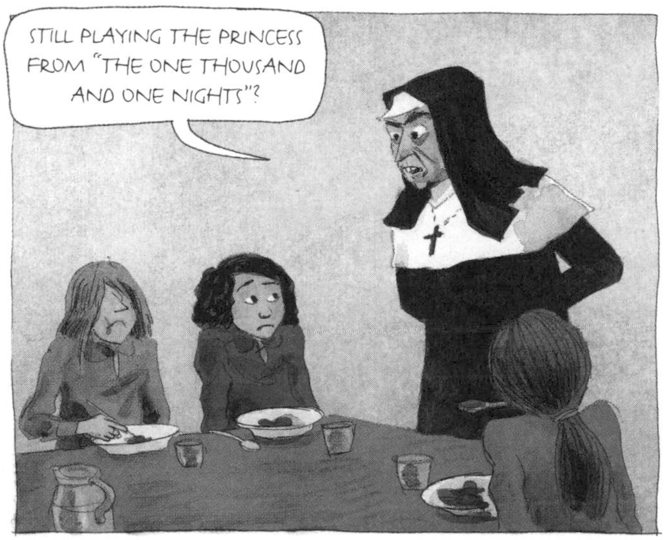
STILL PLAYING THE PRINCESS FROM "THE ONE THOUSAND AND ONE NIGHTS"?

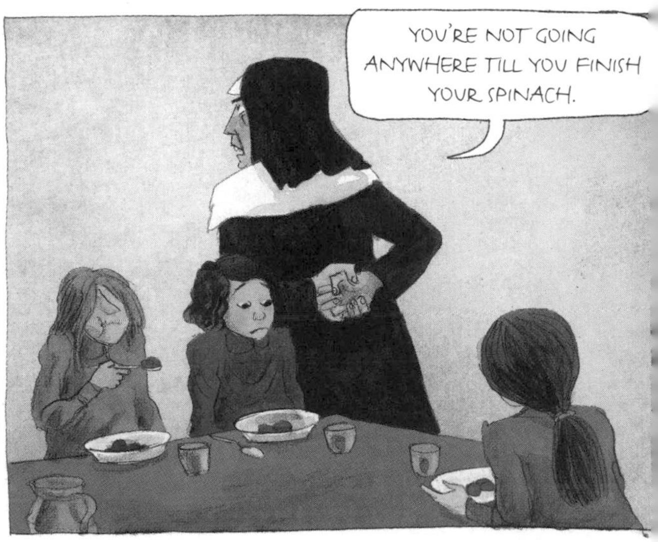
YOU'RE NOT GOING ANYWHERE TILL YOU FINISH YOUR SPINACH.

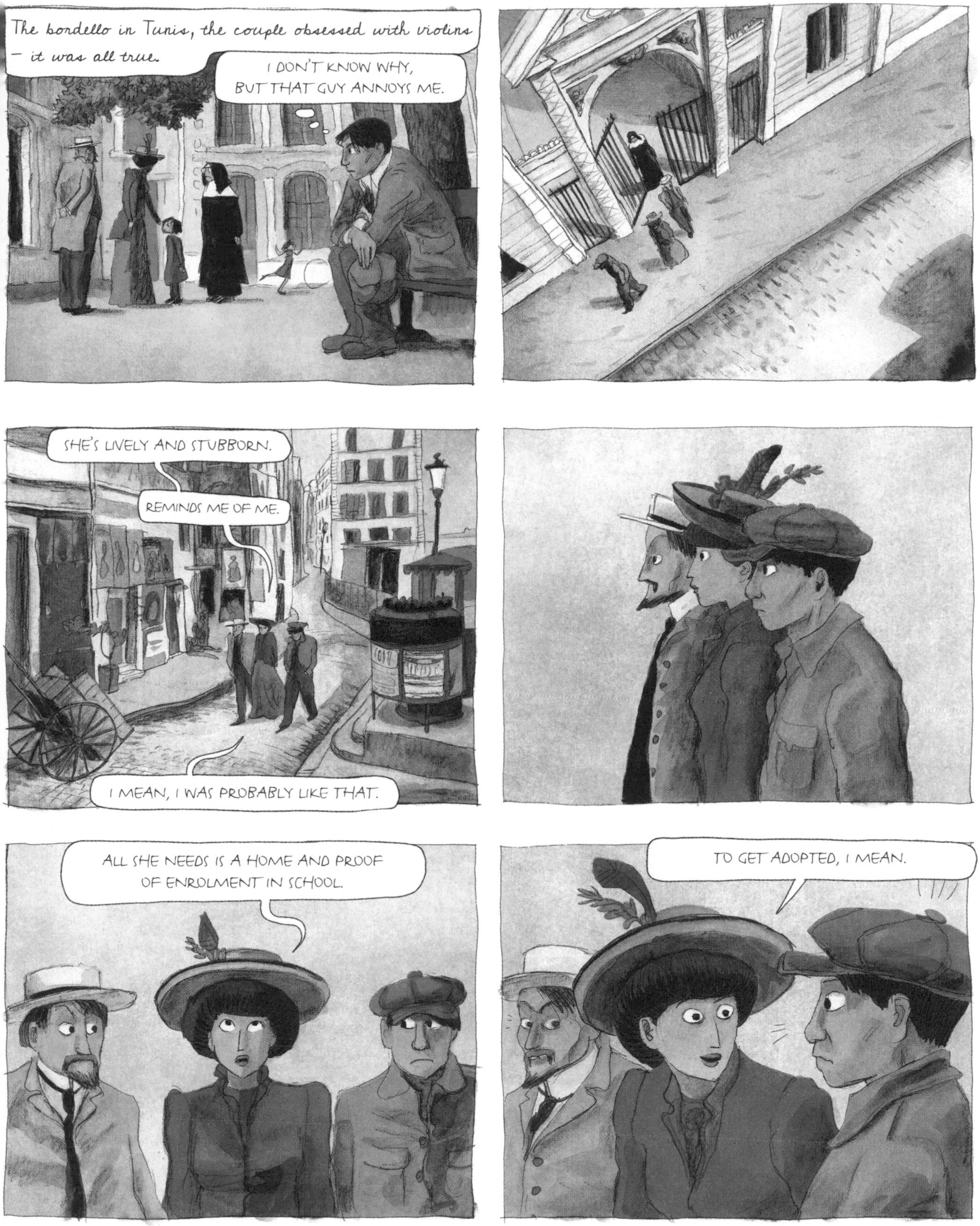

The bordello in Tunis, the couple obsessed with violins – it was all true.
I DON'T KNOW WHY, BUT THAT GUY ANNOYS ME.
SHE'S LIVELY AND STUBBORN.
REMINDS ME OF ME.
I MEAN, I WAS PROBABLY LIKE THAT.
ALL SHE NEEDS IS A HOME AND PROOF OF ENROLMENT IN SCHOOL.
TO GET ADOPTED, I MEAN.

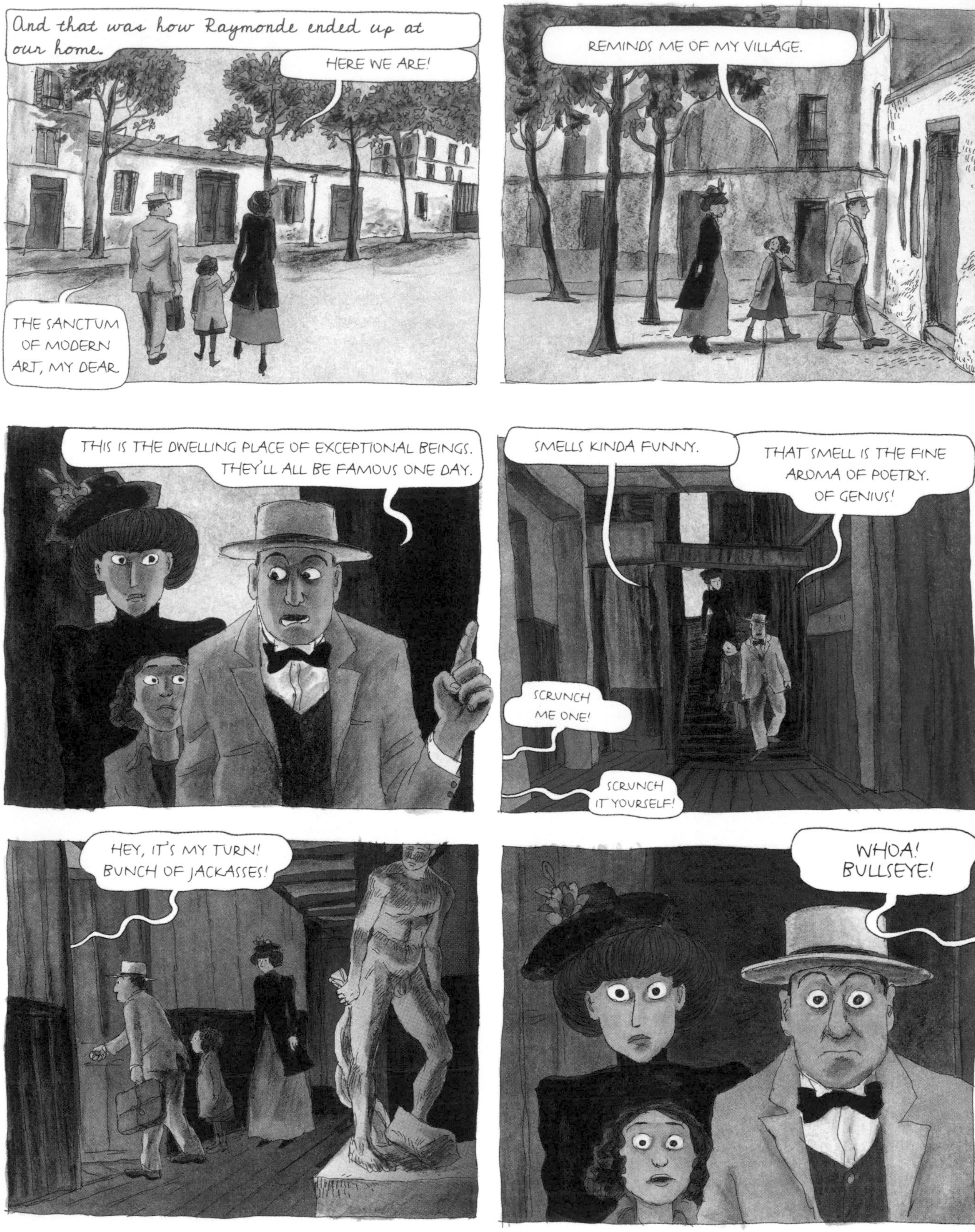

And that was how Raymonde ended up at our home.
HERE WE ARE!
THE SANCTUM OF MODERN ART, MY DEAR
REMINDS ME OF MY VILLAGE.
THIS IS THE DWELLING PLACE OF EXCEPTIONAL BEINGS. THEY'LL ALL BE FAMOUS ONE DAY.
SMELLS KINDA FUNNY.
THAT SMELL IS THE FINE AROMA OF POETRY. OF GENIUS!
SCRUNCH ME ONE!
SCRUNCH IT YOURSELF!
HEY, IT'S MY TURN! BUNCH OF JACKASSES!
WHOA! BULLSEYE!

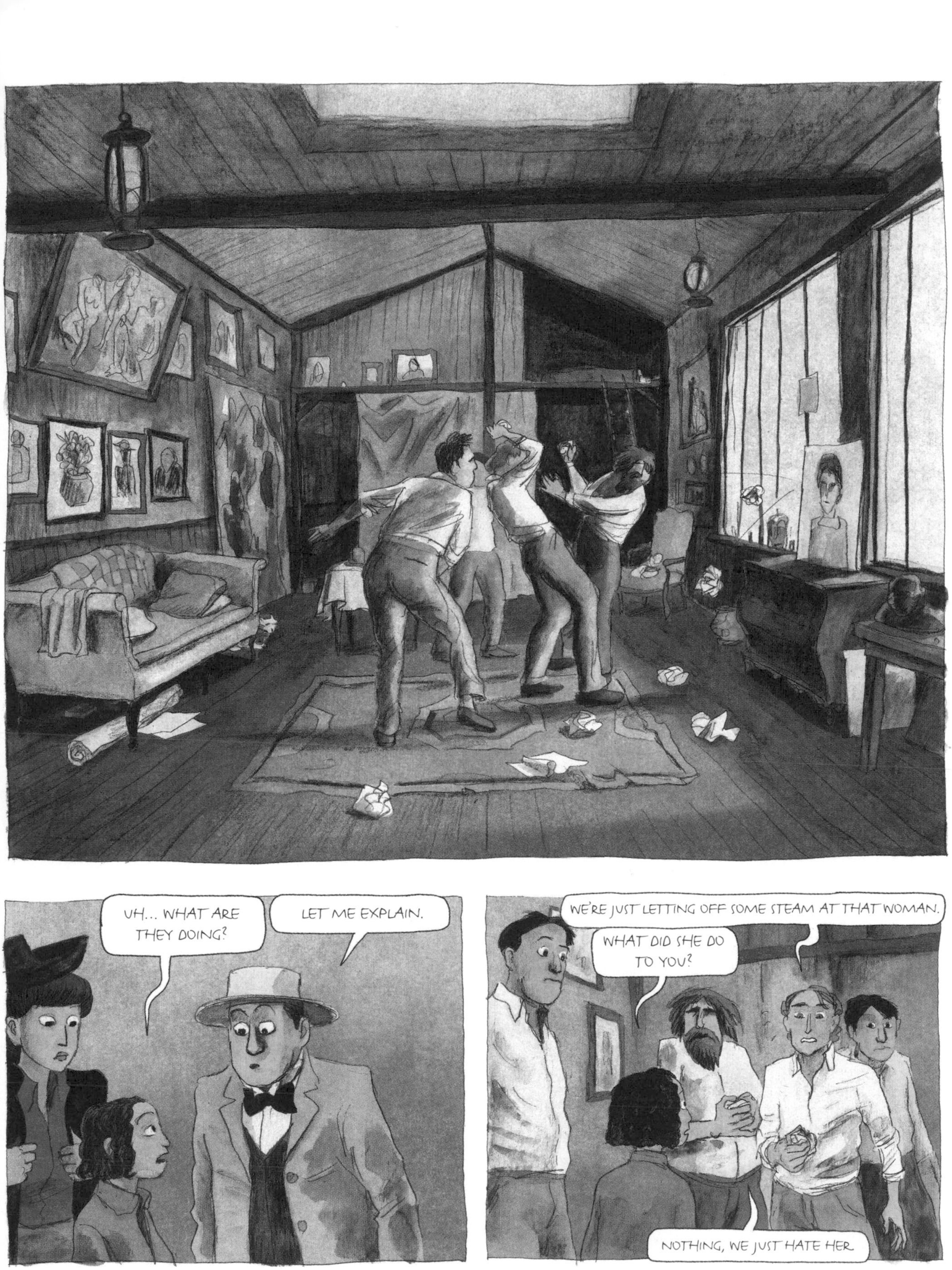
UH... WHAT ARE THEY DOING?
LET ME EXPLAIN.
WE'RE JUST LETTING OFF SOME STEAM AT THAT WOMAN.
WHAT DID SHE DO TO YOU?
NOTHING, WE JUST HATE HER.

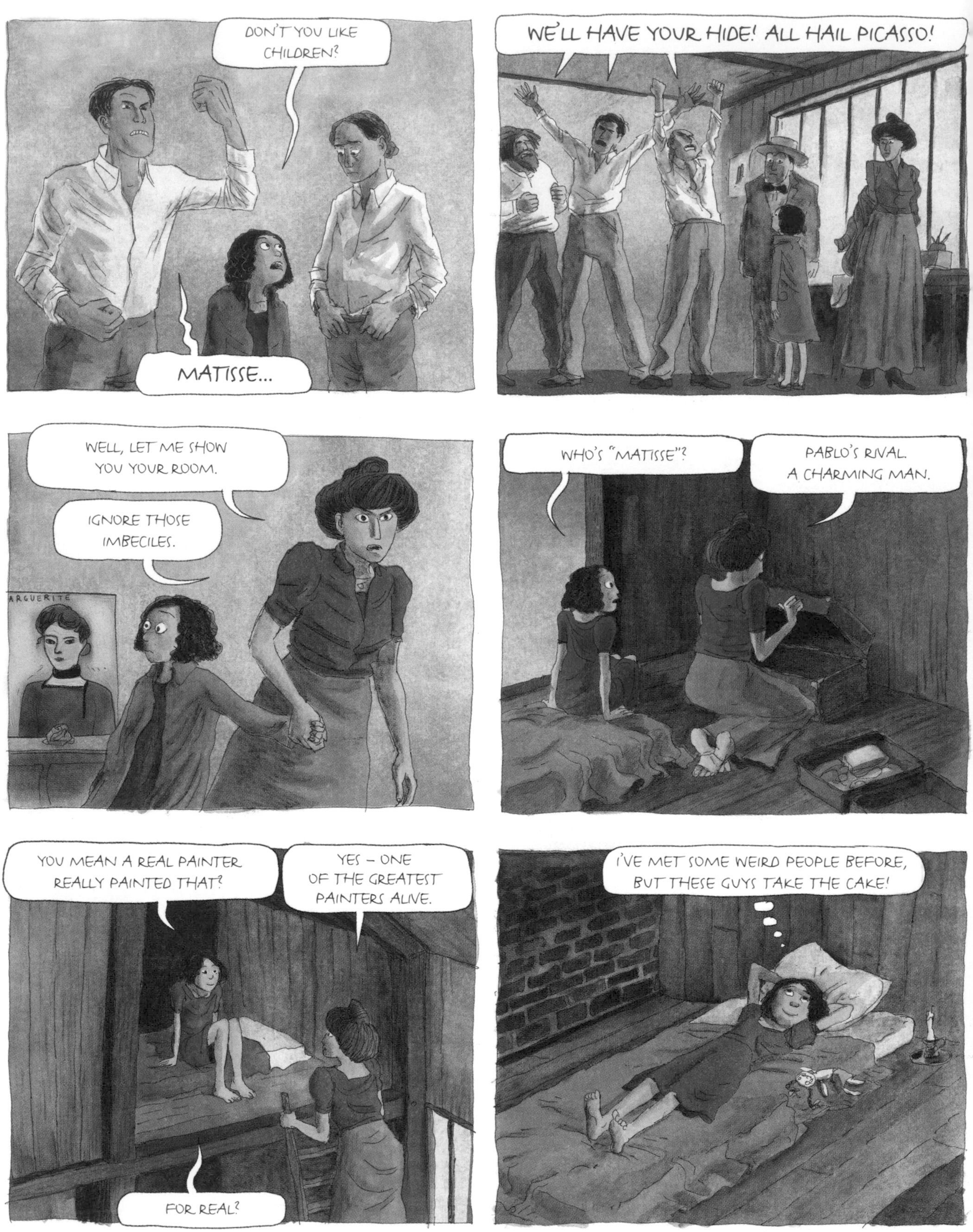
DON'T YOU LIKE CHILDREN?
MATISSE...
WE'LL HAVE YOUR HIDE! ALL HAIL PICASSO!
WELL, LET ME SHOW YOU YOUR ROOM.
IGNORE THOSE IMBECILES.
ARGUERITE
WHO'S "MATISSE"?
PABLO'S RIVAL. A CHARMING MAN.
YOU MEAN A REAL PAINTER REALLY PAINTED THAT?
YES – ONE OF THE GREATEST PAINTERS ALIVE.
FOR REAL?
I'VE MET SOME WEIRD PEOPLE BEFORE, BUT THESE GUYS TAKE THE CAKE!

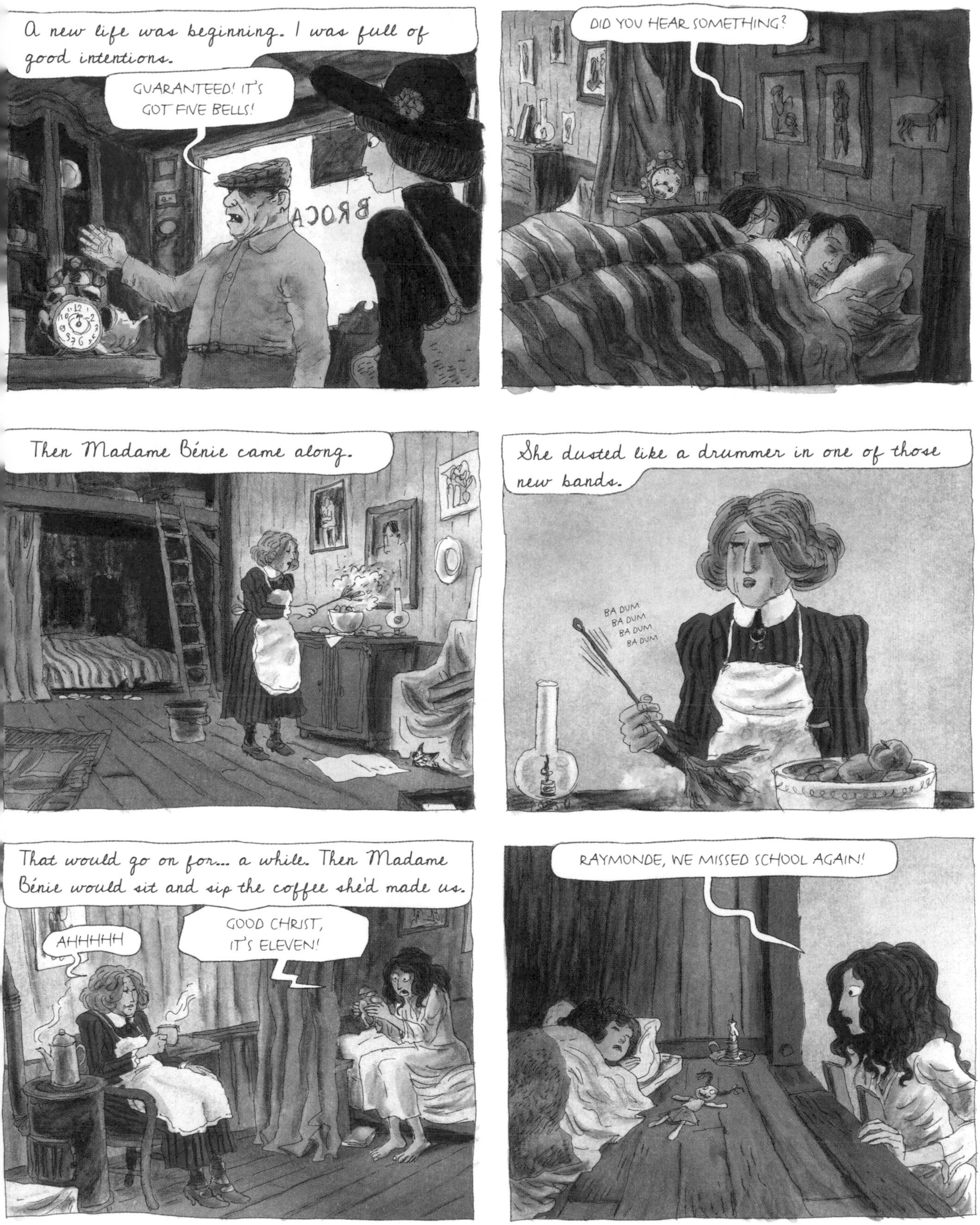
A new life was beginning. I was full of good intentions.
GUARANTEED! IT'S GOT FIVE BELLS!
BROCA
DID YOU HEAR SOMETHING?
Then Madame Bénie came along.
She dusted like a drummer in one of those new bands.
BA DUM BA DUM BA DUM BA DUM
That would go on for... a while. Then Madame Bénie would sit and sip the coffee she'd made us.
AHHHHH
GOOD CHRIST, IT'S ELEVEN!
RAYMONDE, WE MISSED SCHOOL AGAIN!

Raising a child was just a long string of chores. The worst part was making meals at set times.

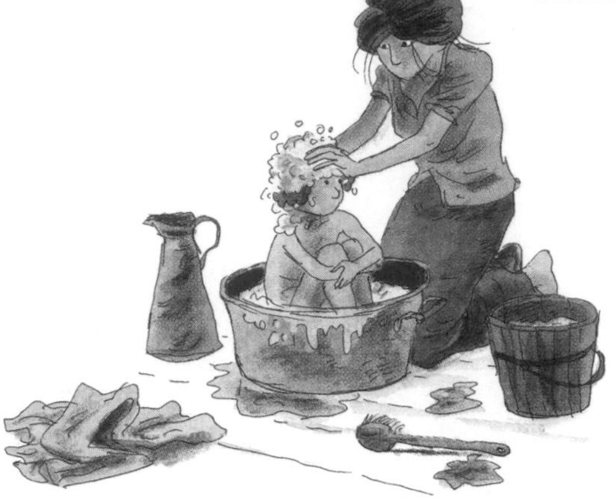

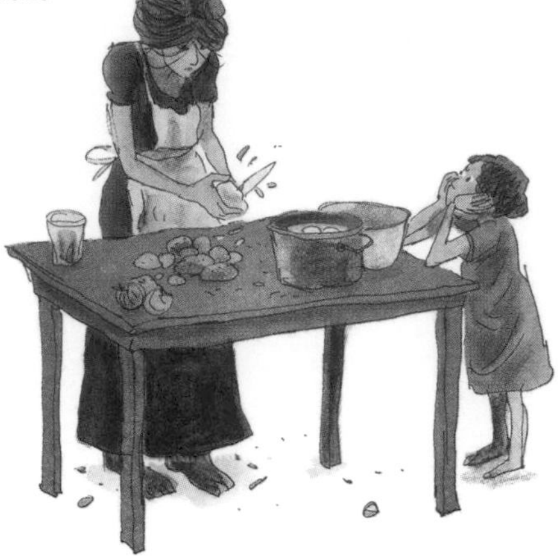

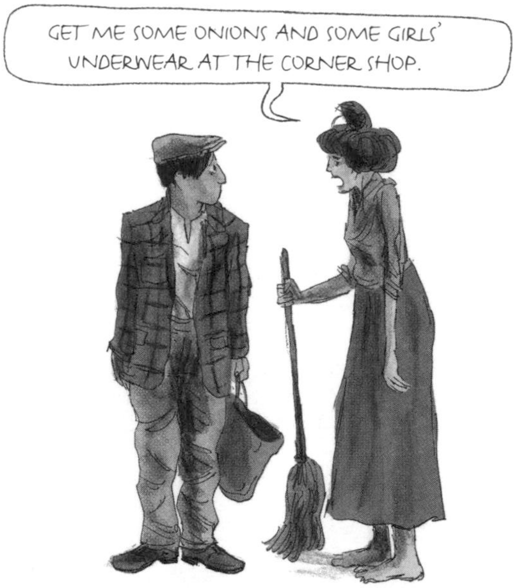
GET ME SOME ONIONS AND SOME GIRLS' UNDERWEAR AT THE CORNER SHOP.

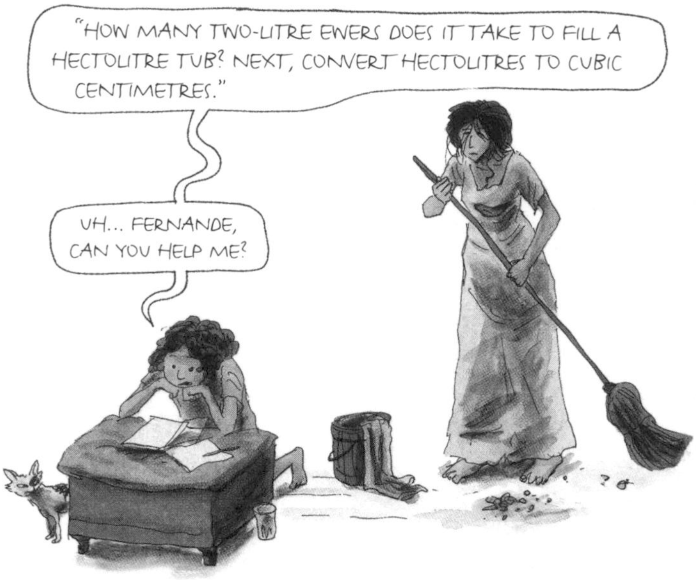
"HOW MANY TWO-LITRE EWERS DOES IT TAKE TO FILL A HECTOLITRE TUB? NEXT, CONVERT HECTOLITRES TO CUBIC CENTIMETRES."
UH... FERNANDE, CAN YOU HELP ME?

After a month, I was totally pooped. And they say motherhood makes you bloom.

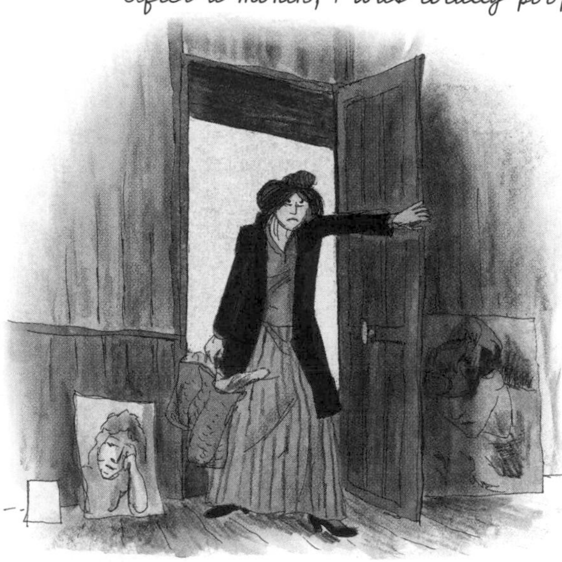

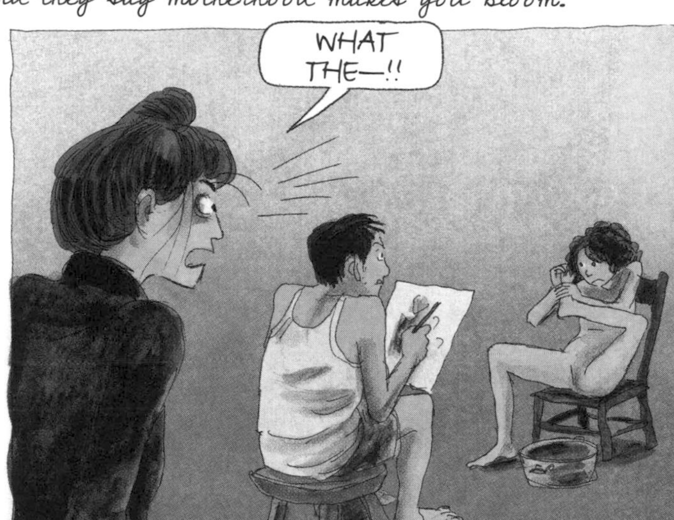
WHAT THE—!!

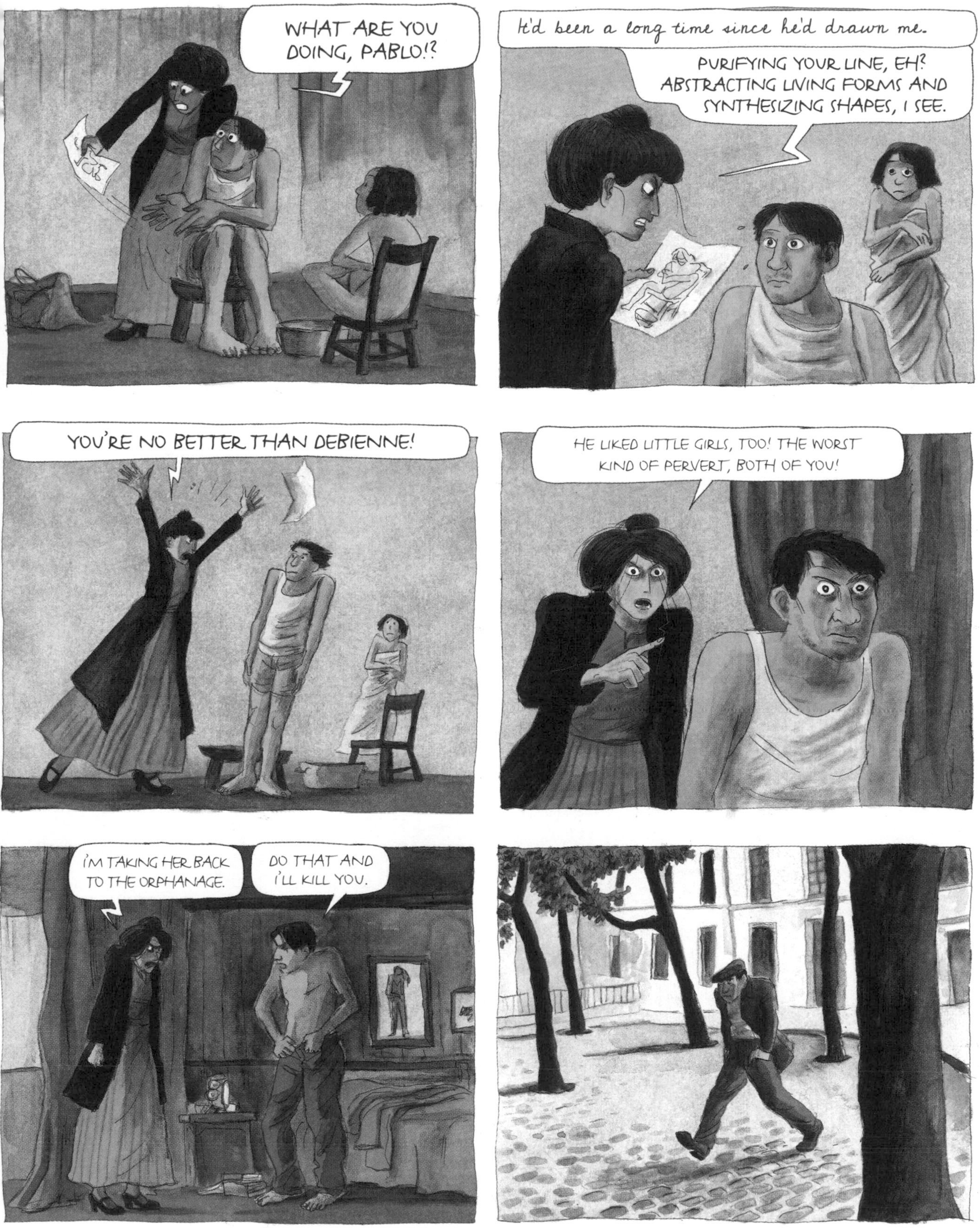
WHAT ARE YOU DOING, PABLO!?
It'd been a long time since he'd drawn me.
PURIFYING YOUR LINE, EH? ABSTRACTING LIVING FORMS AND SYNTHESIZING SHAPES, I SEE.
YOU'RE NO BETTER THAN DEBIENNE!
HE LIKED LITTLE GIRLS, TOO! THE WORST KIND OF PERVERT, BOTH OF YOU!
I'M TAKING HER BACK TO THE ORPHANAGE.
DO THAT AND I'LL KILL YOU.

Bourse-Louvre-Trocadéro
THAT WOMAN IS IMPOSSIBLE.
SHE'S GONNA DRIVE ME CRAZY.

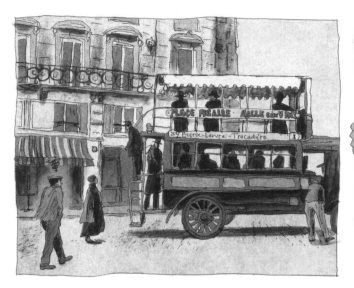

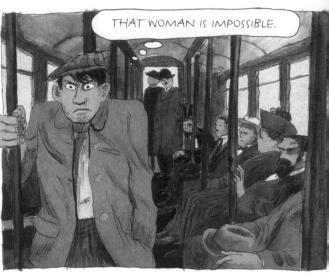

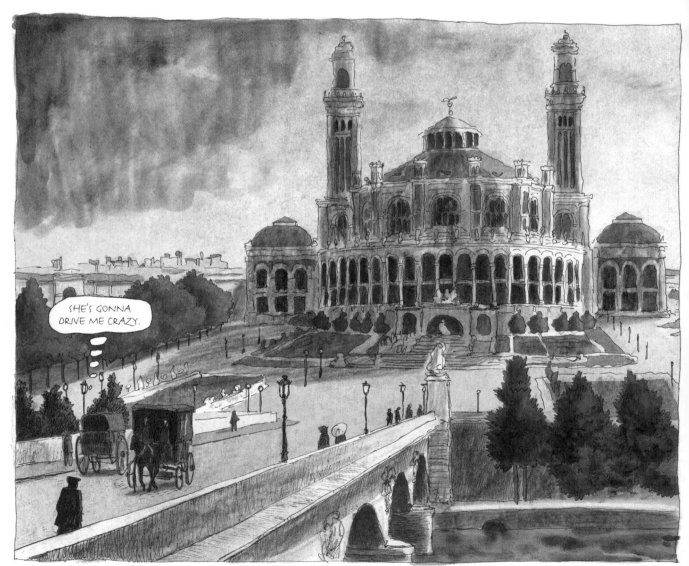

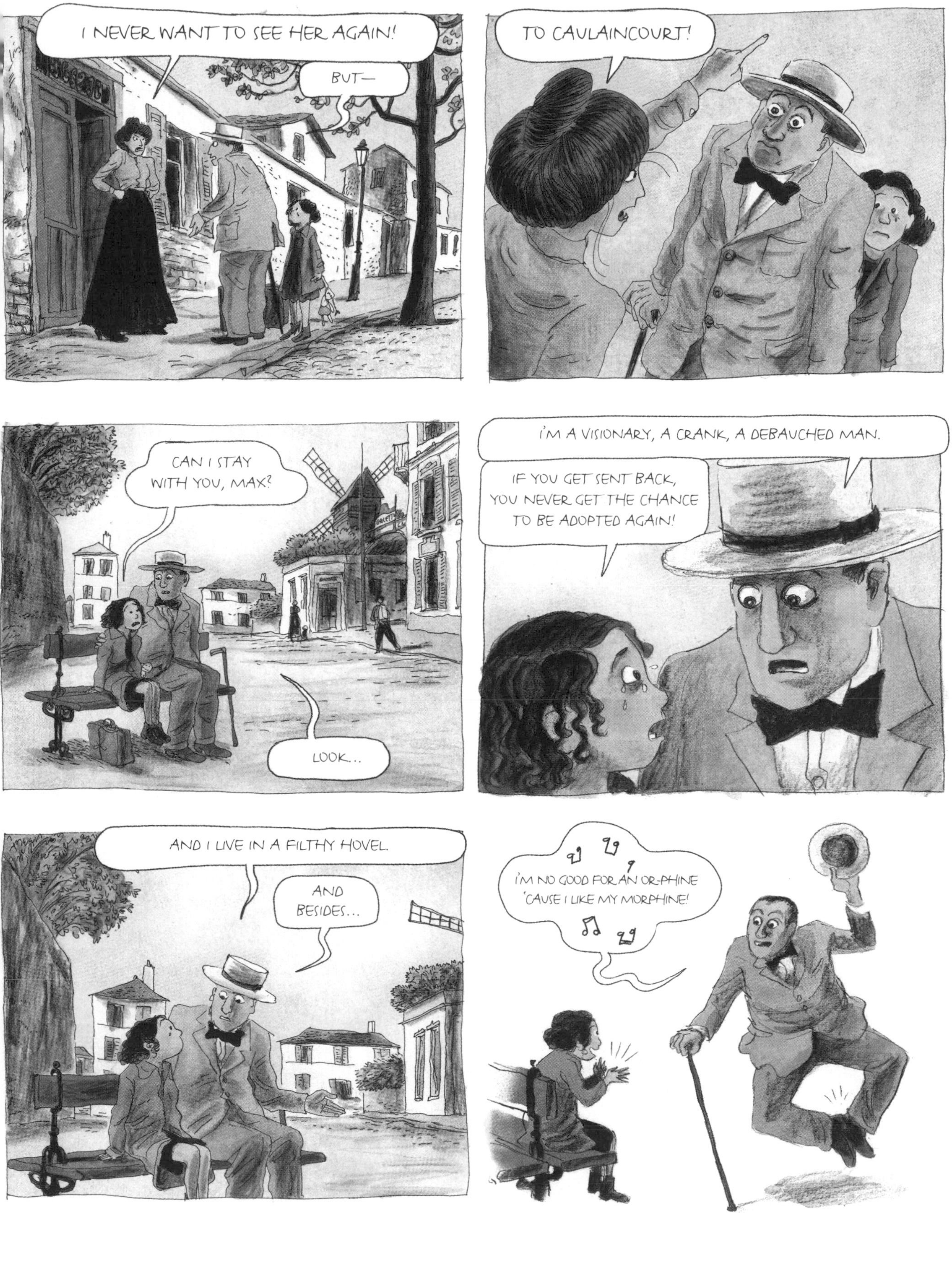
I NEVER WANT TO SEE HER AGAIN!
BUT—
TO CAULAINCOURT!
CAN I STAY WITH YOU, MAX?
LOOK...
I'M A VISIONARY, A CRANK, A DEBAUCHED MAN.
IF YOU GET SENT BACK, YOU NEVER GET THE CHANCE TO BE ADOPTED AGAIN!
AND I LIVE IN A FILTHY HOVEL.
AND BESIDES...
I'M NO GOOD FOR AN OR-PHINE
'CAUSE I LIKE MY MORPHINE!

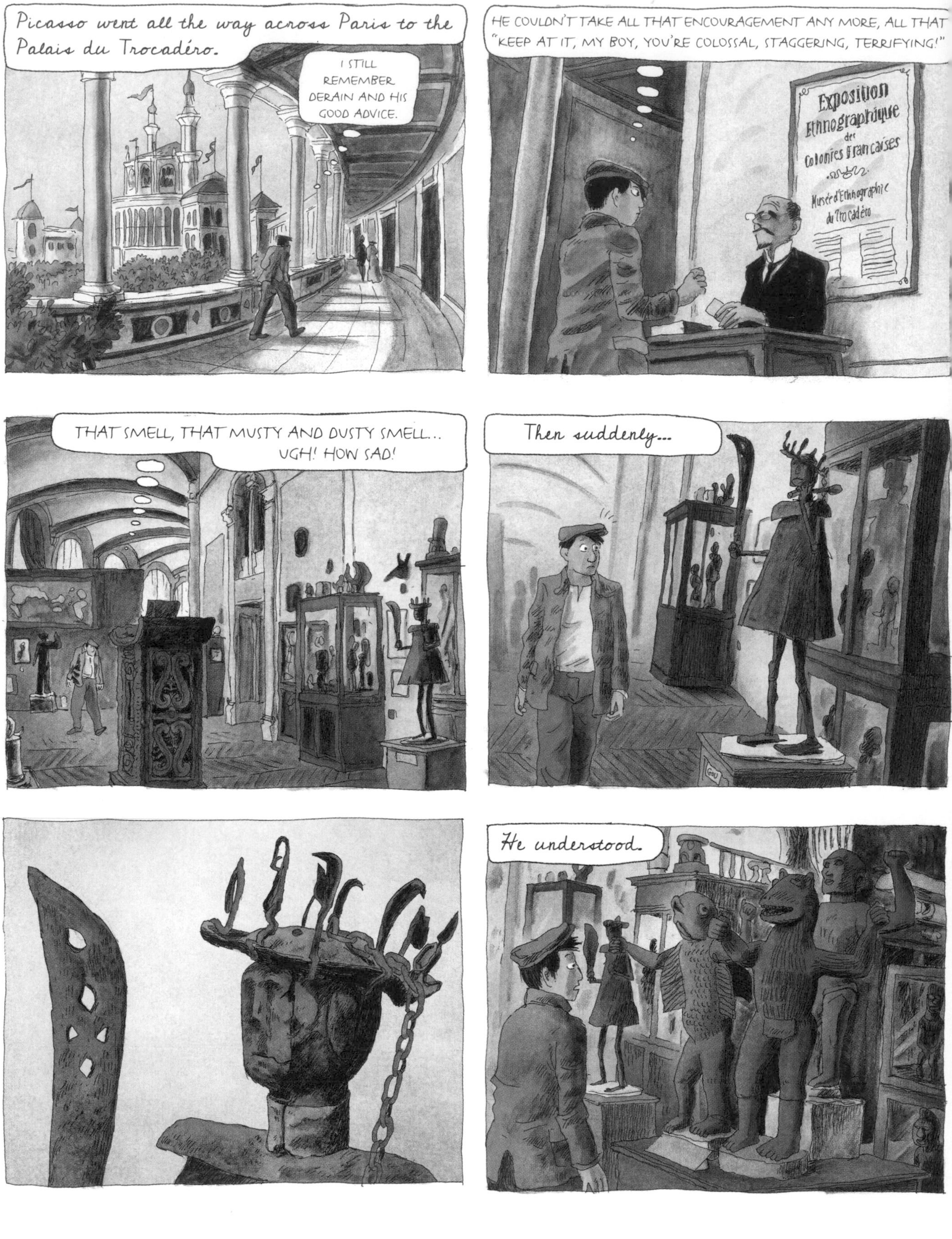
Picasso went all the way across Paris to the Palais du Trocadéro.
I STILL REMEMBER DERAIN AND HIS GOOD ADVICE.
HE COULDN'T TAKE ALL THAT ENCOURAGEMENT ANY MORE, ALL THAT "KEEP AT IT, MY BOY, YOU'RE COLOSSAL, STAGGERING, TERRIFYING!"
Exposition Ethnographique des Colonies Françaises
Musée d'Ethnographie du Trocadéro
THAT SMELL, THAT MUSTY AND DUSTY SMELL... UGH! HOW SAD!
Then suddenly...
He understood.

THAT WE MAY FEAR OUR ENEMY NO MORE, LET US SCULPT OUR WORST NIGHTMARE.

THAT'S THE ANSWER: AN EXORCISM!

FORGE A WEAPON AGAINST FERNANDE, AND I'LL BE PROOF AGAINST HER CHARMS. BREAK THE SPELL!

When he returned, Picasso transformed his "bordello".

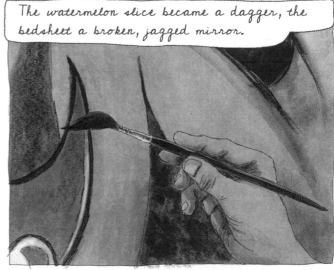

The watermelon slice became a dagger, the bedsheet a broken, jagged mirror.

"ONE EVENING I TOOK BEAUTY IN MY ARMS. AND FOUND HER BITTER AND SWORE AT HER."

RIMBAUD?

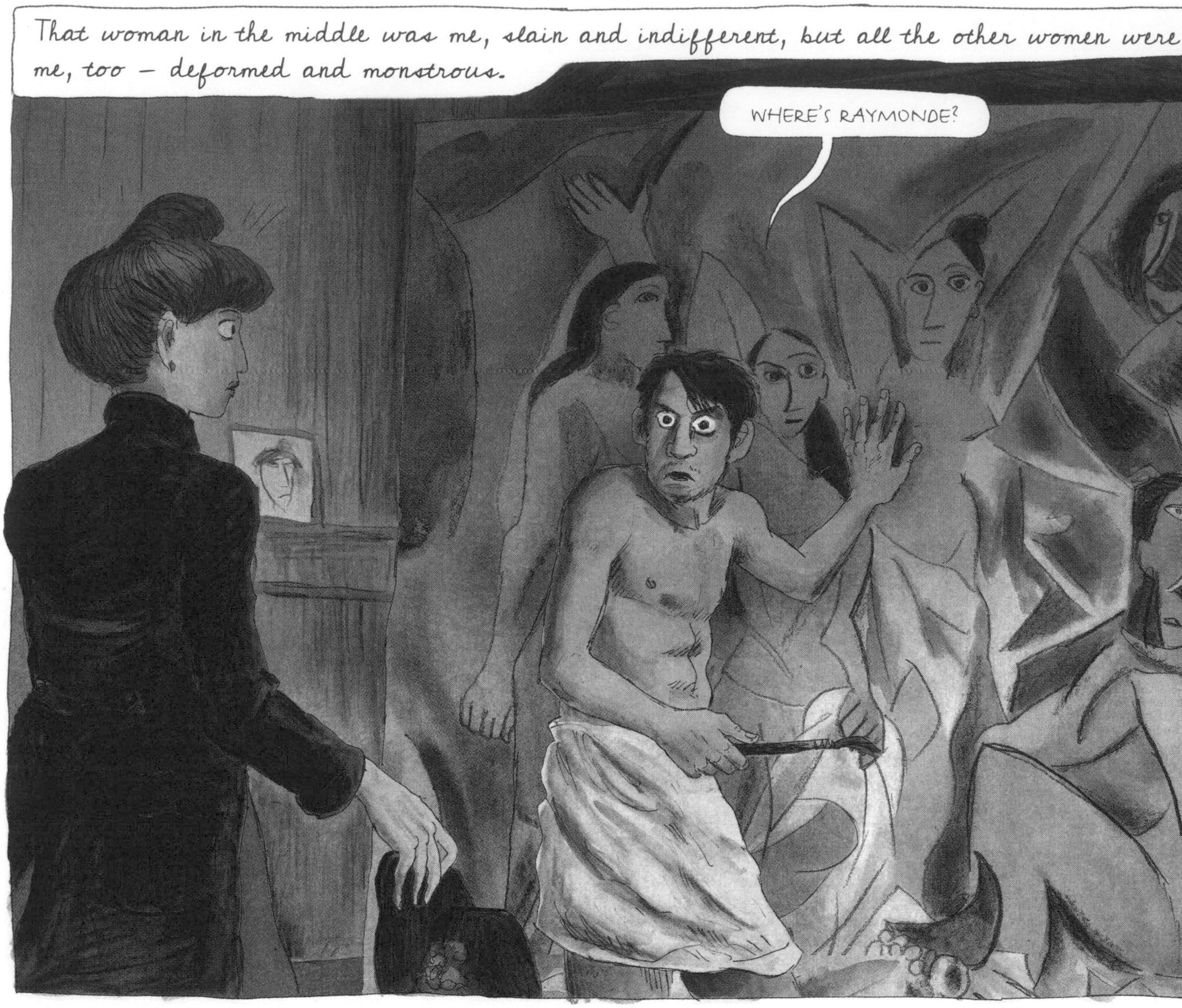
That woman in the middle was me, slain and indifferent, but all the other women were me, too – deformed and monstrous.
WHERE'S RAYMONDE?

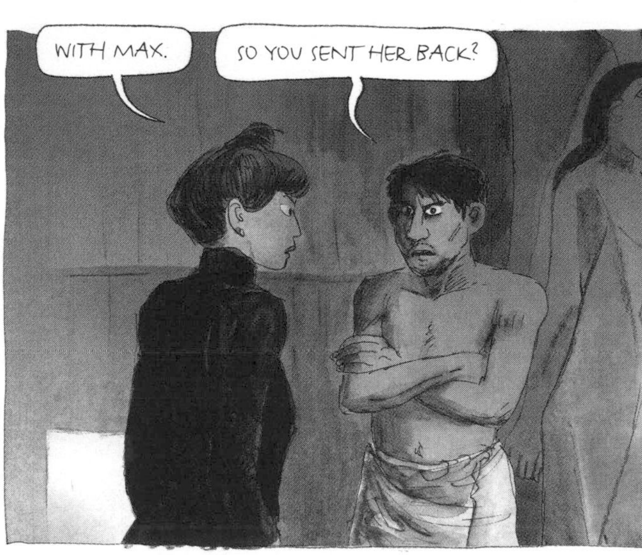
WITH MAX.
SO YOU SENT HER BACK?

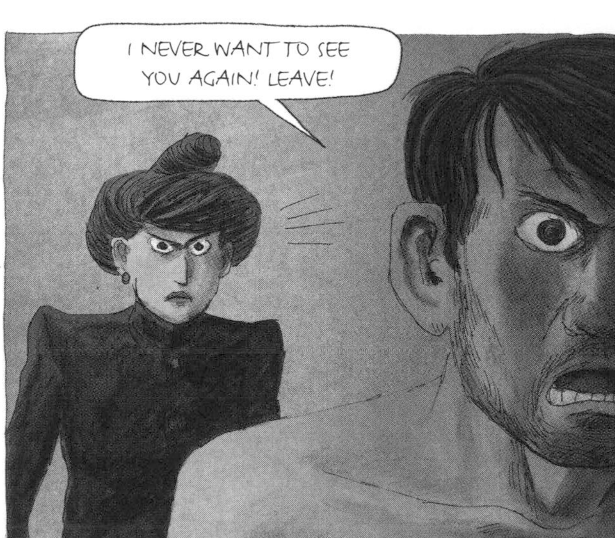
I NEVER WANT TO SEE YOU AGAIN! LEAVE!

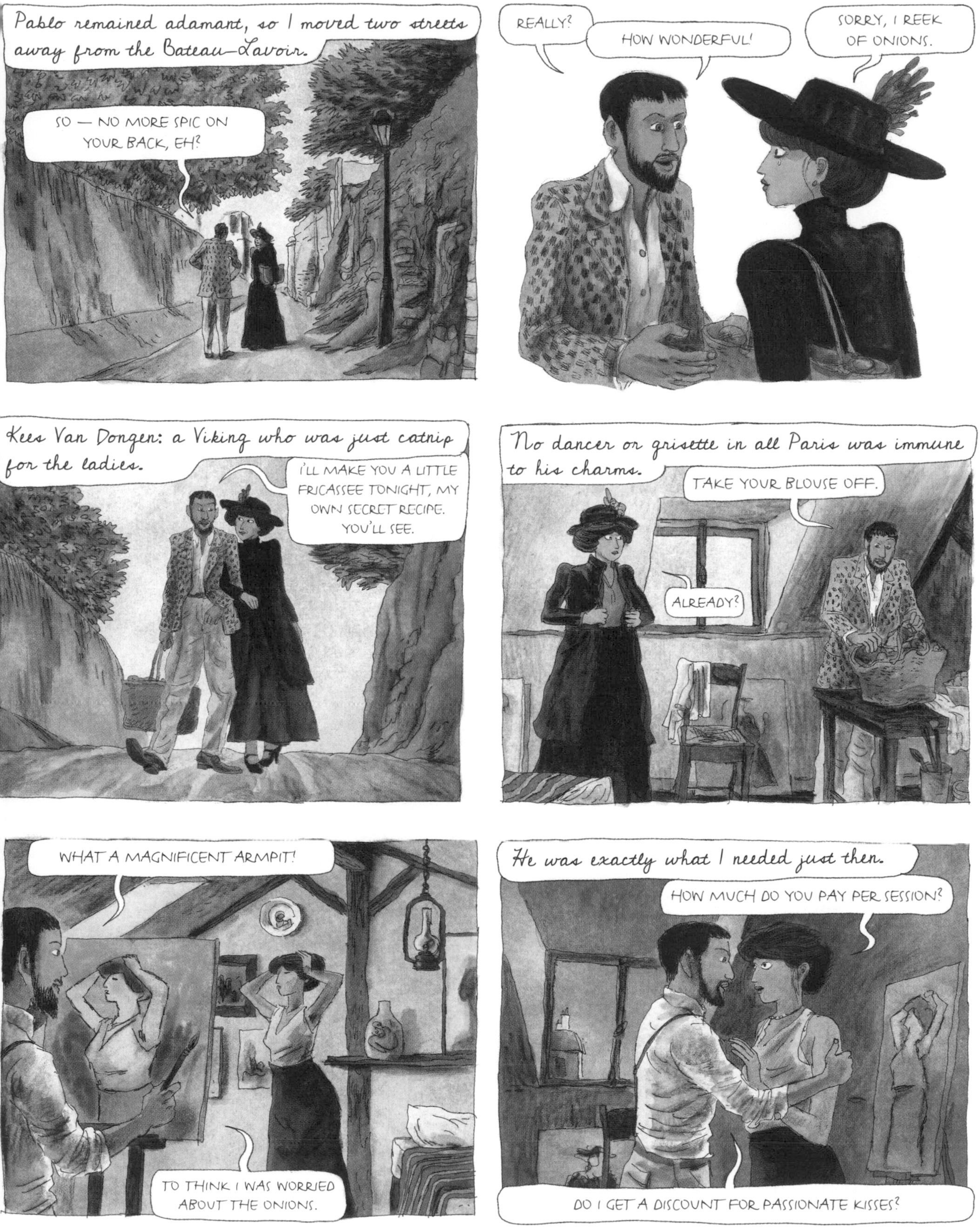

Pablo remained adamant, so I moved two streets away from the Bateau-Lavoir.
SO — NO MORE SPIC ON YOUR BACK, EH?
REALLY?
HOW WONDERFUL!
SORRY, I REEK OF ONIONS.
Kees Van Dongen: a Viking who was just catnip for the ladies.
I'LL MAKE YOU A LITTLE FRICASSEE TONIGHT, MY OWN SECRET RECIPE. YOU'LL SEE.
No dancer or grisette in all Paris was immune to his charms.
TAKE YOUR BLOUSE OFF.
ALREADY?
WHAT A MAGNIFICENT ARMPIT!
TO THINK I WAS WORRIED ABOUT THE ONIONS.
He was exactly what I needed just then.
HOW MUCH DO YOU PAY PER SESSION?
DO I GET A DISCOUNT FOR PASSIONATE KISSES?

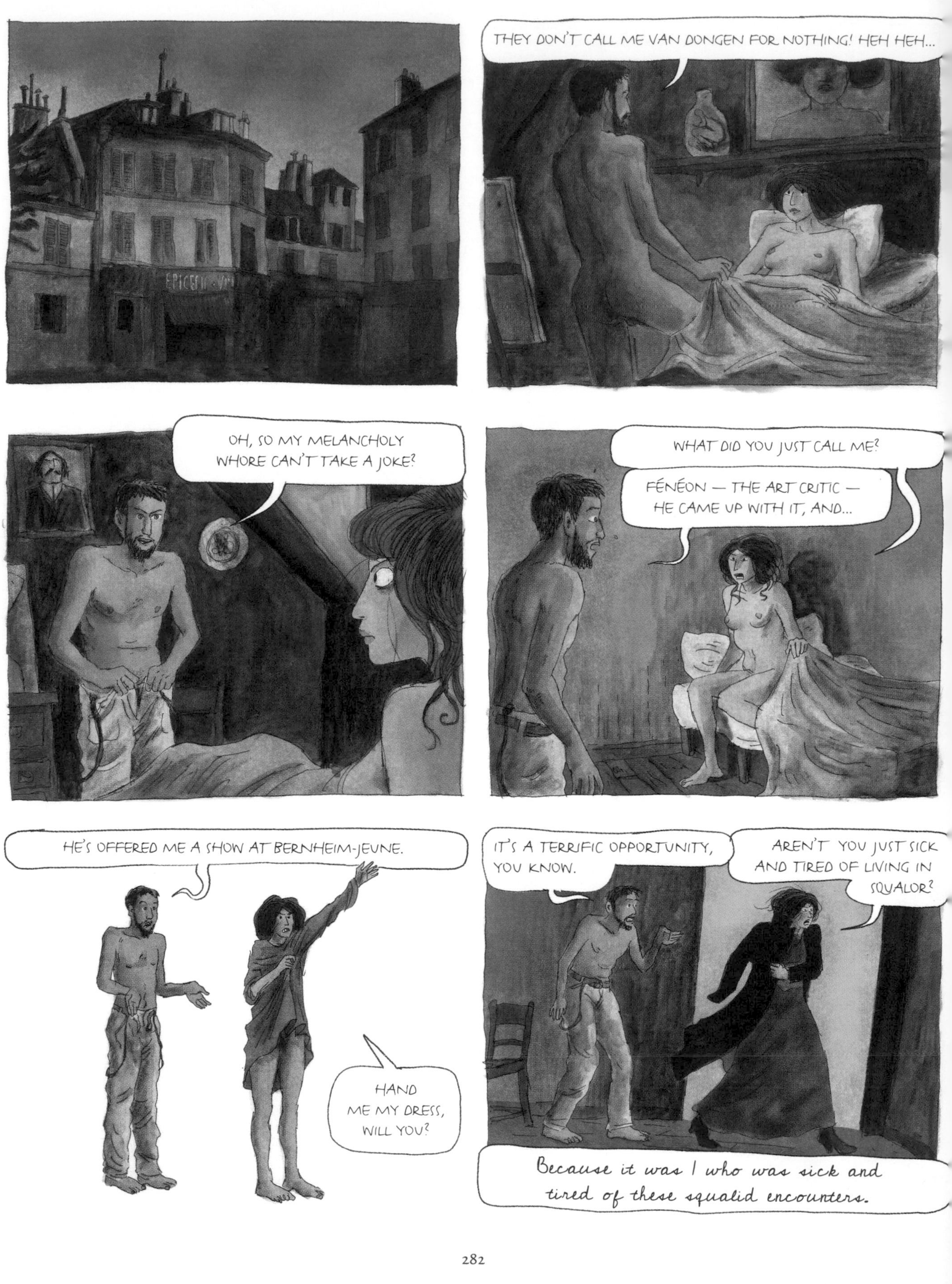
THEY DON'T CALL ME VAN DONGEN FOR NOTHING! HEH HEH...
OH, SO MY MELANCHOLY WHORE CAN'T TAKE A JOKE?
WHAT DID YOU JUST CALL ME?
FÉNÉON — THE ART CRITIC — HE CAME UP WITH IT, AND...
HE'S OFFERED ME A SHOW AT BERNHEIM-JEUNE.
HAND ME MY DRESS, WILL YOU?
IT'S A TERRIFIC OPPORTUNITY, YOU KNOW.
AREN'T YOU JUST SICK AND TIRED OF LIVING IN SQUALOR?
Because it was I who was sick and tired of these squalid encounters.

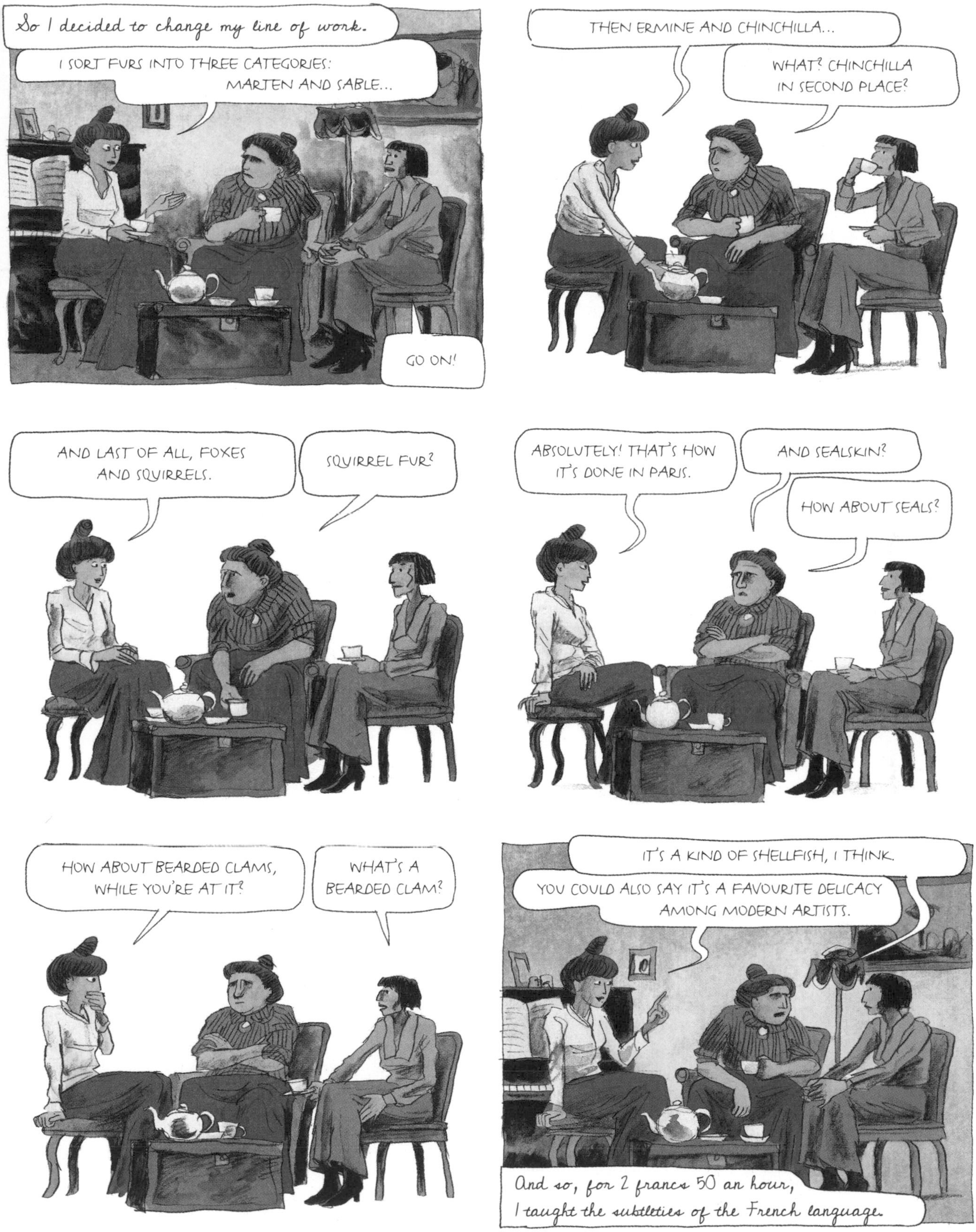
So I decided to change my line of work.
I SORT FURS INTO THREE CATEGORIES: MARTEN AND SABLE...
GO ON!
THEN ERMINE AND CHINCHILLA...
WHAT? CHINCHILLA IN SECOND PLACE?
AND LAST OF ALL, FOXES AND SQUIRRELS.
SQUIRREL FUR?
ABSOLUTELY! THAT'S HOW IT'S DONE IN PARIS.
AND SEALSKIN?
HOW ABOUT SEALS?
HOW ABOUT BEARDED CLAMS, WHILE YOU'RE AT IT?
WHAT'S A BEARDED CLAM?
IT'S A KIND OF SHELLFISH, I THINK.
YOU COULD ALSO SAY IT'S A FAVOURITE DELICACY AMONG MODERN ARTISTS.
And so, for 2 francs 50 an hour,
I taught the subtleties of the French language.

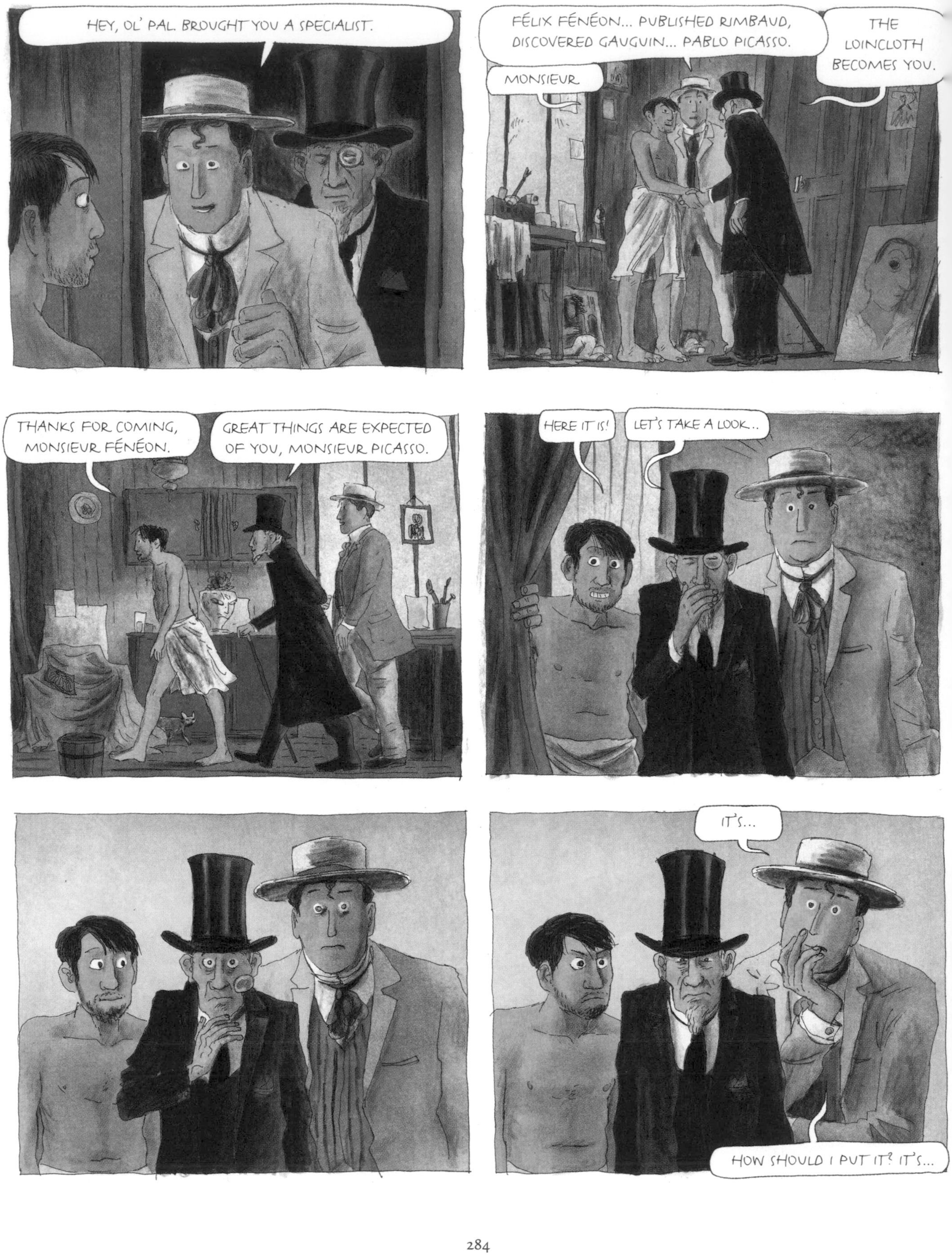
HEY, OL' PAL. BROUGHT YOU A SPECIALIST.
FÉLIX FÉNÉON... PUBLISHED RIMBAUD, DISCOVERED GAUGUIN... PABLO PICASSO.
MONSIEUR.
THE LOINCLOTH BECOMES YOU.
THANKS FOR COMING, MONSIEUR FÉNÉON.
GREAT THINGS ARE EXPECTED OF YOU, MONSIEUR PICASSO.
HERE IT IS!
LET'S TAKE A LOOK..
IT'S...
HOW SHOULD I PUT IT? IT'S...

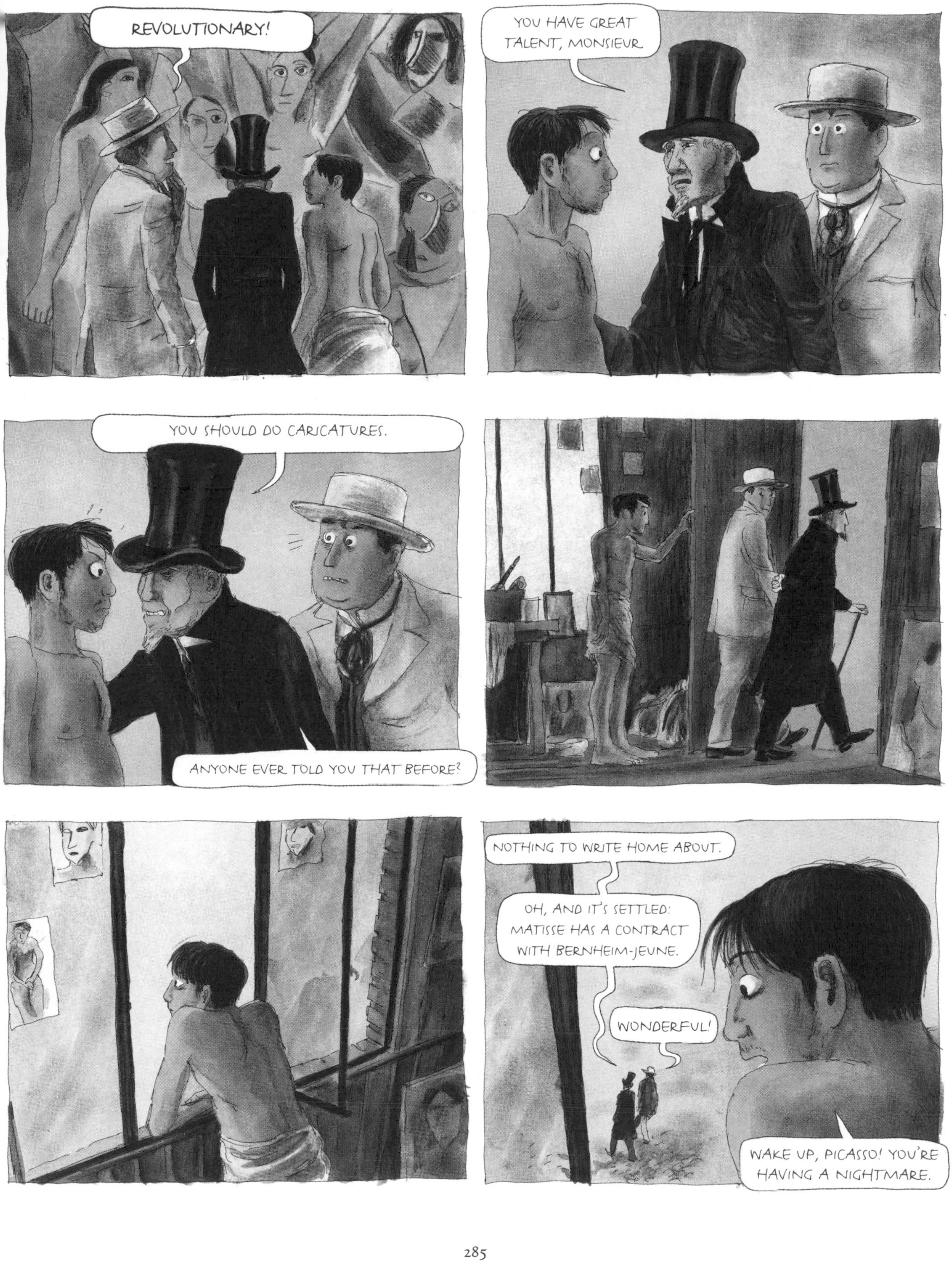
REVOLUTIONARY!
YOU HAVE GREAT TALENT, MONSIEUR
YOU SHOULD DO CARICATURES.
ANYONE EVER TOLD YOU THAT BEFORE?
NOTHING TO WRITE HOME ABOUT.
OH, AND IT'S SETTLED: MATISSE HAS A CONTRACT WITH BERNHEIM-JEUNE.
WONDERFUL!
WAKE UP, PICASSO! YOU'RE HAVING A NIGHTMARE.

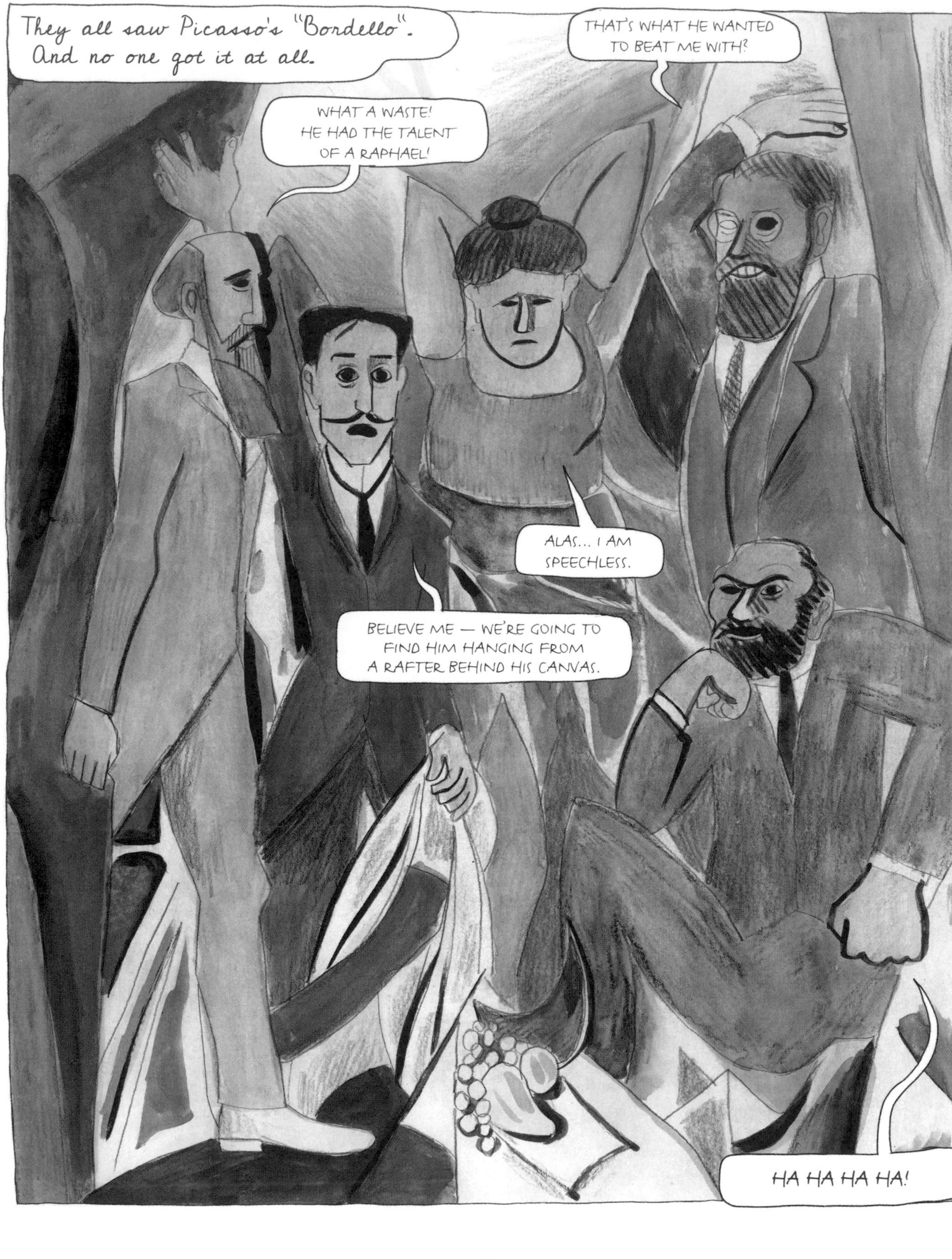
They all saw Picasso's "Bordello". And no one got it at all.
THAT'S WHAT HE WANTED TO BEAT ME WITH?
WHAT A WASTE! HE HAD THE TALENT OF A RAPHAEL!
ALAS... I AM SPEECHLESS.
BELIEVE ME — WE'RE GOING TO FIND HIM HANGING FROM A RAFTER BEHIND HIS CANVAS.
HA HA HA HA!

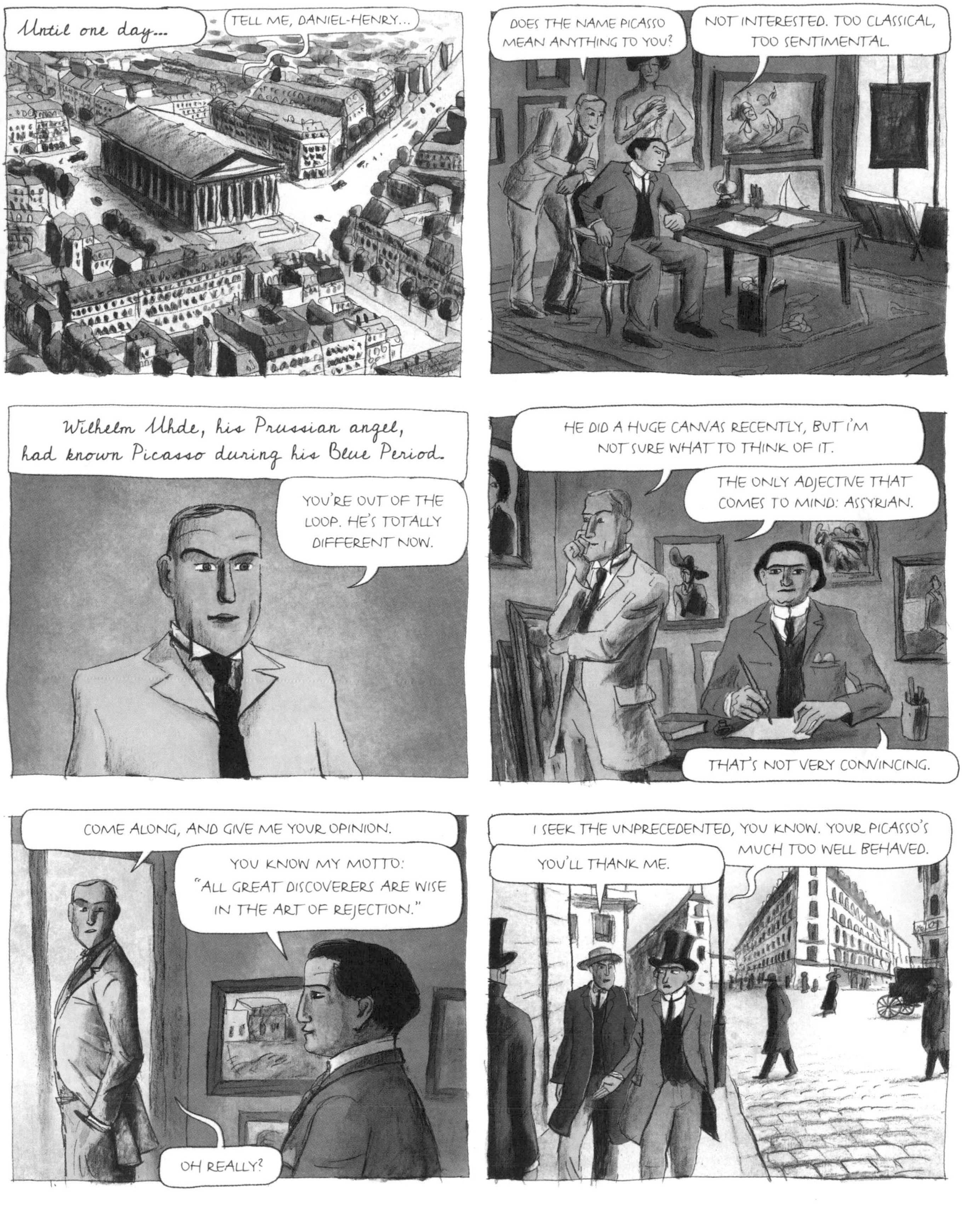
Until one day...
TELL ME, DANIEL-HENRY...
DOES THE NAME PICASSO MEAN ANYTHING TO YOU?
NOT INTERESTED. TOO CLASSICAL, TOO SENTIMENTAL.
Wilhelm Uhde, his Prussian angel, had known Picasso during his Blue Period.
YOU'RE OUT OF THE LOOP. HE'S TOTALLY DIFFERENT NOW.
HE DID A HUGE CANVAS RECENTLY, BUT I'M NOT SURE WHAT TO THINK OF IT.
THE ONLY ADJECTIVE THAT COMES TO MIND: ASSYRIAN.
THAT'S NOT VERY CONVINCING.
COME ALONG, AND GIVE ME YOUR OPINION.
YOU KNOW MY MOTTO: "ALL GREAT DISCOVERERS ARE WISE IN THE ART OF REJECTION."
OH REALLY?
I SEEK THE UNPRECEDENTED, YOU KNOW. YOUR PICASSO'S MUCH TOO WELL BEHAVED.
YOU'LL THANK ME.

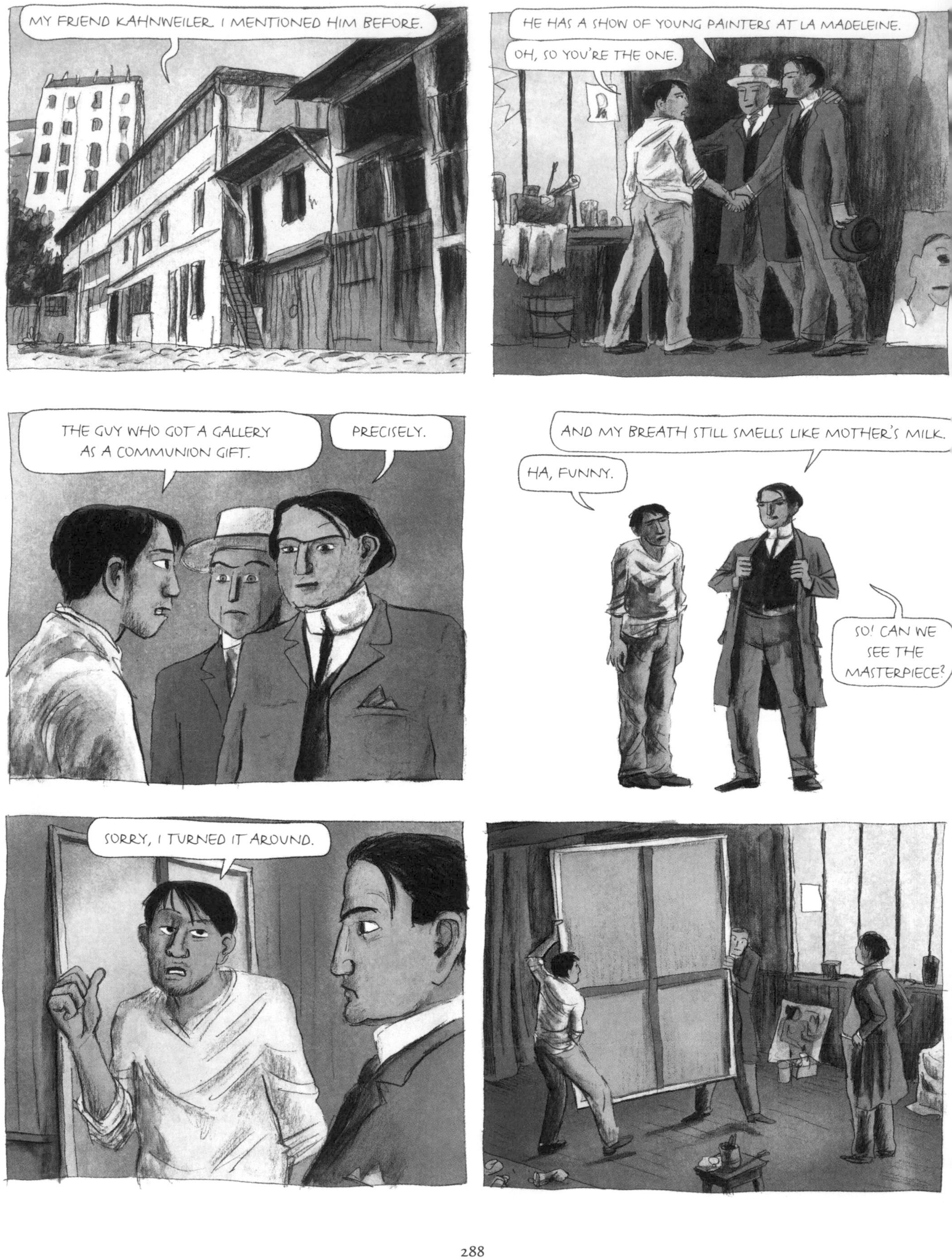
MY FRIEND KAHNWEILER. I MENTIONED HIM BEFORE.
HE HAS A SHOW OF YOUNG PAINTERS AT LA MADELEINE.
OH, SO YOU'RE THE ONE.
THE GUY WHO GOT A GALLERY AS A COMMUNION GIFT.
PRECISELY.
AND MY BREATH STILL SMELLS LIKE MOTHER'S MILK.
HA, FUNNY.
SO! CAN WE SEE THE MASTERPIECE?
SORRY, I TURNED IT AROUND.

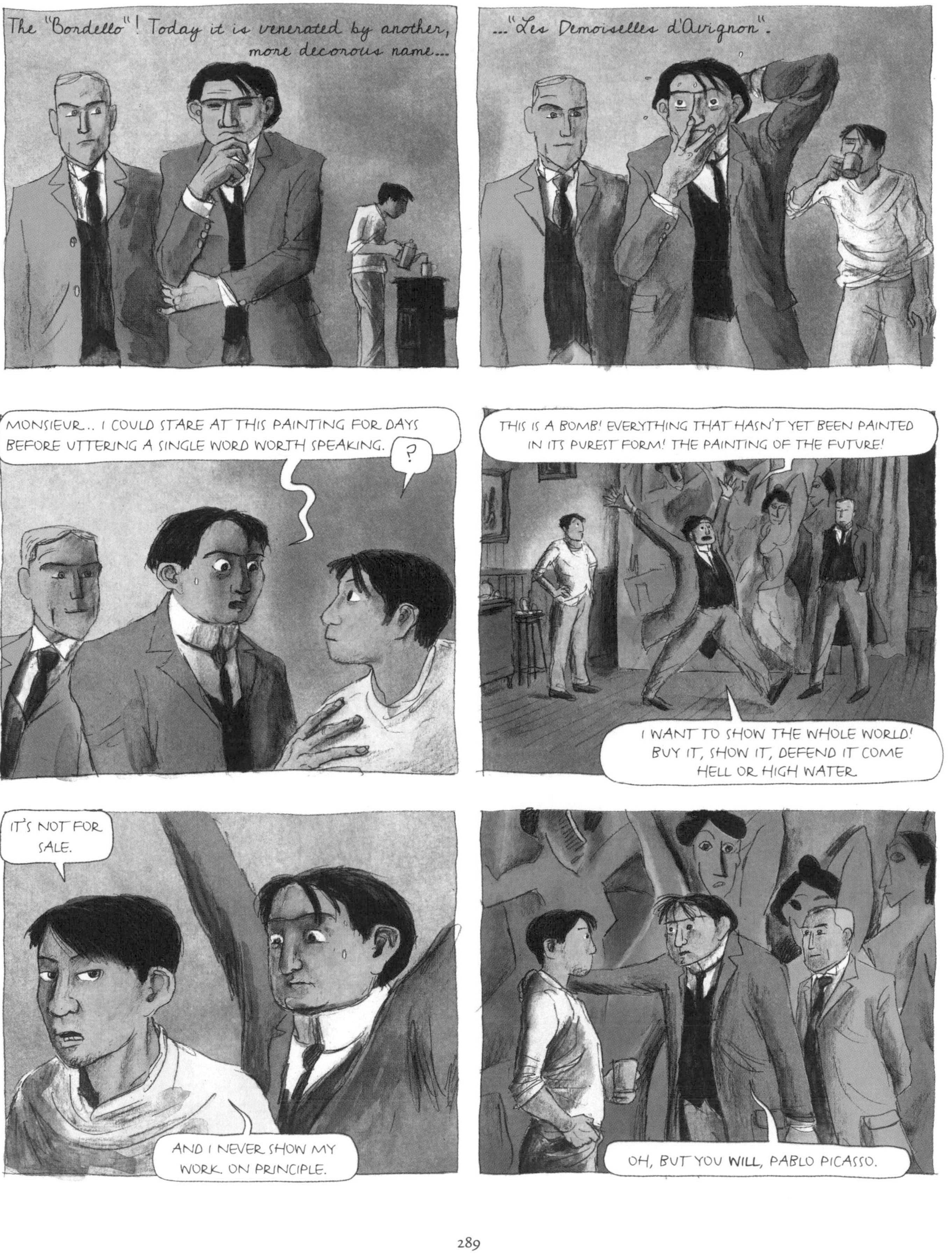
The "Bordello"! Today it is venerated by another, more decorous name....
..."Les Demoiselles d'Avignon".
MONSIEUR... I COULD STARE AT THIS PAINTING FOR DAYS BEFORE UTTERING A SINGLE WORD WORTH SPEAKING.
?
THIS IS A BOMB! EVERYTHING THAT HASN'T YET BEEN PAINTED IN ITS PUREST FORM! THE PAINTING OF THE FUTURE!
I WANT TO SHOW THE WHOLE WORLD! BUY IT, SHOW IT, DEFEND IT COME HELL OR HIGH WATER.
IT'S NOT FOR SALE.
AND I NEVER SHOW MY WORK. ON PRINCIPLE.
OH, BUT YOU WILL, PABLO PICASSO.

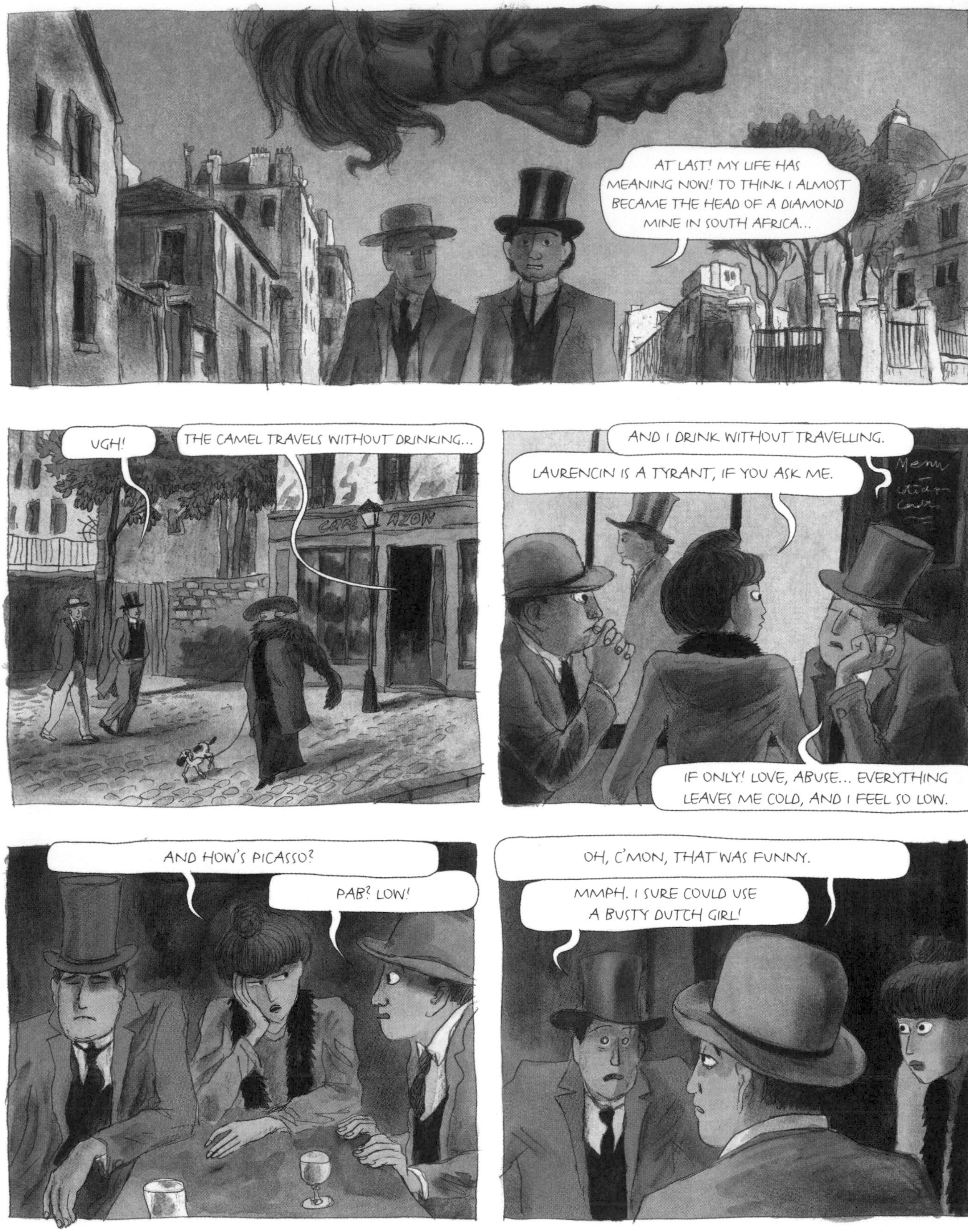
AT LAST! MY LIFE HAS MEANING NOW! TO THINK I ALMOST BECAME THE HEAD OF A DIAMOND MINE IN SOUTH AFRICA...
UGH!
THE CAMEL TRAVELS WITHOUT DRINKING...
AND I DRINK WITHOUT TRAVELLING.
LAURENCIN IS A TYRANT, IF YOU ASK ME.
IF ONLY! LOVE, ABUSE... EVERYTHING LEAVES ME COLD, AND I FEEL SO LOW.
AND HOW'S PICASSO?
PAB? LOW!
OH, C'MON, THAT WAS FUNNY.
MMPH. I SURE COULD USE A BUSTY DUTCH GIRL!

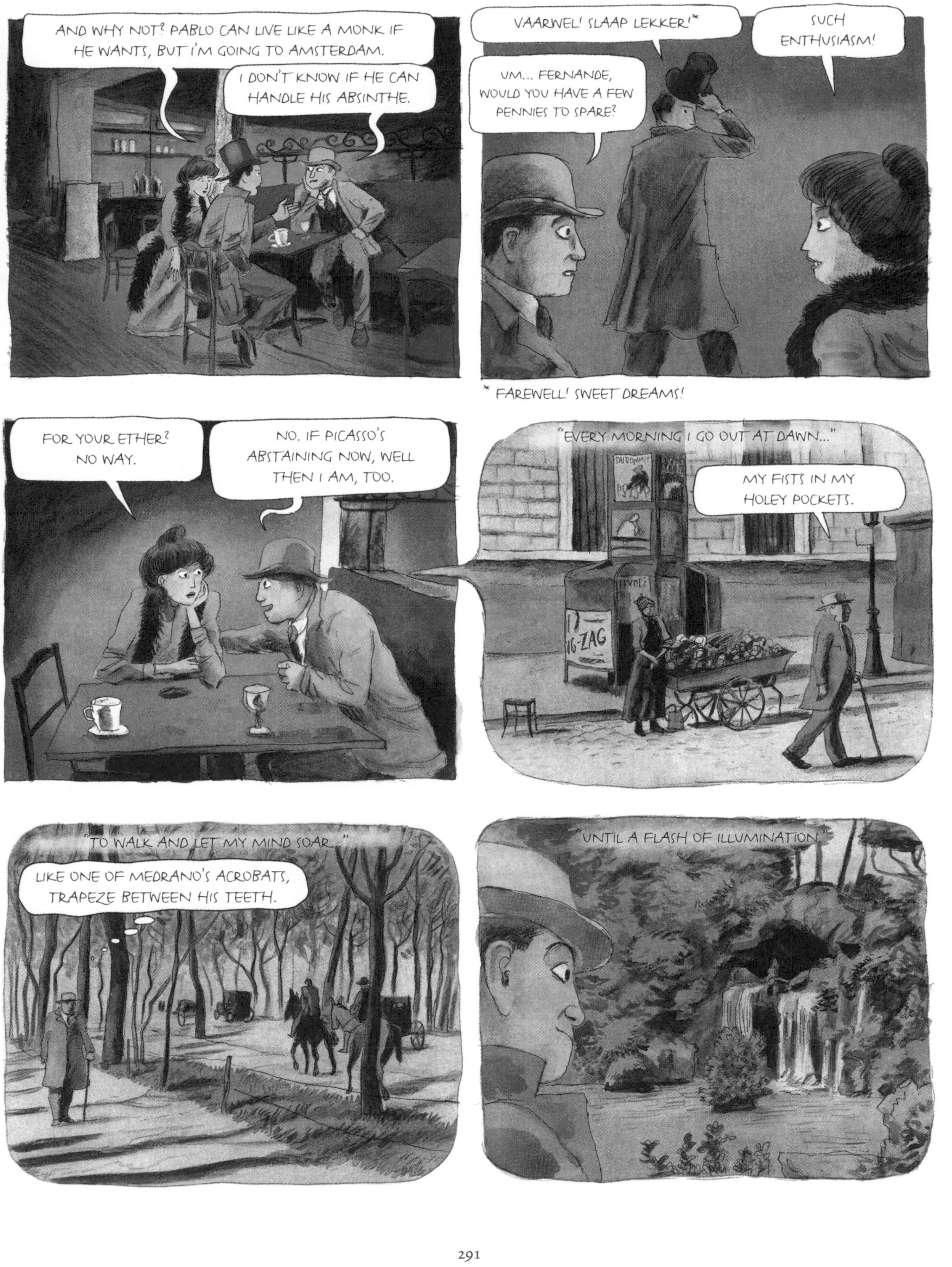
AND WHY NOT? PABLO CAN LIVE LIKE A MONK IF HE WANTS, BUT I'M GOING TO AMSTERDAM.
I DON'T KNOW IF HE CAN HANDLE HIS ABSINTHE.
VAARWEL! SLAAP LEKKER!*
UM... FERNANDE, WOULD YOU HAVE A FEW PENNIES TO SPARE?
SUCH ENTHUSIASM!
* FAREWELL! SWEET DREAMS!
FOR YOUR ETHER? NO WAY.
NO. IF PICASSO'S ABSTAINING NOW, WELL THEN I AM, TOO.
"EVERY MORNING I GO OUT AT DAWN..."
MY FISTS IN MY HOLEY POCKETS.
"TO WALK AND LET MY MIND SOAR..."
LIKE ONE OF MEDRANO'S ACROBATS, TRAPEZE BETWEEN HIS TEETH.
"UNTIL A FLASH OF ILLUMINATION."

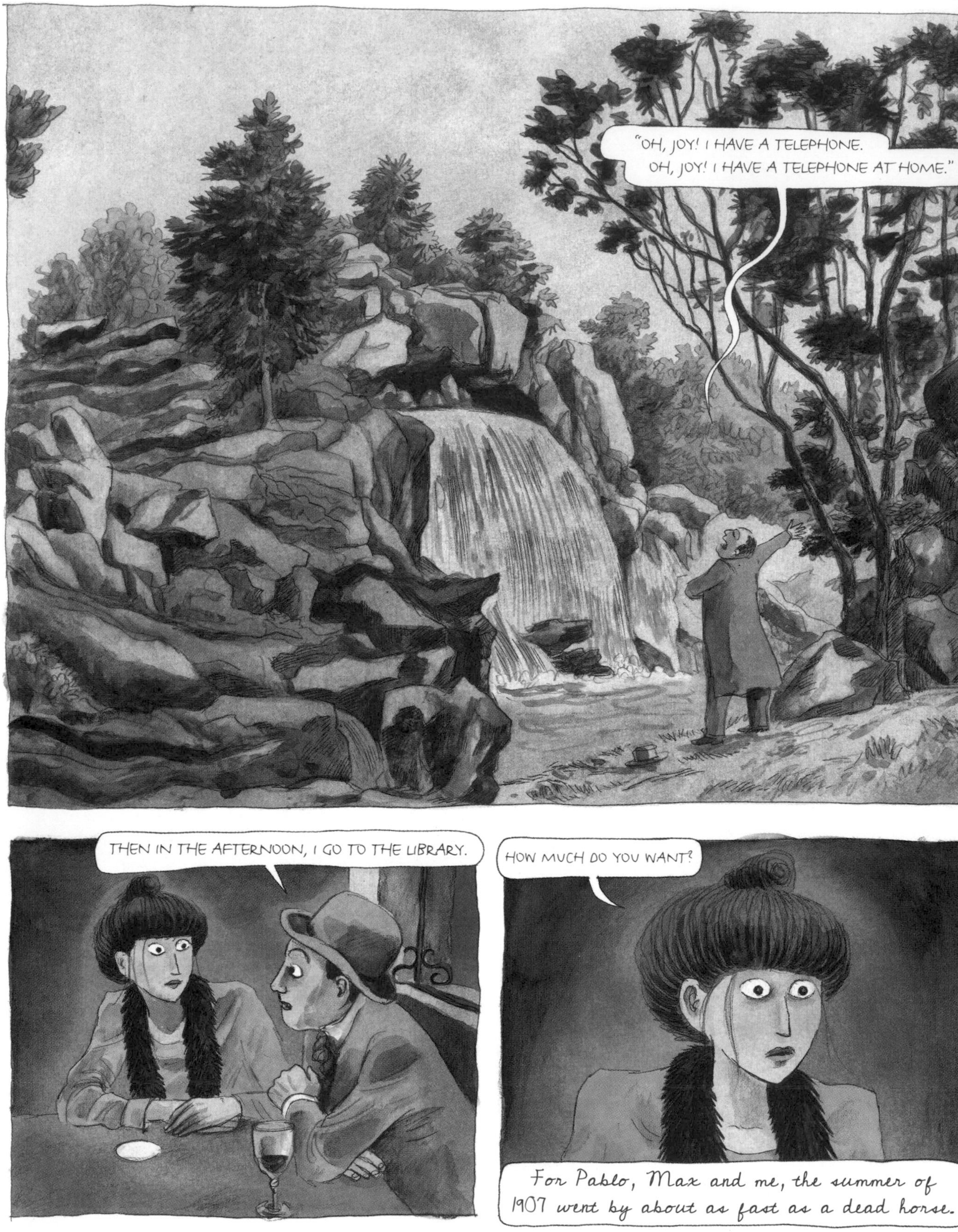
"OH, JOY! I HAVE A TELEPHONE.
OH, JOY! I HAVE A TELEPHONE AT HOME."
THEN IN THE AFTERNOON, I GO TO THE LIBRARY.
HOW MUCH DO YOU WANT?
For Pablo, Max and me, the summer of 1907 went by about as fast as a dead horse.

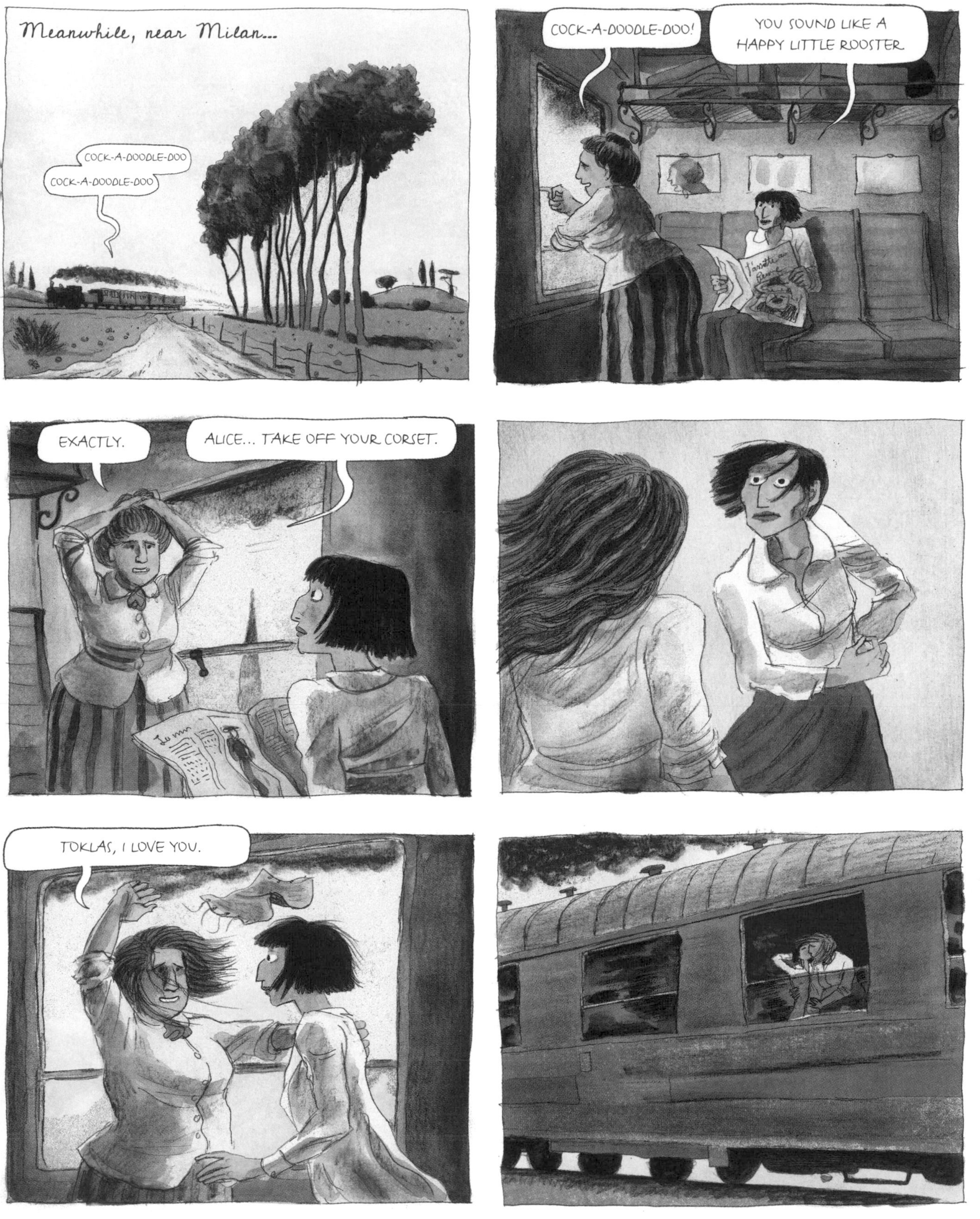
Meanwhile, near Milan...
COCK-A-DOODLE-DOO
COCK-A-DOODLE-DOO
COCK-A-DOODLE-DOO!
YOU SOUND LIKE A HAPPY LITTLE ROOSTER.
EXACTLY.
ALICE... TAKE OFF YOUR CORSET.
TOKLAS, I LOVE YOU.

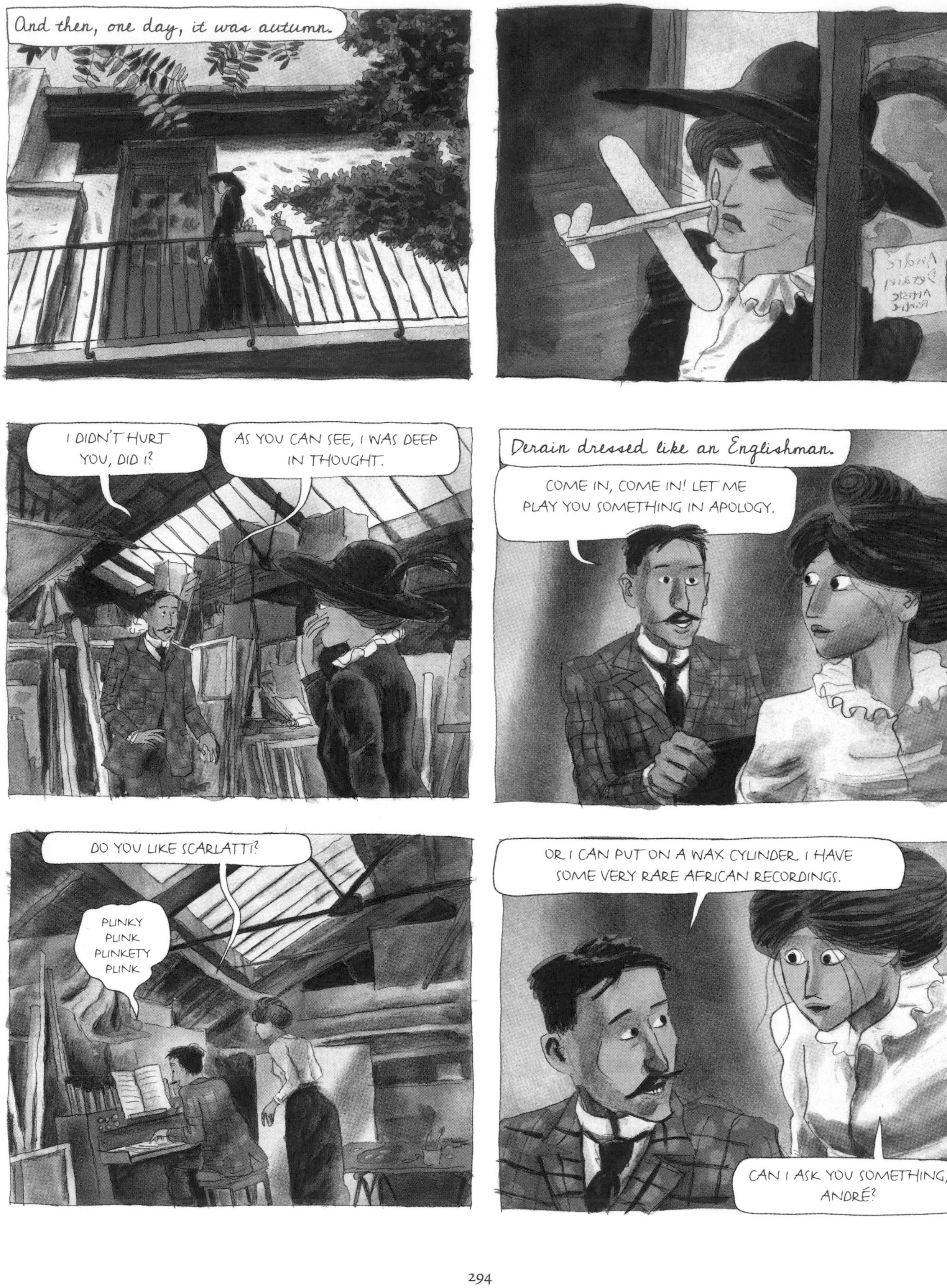
And then, one day, it was autumn.
I DIDN'T HURT YOU, DID I?
AS YOU CAN SEE, I WAS DEEP IN THOUGHT.
Derain dressed like an Englishman.
COME IN, COME IN! LET ME PLAY YOU SOMETHING IN APOLOGY.
DO YOU LIKE SCARLATTI?
PLINKY PLINK PLINKETY PLINK
OR I CAN PUT ON A WAX CYLINDER. I HAVE SOME VERY RARE AFRICAN RECORDINGS.
CAN I ASK YOU SOMETHING, ANDRÉ?

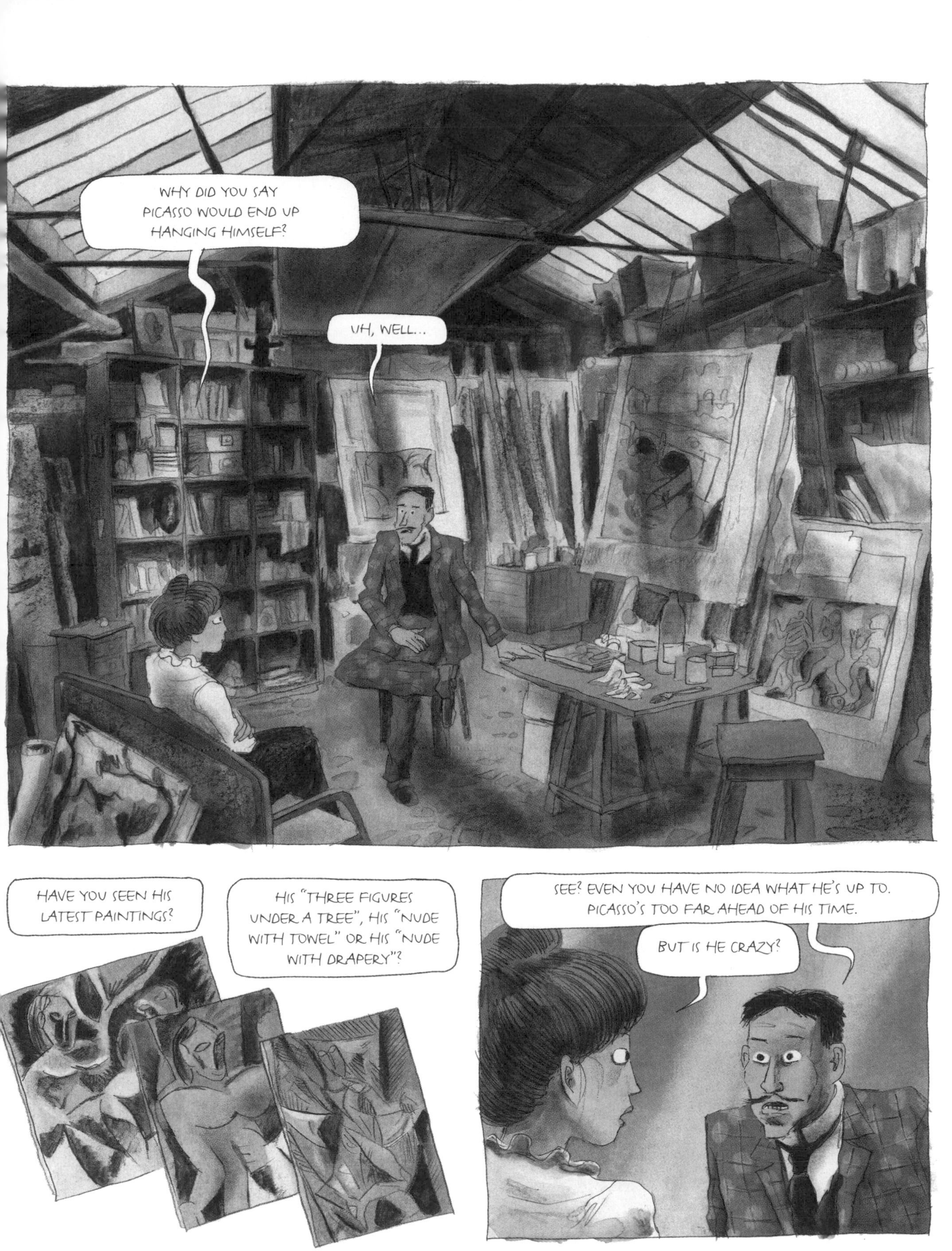
WHY DID YOU SAY PICASSO WOULD END UP HANGING HIMSELF?
UH, WELL...
HAVE YOU SEEN HIS LATEST PAINTINGS?
HIS "THREE FIGURES UNDER A TREE", HIS "NUDE WITH TOWEL" OR HIS "NUDE WITH DRAPERY"?
SEE? EVEN YOU HAVE NO IDEA WHAT HE'S UP TO. PICASSO'S TOO FAR AHEAD OF HIS TIME.
BUT IS HE CRAZY?

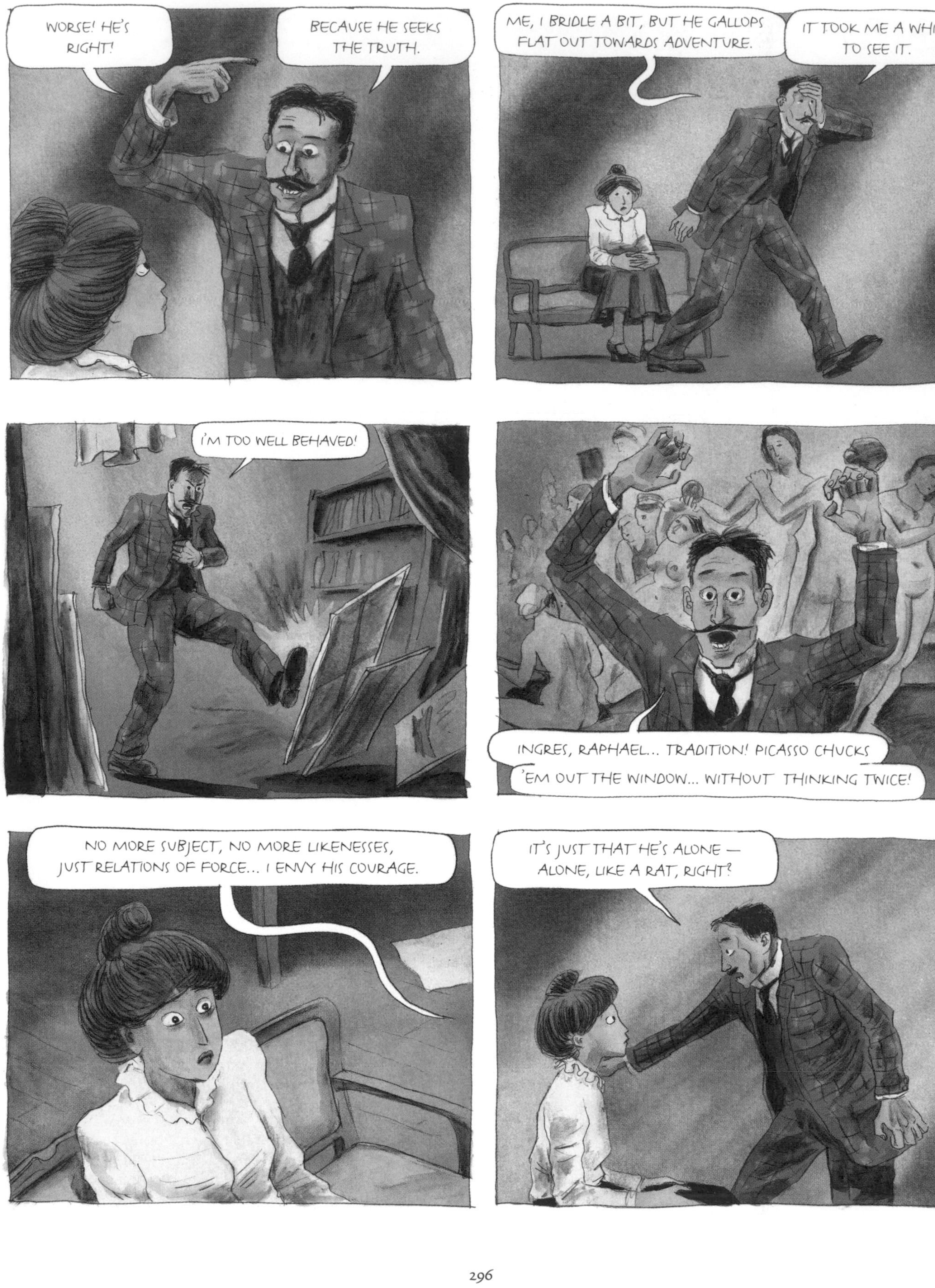
WORSE! HE'S RIGHT!
BECAUSE HE SEEKS THE TRUTH.
ME, I BRIDLE A BIT, BUT HE GALLOPS FLAT OUT TOWARDS ADVENTURE.
IT TOOK ME A WHILE TO SEE IT.
I'M TOO WELL BEHAVED!
INGRES, RAPHAEL... TRADITION! PICASSO CHUCKS 'EM OUT THE WINDOW... WITHOUT THINKING TWICE!
NO MORE SUBJECT, NO MORE LIKENESSES, JUST RELATIONS OF FORCE... I ENVY HIS COURAGE.
IT'S JUST THAT HE'S ALONE — ALONE, LIKE A RAT, RIGHT?

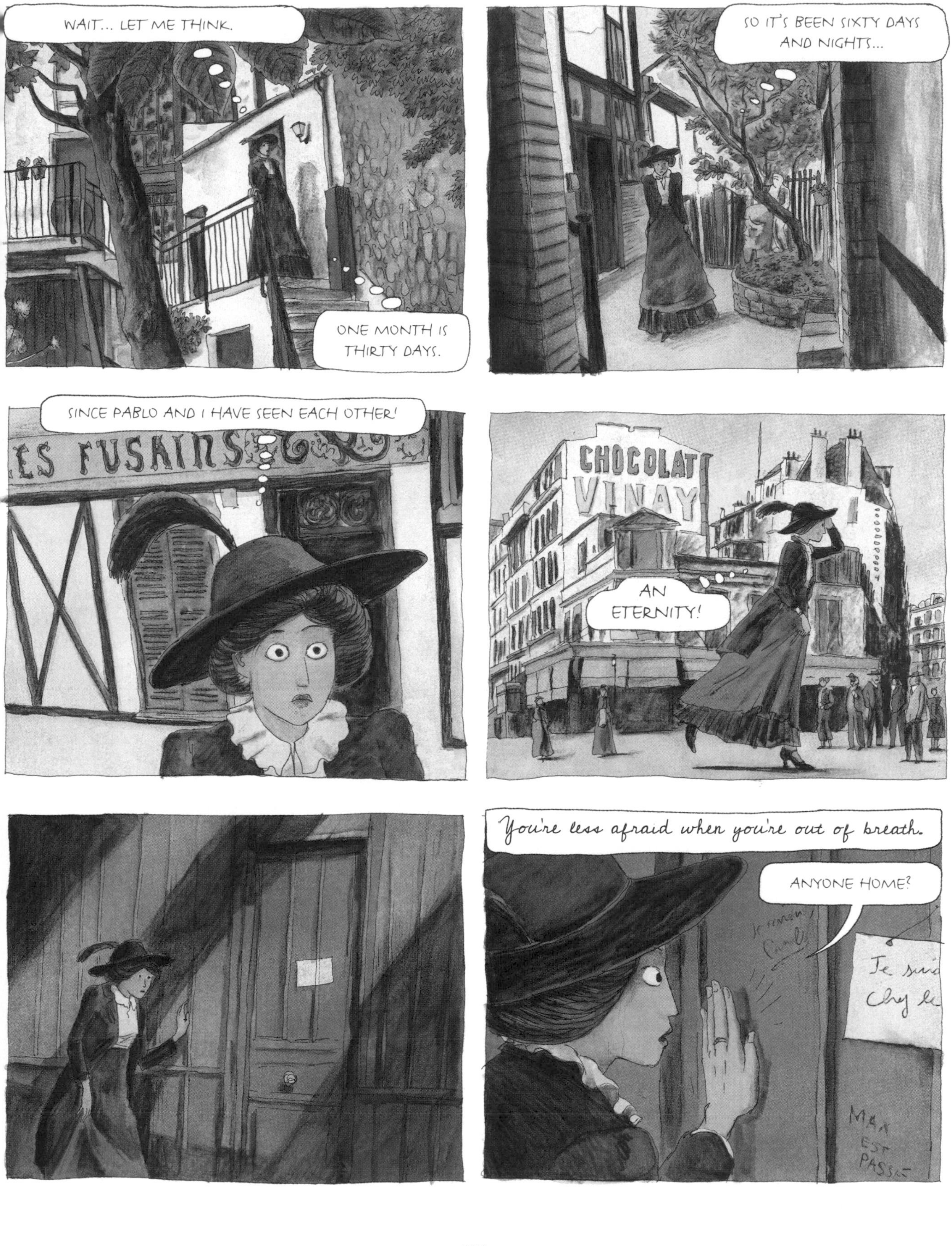
WAIT... LET ME THINK.
ONE MONTH IS THIRTY DAYS.
SO IT'S BEEN SIXTY DAYS AND NIGHTS...
SINCE PABLO AND I HAVE SEEN EACH OTHER!
ES FUSAINS
CHOCOLAT VINAY
AN ETERNITY!
You're less afraid when you're out of breath.
ANYONE HOME?
MAX EST PASSÉ

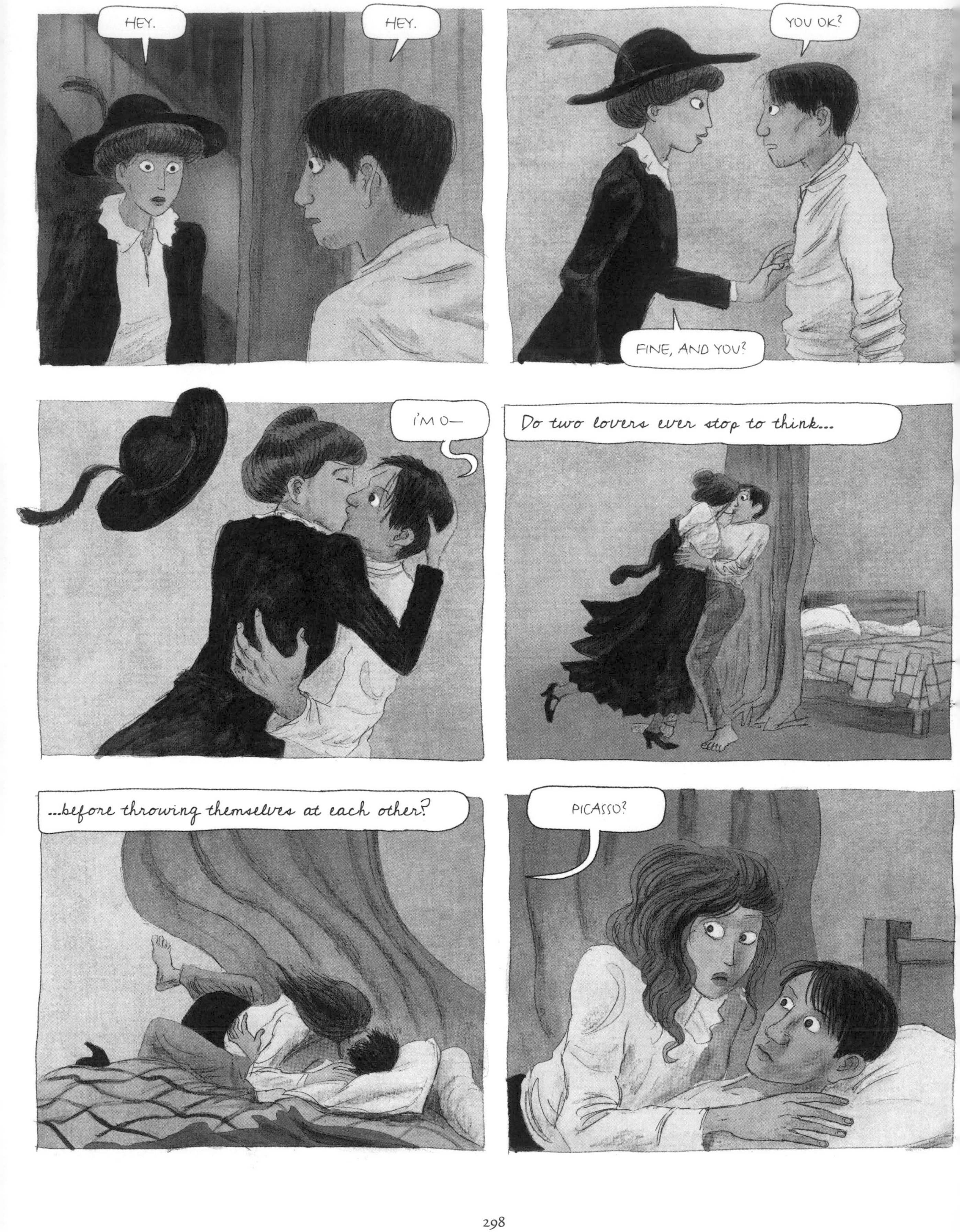
HEY.
HEY.
YOU OK?
FINE, AND YOU?
I'M O—
Do two lovers ever stop to think...
...before throwing themselves at each other?
PICASSO?

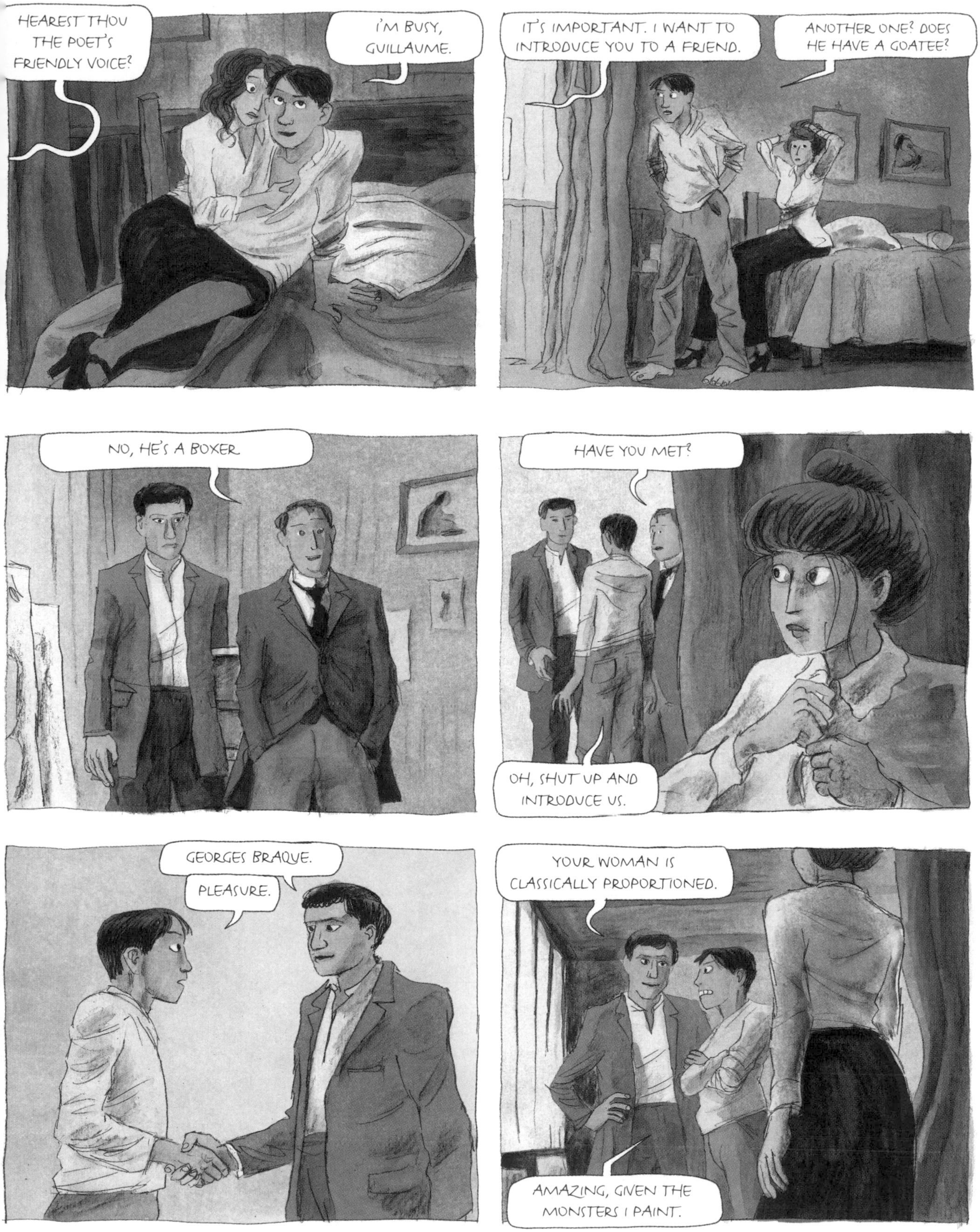
HEAREST THOU THE POET'S FRIENDLY VOICE?
I'M BUSY, GUILLAUME.
IT'S IMPORTANT. I WANT TO INTRODUCE YOU TO A FRIEND.
ANOTHER ONE? DOES HE HAVE A GOATEE?
NO, HE'S A BOXER.
HAVE YOU MET?
OH, SHUT UP AND INTRODUCE US.
GEORGES BRAQUE.
PLEASURE.
YOUR WOMAN IS CLASSICALLY PROPORTIONED.
AMAZING, GIVEN THE MONSTERS I PAINT.

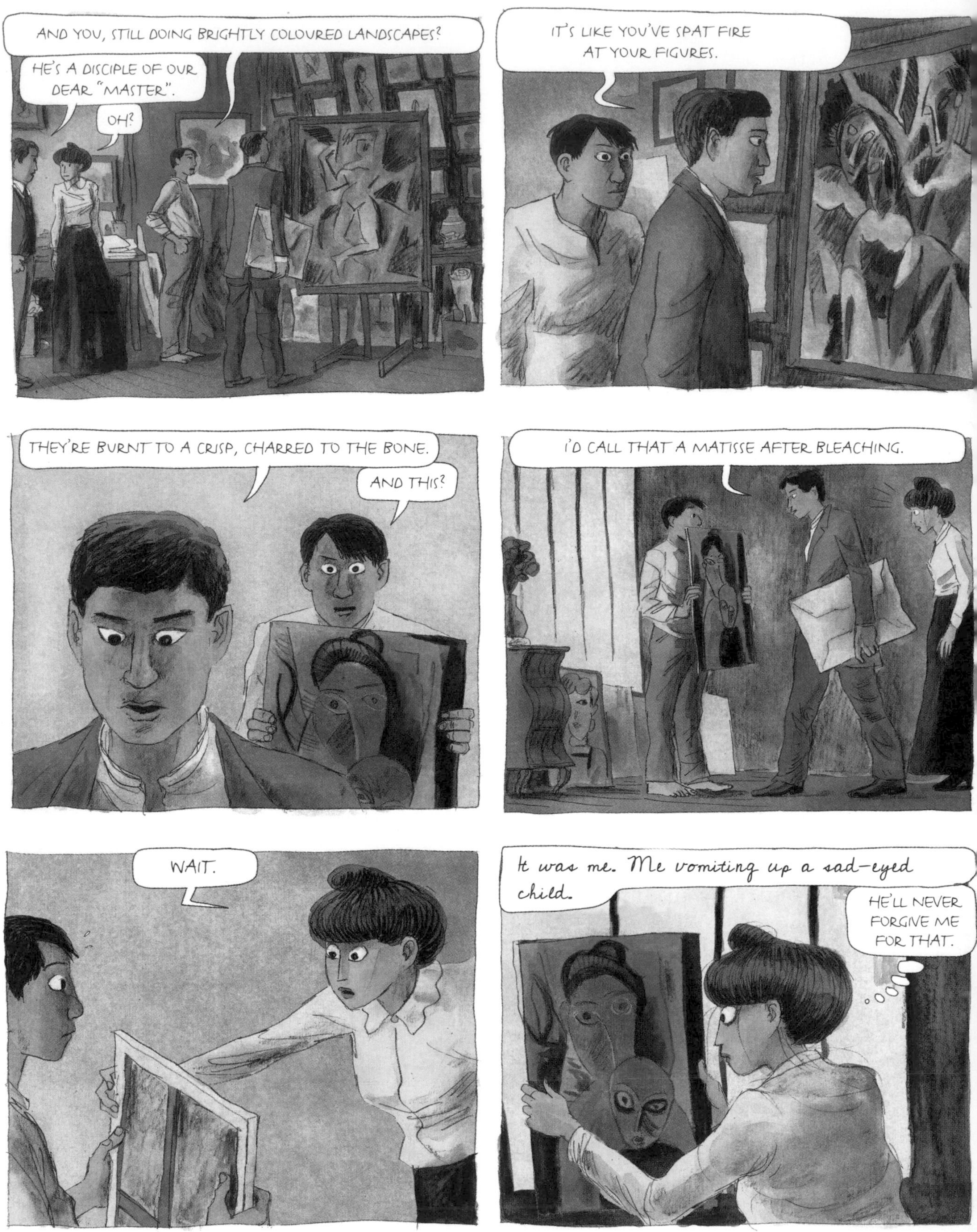
AND YOU, STILL DOING BRIGHTLY COLOURED LANDSCAPES?
HE'S A DISCIPLE OF OUR DEAR "MASTER".
OH?
IT'S LIKE YOU'VE SPAT FIRE AT YOUR FIGURES.
THEY'RE BURNT TO A CRISP, CHARRED TO THE BONE.
AND THIS?
I'D CALL THAT A MATISSE AFTER BLEACHING.
WAIT.
It was me. Me vomiting up a sad-eyed child.
HE'LL NEVER FORGIVE ME FOR THAT.

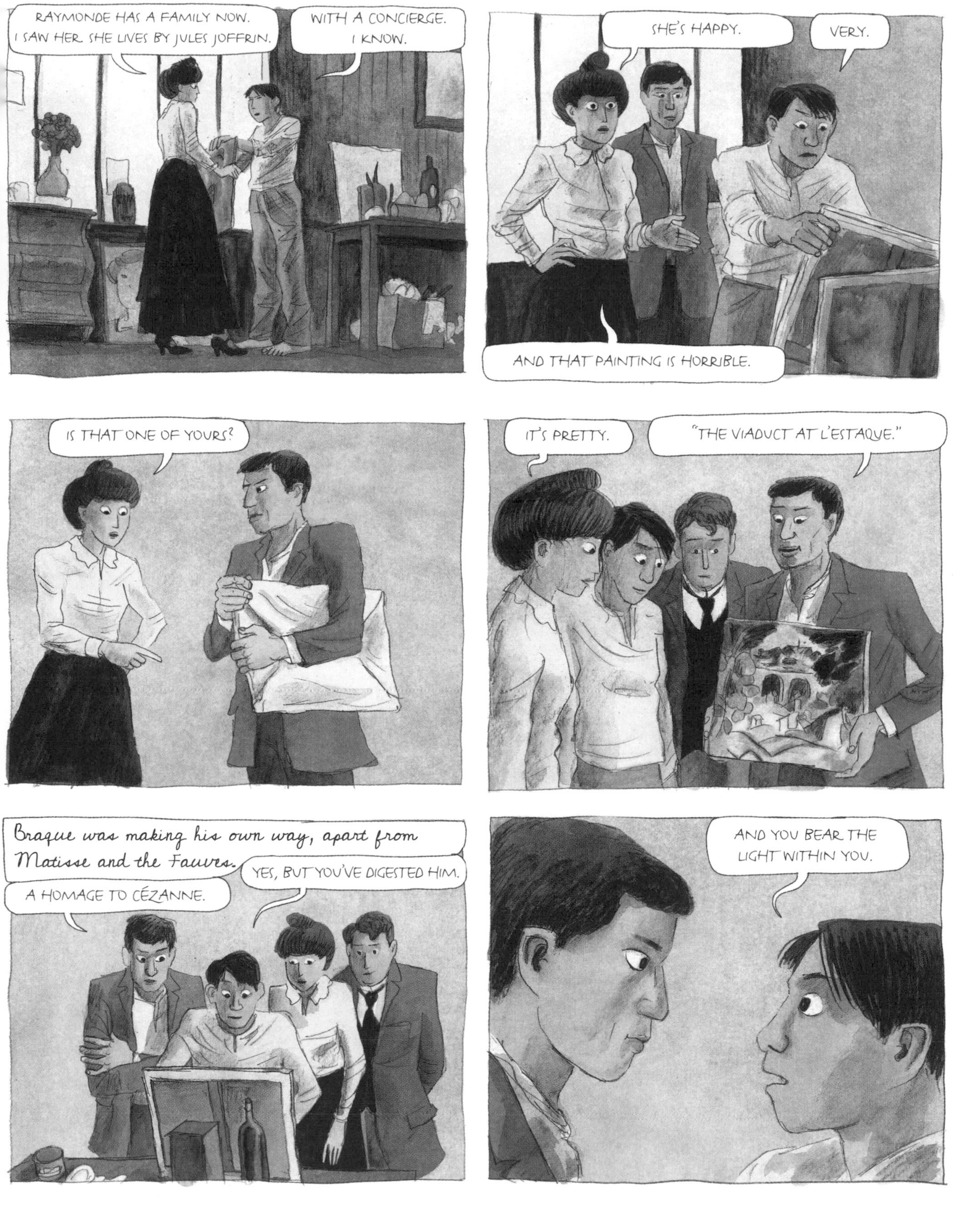
RAYMONDE HAS A FAMILY NOW. I SAW HER. SHE LIVES BY JULES JOFFRIN.
WITH A CONCIERGE. I KNOW.
SHE'S HAPPY.
VERY.
AND THAT PAINTING IS HORRIBLE.
IS THAT ONE OF YOURS?
IT'S PRETTY.
"THE VIADUCT AT L'ESTAQUE."
Braque was making his own way, apart from Matisse and the Fauves.
A HOMAGE TO CÉZANNE.
YES, BUT YOU'VE DIGESTED HIM.
AND YOU BEAR THE LIGHT WITHIN YOU.

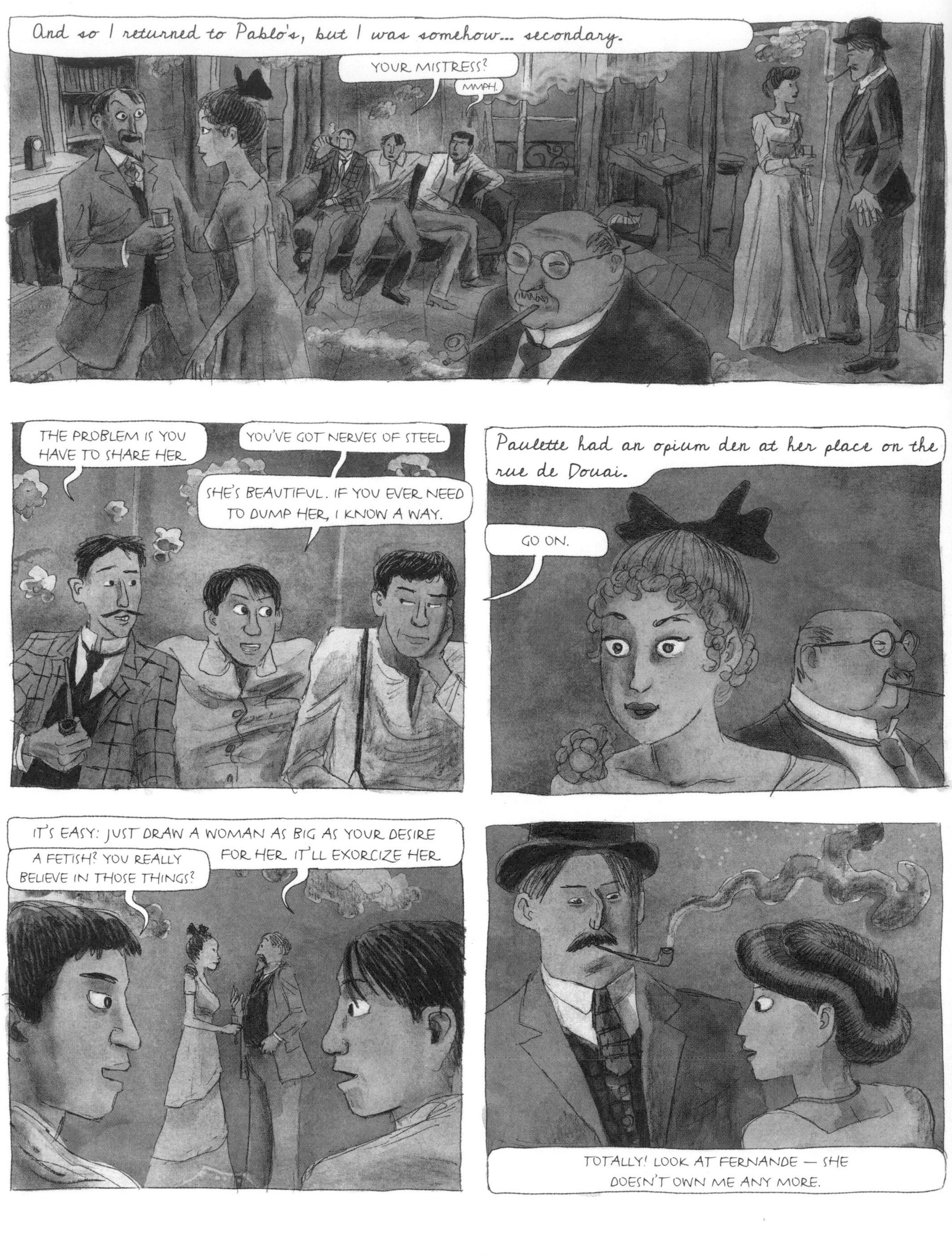
And so I returned to Pablo's, but I was somehow... secondary.
YOUR MISTRESS?
MMPH.
THE PROBLEM IS YOU HAVE TO SHARE HER
YOU'VE GOT NERVES OF STEEL.
SHE'S BEAUTIFUL. IF YOU EVER NEED TO DUMP HER, I KNOW A WAY.
Paulette had an opium den at her place on the rue de Douai.
GO ON.
IT'S EASY: JUST DRAW A WOMAN AS BIG AS YOUR DESIRE FOR HER. IT'LL EXORCIZE HER.
A FETISH? YOU REALLY BELIEVE IN THOSE THINGS?
TOTALLY! LOOK AT FERNANDE — SHE DOESN'T OWN ME ANY MORE.

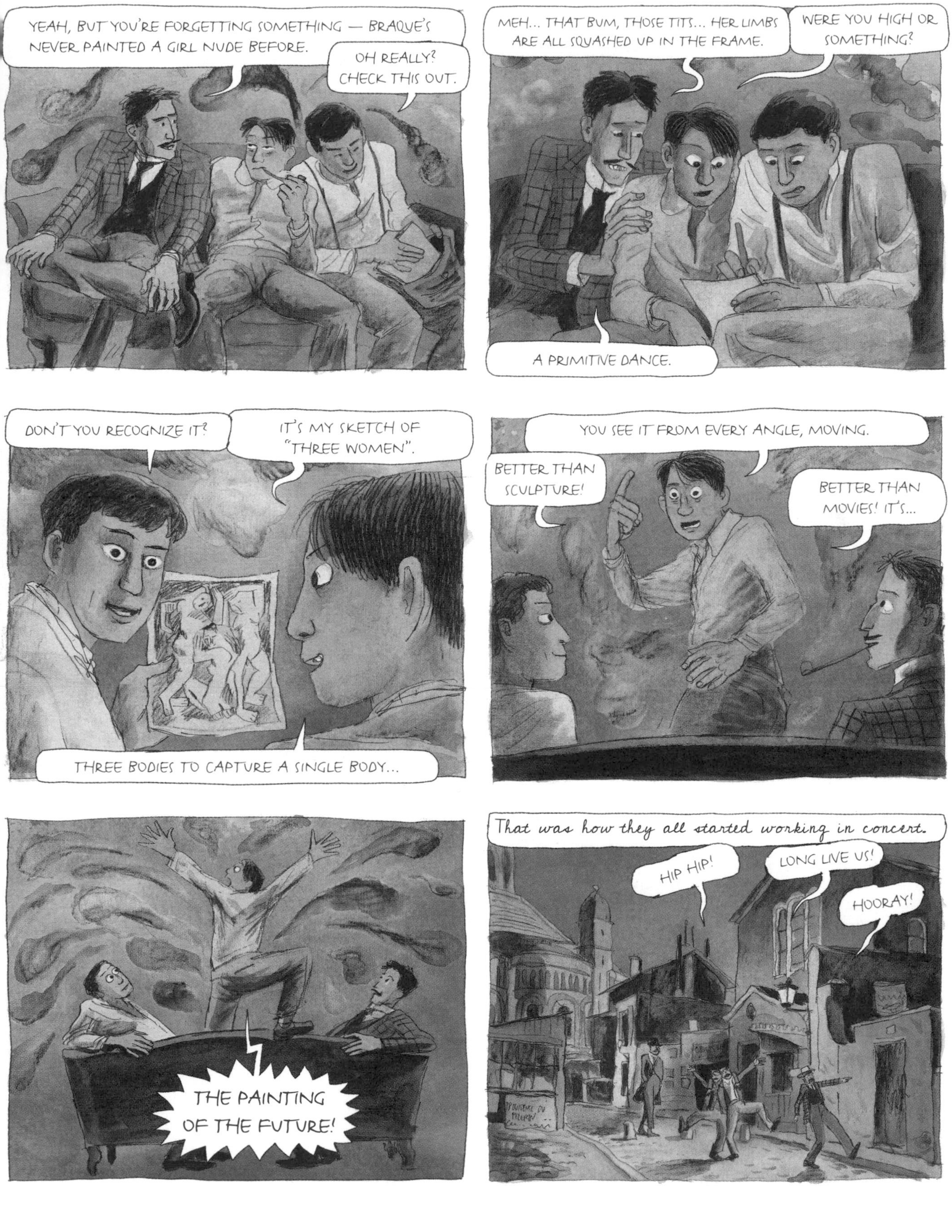
YEAH, BUT YOU'RE FORGETTING SOMETHING — BRAQUE'S NEVER PAINTED A GIRL NUDE BEFORE.
OH REALLY? CHECK THIS OUT.
MEH... THAT BUM, THOSE TITS... HER LIMBS ARE ALL SQUASHED UP IN THE FRAME.
WERE YOU HIGH OR SOMETHING?
A PRIMITIVE DANCE.
DON'T YOU RECOGNIZE IT?
IT'S MY SKETCH OF "THREE WOMEN".
THREE BODIES TO CAPTURE A SINGLE BODY...
YOU SEE IT FROM EVERY ANGLE, MOVING.
BETTER THAN SCULPTURE!
BETTER THAN MOVIES! IT'S...
THE PAINTING OF THE FUTURE!
That was how they all started working in concert.
HIP HIP!
LONG LIVE US!
HOORAY!

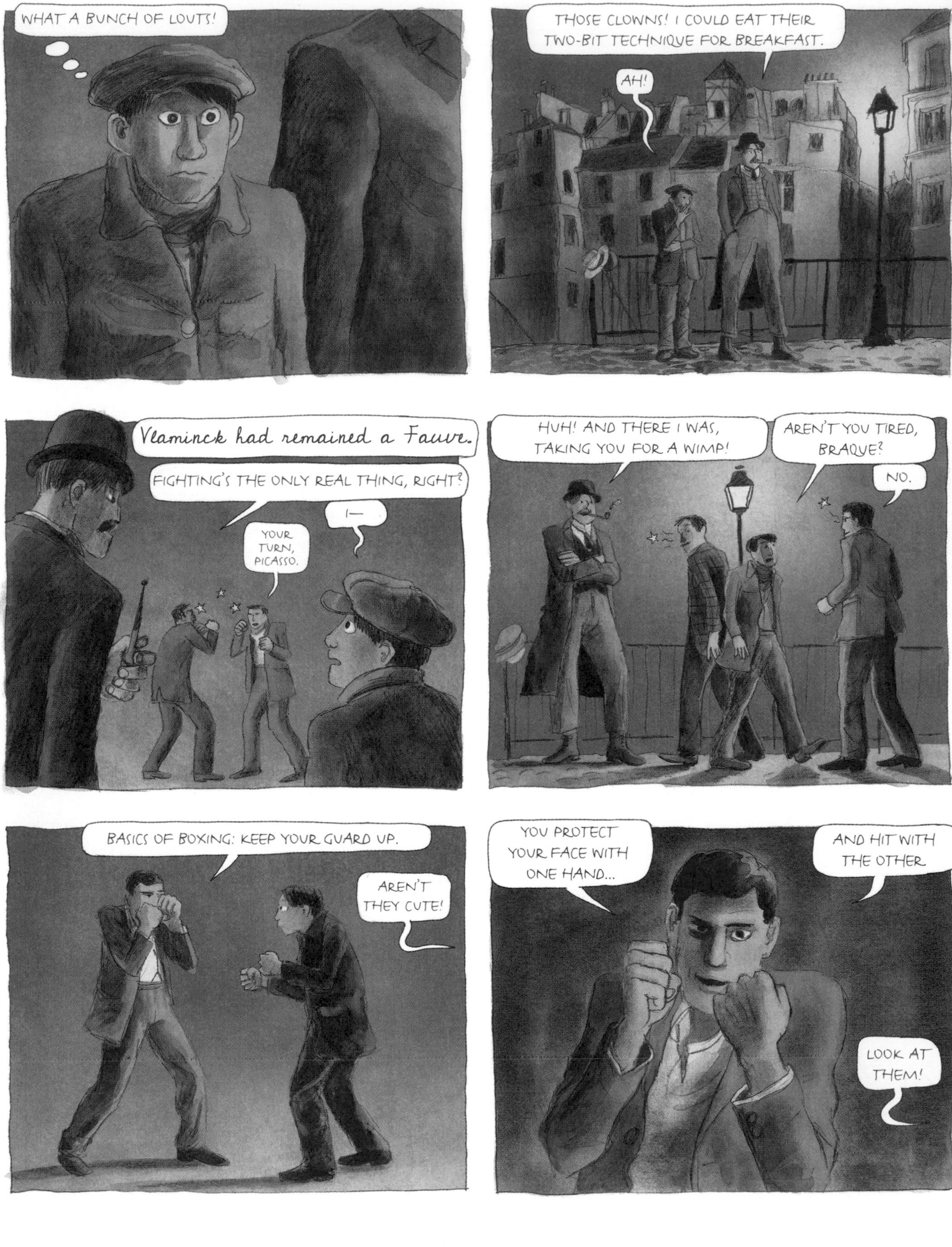
WHAT A BUNCH OF LOUTS!
THOSE CLOWNS! I COULD EAT THEIR TWO-BIT TECHNIQUE FOR BREAKFAST.
AH!
Vlaminck had remained a Fauve.
FIGHTING'S THE ONLY REAL THING, RIGHT?
I—
YOUR TURN, PICASSO.
HUH! AND THERE I WAS, TAKING YOU FOR A WIMP!
AREN'T YOU TIRED, BRAQUE?
NO.
BASICS OF BOXING: KEEP YOUR GUARD UP.
AREN'T THEY CUTE!
YOU PROTECT YOUR FACE WITH ONE HAND...
AND HIT WITH THE OTHER
LOOK AT THEM!

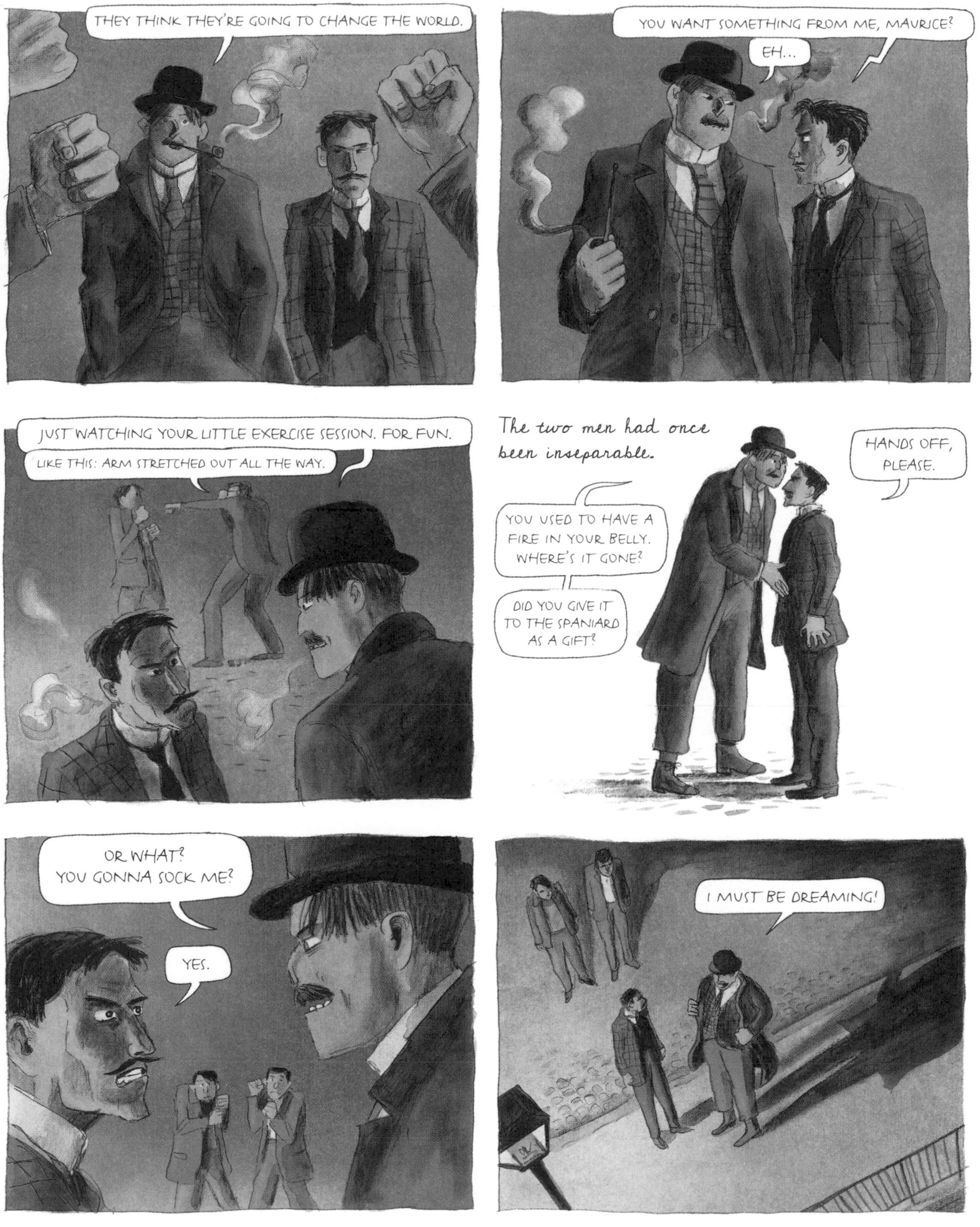
THEY THINK THEY'RE GOING TO CHANGE THE WORLD.
YOU WANT SOMETHING FROM ME, MAURICE?
EH...
JUST WATCHING YOUR LITTLE EXERCISE SESSION. FOR FUN.
LIKE THIS: ARM STRETCHED OUT ALL THE WAY.
The two men had once been inseparable.
YOU USED TO HAVE A FIRE IN YOUR BELLY. WHERE'S IT GONE?
DID YOU GIVE IT TO THE SPANIARD AS A GIFT?
HANDS OFF, PLEASE.
OR WHAT? YOU GONNA SOCK ME?
YES.
I MUST BE DREAMING!

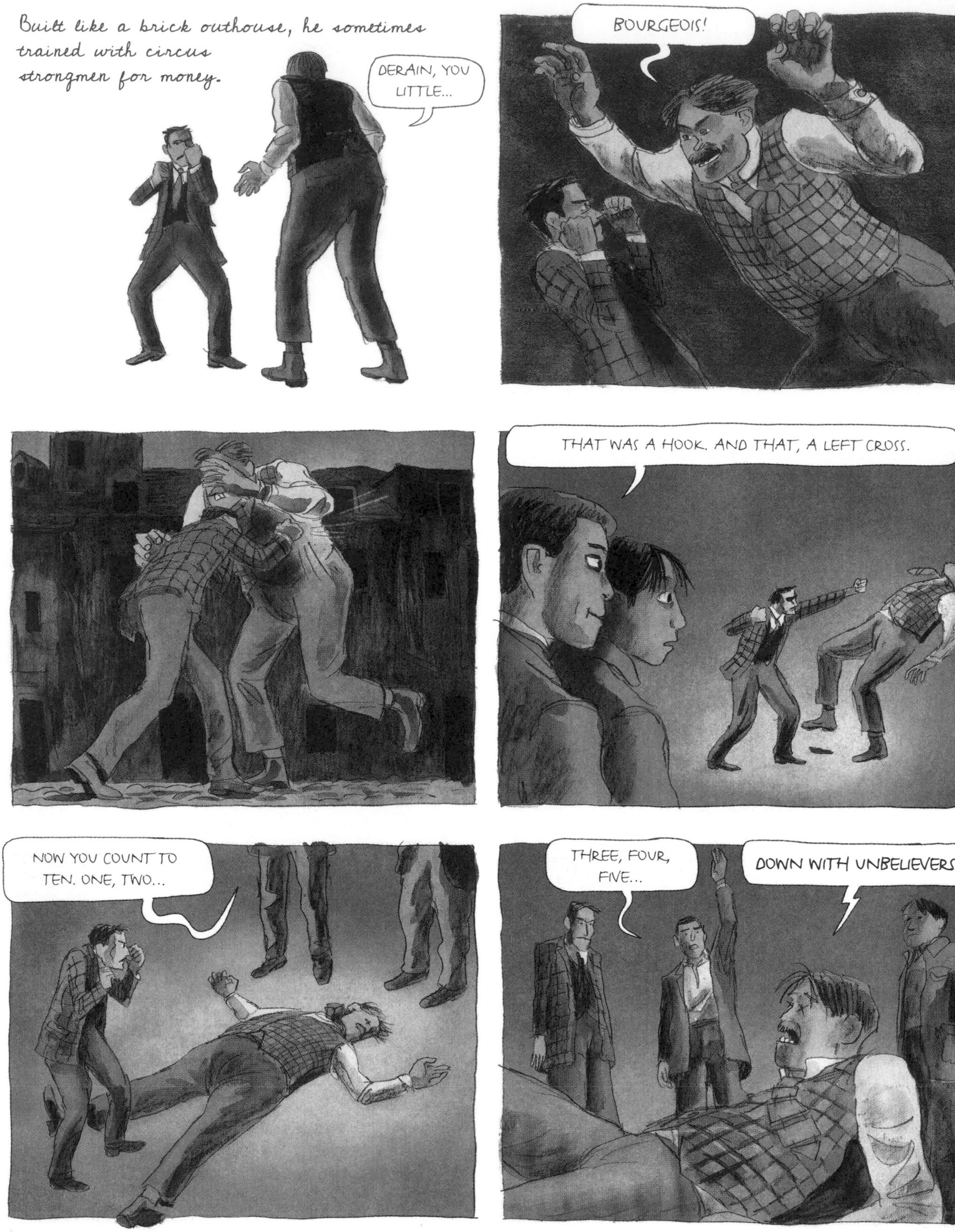
Built like a brick outhouse, he sometimes trained with circus strongmen for money.
DERAIN, YOU LITTLE...
BOURGEOIS!
THAT WAS A HOOK. AND THAT, A LEFT CROSS.
NOW YOU COUNT TO TEN. ONE, TWO...
THREE, FOUR, FIVE...
DOWN WITH UNBELIEVERS!

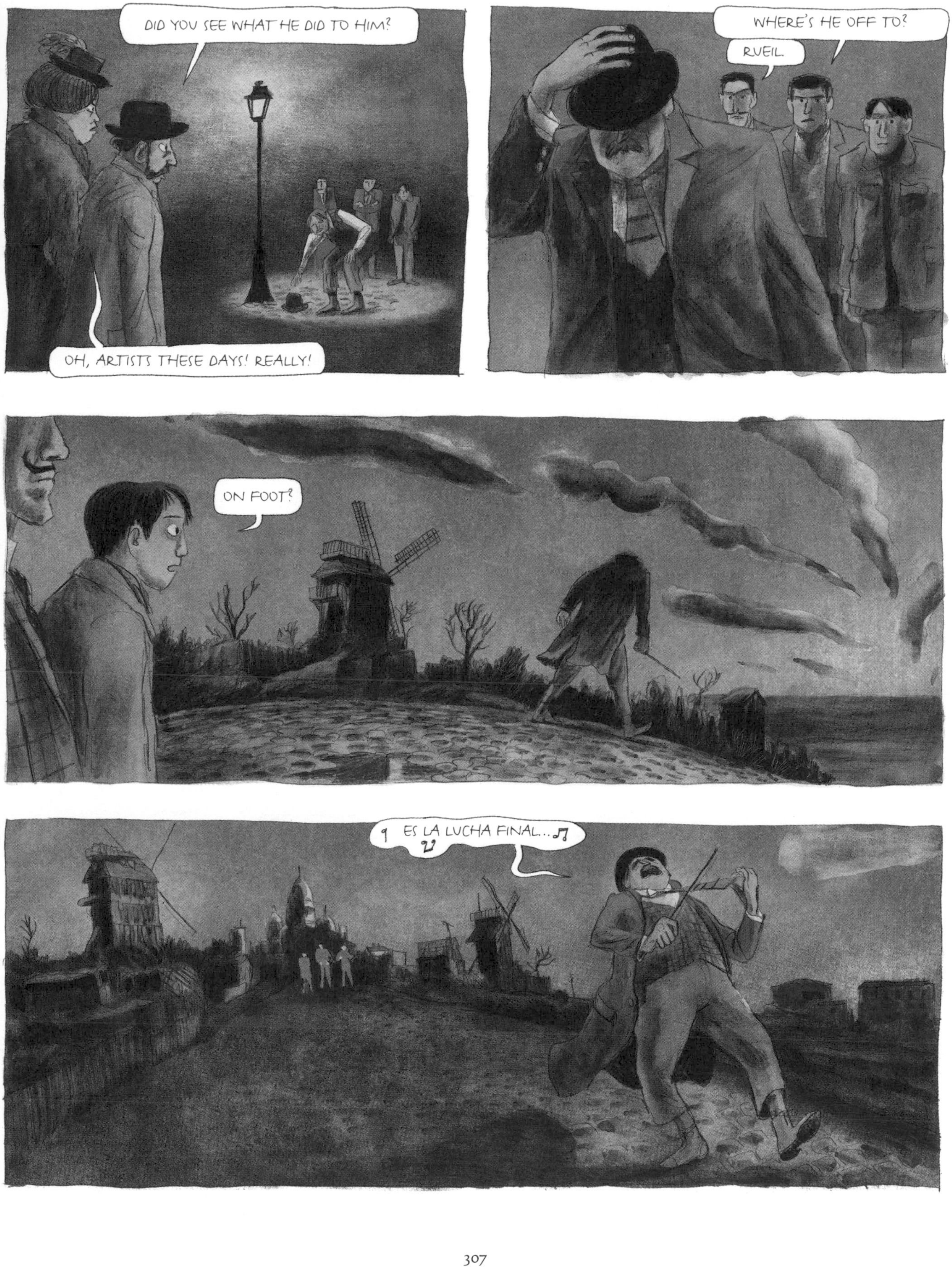
DID YOU SEE WHAT HE DID TO HIM?
OH, ARTISTS THESE DAYS! REALLY!
WHERE'S HE OFF TO?
RUEIL.
ON FOOT?
ES LA LUCHA FINAL...

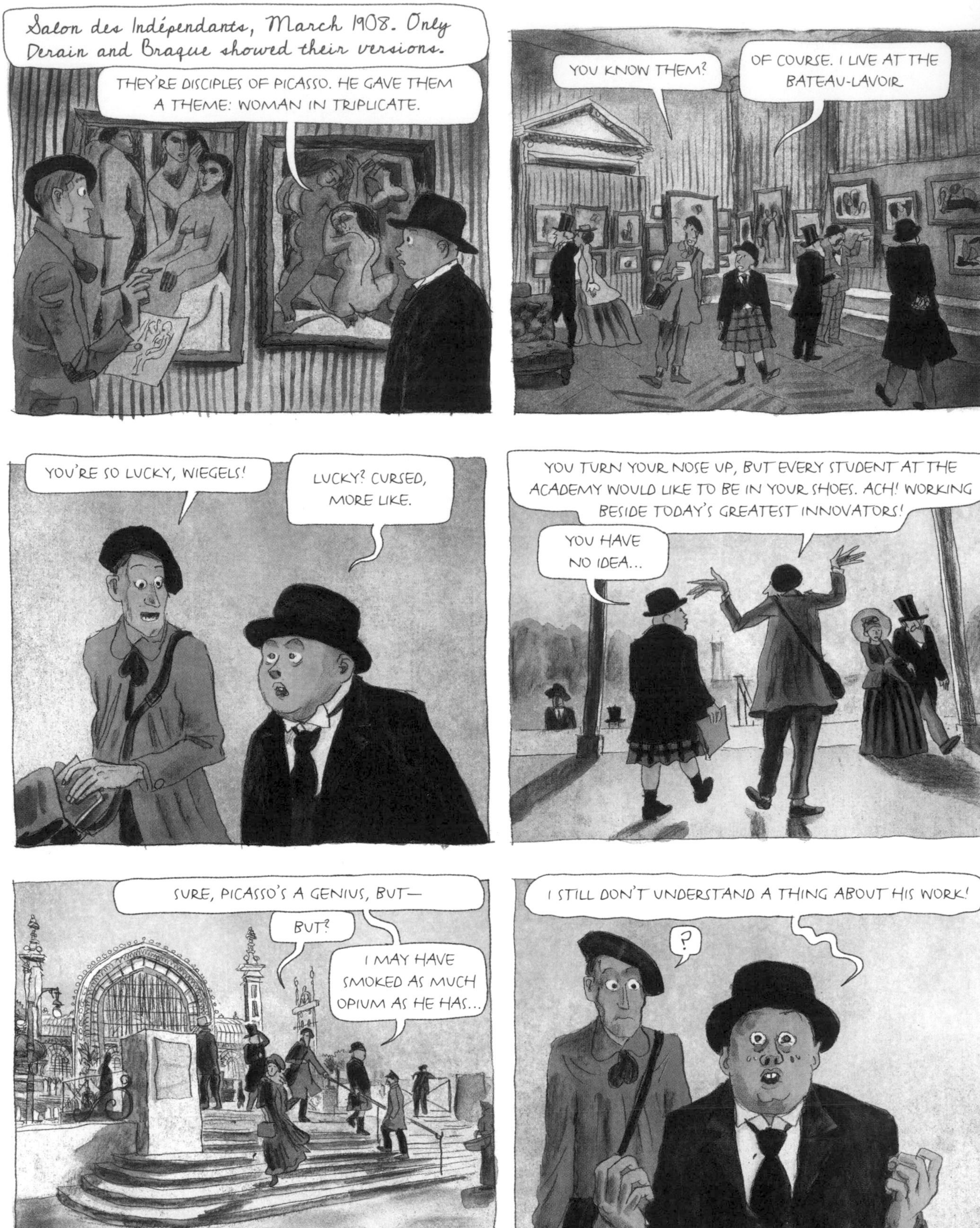
Salon des Indépendants, March 1908. Only Derain and Braque showed their versions.
THEY'RE DISCIPLES OF PICASSO. HE GAVE THEM A THEME: WOMAN IN TRIPLICATE.
YOU KNOW THEM?
OF COURSE. I LIVE AT THE BATEAU-LAVOIR
YOU'RE SO LUCKY, WIEGELS!
LUCKY? CURSED, MORE LIKE.
YOU TURN YOUR NOSE UP, BUT EVERY STUDENT AT THE ACADEMY WOULD LIKE TO BE IN YOUR SHOES. ACH! WORKING BESIDE TODAY'S GREATEST INNOVATORS!
YOU HAVE NO IDEA...
SURE, PICASSO'S A GENIUS, BUT—
BUT?
I MAY HAVE SMOKED AS MUCH OPIUM AS HE HAS...
I STILL DON'T UNDERSTAND A THING ABOUT HIS WORK!
?

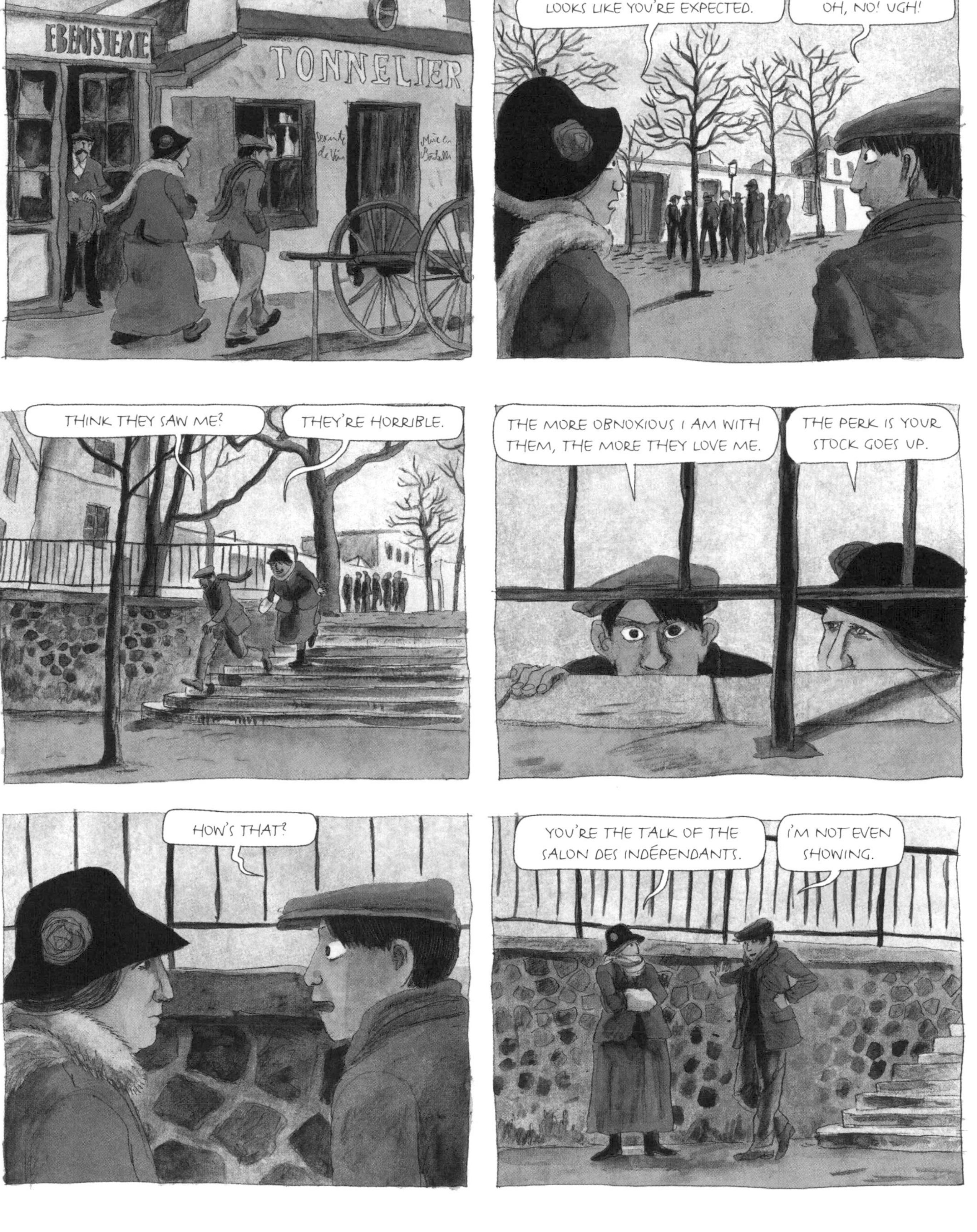
EBENISTERIE
TONNELIER
LOOKS LIKE YOU'RE EXPECTED.
OH, NO! UGH!
THINK THEY SAW ME?
THEY'RE HORRIBLE.
THE MORE OBNOXIOUS I AM WITH THEM, THE MORE THEY LOVE ME.
THE PERK IS YOUR STOCK GOES UP.
HOW'S THAT?
YOU'RE THE TALK OF THE SALON DES INDÉPENDANTS.
I'M NOT EVEN SHOWING.

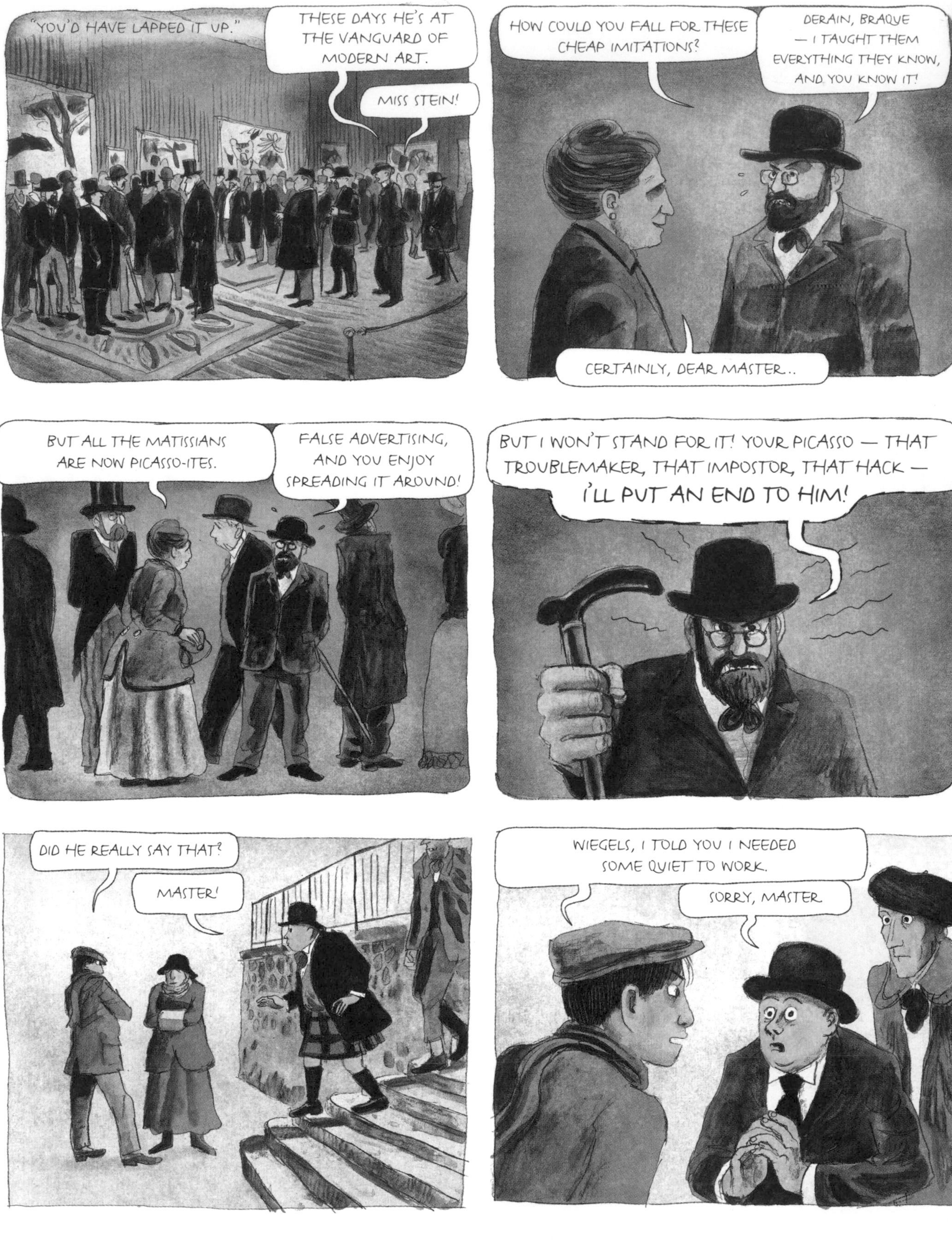
"YOU'D HAVE LAPPED IT UP."
THESE DAYS HE'S AT THE VANGUARD OF MODERN ART.
MISS STEIN!
HOW COULD YOU FALL FOR THESE CHEAP IMITATIONS?
DERAIN, BRAQUE — I TAUGHT THEM EVERYTHING THEY KNOW, AND YOU KNOW IT!
CERTAINLY, DEAR MASTER..
BUT ALL THE MATISSIANS ARE NOW PICASSO-ITES.
FALSE ADVERTISING, AND YOU ENJOY SPREADING IT AROUND!
BUT I WON'T STAND FOR IT! YOUR PICASSO — THAT TROUBLEMAKER, THAT IMPOSTOR, THAT HACK —
I'LL PUT AN END TO HIM!
DID HE REALLY SAY THAT?
MASTER!
WIEGELS, I TOLD YOU I NEEDED SOME QUIET TO WORK.
SORRY, MASTER.

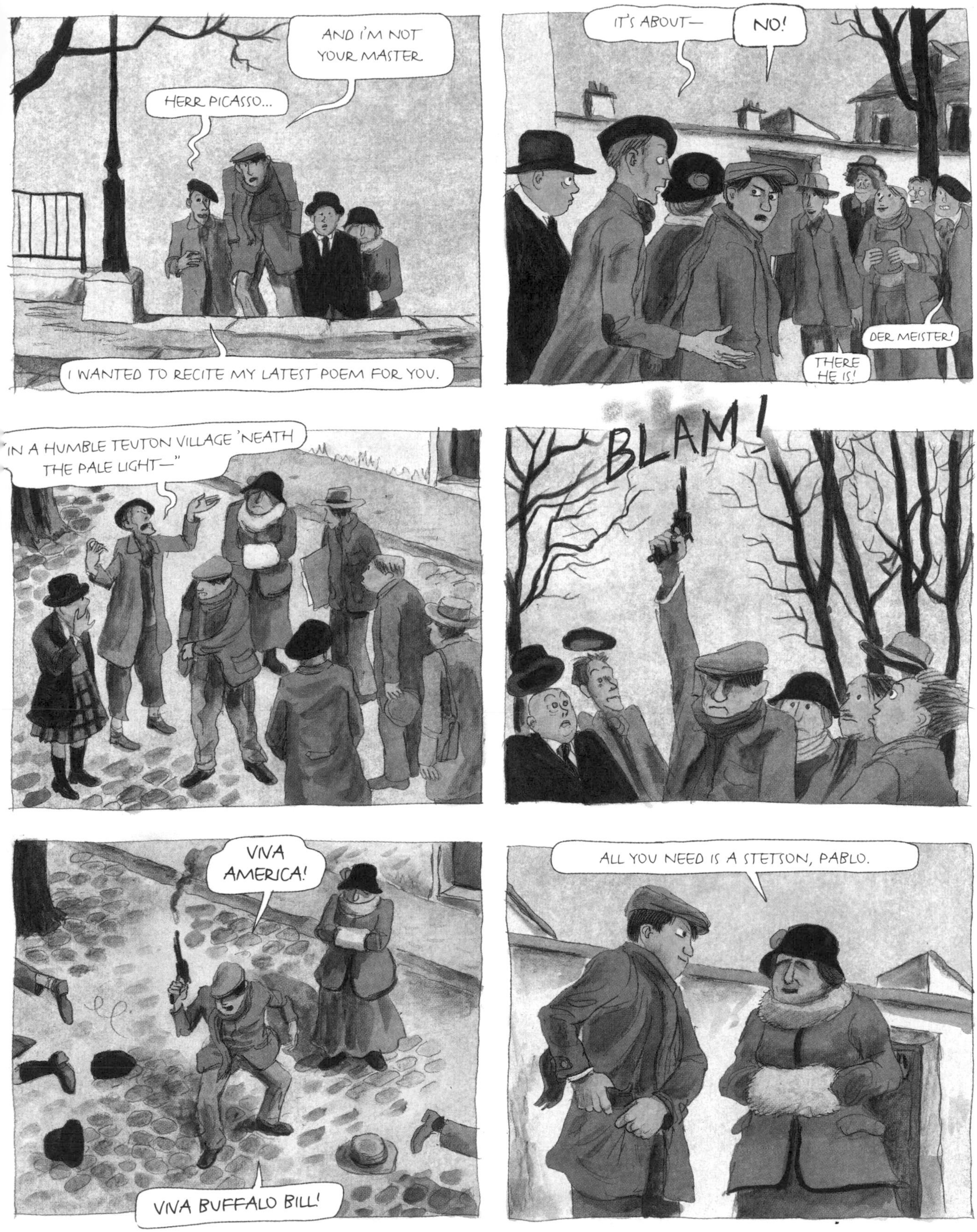
HERR PICASSO...
AND I'M NOT YOUR MASTER
I WANTED TO RECITE MY LATEST POEM FOR YOU.
IT'S ABOUT—
NO!
DER MEISTER!
THERE HE IS!
"IN A HUMBLE TEUTON VILLAGE 'NEATH THE PALE LIGHT—"
BLAM!
VIVA AMERICA!
VIVA BUFFALO BILL!
ALL YOU NEED IS A STETSON, PABLO.

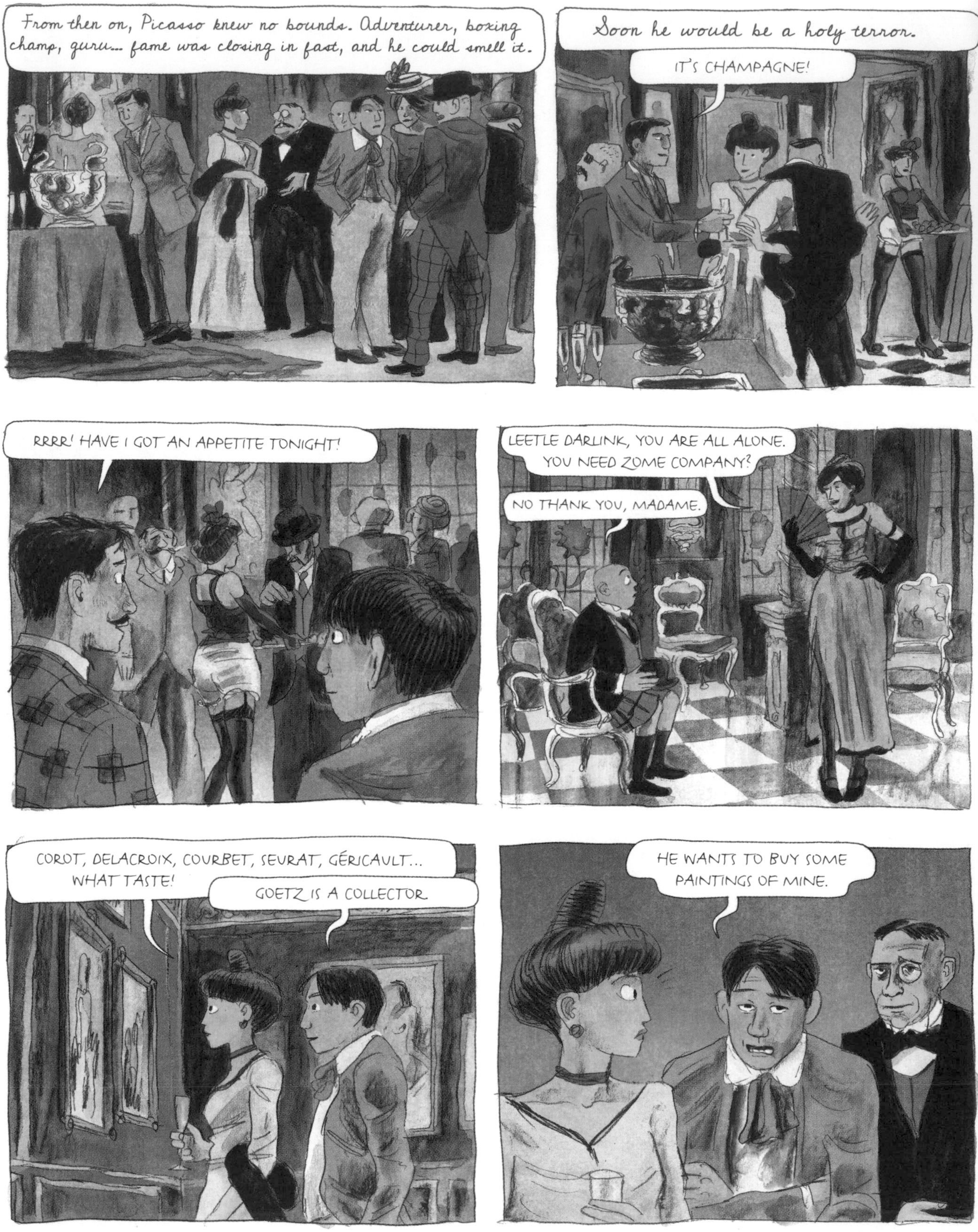
From then on, Picasso knew no bounds. Adventurer, boxing champ, guru... fame was closing in fast, and he could smell it.
Soon he would be a holy terror.
IT'S CHAMPAGNE!
RRRR! HAVE I GOT AN APPETITE TONIGHT!
LEETLE DARLINK, YOU ARE ALL ALONE. YOU NEED ZOME COMPANY?
NO THANK YOU, MADAME.
COROT, DELACROIX, COURBET, SEURAT, GÉRICAULT... WHAT TASTE!
GOETZ IS A COLLECTOR.
HE WANTS TO BUY SOME PAINTINGS OF MINE.

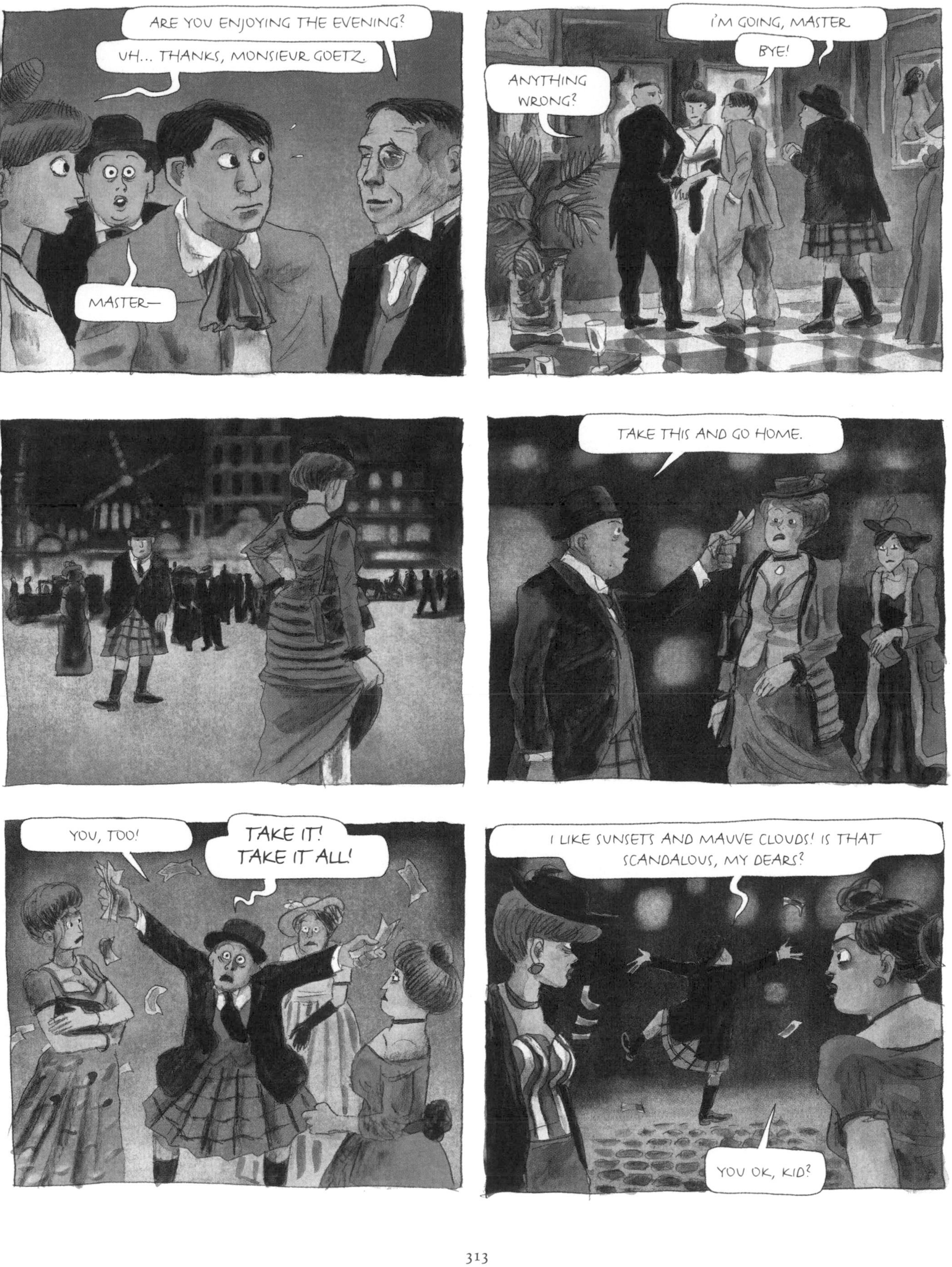
ARE YOU ENJOYING THE EVENING?
UH... THANKS, MONSIEUR GOETZ.
MASTER—
I'M GOING, MASTER
BYE!
ANYTHING WRONG?
TAKE THIS AND GO HOME.
YOU, TOO!
TAKE IT! TAKE IT ALL!
I LIKE SUNSETS AND MAUVE CLOUDS! IS THAT SCANDALOUS, MY DEARS?
YOU OK, KID?

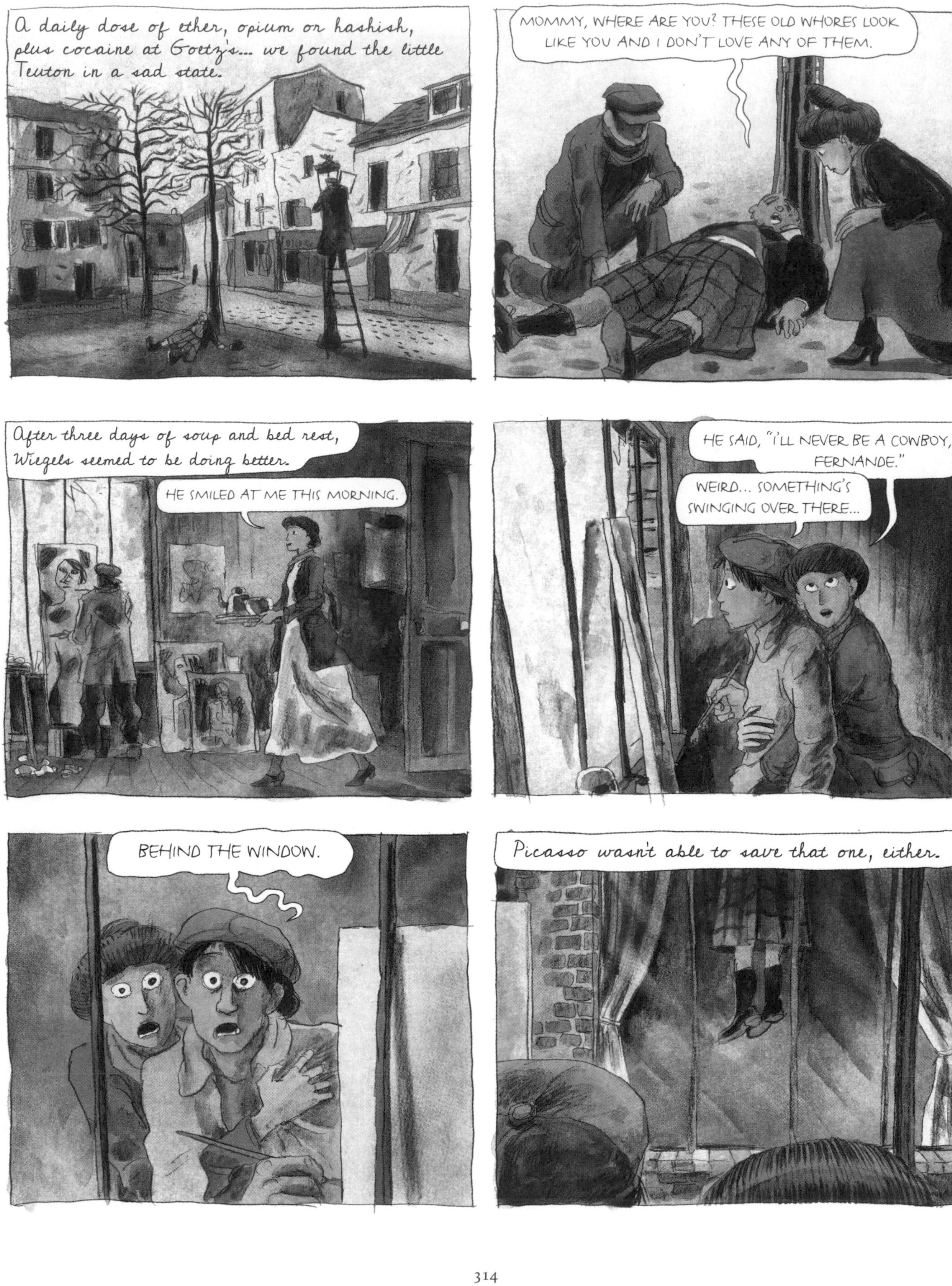
A daily dose of ether, opium or hashish, plus cocaine at Goetz's... we found the little Teuton in a sad state.
MOMMY, WHERE ARE YOU? THESE OLD WHORES LOOK LIKE YOU AND I DON'T LOVE ANY OF THEM.
After three days of soup and bed rest, Wiegels seemed to be doing better.
HE SMILED AT ME THIS MORNING.
HE SAID, "I'LL NEVER BE A COWBOY, FERNANDE."
WEIRD... SOMETHING'S SWINGING OVER THERE...
BEHIND THE WINDOW.
Picasso wasn't able to save that one, either.

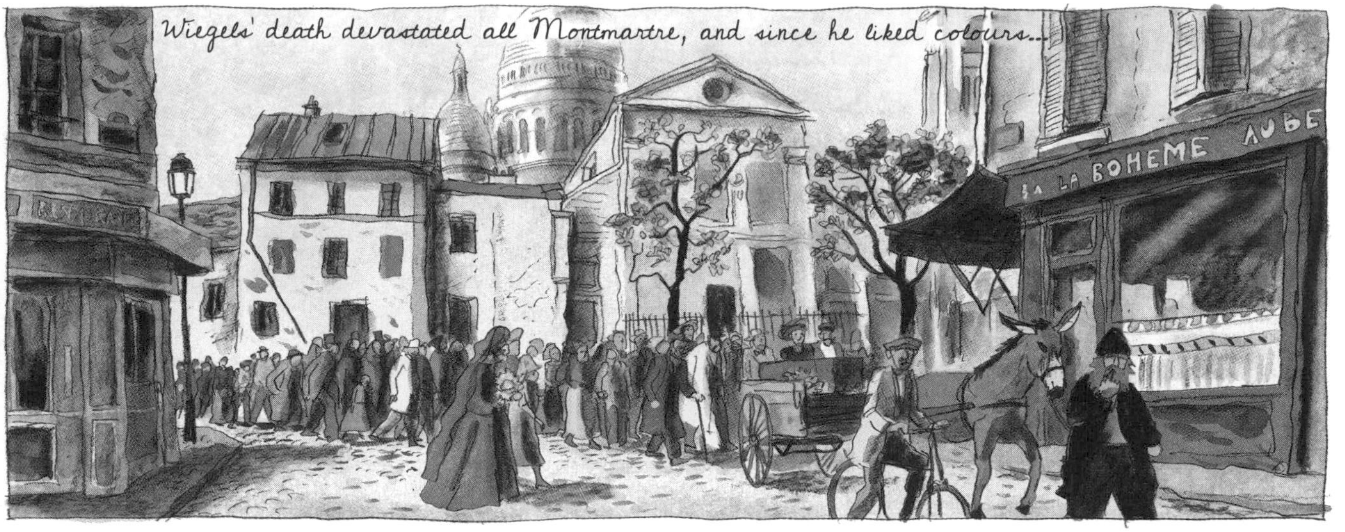
Wiegels' death devastated all Montmartre, and since he liked colours...
LA BOHEME
AUBE

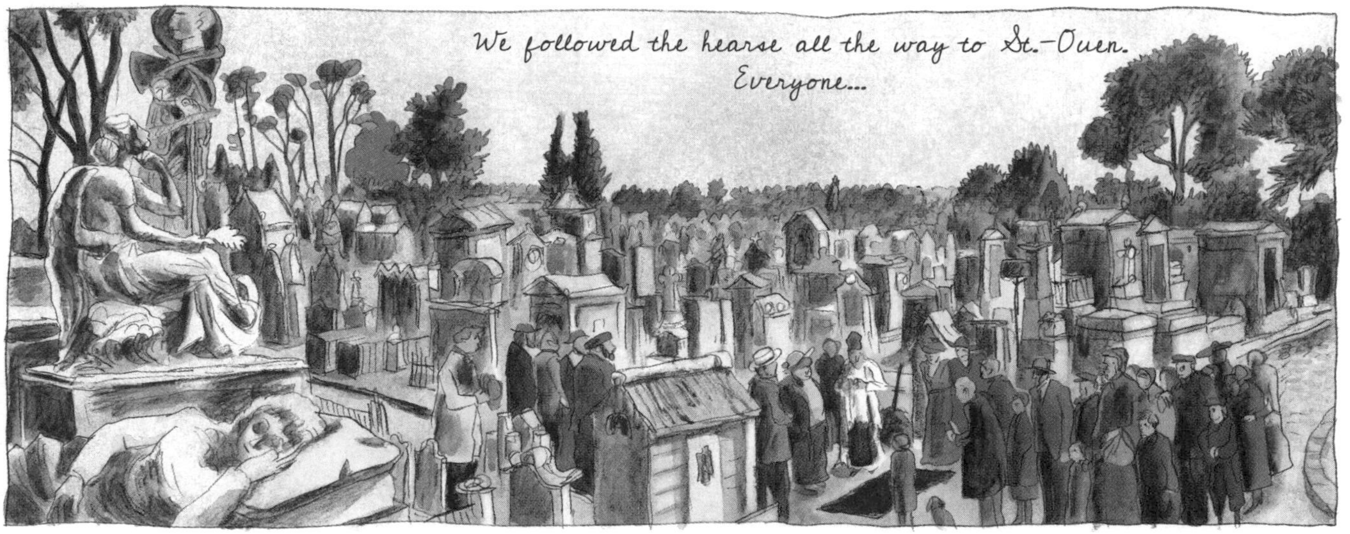
We followed the hearse all the way to St.-Ouen.
Everyone...

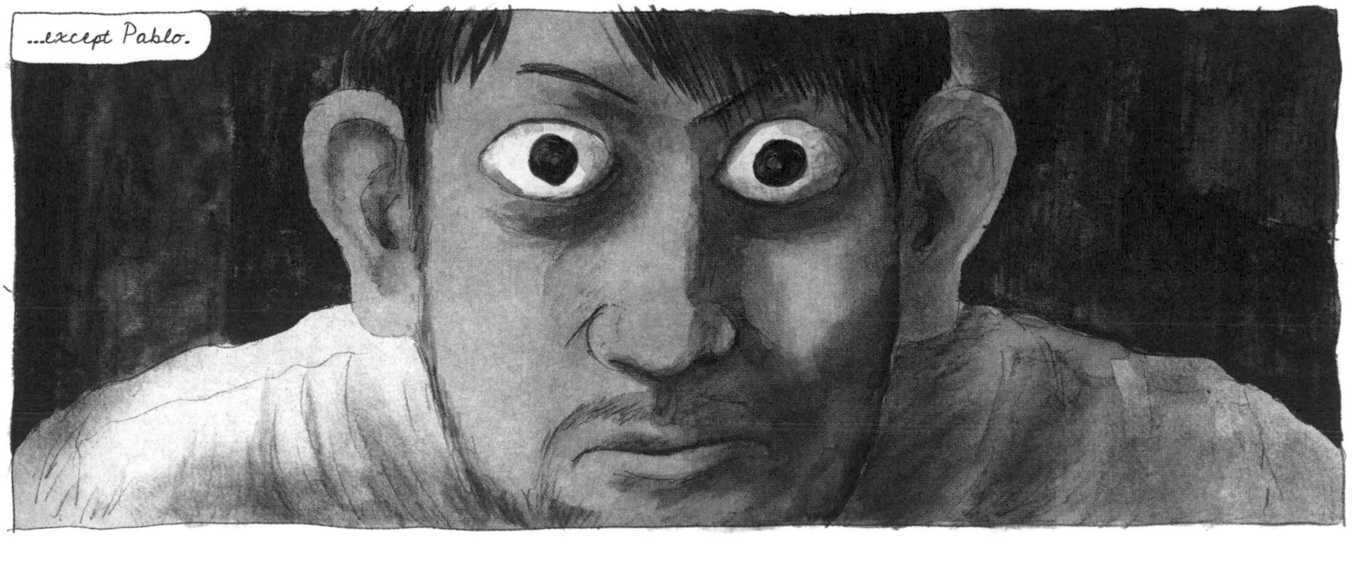
...except Pablo.

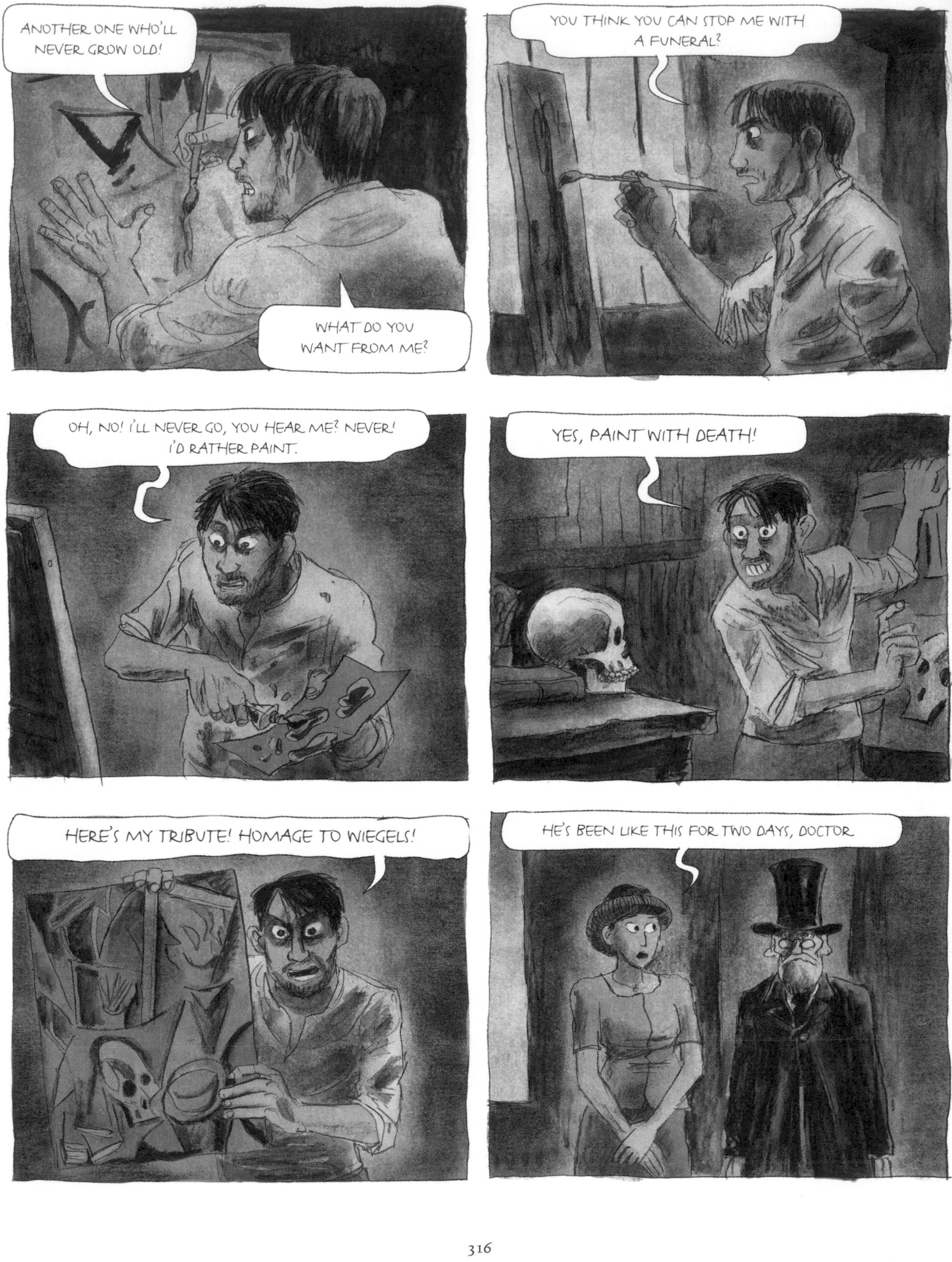
ANOTHER ONE WHO'LL NEVER GROW OLD!
WHAT DO YOU WANT FROM ME?
YOU THINK YOU CAN STOP ME WITH A FUNERAL?
OH, NO! I'LL NEVER GO, YOU HEAR ME? NEVER! I'D RATHER PAINT.
YES, PAINT WITH DEATH!
HERE'S MY TRIBUTE! HOMAGE TO WIEGELS!
HE'S BEEN LIKE THIS FOR TWO DAYS, DOCTOR

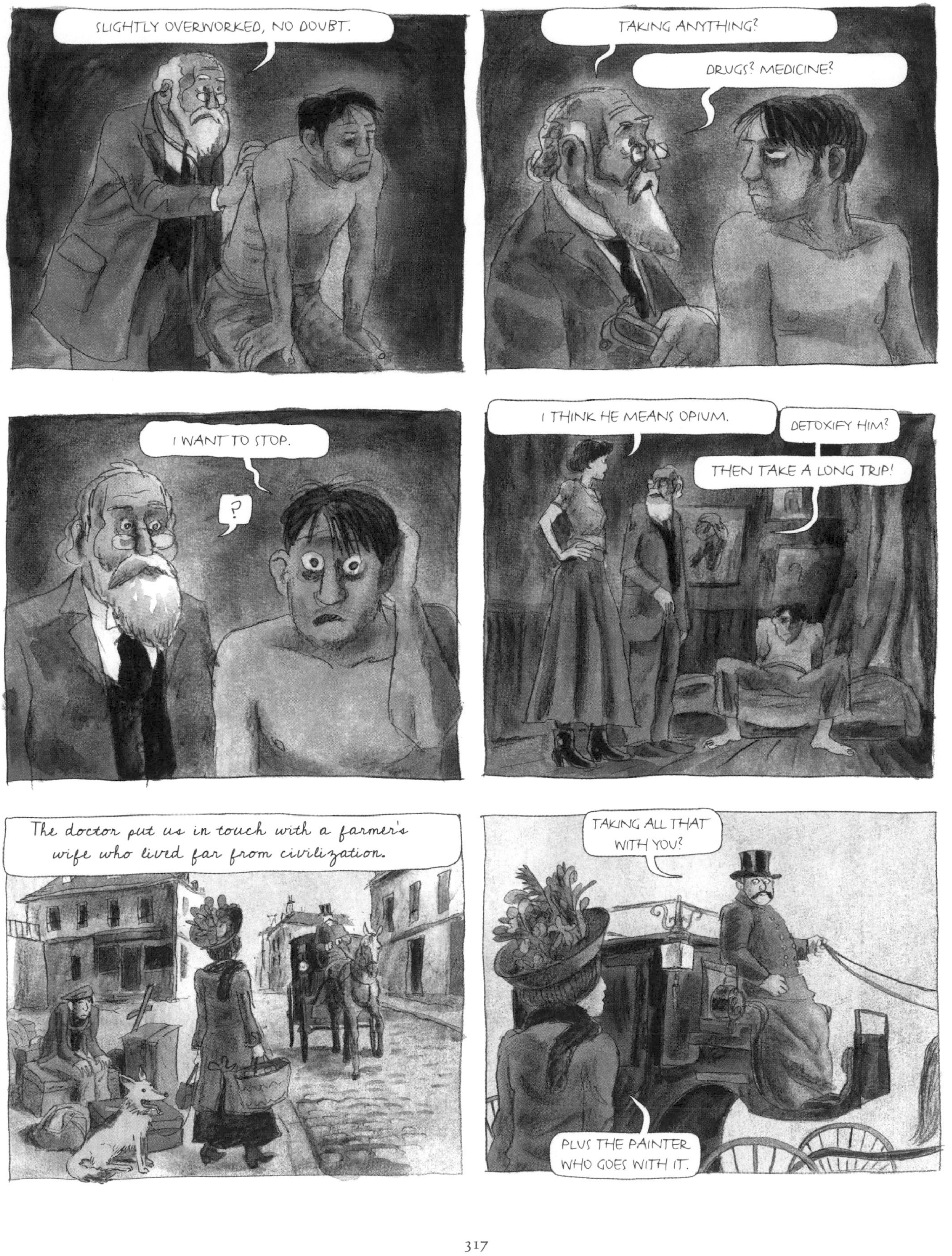
SLIGHTLY OVERWORKED, NO DOUBT.
TAKING ANYTHING?
DRUGS? MEDICINE?
I WANT TO STOP.
?
I THINK HE MEANS OPIUM.
DETOXIFY HIM?
THEN TAKE A LONG TRIP!
The doctor put us in touch with a farmer's wife who lived far from civilization.
TAKING ALL THAT WITH YOU?
PLUS THE PAINTER WHO GOES WITH IT.

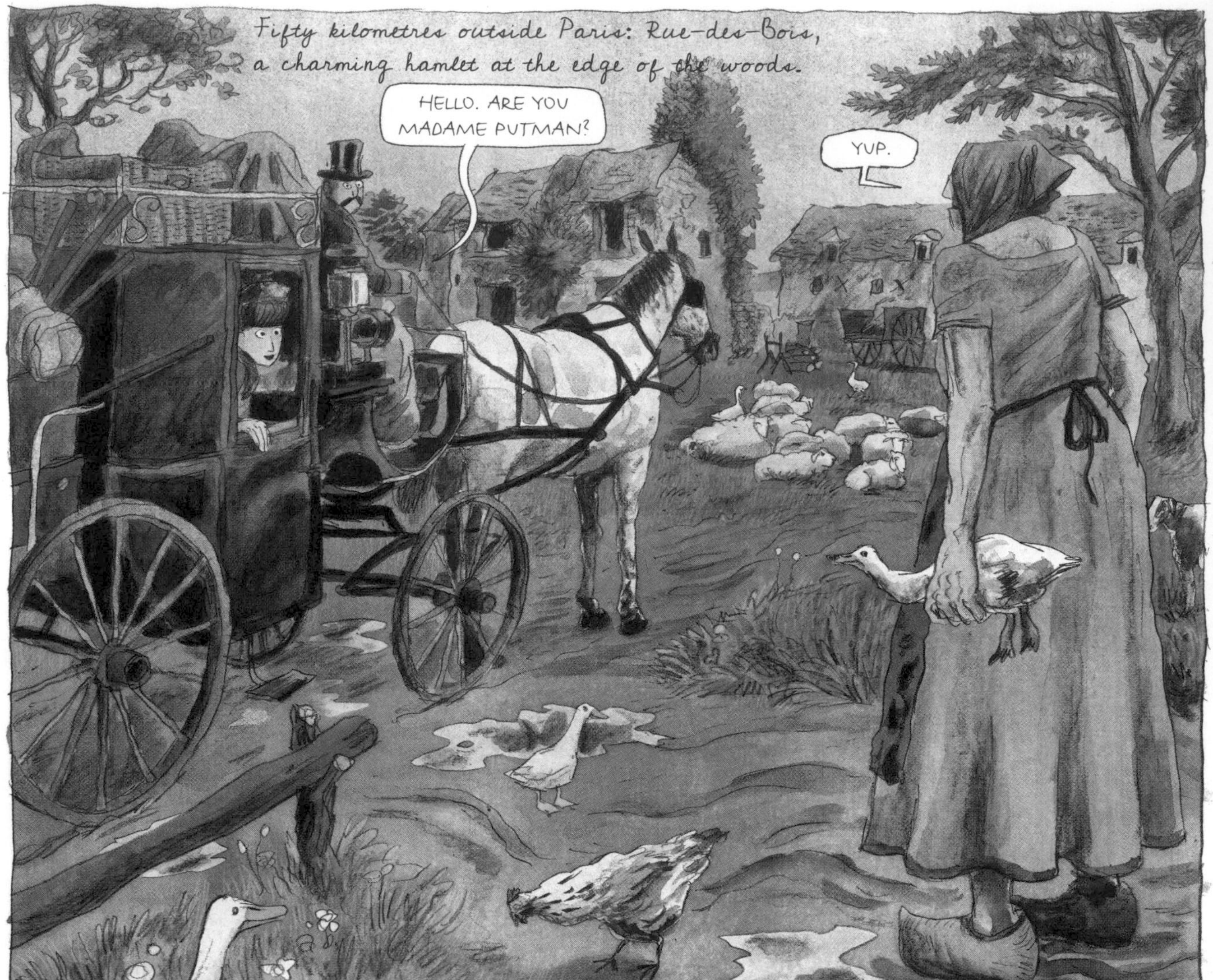
Fifty kilometres outside Paris: Rue-des-Bois, a charming hamlet at the edge of the woods.
HELLO. ARE YOU MADAME PUTMAN?
YUP.

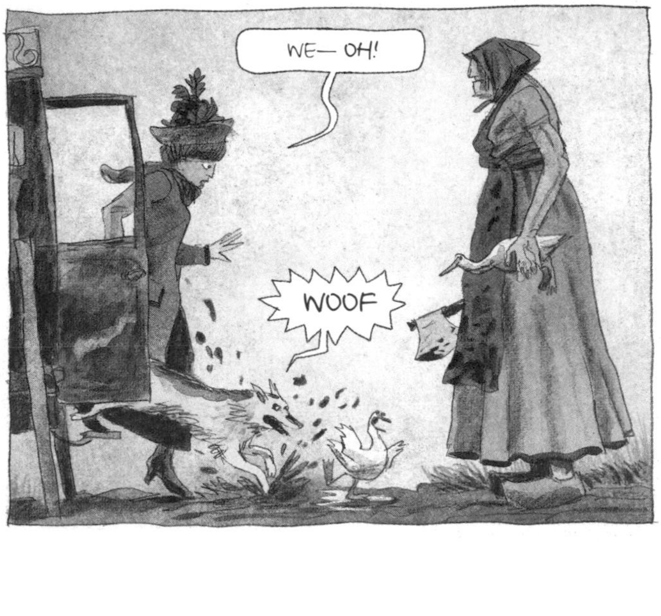
WE— OH!
WOOF

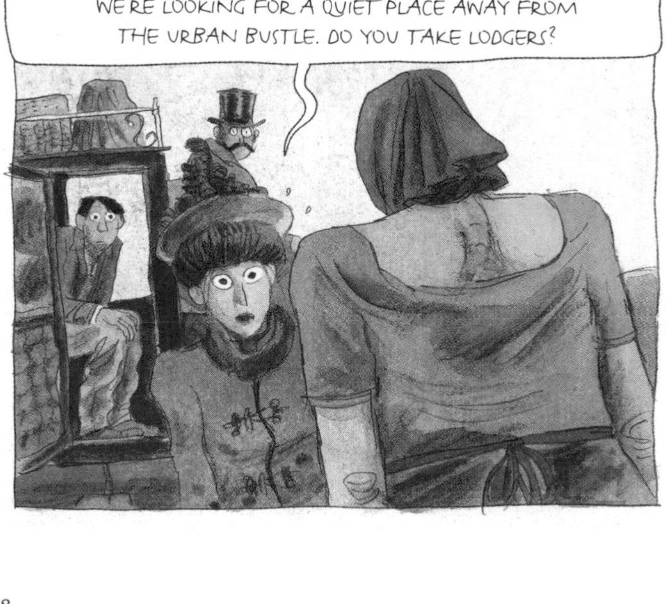
WE'RE LOOKING FOR A QUIET PLACE AWAY FROM THE URBAN BUSTLE. DO YOU TAKE LODGERS?

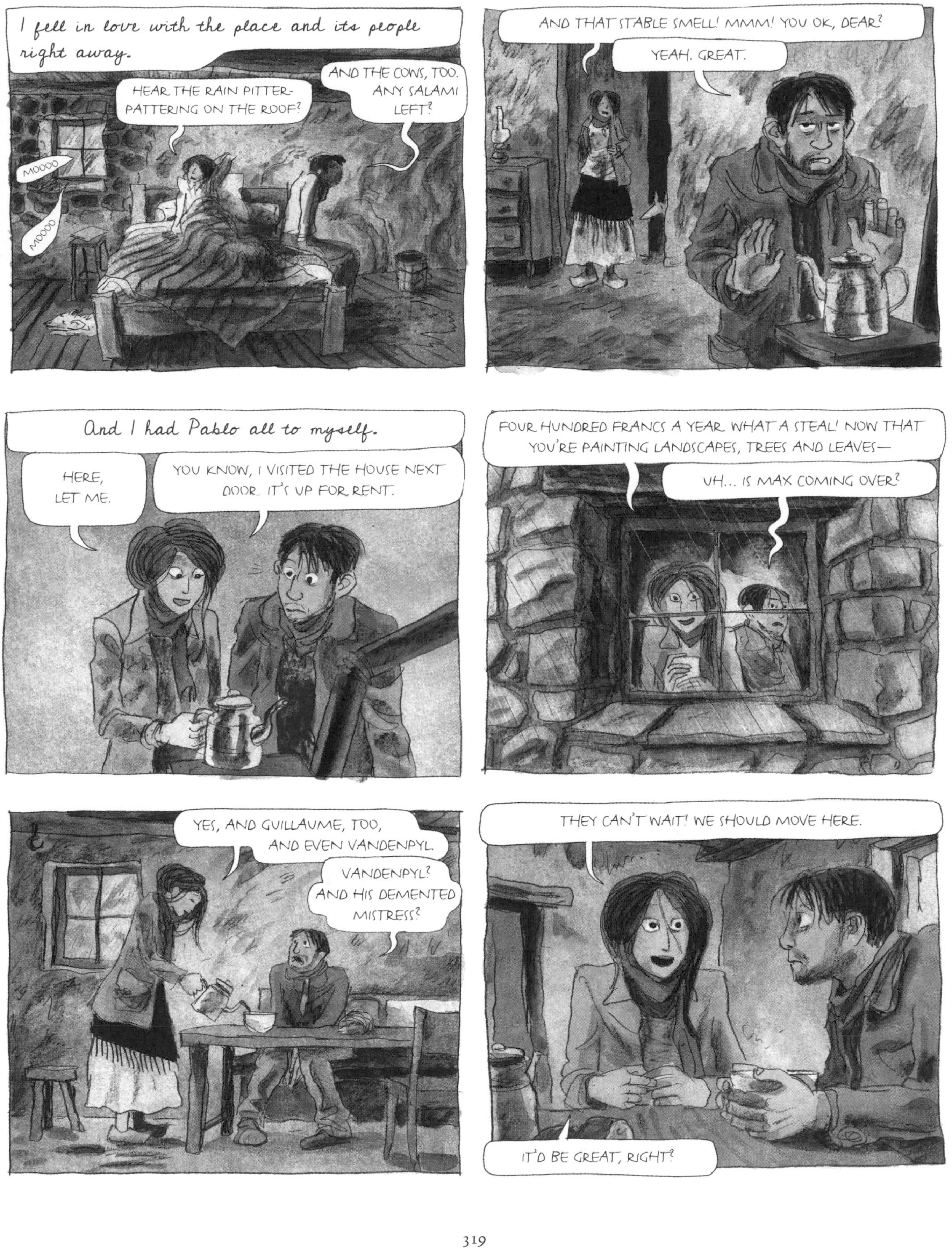
I fell in love with the place and its people right away.
HEAR THE RAIN PITTER-PATTERING ON THE ROOF?
AND THE COWS, TOO. ANY SALAMI LEFT?
MOOOO
MOOOO
AND THAT STABLE SMELL! MMM! YOU OK, DEAR?
YEAH. GREAT.
And I had Pablo all to myself.
HERE, LET ME.
YOU KNOW, I VISITED THE HOUSE NEXT DOOR. IT'S UP FOR RENT.
FOUR HUNDRED FRANCS A YEAR. WHAT A STEAL! NOW THAT YOU'RE PAINTING LANDSCAPES, TREES AND LEAVES—
UH... IS MAX COMING OVER?
YES, AND GUILLAUME, TOO, AND EVEN VANDENPYL.
VANDENPYL? AND HIS DEMENTED MISTRESS?
THEY CAN'T WAIT! WE SHOULD MOVE HERE.
IT'D BE GREAT, RIGHT?

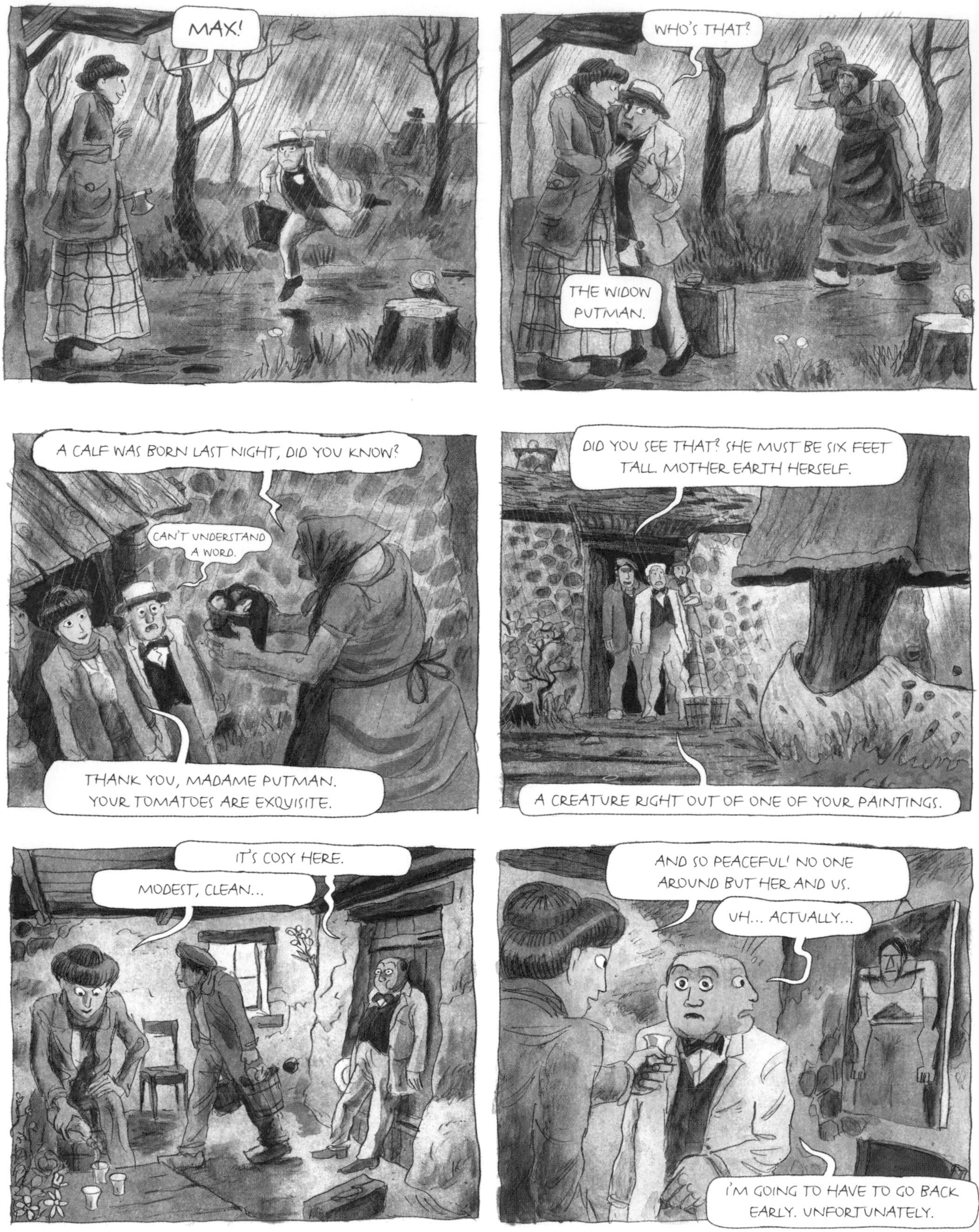
MAX!
WHO'S THAT?
THE WIDOW PUTMAN.
A CALF WAS BORN LAST NIGHT, DID YOU KNOW?
CAN'T UNDERSTAND A WORD.
THANK YOU, MADAME PUTMAN. YOUR TOMATOES ARE EXQUISITE.
DID YOU SEE THAT? SHE MUST BE SIX FEET TALL. MOTHER EARTH HERSELF.
A CREATURE RIGHT OUT OF ONE OF YOUR PAINTINGS.
IT'S COSY HERE.
MODEST, CLEAN...
AND SO PEACEFUL! NO ONE AROUND BUT HER AND US.
UH... ACTUALLY...
I'M GOING TO HAVE TO GO BACK EARLY. UNFORTUNATELY.

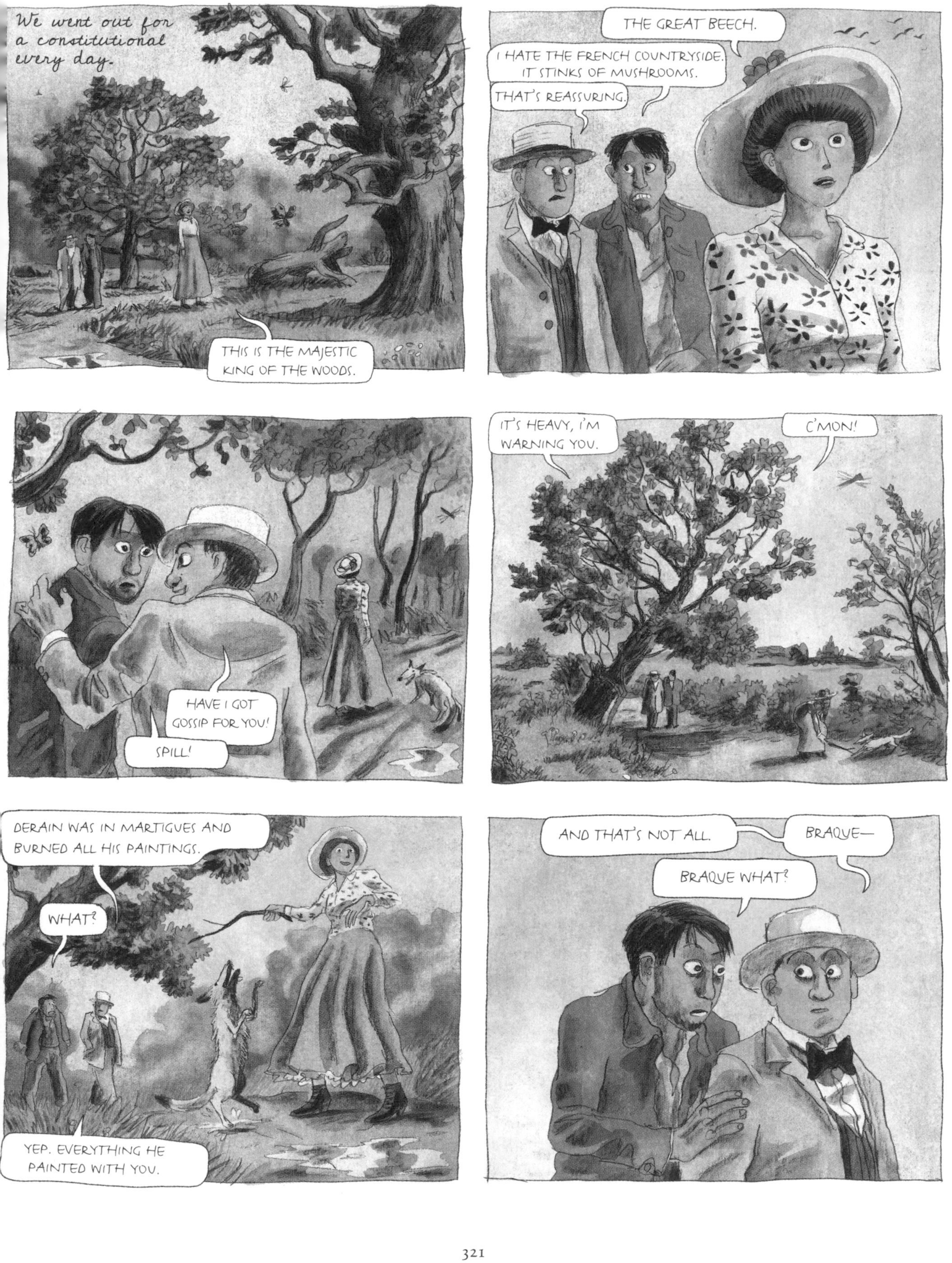
We went out for a constitutional every day.
THIS IS THE MAJESTIC KING OF THE WOODS.
THE GREAT BEECH.
I HATE THE FRENCH COUNTRYSIDE. IT STINKS OF MUSHROOMS.
THAT'S REASSURING.
HAVE I GOT GOSSIP FOR YOU!
SPILL!
IT'S HEAVY, I'M WARNING YOU.
C'MON!
DERAIN WAS IN MARTIGUES AND BURNED ALL HIS PAINTINGS.
WHAT?
YEP. EVERYTHING HE PAINTED WITH YOU.
AND THAT'S NOT ALL.
BRAQUE—
BRAQUE WHAT?

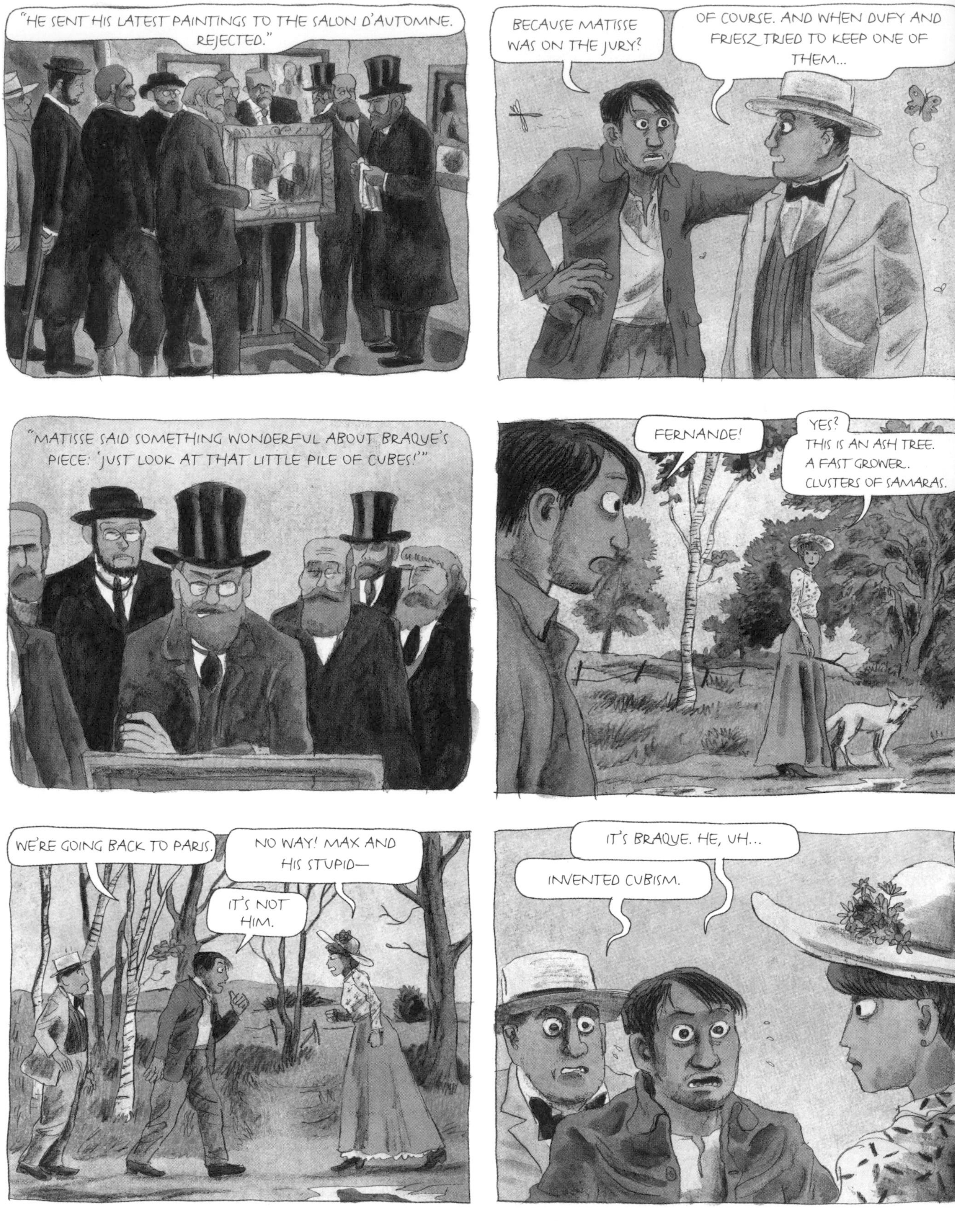
"HE SENT HIS LATEST PAINTINGS TO THE SALON D'AUTOMNE. REJECTED."
BECAUSE MATISSE WAS ON THE JURY?
OF COURSE. AND WHEN DUFY AND FRIESZ TRIED TO KEEP ONE OF THEM...
"MATISSE SAID SOMETHING WONDERFUL ABOUT BRAQUE'S PIECE: 'JUST LOOK AT THAT LITTLE PILE OF CUBES!'"
FERNANDE!
YES? THIS IS AN ASH TREE. A FAST GROWER. CLUSTERS OF SAMARAS.
WE'RE GOING BACK TO PARIS.
NO WAY! MAX AND HIS STUPID—
IT'S NOT HIM.
IT'S BRAQUE. HE, UH...
INVENTED CUBISM.

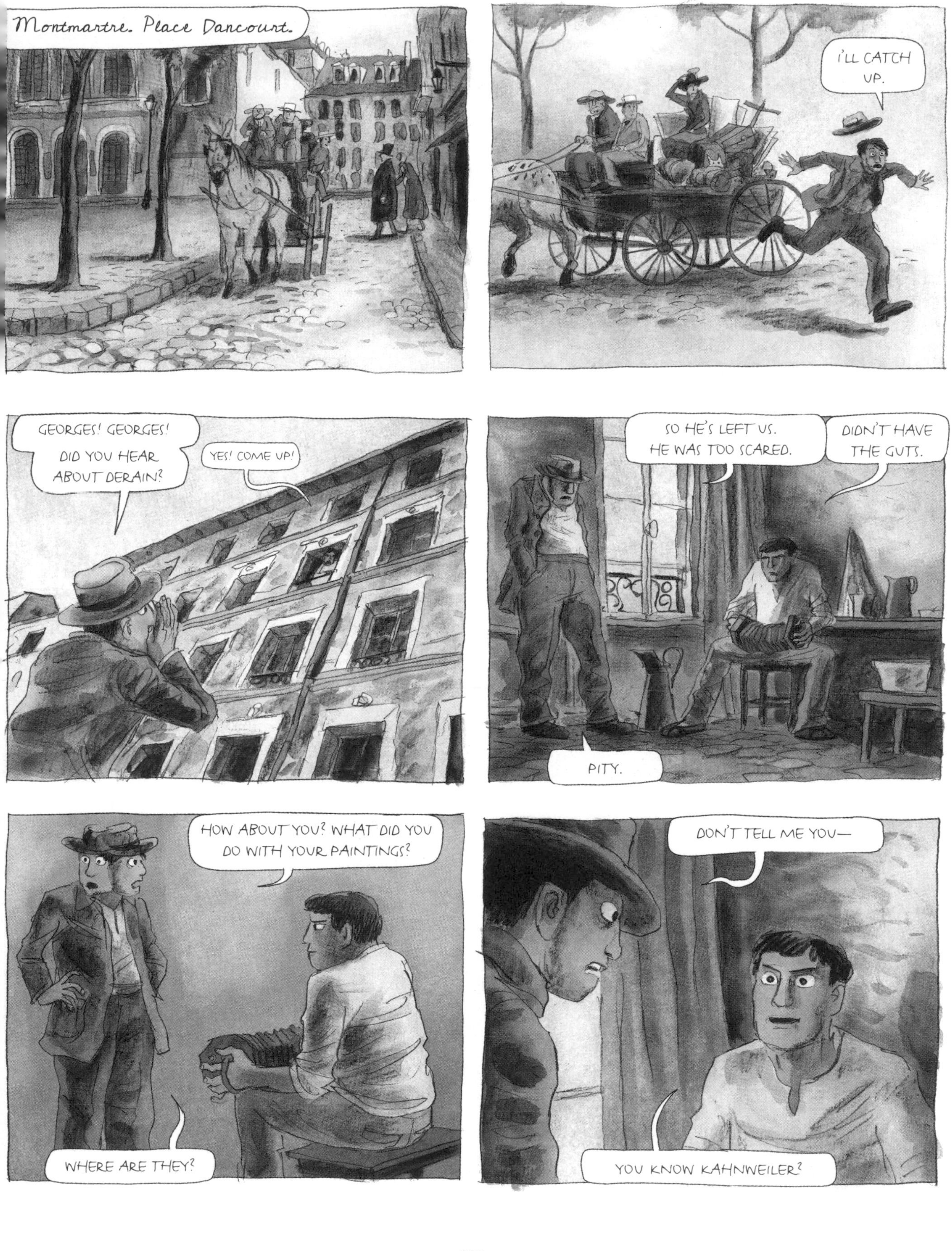
Montmartre. Place Dancourt.
I'LL CATCH UP.
GEORGES! GEORGES! DID YOU HEAR ABOUT DERAIN?
YES! COME UP!
SO HE'S LEFT US. HE WAS TOO SCARED.
DIDN'T HAVE THE GUTS.
PITY.
HOW ABOUT YOU? WHAT DID YOU DO WITH YOUR PAINTINGS?
WHERE ARE THEY?
DON'T TELL ME YOU—
YOU KNOW KAHNWEILER?

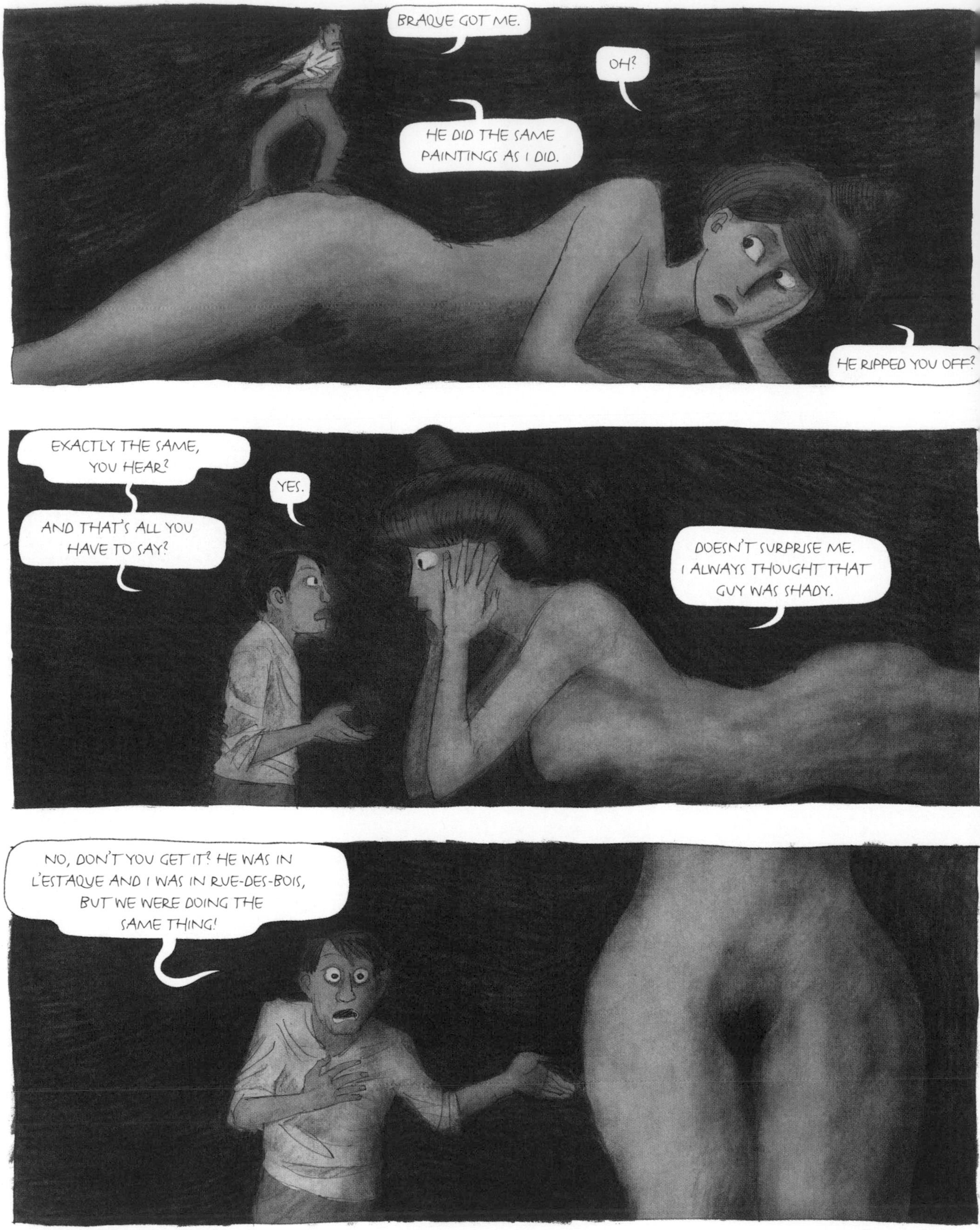
BRAQUE GOT ME.
OH?
HE DID THE SAME PAINTINGS AS I DID.
HE RIPPED YOU OFF?
EXACTLY THE SAME, YOU HEAR?
YES.
AND THAT'S ALL YOU HAVE TO SAY?
DOESN'T SURPRISE ME. I ALWAYS THOUGHT THAT GUY WAS SHADY.
NO, DON'T YOU GET IT? HE WAS IN L'ESTAQUE AND I WAS IN RUE-DES-BOIS, BUT WE WERE DOING THE SAME THING!

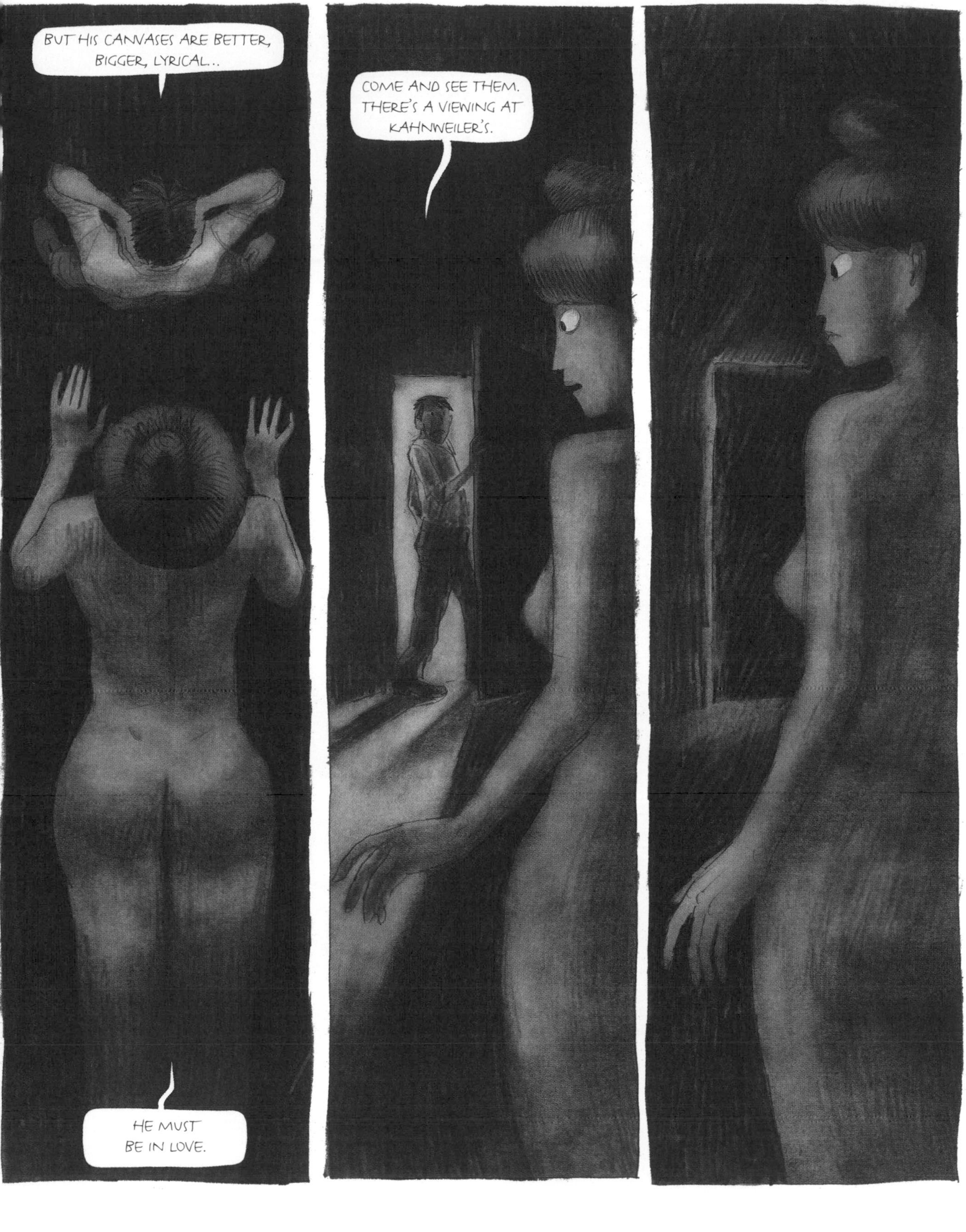

BUT HIS CANVASES ARE BETTER, BIGGER, LYRICAL...
HE MUST BE IN LOVE.
COME AND SEE THEM. THERE'S A VIEWING AT KAHNWEILER'S.

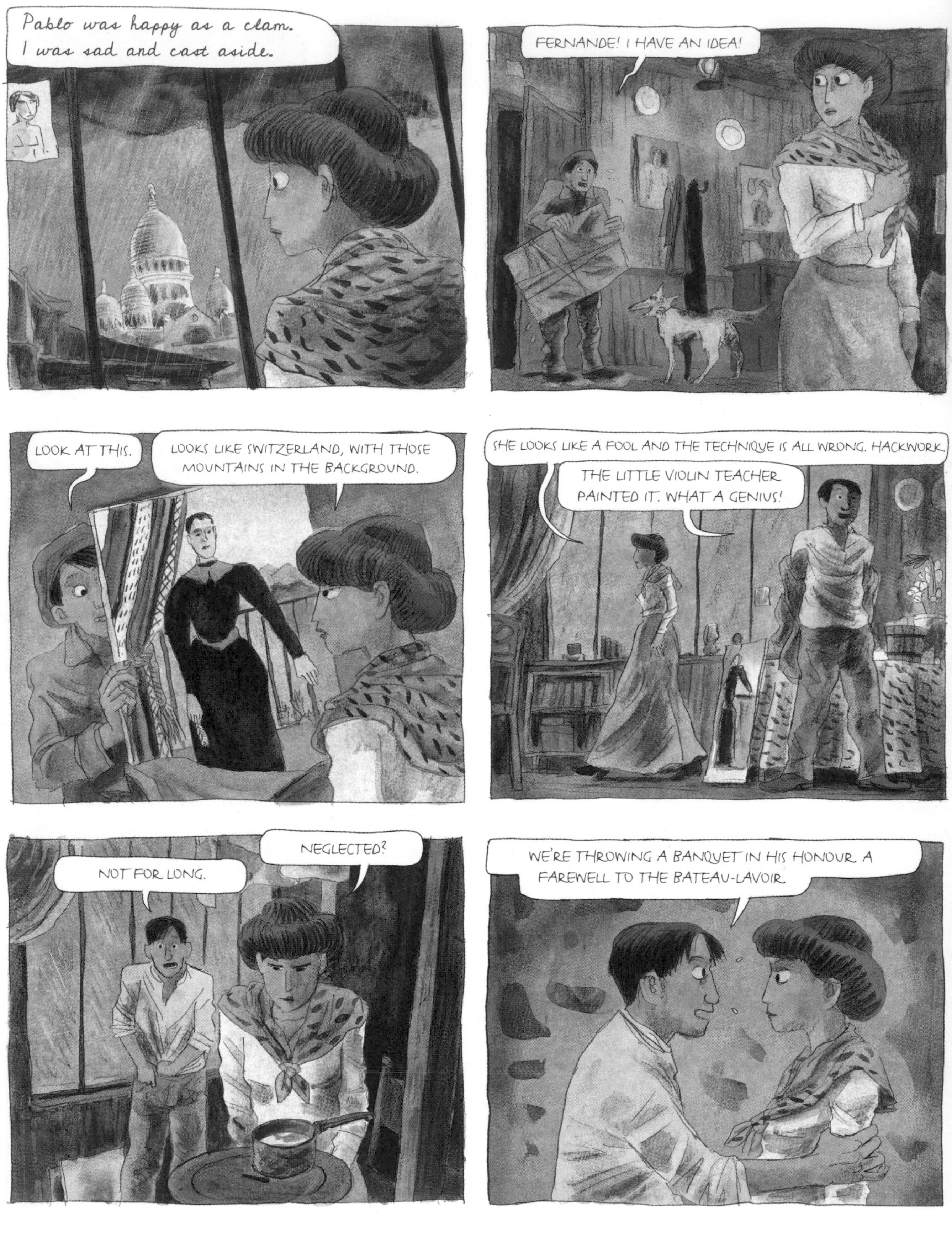
Pablo was happy as a clam.
I was sad and cast aside.
FERNANDE! I HAVE AN IDEA!
LOOK AT THIS.
LOOKS LIKE SWITZERLAND, WITH THOSE MOUNTAINS IN THE BACKGROUND.
SHE LOOKS LIKE A FOOL AND THE TECHNIQUE IS ALL WRONG. HACKWORK.
THE LITTLE VIOLIN TEACHER PAINTED IT. WHAT A GENIUS!
NEGLECTED?
NOT FOR LONG.
WE'RE THROWING A BANQUET IN HIS HONOUR. A FAREWELL TO THE BATEAU-LAVOIR.

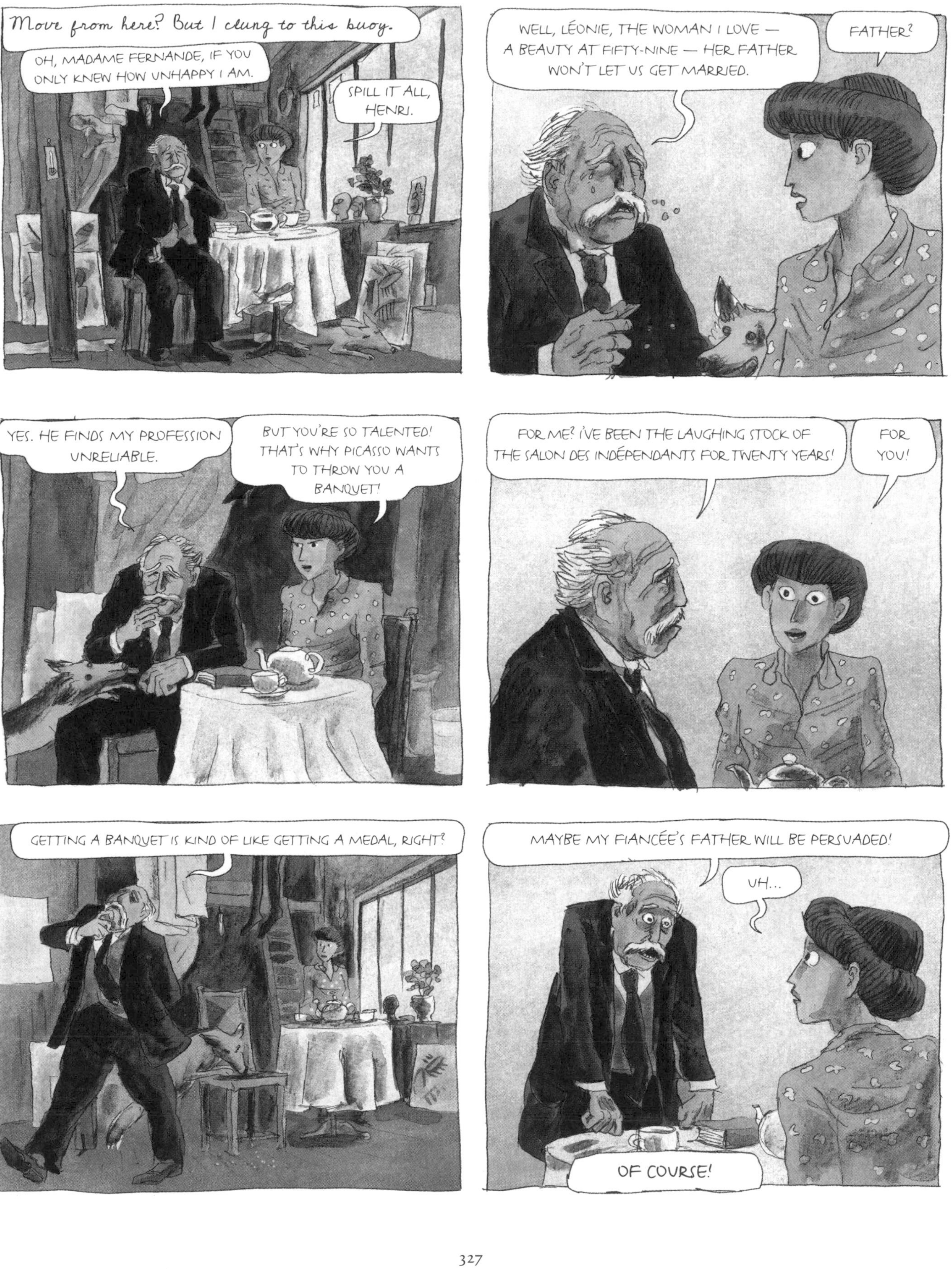
Move from here? But I clung to this buoy.
OH, MADAME FERNANDE, IF YOU ONLY KNEW HOW UNHAPPY I AM.
SPILL IT ALL, HENRI.
WELL, LÉONIE, THE WOMAN I LOVE — A BEAUTY AT FIFTY-NINE — HER FATHER WON'T LET US GET MARRIED.
FATHER?
YES. HE FINDS MY PROFESSION UNRELIABLE.
BUT YOU'RE SO TALENTED! THAT'S WHY PICASSO WANTS TO THROW YOU A BANQUET!
FOR ME? I'VE BEEN THE LAUGHING STOCK OF THE SALON DES INDÉPENDANTS FOR TWENTY YEARS!
FOR YOU!
GETTING A BANQUET IS KIND OF LIKE GETTING A MEDAL, RIGHT?
MAYBE MY FIANCÉE'S FATHER WILL BE PERSUADED!
UH...
OF COURSE!

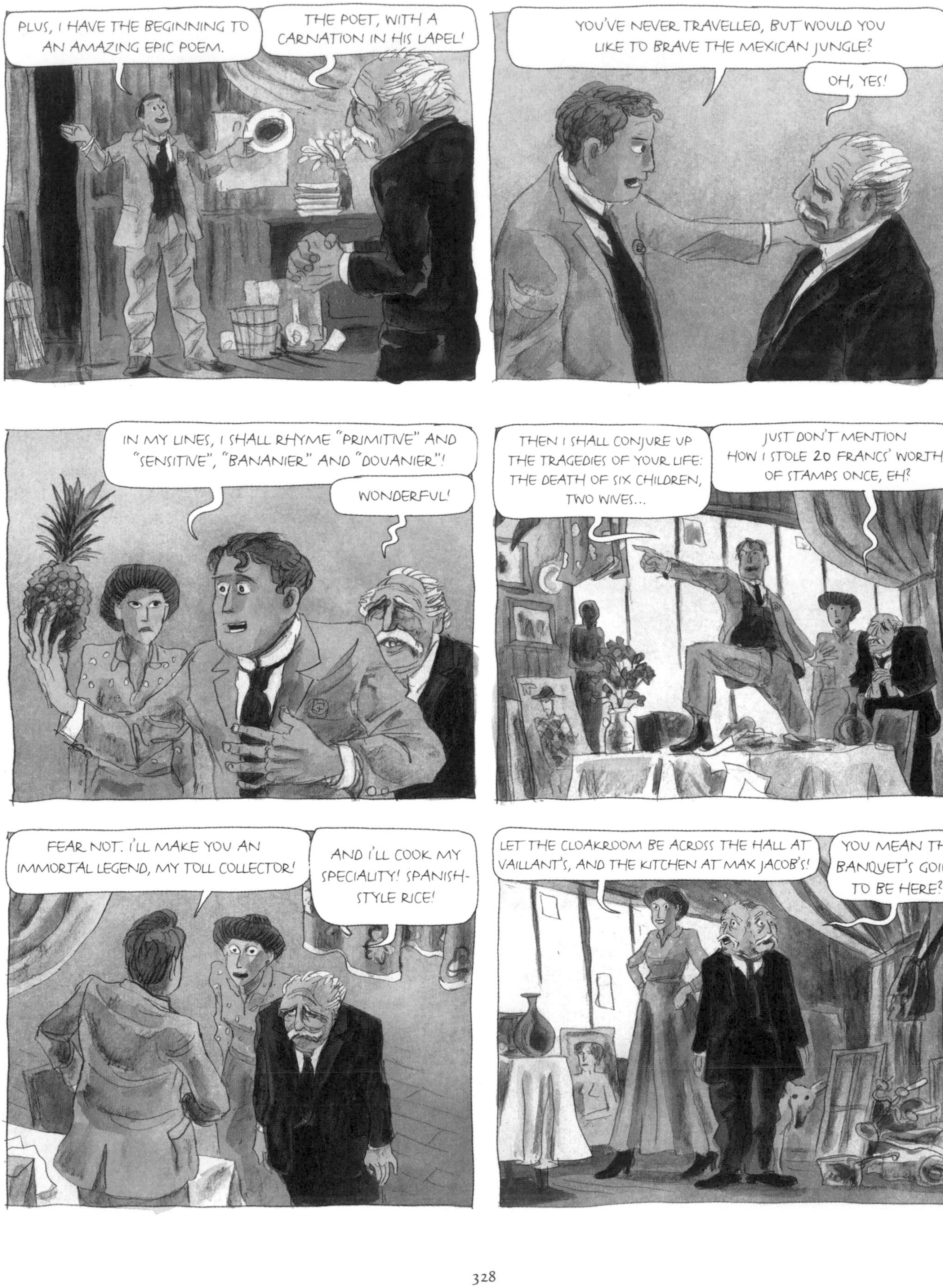
PLUS, I HAVE THE BEGINNING TO AN AMAZING EPIC POEM.
THE POET, WITH A CARNATION IN HIS LAPEL!
YOU'VE NEVER TRAVELLED, BUT WOULD YOU LIKE TO BRAVE THE MEXICAN JUNGLE?
OH, YES!
IN MY LINES, I SHALL RHYME "PRIMITIVE" AND "SENSITIVE", "BANANIER" AND "DOUANIER"!
WONDERFUL!
THEN I SHALL CONJURE UP THE TRAGEDIES OF YOUR LIFE: THE DEATH OF SIX CHILDREN, TWO WIVES...
JUST DON'T MENTION HOW I STOLE 20 FRANCS' WORTH OF STAMPS ONCE, EH?
FEAR NOT. I'LL MAKE YOU AN IMMORTAL LEGEND, MY TOLL COLLECTOR!
AND I'LL COOK MY SPECIALITY! SPANISH-STYLE RICE!
LET THE CLOAKROOM BE ACROSS THE HALL AT VAILLANT'S, AND THE KITCHEN AT MAX JACOB'S!
YOU MEAN THE BANQUET'S GOING TO BE HERE?!

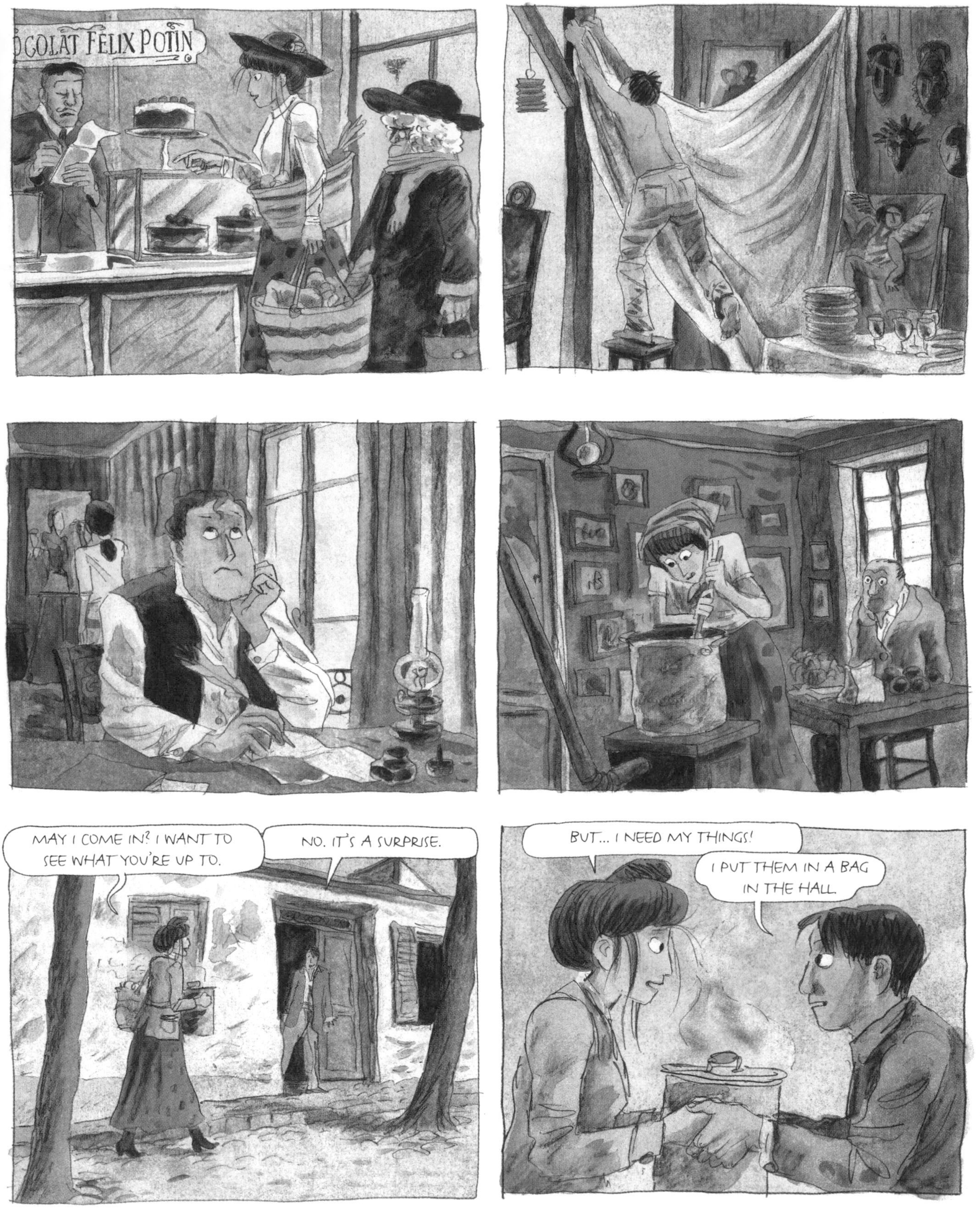
OCOLAT FELIX POTIN
MAY I COME IN? I WANT TO SEE WHAT YOU'RE UP TO.
NO. IT'S A SURPRISE.
BUT... I NEED MY THINGS!
I PUT THEM IN A BAG IN THE HALL.

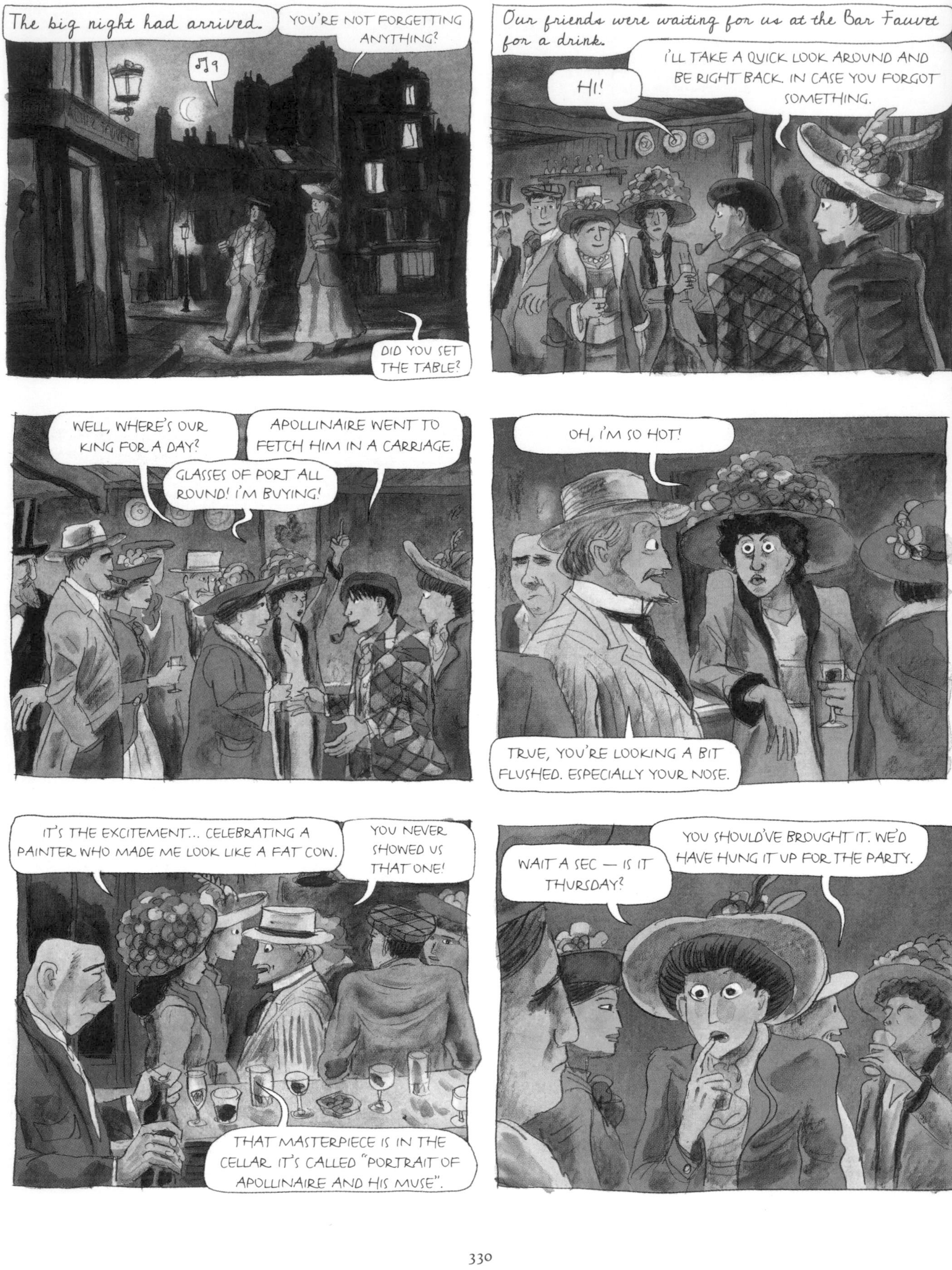
The big night had arrived.
YOU'RE NOT FORGETTING ANYTHING?
DID YOU SET THE TABLE?
Our friends were waiting for us at the Bar Fauvet for a drink.
HI!
I'LL TAKE A QUICK LOOK AROUND AND BE RIGHT BACK. IN CASE YOU FORGOT SOMETHING.
WELL, WHERE'S OUR KING FOR A DAY?
APOLLINAIRE WENT TO FETCH HIM IN A CARRIAGE.
GLASSES OF PORT ALL ROUND! I'M BUYING!
OH, I'M SO HOT!
TRUE, YOU'RE LOOKING A BIT FLUSHED. ESPECIALLY YOUR NOSE.
IT'S THE EXCITEMENT... CELEBRATING A PAINTER WHO MADE ME LOOK LIKE A FAT COW.
YOU NEVER SHOWED US THAT ONE!
THAT MASTERPIECE IS IN THE CELLAR. IT'S CALLED "PORTRAIT OF APOLLINAIRE AND HIS MUSE".
WAIT A SEC — IS IT THURSDAY?
YOU SHOULD'VE BROUGHT IT. WE'D HAVE HUNG IT UP FOR THE PARTY.

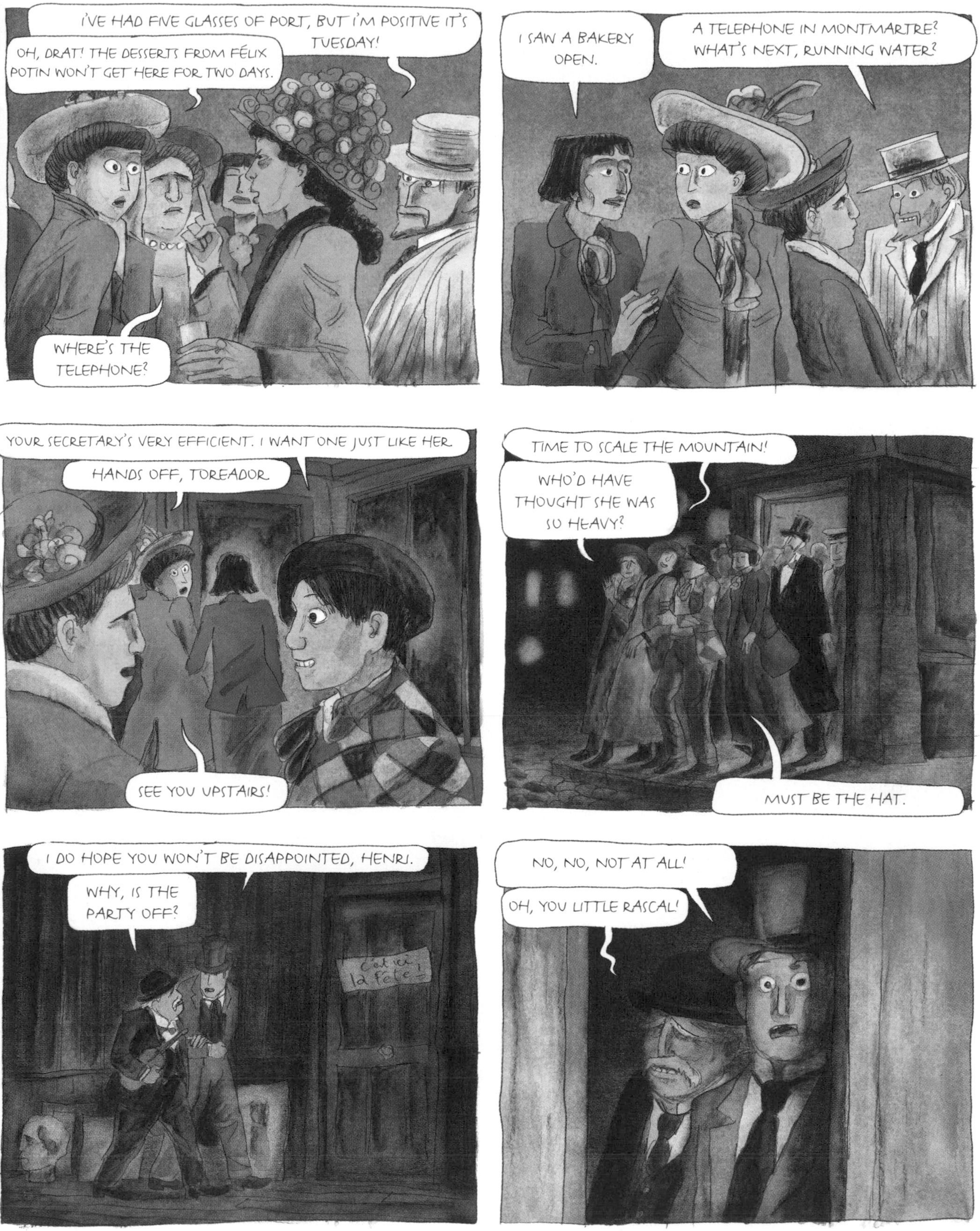
I'VE HAD FIVE GLASSES OF PORT, BUT I'M POSITIVE IT'S TUESDAY!
OH, DRAT! THE DESSERTS FROM FÉLIX POTIN WON'T GET HERE FOR TWO DAYS.
WHERE'S THE TELEPHONE?
I SAW A BAKERY OPEN.
A TELEPHONE IN MONTMARTRE? WHAT'S NEXT, RUNNING WATER?
YOUR SECRETARY'S VERY EFFICIENT. I WANT ONE JUST LIKE HER
HANDS OFF, TOREADOR
SEE YOU UPSTAIRS!
TIME TO SCALE THE MOUNTAIN!
WHO'D HAVE THOUGHT SHE WAS SO HEAVY?
MUST BE THE HAT.
I DO HOPE YOU WON'T BE DISAPPOINTED, HENRI.
WHY, IS THE PARTY OFF?
C'est ici la fête!
NO, NO, NOT AT ALL!
OH, YOU LITTLE RASCAL!

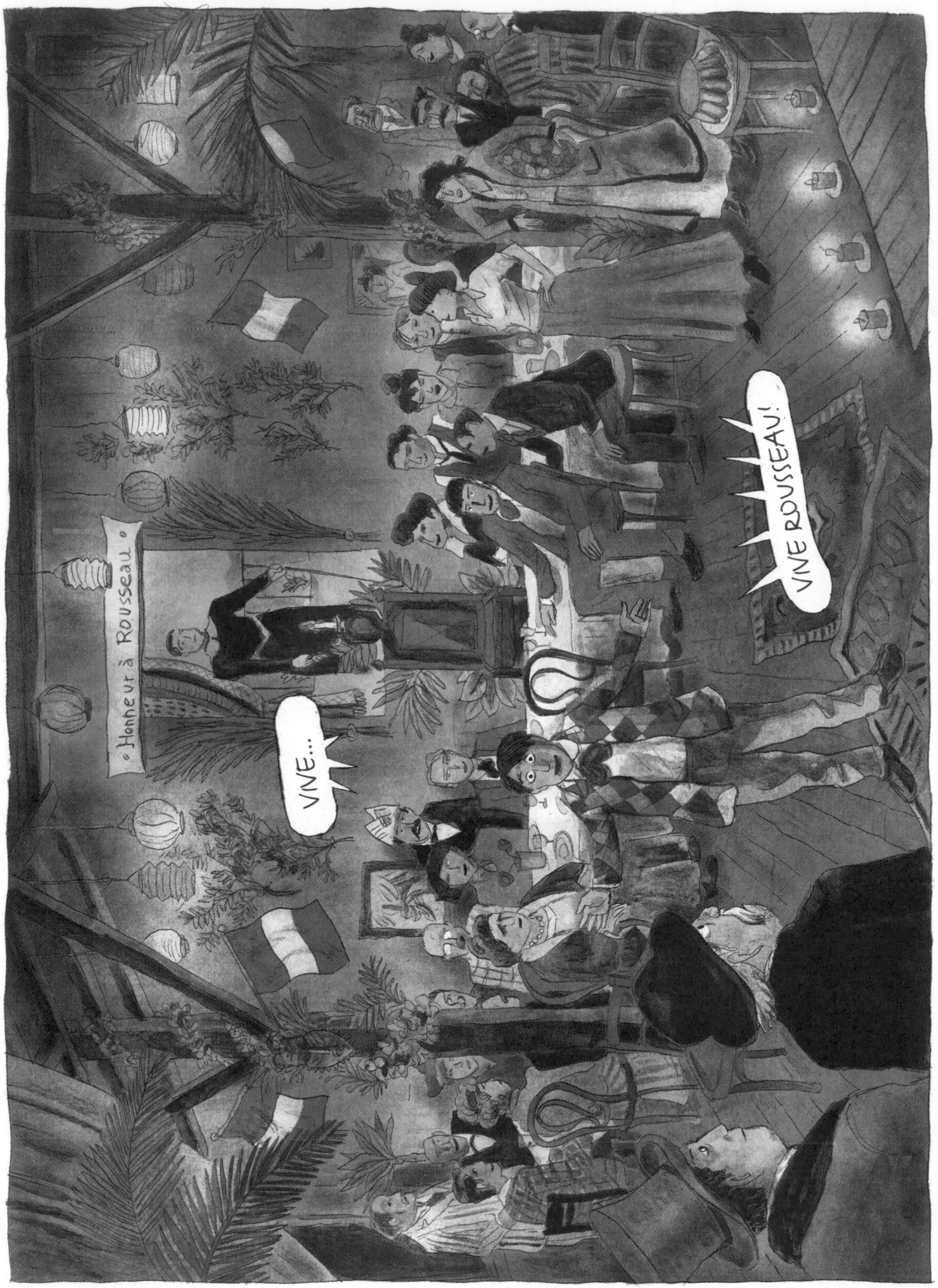
Honneur à Rousseau
VIVE...
VIVE ROUSSEAU!

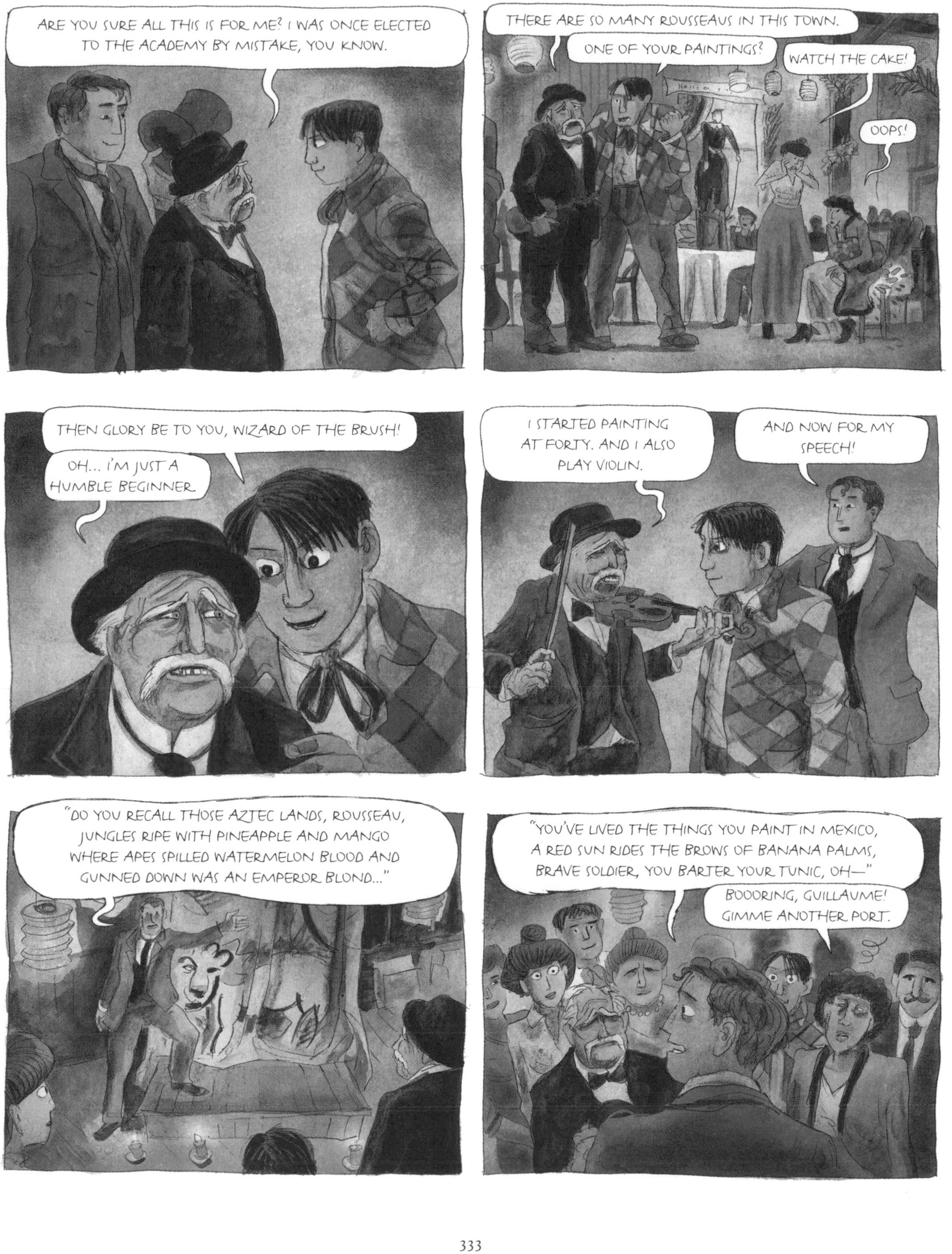
ARE YOU SURE ALL THIS IS FOR ME? I WAS ONCE ELECTED TO THE ACADEMY BY MISTAKE, YOU KNOW.
THERE ARE SO MANY ROUSSEAUS IN THIS TOWN.
ONE OF YOUR PAINTINGS?
WATCH THE CAKE!
OOPS!
THEN GLORY BE TO YOU, WIZARD OF THE BRUSH!
OH... I'M JUST A HUMBLE BEGINNER.
I STARTED PAINTING AT FORTY. AND I ALSO PLAY VIOLIN.
AND NOW FOR MY SPEECH!
"DO YOU RECALL THOSE AZTEC LANDS, ROUSSEAU, JUNGLES RIPE WITH PINEAPPLE AND MANGO WHERE APES SPILLED WATERMELON BLOOD AND GUNNED DOWN WAS AN EMPEROR BLOND..."
"YOU'VE LIVED THE THINGS YOU PAINT IN MEXICO, A RED SUN RIDES THE BROWS OF BANANA PALMS, BRAVE SOLDIER, YOU BARTER YOUR TUNIC, OH—"
BOOORING, GUILLAUME! GIMME ANOTHER PORT.

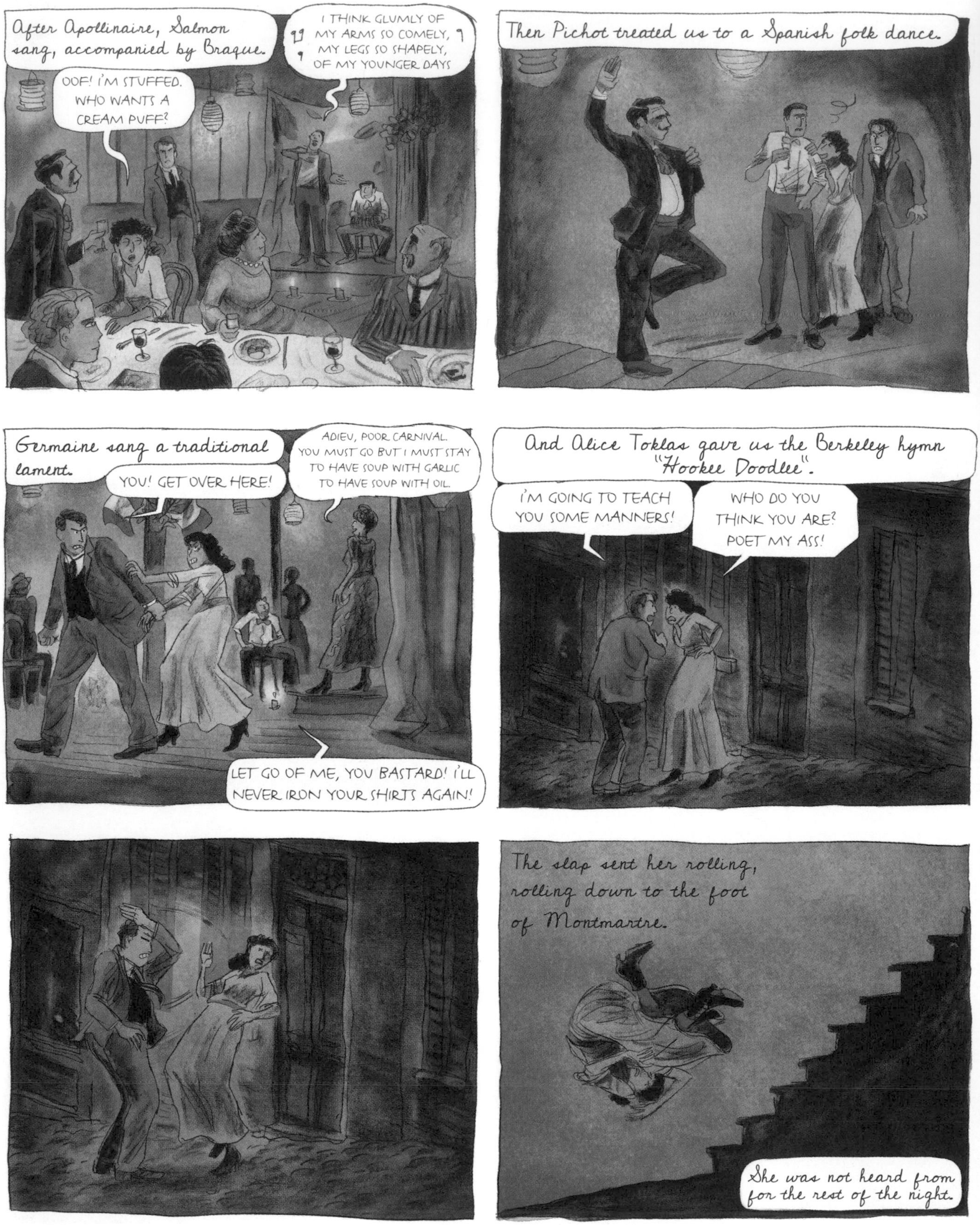
After Apollinaire, Salmon sang, accompanied by Braque.
I THINK GLUMLY OF MY ARMS SO COMELY, MY LEGS SO SHAPELY, OF MY YOUNGER DAYS
OOF! I'M STUFFED. WHO WANTS A CREAM PUFF?
Then Pichot treated us to a Spanish folk dance.
Germaine sang a traditional lament.
YOU! GET OVER HERE!
ADIEU, POOR CARNIVAL. YOU MUST GO BUT I MUST STAY TO HAVE SOUP WITH GARLIC TO HAVE SOUP WITH OIL.
LET GO OF ME, YOU BASTARD! I'LL NEVER IRON YOUR SHIRTS AGAIN!
And Alice Toklas gave us the Berkeley hymn "Hookee Doodlee".
I'M GOING TO TEACH YOU SOME MANNERS!
WHO DO YOU THINK YOU ARE? POET MY ASS!
The slap sent her rolling, rolling down to the foot of Montmartre.
She was not heard from for the rest of the night.

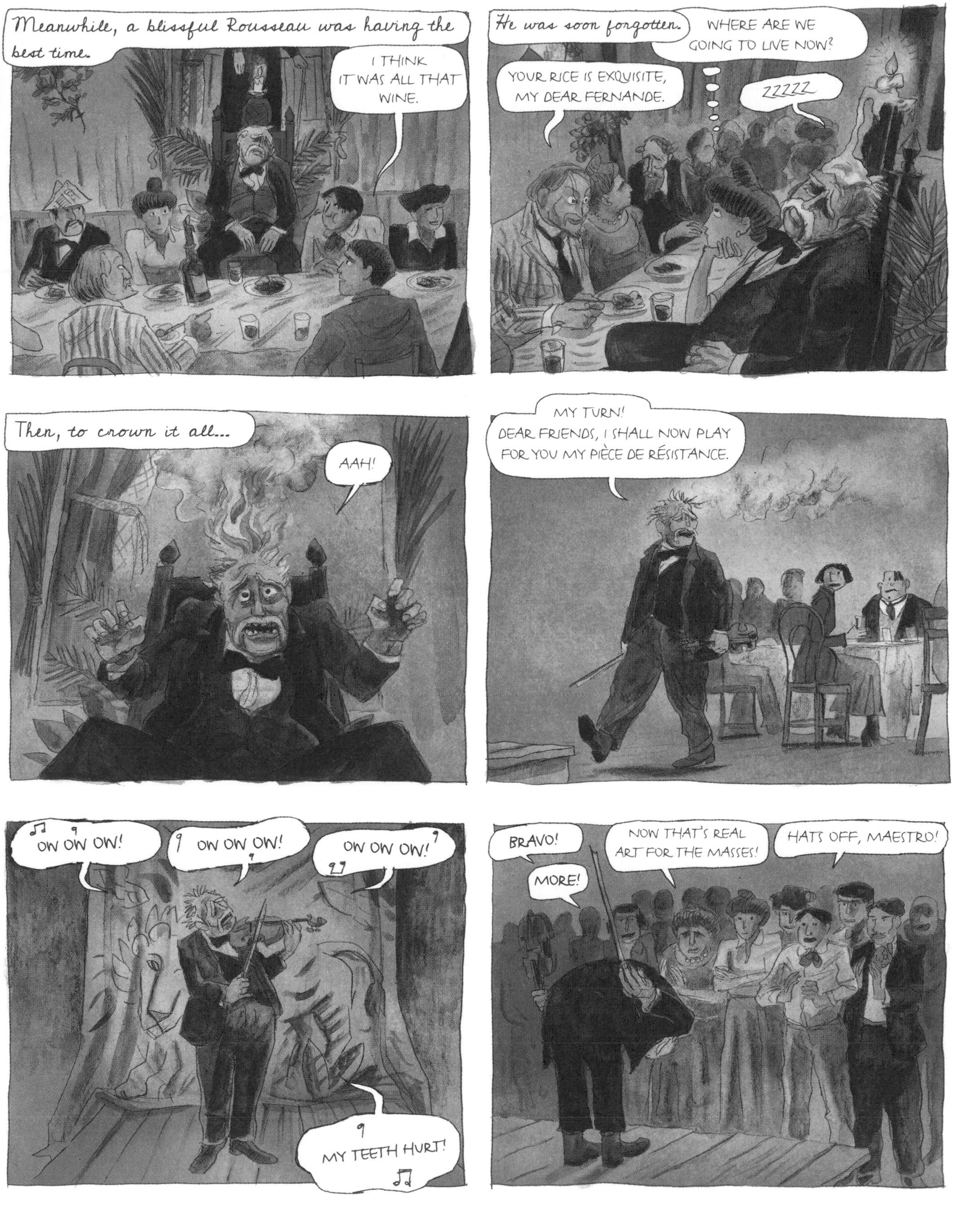
Meanwhile, a blissful Rousseau was having the best time.
I THINK IT WAS ALL THAT WINE.
He was soon forgotten.
WHERE ARE WE GOING TO LIVE NOW?
YOUR RICE IS EXQUISITE, MY DEAR FERNANDE.
ZZZZZ
Then, to crown it all...
AAH!
MY TURN! DEAR FRIENDS, I SHALL NOW PLAY FOR YOU MY PIÈCE DE RÉSISTANCE.
OW OW OW!
OW OW OW!
OW OW OW!
MY TEETH HURT!
BRAVO!
MORE!
NOW THAT'S REAL ART FOR THE MASSES!
HATS OFF, MAESTRO!

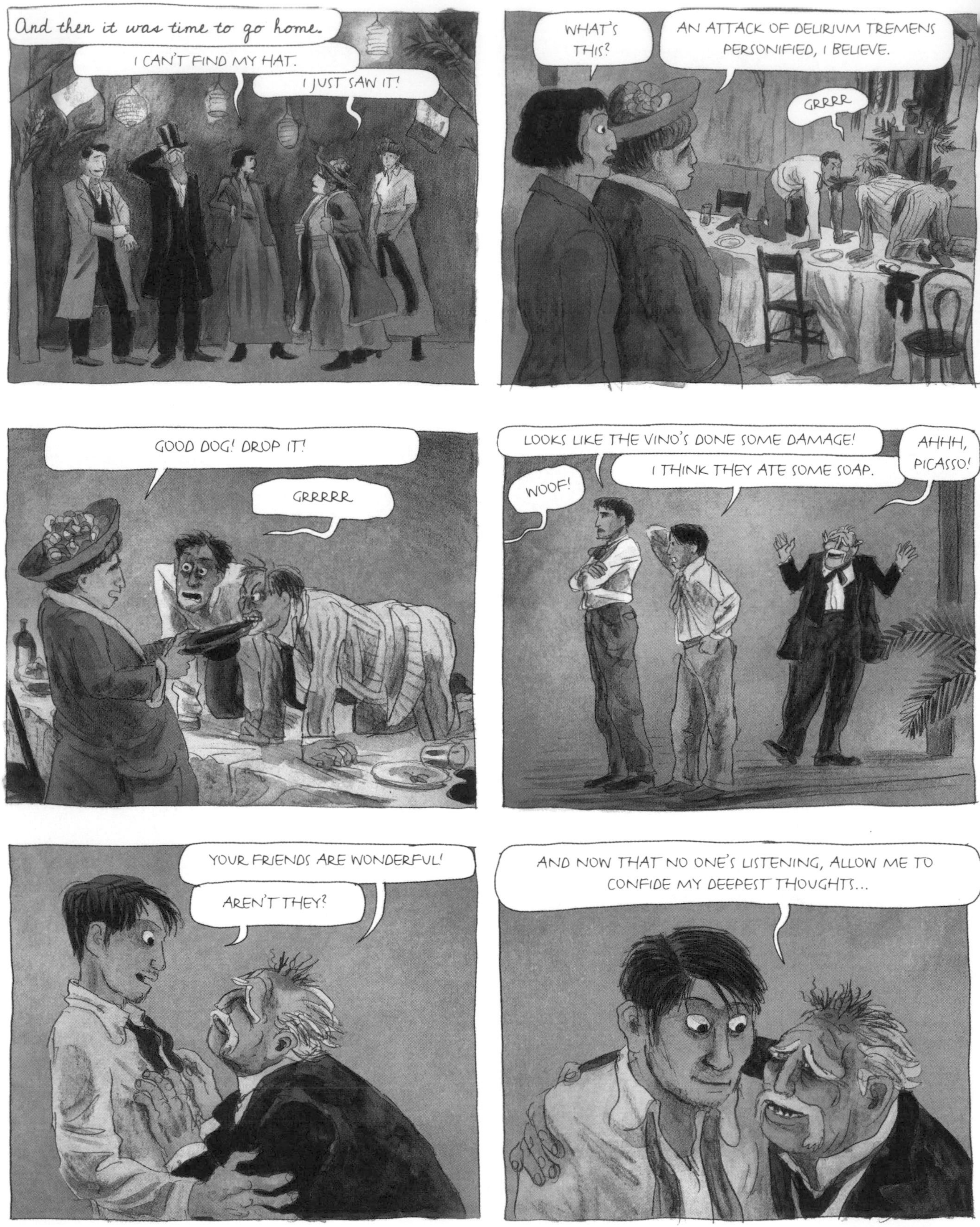
And then it was time to go home.
I CAN'T FIND MY HAT.
I JUST SAW IT!
WHAT'S THIS?
AN ATTACK OF DELIRIUM TREMENS PERSONIFIED, I BELIEVE.
GRRRR
GOOD DOG! DROP IT!
GRRRRR
LOOKS LIKE THE VINO'S DONE SOME DAMAGE!
WOOF!
I THINK THEY ATE SOME SOAP.
AHHH, PICASSO!
YOUR FRIENDS ARE WONDERFUL!
AREN'T THEY?
AND NOW THAT NO ONE'S LISTENING, ALLOW ME TO CONFIDE MY DEEPEST THOUGHTS...

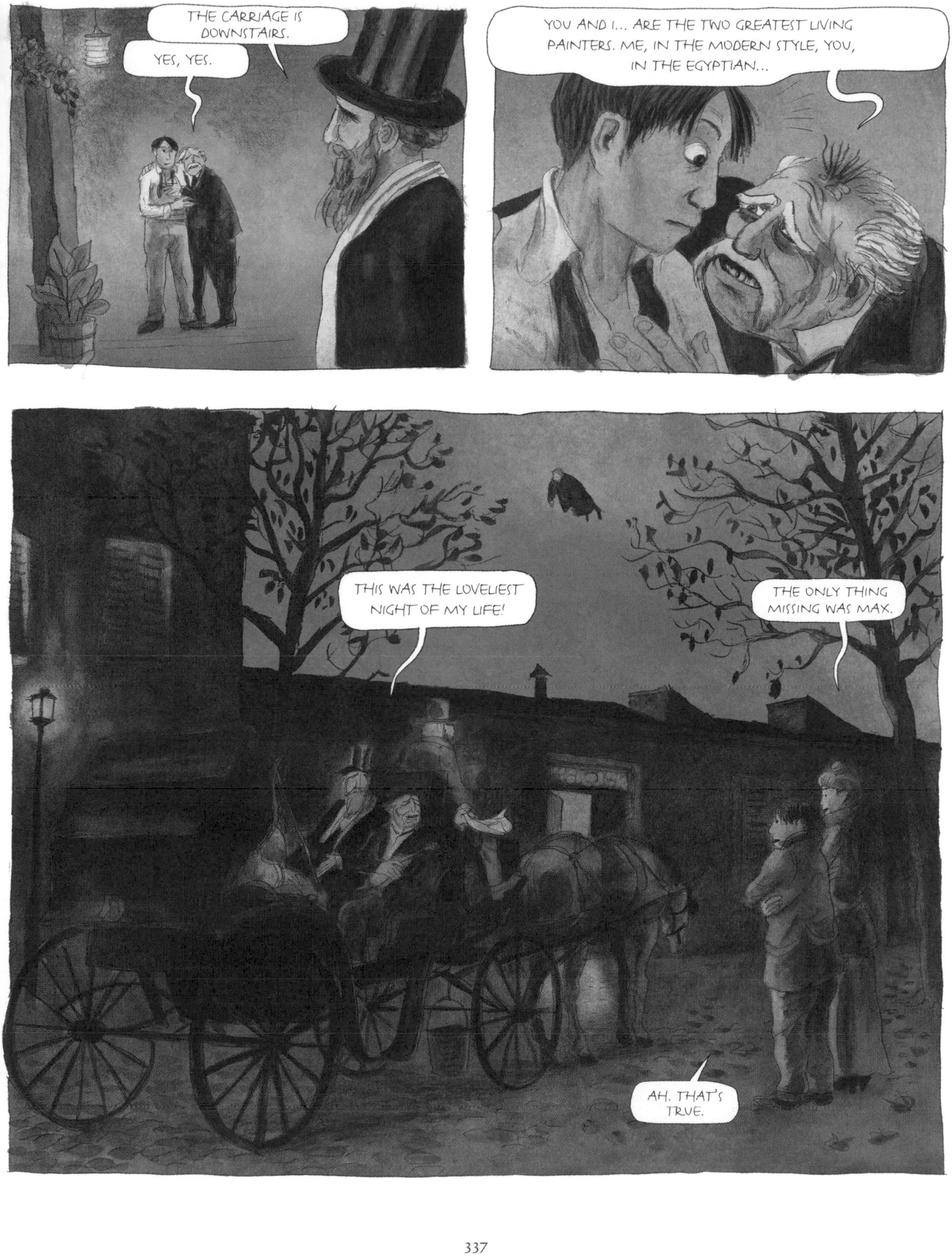
THE CARRIAGE IS DOWNSTAIRS.
YES, YES.
YOU AND I... ARE THE TWO GREATEST LIVING PAINTERS. ME, IN THE MODERN STYLE, YOU, IN THE EGYPTIAN...
THIS WAS THE LOVELIEST NIGHT OF MY LIFE!
THE ONLY THING MISSING WAS MAX.
AH. THAT'S TRUE.

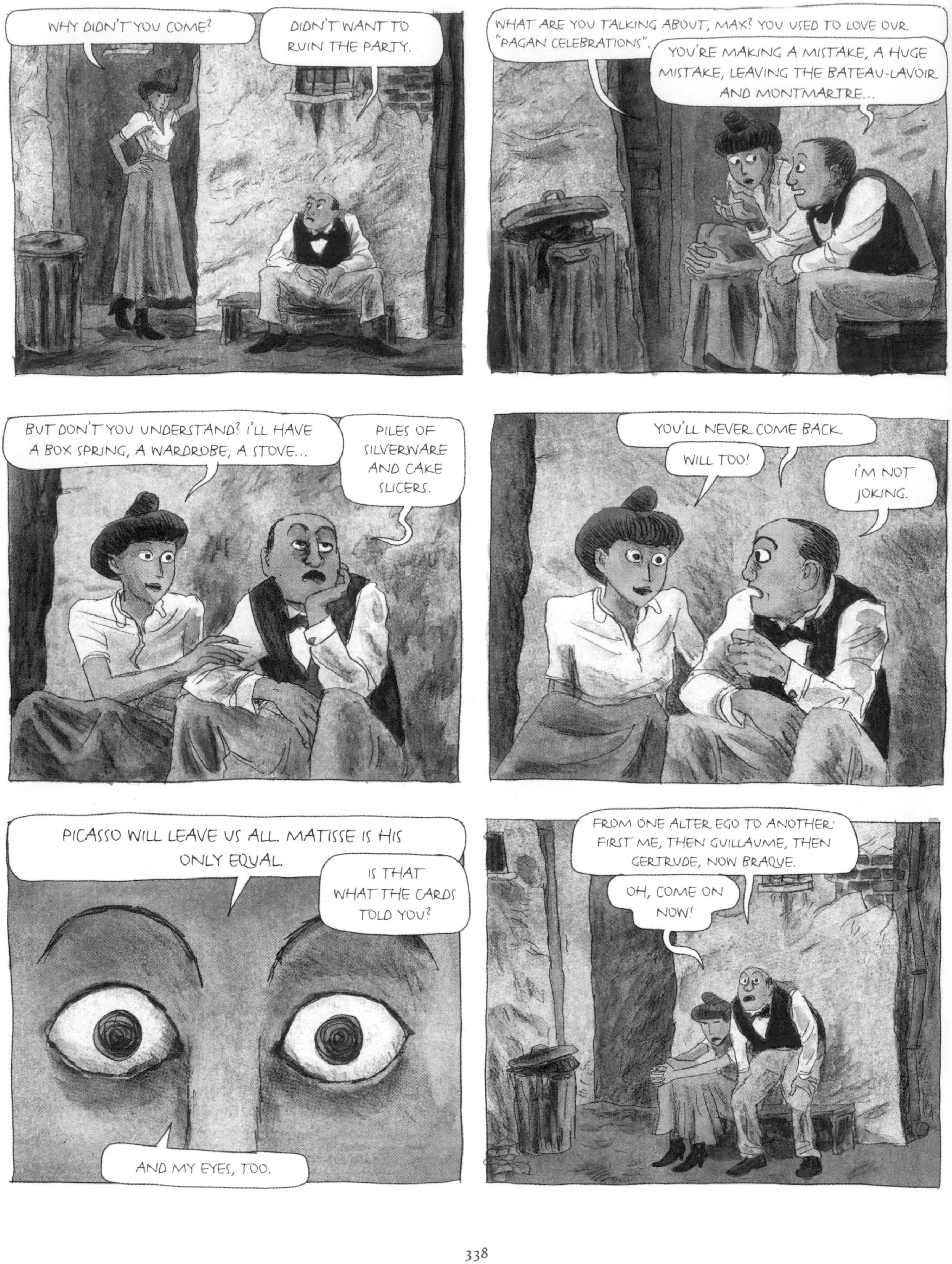
WHY DIDN'T YOU COME?
DIDN'T WANT TO RUIN THE PARTY.
WHAT ARE YOU TALKING ABOUT, MAX? YOU USED TO LOVE OUR "PAGAN CELEBRATIONS".
YOU'RE MAKING A MISTAKE, A HUGE MISTAKE, LEAVING THE BATEAU-LAVOIR AND MONTMARTRE...
BUT DON'T YOU UNDERSTAND? I'LL HAVE A BOX SPRING, A WARDROBE, A STOVE...
PILES OF SILVERWARE AND CAKE SLICERS.
YOU'LL NEVER COME BACK.
WILL TOO!
I'M NOT JOKING.
PICASSO WILL LEAVE US ALL. MATISSE IS HIS ONLY EQUAL.
IS THAT WHAT THE CARDS TOLD YOU?
AND MY EYES, TOO.
FROM ONE ALTER EGO TO ANOTHER: FIRST ME, THEN GUILLAUME, THEN GERTRUDE, NOW BRAQUE.
OH, COME ON NOW!

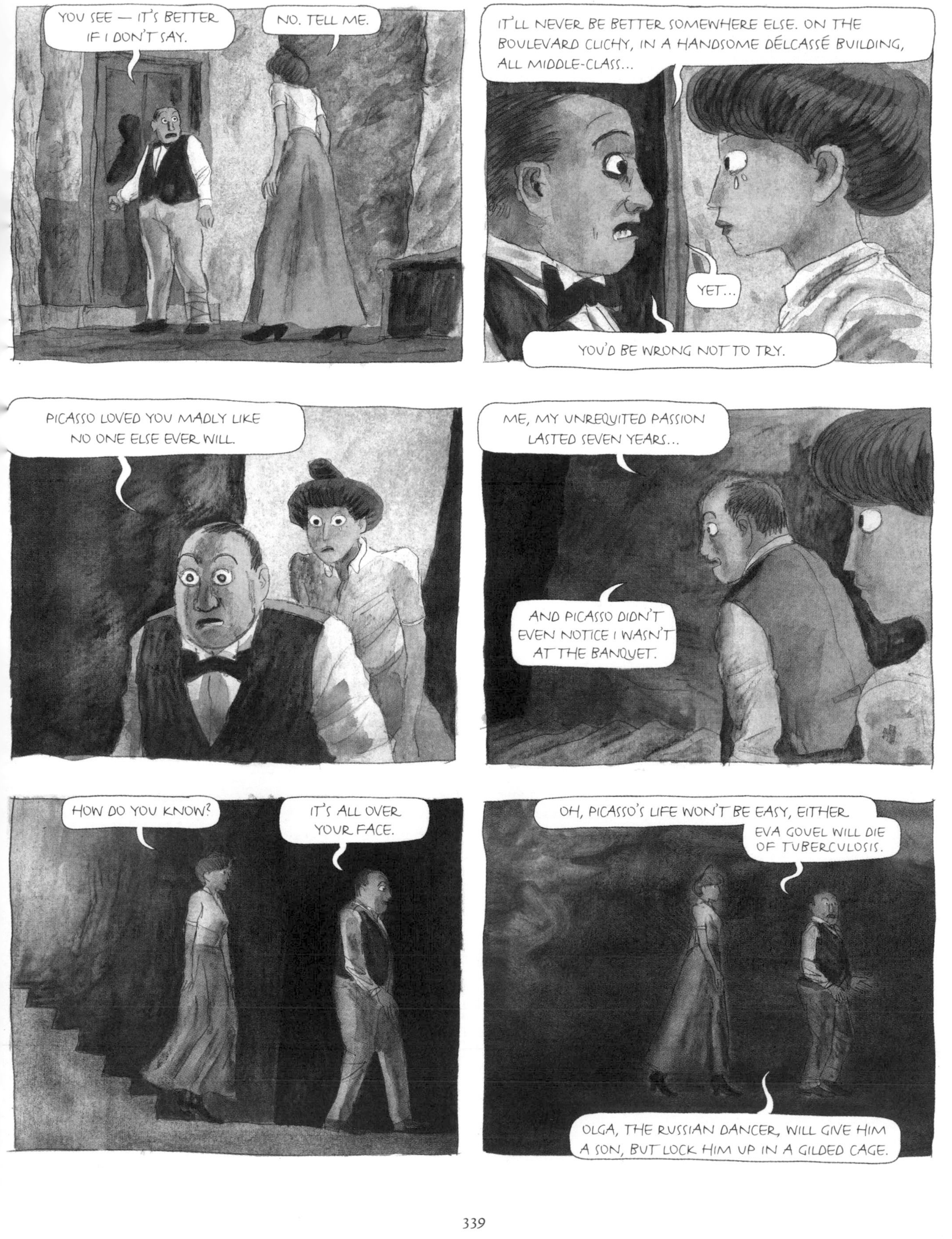
YOU SEE — IT'S BETTER IF I DON'T SAY.
NO. TELL ME.
IT'LL NEVER BE BETTER SOMEWHERE ELSE. ON THE BOULEVARD CLICHY, IN A HANDSOME DÉLCASSÉ BUILDING, ALL MIDDLE-CLASS...
YET...
YOU'D BE WRONG NOT TO TRY.
PICASSO LOVED YOU MADLY LIKE NO ONE ELSE EVER WILL.
ME, MY UNREQUITED PASSION LASTED SEVEN YEARS...
AND PICASSO DIDN'T EVEN NOTICE I WASN'T AT THE BANQUET.
HOW DO YOU KNOW?
IT'S ALL OVER YOUR FACE.
OH, PICASSO'S LIFE WON'T BE EASY, EITHER
EVA GOUEL WILL DIE OF TUBERCULOSIS.
OLGA, THE RUSSIAN DANCER, WILL GIVE HIM A SON, BUT LOCK HIM UP IN A GILDED CAGE.

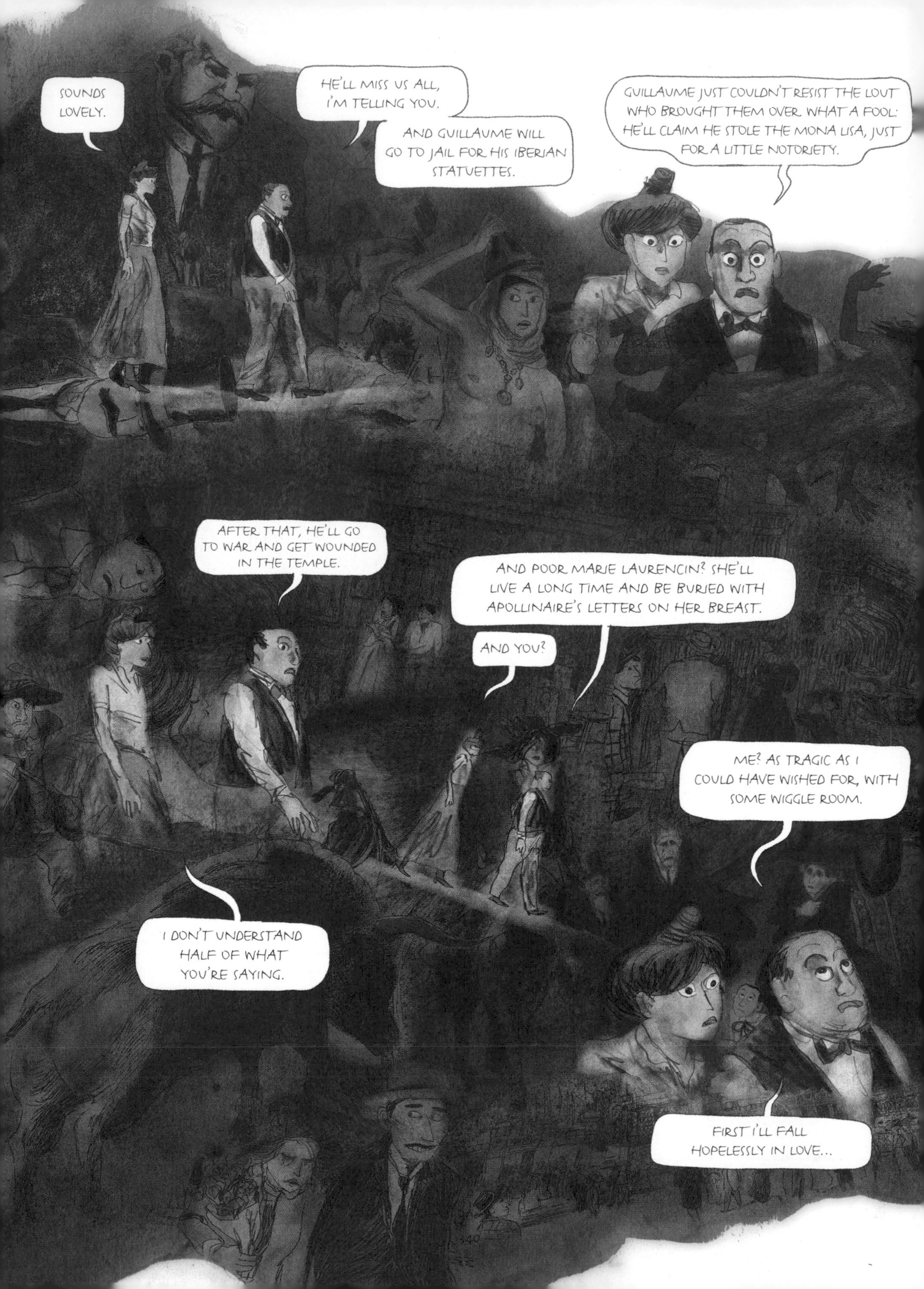
SOUNDS LOVELY.
HE'LL MISS US ALL, I'M TELLING YOU.
AND GUILLAUME WILL GO TO JAIL FOR HIS IBERIAN STATUETTES.
GUILLAUME JUST COULDN'T RESIST THE LOUT WHO BROUGHT THEM OVER. WHAT A FOOL: HE'LL CLAIM HE STOLE THE MONA LISA, JUST FOR A LITTLE NOTORIETY.
AFTER THAT, HE'LL GO TO WAR AND GET WOUNDED IN THE TEMPLE.
AND POOR MARIE LAURENCIN? SHE'LL LIVE A LONG TIME AND BE BURIED WITH APOLLINAIRE'S LETTERS ON HER BREAST.
AND YOU?
ME? AS TRAGIC AS I COULD HAVE WISHED FOR, WITH SOME WIGGLE ROOM.
I DON'T UNDERSTAND HALF OF WHAT YOU'RE SAYING.
FIRST I'LL FALL HOPELESSLY IN LOVE...

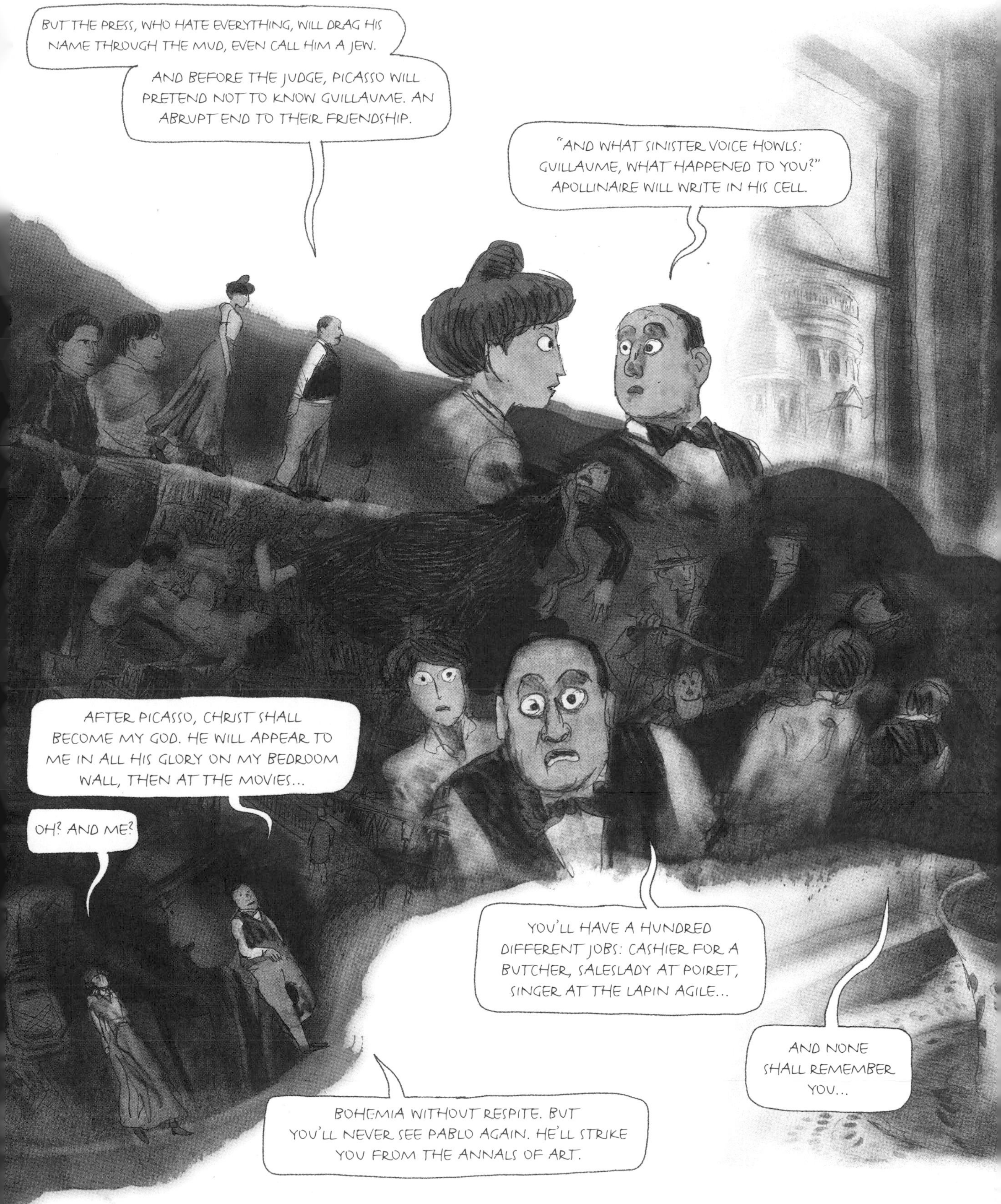
BUT THE PRESS, WHO HATE EVERYTHING, WILL DRAG HIS NAME THROUGH THE MUD, EVEN CALL HIM A JEW.
AND BEFORE THE JUDGE, PICASSO WILL PRETEND NOT TO KNOW GUILLAUME. AN ABRUPT END TO THEIR FRIENDSHIP.
"AND WHAT SINISTER VOICE HOWLS: GUILLAUME, WHAT HAPPENED TO YOU?" APOLLINAIRE WILL WRITE IN HIS CELL.
AFTER PICASSO, CHRIST SHALL BECOME MY GOD. HE WILL APPEAR TO ME IN ALL HIS GLORY ON MY BEDROOM WALL, THEN AT THE MOVIES...
OH? AND ME?
YOU'LL HAVE A HUNDRED DIFFERENT JOBS: CASHIER FOR A BUTCHER, SALESLADY AT POIRET, SINGER AT THE LAPIN AGILE...
AND NONE SHALL REMEMBER YOU...
BOHEMIA WITHOUT RESPITE. BUT YOU'LL NEVER SEE PABLO AGAIN. HE'LL STRIKE YOU FROM THE ANNALS OF ART.

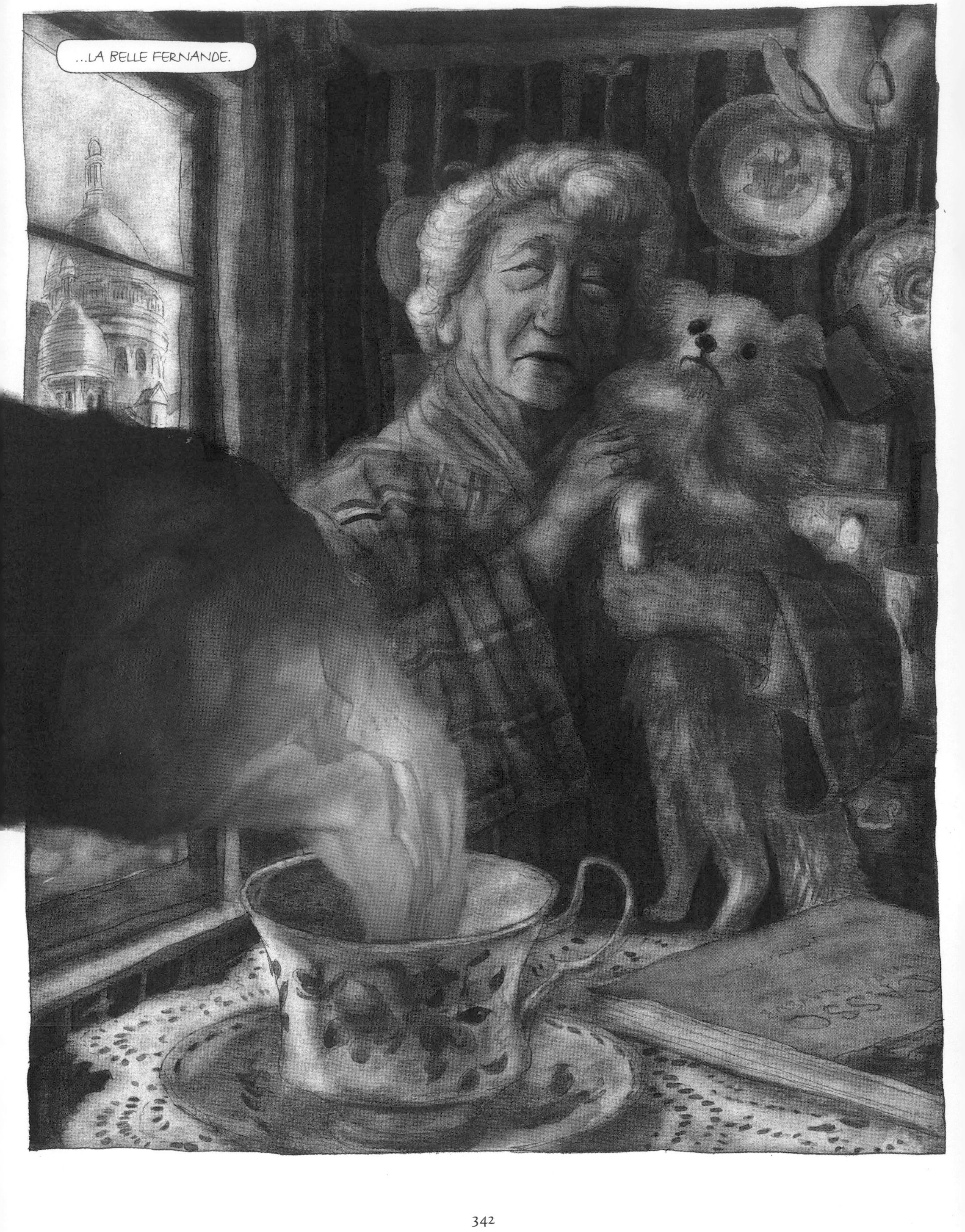
...LA BELLE FERNANDE.

Also available in the **ART MASTERS** series:

VINCENT
by Barbara Stok

ISBN 978-1-906838-79-9
Paperback, 144 pages
RRP: UK £12.99 US $19.95 CAN $21.95
Available in all good bookshops